THE
unofficial **GUIDE**®
ᵀᴼPáris

6TH EDITION

THE *unofficial* GUIDE®

ᵀᵒParis

6TH EDITION

DAVID APPLEFIELD

WILEY

For Julia, Alexandre, Anna, and Ernesto

Please note that prices fluctuate in the course of time and travel information changes under the impact of many factors that influence the travel industry. We therefore suggest that you write or call ahead for confirmation when making your travel plans. Every effort has been made to ensure the accuracy of information throughout this book, and the contents of this publication are believed correct at the time of printing. Nevertheless, the publishers cannot accept responsibility for errors or omissions, for changes in details given in this guide, or for the consequences of any reliance on the information provided by the same. Assessments of attractions and so forth are based upon the author's own experience, and, therefore, descriptions given in this guide neces-sarily contain an element of subjective opinion, which may not reflect the publisher's opinion or dictate a reader's own experience on another occasion. Readers are invited to write the publisher with ideas, comments, and suggestions for future editions.

Published by:
John Wiley & Sons, Inc.
111 River Street
Hoboken, NJ 07030

Produced by Menasha Ridge Press

Cover design by Michael J. Freeland

Interior design by Vertigo Design

For information on our other products and services or to obtain technical support, please con-tact our Customer Care Department within the United States at 877-762-2974, outside the United States at 317-572-3993, or by fax at 317-572-4002.

John Wiley & Sons, Inc., also publishes its books in a variety of electronic formats. Some con-tent that appears in print may not be available in electronic formats.

ISBN 978-0-470-53745-9

Manufactured in the United States of America

5 4 3 2 1

CONTENTS

LIST *of* MAPS

ABOUT *the* AUTHOR

David Applefield is a media specialist, writer, lecturer, and editor from Boston who has lived in Paris for more than 25 years. He publishes the popular Paris Web site **paris-anglo.com** and is the author of *Paris Inside Out*. His fiction includes *Once Removed* and *On a Flying Fish*. Applefield represents the *Financial Times* in West Africa.

ACKNOWLEDGMENTS

I WOULD LIKE TO THANK LIZ SCHWARZ for her excellent fact-checking, and the many readers who took the time to share their Paris experiences with me.

—David Applefield

THE *unofficial* GUIDE®
ᵀᴼParis

6TH EDITION

INTRODUCTION

WELCOME *to* UNOFFICIAL PARIS

BONJOUR (bohn-**jzoor**), YOU'RE A LUCKY PERSON. I say that in every edition of this guide. My opinion on Paris remains resolute. Visiting Paris is always a privilege. Why? Because a trip to Paris is not only about visiting the place—it's a state of mind. That's what Paris is for. It's a costume party of the soul with an outrageous caterer. And it's all unofficial. When you are having fun and catch yourself having fun, that's an unofficial moment. Unplanned pleasure. The trip may be planned, but the moment commands its own magic. Paris is perfect for such moments.

Following 9/11 and the U.S. involvement in Iraq, some tourists expressed concern about tensions between France and the United States. Such concerns are wholly irrelevant now. Franco-American relations are excellent, and with the election of President Barack Obama, the prestige of being an American in the world has been greatly restored. As a visitor to Paris, you should not feel any negative impact of geopolitics. You will have a wonderful time in Paris. Anybody who tells you that the French don't like Americans or who makes other toxic generalities simply doesn't know France. I have been in Paris for more than 25 years, and I am willing to risk my credibility on this.

Truly, you do not need a highly programmed schedule to indulge in the riches of the City of Light. Simple things like strolling along the banks of the Seine River, for example, or whiling away an hour or two in a picturesque café with a glass of red wine, produce genuine and original delight no matter the time of year or hour of day (or night). Alone, with a friend or your spouse, or even the whole family, the experience of being in Paris is always singular and personal. It's as if the city marks you on the forehead and you become one of its children, destined to come back to redo the things you loved doing and seeing the last time. So, in essence, much of the myth becomes real and the clichés are rooted in fact—when you know what you're doing. Which, of course, is where *The Unofficial Guide to Paris* comes in.

Although it takes only a moment to fall in love with Paris, you need to be energetic, curious, well informed, well prepared, poised in psychic elegance, and yet wholly spontaneous to really know it. And if you can't be all of these things? Well then, you'll have to settle for simply being in love.

Paris is not only the capital of France, it is also the northern capital of the Latin spirit. It's where the soul meets the body and the mind meets the heart. It's where you lovingly do the "wrong" things for the right reasons, like eating sinfully rich and expensive desserts, buying silk, kissing in public, learning to drink Calvados, and ignoring the clock. Paris is not a city to be overly rational in. And yet it's also the hub of high intellect and culture, where matters of theory consume people in cafés, and style and form take on greater importance than practicality and price. Be forewarned: Paris continues to grow increasingly expensive as a weak dollar buys fewer and fewer euros, but don't let money ruin your trip. You can experience many of Paris's pleasures for very little money and often for free. Once in Paris, your billfold will disengage from your conscience and attach itself to your spirit. You won't give another thought to what you are spending until you arrive home and have to pay off your credit card. Of course, we will scrupulously try to protect your pocketbook at each turn of your visit, but in the end, don't be surprised to discover that you've reevaluated the relationship between money and value.

Although a Catholic country (but not too Catholic; church and state were officially separated in 1905), the French don't live for tomorrow. There may be an afterlife, but what really counts is dinner this evening and that concert tomorrow night, sexy shoes, and strong coffee. In Paris, let your motto be *carpe diem!*

Even as a visitor to this city, you will walk a tightrope between the finest relics of the past and the sophistication of the moment. When you approach your stay with the openness needed to become a surrogate Parisian, the city reveals its curious ability to seduce, and you'll suddenly find yourself on one of Paris's gilded bridges asking yourself if maybe you shouldn't give up your job back home and become a watercolorist on the Left Bank, or a chef or poet, or write that novel. The question is perfect to rejuvenate the soul! But don't panic; there's no need to decide right away. Duck into a bistro for a glass of Bordeaux. And dream a bit. Being a traveler in Paris is a never-ending odyssey; actually, you don't visit Paris, you end up having a relationship with it over the course of your life. And this is by far the best way to enjoy the city as a visitor. Although you're not a Parisian, we urge you to feel like one. Paris belongs to its visitors during the days they are here, and beyond. You're not a stranger. You become part of your host city, and you will come back to revisit those special feelings as often as you can. This is the Paris we encourage you to discover. The real Paris—and its culture, which lies richly embedded in the art and architecture, the cuisine and wine, the perfume and fashions, the language and music, and, of course, the gestures of the people.

But like all good things, Paris is also complex, and Parisians can be complicated. The truth remains that although Paris is one of the world's most visited places, it is also one of its most misunderstood cities. Media and government spin have left France and the French battling to prove their historically unwavering adoration of the Anglo-American people and culture. So if you're worried about being judged or disliked, push that aside. You will have a wonderful and safe visit to Paris and the rest of France.

Even so, a rapid wave of crass commercialism, indicative of corporate globalization everywhere, has not spared the French capital, and the frenzy of contemporary life encroaches on the city's deep, indigenous charm. The impatience of a people consumed by a deeply reserved public self often translates wrongly as rudeness. The sense of independence and national pride, characteristic of the French, is often perceived as arrogance or intolerance. Most often you'll think you're witnessing cool indifference, but in reality there is lots going on beneath that disinterested glare that Parisians often show tourists. The insistence on local ways being combined with a love of form and an obsession with procedure can be particularly difficult for Anglo-Saxons to comprehend. In the street or at the dinner table, in a taxi or at your hotel, you may find that the way things are done in Paris is disorienting or, worse, defies logic. Yes, but it's your logic, not theirs. You might not understand why you can't have lunch at 3 p.m. or dinner at 6 p.m. You'll question why that Right Bank gift shop won't give you a refund, and you'll want to pull your hair out wondering why the bank won't open another teller when there are 13 people waiting in line to change money. In the larger realm of a Paris visit, these are small things that can be elegantly and calmly avoided by simply knowing in advance and planning around the cultural sticking points. This "knowing"—the key to *The Unofficial Guide to Paris*—will be your ticket to understanding. And let's face it, along with having accurate expectations, understanding your destination is the magic formula for a satisfying visit anywhere. Making you feel at home from the moment you set foot on French soil, while packing your mental luggage with a treasure chest of otherwise unavailable tips, inside information, and smart little tricks of the Paris trade, has been both our raison d'être and pleasure. So *bienvenue à Paris* (welcome to Paris) and *on y va*—let's get going. We have lots to see and do.

ABOUT *this* GUIDE

WHY UNOFFICIAL?

WELCOME TO *The Unofficial Guide to Paris*. The structure and organization of this guide has been specifically conceived for Paris while maintaining the orientation of the other *Unofficial Guides*. We have made a special effort to turn over every stone in your path, to open doors, to anticipate the questions and obstacles that foreign travel to Paris may present. As always, this guide sets out to represent your interests and save you time, money, and effort so that in the three, five, or seven days you have in Paris, you won't waste half of your time just figuring out how things work. Above all, we have attempted to bring you close to the best and most authentic aspects of a mythic place. Paris is not New York or Tokyo, and we want you to find the most Parisian parts of Paris.

Much of the information in this guide is not found elsewhere. When possible we've included details tailored to your needs and expectations. We've thought in advance about what Paris is like if you're traveling with children, if you're on a limited budget, if you're a single woman, if you're gay, if your French is dreadful. . . . The inside track of experiencing Paris is the product of more than 25 years of hands-on, on-site research. Having said that, the needs of international travelers change and vary, as do the conditions of hotels, the quality of restaurants, and the prices of everything. With humility and curiosity we invite you to tell us what you have found most helpful, what we might want to include in subsequent editions, and where our recommendations need to be reexamined. Thank you, or *merci* (mair-**see**).

ABOUT *UNOFFICIAL GUIDES*

READERS CARE ABOUT AUTHORS' OPINIONS. The authors, after all, are supposed to know what they are talking about. This, coupled with the fact that the traveler wants quick answers (as opposed to endless alternatives), dictates that authors should be explicit, prescriptive, and, above all, direct. The authors of the *Unofficial Guides* try to do just that. They spell out alternatives and recommend specific courses of action. They simplify complicated destinations and attractions and allow the traveler to feel in control in the most unfamiliar environments. The objective of the *Unofficial Guide* authors is not to give the most information or all of the information, but to offer the most accessible, useful information. Of course, in a city like Paris there are many hotels, restaurants, and attractions that are so closely woven into the fabric of the city that to omit them from our guide because we can't recommend them would be a disservice to our readers. We have included all the famous haunts, giving our opinion and experience of them, in the hope that you will approach (or avoid) these institutions armed with the necessary intelligence.

An *Unofficial Guide* is a critical reference work; it focuses on a travel destination that appears to be especially complex. Our authors and research team are completely independent from the attractions, restaurants, and hotels we describe. *The Unofficial Guide to Paris* is designed for individuals and families traveling for the fun of it and for those on business, and will be especially helpful to those hopping across the pond for the first time. The guide is directed at value-conscious, consumer-oriented adults who seek a cost-effective, though not spartan, travel style.

Special Features

- Handy pronunciation key for essential French words.
- Friendly introductions to key Paris neighborhoods.
- "Best of" listings giving our well-qualified opinions on everything from croissants to trips on the Seine.
- Listings that are keyed to your interests so you can pick and choose.
- Advice to sightseers on how to avoid the worst crowds; advice to business travelers on how to avoid traffic and excessive costs.
- Recommendations for lesser-known sights that are off the well-beaten tourist path but no less worthwhile.
- A district (arrondissement) system and maps to make it easy to find places you want to go and avoid places you don't.
- A hotel section that helps you narrow down your choices quickly, according to your needs and preferences.
- Shorter listings that include only those restaurants, clubs, and hotels we think are worth considering.
- A district section that tells you what you can do in a particular area, with "rain dates" to cover the need to make a quick change in plans.
- Insider advice on best times of day (or night) to go places.
- A table of contents and detailed index to help you find things fast.

HOW THIS GUIDE WAS RESEARCHED AND WRITTEN

IN PREPARING THIS WORK, we've taken little for granted. We try to regain the innocence of a first-time visitor and anticipate every area of surprise, confusion, and curiosity. Each hotel, restaurant, shop, and attraction has been visited by trained observers who conducted detailed evaluations and rated each according to formal criteria. We've conducted hundreds of informal interviews with tourists of all ages and backgrounds to determine what they enjoyed most and least during their Paris visit.

While our observers are independent and impartial, they are "ordinary" travelers. Like you, they visited Paris as tourists or business travelers, noting their satisfaction or dissatisfaction.

The primary difference between the average tourist and the trained evaluator is the evaluator's skills in organization, preparation, and observation. The trained evaluator is responsible for much more than simply observing and cataloging. Observer teams use detailed checklists to analyze hotel rooms, restaurants, nightclubs, and attractions. Finally, evaluator ratings and observations are integrated with tourist reactions and the opinions of patrons for a comprehensive profile of each feature and service.

In compiling this guide, we recognize that a tourist's age, background, and interests will strongly influence his or her taste in Paris's wide array of attractions and will account for a preference for one sight or museum over another. Our sole objective is to provide the reader with sufficient description, critical evaluation, and pertinent data to make knowledgeable decisions according to individual tastes.

LETTERS, COMMENTS, AND QUESTIONS FROM READERS

WE EXPECT TO LEARN FROM BOTH OUR MISTAKES and the input of our readers, and to improve with each new book and edition. Many of those who use the *Unofficial Guide* write to us asking questions, making comments, or sharing their own discoveries or lessons learned on their trips. We appreciate all such input, both positive and critical, and encourage our readers to continue writing. Readers' comments and observations will frequently be incorporated into revised editions of the *Unofficial Guide* and will contribute immeasurably to its improvement.

How to Write the Author

David Applefield
The Unofficial Guide to Paris
P.O. Box 43673
Birmingham, AL 35243
unofficialguides@menasharidge.com

When you write, be sure to put your return address on both your letter and the envelope; sometimes envelopes and letters get separated. And remember, our work takes us out of the office for long periods of time, so forgive us if our response is delayed.

Reader Survey

At the back of the guide you will find a short questionnaire, which you can use to express opinions about your Paris visit. Clip the questionnaire along the dotted lines and mail it to the address on the preceding page.

HOW *This* GUIDE *Is* ORGANIZED:
By Subject and Geographic Districts (Arrondissements)

WE HAVE ORGANIZED THIS GUIDE in the order in which you will need it. Thus, Part One, **Understanding Paris,** gives a quick tutorial on the French language, explains how numbers and prices are handled, and gives a brief history of the city. Part Two provides an in-depth discussion for **Planning Your Visit**—essentially, all you can do before leaving home. Part Three covers in detail your first major decision: which of the **Accommodations** to stay in. Part Four, **Arriving, Getting Oriented, and Departing,** walks you through your first and last days, two of the most stressful travel days of any trip. Part Four also investigates all your special needs for the journey—doctors, babysitters, facilities for the disabled, telephone and e-mail services, and so on. The next section, Part Five, is your guide to **Getting Around** the city and its environs, whereas in Part Six, **Sightseeing, Tours, and Attractions,** we'll show you how to plan your days and offer detailed profiles of Paris's most important attractions. Of course, you must eat, so Part Seven, **Dining and Restaurants,** takes you on a gourmet tour of some of the best restaurant choices. Since shopping is the second-most favorite activity of many travelers, Part Eight, **Shopping,** takes you by the arm into the best boutiques and suggests what gifts your friends back home will love. Part Nine, **Exercise and Recreation,** tells you how to stay in shape and relax. Lastly, Part Ten anticipates your evening activities and outlines the major cultural and entertainment options and key nightlife under the heading **Entertainment and Nightlife.**

Paris has the built-in convenience of being organized into 20 districts, called *arrondissements* (ahron-dees-**mohn**), each with its own mayor and municipal council. Every Paris address indicates the arrondissement in which the establishment is found, so we've preserved these geographic borders as a way of organizing this guide. However, note that Paris also has several neighborhoods and regions dating back hundreds of years in some cases, and these may overlap several arrondissements. Detailed explanations of both the neighborhoods and the arrondissement system follow below. If you can keep the organization of arrondissements in mind while remembering the general locations of the neighborhoods, you'll have no problem navigating the City of Light. Voilà! And bon voyage!

HOTELS

THERE ARE HUNDREDS OF DECENT HOTELS IN PARIS, but the criteria you use to choose a hotel in Paris is different than North American criteria. Size of hotel, size of room, star ratings, location, price, aesthetics, convenience to public transportation, organization of the bathroom (does the room have a shower?), breakfast, service, credit cards, view, and more all need to figure into your decision. We've explained most of the nuances so you may proceed with confidence.

ATTRACTIONS (MUSEUMS, MONUMENTS, PARKS, CHURCHES, LANDMARKS)

HERE, INSTEAD OF LONG AND DRAWN-OUT HISTORIES, you'll find concise overviews highlighting the key things to see and the best ways to see them. Our fundamental goal is for you to be able to figure out what is there to see and then decide if and when you'll be adding it to your itinerary. Additionally, if you pass by a huge and impressive building or monument, we want to make sure you'll be able to find a handy description of it in this guide.

RESTAURANTS (BISTROS, BRASSERIES, CAFÉS)

NOT ONLY DO WE PROVIDE A BOUQUET of choice restaurants in Paris—cuisine is such an integral part of experiencing Paris that we've also covered the entire culture of food and drink in great detail. Since you will probably eat a dozen or more restaurant meals during your stay, and since not even you can predict what you might be in the mood for on Saturday night, you can browse through our detailed profiles of some of the best restaurants and best-value places to eat in the city. There's an abundance of restaurants, so knowledge is the key to eating well at fair prices.

ENTERTAINMENT AND NIGHTLIFE (CLUBS, BARS, CABARETS)

THE PARIS NIGHTLIFE SCENE IS VIBRANT, VARIED, and constantly rejuvenating itself. With only a limited number of evenings, it's important to select well what you do and where you go after dinner. Nighttime cultural events have been included here in the bar-and-club scene. Other cultural events are found in Part Six, Sightseeing, Tours, and Attractions. Since one usually selects clubs or nightspots, like restaurants, spontaneously after arriving in Paris, we believe detailed descriptions are warranted and helpful. Our selections include the famous and celebrated as well as the latest and trendy, for both the young and immortal, and the less-than-young and mortal.

NEIGHBORHOODS AND ARRONDISSEMENTS

ONCE YOU'VE DECIDED WHERE YOU'RE GOING, getting there becomes the issue. To help you do that, we have presented Paris in terms of its historic neighborhoods (and which arrondissements they encompass), which we have briefly described here to give you a quick idea of what they're about.

Fortunately, Paris is a very compact city, and you'll find that it's easy to walk from the Marais to Châtelet and from the Latin Quarter or Saint-Germain-des-Prés to Montparnasse. We've provided an overview of Paris's main sections or areas worth exploring, and they often cross over into more than one arrondissement.

Latin Quarter—5th arrondissement
(Central Paris, Left Bank, from the Seine to Port Royal, Boulevard Saint-Michel to Jardin des Plantes)

This is Paris's spiritual center. The fountain at Saint-Michel is Paris's best-known meeting spot. The area is replete with bookstores, students, cafés, boutiques, churches, and small hotels. Intellectual life finds its roots here, with the Sorbonne at the symbolic center. The narrow pedestrian streets are especially lively at night, replete now with inexpensive Greek and North African restaurants. The Luxembourg Gardens require at least an hour of your leisure time. If you're not staying in this area, plan to spend some time walking around both during the day and in the evening.

The Marais—3rd arrondissement
(Central Paris, Right Bank, from the Seine at Hôtel de Ville to République, the Bastille to rue Beaubourg)

Probably Paris's most quaint and charming area, the Marais is steeped in character and history. *Marais* means lowland or swamp, and this is in keeping with the area, which is flat and extends from the Seine on the Right Bank. Home of the traditional Jewish community, the Marais has also emerged as the seat of gay Paris. Filled with wonderful small streets with lovely facades and doorways, the area hosts some of Paris's best museums, hotels, and shops. Place de Vosges cannot be missed.

Châtelet–Les Halles—1st and 2nd arrondissements
(Central Paris, Right Bank, from Place du Châtelet to Réamur-Sébastopol, between the Louvre and Hôtel de Ville)

The traditional market area for the city, today Châtelet–Les Halles represents the commercial core of Paris. Busy and loud, this area hosts the

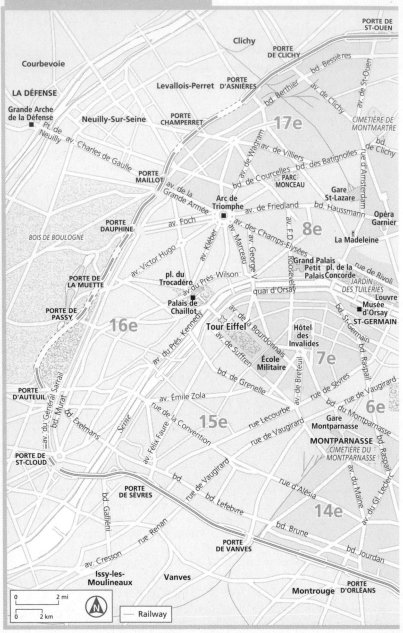

Paris Arrondissements

PORTE DE
ST-OUEN

Courbevoie

Clichy

PORTE
DE CLICHY

bd. Bessières

LA DÉFENSE

Levallois-Perret

PORTE
D'ASNIÈRES

bd. Berthier

av. de Clichy

CIMETIÈRE DE
MONTMARTRE

Grande Arche
de la Défense

Neuilly-Sur-Seine

PORTE
CHAMPERRET

17e

av. de S-O-uen

bd.
de Clichy

Pt. de
Neuilly

av. Charles de Gaulle

PORTE
MAILLOT

av. de la
Grande Armée

av. de Wagram

av. de Villiers

bd. de Courcelles

bd. des Batignolles

rue d'Amsterdam

PARC
MONCEAU

Gare
St-Lazare

Opéra
Garnier

Arc de
Triomphe

av. de Friedland

bd. Haussmann

La Madeleine

PORTE
DAUPHINE

av. Foch

av. des Champs-Élysées

8e

BOIS DE BOULOGNE

av. Victor Hugo

av. Kléber

av. Marceau

av. George V

av. F.D. Roosevelt

Grand Palais
Petit pl. de la
Palais Concorde

rue de Rivoli

PORTE DE
LA MUETTE

pl. du
Trocadéro

av. du Prés. Wilson

quai d'Orsay

JARDIN
DES TUILERIES

Louvre
Musée
d'Orsay
ST-GERMAIN

PORTE DE
PASSY

Palais de
Chaillot

Tour Eiffel

av. de la Bourdonnais

Hôtel
des
Invalides

bd. St-Germain

bd. Raspail

16e

av. du Prés. Kennedy

av. de Suffren

École
Militaire

7e

PORTE
D'AUTEUIL

av. du Général Sarrail

bd. Murat

bd. Exelmans

Seine

av. Émile Zola

rue de la Convention

bd. de Grenelle

av. de Breteuil

rue de Sèvres

bd. du Montparnasse

rue de Vaugirard

6e

PORTE DE
ST-CLOUD

av. Félix Faure

15e

rue Lecourbe

rue de Vaugirard

Gare
Montparnasse

bd. Raspail

MONTPARNASSE

CIMETIÈRE DU
MONTPARNASSE

bd. Galliéni

PORTE
DE SÈVRES

rue de Vaugirard

bd. Lefebvre

rue d'Alésia

av. du Maine

av. du Gl. Leclerc

14e

rue Renan

bd. Brune

bd. Jourdan

av. Cresson

PORTE
DE VANVES

Issy-les-
Moulineaux

Vanves

Montrouge

PORTE
D'ORLÉANS

0 _____ 2 mi
0 _____ 2 km

N

— Railway

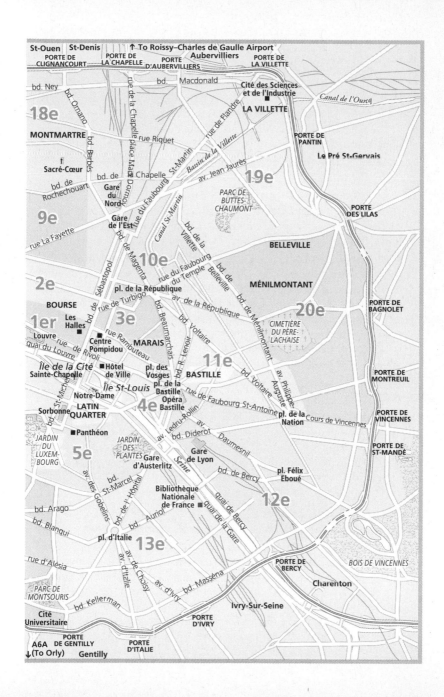

Pompidou Center, Hôtel de Ville, and the Halles shopping mall. Filled with cafés, shops, movie houses, restaurants, galleries, and hotels, this is also the transportation hub for subway and RER transfers.

Île Saint Louis, Île de la Cité—*1st and 4th arrondissements* (Central Paris, the Two Islands, Notre-Dame and Environs)

Paris's two islands in the center of the city afford visitors a taste of medieval Paris, mixed with both 17th-century mansions and contemporary sophistication. Visits to Notre-Dame and Sainte-Chapelle are musts. Ice cream at Berthillon on the Île Saint Louis shouldn't be overlooked.

Saint-Germain-des-Prés—*6th arrondissement* (Central Paris, Left Bank, Boulevard Saint-Germain-des-Prés, between Saint-Michel and Musée d'Orsay, from the Seine to Jardin du Luxembourg and Sèvres-Babylone)

Chic shopping meets the best of Parisian literary and artistic elements. The famous cafés Les Deux Magots and La Hune nourished many of the last century's greatest writers and thinkers, such as Jean-Paul Sartre and Simone de Beauvoir. Explore the back streets between Boulevard Saint-Germain and the Seine for a sampling of avant-garde galleries and bookstores. La Palette is the area's best watering hole for the culturally inclined. There are scores of excellent and charming hotels and restaurants here, but be prepared to pay for quality and style.

Bastille/République—*11th arrondissement* (Place de la Bastille, Gare de Lyon, Nation, République, Oberkampf)

Centered around the new Bastille Opéra, this once-poor and bohemian area is now the pulse of Paris nightlife. The rue de Lappe and rue de la Roquette reflect the tone and tempo of the city's music and bar scene. Artists and craftspeople have their workshops in the many alleys and courtyards of the area. Oberkampf is the latest area to explode with hopping nightlife.

Champs-Élysées/Concorde—*1st and 8th arrondissements* (Louvre to the Arc de Triomphe, Place de la Concorde, Madeleine, Place Vendôme)

Much of Paris's reputation comes from the aristocratic splendor and chic grandeur of the world's most famous avenue. It's worth a stroll, but not too much more. The area is expensive and somewhat ruined by the arrival of international clothing and fast-food chains. The walk between the Arc de Triomphe at Étoile and Place de la Concorde, where Marie-Antoinette lost her head, will be memorable, day or night. The Louvre and the Tuileries Gardens, included in this area, are essential stops for all Paris visitors.

Invalides/Eiffel Tower—*7th arrondissement*
(Right Bank from Musée d'Orsay to Eiffel Tower, Trocadéro on the Left Bank, Assemblée Nationale to Duroc)

Characterized by officialdom, government ministries, and upper-class respectability, this area nonetheless houses the world's most famous landmark, the Eiffel Tower. Les Invalides is Napoléon's resting place, and the Orsay Museum is the place to visit the Impressionists and the best examples of Art Deco. The area is quiet at night and sometimes a bit too sedate for visitors wishing for the excitement of street life.

Montparnasse—*14th arrondissement* (Left Bank between Denfert-Rochereau and Jardin du Luxembourg and Port-Royal)

Famous for its large and brassy brasseries—La Coupole, Le Dôme, Le Sélect, La Closerie des Lilas—Montparnasse provided shelter for artists, writers, and bohemians after the First World War. Although upscale and pricey today, these cafés continue to attract the cultural crowd and are worth visiting. The area is filled with small hotels, regional restaurants (Breton crêpes shops), and stores. Go up the Tour Montparnasse, Paris's only skyscraper. The view is breathtaking. Also visit Sartre, Beauvoir, and Beckett in the Montparnasse Cemetery.

Grands Boulevards—*10th arrondissement*
(Right Bank between Strasbourg-Saint-Denis and Miromesnil, Opéra, la Bourse, and Covered Arcades)

Once the showcase of Haussmann's 19th-century renovated Paris, today the area is alive with a mixture of financial institutions, old theaters, seedy back streets, wonderful arcades with tea salons and antiques, and large immigrant communities. Behind the Opéra Garnier you'll find Paris's leading department stores, Les Galeries Lafayette and Le Printemps.

Montmartre—*18th arrondissement*
(between Grands Boulevards and Sacré Cœur, Pigalle, Clichy)

At the northern edge (or top) of the city lies Montmartre. Once a village unto itself, today it attracts both Parisians and visitors for its charming little streets around the striking Sacré Cœur Basilica, its tiny restaurants, and art-lined Place du Tertre. Down below, you'll find the Moulin Rouge and other venues of cabaret and burlesque. Pigalle is dotted with porn shops and sex shows. Place Blanche is celebrated for its prostitutes and transvestites. It's safe to walk around day or night, but hang on to your purses and wallets. In the summer, the area is overrun with busloads of tourists from Germany, England, and Holland.

Outer Arrondissements

Here we have grouped other hotels, restaurants, attractions, and nightlife worth visiting that fall outside the inner arrondissements. Since this covers a large area that even extends outside Paris at times, note that there is no map of this region.

THE ARRONDISSEMENTS

TO FIND A PARIS ADDRESS, YOU NEED TO KNOW that the city of Paris is organized into 20 districts called arrondissements. Each arrondissement is its own political entity, with a mayor and district government. The arrondissement is built into every Paris address, much like American ZIP codes. Every Paris postal code address begins with 75, the number of the state or department, followed by the arrondissement number. So it's easy to know the general area in which a hotel or restaurant is located by simply paying attention to the postal code. For example, 75001 indicates the 1st arrondissement of Paris, and 75020 is the 20th arrondissement of Paris. Easy!

unofficial **TIP**
The arrondissements are organized starting in the middle of the city and circling like a whirlpool clockwise. With a simple map, you'll be able to situate yourself easily.

A quick tip on French addresses: Street numbers running north–south begin at the Seine and increase as they move away from it. Odd and even numbers on a street do not always fall opposite or even very near each other. If you see a street address with the letters *bis* or *ter* after the number, the address is located next to that number or before the next number. Finally, the French are accustomed to adding a comma after the number in the street address. Example: 23, rue de Rivoli.

Okay, so Paris has arrondissements, but how are they different? Well, it's hard to characterize the arrondissements in simple terms, and it's especially dangerous to overgeneralize about what you'll find in which. There are extremely charming spots in almost every area of Paris, and every arrondissement enjoys subway (Métro) access. Unlike other large cities, Paris is very dense and the distances are not overwhelming. The distance between subway stops in Paris represents a five- to ten-minute walk. The scale of Paris permits active visitors to cross most of the city by foot.

Left Bank/Right Bank

You may have heard of Paris's Left Bank (*Rive Gauche,* reeve **gowsh**) and Right Bank (*Rive Droite,* reeve **dwaht**), but you haven't a clue as to the difference between them or which is a better address. Let's start here. In short, the Seine River cuts Paris in half, along an east–west axis. The southern side of the river is the Left Bank (*Rive Gauche*), whereas the northern side is the Right Bank (*Rive Droite*). Although traditionally the Left Bank was more bohemian and proletarian—housing the famous Latin Quarter (*Quartier Latin,* car-**tee-yay** lah-**tahn**) area, so called because of its student population who studied Latin—today it's impossible to generalize or identify major differences. The Left Bank today can be as upscale as the traditionally more bourgeois Right Bank. You may decide to stay on the Left Bank, but there are equally attractive offerings on the Right Bank. So although some people prefer one over the other, there are great locations to be found on both sides of the river.

On BEING a "TOURIST"

ALTHOUGH WE'VE TRIED TO AVOID referring to our readers as "tourists," we do use the term throughout the book. There is no shame in being a tourist. A tourist is simply a person who travels for pleasure, and we assume that's what you are. In fact, the best way to visit Paris is as a tourist. The negative images the word conjures come from the early days of group travel, when Europe became accessible to culturally insensitive mobs. Hence, the term "ugly tourist." Today, you won't be confused with one of them, and we're bringing the word back into fashion.

UNDERSTANDING *LES BISES*

FOR SOME UNEXPLAINED REASON the French are world-renowned for their kiss, the open-mouthed version that humans everywhere find so pleasurable. Parisians find the anglicized nomenclature very curious, though, in that any other kind of kiss, well, just ain't a kiss. *Les bises* (lay **beez**), however, that funny but tender ritual of planting a succession of tiny pecks on the right and then left cheek of the man or woman you are greeting, is tantamount for Parisians to the Anglo-Saxon handshake or backslap. Getting this banal but endearing form of hello and goodbye down pat isn't quite as easy as it looks. Each Parisian has his or her habit, style, and number, ranging between two and four. Most true Parisians practice the even number two and start on the recipient's right cheek, not too close to the mouth. Remember, *les bises* are not kisses; these greeting-pecks signify only a polite affection that's reserved for friends, close acquaintances, familiar colleagues, family, and extended family. Parisians who have migrated from the south of France or other provinces may tend to use the more loquacious and elaborate succession of three or four kisses. This varies according to culture, region, or individual preference and personality, and it'll take you plenty of time to coordinate the habit of, let's say, your two left-right combo, with your good neighbor's left-right-left trilogy. Come into a room with 11 cousins and three sets of close friends and their flock of kids, and be prepared to buckle down for a good ten minutes of facial gymnastics. Just do it, or you'll never get to the apéritifs. As you'll quickly see, a Parisian instantly

Fast Facts about France and Paris

Capital of France Paris. The country is a republic, divided into 22 regions of which the Île de France is one with Paris at its center. Within these 22 regions there are 96 states or *départements*.

Population of France 64,300,000.

Population of Paris 2.2 million in Paris, almost 12 million in the greater Paris area (Île de France).

French National Independence Day 14 July, dating back to 1789 when the Bastille was stormed and independence was won from the monarchy.

Voting Age 18. Driving age: 18. Drinking age: 18 (16 for beer and wine).

Chief of State President, elected by popular vote for a five-year term.

Religion 64% Roman Catholic, 2% Protestant, 0.6% Jewish, 3% Muslim, 27% nonaffiliated.

Store Hours Generally 9 a.m. to 7 p.m., with some closing during the lunch hours.

Banking Hours Although these vary from bank to bank, hours are most often 9 a.m. to 4 p.m. or 5 p.m., Monday through Friday. Some branches are closed from noon or 12:30 p.m. to 1:30 p.m. or 2 p.m., and others are open on Saturday or Saturday morning.

Time Paris is on Greenwich Mean Time (GMT) + 1. So 6 p.m. in Paris is noon in New York and 9 a.m. in Los Angeles. (Caution: Clocks are not pushed ahead and set back on the same days as in North America, so each year there are a few weeks in which Paris time is either 5 or 7 hours ahead of the U.S. east coast.)

Electric Current 220 W.

Official Language French. (English is spoken in large hotels, many businesses, and in the tourist trade. There are more than 100,000 permanent Anglo-American residents in Paris.)

Currency The euro, which replaced the French franc in January 2002.

Geographic Location 48°58' N latitude, 2°27' E longitude.

Size of Country Approximately the size of Texas.

learns that his wife's friend Camille from Avignon always plants three quick ones, while her husband Jean-Claude, who rarely leaves his native 16th arrondissement, never exceeds two rather indifferent cheek-graces while steering his lips up and away à la Chirac like any good bourgeois. Form, as you know, is everything in Paris, and so much of French form—language, gestures, attitudes, responses, even politics—begins poutfully with the lips. Don't forget, there is nothing ambiguous about *les bises,* and certainly nothing sexual about the

PUBLIC HOLIDAYS

January 1 New Year's Day (*Jour de l'An*)

Easter (*Pâques*), Easter Monday (*Lundi de Pâques*)

May 1 Labor Day (May Day) (*Fête du Travail*)

May 8 VE Day (Victory in Europe)

Ascension Day (*Ascension*) sixth Thursday after Easter

Pentecost (*Pentecôte*)

Whit Monday second Monday after Ascension (*Lundi de Pentecôte*)

July 14 Bastille Day (*Fête Nationale*)

August 15 Assumption (*Assomption*)

November 1 All Saints' Day (*Toussaint*)

November 11 Remembrance Day (Armistice 1918)

December 25 Christmas Day (*Noël*)

practice, so don't assume someone has a crush on you, wants to take you to bed, is giving you a gay message, or is trying to get you excited with his or her sweet *eau de cologne* by simply gracing your cheeks with *les bises*. You'll know when that happens. What's interesting to note here is that the French are simply used to and comfortable with close personal contact. They are not bothered by human proximity or touching. They don't require the same distance Anglo-Americans insist upon when talking. So take it from someone who has dished out at least 21,000 pairs of *bises* and has shaken hands 390,000 times (often with the exact same Parisians) in 20-odd years in the French capital—practice *les bises* before arriving. Toss your head, convey confidence, steer your lips noiselessly in the direction of the ears, and for heaven's sake, keep it dry!

A final word to the wise: when in doubt, keep shaking hands. Don't start shelling out these friendly doses of "non-kisses" until you get the green-light feeling from the initiating Parisian acquaintance. Otherwise you risk being perceived as too familiar too quick, which can be a real turnoff in Paris. When the *bises* time is right, however, be consistent and repeat the ritual every time you come and go; otherwise, you'll offend. And that, *mes amis,* is a whole other lesson.

COMMAS VERSUS DECIMAL POINTS

IN THIS GUIDEBOOK, numbers are expressed in the fashion familiar to you, where one hundred dollars and fifty cents is written $100.50, and so on. However, in writing numbers and prices, the French use commas where you use decimal points. So, in French, $100.50 would be written $100,50. The euro maintains this style. So be careful with numbers, especially when it's time to pay.

PART ONE

UNDERSTANDING PARIS

A **BRIEF HISTORY** *of* **PARIS**

ONE OF THE GREAT ADVANTAGES OF VISITING PARIS is the close-ness to history that the experience offers. Everywhere you look you're reminded of what transpired here in an earlier epoch, from the Romans and the Gauls through the Prussians and the Germans, the American liberators in the 1940s all the way to Lance Armstrong's seventh Tour de France win in 2005. As a basic crutch for orienting yourself to the city and its traditions, here is an overview of Paris's colorful history. According to the travel writer Robert Cole, the Parisian view of its own history is the reverse of "all roads lead to Rome." Everything great in France began in Paris and spread outward.

LES PARISII **AND THE ROMANS**

THE FIRST SETTLERS ON THE LARGEST ISLAND in the Seine (now Île de la Cité) were the Parisii, a community of Celtic fishermen and boat people governed by Druidic religious practices, who arrived dur-ing the third century BC. In the year 52 BC, the Romans arrived and began constructing the first buildings on the Left Bank of the river up the hill that consists of today's Montagne Sainte-Geneviève, in the 5th arrondissement. Here, as well, were the ruins of the Cluny Baths and the Arènes de Lutèce, where Julien was proclaimed emperor in AD 360. The Romans named their settlement Lutetia Parisiorum, which lent itself to the legend that the city was founded by Helen of Troy's lover, Paris. After refusing to send delegates to Julius Caesar's Assembly of Gaul, the Celts revolted against Roman domination and set fire to the city and bridges, but they were ultimately crushed by Caesar's legion, which camped at the site of today's Louvre. Lutetia spread to the Left Bank, which took on the name the Latin Quarter.

BARBARIAN INVASIONS

THREATENED BY ATTILA THE HUN (and subsequently saved by the visionary Christian Geneviève, who was made patroness of the city) and the warring Francs, the town began to take on wings as the Frank King Clovis declared it his capital and his official residence in 508. It is believed that the site of present-day Paris was a stopping-off point between Marseilles and Britain along an ancient trading route. Abbeys and chapels flourished on both the Right Bank and the Left, as witnessed by Saint Germain L'Auxerrois and Saint-Germain-des-Prés, and the city took on a unique religious importance. The western Frank kingdom of Neustria was referred to by the end of the ninth century as Francia, which became France. Over time, the residents of Francia looked to the governors of this kingdom for political direction. Hugh Capet emerged as ostensibly the first king of Francia and the founding monarch to rule France.

CHARLEMAGNE

OVER THE NEXT FOUR CENTURIES, Paris was occupied and deserted by the Merovingians and by Charlemagne and raided by the Normans. It wasn't until near the end of the first millennium, under the Capetian dynasty, that Paris gained importance as a royal capital and urban economic center. Under the reign of Philippe-Auguste, a wall was erected around the city. The principal streets were paved in cobblestone (*pavé* in French), and the first bridges joining the Right and Left banks were built. Notre-Dame was erected on Île de la Cité in 1163, and the university sector on the Left Bank was conceived in 1215, with the Université de Paris becoming the primary theological and philosophical center in medieval Christianity. Here was where Bonaventure, Thomas Aquinas, and others taught. The Palais Royal functioned as the political core of the capital. Flourishing because of its floating merchants (represented on Paris's coat of arms) and a vibrant silver market, Paris had grown to more than 100,000 inhabitants by the 13th century, becoming the largest city in the western Christian world.

RENAISSANCE AND THE REFORMATION

INSURRECTIONS FOLLOWED, and the 1300s were marred by massacres and invasions by regional tribes. Joan of Arc besieged the city in 1429 while Paris was under the rule of the English, and in 1438 the legitimate monarch Charles VII took control.

It wasn't until François I, known as a Renaissance prince and patron of the arts, that Paris became the official residence of the king. Renaissance structures replaced medieval ones, and Paris witnessed the construction of its Hôtel de Ville, the Tuileries, and the Pont Neuf, Paris's first stone bridge.

The 1500s were bloodied by religious wars (the Huguenots' Protestant

Reformation) and a devastating famine (1589), forcing King Henri III, who was later assassinated, to flee. Henri of Navarre proclaimed himself Henri IV (1589–1610) and assumed the reins of the city; under Henri IV, major architectural additions—the Place de Vosges, place Dauphine, l'Horloge—were commissioned. Under Louis XIII the city experienced the construction of new areas—the Marais, the Bastille, and Saint Honoré—walled in along a periphery that vaguely followed today's Grands Boulevards. The Île Saint Louis was refurbished, and new communities sprung up on the Left Bank, especially near the Luxembourg Gardens, which were built by Marie de' Medici.

LOUIS XIII AND LOUIS XIV

PARIS'S IMPORTANCE AS A CULTURAL CENTER GREW as the Royal Imprimerie was built and the Académie Française was established. The powerful Cardinal Richelieu left his administrative mark on the style and form of government under Louis XIII (he's buried in the chapel of the Sorbonne). Nonetheless, Louis XIV (the Sun King), known for his maxim "The State Is Me," preferred his château in Versailles. But to glorify the monarchy, under the auspices of the famed Colbert, great additions were made to Paris: the colonnade of the Louvre, Les Invalides, the arches at the Portes Saint Denis and Saint Martin, the Place Vendôme, and many other points of great architectural beauty.

The arts and music flourished in the city, and the logical next step in urban development was the creation of the café, a place for intellectuals, writers, and artists to meet. The 18th century saw the opening of the first restaurants, le Procope and la Régence, and the first theaters, l'Odéon and the Comédie Française. Business, banking, and commerce gained an increasingly important foothold, and property prices rose steadily. Interest and development of the law as a discipline mounted. A group of thinkers called the Encyclopédistes met and gained influence, contending that all knowledge was finite and could be catalogued and distributed. The city expanded to the west and north, and by the time of the French Revolution in 1789, the population had risen to 650,000 within the city walls.

THE FRENCH REVOLUTION

KING LOUIS XVI AND HIS FAMOUS WIFE, the Austrian-born Marie Antoinette (of "Let them eat cake" fame), ascended the throne in 1774. At first popular, the couple made rather damning public-relations errors, and those, combined with harsh conditions, food shortages, and inept governing, sparked public revolts and riots. Inspired by the American Revolution and the ideological concept of the Universal Declaration of Human Rights, revolution broke out. Louis XVI and Marie Antoinette were guillotined at the Place de la Concorde, renamed the Place de la Révolution. *"Liberté, Egalité, Fraternité"* became the motto of the Republic.

The Bastille prison was stormed on July 14, 1789, the start of the

French Revolution. It's been the *Fête nationale* since. The First Republic dates from 1791 to 1799 and was followed by the reign of Napoléon Bonaparte, under a regime called the Consulat (echoing the Romans). The monarchy returned to power from 1815 to 1848 with the Bourbons. From 1848 until 1852 France entered its Second Republic, with Louis-Napoléon Bonaparte (the nephew) at the helm. The next 20 years are called the Second Empire. Then in 1871 the French installed the Third Republic and ended the monarchy for good.

NAPOLÉON I (NAPOLÉON BONAPARTE)

NAPOLÉON'S VISION WAS TO MAKE PARIS the capital of Europe, and he proceeded to build the Arc de Triomphe and the column at Place de la Vendôme and opened the Ourcq canal, bringing drinking water into the city. The markets, public high schools (*lycées*), and slaughterhouses were developed. The Madeleine and the Pantheon were built, and the sewer system was installed. Napoléon's reign marked the First Empire. This popular general as emperor profoundly modified the legal code and administrative structure of France. After an eventful rise and fall from power, Napoléon regained power in 1815 only to be defeated the same year at the Battle of Waterloo. He abdicated and was sent by the British to the island of Saint-Hélène, where he died in 1821. His son, Napoléon II, succeeded him.

It was the Second Empire, under Napoléon III (Louis-Napoléon Bonaparte, the nephew of Napoléon I), that gave Paris its new look, with the creation of a centralized administration and economic, social, and cultural services. The period was characterized by the writings of Honoré de Balzac and Victor Hugo, as well as Alexandre Dumas, Musset, and Nerval, and the music of Rossini, Chopin, Liszt, Wagner, and Offenbach.

HAUSSMANN AND THE NEW PARIS

IN 1860, PARIS WAS ORGANIZED INTO 20 arrondissements, each with its own mayor and city government. To address urban development and questions of security, the urban planning of the city was overhauled and remodeled by the celebrated architect Haussmann, who conceived the wide boulevards (rue de Rivoli, avenue de l'Opéra) and the wide sidewalks in the upper-class areas, driving the hordes of working-class poor into the outer districts, primarily to the east. Vast parks on both sides of the city were created, Bois de Vincennes (for the poor) and Bois de Boulogne (for the rich), and numerous new bridges and the Opéra Garnier were erected.

COMMUNE DE PARIS

RAPID GROWTH OF INDUSTRIAL ACTIVITY helped contribute to the city's mounting population—1.8 million inhabitants by the year 1871. An imbalance of the social and economic classes ensued, and in 1830 and 1848 popular uprisings ripped through the capital,

French Periods and Rulers

The Gallo-Roman Period 3rd century BC to AD 360

Gallo-Romans build the City of Lutetia in AD 1.

Early Middle Ages 450–885

Clovis makes Paris his capital. Charlemagne abandons Paris.

The Capetians 12th century–1300

Notre Dame and Sorbonne are built.

The Valois 1337–1590

Charles V builds the Bastille and a wall around Paris. Henri VI is crowned king of France.

The Bourbons 1590–1790

Henri IV converts to Catholicism. Île de St. Louis is developed. Treaty of Versailles is signed.

The French Revolution and First Empire 1789–1814

Louis XVI adopts red, white, and blue as the colors of France. Louis XVI is executed. Napoléon Bonaparte creates the police system. Napoléon is coronated at Notre-Dame.

The Restoration 1815–1848

Battle of Waterloo. The Fall of Louis-Philippe.

The Second Republic 1848–1870

World Exhibitions in 1855 and 1867. Town planning is undertaken by Baron Haussmann.

The Third Republic 1870–1940

Napoléon III goes into exile. The Paris Commune is suppressed. World Exhibition at the new Eiffel Tower. First Métro line opens in 1900. Paris is occupied by the Germans in June 1940. Liberation of Paris, August 25, 1944.

The Fourth Republic 1946–1958

De Gaulle forms provisional government. Second wave of expatriate writers and artists settles in Paris. France confronted with Algerian war for independence.

The Fifth Republic 1958–present

General strikes in 1968. Building of the Périphérique in 1973. Pompidou Center opens in 1977. Socialist President Mitterrand wins in 1982. Jacques Chirac elected in 1995. Nicolas Sarkozy elected in 2007.

culminating in the celebrated and dramatic revolution, between March and May 1871, of the Commune de Paris, immortalized by Hugo's *Les Misérables*. The Prussians then besieged the city.

THE THIRD REPUBLIC

THE THIRD REPUBLIC (1870–1940) followed this time of unrest, and prosperity and economic stability retook the city as marked by the

Exposition of 1889 and the construction of the Eiffel Tower. The construction of the Grand Palais and the Petit Palais followed, as did the building of the Alexandre III bridge. In 1886 Bartoldi's Statue of Liberty, a gift from the people of France to the people of the United States, was transported and installed in New York's harbor. In 1889 the Moulin Rouge opened in Clichy.

The Impressionist painters Renoir, Monet, Sisley, and Pissarro portrayed the day in attractive and gay colors and scenes, and by the beginning of the 20th century, Paris had established itself as the international capital of art, attracting painters from around the world to such noted centers of cultural life as Toulouse-Lautrec's Montmartre, the Bateau Lavoir, and La Ruche. Cabarets opened, and the Sacré Cœur Basilica was erected.

WORLD WAR I

THE BATTLE OF THE MARNE, in which, for lack of transport, Paris taxis carried troops to the battlefield, saved Paris in the early days of World War I. The peace treaty to end the war was signed in Paris. Following World War I, the city's geographic boundaries moved outward as the new building material, concrete, was introduced. With the Russian Revolution, Paris was inundated with eastern aristocratic expatriates, who contributed to the rapid growth of bistros (the Russian word for "rapid," suggesting fast food).

BETWEEN THE WARS

NEW CAFÉS OPENED ON THE BOULEVARDS, and the area of Montparnasse became a magnet for artistic and literary life, with disillusioned souls settling in Paris to write, paint, and drink. The city became the studio for André Breton, Jean Cocteau, Louis Aragon, Paul Éluard, Pablo Picasso, and the writers James Joyce, Ernest Hemingway, and Gertrude Stein, the core of expatriates who came to be known as the Lost Generation. Art Deco flourished, and the Paris Métro expanded.

WORLD WAR II

RIGHT-WING EXTREMISTS began gaining attention as fascism grew in Europe, generating the need for the creation of the workers party, the Front Populaire, in 1936.

In June 1940 the German *Wermacht* marched through the Arc de Triomphe and began the Occupation of Paris. France was partitioned, and Philippe Pétain led the Vichy Government. By July 1942 large numbers of French Jews had been gathered up and deported to Nazi concentration camps, and France saw a political and social rift between the Resistance fighters and those who collaborated with the Germans, a wound from which the country has never fully healed. In August 1944 General Charles de Gaulle and his army marched down the Champs-Élysées, marking the Liberation of Paris.

THE FOURTH REPUBLIC

THE FOURTH REPUBLIC WAS CREATED when Charles de Gaulle formed a provisional government. Paris stabilized and regained its position as the capital of fashion, style, and art. A second wave of expatriate writers and artists settled in the City of Light, repelled by the repressiveness and conservative mood in the postwar United States. In the late 1950s and 1960s, the Saint-Germain-des-Prés area of Paris became the headquarters of leading French intellectuals, led by the existentialist Jean-Paul Sartre and Simone de Beauvoir.

Handicapped by its colonial past, especially in North Africa, France was violently confronted with the Algerian war for independence. This conflict brutally divided the country and led to the collapse of the Fourth Republic and the popular demand that Charles de Gaulle restructure the government.

THE FIFTH REPUBLIC

CHARLES DE GAULLE WAS CALLED UPON to form the Fifth Republic of France. In 1965 de Gaulle pulled France out of NATO. In May 1968 general strikes and student protests against the outdated administration of President de Gaulle crippled the country; rioting broke out in the Latin Quarter, and the country came to a halt. De Gaulle was forced to step down and was succeeded by Georges Pompidou.

THE SOCIALIST YEARS

IN 1982 SOCIALIST LEADER FRANÇOIS MITTERRAND was elected president of France, beginning a 14-year period of Socialist domination of French politics. Selected French industries were nationalized. Mitterrand launched his great spending spree on major architectural legacies, as all French presidents do. I. M. Pei was commissioned to renovate the Louvre, and his controversial Pyramid was inaugurated for the bicentennial of the French Revolution in 1989; the new Bastille Opéra opened as well. The Grande Arche at La Defénse was inaugurated.

In 1994 the Eurotunnel connecting France and England began commercial service. France signed the Treaty of Maastricht, an important commitment toward the goal of a unified Europe. In 1996 Mitterrand died in office.

TURN OF THE MILLENNIUM

JACQUES CHIRAC, THE MAYOR OF PARIS at that time and the leader of the conservative Right Wing RPR Party (which became today's UMP—*Union pour un movement populaire*), was elected president of France after Mitterrand's death. The euro, the single currency of the European Union, was adopted as the official money of France and ten other European countries. In 1997 Chirac called for new elections and ended up in a coalition government, with Socialist Lionel Jospin as prime minister. In 1999 France participated in the NATO war on Yugoslavia while attempting to maintain a sense of political and economic independence from the United States and its model for globalization. The Right Wing was weakened by scandals and infighting, and the political future of French government seemed uncertain. Jospin ran for president in the 2001 presidential elections, was surprisingly beaten in the first round by the xenophobic right-winger Jean-Marie Le Pen, and retired from politics. President Chirac beat Le Pen in a landslide in the second round; he then went on to win the legislative elections and selected the relatively unknown Jean-Pierre Raffarin to form a solid right-central government. In 2002 the euro replaced French banknotes and coins.

Following the terrorist attacks of September 11, 2001, in the United States, Chirac and the French nation opposed President Bush's unilateral decision to invade Iraq, threatening to use France's veto in the United Nations if a second resolution came to a vote. This set off a rabid wave of anti-French media and public sentiment in the United States, which affected tourism in France. Most of the Franco-American tension had subsided by 2003.

We are now in a new period of Franco-American political cooperation, and the real tension comes in the form of economic trade wars between Brussels and Washington, D.C., with the Chinese commercial potential hovering above. The traumatic defeat of the May 2005 French referendum on the European Union Constitution fractured the political alliances of the country and perplexed both the Right and Left. President Chirac, who had put all his eggs in the OUI column, took a solid hit and was obliged to reshuffle his cabinet, replace Raffarin with Dominique de Villepin as prime minister, and elevate his youthful rival Nicolas Sarkozy to Minister of the Interior. Nicolas Sarkozy was elected president in 2007. He defeated Ségolène Royal, the Socialist opponent, in a heated campaign.

Sarkozy is the first president of France born after World War II. De Villepin was discredited in a lingering scandal called Clearstream. President Sarkozy has increased the centralized power of the executive branch of government and aimed to give France an increasingly influential role in both European and international politics. He solidified his power base by assembling a variety of French political stars from all parties to form his cabinet. Early in office, Sarkozy divorced his wife, Cécilia (who then married events empresario Richard Attias), and quickly married the glamorous and talented singer Carla Bruni.

The LANGUAGE: *Français*

IN PARIS ONE SPEAKS FRENCH (*Français* [frahn-**say**]). So much of your experience will be flavored by your ability to communicate. If you speak some French, so much the better; your linguistic abilities will be applauded. If you have a notion of French, use it. Abandon all fears of seeming ridiculous. You'll be commended for your effort and respected by Parisians for not automatically assuming that everyone on earth must speak English. If your French is as clumsy as a six-pack of Coke falling down the stairs, try anyway, and use your hands. Point. Smile. Shrug your shoulders. Do anything but fall into the "get me some ketchup, *garçon*" mindset.

unofficial **TIP**
The worst attitudinal error you can make in Paris is to convey either ignorance or arrogance when it comes to the language. It's OK that you don't speak French, but look apologetic about it.

The French take their language and culture seriously and are constantly reminded of their dwindling influence in the world. It wasn't all that long ago that French was the official diplomatic language internationally. Fortunately, both the tourists and the Parisians have made major headway over the last generation in gaining language skills. More tourists handle themselves well in French today than was true 20 years ago. And, similarly, more Parisians can get by in English today, recognizing the international need for a universal language (and understanding that it is no longer French), and enjoy doing so.

At the bare minimum, arrive with a few humble, rehearsed phrases proving that your French at least includes *bonjour, au revoir, merci, rendez-vous*, and *combien*.

GETTING LINGUISTICALLY EQUIPPED: PARLEZ-VOUS FRANÇAIS?

YOU MIGHT KNOW SOME FRENCH or may be willing to give it a try, but knowing a word and being able to say it are two different things. French pronunciation can be daunting in that some letters are silent and lots of words are not pronounced as spelled. The worst is when words in French are the same as in English, but you can't make them sound right. Try pronouncing the French for hospital, *hôpital*—it's pronounced "**oh**-pee-tal." How *beaucoup* ends up sounding like "bo-**kew**" is beyond most tourists' imaginations. The toilet becomes "twa-**let**," instead of the English "**toy**-lit." Many guidebooks offer travelers lists of terms and phrases, but without the articles that precede them and, more importantly, easy-to-use phonetic transcriptions, you might as well give up before you contort your mouth and lips into incomprehensible sounds. It won't come out as recognizable French.

So—for those who need it—we have included next to each French word in italics a transcription of the sound.

unofficial **TIP**
We have added a pronunciation guide only to words that you most likely might need to pronounce.

The syllable that is in bold is the one that you stress. *D'accord?* (dac-**core**?) All right? We just want you to be able to look at a cluster of letters, pronounce it, and have someone rush off to fetch you another towel or bring you the salt and pepper. Just read these transcriptions out loud as if they were in English. Purse your lips, raise your shoulders, and let the music and passion take over. You're speaking French.

SURVIVAL FRENCH

START OUT BY BEING ABLE TO ASK IN FRENCH whether the person in front of you speaks English. To be safe, start every sentence with either *pardon* (pahr-**dohn**) or *excusez-moi* (excuse-**say mwah**). *Parlez-vous anglais?* You'll get as an answer either *oui, un peu,* or *non, pas du tout* (yes, a little, or no, not at all). If you get the latter, you'll want to set the record straight right away that you also do not speak French. *Moi non plus. Je ne parle pas français.* Or, *je parle un peu* (I speak a little bit). *Merci,* of course, is thank you, and *merci beaucoup* is thank you very much.

Get in the habit quickly of greeting your hotel concierge or the chambermaid with *Bonjour, monsieur* or *Bonjour, madame.* On your second day try adding *Comment allez-vous?* (**co**-mo tah-**lay voo**) or *Comment ça va?* (**co**-mo sah **vah**), which means, how are you? They'll be impressed. But be warned: Do not ask people on the street who you have not already met, *Comment ça va?* They'll probably ignore you anyway, thinking you're weird. Strangers usually do not talk to each other. Yes, you can err on the friendly side.

Remember that French is far more formal than English, and the rules of language need to be respected. A basic difference between English and French is that French uses the *tu* and *vous* form for "you." When addressing anyone other than a close friend, family member, or child, you should use only the *vous* form. French people who work together in the same office for years do not change over to the *tu* form. So don't initiate familiarity; let the French person do it. In any case, most Parisians understand that Americans and their language are naturally casual and familiar, so tourists are usually excused for their innocent murder of French formalities.

When greeting or taking leave of someone, don't be surprised if a hand is extended your way. Shake it. You may repeat this formal act with the same person several times in the same day. For a note on *les bises,* that charming succession of little kisses that Parisians are always giving each other, see the Introduction.

Saying Hello and Goodbye

Bonjour, madame (bohn **jzoor** ma-**dahm**).
Au revoir, madame (oh rev-**war** ma-**dahm**).
Bonjour, monsieur (bohn-**jzoor** miss-**yiuh**).
Au revoir, monsieur (oh rev-**war** miss-**yiuh**).

(These days, when you don't know the marital status of a woman, use *madame* instead of *mademoiselle.*)

A more casual greeting is simply *Salut* (sah-**loo**).

Myths and Misnomers

- The French do not hate Americans, though they are often passionate about politics both in public and private. In fact, the French love affair with American contemporary culture is vast. You'll never be the object of any blatant and personalized display of anti-Americanism, unless of course you are wearing a loud button on your shirt: WE LOVE THE DEATH PENALTY. Not a popular opinion in Europe.

- French fries are really Belgian in origin and are simply called *les frites* in French. The way of cutting potatoes into thin strips was originally French.

- The French have no idea what French dressing is. The most common salad dressing is called *vinaigrette,* resembling Americans' Italian dressing.

- The French don't think of French bread as particularly French. It's just a *baguette* or stick of bread.

- French cuffs don't mean a thing in France. They're *manchette*.

- There is no such thing in France as the French kiss. Open-mouthed tongue kissing has no national boundaries, and aside from *les bises,* the formal greeting that marks most encounters, it is really the only kind of kissing that counts here.

- French windows are just normal windows for the French.

- Don't look for a French harp. It doesn't exist in France. The same is true for the French knot and French omelet.

- French pastry in France is just *pâtisserie*.

- Of course, French toast, having nothing to do with France, is called *pain perdu* (lost bread).

Other Useful Phrases

Enchanté (or *enchantée* if a woman is talking) (on-shahn-**tay**) means pleased to meet you.

Je suis ravi (or *ravie*) *de faire votre connaissance* (dzjuh **swee** ra-**vee** duh **fair** voh-tra ko-ness-**sahnz**) means pleased to make your acquaintance (very formal). You'll either impress them or make them laugh.

Combien ça coûte (**comb**-bee-**yen** sah **coot**). How much does it cost?

Ooh la la! (Yes, people do say this when impressed or surprised.)

NUMBERS *and* PRICES: *The Euro*

AS IS ALWAYS TRUE, NUMBERS CHANGE—phone and fax numbers, opening and closing times, and especially prices. For those of you

Myths and Misnomers: Part 2

The French, however, have their own misnomers for you:

- A *café américain* is a full cup of weak coffee, American style. (We agree, Starbucks has improved the item a lot. Speaking of Starbucks, they've achieved an invasion of Paris, about which the locals seem pretty blasé.)

- A *bar américain* is the kind of bar you stand up and drink at.

- A *cuisine américaine* is a kitchen with a center counter or bar, open and roomy; in other words, a kitchen.

- A *voiture américaine* is a big car like a Cadillac.

- *Homard à l'américaine* is lobster cooked with tomatoes and shallots, as is never done in America.

- And novels that are *traduit de l'américain* means that they are translated from American (as opposed to English), as if American were its own language.

who have really been out of the loop, the French franc has been replaced. Where we describe pretravel purchases or services and products with U.S. list prices, we have included U.S. dollar prices. Everything else is in euros only.

To make conversion easy for you, we suggest that you consult before or during your Paris visit the Web site **xe.com** for up-to-the-minute conversion rates. You can print out your own handy guide, and this will help you figure out prices while shopping. As of this writing, 1 euro is about $1.45, or think of a U.S. dollar as about €0.68. Expect fluctuations. Although some *Unofficial Guide to Paris* financial insiders believe that the euro will slide back a bit, especially after the financial crisis of 2008, expect the dollar to remain weak. Make sure you check rates before making reservations and purchases, and remember, your holiday may either cost you a third more than you had hoped or require that you make a few adjustments or sacrifices. One way or another, do not let a hundred bucks spoil an otherwise fantastic stay in Paris.

unofficial **TIP**
To get a quick idea if something in euros is expensive, think of the conversion as one-to-one, one U.S. dollar is one euro, and then fine-tune according to the exchange rate. Or think of the cost of something in euros as the price in dollars before you add the tip or sales tax.

PART TWO

PLANNING *your* VISIT

HOW FAR *in* ADVANCE SHOULD YOU PLAN?

WELL, IT DEPENDS. The earlier you get started and pick your dates, the better. In general, trips should be organized and booked at least three to four months before the departure date; however, spontaneous and flexible travelers have the advantage of landing great last-minute deals. Count on spending a few torturous hours on hold on the telephone as well as a fair amount of time online. Continental Airlines, for example, offered a summer special, Newark–Paris round-trip for under $500, but travelers only had three weeks to make a reservation and pay. If you hope to travel at peak times—holiday seasons, Christmas, Easter, or during school vacations—you should reserve your airline tickets at least six months in advance, or as soon as you know your dates. Some classy tour operators in the United States pitch short trips, even weekends to Paris, which is a bit easier from the East Coast, where the flights are as little as six hours and the time difference is six hours. In any case, the sooner you book your dates and buy your plane tickets, the less stress you will feel! And that's worth a lot. If you are a privileged frequent flyer member and belong to a gold or platinum club connected to a frequently used airline, don't hesitate to use hotline or club member phone numbers. You'll save time and aggravation.

When to go? This is somewhat personal. Some seasoned travelers enjoy the spring and early summer best, and others swear by the fall. Personally, I love all seasons in Paris, even the gray and wet months of winter. Keep in mind this: France is divided into three school zones, each setting its own scholastic calendar. Dates change from year to year and are announced as early as three years in advance. For exact dates, inquire at your closest French consulate or travel office and indicate that it is the Paris region that concerns you. Dates are also given on the Web site of the French national tourist office: **us.franceguide.com/practical-information.**

The highways, train stations, airports, and ski slopes are jammed with vacationing families during the school breaks. Paris proper can actually be less congested. Reserved train seats between Paris, the mountain areas, and the south of France get snapped up quickly for these periods, so be forewarned if you plan on heading out of Paris or hope to get into the city then. The primary dates are Toussaint (the last weekend in October and first week in November), Christmas (December 18 or so until about January 4), winter break (February 19 or so until about March 8), spring break (mid-April to about May 3), and of course summer vacation (end of June to early September). Avoid arrivals and departures on the first and last days of the school holidays. You can reserve train tickets on the Internet and hold them with a credit card up until the time you travel. And you can cancel without penalty. A very useful tip.

We recommend visiting Paris in the off-season when possible, but this requires a different mental outlook since the weather can often be dark, chilly, and/or wet. Otherwise, Paris is glorious in April, May, June, and September to mid-October, but the prices are highest then, and hotels in the early fall are often booked up. There are mixed opinions on visiting Paris in August, but we tend to like it. The pace is slower, and the city is less congested. The weather can be uncomfortably hot, but usually it is manageable, and good deals can be had on hotel rooms. The summer of 2003 was unforgettably torrid—the hottest summer in 40 years—and with the absence of air-conditioning, travel was not fun, and cities were dangerous for elderly people left alone. But the experience has helped make the French better prepared for intense heat.

unofficial **TIP**
There is a lot more air-conditioning in France these days, but if you are an air-conditioning freak, you'll find Paris to be absurdly under-cooled.

Try to avoid traveling on the last few days of July and first few days of August, when a massive exodus of excited Parisians flee the city for their annual summer vacations. Although less so than before, most Parisians still leave the city at the same time, and, should you travel on these dates, you're certain to be caught up in a hectic crosscurrent of agitated travelers excited about leaving or irritated about returning. July 15 and August 15 are also very busy travel days in France and should be avoided when possible. If you can't avoid these heavy traffic days, keep in mind that the crowds will be heavy. Traffic on the autoroutes will be dense. If you must travel on these dates, just give yourself more time, bring cool drinks, and adjust your mental outlook. It's fun being caught up in the midst of the French holiday rush, isn't it?

unofficial **TIP**
Be careful not to lose an attractive deal by forgetting to confirm the reservation before the expiration date (and hour, usually midnight).

Making early plane and hotel reservations will guarantee you seats on the dates you've chosen and rooms in your hotel of choice. Although travel professionals specializing in cut-rate trips warn that booking too early precludes your getting the best deals and bargains, we feel that as soon as you know your dates, you should start your research for either a package tour or an affordable airfare and book it. Your time and peace of mind are worth a lot. Airlines will usually hold seats on that date and at that price for several days. This buys you time without obliging you to commit immediately. Usually you can extend the holding date by a few days by simply asking, but this depends on the restrictions attached to the special fare and the cooperative spirit of the salesperson. Your travel agent will be better at making and holding a reservation in your name than you may be yourself. You can hold several reservations at the same time, which will enable you to continue your search for the best dates, prices, and conditions. The best deals often require that you commit immediately and pay with a credit card. Cancellations and changes are subject to penalties. With the higher prices of oil and airfares, airlines are getting increasingly strict about changes and penalties.

WHEN *to* GO

YOU SHOULD CONSIDER THE PRICE, the weather, and your mental outlook. The first two are absolutes, but the last is a bit harder to judge. As mentioned above, seasoned travelers who wish to spend lots of time inside great museums, theaters, restaurants, cafés, and hotels may truly find off-season Paris trips more enjoyable. The weather may be grim, but your experience may remain untainted by wind and clouds, so November through March may make sense. There are great airfare deals and lower hotel rates for the courageous or romantic who visit Paris during these months. Even so, first-time visitors are advised to opt for early summer or September, when Paris puts on its prettiest face.

unofficial **TIP**
The French love to discuss politics, and if you can talk about ideas without getting personal, you'll enjoy the quality of the public debate.

PRICE

HIGH SEASON IN PARIS runs from April 1 or Easter Sunday through June 30, September 1 through October 31, and the week between Christmas and New Year's Day. This is when prices are at their highest and availability is at its lowest. Low season runs from November 1 through March 31, with a slight rise between early July and August 31. The "TOs" (tour operators) call this summer variation the shoulder season.

There are ways to defend yourself during high season and peak weeks, so don't use only "season" as your guide for travel dates. One tourist tells us that he prefers the off-season because it's very affordable, "plus you don't sweat climbing the stairs at the Notre-Dame and Sacré Cœur! The spring and fall in Paris are particularly pleasant, and the Champs-Élysées and other noted shopping areas are beautifully illuminated around Christmas. And the competition for sidewalk café table space is purely Parisian." What you lose in climate, you'll gain in atmosphere.

unofficial **TIP**
Don't forget that prices soar during international trade shows and conferences like the Prêt-à-Porter fashion extravaganza and the International Aeronautics Show at Le Bourget. Hotels fill up quickly. The Web site **salonsparis.ccip.fr** lists all trade shows and their dates.

WEATHER

THE PLEASURES OF PARIS TRANSCEND its meteorological conditions. There's a lot to say about Paris's weather and seasons, and it's not all great news. It's wholly possible to have a great time in the grayest months. Knowing what to expect in advance is the key.

The summers are hot but bearable; the winters are long and gray, cold and wet, but usually not freezing. September and October, like April through June, can be divine. In August many Parisians clear out for the long summer holiday, which makes the city less congested and more manageable for a visit. There are fewer Parisians in Paris, but there are also fewer people in general, and the city is calmer. And although there are fewer Parisians, there are actually lots of French tourists, so you'll be sharing restaurants and cafés with French people, who are not all Parisians. There are fewer restaurants open, but there are still many. August can be hot, but the quality of the daylight and the shade on the sidewalk cafés are sources of great comfort. Paris in August can be surprisingly pleasant.

unofficial **TIP**
Some guidebooks will tell you that all you see in Paris in August is other tourists; this is not our experience.

It's the grayness (*grisaille* [greez-**eye**]) of winter that tends to haunt the moods of the locals. It takes a cheery outlook, a decent pair of waterproof walking shoes, a handy umbrella, and an interesting itinerary to claim victory over the Parisian weather between the late fall and early spring. One tip is to wear wool and silk to resist Paris's particularly penetrating winter chill. Clearly, the Paris you visit in June will not feel like the Paris of January. One of the great advantages to off-season travel is that the city feels more authentic; there are fewer visitors, the lines are shorter, and, of course, hotel prices are reduced. And the food in the colder months tends to be particularly savory. French onion soup *au gratin* (oh gra-**tahn**) is always good, but it's even better in the heart of winter. The same goes for hot chocolate.

Check weather conditions in Paris before leaving for your trip at **weather.com** or **weather.edition.cnn.com,** which both provide an

PARIS AVERAGE TEMPERATURE		
MONTH	CENTIGRADE	FAHRENHEIT
January	2°–6° C	35°–43° F
February	2°–8° C	35°–46° F
March	4°–11° C	39°–52° F
April	7°–15° C	45°–59° F
May	10°–19° C	50°–66° F
June	13°–22° C	55°–72° F
July	15°–24° C	59°–75° F
August	15°–23° C	59°–73° F
September	12°–21° C	54°–70° F
October	9°–16° C	48°–61° F
November	5°–10° C	41°–50° F
December	3°–7° C	37°–45° F

8- to 10-day extended forecast. You can also call Paris for weather conditions (in French): from the United States call ☎ 011 33 8 92 68 02 75.

It rarely snows in Paris, but the city does get flurries that stick for a few hours once or twice each winter. Parisians get all excited by the white flakes, and the inexperienced Parisian drivers slide around the roads like foolish seals. More often there is rain or sleet. Each

PARIS RAINFALL			
MONTH	NUMBER OF RAINY DAYS	MONTHLY RAINFALL	AVERAGE HOURS OF SUNSHINE PER DAY
January	10	55 mm (2.2 in.)	2
February	9	45 mm (1.8 in.)	3
March	7	30 mm (1.2 in.)	5
April	6	40 mm (1.6 in.)	6
May	8	50 mm (2 in.)	7
June	9	50 mm (2 in.)	8
July	8	55 mm (2.2 in.)	8
August	8	60 mm (2.4 in.)	7
September	8	50 mm (2 in.)	6
October	8	50 mm (2 in.)	4
November	8	50 mm (2 in.)	2
December	9	50 mm (2 in.)	1

summer a hot-weather hail hits the city for an hour or so, and ice balls create a strange cacophony on the metal roofs of the city. The heat in the summer can build, and Paris air gets heavy and diesel-laden. We'll tell you later how to avoid urban heat waves.

PACKAGE DEALS *and* TRAVEL AGENTS

EVERYONE WANTS TO PAY AS LITTLE AS POSSIBLE, face as few hassles as possible, and have the most authentic experience possible. But to get all this, should you leave the planning to someone else and buy a package deal to Paris, or should you piece it together yourself? Unfortunately, according to knowledgeable insiders, three-fourths of all the agents and packagers selling trips to France today do not really know enough about Paris or what they are selling. We met a poor couple who had been sold a Mont Saint-Michel road trip as an add-on to their three-day Paris stay. Thirty minutes out of Paris they asked their driver if they were almost there. Mont Saint-Michel is in Normandy, a four-hour drive each way. They spent eight hours in a car and two hours at the scenic coastal monastery. With only three days in Paris, a third of their time was sacrificed for this interesting but misplaced excursion. They couldn't have known. Their travel agent back home blindly bought the wonderful-sounding trip from a packager.

unofficial **TIP**
Note that the preferred month for visiting Paris is August for the Brits, June for the Americans, and May for the Germans. September, October, May, and June have the most foreign visitors in Paris.

These kinds of things happen with Paris plans too. The travel market to France is so large that all sorts of packages at all sorts of prices are sold, and the results are at best unpredictable. The success of your package deal depends greatly on the quality and size of the tour operator, your self-confidence, and your degree of experience in international travel. There are so many variables involved, such as the price of the room, the location of the hotel, the number of stars, the number of nights, the excursions included, airport transfers, and whether or not passes and meals are included, that it's really difficult to know if you're getting good value or, more importantly, what you want. We noticed that the photos do not always correspond with the actual hotels being advertised, and that the photos that are used can be misleading. The tour operator gives itself the option to place you in "a similar hotel" to the one mentioned in the catalog, and there are plenty of blackout periods, plus weekend surcharges and other fine print. You really have no control over what you'll end up with.

Knowledge is power. When selecting a package from a brochure, be aware of the pitfalls. The tour operator will not be available to answer specific questions once you're in Paris. The hotel you'll end up in depends on available inventory just before your travel dates.

If you are pitched a package deal by a travel agent, aside from the obvious questions—what's included in the package, how much free time will you have, and how large are the groups—ask specific questions:

- What is the nearest Métro station to the hotel?
- Which restaurants near the hotel can you recommend?
- How far is the hotel from the Louvre?
- How many others will be on the bus? How long does it take to get to our destination?
- How many people have you booked on this trip in the past year? Could I talk to or e-mail some of them?

If any of these draw blank looks, move on. These are not the right people for you. If you do need others to help make your Paris plans, consider this: Unless you're extremely budget sensitive and you find a real all-inclusive steal, work with a small, personalized tour operator who has a love affair with France—or do it yourself. You'll enjoy greater freedom and mobility, you'll eat whatever and wherever you choose, you'll increase your chances of staying in a charming spot, and you'll be pleased with yourself for opting for greater adventure. If you are already an expert on Paris and don't mind staying in a more commercial hotel, check out the packages.

Whether you like package tours or not, they can offer hotel accommodations, meals, and airport transfers, along with airfare, for not much more (and sometimes less) than you'd otherwise pay for the airfare alone. However, don't be lazy. Do the math. The package price may not be cheaper than if you pieced it together yourself. Often, however, it is, and the savings may be worth losing some charm. Admittedly, the greatest attraction is not having to make the arrangements yourself. If savings are more motivating than location, you don't have the time or energy to make a few calls, and you don't mind being in a large, touristy hotel, you may choose the package deal and be quite satisfied.

At the minimum, you can learn a lot from examining the packages and then deciding to book on your own or opting for a smaller, specialized tour operator. Otherwise, use one of the recommended tour operators we mention or one who comes highly recommended by friends who have been to Paris and with whom you

unofficial **TIP**
We suggest avoiding the huge packagers who sell volume, not quality.

share similar tastes. Note that there are escorted tours and individual or self-driven tours; choose according to the level of independence you require or prefer.

Your trip to Paris has to be special—you want every moment to be a treasure. You want to feel immersed in the local culture and seduced by its style and beauty, so don't be too quick to sacrifice splendor and control for a few dollars or a few hours of research. Many of us frequent travelers firmly believe that planning the trip is half the fun!

If your local travel agent is particularly knowledgeable about Paris, by all means work with him or her. If he regularly sends customers to a favorite little hotel in the Latin Quarter that he has been to himself, fine, do it, follow his lead. If he works with a great tour operator and can get you an attractive deal in a charming two- or three-star hotel, certainly consider it. But

unofficial **TIP**
If the travel agent doesn't have special Parisian knowledge, experience, and contacts, research and reserve the trip yourself.

chances are, although travel agents book a lot of people to Paris, they often do not know the ins and outs of Parisian tourism. Local travel agents buy trips from big packagers with lots of marketing muscle and a lot of "product" to push. This is not likely to lead you to a delightful excursion. If you end up in a high-rise hotel in the 15th arrondissement or near the *périphérique,* you will have missed the real charm that Paris has to offer—and although you might enjoy a view of the Seine, you may not realize that you could have done a lot better. Many travelers come back and teach their travel agents a thing or two.

A compromise is to have your travel agent book the trip that you have researched yourself. Try one of the hotels that we profile and let the professionals do their job. That way you know what you're getting, but you don't have the hassle of making reservations and confirmations.

For more details on Paris lodging, see Part Three, Accommodations.

FINDING A PACKAGE TOUR, TOUR OPERATOR, OR CONSOLIDATOR

PACKAGES ARE PUT TOGETHER in a variety of ways by their vendors. Wholesalers tend to purchase blocks of airfares, hotel rooms, or tour slots in advance with the intention of assembling them into various package configurations, sometimes with an eye toward particular dates, events, or groups. They may start bulk-buying the various package components a year in advance of their use, which allows them to get good prices to pass along to the customer. Consolidators, on the other hand, work a much narrower margin of time. These operators purchase airplane seats or other travel products that are in danger of going unsold, negotiating discounted rates with the airlines (or hotels, and so on) based on the perishability of the product. Both approaches have their advantages, and many companies use both to some degree.

Consult brochures published by the French government tourist office, Maison de la France. Take a look at the online EZ Reference Guide, which includes everything from U.S. tour operators, charter-flight companies, bed-and-breakfasts, château stays, villa rentals, and youth hostels, to ski trips, barging, canal cruises, guide services, festival tours, bike tours, golf tours, horseback-riding trips, and even ballooning excursions. More general information on France and its regions is available in their annual publication "FranceGuide," which can be downloaded from the Web site **us.franceguide.com** or ordered from their hotline ☎ 514-288-1904.

Check the Travel Section of Your Local Newspaper

Do this regularly to see who's offering specials to Paris. Wholesalers, charter companies, and the major airlines dangle Paris teasers to attract attention. Also be on the lookout for travel and tourism trade shows in your area.

Surf the Web

The Internet, as cybernauts already know, is a jungle in which all things are found. But the tangle of information can be overwhelming, confusing, and unreliable, as well as incredibly helpful. If you're inclined to explore, here is a presifted list of Web addresses at which package tours to Paris may be found and examined:

PARIS PACKAGE TOURS ON THE WEB	
aavacations.com	lowestfare.com
france.com	orbitz.com
frenchexperience.com	uniquefrance.com
go-today.com	virgin-vacations.com

Suggested Tour Operators

In the spirit of saving you time, energy, and money as well as sparing you any feelings of disappointment, we have assembled a group of highly reliable and top-quality outfits offering travel services and trips to Paris. Again, we believe that it's better to insist on high-quality from the start if you want a truly memorable experience in a particularly Parisian way.

We've selected the following tour operators specializing in Paris and France based on the quality of the tours, not the price. In general, they do not provide "low-end" budget travel but can be considered reasonable in terms of the price-to-quality ratio.

BIKE RIDERS P.O. Box 130254, Boston, MA 02113; ☎ 617-723-2354 or 800-473-7040; fax 617-723-2355; info@bikeriderstours.com; **bikeriderstours.com.** They have excellent self-guided bicycling tours in Burgundy, as well as guided tours in the Loire, Dordogne, Corsica, and Provence. A great combination with your Paris stay.

CHEMIN CACHÉ 34 rue des Bourdonnais, Paris 75001; ☎ 06 30 71 81 48; contact@mycustom-trips.com. Operated by Canadian-born Katherine Robitaille and her French husband, Vincent Bruneau, Chemin Caché creates tailor-made, private vacations in Paris and throughout France. They cater to the traveler's specific interests while offering a unique insight into French life and culture.

ESSENTIAL EUROPE ☎ 514-285-8758 or 866-285-8758; fax 514-285-9128; info@eetvl.com; **essentialfrance.com**. Essential Europe is the brainchild of Magali Deur and Kim Chisholm, seasoned travelers and highly experienced professionals specializing in sending North Americans to Paris and the French provinces. Based in Boston and Montreal, Essential Europe transforms a client's idea or dream into a comprehensible itinerary.

THE FRENCH EXPERIENCE 370 Lexington Avenue, New York, NY 10017; ☎ 212-986-3800 or 800-283-7262; fax 646-349-3276; **french experience.com**. High-quality trips for individuals and groups to Paris and the provinces.

FINDING AIRFARE DEALS *and* MAKING RESERVATIONS

IF YOU'RE PLANNING YOUR OWN TRIP, start by securing your airline reservations. With your travel dates determined, you can then proceed to plan the rest of your trip.

START WITH YOUR LOCAL TRAVEL AGENT

IF HE OR SHE CAN LAND YOU A NONSTOP OR DIRECT FLIGHT to Paris on your selected dates at a fare that is within your budget, take it. Tell your travel agent in advance what you're looking for.

Give your travel agent a range of possible dates and an idea of your top dollar. Tell him or her if you're willing to fly on a charter flight, if you'd consider changing planes in another city, what frequent-flyer programs you use, and anything else that might give your schedule and itinerary more flexibility. Lastly, give your travel agent a deadline, like "I need to hear back from you by Friday." Good travel agents are like magicians. Unfortunately, today many know only how to sell tickets.

SKIM THE TRAVEL SECTION OF YOUR LOCAL PAPER

THIS IS WHERE SPECIALS EMERGE, but you have to move quickly. Often, there are only a few tickets available at the price offered, and they're snapped up even before the paper comes out. Jockeying for great deals, especially during the peak season, can be nightmarish. Airline restrictions, blackout dates, and other airline rules can be enough to spoil the journey before you leave.

SURFING FOR INEXPENSIVE AIRFARE

THE INTERNET TODAY IS SO RICH—and poor—in travel offers that we're unable to predict what you'll find. You might get lucky. But don't

KEY WEB SITES FOR AIR-TRAVEL RESERVATIONS	
bestfares.com	kayak.com
bookingbuddy.com	lowestfare.com
cheapertravel.com	orbitz.com
cheaptickets.com	priceline.com
dialaflight.com	sidestep.com
economytravel.com	sky-tours.com
expedia.com	travelocity.com
fareplanet.com	

make yourself crazy by becoming obsessive about the prices—they change quickly. To compare fares and stalk good deals, try the popular Web sites **lastminutetravel.com, sidestep.com, cheapair.com, cheaptickets.com,** and the French travel search engine, **liligo.com**. Air France posts specials at one minute after midnight every Wednesday morning. In fact, it is our experience that you'll do better, and have more choices, on the French or international sites than on those that are U.S. based and cater primarily to North Americans. The downside may be the language, but it doesn't take a lot to figure out how to punch in your city and travel dates and convert the fare from euros to dollars. Try it.

Remember, as a security measure when buying online, always use secure Web sites (signified by a closed "lock" in the bottom corner of your Web browser or "https://"—the "s" is for secure—in the address), and buy your tickets with a credit card. Double-check to make sure that the name you submit for each ticket matches the name on each passenger's passport exactly. When making long-distance purchases, it is difficult to make changes after you've received your tickets. So if you prefer to shop online, be sure to call customer service to make the reservation so that you can receive a paper ticket by mail. And give yourself plenty of time to receive tickets, vouchers, and so on by mail well before your departure date.

Closer to home, many travelers recommend Microsoft's Expedia (**expedia.com**) as an excellent means of at least pricing fares. The site also has a "fare alert" feature on its flights page that e-mails you if fares drop below a designated price. Travelocity (**travelocity.com**) and others do this too, and it is a very useful feature. Leave no stones unturned.

*un*official **TIP**
We like the London-based outfit called Dial-a-Flight (**dialaflight.com**), which offers excellent service along with some remarkable fares.

Priceline (**priceline.com**) advertises nationally, both online and via its toll-free number (call ☎ 800-774-2354). You submit a price that you're willing to pay for a given destination, with a credit card number. If Priceline can get the tickets at your price, they do, and they'll debit your credit card immediately. It's a great concept, but you should be very careful. There are all sorts of conditions and disclaimers to this type of sale—not the least of which is that you may have to make numerous stopovers to reach your destination (a flight to Paris via New York, Reykjavik, and London may not be what you had in mind). Much of the pleasure of traveling to Paris is the expectation and period of preparation. If there is a risk that your plans are going to get wiped out, or that you'll have to spend 18 hours on multiple flights to get there, then the potential savings are hardly worth it. Also, you will not earn frequent-flyer miles when using Priceline to book tickets. If you need personal service and hand-holding, this, and the many other massive database sites with limited personal service, won't be the best route for you.

CALL THE AIRLINES DIRECTLY

BE READY TO BE PUT ON HOLD for intolerable lengths of time. If your travel dates are inflexible, you'll be limited to the normally expensive published fares. If you are flexible, insist on hearing about all their specials. The airlines put up promotional offers all the time. These deals change frequently and are often very limited and carry contorted restrictions, blackout dates, minimum-stay requirements, and the like. Ask, ask, ask. One option is to consider other cities of arrival, like Brussels or Geneva, or other cities of departure. Keep asking. If you hit a dud salesperson, thank him or her, hang up, and call back—someone else with the same airline might be savvier. This happens all the time. Don't wait for the airline to be creative. Ask: "If

Air Canada	☎ 888-247-2262 (U.S. and Canada)
Air France	☎ 800-237-2747
Air India	☎ 800-223-7776
Air Tahiti Nui	☎ 877-824-4846
Air Transit	☎ 877-872-6728
American Airlines	☎ 800-433-7300
Continental	☎ 800-231-0856
Corsairfly	☎ 877-940-0149
Delta Airlines	☎ 800-221-1212
Egyptair	☎ 800-334-6787
Icelandair	☎ 800-223-5500
Northwest Airlines	☎ 800-225-2525
Openskies	☎ 866-581-3596
United Airlines	☎ 800-538-2929
US Airways	☎ 800-428-4322
Virgin Atlantic	☎ 800-821-5438

I were to fly from Philadelphia, do you have any specials?" or "If we leave on a Saturday instead of Monday, isn't the fare lower?" or "Do you have any discounts?" Determination and a proactive attitude can often lead to new options and fare reductions.

If you get a particularly helpful and knowledgeable sales representative on the phone, ask if he or she has a direct number or an alternative number so you don't have to hold for another 20 minutes when you call the airline back. In this era of not-so-great customer service, you have to defend yourself!

Start at the airline's Web site to check destinations and schedules. Think slightly out of the box as well. By leaving from Philadelphia instead of New York, you widen the field of choices and fares. By flying to Paris via London, Brussels, Amsterdam, or Frankfurt, you also widen your choices, your schedule possibilities, and the potential for promotional fares. You increase the hours of travel, but this might not bother you. Or you could end up planning a day or two in another European city.

If you see two flights listed for the exact same time and destination—for example, Air France and Continental or Delta—don't get confused. This is the same plane, but it takes two flight numbers (code sharing) and is sold separately by both companies. Ask if you're flying on the airline that is selling you the ticket. Frequent-flyer miles are applied to the company that issues the ticket.

Note: It is wise to sign up for the airlines' online newsletters. The airlines are actively attempting to lure passengers into buying tickets online and are offering good deals to help change consumer habits. Register on the airlines' Web sites, and you'll receive the latest offers by e-mail. Paris is often on the list of destinations.

GATEWAYS IN NORTH AMERICA The following cities have nonstop service to and from Paris:

Atlanta	Cincinnati	Miami	Quebec
Boston	Dallas	Montreal	San Diego
Calgary	Detroit	New York	San Francisco
Charlotte	Houston	Newark	Toronto
Chicago	Los Angeles	Philadelphia	Washington, D.C.

TRICKS FOR CHEAP AIRFARE

Alternative Destinations: Connecting to Paris

You can investigate flying via another European city, either to save money or to simply find a flight when all the nonstop flights are booked solid. There are advantageous fares to Paris on regularly scheduled flights on major airlines if you are willing to change planes and spend a few extra hours in transit. Your baggage gets checked straight through to Paris. Examples of alternatives include British

Airways via London, KLM via Amsterdam, Lufthansa via Frankfurt, Swiss via Geneva or Zurich, Aer Lingus via Dublin or Shannon, TAP via Lisbon, Iberia via Madrid, SAS via Copenhagen, and Icelandair via Reykjavik. A stopover and plane change at some obscenely early morning hour will translate into a few extra hours of travel time and even redder eyes, but the savings may be worth it. Some people get a kick out of at least seeing the airport in a new country and use the time to peruse the airport shops. Amsterdam's Schiphol Airport, in particular, offers good shopping.

Couriers

Call the international courier companies in your city and ask if they are taking volunteers. (Check the Yellow Pages for couriers.) Some offer a two-week round-trip ticket for next to nothing. The hitch is that you cannot take any check-in luggage with you, since you will be checking in baggage for the courier company. But if you're a savvy packer, this can be a very inexpensive way to get to Europe.

Consider London

With the Eurostar train and the Eurotunnel connecting the United Kingdom and the continent, it's just over two hours to Paris's Gare du Nord from London's revamped Saint Pancras Station. This means that if all else fails, or if you'd like to spend a few days in London on either side of your Paris visit, you could consider flying into London's Heathrow or Gatwick airports from North America, make the easy train commute to London's Saint Pancras Station, and then head on to Paris. British Airways has about seven flights per day between New York's JFK and London. Bookings can be made online at **eurostar.com** or by calling the bilingual direct line at ☎ 011 44 12 33 61 75 75. In Paris, call ☎ 08 92 35 35 39. Special deals start from about €80 return.

THE PARIS AIRFARE GAME

THE RANGE OF AIRFARES is all over the map these days, and with the price of fuel skyrocketing (sorry for the pun), the increases have been staggering, but to give you a ballpark figure for a round-trip ticket from the East Coast of the United States to Paris, expect to pay between $900 and $1,200 in off-peak periods and up to $1,500 per person in economy class during the summer and high-season, peak periods. Availability, special offers, frequent-flyer miles, and advance reservations and payment will all affect the fares you'll be quoted. Remember, there are often no two people on the same plane who paid the exact same price for their ticket. If you're being quoted only the expensive fares in this range, keep looking. Use the Web. Call tour operators. Ask more than one travel agent.

unofficial **TIP**
If you have the flexibility to travel off-season, you'll be able to land better fares then.

Ticket Consolidators

There are plenty of outfits offering cut-rate plane tickets to every city on earth. If you are accustomed to using one and have had positive experiences, by all means continue to rely on this service when buying your Paris tickets.

Otherwise, be careful. Consolidators buy up blocks of tickets to resell at cut prices. This helps airlines reduce the number of empty seats. Sometimes you are asked to pay before you receive your tickets, or you are issued vouchers that you exchange for your tickets at the airport. Inquire about the reliability of the outfit before you commit, and use only credit cards to pay. Smart travelers call airlines directly to reconfirm their reservations and secure seat assignments.

Low-cost Airlines

Check out the Canadian operator Air Transit (**airtransit.com**) and the French company Corsairfly (**corsairfly.com**), which offer flights to Paris from a number of Canadian cities.

Paris Travel Agents

Although you may be originating on the other side of the world, Paris-based travel agents can often provide better fares and better service than you can find at home. Check out:

MA MAISON DES ÉTATS UNIS 3, rue Cassette, 75006; ☎ 01 53 63 13 43; fax 011 33 1 42 84 23 28; **maisondesetatsunis.com.**

NOUVELLES FRONTIÈRES ☎ 011 33 1 49 2065 87; **nouvelles-frontieres.fr.**

Choosing an Airline

If you have a choice of airlines, try to fly Air France. Why? As soon as you step onto an Air France flight, you'll feel the cultural difference. You'll be in a tiny piece of France, served by a French crew that's dressed in French tailored suits and silk scarves, wearing French haircuts and eau de cologne, and offering flutes of French Champagne and wine (on Air France the Champagne is offered for free). The in-flight entertainment and menu will be in French and in English, and the style and quality of the food will clearly be French. This is a great way to start getting into the mood of Paris even before you arrive. Plus, Air France has an excellent safety record, and many international travelers in these troubled times prefer the psychological comfort of flying with a carrier that is not American. Air France's 2005 accident on the runway at Toronto Airport was horrific, but the fact that the well-trained crew evacuated all 308 passengers safely in 90 seconds speaks well for the company.

After the Concorde crash in Paris in 2000, spoiling an otherwise perfect record, Air France finally decided to put those wonderful planes in mothballs. No more three-and-a-half-hour flights between Paris and New York. The Concorde is history. The new generation of super jets includes the Airbus 380 (in service since 2007) and the future Boeing Dreamliner.

Choosing an Airport: Roissy–Charles de Gaulle or Orly

Paris has two international airports. Unlike cities such as London, Washington, D.C., and New York, where the choice of airport can make a huge difference in your travel time, comfort, and expense, Paris's two airports are both close to the city and easily accessible by public transportation and taxi. It really does not matter which you arrive at. More important than the airport are the airfares and the arrival times. We prefer the Air France flights from Newark and Boston because they leave the United States in the early evening and arrive in the early morning Paris time. If you do have a choice of airport, remember that Orly is a bit closer to central Paris than Roissy–Charles de Gaulle, although the difference is negligible.

If you know where you'll be staying at the time you make your plane reservations, you may choose the airport that's more convenient to your hotel. One reader tells us that she always flies into Roissy–Charles de Gaulle and stays in a small hotel near Les Invalides, because the Air France airport bus stops there and she can easily walk to her hotel. Airlines are known to change their arrivals and departures from one airport to the other, so be sure to note at which airport you'll be arriving. In 1999, for instance, American Airlines moved operations from Orly to Roissy–Charles de Gaulle. Paris also has a smaller regional airport, Beauvais, which the budget airlines use for inter-European flights.

Other Things to Consider before Leaving Home

- Renting a car. If you decide to rent a car, make sure you reserve one before leaving home—U.S. rates may be substantially lower than those in France. See details in Part Five, Getting Around.
- Buying train passes or making train reservations. See details in Part Five, Getting Around.
- Prepurchasing a Paris Visite public transportation pass for 1, 2, 3, or 5 consecutive days. See details in Part Five, Getting Around.
- Prepurchasing a Paris Museum and Monument pass for 1, 2, or 5 days. See details in Part Six, Sightseeing, Tours, and Attractions.
- Prepurchasing theater, music, opera, or sporting-event tickets before leaving home. Check out Divento at **divento.com** or call ☎ 800-820-9306 and the "Organize your Trip" pages of the French tourist office Web site: **franceguide.fnacspectacles.com.**
- Prepurchasing Paris and France maps from Michelin at **michelin travel.com** or by calling ☎ 800-432-627. You can also check and print road itineraries from their excellent Web site, **viamichelin.com.**
- Reserving a cell phone or SIM card for use in France. Note that all GSM cell phones will work in France. Make sure you ask your cell-phone

operator back home to activate your international service before traveling. You can also purchase an inexpensive cell phone without a subscription and buy a prepaid phone card to use in France. See Cell Phones later in this chapter.

- Reserving a babysitter in advance. Consult the listings in Part Four, Arriving, Getting Oriented, and Departing.

REDUCING *the* CONFUSION *of* CHOICE

IT'S EASY OBTAINING TRAVEL INFORMATION on Paris. In fact, you may suffer the opposite problem; there is so much written on Paris that it is hard to determine what's helpful and, in the case of conflicting information, who's right. By scanning the travel section of your local bookstore or surfing the Web, you'll certainly notice that Paris information is wildly abundant. In 1998 we found 2 million references to Paris on the AltaVista search engine alone. Today, a word search on Paris, France, in Google offers you more than 80 million references! You don't need or want 1,000 hotel rooms; you want a few reliable suggestions and tips that correspond to your needs and interests. Ultimately, all you really want is help in making sure that you'll have a great time. We've attempted to sort this out for you, to weed back the "confusion of choice" and spare you the glut of less-than-useful and often contradictory information and advice littering the market.

unofficial **TIP**
If you're using the Internet to gather information, visit **francetourism.com**, **franceguide.com**, and **parisinfo.com** for general information on France and Paris.

MAISON DE LA FRANCE (FRENCH GOVERNMENT TOURIST OFFICE)

THE MOST COMPLETE AND THOROUGH SOURCE of basic travel information on Paris is the French Government Tourist Office, known as the **Maison de la France.** A phone center in Montreal fields your questions and requests for brochures and has replaced the more personalized service travelers used to get. In addition, we've found that receiving printed information can take up to a month, so start inquiring early. The "France-on-Call" hotline in the United States is ☎ 514-288-1904. The Maison de la France addresses are:

IN THE UNITED STATES
- **Chicago**
  205 North Michigan Avenue, Suite 3770, Chicago, IL 60611-2819
  ☎ 514-288-1904; **info.chicago@franceguide.com**
- **Los Angeles**
  9454 Wilshire Boulevard, Suite 210, Beverly Hills, CA 90212-2967

☎ 514-288-1904; fax 310-276-2835;
info.losangeles@franceguide.com
* **New York**
  825 Third Avenue, 29th floor (entrance on 50th Street), New York, NY 10022
  ☎ 514-288-1904; fax 212-838-7855; **info.us@franceguide.com**

IN CANADA
* 1800 Avenue McGill College, Suite 1010, Montreal, Quebec H3A 3J6
  ☎ 514-288-2026; fax 514-845-4868; **canada@franceguide.com**

IN THE UNITED KINGDOM
* Lincoln House, 300 High Holborn, London WC1V 7JH
  ☎ 0906 8244 123; fax 0207 061 6646; **info.uk@franceguide.com**

THE ALLIANCE FRANÇAISE

THE **Alliance Française** (4101 Reservoir Road NW, Washington, D.C. 20007; ☎ 202-944-6353; fax 202-944-6347; **alliance-us.org**) is a great source of cultural and linguistic information and overall support for Paris-bound travelers. It's also sure to both propel you into the world of French culture before your Paris journey and help you maintain your contact with your Parisian experience after your return. This century-old worldwide network is, according to its brochure, "dedicated to promoting awareness, understanding, and appreciation of the French language and culture."

Go to their Web site for a list of 117 chapters and French schools throughout the United States (sometimes this may be just a contact person giving French classes in a small town). Or call or write to get on the Alliance Française mailing list.

FRANCO-AMERICAN CHAMBERS OF COMMERCE

IF YOUR INTEREST IN PARIS goes beyond simple tourism and you're on your way to Paris for professional or commercial reasons, you may have specific questions regarding your mission. The **Franco-American Chambers of Commerce,** founded in 1896 to promote strong relations between the United States and France (with 19 chapters in the United States), could be a key source of pretravel information.

UNITED STATES FRANCO-AMERICAN CHAMBERS OF COMMERCE
* **Atlanta**
  2990 Grandview Avenue, Suite 200, Atlanta, GA 30305
  ☎ 404-846-2500; fax 404-846-2555; **facc-atlanta.com**
* **Boston**
  185 Alewife Brook Parkway, Suite 413, Cambridge, MA 02138
  ☎ 617-520-2121; fax 617-520-2144; **faccne.org**
* **Charlotte**
  P.O. Box 12328, Charlotte, NC 28220
  ☎ 704-225-3910; fax 704-771-1528; **faccnc.com**

- **Chicago**
  35 East Wacker Drive, Suite 670, Chicago, IL 60601
  ☎ 312-578-0444; fax 312-578-0445; **facc-chicago.com**
- **Cincinnati**
  2200 PNC Center, 201 East Fifth Street, Cincinnati, OH 45202
  ☎ 513-852-6510; fax 513-852-6511
  france-cincinnati.com
- **Cleveland**
  200 Public Square, Suite 3300, Cleveland, OH 44114
  ☎ 216-274-2354; fax 216-241-2824; **faccohio.org**
- **Dallas–Fort Worth**
  2665 Villa Creek Drive, Suite 214, Dallas, TX 75234
  ☎ 972-241-0111; fax 972-241-0901; **faccdallas.com**
- **Denver**
  8101 East Dartmouth Avenue, Suite 21, Denver, CO 80231
  ☎ 303-695-7818; fax 303-695-5057; **rmfacc.org**
- **Houston**
  5373 West Alabama, Suite 209, Houston, TX 77056
  ☎ 713-960-0575; fax 713-960-0495; **facchouston.com**
- **Los Angeles**
  10390 Santa Monica Boulevard, Suite 130, Los Angeles, CA 90025
  ☎ 323-651-4741; fax 323-651-2547; **frenchchamberla.org**
- **Miami**
  168 NE First Street, Suite 1102, Miami, FL 33131
  ☎ 305-374-5000; fax 305-358-8203; **faccmiami.com**
- **Michigan**
  c/o Clayton & McKervey, P.C, 2000 Town Center, Suite 1800,
  Southfield, MI 48075
  ☎ 248-936-9473; fax 248-208-9115; **faccmi.org**
- **New Orleans**
  World Trade Center, Suite 2938, 2 Canal Street
  New Orleans, LA 70130
  ☎ 504-561-0070; fax 504-592-9999; **facc-la.com**
- **New York**
  122 East 42nd Street, Suite 2015, New York, NY 10168
  ☎ 212-867-0123; fax 212-867-90507; **faccnyc.org**
- **Philadelphia**
  1528 Walnut Street, Suite 2020, Philadelphia, PA 19103
  ☎ 215-545-0123; fax 215-545-0144; **faccphila.org**
- **San Diego**
  964 Fifth Avenue, Suite 235, San Diego, CA 92101
  ☎ 619-544 1445; **france-sandiego.org**
- **San Francisco**
  703 Market Street, Suite 450, San Francisco, CA 94103
  ☎ 415-442-4717; fax 415-442-4621; **faccsf.com**
- **Seattle**
  2200 Alaskan Way, Suite 490, Seattle, WA 98121
  ☎ 206-443-4703; fax 206-448-4218; **faccpnw.org**

- **Washington, D.C.**
  1200 G Street, NW, Suite 800, Washington, DC 20005
  ☎ 202-640-1806; **faccwdc.org**

WHAT *to* PACK

THE BEST PIECE OF ADVICE IS: "Bring less!" Travelers have a terrible tendency to overpack. Some visitors fear that they won't be able to find Tylenol or cornflakes in Europe and decide to bring 'em along. Please, bring only the essentials. Additionally, more stringent regulations concerning safety and security provide all the more reason to pack light. Use luggage that locks but is easy to open and shut and is not overstuffed. There is nothing more stressful than battling luggage as it sprawls over a table at airport security.

Some savvy travelers go so far as to carry just one suitcase small enough to fit into the overhead compartments inside the plane; this saves lots of time on both ends. However, be certain that your bag does fit international size and weight restrictions—and on fully booked flights, you may find your carry-on luggage being checked anyway. Post-9/11 savvy travelers now prefer to check their one piece of luggage and keep carry-ons to a minimum.

Airline restrictions from the United States limit you to two checked-in bags per person with a maximum weight of 50 pounds per bag. Check with your travel agent or carrier for specifics. Some people like to travel with one bag and pack an empty nylon or duffel bag in order to have space for gifts and other purchases for the return flight. This is a great idea—you will definitely have some treasures you will want to lug home from Paris. Otherwise, you can buy disposable, soft, zip-around bags made of indestructible red-white-and-blue nylon cord in all the flea markets and cut-rate shops—you've probably seen them at airports before; they're fairly ubiquitous. This might be your best-value purchase. They cost less than €5 and are perfect for lugging back your great finds (*trouvailles* [**troo**-vye]).

We always advise international travelers to avoid heavy suitcases that do not roll. Bags with shoulder straps and rollers will give you much-needed mobility and will also help you save on taxi fares. If you have one or two bags with rollers, you may opt to get to your hotel via public transportation rather than a taxi and pay around €8 instead of €40 each way!

For some people, packing is an obsessive science. The most amusing tip we've heard in a long time comes from an American woman who writes: "Call me a wasteful American, but I do take older undergarments and socks along and pitch them at the end. This is a great way to clean out your drawer, create suitcase room along the way, and avoid a pile of laundry upon return." But if there is any city in the world in which you'll feel like wearing your fanciest or most risqué underwear, it'll be Paris!

Other packing tips: Take along photocopies of your passports, credit cards, and other important papers, to be left in your hotel room in case you lose the originals (also leave copies of this information at home or with a family member). Avoid taking along anything electric, unless it's dual-voltage or adaptable; otherwise you'll have problems with the current. You'll also risk delays at security checkpoints in the airports. Most hotels (even one-stars) provide hair dryers.

Cordless shavers are handy. Bring a small solar calculator for quick currency conversions while shopping. Note that all of France uses 220–230 volts AC (not the North American 110 volts). Electrical current alternates at 50 cycles, not the 60 in use in America. If you are bringing shavers, travel irons, hair dryers, or whatever, make sure that they are adapted for the European current. Otherwise, you'll need a voltage transformer, which is bulky and heavy and not worth the trouble to carry. Remember, too, that the outlet prongs are shaped differently, and your appliances won't fit into French wall outlets without adapters. You'll need an adapter plug, which costs only about $3 and is easily found at Radio Shack, appliance and travel shops, and even in the luggage sections of all-purpose stores like K-Mart and Wal-Mart. You'll also need one if you're planning on plugging in a laptop computer or charging the batteries of your video camera.

Many travelers carry an extra pair of eyeglasses, medication (with a prescription and its generic name), and valuables on their person instead of checking this in luggage. Smart.

unofficial **TIP**
Bring along a few extra identity photos of yourself. These come in handy when you need to get a train pass, a senior-citizens discount card, a permit to fish in the Seine, or whatever else crops up.

If you need some quick extra-baggage capacity, the duty-free liquor shops at both Roissy–Charles de Gaulle and Orly airports sell an excellent blue tote bag marked "Aeroboutique Duty Free Paris" for €6. It's strong, insulated, and not too ugly.

With the more stringent security enforced for carry-on luggage, you must be careful to put the following items in your check-in luggage: scissors, pen knives, razors or razor blades, or any other sharp object that could conceivably be used as a weapon. Visit **tsa.gov** for a more complete and up-to-date list of items prohibited in carry-ons.

CELL PHONES

CHECK WITH YOUR PHONE COMPANY to find out if your cell phone will work in France. If it's not a multiband GSM phone, it won't (France uses a GSM system). If it works, you'll have to select the carrier you wish to use—Orange (France-Telecom), SFR, or Bouygues. The coverage is about the same, and the rate schedules are usually torturously complicated. The roaming charges will kill you, but at least you'll be accessible. A better solution is bringing a prepaid phone card with you from any of the large U.S. companies, which allows you to dial into a local number and make your calls on the prepaid card. You can also rent or purchase a cell phone with a prepaid French SIM card before you travel from Cellular Abroad (**cellularabroad.com**; ☎ 800-827-3020) or Telestial (**telestial.com**; ☎ 800-707-0031). Incoming calls and SMS are free; calls to the United States are from €0.18 per minute, and each text is about €1.

PASSPORTS AND VISAS

AS IS TRUE WITH ALL INTERNATIONAL TRAVEL, when visiting France you must be in possession of a valid passport. Note that the date of expiration should be sooner than three months after the date of your expected return. Citizens of the United States, Canada, Britain, and other European Union countries do not need a visa for France. Upon entry into France, your passport will be stamped, enabling you to stay in the country for up to three months. If you hold a passport from another country, make sure to inquire about visa requirements at the closest French consulate. It is always a good idea to leave a copy of the information page of your passport at home and put a second one in your luggage. That way, in case your passport is lost or stolen, you will facilitate its replacement by showing this photocopy at your consulate in Paris. And now, most countries have complied with U.S.-driven regulations for hi-tech passports and are issuing chip-embedded identity-recognition devices and/or biometric data. Inquire, especially if you have an old passport that is about to expire. You might find yourself stuck or delayed.

unofficial **TIP**
You do not need an International Health Certificate to enter France from the United States, although if you plan to continue your journey to another country, you should inquire with that country's consulate before leaving home.

Do not wait too long to apply for a new passport or renew an old one. Routine applications are processed within four to six weeks of receipt, and expedited requests are processed within three weeks. If you need your passport within two weeks, you need to schedule an appointment to apply in person at one of the 13 regional passport agencies.

French Consular Offices

For all other administrative, commercial, and legal issues, contact the French Consular office nearest you. The French government posts travel and administrative information at **info-france-usa.org**.

FRENCH CONSULAR OFFICES IN THE UNITED STATES
- **Atlanta**
  3475 Piedmont Street NE, Atlanta, GA 30305
  ☎ 404-495-1660; fax 404-495-1661; **consulfrance-atlanta.org**
- **Boston**
  Park Square Building, 31 St. James Avenue, Suite 750,
  Boston, MA 02116
  ☎ 617-832-4400; fax 617-542-8054; **consulfrance-boston.org**

- **Chicago**
  Olympic Center, 205 North Michigan Avenue,
  Chicago, IL 60601
  ☎ 312-327-5200; fax 312-327-5201; **consulfrance-chicago.org**
- **Houston**
  777 Post Oak Boulevard, Suite 600, Houston, TX 77056
  ☎ 713-572-2799; fax 713-572-2911; **consulfrance-houston.org**
- **Los Angeles**
  10390 Santa Monica Boulevard, Suite 410, Los Angeles, CA 90025
  ☎ 310-235-3200; fax 310-479-4813
  consulfrance-losangeles.org
- **Miami**
  Espirito Santo Plaza, 1395 Brickell Avenue, Suite 1050,
  Miami, FL 33131
  ☎ 305-403-4150; fax 305-403-4151; **consulfrance-miami.org**
- **New Orleans**
  1340 Poydras Street, Suite 1710, New Orleans, LA 70112
  ☎ 504-569-2870; fax 504-569-2871
  consulfrance-nouvelleorleans.org
- **New York**
  934 Fifth Avenue, New York, NY 10021
  ☎ 212-606-3600; fax 212-606-3620
  Visas: 10 East 74th Street
  ☎ 212-606-3601; **consulfrance-newyork.org**
- **San Francisco**
  540 Bush Street, San Francisco, CA 94108
  ☎ 415-397-4330; fax 415-433-8357
  consulfrance-sanfrancisco.org
- **Washington, D.C.**
  French Chancery, 4101 Reservoir Road NW, Washington, DC 20007
  ☎ 202-944-6195; fax 202-944-6148
  Visas: ☎ 202-944-6200; **consulfrance-washington.org**

IN CANADA
- **Moncton/Halifax**
  777 rue Main, Suite 800, Moncton, NB E1C 1E9
  ☎ 506-857-4191; fax 506-858-8169
  consulfrance-moncton.org
- **Montreal**
  General Consulate, 1501 Mc Gill College, 10th Floor,
  Montreal, Quebec H3A 3M8
  ☎ 514-878-4385; fax 514-878-3981
  consulfrance-montreal.org
- **Toronto**
  General Consulate, 2 Bloor Street East, Suite 2200
  Toronto, ON M4W 1A8
  ☎ 416-847-1900; fax 416-847-1901; **consulfrance-toronto.org**

- **Vancouver**
  General Consulate, 1130 West Pender Street, Suite 1100,
  Vancouver, BC V6E 4A4
  ☎ 604-681-4345; fax 604-681-4287
  consulfrance-vancouver.org

IN THE UNITED KINGDOM
- **London**
  General Consulate, 6A Cromwell Road, London SW7 2EW
  ☎ 0207-073-1250; **consulfrance-londres.org**
- **Edinburgh/Glasgow**
  General Consulate, 11 Randolph Crescent, Edinburgh EH3 7TT
  ☎ 0131-225-7954; fax 0131-225-8975
  consulfrance-edimbourg.org

TRAVEL RESTRICTIONS

IF YOU'RE WONDERING WHETHER FRANCE has any restrictions as to what you can bring into the country as a tourist, you can relax. France has comparatively few travel restrictions. You can strut past customs inspectors with a pair of Irish setters and not be questioned (although you do need health certificates for bringing pets into the country). As long as your passport is valid and you're not carrying massive amounts of electronic equipment, customs and immigration inspectors at Paris's two main airports are relatively lax. There are no restrictions on cameras or film you bring in, as long as they are for your own use. You may bring with you any reasonable gifts, and as in the United States, up to the equivalent of $10,000 in cash or negotiable instruments without having to declare it. You are limited to 200 cigarettes or 50 cigars or 100 cigarillos or 250 grams of tobacco, along with one liter of alcohol and two liters of wine (but no one brings wine to France!). Legally, you cannot import gold other than your own personal jewelry. And don't bring in pirated or knock-off brand clothing or anything made of ivory, endangered species, or exotic wood.

unofficial **TIP**
For absolute assurance, you may want to stick photocopies of any invoices or receipts for expensive video, photographic, or computer equipment that you are traveling with into your carry-on luggage.

HOW TO DRESS

PARISIANS TEND TO DRESS NICELY and more formally than their North American counterparts, so when in doubt, err on the dressy side. The line between being dressed up and being simple and elegant, as Parisians often are, is a fine one. The French way of dressing includes subtleties and nuances that are often hard for visitors to grasp quickly. The choice of brooch, the tasteful belt, the shoes, the fabric of your vest, the shape of buttons, and a pair of unique earrings all make a difference. Elegance in France is not necessarily eye-catching; it's often the opposite, the art of understatement. To be

unofficial **TIP**
We suggest that you find
for yourself a balance
between looking good and
being looked at.

comfortable, don't overdress in formal evening wear when going to a Paris restaurant.

In the summer months, you'll rarely see
Parisians bopping around town in shorts,
although women often wear short skirts.
There's no stigma about wearing shorts when
it's 90° F and you're sightseeing, but as a rule the French don't look
favorably on irreverent casualness or sloppiness. They have their own
casual look called *decontracté* (relaxed), but it is always stylish. So
if blending in is important to you, here are some tips on style. In the
winter months, you probably won't want to wear a ski jacket or down
parka in the city unless you're going skiing. An overcoat or leather
jacket with some warm but not too bulky sweaters is best. The French
wear scarves and shawls religiously, and you may even want to buy
yourself something French and silky while you're here. A portable
umbrella is always a good idea, and chances are that you'll be using
it if you're traveling in the fall, winter, or early spring.

Gentlemen, you may decide to throw a tie and jacket into your
luggage, but you should note that French elegance and proper dress
do not usually oblige you to wear a tie and jacket. Even French com-
mentators on television do not wear ties. The fanciest restaurants
will shun jeans but usually do not require ties.

Bring your favorite toiletries with you. Although you'll find everything you need in Paris, American products tend to be more costly,
and it's a shame to have to pay $8 for shaving
cream when you could bring yours along for
$2. But, then again, you'll find great—if not
better—French equivalents to almost anything you need in your local Monoprix. In
the hot months, a great item to pick up is a
spray can of Evian mineral water, sold in pharmacies. Not only will
this keep you cool, it helps keep you from dehydrating on the airplane
ride back home. It's better than air-conditioning.

unofficial **TIP**
Jeans are worn frequently,
and women even wear
them to the office.

A Word on Tourist Garb

Although Americans (and Europeans) love to wear sneakers, if you
want to feel less conspicuous as a visitor, try bringing along very
comfortable walking shoes instead of Nikes or Reeboks (unless you
plan to jog). Since Paris gets a fair amount of seasonal rain, shoes
that keep water out are advisable.

Fannypacks and baseball caps (unless you're a hip-hopper) both
single you out as a tourist. If that's your preference, go ahead—
fannypacks, in particular, are good at keeping your valuables safe
(though it's best to wear a shirt or windbreaker over the bag, as
some purse snatchers are very adept at unfastening the clasps of
fannypacks' belts). Small daypacks are equally useful and more discreet. Women should opt for an oversize tote bag to use instead of a

purse. These are ideal for storing all the necessities you might need for a day on the town—an umbrella, water bottle, map, sunglasses, and the small purchases you're likely to make throughout the day.

Savvy travelers like black clothing. Black goes with everything and hides dirt. Black shoes are always appropriate and are easy to clean. One smart tourist admits that she's "a true shoe hound but can go an entire week on one pair of black shoes in Paris."

For those of you traveling in the winter months, listen up. If you have a tendency to get cold walking outside in the winter but hate it when you roast in department stores, be sure to dress in layers.

ESTIMATING YOUR BUDGET: A BALLPARK IDEA

TO BUDGET YOUR TRIP, use the following information as a rough indicator for the basics, per person, noting that there are great variations in the costs of hotel rooms, wining and dining, and shopping preferences. Estimates are based on two people traveling for a week, neither depriving themselves of normal comfort nor saying no to the little purchases during the day that make foreign travel a delight. Airfare and airport transfers are not included as part of the total per day per person.

Airline tickets	$1,500
Airport transfers	$80
Hotel room (based on a modern and comfortable three-star hotel, per person, per night)	$160
Meals (lunch and dinner, good but not starred restaurants)	$160
Métro/museum passes	$30
Miscellaneous	$80
Total	**$430/per day per person**

How Much Cash to Carry?

As much as you can! No, really, the amount of cash you bring is totally subjective, depending on how much you tend to spend and what you plan to buy. Since your airplane tickets, hotel room, and much of your wining, dining, and entertainment can be paid by credit card, you won't need large amounts of cash. A mix of euros and U.S. cash, a major credit card, and perhaps major traveler's checks in small denominations in either U.S. dollars or euros is preferable.

It is relatively easy to get cash out of Cirrus- and Plus-affiliated ATMs in Paris by using your VISA or MasterCard, or your bank's ATM card. American Express also has a limited number of its own ATMs. Most Paris banks are on the Cirrus or Plus system and even offer instructions in English. Remember to bring your PIN (four-digit number) with you—your PIN for international-banking access may be different than the one you use every day at home, so ask your

unofficial **TIP**
The American dollar is little recognized and has no appeal to French merchants; don't try to use dollars to pay or think that a U.S. $50 or $100 bill is going to impress anyone.

bank for this information before leaving the country. Some banks are slow in processing these requests, so plan on asking about this at least a month prior to your departure. We advise having a second card with you in case a Paris machine eats one card and you cannot recover it right away. You may want to request a second copy of the same card and keep one in a safe place in case the magnetic strip on the other card becomes defective. Also note that Visa and MasterCard charge up to 3 percent on overseas purchases.

When possible, you'll want to show up in Paris with at least €200 in cash in your pocket in case you need to pay a taxi or get something to eat before you can change money. Ask your local bank if they can get you some euros before you leave—as a service, they usually will. But don't buy too much. U.S. exchange rates on foreign funds are usually lower, and unless you have easy access to a major foreign-currency dealer in a large American city, you'll do a lot better waiting to change most of your money in Paris. Call a foreign-currency dealer in the city nearest you to inquire about rates and commissions. You can check prevalent exchange rates in the business section of most newspapers, but note that these are the bank-to-bank rates. Expect to get about 10 percent less.

Exchange rates at ATMs tend to be better than those offered at Parisian banks. When using a debit card, your bank at home will charge you between $2 and $5 per transaction or a small percentage of the amount withdrawn. Inquire first with your bank or credit-card company what the fees are for withdrawing funds from an ATM abroad. Most credit-card companies consider overseas ATM withdrawals as "cash advances" and start charging you a steep interest rate from the day of withdrawal until the day the next statement is paid. Be sure you know what these often hidden fees are before you use them, so that you're not surprised by the costs on your statement when you get home. To avoid these interest fees, consider simply prepaying a sum of money to your credit-card company and traveling with a credit balance. Then your cash advances won't cost you a cent in interest.

unofficial **TIP**
If you can't get euros before you arrive in Paris, do change a small amount of currency into euros at the airport—you'll need it for the taxi, bus, or other small items on your way into Paris.

One little trick that we have shared with our readers in the past is the purchase of euro coins (as opposed to paper currency) at the airport or at an exchange office before traveling. You can often buy coins at a much better exchange rate simply by asking for them. It's a bit inconvenient to carry a packet of coins, but the savings in the exchange rate may be enough to buy you a sandwich or drink, and you may need the coins upon arriving for tips, Métro tickets, telephone cards, and small items like newspapers, candy, or water. The one- and two-euro coins are your best bet. If you still have some French franc notes from a previous visit, you will be able to exchange them for euros at the Banque de France (39, rue Croix des Petits Champs, Paris 75001) until 2012.

When returning home, we recommend that you either save your coins and keep them for your next visit or, if you have the option, leave them for the World Wildlife Fund or UNICEF.

When carrying American cash, preferably in crisp $20 or $100 denominations ($50 bills are often confused for other denominations), you may find it useful knowing that there are a number of 24-hour cash machines in Paris that convert foreign banknotes into local currency. This can be a real lifesaver late at night when you need taxi money or cash to pay for a late round of cognacs.

PART THREE

ACCOMMODATIONS

UNDERSTANDING *Your* OPTIONS

LATER IN THIS CHAPTER, you'll find a broad selection of profiled hotels from which to choose. But before you make a reservation, you need to get a handle on where in Paris you want to stay and how much you're willing to pay. A basic understanding of the Paris hotel scene and the various types of lodging available will also be helpful. We understand that your choice of lodging is perhaps the single most important detail of your trip. Your hotel room, after all, will be your point of contact with the city, your base camp, and your home away from home. To be fair, the French have attempted to adapt hotel conditions when possible to the standards and expectations of their guests. But your cultural sensitivity should always be turned on, which means you should not expect the same size rooms in Paris as you might in Atlanta or Sydney.

By North American standards, many Paris hotel rooms are generally small, sometimes painfully so. You may find yourself in a tastefully decorated room in the Latin Quarter where you can barely walk around the outside of your bed. The closet might be cramped, and the shower may demand a gymnast's flexibility to maneuver inside. Also, in France, bigger does not necessarily mean better. So what you give up in space, you might gain in décor or view or taste. The key to being satisfied is not to settle for less but to think differently. A small room can often be especially cozy and secure-feeling. The décor may convey quality and elegance, and the location of the hotel may be sublime. So overlook the expectations whose validity is solely rooted in what you'd demand back home.

In the one-, two-, and even some three-star establishments, bath towels may seem like washcloths, and you may have to crane your neck to see the little TV suspended in the corner of the room. Of course, if you're really claustrophobic or unhappy with your lodging, ask if there is another room available. The hotel manager may have put you in a room with the best view, while you may prefer a larger room with a nondescript view or with a shower in the hall. Just ask.

Often the largest rooms are not the best rooms. Sometimes they are on the top floor and there is no elevator. Sometimes they are on the ground floor and open out into a small courtyard. Sometimes they are designed for three people and have three twin beds. Decide what's most important to you.

THE HOTEL SCENE

THE GOOD NEWS IS THAT PARIS ENJOYS A wealth of wonderful hotels of immense charm and enchantment at relatively affordable rates, and you're on your way to staying in one! The wealth of choices, in fact, is overwhelming, and your key to ending up in the right place depends mostly on you and your priorities— location, style, needs, and, of course, price.

> *unofficial* **TIP**
> There is no reason at all to settle for accommodations that do not charm and delight you, that do not meet your needs, and in which you don't feel like a special person.

The fact that the city is so old and dense and is bound by strict building codes has protected Paris from the development of numerous large hotels inside the city, which has protected the smaller hotels. Most Paris hotels have fewer than 60 rooms and are independently owned or family-run, even the ones that belong to a group or network. And it is the attitude of independence that characterizes many Parisian hotels.

The little independent hotels with character offer you personality and originality. What you don't get is the predictability of chains or the consistency of standards and generic tastes. For this reason, it's hard to judge hotels according to North American standards. A lovely hotel with 16 rooms in the Marais, built in the 17th century and decorated in Louis XIV–style original furniture, may not have an elevator, and most likely does not have air-conditioned rooms, ice machines, or even a bellboy. It's the perfect spot for a couple who loves this kind of place, but cramped and impractical for another who needs plenty of space to spread out their luggage or do their daily in-room exercises.

When North American travelers are asked about their hotel, most begin by saying, "It's clean." Rest assured, most Paris hotels are clean, well kept, and safe. The plainest and cheapest ones, even the few shabby ones, are by and large clean and safe. So you can base your criteria on other things, like location, aesthetics, and price. The kind of places you'd never consider staying in American cities are cost-effective "finds" in Paris.

LOCATION

VISUALIZE THE CITY AS AN EGG laying on its side, with the Seine River flowing east–west (like a crack in the egg), starting in the southeast, heading through central Paris, and then sloping down and out of the city to the southwest. An inner ring-road called the PC or *petite ceinture* encircles the city, and a fast-moving and often congested beltway called the *périphérique* divides the city from the encroaching suburbs (*les banlieues proches*). Major highways (*autoroutes*) feed into the *périphérique* from all directions at various ports of entry (*les portes de Paris*) or gateways into the city. The A1 and A3 lead north to Roissy–Charles de Gaulle Airport and onward to the north of France, the English Channel, and Brussels. The A4 leads east to Disneyland Paris (27 miles from Paris) and onward to the east of France and then Germany. The A6 leads south to Orly Airport, and then southward to Lyon and the south of France. The A10 branches off to Chartres and Orleans. The A13 runs through the Bois de Boulogne, west toward Versailles, and then out toward Normandy and Brittany.

All road signs in France list distances in kilometers, and distances to Paris are measured from the heart of the city, Notre-Dame Cathedral, also known as "kilometer zero." France is a highly centralized country, with Paris located at the geographic and administrative center of the whole.

unofficial **TIP**
Seasoned travelers or affirmed Paris aficionados may opt for a small hotel in a less central arrondissement and use the savings to splurge on good restaurants. We like the ones around Père Lachaise cemetery. Far from the center. But it all depends on you!

Most visitors who book their own trip to Paris prefer to stay in the more central neighborhoods that are known for their liveliness and character: the Latin Quarter, the Marais, Châtelet–Les Halles, Île Saint Louis–Île de la Cité, Saint-Germain-des-Prés, Bastille/République, Opéra, Champs-Élysées–Concorde, Invalides–Eiffel Tower, or Montparnasse.

While there are scores of perfectly comfortable hotels that may offer excellent value outside these areas, the great advantage to being here is that you know in advance that you'll find charming restaurants, shops, and animated street life within a short walk.

Prime Areas

The most centrally located arrondissements are the 1st, 2nd, 3rd, 4th, 5th, 6th, and 7th, with the 4th, 5th, and 6th probably being the choicest. But being quaint comes with its price. Again, these generalizations are too broad to be wholly fair. Simply put, if you find a package tour offering seven nights at a hotel in, say, the 15th arrondissement, don't expect to be centrally located or in a small and charming hotel. Since the Eiffel Tower borders the 7th and the 15th arrondissements, a hotel brochure may boast of rooms with a view of the Tower. This may seduce you, but a view of the Eiffel Tower is not the only, or most important, criterion for selecting your hotel. In fact, if you'd like to be in an area with the sounds and smells of Parisian street life, don't be motivated by famous monuments. Similarly, the Champs-Élysées area is world-famous and glitzy and certainly worth a good, long stroll, but it's ultimately a rather boring and overpriced area to stay in. Again, there are exceptions to the rule.

Smart travelers who are not loaded down with luggage can save time and money by selecting hotels that are an easy walk from either an RER stop or an Air France Airport bus stop. Staying near RER stations while being in central Paris affords you easy access to the Eurostar to and from London and the Thalys fast trains for Brussels and Amsterdam, as well as to and from both airports. The same advice may apply for selected metro stops that are near train stations connecting travelers to the airports. See the hotel profiles later in this chapter for hotels situated within walking distance of Gare du Nord, Châtelet–Les Halles, Luxembourg, Port-Royal, or Denfert-Rochereau.

unofficial **TIP**
On the whole, beware of flashy offerings near easily recognizable sights. Think of atmosphere instead of tourist attractions.

TYPES *of* LODGING

ONCE YOU HAVE AT LEAST A GENERAL IDEA of location, you should determine what kind of lodging best suits your needs and budget. Alternatives include large and small hotels (either part of a recognizable chain or independent), furnished apartments, or hostels.

SMALL VERSUS LARGE HOTELS

WE LOVE THE SMALL PARISIAN HOTELS that have charm, character, style, and ambience, and represent the essence of Paris. Some larger hotels, such as the Lutétia, the Crillon, and the Raphaël, also capture Parisian authenticity and grandeur, but at memorable prices! In any event, there's nothing worse than finding yourself in a nondescript hotel room that could be anywhere from Indianapolis to Singapore. You want to feel Paris in the style and décor of your hotel from the moment you walk into the lobby.

HOTEL CHAINS VERSUS INDEPENDENTS

THE INTERNATIONAL CHAINS you are familiar with—Holiday Inn, Hilton, and Sheraton, to name a few—are available in Paris and may afford you some preliminary comfort. The Best Western chain has franchised its name to a lot of small but high-quality hotels, which may offer you a mixture of international standards and local charm. You'll be able to reserve with an 800 number, and you'll recognize their logo as your taxi approaches, but often the overseas versions of the chain differ markedly from their domestic cousins,

Best Western	☎ 800-780-7234
Hilton Hotels	☎ 800-445-8667
Hyatt Hotels	☎ 888-591-1234
Sheraton	☎ 800-325-3535
Westin Hotels	☎ 800-937-8461

and you may be surprised. This, incidentally, cuts both ways. Best Westerns in Paris, as we said, are sometimes upscale establishments in swanky neighborhoods and sometimes simpler hotels on quiet back streets. The Holiday Inns in Paris command greater status than their North American counterparts and tend to be more expensive. Often the hotel chain buys or franchises the name and reservation system to independent Paris hotels. Thus, travelers expecting the consistency of a known brand are often amazed by the diversity found among the chain's Paris locations. An exception is the Hilton, which complies with Hilton standards worldwide and is in a location that is impressive (at the foot of the Eiffel Tower), but it isn't too convenient or very Parisian.

Even with the diversity and charm characteristic of some Paris chain hotels, we remain partial to the independents, including more of them than chain hotels in our detailed hotel profiles later in this section. If, however, you want to check out the Paris rates and availability at the chain hotels, here are the 800 numbers in North America:

ABOUT FRENCH HOTEL CHAINS

THERE ARE A NUMBER OF FRENCH CHAINS found all over France that you might not have heard of.

ACCOR This French megachain owns four major chains—**Ibis, Mercure Hotels, Novotel,** and the more upscale **Hotel Sofitel** and **Pullman**—totaling some 4,000 hotels worldwide. They also own a number of budget chains, including **Hotel F1,** and **Etap.** The toll-free number for Accor's Reservations Centre in the USA and Canada is ☎ 800-515-5679, and their Web site is **accorhotels.com.**

CONCORDE HOTELS Definitely the chain of prestige, Concorde has six renowned hotels in Paris with rooms ranging from €165 to €800 per night. Call ☎ 800-888-4747 toll-free in the USA and Canada or visit **concorde-hotels.com.**

RELAIS & CHÂTEAUX These famed hotels and restaurants, some of the most exclusive properties in the world, have an elegant Web site where you can download a catalog free of charge or else order a copy (free except postage) from the toll-free number in the United States, ☎ 800-735-2478. Visit **relaischateaux.fr.**

TIMHÔTEL This and other chains like **Libertel** have brought a number of small and decent hotels under one umbrella and given a face-lift to smaller hotels that merit greater attention. Timhôtel has 19 hotels, all within Paris, and all typically Parisian. All are two- and three-star hotels and have on average 50 rooms, ranging from about €90 to €230 a night for two people. These prices are for Internet bookings; a reservation made by phone will cost about €20 more per night. These represent a good compromise between the big chains and the independents. You can reserve a room and consult their catalog at **timhotel.com**, or call a hotel directly (the numbers are on the Web site); there is no central reservations number.

Other major French chains include **Kyriad, Campanile, Balladins, Bonsaï,** and **Première Classe,** many of which you'll find at exits on the large, interstate-type freeways around Paris.

SOME HAVE STARS, SOME HAVE NONE UPON THARS

DR. SEUSS'S STAR-BELLIED SNEETCHES aren't the only ones obsessed with stars (Seuss even spent time in Paris, in the 1920s, mingling with the likes of Ernest Hemingway and Gertrude Stein). The stars you see posted on Paris hotels are assigned according to fixed minimum criteria set by legislation. One hotel owner explained that the "stars are a classification system but are not a reference of quality." It is interesting to note that the official criteria include:

1. Number of rooms
2. Size of the reception area
3. Number of entrances
4. Number of elevators
5. Heating and air-conditioning
6. Round-the-clock hot water
7. Public telephones
8. Switchboard and in-room telephones
9. Blinds or shutters on windows
10. Soundproofing
11. Size of rooms (for example, a room in a two-star hotel must be at least 9 square meters—97 square feet—while in a four-star the minimum is 12 square meters—129 square feet)
12. Number of suites
13. Cooking facilities
14. Percentage of rooms with in-room sinks and bathrooms
15. Number of out-of-room bathrooms
16. In-room lamps
17. Electrical outlets
18. Hall lighting
19. Linguistic abilities of receptionists
20. In-room breakfast service
21. Disabled access

Note: One square meter equals about 11 square feet; thus, to convert square meters into square feet, multiply the number of square meters by 11. Example: 10 square meters equals approximately 110 square feet.

Tourist hotels are approved and examined by the French government. There are five official categories determined according to the facilities, the area, and the services provided.

In 2008 the famous star system of rating hotels was wholly revamped, since the old system was considered obsolete and misleading. The government also revitalized its €1.5 billion investment plan for the modernization of the nation's hotels in order to keep France attractive in tourism. The new classification has 233 criteria, some of which are required and some of which are optional, ranging from Internet access, quality of service, and commitment to sustainable development. The new rankings, assigned for five years following a visit by industry professionals, range from one to five stars and are voluntary. This is a positive change for France since the old ranking system hadn't been updated in more than 20 years. When reserving a hotel room you may wish to ask if the hotel's star rating is based on the new system.

The Former Two- and Three-Star Hotels

Paris, according to the Paris Tourist Office's November 2008 statistics, currently has 1,465 *hôtels classés* (one-, two-, three-, and four-stars), totaling more than 76,000 rooms within the city limits. In 2006, prior to the updated star-rating system, 1,400 of these were two- and three-star hotels, the ones best adapted for most travelers' needs and desires. The occupancy rate for Paris hotels averages 77 percent, although many of our favorite hotels are full (*complet*) most of the year and require reservations at least several months in advance.

Former One-Stars, Inexpensive Choices, and Hostels

If you'd like to spend as little on accommodations as possible in order to make your trip economically feasible, or if you want to free up money for fine dining or gifts, you'll be pleased to know that Paris has several hundred small hotels with one or no stars, offering clean and simple rooms, with and without showers and toilets in the room. As the star-rating system has been modernized, it is not yet clear what will happen to the rating of these establishments. But, note that on the whole they represent good value for the budget-conscious traveler not bothered by modest accommodations. In general, however, be cautious, especially with those hotels situated in expensive areas. Although all are safe and most are clean, standards are variable, comfort is minimal, and some are not too charming.

There are still a few hundred *hôtels non classés* (without stars) and one-star hotels, although they are disappearing rapidly. The Tourist Office, though, indicates that the number of un-starred hotels has actually increased by nearly 60 percent. Curious travelers will note that this is certainly due to the responsibilities and cost of earning and keeping those stars. Those with few stars that we profile later in this chapter are some of the best economical choices in the city.

Students and low-budget travelers have lots of choices in Paris. There are a number of fine hostels in Paris, as well as student residences. See Alternative Lodging Options below.

ALTERNATIVE LODGING OPTIONS

Furnished Apartments

A number of small companies in Paris offer fine apartments for rent by the week and month. It is a sure way of living like a Parisian while feeling at home. This may not be the best solution for inexperienced travelers, but it certainly is an interesting housing option. We know several small firms well that we can comfortably recommend. Glenn Cooper's **Rentals in Paris** (New York phone and fax ☎ 516-977-3318; Paris ☎ 06 11 32 60 92; abby@ rentals-paris.com; **rentals-paris.com**), with 27 high-quality apartments, is one of the best. A

unofficial **TIP**
For stays of a week or longer you can have your own furnished apartment in central Paris for less than you would pay at many hotels. This choice is particularly attractive when traveling with a family, a small group of friends, or two or more couples. Reserve as far in advance as possible.

native New Yorker and graduate of Wharton Business School, Cooper opted to start this family-run business because he loves Paris and has a passion for things French. Although his flats are not inexpensive, the attention to detail, his American staff, and the elegant accommodations assure guests a memorable stay. Cooper offers a nice selection of upscale apartments, including studios, one-bedrooms, and two-bedrooms, all located in the prime areas for Paris tourism and business travel (1st, 2nd, 3rd, 4th, 5th, 6th, 7th, 14th, 16th, and 18th arrondissements). Count on €700–€1,800 per week or €2,100–€5,400 per month. All of Cooper's apartments can be viewed on his Web site, along with an online calendar to check availability.

A longtime favorite of ours is **RothRay Rentals** (10, rue Nicolas Flamel, 75004; ☎ 01 48 87 13 37; fax 01 42 78 17 72; rothray@online.fr; **rothray.com**) in Paris. "If you've stayed in your own apartment in Paris, you'll have a hard time going back to a hotel," claims the British codirector of RothRay, Ray Lampard, whose small but top-rate collection of elegant apartments in central Paris is the object of many rave reviews.

The West Coast newsletter *Paris Notes* published an interesting feature on short-term apartment rentals, weighing the pros and cons of this lodging option. According to them, if you are staying less than a week, go to a hotel. For two weeks or a month or longer, keep reading. If your main motivation is to save money, proceed carefully, because savings depends on the number of people in your party and whether you plan on cooking at home. If you never cook, think again. On the other hand, if you're a family of four or five, two or more couples, or a small group of friends, the prospect of sharing a large 17th-century apartment with beamed ceilings and a view of Notre-Dame can be very tempting and ultimately more comfortable and economical than taking hotel rooms. If you fear that the scale and aesthetics of old Paris buildings, kitchens, bathrooms, and the like may be too alienating or too much of a hassle—or you've decided not to have any dishes to wash in Paris—you might consider this option for another trip.

RothRay's ten centrally located apartments are both well selected and impeccably maintained. With apartments chosen for both business travelers and discriminating tourists, it focuses only on the "heart of Paris," the Marais and the Châtelet–Les Halles area, from where you can walk to almost everything. RothRay has limited inventory, a highly loyal following, and a seven-day minimum, so the only downside is that they fill up quickly. It requires only a 25 percent refundable deposit, and payment can be made by personal check in your own currency. Daily rates range from €110 to €120, but if you consider that their top-priced apartment, located on rue Saint-Germain l'Auxerrois, is an 18th-century fifth-floor duplex with two double bedrooms, a large living room, kitchen, full bathroom, washing machine, and terrace, you see that the economics make sense. Reserve as far in advance as possible.

A third furnished rental option is Theo Kilgore's **Paris Apartment Search** (5, rue Villedo, 75001; ☎ 01 55 35 05 45; fax 01 55 35 05 46; t.kilgore@free.fr; **parisapartmentsearch.com**), which offers a wide range of accommodations from studios to five-bedroom luxury flats. Theo is a personable and accommodating American with lots of experience and a wealth of Paris-specific knowledge. The advantage of this firm is its willingness to find lower- and reduced-price options.

Other reliable apartment-rental agencies include:

At Home in Paris ☎ 01 42 12 40 40; fax 01 42 12 40 48
info@athomeinparis.fr; **athomeinparis.fr**

France Appartements ☎ 01 56 89 31 00; fax 01 56 89 31 01
info@rentapart.com; **rentapart.com**

Apartment Living in Paris ☎ 01 45 67 27 90; fax 01 45 66 60 90
apartment.living@free.fr; **apartment-living.com**

Paris Appartments Services ☎ 01 40 28 01 28; fax 01 40 28 92 01
info@paris-apts.com; **paris-apts.com**

Servissimo ☎ 01 43 29 03 23; fax 01 43 29 53 43
info@servissimo-paris.com; **servissimo-paris.com**

For longer-term apartment rentals (one-month minimum) of the highest quality, many professionals consult **De Circourt Associates** ☎ 01 43 12 98 00; fax 01 43 12 98 08; circourt@ homes-paris.com; **homes-paris.com.**

U.S. Apartment Rental Services for Paris

Paris Notes named **Chez Vous** the "Best American-based Paris Specialists" and recognized **France for Rent** for their knowledgeable U.S.-based French staff.

Chez Vous 1001 Bridgeway, PMB 245, Sausalito, CA 94965; ☎ 415-331-2535; fax 415-331-5296; bonjour@chezvous.com; **chezvous.com.**

France for Rent 1505 Bridgeway, Suite 114, Sausalito, CA 94965; ☎ 415-642-1111; info@franceforrent.com; **franceforrent.com.** Their Web site will allow you to visualize what a Paris apartment looks like.

This company manages its own Paris properties:
France Homestyle ☎ 206-325-0132; fax 206-328-3673; info@francehomestyle.com; **francehomestyle.com.**

The **Paris-Anglophone** Web site **paris-anglo.com** offers a housing section, Housing in France, on its home page.

HOSTELS IN PARIS

YOUNG TRAVELERS, STUDENTS, and budget travelers may opt to stay in one of Paris's hostels (*auberge de jeunesse*). This is another way of experiencing Paris and a totally worthwhile option if you have to do Paris on the cheap. There are a number of centrally located hostels run by organizations such as MIJE, BVJ, and the YMCA. Here is a selection:

- **BVJ Louvre**
  20, rue Jean-Jacques Rousseau, 75001
  ☎ 01 53 00 90 90; bvj@wanadoo.fr; **bvj-hotel.com**
  Métro: Louvre
- **BVJ Quartier Latin**
  44, rue des Bernardins, 75005
  ☎ 01 43 29 34 80; bvj@wanadoo.fr; **bvj-hotel.com**
  Métro: Maubert-Mutualité
- **UCJG–YMCA**
  14, rue Trévise, 75009
  ☎ 01 47 70 90 94; ymca_ucjg.paris@wanadoo.fr
  perso.orange.fr/ymca_ucjg.paris
  Métro: Cadet
- **Fédération Unie des Auberges de Jeunesse**
  (4 hostels in the Paris area)
  Central Booking Office: 27, rue Pajol, 75018
  ☎ 01 44 89 87 27; fuaj@fuaj.com; **fuaj.org**
  Métro: La Chapelle
- **MIJE Fauconnier**
  11, rue du Fauconnier, 75004
  ☎ 01 42 74 23 45; info@mije.com; **mije.com**
  Métro: Saint-Paul

- **MIJE Fourcy**
  6, rue Fourcy, 75004
  ☎ 01 42 74 23 45; info@mije.com; **mije.com**
  Métro: Saint-Paul
- **MIJE Maubisson**
  12, rue des Barres, 75004
  ☎ 01 42 74 23 45; info@mije.com; **mije.com**
  Métro: Hôtel-de-Ville
- **Three Ducks Hostel**
  6, place Étienne-Pernet, 75015
  ☎ 01 48 42 04 05; backpack@3ducks.fr; **3ducks.fr**
  Métro: Félix-Faure
- **Young & Happy Hostel**
  80, rue Mouffetard, 75005
  ☎ 01 47 07 47 07; smile@youngandhappy.fr;
  youngandhappy.fr
  Métro: Monge

WEB ADDRESSES FOR PARIS LODGING

ONE OF THE MOST COMPREHENSIVE and useful Web addresses for Paris hotel-hunting is Jean-Noel Frydman's **france.com,** which lists hundreds of good choices and offers direct, online reservations and lots of related travel services.

HOTEL SITES	
booking.com	**hotelsupermarket.com**
france-hotel-guide.com	**lastminute.com**
frenchexperience.com	**paris-anglo.com**
hotelnetdiscount.com	**travel-in-france.com**
hotels.com	**viamichelin.com**
leshotelsdeparis.fr	

APARTMENT SITES	
france-apartment.com	**homerental.fr**
guestapartment.fr	**locaflat.com**

HOSTEL SITES	
hostels.com	**hostelworld.com**
hostelbookers.com	

SPECIALIZED AND UNUSUAL ACCOMMODATIONS

HERE ARE SOME TYPES OF LESSER-KNOWN accommodations that allow you to see France from a different perspective. *Note:* These mostly apply to areas outside of Paris.

COUNTRY RESIDENCES/GÎTES The French love *gîtes* (je-**heet**), more than 56,000 individually owned, fully equipped accommodations in rural villages and in the countryside. Classified according to standards of comfort ranging from one to four *épis* (ears of wheat), *gîtes* can be rented for weekends, by the week, or by the month. There are too many properties for a complete directory guide, so the organization now publishes annual guides of only new *gîtes* and *Gîtes de Charme*. They are available at Gîtes de France (56, rue Saint-Lazare, Paris 75009) by calling ☎ 01 49 70 75 75, in local bookshops, and online. See the full catalog of properties at **gites-de-france.fr**; info@gites-de-france.fr.

EFFICIENCY APARTMENTS/RÉSIDENCES DE TOURISME A tourist residence is a block of fully equipped apartments available for rent by the week or month, offering the services of a hotel and the privacy and price of an apartment. For information, contact the **Syndicat National des Résidences de Tourisme** (**snrt.fr;** ☎ 01 47 38 35 60; fax 01 47 38 35 61; snrt@snrt.fr). The advantage of an efficiency apartment is that you have a full apartment to yourselves. At times, though, these *résidences* feel a bit like dolled-up dorms or classy retirement homes.

One firm called **Parissimo Apartments** (**parissimo.fr;** ☎ 01 45 51 11 11; fax 01 45 55 55 81) rents individual apartments in wonderful old buildings. Stay in an edifice erected by the famous architect and city planner Haussmann or in a 120-square-meter apartment with a 50-square-meter terrace with a jacuzzi! It's large enough for the whole family or two or three couples. The €130–€150 daily rate is often in the same ballpark as the rate for a three-star hotel. Other choices include **Citadines** (**citadines.com**), **Adagio** (**adagio-city.com**) and **ParisAppartHotel** (**parisapparthotel.com**).

BED-AND-BREAKFASTS/CHAMBRES D'HÔTES In 2005 the City of Paris launched a new quality charter for bed-and-breakfast accommodations (*chambres d'hôtes*) under the logo "Hôtes Qualité Paris." A selection of approved companies can be found on the Paris Tourism Office's Web site, **parisinfo.com.**

CAMPING There is essentially no camping in Paris proper, although some travelers admit to pitching a tent in the Bois de Vincennes and Bois de Boulogne. We strongly advise you to *not* do this. The *bois* are now spotted with homeless people who've opted for tent-living in the woods. There are a few caravan (RV) campsites on the edges of Paris. Camping in France is forbidden on beaches, beside roads, on listed sites, and in reserves and natural parks, except in special areas set up for the purpose. For an official guide to campsites, contact the **Fédération Française de Camping-Caravaning,** ☎ 01 42 72 84 08; fax 01 42 72 70 21; **ffcc.fr;** info@ffcc.fr.

Staying in a Private Home or with Parisian Friends

If you have friends who live in Paris or have the opportunity to stay in the apartment or house of Parisians, you'll want to know something about local habits, customs, and practices. Of course, as in any city and culture, your experience will depend on the kind of people you stay with, their personalities, their economic bracket, their age, and their general openness. On the whole, be warned that Parisians tend to be more formal than you may be used to, and they certainly will take longer to "warm up" or joke around than perhaps you would if receiving French people at your home. This is not being unfriendly; it is being reserved, respectful, and tastefully timid. Don't count on Parisians to be gregarious backslappers. However, when they get comfortable with you, you'll find many locals to be natural *bon vivants*, and you just might end up friends for life. Parisians often find that Americans are too friendly too quickly, and that ultimately this kind of chummy contact is superficial.

If you're renting a room in an apartment shared with the host family, you'll want to remember a few simple rules.

- Don't expect large bath towels.
- If you're invited for dinner, always bring something, usually a nicely wrapped bouquet of flowers (tell the florist that they're *pour offrir* [pour off-**reer**]—flowers for personal consumption are wrapped in plain paper, and flowers that are being given to someone as a gift are dolled up for the same price). A decent bottle of wine or Champagne is standard. By decent, we mean that you should spend at least €20. Don't bring a bottle of table wine (*vin de table*) or any bottle with a plastic cork or with blue metal wrapping over the cork. Trust us. Even simple, unpretentious, and modest Parisians know a thing or two about wine. Small gifts from home are highly appreciated, and if you happen to think of it in advance, a bottle of Californian wine will be greeted with pleasant curiosity.
- After dinner, you may offer to help with the dishes, but there is a good chance that you will not be encouraged to enter the kitchen or be invited to help out, so although you'll want to be polite, don't be overly insistent.
- Be prepared to spend a lot more time sitting around the table at the end of the meal, drinking coffee, eating clementines, sipping cognac or Calvados, and talking than you'd ever think of doing back home. (If you care for a smoke, you'll now have to use the sidewalk!) This is one of the great pleasures of being in Paris—eating, drinking, and talking.
- In French, the bathroom sink and the kitchen sink, the *lavabo* and *évier*, respectively, should not be confused.
- Don't take really long showers; be conscious of water consumption and hot-water quantities, especially in the colder months, and try not to create puddles on the floor even though shower curtains are either absent or skimpy. Laundry is not done as often or as easily as back home. Lots of people don't have automatic dryers and still hang laundry in the bathroom.

HOTELS *for* BUSINESS TRAVELERS

BUSINESS TRAVELERS WANT TO BE NEAR AIRPORTS, train stations, business centers, commercial districts, convention halls, or conference centers. Business travelers want comfort and convenience, business amenities like computer connections, fax and e-mail facilities, and meeting rooms. Paris, which is well equipped for the business traveler, has the wonderful ability to meet both your professional and personal needs without compromising either.

Hotel prices sometimes double during major trade shows or salons such as the Prêt-à-Porter fashion week and the aeronautics show at Le Bourget Airport, which attracts big rollers from around the world. You may be surprised to see that not only is it harder getting a room, but room rates also jump on these days. If you haven't been alerted to rate changes, do not agree to pay the higher rate. Check your bill. Using the housing services offered by a convention center or trade show may also result in higher-than-necessary room rates. Unsuspecting travelers, often on expense accounts, bear the brunt.

PARIS'S MAJOR CONFERENCE CENTERS

FOR A LIST OF PARIS TRADE SHOWS, contact your local Franco-American Chamber of Commerce (see list in Part Two, Planning Your Visit), **eventseye.com,** or **comexposium.com.**

For business services provided by the Chamber, visit "Doing Business in France" at **paris-anglo.com** or **ccip.fr.** More than 60 of all the major trade shows in Paris are organized by Reed Exhibitions (☎ 01 47 56 50 00; fax 01 47 56 14 40; info@reedexpo.fr; **reedexpo.fr**).

unofficial **TIP**
Inflated prices are often tacked onto standard rack rates during conferences or shows.

VIPARIS Call ☎ 01 40 68 22 22 to rent offices and showrooms. Viparis manages ten exhibition venues in the Paris area, including Porte de Versailles, CNIT La Défense and Paris Nord Villepinte. Organization of exhibitions, expositions, trade shows, fairs, seminars, and congresses. Visit **viparis.com** for more information.

HOTELS AT THE AIRPORTS

NOT ONLY PROFESSIONALS PREFER to stay at or near the airport. Conservative tourists unfamiliar with Paris may feel more secure staying within eyesight of the runway and their returning flight. Unless you're in Paris only for an overnight stay or a quick transfer, we advise travelers to venture into the city rather than staying at or near either airport. The city is not prohibitively far, and access is relatively easy and affordable. The areas around both airports

ROISSY–CHARLES DE GAULLE AIRPORT HOTELS		
★★★★	Hilton	☎ 01 49 19 77 77
★★★★	Sheraton	☎ 01 49 19 70 70
★★★★	Sofitel	☎ 01 49 19 29 39
★★★	Novotel	☎ 01 30 18 20 00
★★	Ibis	☎ 01 49 19 19 19
ORLY AIRPORT HOTELS		
★★★★	Holiday Inn	☎ 01 49 78 42 00
★★★	Novotel Orly	☎ 01 45 12 44 12
★★	Ibis Orly	☎ 01 56 70 50 50
★★	Citôtel La Rotonde	☎ 01 69 38 97 78
—	B&B Hotel	☎ 08 92 78 29 29

are not pretty, and the hotels are not particularly impressive or economical.

If you still want to sleep at the airport and commute into town, here is a list of airport hotels. Pay special attention to our comments on obtaining the best possible rates. If you arrive at either Roissy–Charles de Gaulle or Orly without hotel reservations, proceed to the **Aeroport de Paris (ADP) Espace Tourisme** located at Roissy Terminals 1, 2C, 2D, and 2F, and at Orly Ouest. Their reservation service for same-day hotel reservations will obtain significant discounts for you. We discovered that by picking up the direct airport hotel phone we were quoted a rate that was only about €8 more than when we had the information stand book the room for us, and 50 percent lower than if we had just walked into the Sofitel Roissy Hotel ourselves ten minutes later without a reservation. So give yourself a few minutes to figure out how to get the same thing for the least amount of money.

RATES, RULES, *and* RECOMMENDATIONS

AS A ROUGH APPROXIMATION, you can spend as little as €70 for a double room with a shower in a modest hotel, not necessarily centrally located but certainly 10 to 20 minutes from the center of Paris. In the center of town, a very comfortable, newly renovated hotel room with a good dose of charm and style will cost you between €150 and €220. There is a lot of diversity in this range. Larger, more elegant hotels offer double rooms from about €250, whereas spacious, top-of-the-luxury-line hotel rooms or suites can easily run €600–€1,200 a night. Ouch!

The hotel industry in Paris, as everywhere, is driven by a commercial need to fill available rooms. Only since the early 1990s have hotel owners been free to set prices at will. With the invention of what insiders call "yield management," many hotels are constantly manipulating prices to do just that. Even the smaller, family-run establishments are obliged to play this game in order to survive—especially during the low season. Consequently, room rates are known to fluctuate like stock-market prices. If you've entrusted your travel agent or have reserved via one of the knowledgeable and quality-oriented tour operators serving Paris, you can sleep comfortably.

The published "rack rates," the ones hung on the board behind the front desk, are the highest possible rates you can be charged. French law stipulates that hotels cannot announce a price and then charge a higher one, so to protect themselves hotels announce the maximum but are prepared in most cases to sell rooms for less. If you book way ahead, you'll avoid headaches and stress, but you'll get booked at the highest published price. Late reservations yield the possibility of a better rate but present the stress of finding your first choice fully booked (*complet* [comb-**play**]). Last-minute reservations are not only subject to availability but also require a bit of finesse to negotiate. The unsuspecting traveler

> *un*official **TIP**
> Beware: You may be quoted different prices for the same room at the same or different times of the year.

with a naive look (or telephone voice) will be quoted one price, while the savvy traveler poses a succession of key questions and ends up saving $30 to $50 per night on a room in a three- or four-star hotel. You can walk into a hotel and be quoted $100 a night or call ten minutes before arriving and obtain the same room for $60 or $70, if there is availability. It's that wild. According to the hotel-booking service at Roissy–Charles de Gaulle Airport, for example, the Sheraton Hotel quotes different rates every hour!

We don't think you should spend endless hours jockeying to save a few bucks, but we do want you to be able to obtain the best-quality room that meets all your needs for the best possible price. A $40 savings a night amounts to $280 per week; that's enough to buy you a very memorable meal, an extra night in a château, or a great pair of French shoes.

In addition to displaying the highest rates, there are a number of other "rules" that French hotels must abide by and a few that you must follow:

- Prices displayed outside the hotel and in bedrooms must be inclusive of all charges and taxes. A surcharge can be levied for an extra bed or for breakfast.
- Rooms must usually be left by noon on the day of departure, but this can be flexible.
- Rates are usually quoted for a double room (two people).

- Rates include service and value-added tax (VAT), but not always the *taxe de séjour* (hotel tax), which is less than €2 per night for each guest over the age of 13.

- Guests are expected to arrive at their hotel no later than 8 p.m. If you have only a telephone reservation without a deposit, the hotel is not required to hold the room after 7 p.m., so call ahead if you are going to be later than you indicated. To avoid misunderstandings from the start, it is best to let the hotel know your approximate arrival time, especially if you expect to arrive after 7 p.m.

- If guests arrive before 7 p.m. on the day of a confirmed reservation and find that no rooms are available, the hotel is obligated to find them a room at a comparable price.

- Paris hotels are increasing their use of e-mail and the Internet. Many are letting online companies handle reservations, referrals, and payment. It's advisable that you bring paper copies of your e-mail confirmations with you, just in case.

Alain-Philippe Feutré, past president of the French Hotels Syndicate, has been devoted to increasing the quality of service afforded to tourists and helping inform visitors about the hotel conditions in Paris. Monsieur Feutré offers the following insights and advice.

Americans and Britons make up the largest part of the Paris hotel clientele and thus are very important to hotel owners who are in general eager to please. Don't select a hotel just because you like the sound of the name, or a descriptor affixed to the name. "Everyone [for example] is using the term *hôtel de charme* these days. Insist on seeing photos or reading a detailed description of the hotel you're considering. Ask how many rooms the hotel has. If there are 150 rooms, it is not a *hôtel de charme*!" Locations can be misleading as well. A hotel called Notre-Dame or Tour Eiffel may not be near Notre-Dame or the Eiffel Tower at all.

In terms of size, you should be clear that almost any hotel with character and charm in central Paris will have small rooms. "This is a matter of history and architecture," Monsieur Feutré explains. "It's better that people know this in advance. I prefer that guests who need a large room go to the Hilton and maintain their positive attitude about Paris than end up in a small room and be unhappy."

When asked about the amount of English that is spoken in Paris hotels, he replied, "*Ça vient!*" (We're getting there!) "In the luxury hotels there's no problem with language. And in almost all the smaller ones, at least the receptionist speaks some English. We recognize the need. But one point that disappoints us is that very few Americans make an effort to communicate in French. Isn't trying to understand something about the place they are visiting one of the reasons people travel? It's appreciated when you arrive with at least a few words of our language."

Regarding special services, disabled access, allergies to smoke, and the like, Monsieur Feutré stated that you should clearly make your request in advance. The Paris Tourism Office has a list of more than 300 hotels with disabled access, yet only 15 hotels in the Greater Paris area are sufficiently adapted to have been awarded the "Tourisme & Handicap" label from the authorities.

Although previously renowned for its cigarette smoke, France has made real progress in this area. In January 2008 smoking was banned in all enclosed public spaces, including hotels. Apparently, more than 70 percent of French people support this, and the law has worked like a gem.

Commenting on recent trends, Monsieur Feutré says, "Travelers are more prone to negotiate the rate. They tend to reserve at the last minute. Clients treat hotels today like the airlines. We experience no-shows without cancellations. We need both clients and hotels to act responsibly in order to preserve the quality of service."

With regard to reservations and deposits, there are plenty of interesting ambiguities that need to be spelled out. Legally, in France, holding a reservation with a credit-card number is not a true guarantee for either the hotel or the client. The only way to make sure that a reservation is guaranteed is for the client to instruct the hotel in writing to debit the card (usually the price of one night). With the authorization to debit the card and the transaction going through, the hotel is obliged by law to respect its commitment. If the hotel doesn't debit the card, it can't know if the card is valid and is not bound to respect the reservation. The same is true if a hotel holds your check until arrival. If your check is not cashed, the deposit is considered *les ahrres* (a refundable deposit), which is not binding. You should stipulate when you reserve by fax or e-mail that you are sending an *accompte* (deposit), which will not be refunded unless you cancel by a certain date. Monsieur Feutré says, "I advise guests to put in writing the cancellation date. Otherwise, a reservation held by an uncashed check or undebited credit card could be cancelled at the last minute by the hotel. Imagine if a hotel has 20 free rooms and a tour operator comes around and offers to buy 25. The hotel will sacrifice yours to sell all the empty rooms in a group. When you arrive, the manager may say, 'I'm sorry, but there has been a flood.'"

MAKING RESERVATIONS FROM HOME

HAVING CONSIDERED THE TYPE OF ACCOMMODATION, location, and price, you're ready to choose a specific lodging property and reserve. Review our profiles later in this chapter for detailed suggestions.

The most efficient means of reserving a hotel room in Paris today is by e-mail. If you are writing directly to the hotel, make sure you note the type of room you want, the number of guests, your preference of a bed for one person or a bed for two people, your date of arrival and

unofficial **TIP**
Note that the French write dates differently than you may be used to: day/ month/year. So, 3/5/2010 is May 3, 2010, not March 5, 2010!

departure, and your estimated time of arrival. We usually wait to send the credit-card number until after the hotel has confirmed the availability and price of the room. Print this confirmation e-mail and bring it with you.

The second-most efficient means of reserving is by sending a fax. Again, simply state your dates of arrival and departure, the number of guests, and any special needs or requests; for example, one large bed, two single beds, with bath or shower, if you prefer lower floors or upper floors, and so on. The smaller French hotels do not distinguish between queen- and king-size beds. If you want a big bed for yourself or are sharing a bed, just use the term *un grand lit* (ah gran lee). *Note:* Don't offer your credit-card number until after you obtain the information you've requested.

If you are reserving a hotel room on your own by telephone or fax, make sure to ask for the best room rate available and be sure that the rate you've been quoted includes all taxes and services (as required by French law). Ask if the breakfast (*petit déjeuner*) is included or not.

unofficial **TIP**
The longer you stay, the greater the chance for a discount off the rack rate.

If not, ask if the breakfast can be included for the same price. Chances are, if the hotel is not full, you'll win on this point. Specify if you want a full bathroom (*salle de bain*) with shower (*douche*) or bath (*bain*). Rooms with showers tend to be between €10 and €20 cheaper than those with bathtubs, so if you prefer a shower in any case, you'll save a bit. Watch out, though. Showers, mostly with handheld nozzles, are quaint but may not be up to your standards. The point here is to inquire on all your room options. In the smaller hotels, sometimes a room that is quieter but less scenic is cheaper, which may suit you fine. You will most likely be quoted prices in euros, so note the prevailing exchange rate. If you're planning to pay by credit card, ask for a euro rate, because your card will be charged in euros but debited in dollars.

If the hotel has a lot of empty rooms, you may obtain a better rate by simply asking for one. One Paris concierge tells us that he regularly offers a deep discount of up to 50 percent off the posted rate when he has empty rooms. Before being quoted a price, you will often be asked how many nights you'll be staying. If you're not sure, intimate that you may want to stay longer. To persuade you or entice you, the hotel may quote a reduced rate. On the other hand, in high season you'll probably get a "take it or leave it" response.

You have other options, though. Your local travel agent may be able to obtain a better rate for you. You may manage to have the breakfast included in the rate when normally it is not. Ask. You may be able to have parking thrown in if you're driving. You may be able to obtain an extra bed without charge, or not be charged for your children. You must ask, and ask again. Parisians tend to be gun-shy when it comes to asking for discounts or advantages. It's not in their culture, but it is in yours, and hotel reservation people and sales agents know this. So ask, always ending with *s'il vous plaît* and *merci beaucoup*, and *c'est gentil* when you've obtained something. "C'est gentil" means "that's nice," and it conveys that you are appreciative of the effort that has been made to please you. Form is important!

Never get angry or huffy when dealing with Parisians in the service sector. You will not help your cause. Don't try to go over someone's head or ask for a supervisor. This, likewise, will not bring you greater satisfaction and can easily make matters worse. No one fears for his job in France, and supervisors almost always defend their own hierarchy. Furthermore, you may be speaking to the owner or manager already. Take on a rather apologetic tone and start again. Parisians need to be stroked and seduced, or else they don't seem to care or respond. Small, charming hotels usually provide charming personnel but are also proud of their independence. You may not be used to having to adopt an apologetic tone when you are the paying customer, but it's like that in Paris. In France, as elsewhere, the customer's money is king, but the customer himself, well, he's only a high-ranking serf holding a wallet. Also note that the French are not as telephone-oriented as North Americans; you may find the telephone service or manners of people on the phone to be inadequate. Often this is just a cultural difference and not rudeness.

So let's recap the reservations process. If your travel agent handles this for you, he or she should be no less thorough.

1. Reservations should be in writing (letter, fax, or e-mail). Usually, hotels will ask that you either send a deposit to hold the reservation or give a credit-card number. Most of the time, personal checks will not be cashed nor credit cards debited until your arrival. A hotel may ask for a 25 percent deposit, but usually all you need to send or agree to is the cost of the first night as the deposit. With some hotels you may send a U.S.-dollar check with instructions that the hotel hold this until your arrival. As per Monsieur Feutré's advice, make sure you have a clear written understanding about when the hotel should debit your credit card or cash your deposit check.

2. Make sure your reservation, room rate, receipt of deposit, and conditions for cancellations are confirmed in writing by the hotel management. Bring the confirmation with you.

3. If you do not show up or do not cancel in advance, the deposit will not be refunded. Legally, you could be held responsible for the cost of your entire stay, but this never happens. Out of consideration, call to cancel once you know for sure you're not coming. If the hotel cancels your reservation or does not hold your room (after debiting your credit card

or cashing your deposit check), the law states that the hotel must pay you double the amount of the deposit.

ARRIVING WITHOUT RESERVATIONS

SURE, YOU CAN DO IT. Plenty of travelers do. But be aware that there are five distinct disadvantages and one great advantage.

Disadvantages

1. You may arrive on a day the city is packed due to a trade show or sports event.
2. You'll lose time tracking down a hotel, making phone calls, figuring out how to find the hotel, and so on.
3. You'll have less bargaining power in terms of choice and price by reserving on the day you arrive.
4. You may arrive early in the morning or late at night and have difficulty connecting with a hotel of your choice.
5. You may be too tired to deal with the hassle and end up checking into a hotel at the airport, overpaying, and missing the charm of your first night in Paris. If you change hotels you'll have to settle in twice. Not fun.

Advantage

A little-known tip for the more flexible, spontaneous traveler: You can pick up excellent deals on hotel rooms by booking at the well-marked **Aéroport de Paris (ADP) Information Stands–Espace Tourisme** at both airports and in all terminals. There is no sign indicating that hotel reservations are made here, and the ADP makes no attempt to publicize this or the amazing fact that between 100 and 200 excellent hotels fax the airport each morning, offering their available rooms at savings that can run up to 50 percent! Reservations must be made for one or more nights beginning on the day you reserve (arrive). The Information Stand staff will make the call for you, give you a confirmation voucher, and instruct you on how to get to your hotel. You pay 12 percent of the first night's rate as a deposit on the spot (cash or credit card), which the ADP keeps as its commission. The 12 percent is deducted from your hotel bill.

unofficial **TIP**
Reserve hotel rooms at terrific savings upon arrival in Paris at the ADP Information Stands in the airports.

It's better to have an idea of where you'd like to stay and the type of hotel before you ask, but the staff here is very friendly and helpful and speaks good English, if you need advice. We called the Sofitel airport hotel for a room for two and were quoted €15 more than if the Information Stand, ten feet away, had made the reservation for us! Try both, and take the best offer. Although the Information Stand is cobranded with the Office de Tourisme de Paris and ADP, the relationship between the two is ambiguous, and the ADP, curiously, offers a much more dynamic and advantageous hotel service than the Paris Tourism Office.

The main Paris Tourism Office in the city is located at 25, rue des Pyramides, in the 1st arrondissement at Métro Pyramides. There are also seven smaller welcome centers throughout the city at locations such as the Carrousel du Louvre and three of the Paris train stations. Check the Web site (**parisinfo.com**) for other addresses. A word of warning: Although they distribute lots of pamphlets and brochures, we've been told that their staff has been instructed not to spend more than two minutes per tourist inquiry. Reservations can be made by credit card at the tourist offices or through their Web site above, with substantial reductions offered for online bookings.

The PARISIAN HOTEL ROOM

FIRST OF ALL, IN FRANCE THE GROUND FLOOR of a building is called the *rez-de-chaussée* (ray duh show-say) (RC) and not the first floor. What you think of as the second floor is in France the first floor, the *premier étage* (preh-mee-**ay** ay-**tadj**). So if your hotel room is on the fourth floor, be prepared to go to the fifth floor—not a problem when there is an elevator, but a bit tough on the thighs and calves when there is not. Most hotels are equipped with elevators, but the smaller and more modest ones may still rely on the good old stairs, which is something to consider if you have a back problem or suffer from asthma. A few flights of carpeted stairs, though, may help you get your daily exercise while reducing your personal carbon footprint.

Don't be disturbed if you are asked for your passport when you check in. This is a common, legal formality. You'll get your passport returned either right away or a little while later. There is no stigma whatsoever about unmarried couples checking into hotels together. In fact, Parisians are not at all judgmental when it comes to questions of the heart or body. Public affection is widespread and is discreetly applauded.

ELEVATORS

TO REACH THE UPPER FLOORS IN SMALL HOTELS you'll either have to walk or squeeze into an elevator (*ascenseur* [ah-sen-**soor**]) that may be reminiscent of the marvels of Houdini. These devices were adapted to the small spaces available in the stairwells of old buildings. Luggage goes up by itself or piece by piece. Claustrophobics might opt for the stairs.

Both in hotels and apartments, don't be alarmed when the lights go off on the stairway when you're in the corridor or climbing up arching steps. All Paris buildings' lights are on electric timers. Most Europeans have been energy-conscious since electric power was invented.

BEDS

FRENCH BEDDING ON THE WHOLE is very comfortable, although there are a few details that will seem unusual, such as the shape of the pillows—square instead of rectangular. Made beds often have long sausage-like pillows maintaining a neat round form. These are great when sitting up and reading, but when it's time to catch some Zs, substitute the soft and square pillow (often feather-stuffed) you'll find in the closet to avoid getting a stiff neck.

Many European hotel beds are equipped with a duvet (a sort of down comforter) instead of the more traditional sheets and blankets. If you find a duvet too hot to sleep under, you have two alternatives: you can ask the hotel to provide sheets and blankets (sometimes available, sometimes not), or you can take the duvet out of its light-weight case and use the case for a sheet.

Other than in the expensive luxury hotels, double beds will not be as large as king size. Double rooms come with either a double bed or two twin beds, so state your preference when you reserve. Single rooms often come with single beds, unlike in American hotels, where you pay for a single but get a big bed anyway.

BATHROOMS

HOTEL BATHROOMS (*salles de bain* [**sahl** duh **bahn**]) in Paris are full of surprises. You may be enthralled or you may burst into fits of laughter. One travel editor stayed in a modest but tasteful older hotel in the 9th arrondissement and found his bathroom "large enough to play racquetball in." At the other extreme, a woman from Boston got stuck in the narrow tub of her hotel bathroom in the Latin Quarter.

Most newly renovated hotels have redone the plumbing and opted for international standards, including big mirrors, recessed lighting, built-in hair dryers (or at least the right electrical plugs), and Formica or stone countertops. In many hotels these concessions to style are meant to compensate for lack of space. Hotel rooms with bathtubs are slightly more expensive than those with showers.

SHOWERS VERSUS BATHTUBS

ONE OF THE MOST CULTURALLY CONFLICTED details in the Anglo-Franco worlds revolves around *la douche,* the shower.

It's rather amusing how humorless and inflexible North Americans can be when it comes to their morning shower. You may relish every variation of goose liver, but when it comes to that morning ritual, there's little room for experimentation. You want to turn on the hot water and stand blissfully and unthinkingly beneath a pulsating showerhead until life returns to your body. The French see the shower as a hygienic, practical event attached to contemporary life; North Americans approach their ritual as a daily renaissance.

In essence, the Parisian bathroom is what it says, a "bath" room, and the shower part is a historical add-on, a bastardization of the source. Anyone who has showered in France knows just how much dexterity one needs—and the naked gymnastics required—to hang onto the nozzle (*pommeau de douche*) with one hand and lather up with the other, while keeping the water inside the confines of the often short and squatty bathtub (*baignoire*). The showerhead,

unofficial **TIP**
Before hosing yourself down in your Parisian *douche,* don't get confused: the F is for *froid* (cold) and the C is for *chaud* (hot).

as an object, virtually does not exist in French households, and the stall shower (*cabine de douche*) is not commonly found. Considering that many Parisian buildings were first constructed in the 16th and 17th centuries, bathroom plumbing of any kind is an afterthought.

So approach your Parisian hotel visit forewarned. Your *salle de bain* will include a sink, a *bidet* (but that's another story), and a bathtub (which in most cases, but not all, will be equipped with the handheld shower nozzle and a moderately effective shower curtain). The shower curtain rod often poses a major architectural problem with the high ceiling and round-shouldered tubs. Some Parisians will tell you that you should first wet yourself down, then turn off the water and replace the nozzle, then lather yourself up, and finally turn the water back on, grab the nozzle, and rinse yourself with the shower spray. Clearly, they missed the point—but you do save water. Plus, in the winter you freeze.

Additionally, although most Parisian hotels have resolved problems of water pressure, you may not find the water supply abundant enough for your taste. Remember, you can always take a leisurely bath, if there's enough length of tub to stretch out. The larger, newer, and more costly hotels provide perfectly adequate bathtubs . . . usually. The older ones have tried to keep up. Be reassured, though, most four-star hotels have also installed stall showers. Ask for a room with a *douche séparée.* You should note that even these will have the removable, handheld nozzles that hang on a hook. And, more important, rooms with stall showers often do not have bathtubs and are the smaller, less desirable, and cheaper rooms. So beware, you may be sacrificing your lovely view of the Seine or your splendid terrace for the sake of a few vertical drops of H_2O. Wasn't it Marie Antoinette who said, "Let them take showers; kings and queens take baths"?

The tub itself is prone to many interesting variations, since many were installed to fit into a nonstandardized, prearranged space. In older and more modest hotels, you may still find the sitting tub (*sabot,* meaning clog) to be a short porcelain tub with a large inner step on which you are obliged to sit. Although excellent for washing your feet, you neither get a real shower nor a real bath. But they're fun!

If fun is not your thing and you are a stickler for your shower, ask your hotel when reserving if they have rooms with a *cabine de douche* (stall shower) or if the *bain* comes only with a *pommeau de douche.*

One travel writer recently pointed out that Americans should be forewarned about the high calcium levels in Parisian water and the dehydrating results to visitors' skin. Come equipped with skin creams to replenish the epidermal injuries caused by Parisian showers, she suggests.

THE BIDET

YOU MAY BE PERPLEXED on your first trip to a French bathroom to find a curious porcelain structure (with funky plumbing) situated between the sink and the shower. Welcome to the *bidet* (bi-**day**), one of the great icons of French culture.

Historically designed to serve aristocratic women as a hygienic aid, especially after sex, today the *bidet* can be used for lots of things, from relieving the pain of hemorrhoids to hand-washing delicate clothing to soaking your feet. Fresh water enters the fixture through a vertical spray in the center of the bowl, through a flushing rim or integral filler, or through a pivotal spout that delivers a horizontal stream of water. A pop-up drain allows you to fill it with water. It's surprising, but you'll still find these in even newly renovated hotel bathrooms.

THE TOILET

LES TOILETTES (lay twa-**let**) in France are also called the WC (**doub**la **vay-say,** or just vay-say) meaning "water closet," and that's what it is, a closet-sized space with a toilet. The WC (also called *le water*, pronounced lay wah-**tair**) is very often a separate room. Although this may seem odd at first, it's rather practical, and some hotel rooms are still organized this way. Newer ones usually aren't, though. It's always a great travel joy discovering the culturally diverse methods of flushing. For a tour of the nearly extinct "Turkish toilet," see Café and Café Tabac in Part Seven, Dining and Restaurants. The good news is that Parisian toilet paper has joined the 21st century and is no longer known for its abrasive quality.

CLOSETS

A CLOSET IS KNOWN IN FRANCE as a *penderie* (pon-**dree**), armoire (arm-**wahr**), or *placard* (plah-**cahr**). If closet space and drawer space are important to you, state this when you reserve. In the 17th century the built-in closet had not yet been conceived. In older and smaller hotels, it hasn't always been possible to create built-in closets or have enough room for a vestibule. Rooms in smaller hotels may not have closets at all. Rooms without closets generally offer some sort of wardrobe for hanging clothes.

HOTEL CLOCKS AND TIME

FOR MOST OF THE WORLD, a hotel room is a hotel room, but there are nonetheless interesting nuances in each country worth noting. For example, you may not find a clock on the night table in Paris. So bring a travel clock. Almost all the larger hotels are equipped with wake-up call technology, but the smaller ones still use the manual phone call or a knock on the door. To avoid confusion and to avoid missing a train, don't forget that time is counted on the 24-hour clock in France, so 1 p.m. is 13h and 9 p.m. is 21h.

AUTOMATED WAKE-UP CALLS

IF YOU HAVE A DIRECT-DIAL TELEPHONE in your room, you may be able to automatically program an electronically monitored wake-up call from France Telecom by calling **Automated Call Alarm** (*Mémo appel*), a service provided by France Telecom for €0.56 per call. Simply dial 55 and then the time (using the French 24-hour clock) you wish to be awakened, followed by the # sign on your telephone. (For example: Dial 55 and then 0715 plus # to be called at 7:15 a.m.) To cancel or change the wake-up call, repeat these steps and punch in the corrected time. This works from any private telephone in France. Ask at your hotel.

RADIOS

IF YOU'RE USED TO WAKING UP with the radio or love to roam the airwaves late at night, you may have to bring your own radio since your Parisian hotel room may not be equipped with one. If it is, though, see the chart below for the locations of a few key stations you might find interesting or useful.

You may also have access to World Radio Paris, an English-speaking station, through cable and satellite channels. It rebroadcasts a wide range of BBC and NPR programs and is a good source of what's on in Paris.

RADIO STATION	FREQUENCY	CATEGORY
France Inter	87.8 MHz	News, Talk
RFI	89.0	World News, Africa News and Culture
Nostalgie	90.4	Oldies, Top 40, Club
Chérie FM	91.3	Rock, Top 40
France Culture	93.5	Talk, Classical, News
Skyrock	96.0	Loud, commercial, young hip-hop
BFM	96.4	Business news and commentary
ADO FM	97.8	Latest in R&B, hip-hop
Radio Latina	99.0	Latin American, Salsa
Radio Nova	101.5	Top 40, Rap, Club
Fun Radio	101.9	Shock DJ, Top 40
Oui FM	102.3	Top 40, Club
RMC	103.1	Folk, French, Easy
FIP	105.1	Eclectic, great to wake up to
France Info	105.5	News, Talk

NO BIBLE IN THE DRAWER

CHURCH AND STATE OFFICIALLY SEPARATED in France in 1905. Despite the fact that France is predominantly Roman Catholic, there are no prayers in the local schools and few references to God in public life. Your hotel room will not be equipped with a Gideon Bible in the drawer (though sometimes you'll find a four-language New Testament or the like). For a short list of local religious congregations and the times of masses and services in English, see "Religion and Houses of Worship" in Part Four, Arriving, Getting Oriented, and Departing.

A WORD ON NOISE (YOURS AND OTHERS')

PARIS IS LIVELY, and with the liveliness comes noise. Especially on weekends, Parisians go out in hordes and stay out late. Even at 1 a.m. the streets around the Bastille or in the Latin Quarter will be swamped with Parisians out on the town, eating, drinking, coming from the cinemas, and congregating in the cafés. On Friday nights between 11 p.m. and midnight, an astonishing roar may be heard along the Grands Boulevards starting at the Place de la Bastille and heading west. Thousands of motorcyclists on everything from Harleys to mopeds drive en masse around the city, a tradition that dates back several decades. This may be amusing, but it may also be annoying if your hotel room looks out over the street. Some older hotels still do not have soundproofed windows, but this is slowly changing. If you're sensitive to high decibels, ask for a room that looks out onto a courtyard or garden (that is, a room in the back). The view may not be inspiring, but you'll preserve your ability to sleep. To check if a hotel room has been soundproofed or has double-glazed windows, ask if the room is *insonorisée* or if the windows are *double vitrage* (**doob**-la vee-**traj**).

French law stipulates that no one can make loud noises in the street or in their homes after 10 p.m., and on the whole Parisians within apartment houses are cautious about not disturbing their neighbors. So if you're the rowdy one, observe the law and be sensitive to your neighbors.

HEATING AND AIR-CONDITIONING

ALTHOUGH MORE AND MORE HOTELS are adding air-conditioning (*climatisation* [clee-mah-tee-zah-see-yown]) when they renovate, do not automatically count on air-conditioned rooms. In fact, you should generally assume that there is no air-conditioning. The summer heat may be hard to take in small hotel rooms, but even in the hot days of August an open window often does the trick. The only inconvenience is when your room faces a noisy street. If you're sensitive either to the heat or noise, pick either an air-conditioned room or a quiet one. In any case, there are only 20 or 30 days in the entire year when air-conditioning would be needed in Paris. Many smaller hotels, even the top-quality ones, can't justify the expense of installing such systems, especially in 17th- and 18th-century buildings.

Heat is rarely a problem in Parisian hotel rooms, although some travelers complain about rooms being too warm. Heating in French is *chauffage* (show-**fahj**). Radiator is pronounced "rah-dee-a-**tur**."

MINIBARS

THREE-STAR HOTELS AND ABOVE almost always provide a minibar in the room. This is convenient not only for finding a Perrier to quench your thirst but also for storing your own drinks and snacks. The prices of items are itemized and will be 30–40 percent higher than in a grocery store but about the same price as in a café. In the summer, it's a good idea to chill a bottle of water the night before to take with you on your excursion the next day.

MAKING CALLS FROM YOUR HOTEL ROOM

FINDING THE BEST WAY TO CALL HOME from a foreign hotel room has always been a tricky deal and one open to lots of theories and interpretations. Ask the receptionist at your hotel how much you'll be charged to call the United States, and you'll see what we mean. No one really knows for sure. Most hotel computers do the calculating automatically, and the personnel don't have a clue. At the Hotel Westminster we were told to make our call first and we'd see the cost on our bill. At one hotel you'll be told €0.50, per *impulsion,* but no one can tell you how long an *impulsion.* Another will tell you €2.50 a minute . . . they think. To clear this up, see "Calling Home from Your Hotel" in Part Four, Arriving, Getting Oriented, and Departing. The best advice is to avoid calling from your room and use your local or international calling card. You'll have to pay only for the local calls.

WATCHING FRENCH TELEVISION

ALTHOUGH WE SUGGEST that you spend little time in your hotel room and maximum time out and about in Paris, you will savor those cozy moments when resting in the afternoon or lounging late at night on your bed in your hotel room. Aside from reading, or writing postcards, you may find it amusing or enlightening to zap on the television and soak up some of the local programming. You'll note right away several major differences. There are far fewer stations in France than in North America—about 20 free analogue and digital stations, including TF1, France 2, France 3, La Cinq (5), Arte (7), and M6; plus two major subscription cable stations, Canal+ and TPS, which serve up a strong offering of films and international live sporting events such as the U.S. Super Bowl and NBA basketball. If you're up at 7 a.m., you can pick up the previous night's *ABC Nightly News* in English on Canal+.

unofficial **TIP**
Most foreign-language French television, from American sitcoms like *Sex and the City* or *Mad Men* to the English comedy of Rowan Atkinson, is dubbed, and unless you speak French or read lips, you'll find that your familiar programs from home have become incomprehensible.

Anglophone stations, including CNN, CNBC, DW, Fox News, Sky, and BBC, are widely available via cable or satellite at many hotels. Otherwise, it'll be the national stations, which to our thinking are more interesting for Parisian visitors anyway.

You'll also note that there are fewer commercials polluting the airwaves than on U.S. television. And in France the commercials are placed between the programs, instead of interrupting them. You'll enjoy the ads, though; here, the aesthetics and style are as important as the sales message. You'll also see unabashed nudity in everything from a shampoo ad to a movie made for television. The French don't share American sensibilities on this subject and are quick to ridicule Anglo-Saxon Puritanism.

The other difference is the amount of cultural programming in prime-time slots. The French have a fathomless respect for culture. They support and encourage it in many ways, not the least of which is through the increasingly ubiquitous influence of television. In France you can expect to see theater, opera, or ballet on one of the publicly broadcast television stations, even during prime-time scheduling. Arte (**ahr**-tay) is a Franco-Germanic state-funded station broadcast on channel 5 after 7 p.m. until, depending on the programming, 2 or 3 a.m. It often shows English-language movies, documentaries, and performances that are subtitled rather than dubbed in French.

KEYS AND OUTER DOORS

SMALLER HOTELS MAY NOT STAY OPEN all night long. You'll be told to take the *key* (clé [clay]) with you if you plan on returning after midnight. Some hotels have a key for the outer door to the street. Others will provide you with a door code to get in.

LA COUR VERSUS *LA RUE*

ROOMS USUALLY FACE THE STREET or a courtyard or small garden called *la cour* (lah coor). Street-side rooms are usually noisier but may be more scenic. To find out if the room looks out onto the street or courtyard, ask: *Est-ce que la chambre donne sur la rue ou sur la cour?* (Es kuh lah **shahm** dun soo wer la **roo** oow soo wer lah **coor**?)

THE LOBBY

IN THE LOBBY OF MANY PARISIAN HOTELS, you'll find racks of pamphlets aimed at tourists. Although some of this information may interest you, we find most of it distracting. Be careful with appeals from restaurants and nightclubs that are mass-marketed to the tourist industry. Your time and dollars in Paris are precious, and you don't want to waste either.

Most reception areas will have a public telephone and a Paris telephone book, called the *annuaire* (an-nyew-**air**) or *botin* (bow-**tahn**). The Yellow Pages are called the Pages Jaunes (pahj **joan**). Travel agents are listed under *Agents de voyages*. Airlines are *compagnies aériennes*.

TO BREAKFAST OR NOT TO BREAKFAST?

WHEREAS DINNERS ARE ALMOST ALWAYS LONG, Parisian breakfasts tend to be brief, rarely consisting of more than a coffee with milk (*café au lait*), tea, hot chocolate, bread (*baguette* [bah-**get**]), butter (*beurre* [buhr]), and jam (*confiture* [con-fee-**tur**]). You may be offered orange juice or cereal, but these are American add-ons that have only made it onto the Parisian breakfast table in the last decade or so. To this, you may add yogurt, a croissant (kwa-**sohn**), or *petit pain au chocolat* (peh-**tee** pahn oh show-ko-l**ah**).

Parisians are used to what Anglo-Americans call the "Continental breakfast." In people's homes you may be served your coffee in a bowl instead of a cup. This is a tradition in the countryside, which many Parisians embrace, and a habit you'll see practiced in French movies. Only in the last few years have Parisians started to understand the concept of brunch, and a number of local restaurants now offer Sunday brunch specials. Not very French, but part of contemporary Paris these days. The larger hotels are offering buffet breakfasts, too; they are easier to serve.

As for the structure of a French meal, see Part Seven, Dining and Restaurants. For a detailed look at coffee and drinks, see the Café and Café Tabac section, also in Part Seven.

If breakfast is not included, you can decide if you want to have your Continental or buffet breakfast in your hotel or not. And you can decide from day to day. Some guidebooks advise budget-conscious travelers never to take the hotel breakfast unless it's already included in the room rate, but we generally advise travelers to take the breakfast, especially in small hotels—but look at its cost first. Generally, for the extra €5 to €12 you'll spend, you can enjoy a leisurely morning in the breakfast room, drinking a pot of good coffee while munching your morning croissants with raspberry *confiture*. You can get yourself calmly organized for the day, you can easily use the bathrooms, and the croissants you'll be eating come from the same neighborhood *boulangerie* anyway. If you take your breakfast in a local café, be prepared to spend at least the same amount, if not more, especially if you are sitting at a sidewalk table, where the prices are up to twice the price as at the counter inside. The advantage to the breakfast in large hotels is that the buffet-style breakfasts with fruit juice, eggs, bacon, sausage, or cereal allow you to load up and start a full day of sightseeing or business well nourished. Large hotels will often include the buffet breakfast in the price of the room. If not, try to get it included.

HOTEL CONCIERGES

AT THREE- AND FOUR-STAR HOTELS, your hotel concierge or receptionist may become your best ally in Paris. He (they're almost always men) can and will answer almost any of your questions, and when he does not know, he'll know how to find out for you. This is a source of great pride. Your hotel concierge, especially in the bigger and more expensive hotels, should be able to arrange for any of your special needs or desires as well. We've even heard of concierges being able to rent helicopters and schedule racing cars and acupuncture sessions on demand. Most likely your requests will be limited to restaurant reservations, opera tickets, nightclub recommendations, and tour guides, but know that a good concierge is worth every euro of tip you give him. (No need to tip on small and easy requests, but a €5 or €10 bill will be appreciated when the concierge tracks down courtside tickets to the French Open Tennis match at Roland Garros or gets you a table by the window at the Jules Verne restaurant at the Eiffel Tower.) Hotels with one or no stars don't usually have concierges, but the owner or manager should be helpful to you in any case.

APARTMENT CONCIERGES

THE LIVE-IN GUARDIANS OR SUPERINTENDENTS of all Parisian apartment houses are also called concierges. They are usually women or a husband-and-wife team. They clean the building, distribute the daily mail, gossip profusely, and end up being either your buddy or your enemy. If you're staying in an apartment, always be extra nice to concierges. You'll depend on them often, and if you create a good relationship with them, your trip will go a lot more smoothly. If you annoy them, watch out.

HOTEL STAFF

IT'S ALWAYS DANGEROUS TO GENERALIZE. But it is usually true, especially with small hotels, that the night staff may be less capable to answer questions and to make flawless reservations. When calling to make reservations, remember that you will probably receive the most efficient and competent service from the day staff. The best time to get anything administrative done in Paris is between 10 a.m. and noon and 3 p.m. and 5 p.m.

PARIS HOTELS: *Rated and Ranked*

OVERALL RATINGS In the *Unofficial* tradition, we have rated Parisian hotels according to relative quality, convenience of location, tastefulness, state of repair, cleanliness, size of standard rooms, and overall value. We lean toward the charming and small rather than the impersonal and large, while including some larger hotels that have a lot of style and, although expensive, represent good value. Paris has many quaint yet sophisticated establishments often referred to as *hôtels de charme*. Today, as the demographic profile of travelers has risen in terms of age and affluence, a good many of the popular guidebooks focus primarily on these excellent and "charming" places, which, despite their proven quality, tend to be expensive. You would expect a

Hilton or Hyatt to be €200 a night, but you're shocked to find a little hotel with 25 rooms to be the same price, regardless of its charm and history. Many international travelers today are wholly accustomed to and willing to pay between €100 and €150 a night for a good hotel. We have supplied lots of choices that fulfill these expectations. However, we've compiled an original composite of simpler and more economical choices, too, that nonetheless represents quintessential Paris for more modest budgets. You may consider scaling down or adapting your hotel expectations and using the savings for your culinary exploits. Overall star ratings in this guide apply to Paris properties only and do not correspond to ratings awarded by the department of tourism, automobile clubs, or other travel critics.

EUROPEAN CRITERIA Our star ratings have been applied in a European context. Being able to have your breakfast in a quaint garden, for us, is more seductive than eating from a minibar. Lovely watercolor paintings in your room or Louis XVI chairs in the lobby get higher marks from us than the presence of an ice machine. Elsewhere, the ice machine or laundry service may be more important, but not in Paris. So here's a big clue to Parisian happiness: Do not perpetually compare what you find in Paris with what you're used to in San Francisco or Orlando. Things are older in Europe, style is revered more than functionality, and in order to maintain original charm and historically authentic details, modern comforts have been added afterward to catch up to contemporary needs. As mentioned earlier, many luxury

---

★★★★★   **Superior rooms, very high class, *de luxe*   €450–€800**

Tasteful and luxurious. Be prepared to feel like royalty—and insist on it. Hotels in this category are generally not profiled in this guide but listed under Crème de la Crème.

★★★★   **Extremely nice rooms, high class   €180–€400**

What you'd expect at a luxury chain hotel, but with added touches of European elegance. We've profiled a number of those that offer the best value for the high price.

★★★   **Very comfortable rooms   €130–€250**

What you'd expect at a midrange chain hotel but with more style and charm. We focus on numerous hotels in this category. For your information only, we include one- and two-star descriptions, although we recommend the three-, four-, and five-star hotels we highlight.

★★   **Adequate rooms   €80–€120**

Clean, comfortable, and functional without any frills, but in some cases with a surprising amount of character and overall quality. The less interesting two-stars are not mentioned here.

★   **Super budget, rooms of basic comfort   under €70**

Simple rooms with or without toilets or showers in rooms. Often less central, but not necessarily. Safe and clean, though. The ones profiled here represent good value.

unofficial **TIP**
Some of the best housing deals in Paris are the two-stars that are elegantly designed and decorated but don't qualify for three stars and have maintained two-star prices so as not to scare off customers.

Parisian apartments were built before indoor plumbing existed. Elevators in many cases have had to be custom-built to fit into 17th-century stairwells. Bathtubs are often molded into the spaces below mansard ceilings. It's a whole new ballgame, and understanding the ratings depends on your appreciating Parisian culture. In Paris, you're paying not only for the amenities and comfort but also for the elegance or authenticity.

QUALITY RATINGS In addition to overall ratings (which delineate broad categories), we also employ quality ratings. They apply to room quality only and describe the property's standard accommodations. In addition to standard accommodations, many hotels offer luxury rooms and special suites that are not rated in this guide. Our rating scale is ★★★★★ to ★, with ★★★★★ as the best possible rating and ★ as the worst.

VALUE RATINGS We also provide a value rating to give you some sense of the quality of a room in relation to its cost. As before, the ratings are based on the quality of room for the money and do not take into account location, services, or amenities. Our scale is as follows:

★★★★★	An exceptional bargain
★★★★	A good deal
★★★	Fairly priced (you get exactly what you pay for)
★★	Somewhat overpriced
★	Significantly overpriced

A ★★½ room at €110 may have the same value rating as a ★★★★ room at €200, but that does not mean that the rooms will be of comparable quality. Regardless of whether it's a good deal or not, a ★★½ room is still a ★★½ room.

For each hotel we also provide the Paris arrondissement where the property is located.

For travelers who feel that too much of a travel budget is consumed by the cost of a hotel room (in which you don't plan to spend all that much time anyway), we include a number of well-situated, clean, safe, modest, independent, and small no-star, one-star (*hôtels de préfecture*), and two-star hotels. These are nothing fancy, but are wholly reliable for very little money. The last remaining one-star hotels, although inconsistent and risky, are perhaps the unsung heroes of the Paris hotel scene. (It's remarkable that two people can sleep in a safe and clean, admittedly spartan, hotel room with a shower in the room, in central Paris, for under €80.) Each year there are fewer and fewer of these cost-conscious gems, as they either close for good or get bought up, renovated, and gain stars. Some are undoubtedly run-down and funky. Others are fine yet remain unknown or overlooked by the travel agents and travel writers. Without frills, they offer not only the essentials but also their own kind of lowbrow Parisian charm. Plus, a one-star or no-star may be as much as €50 cheaper than the two- and three-star haunts! You'll witness this proletarian style—known in French as *populaire* (pohp-you-**laihr**), as opposed to bourgeois (bore-**jwah**)— in the flowered wallpaper, the bedspreads, the crisp but worn hand towels, the housedress that the patron of the hotel is wearing, and the handwritten notes behind the bathroom door giving you instructions for not flooding the perfectly clean but comically cramped bathtub or shower. It's all up to you. We just want you to have a range of choices. If the no-stars and one-stars scare you off, consider the two-stars, often as good as the three-stars but considerably cheaper. We found a two-star hotel that didn't qualify for a third star only because it didn't have a separate toilet for men and women in the lobby. The two-stars are the most enigmatic category. You can find dull and ugly joints with two stars and absolutely enchanting two-stars with 17th-century décor.

PRICES IN PROFILED LISTINGS

COST ESTIMATES ARE BASED ON the hotel's published rack rates for standard rooms for two people with a full bathroom (usually with a shower, not a bath). Generally, in Paris, you pay by the number of people staying and not simply by the room. (Some hotels have designated "single" rooms that are often smaller.) A general price range appears at the top of each profile, with more detailed information listed under "Pricing."

How Paris Room Rates Are Organized

Most Paris hotels organize their rates in the following way. We've added sample prices. Some maintain the same rack rate year-round; others use high-season and low-season rack rates. For example:

A Word on Paris Hotel Prices

Although Paris is an expensive city, hotel rates tend to be significantly cheaper than those in London or New York. Spending €120 a night for a decent hotel room these days seems like a bargain. For €120 a night in Paris, you cannot only expect a hotel room of good quality in a desirable area, you can demand one. For €140 to €160 a night you can stay in one of Paris's numerous small but very comfortable and utterly charming hotels. In some of the areas highlighted here, it's even difficult to spend more. Likewise, for as little as €60 a night you can stay in a perfectly clean and safe, small and modest hotel. On the high end, Paris's luxury hotels can be wildly extravagant, running €400–€1,000 a night. Most of these are located in the chic 8th and 16th

ROOM	LOW SEASON	HIGH SEASON
Single (one person)	€80	€110
Double with twin beds	€120	€140
Double with "grand lit" (double or king-size bed, often a better room)	€140	€170
Triple	Supplement of €15	
Suites or apartments	€250	€300
Buffet breakfast	€12 (some include breakfast)	Same
Hotel tax	€1.50 per person	Same

arrondissements. Other than in one case—that of the Lutétia, which is particularly beautiful—these ultra-chic establishments have been mentioned under Crème de la Crème below but are not profiled.

DISCOUNTS FOR GUIDEBOOK READERS

IN ORDER TO REMAIN INDEPENDENT and impartial, this guide has not attempted to negotiate special discounts for its readers. However, some French guidebooks have. There is nothing stopping you from asking for the same discount. Hôtel Lévêque in the 7th arrondissement offers free breakfast for readers of Rick Steves's travel guides. You should ask for the free breakfast too. Some of the larger chains offer free miles on frequent-flyer programs, so don't forget to ask for them.

CRÈME DE LA CRÈME

BELOW IS A QUICK SURVEY of Paris's most luxurious hotels. Rates in these 15 establishments run between €400 and €1,000 a night.

BRISTOL (161 rooms) 112, rue Faubourg Saint-Honoré, 75008; ☎ 01 53 43 43 00; fax 01 53 43 43 01; **lebristolparis.com.** Restaurant: Le Bristol.

LE CRILLON (147 rooms) Place de la Concorde, 75008; ☎ 01 44 71 15 00; fax 01 44 71 15 02; **crillon.com.** Restaurants: Les Ambassadeurs and L'Obélisque.

GRAND HÔTEL INTER-CONTINENTAL (470 rooms) 2, rue Scribe, 75009; ☎ 01 40 07 32 32; fax 01 40 07 30 30; **paris.intercontinental.com.** Restaurant: Café de la Paix.

PULLMAN PARIS TOUR EIFFEL (460 rooms) 18, avenue Suffren, 75015; ☎ 01 44 38 56 00; fax 01 44 38 56 10; **pullmanhotels.com.** Restaurant: Pacific Eiffel.

WESTIN PARIS (438 rooms) 3, rue Castiglione, 75001; ☎ 01 44 77 11 11; fax 01 44 77 14 60; **starwoodhotels.com.** Restaurant: Le First Restaurant Boudoir.

HÔTEL LUTÉTIA (231 rooms) (see Hotel Profiles later in this chapter) 45, boulevard Raspail, 75006; ☎ 01 49 54 46 46; fax 01 49 54 46 00; **lutetia-paris.com.** Restaurant: Le Paris.

MEURICE (160 rooms) 228, rue de Rivoli, 75001; ☎ 01 44 58 10 10; fax 01 44 58 10 15; **meuricehotel.com.** Restaurant: Le Meurice.

RENAISSANCE LE PARC TROCADÉRO (116 rooms) 55, avenue Raymond Poincaré, 75116; ☎ 01 44 05 66 66; fax 01 44 05 66 00; **marriott .com.** Restaurant: Le Relais du Parc.

PLAZA ATHÉNÉE (191 rooms) 25, avenue Montaigne, 75008; ☎ 01 53 67 66 65; fax 01 53 67 66 66; **plaza-athenee-paris.com.** Restaurant. Plaza Athénée.

PRINCE DE GALLES (168 rooms) 33, avenue George V, 75008; ☎ 01 53 23 77 77; fax 01 53 23 78 78; **starwoodhotels.com.** Restaurant: Le Jardin des Cygnes.

RAPHAËL (90 rooms) 17, avenue Kléber, 75116; ☎ 01 53 64 32 00; fax 01 53 64 32 01; **raphael-hotel.com.** Restaurant: La Salle à Manger.

LE RITZ (162 rooms) 15, place Vendôme, 75001; ☎ 01 43 16 30 30; fax 01 43 16 31 78; **ritzparis.com.** Restaurant: L'Espadon.

ROYAL MONCEAU (265 rooms) 37, avenue Hoche, 75008; ☎ 01 42 99 88 00; fax 01 42 99 89 90; **royalmonceau.com.** Restaurant: Le Jardin.

SAINT-JAMES PARIS (48 rooms) 43, avenue Bugeaud, 75116; ☎ 01 44 05 81 81; fax 01 44 05 81 82; **saint-james-paris.com.**

SCRIBE (213 rooms) 1, rue Scribe, 75009; ☎ 01 44 71 24 24; fax 01 42 65 39 97; **sofitel.com.** Restaurant: Les Muses.

NOTABLE PARIS LODGING

Best Location

Hôtel de la Place des Vosges
Hôtel le Colbert
Les Rives de Notre-Dame

Best for Bohemians

Hôtel de la Place des Vosges
Hôtel Langlois

Class Acts

Hôtel Clarion Saint-James & Albany
Hôtel le Colbert
Hôtel Lutétia
Hôtel Regina
L'Hôtel

Super Charm

Hôtel de la Bretonnerie
Hôtel des Marronniers
Hôtel des Saints-Pères
Hôtel Duc de Saint-Simon
Hôtel du Champs-de-Mars
Hôtel Parc Saint-Séverin
Les Rives de Notre-Dame

Most Romantic

Hôtel Regina
Hôtel Saint-Louis Marais
L'Hôtel

continued on page 102

How Paris Hotels Compare

HOTEL	OVERALL RATING	QUALITY RATING	VALUE RATING	PRICE	ARRONDISSE-MENT
Hôtel Lutétia	★★★★½	★★★★★	★★★	€600–€5,000	6
L'Hôtel	★★★★½	★★★★★	★★★	€288–€740	6
Hôtel Clarion Saint-James & Albany	★★★★½	★★★★½	★★★★	€425–€585	1
Hôtel Duc de Saint-Simon	★★★★½	★★★★½	★★★	€225–€390	7
Hôtel Regina	★★★★½	★★★★½	★★	€375–€3,160	1
Hôtel de la Bretonnerie	★★★★	★★★★½	★★★★	€135–€215	4
Hôtel des Saints-Pères	★★★★	★★★★½	★★★★	€175–€370	6
Hôtel Saint-Paul le Marais	★★★★	★★★★½	★★★★	€158–€390	4
Hôtel Britannique	★★★★	★★★★½	★★★	€160–€325	1
Hôtel d'Angleterre	★★★★	★★★★½	★★★	€140–€320	6
Hôtel le Colbert	★★★★	★★★★½	★★★	€179–€490	5
Les Rives de Notre-Dame	★★★★	★★★★½	★★★	€150–€550	5
Terrass Hôtel	★★★★	★★★★½	★★★	€280–€410	18
Hôtel de la Place des Vosges	★★★★	★★★★	★★★★★	€90–€200	4
Hôtel des Grandes Écoles	★★★★	★★★★	★★★★★	€115–€140	5
Hôtel du Champ-de-Mars	★★★★	★★★★	★★★★★	€89–€119	7
Hôtel de Notre-Dame Maître-Albert	★★★★	★★★★	★★★★	€122–€165	5
Hôtel Istria	★★★★	★★★★	★★★★	€70–€185	14
Hôtel Parc Saint-Séverin	★★★★	★★★★	★★★	€156–€365	5
Hôtel Langlois	★★★½	★★★★	★★★★★	€110–€190	9

HOTEL	OVERALL RATING	QUALITY RATING	VALUE RATING	PRICE	ARRONDISSE- MENT
Hôtel des Tuileries	★★★½	★★★★	★★★★	€140–€250	1
Hôtel Récamier	★★★½	★★★★	★★★★	€250–€420	6
Timhôtel Jardin des Plantes	★★★½	★★★★	★★★★	€90–€140	5
Welcome Hôtel	★★★½	★★★★	★★★★	€85–€129	6
Grand Hôtel Lévêque	★★★½	★★★½	★★★★★	€69–€144	7
À la Villa des Artistes	★★★	★★★★	★★★★	€199–€240	6
Grand Hôtel Malher	★★★	★★★★	★★★★	€100–€190	4
Hôtel de Lutèce	★★★	★★★★	★★★	€155–€230	4
Hôtel des Deux-Îles	★★★	★★★★	★★★	€165–€195	4
Le Pavillon Bastille	★★★	★★★★	★★★	€195–€390	12
Hôtel du Cygne	★★★	★★★½	★★★★★	€75–€165	1
Hôtel Beaumarchais	★★★	★★★½	★★★★	€75–€199	11
Hôtel des Chevaliers	★★★	★★★½	★★★★	€155–€190	3
Hôtel Favart	★★★	★★★½	★★★★	€97–€200	2
Hôtel Bersolys	★★★	★★★½	★★★	€130–€170	7
Hôtel du Danemark	★★★	★★★½	★★★	€158–€178	6
Hôtel les Jardins du Luxembourg	★★★	★★★½	★★★	€143–€153	5
Hôtel Eugénie	★★★	★★★	★★★★	€115–€165	6
Hôtel Turenne le Marais	★★★	★★★	★★★★	€125–€250	4
Hôtel Brighton	★★★	★★★	★★★½	€180–€365	1
Hôtel Esméralda	★★½	★★★½	★★★★★	€65–€140	5
La Tour d'Auvergne	★★½	★★★½	★★★★	€145–€190	9
Hôtel Bonne Nouvelle	★★½	★★★	★★★★★	€69–€149	2
Hôtel Sévigné	★★½	★★★	★★★★	€68–€111	4

Paris Hotels by Arrondissement

ARRONDISSEMENT/ HOTEL	OVERALL RATING	QUALITY RATING	VALUE RATING	PRICE
1ST ARRONDISSEMENT				
Hôtel Clarion Saint-James & Albany	★★★★½	★★★★½	★★★★	€425–€585
Hôtel Regina	★★★★½	★★★★½	★★	€375–€3,160
Hôtel Britannique	★★★★	★★★★½	★★★	€160–€325
Hôtel des Tuileries	★★★½	★★★★	★★★★	€140–€250
Hôtel du Cygne	★★★	★★★½	★★★★★	€75–€165
Hôtel Brighton	★★★	★★★	★★★½	€180–€365
2ND ARRONDISSEMENT				
Hôtel Favart	★★★	★★★½	★★★★	€97–€200
Hôtel Bonne Nouvelle	★★½	★★★	★★★★★	€69–€149
3RD ARRONDISSEMENT				
Hôtel des Chevaliers	★★★	★★★½	★★★★	€155–€190
4TH ARRONDISSEMENT				
Hôtel de la Bretonnerie	★★★★	★★★★½	★★★★	€135–€215
Hôtel Saint-Paul le Marais	★★★★	★★★★½	★★★★	€158–€390
Hôtel de la Place des Vosges	★★★★	★★★★	★★★★★	€90–€200
Grand Hôtel Malher	★★★	★★★★	★★★★	€100–€190
Hôtel de Lutèce	★★★	★★★★	★★★	€155–€230
Hôtel des Deux-Îles	★★★	★★★★	★★★	€165–€195
Hôtel Turenne le Marais	★★★	★★★	★★★★	€125–€250
Hôtel Sévigné	★★½	★★★	★★★★	€68–€111
5TH ARRONDISSEMENT				
Hôtel le Colbert	★★★★	★★★★½	★★★	€179–€490
Les Rives de Notre-Dame	★★★★	★★★★½	★★★	€150–€550
Hôtel des Grandes Écoles	★★★★	★★★★	★★★★★	€115–€140
Hôtel de Notre-Dame Maître-Albert	★★★★	★★★★	★★★★	€122–€165
Hôtel Parc Saint-Séverin	★★★★	★★★★	★★★	€156–€365
Timhôtel Jardin des Plantes	★★★½	★★★★	★★★★	€90–€140

ARRONDISSEMENT/ HOTEL	OVERALL RATING	QUALITY RATING	VALUE RATING	PRICE
Hôtel les Jardins du Luxembourg	★★★	★★★½	★★★	€143–€153
Hôtel Esméralda	★★½	★★★½	★★★★★	€65–€140
6TH ARRONDISSEMENT				
Hôtel Lutétia	★★★★¼	★★★★★	★★★	€600–€5,000
L'Hôtel	★★★★½	★★★★★	★★★	€288–€740
Hôtel des Saints-Pères	★★★★	★★★★½	★★★★	€175–€370
Hôtel d'Angleterre	★★★★	★★★★½	★★★	€140–€320
Hôtel Récamier	★★★½	★★★★	★★★★	€250–€420
Welcome Hôtel	★★★½	★★★★	★★★★	€85–€129
À la Villa des Artistes	★★★	★★★★	★★★★	€199–€240
Hôtel du Danemark	★★★	★★★½	★★★	€158–€178
Hôtel Eugénie	★★★	★★★	★★★★	€115–€165
7TH ARRONDISSEMENT				
Hôtel Duc de Saint-Simon	★★★★½	★★★★½	★★★	€225–€390
Hôtel du Champ-de-Mars	★★★★	★★★★	★★★★★	€89–€119
Grand Hôtel Lévêque	★★★½	★★★½	★★★★★	€69–€144
Hôtel Bersolys	★★★	★★★½	★★★	€130–€170
9TH ARRONDISSEMENT				
Hôtel Langlois	★★★½	★★★★	★★★★★	€110–€190
La Tour d'Auvergne	★★½	★★★½	★★★★	€145–€190
11TH ARRONDISSEMENT				
Hôtel Beaumarchais	★★★	★★★½	★★★★	€75–€199
12TH ARRONDISSEMENT				
Le Pavillon Bastille	★★★	★★★★	★★★	€195–€390
14TH ARRONDISSEMENT				
Hôtel Istria	★★★★	★★★★	★★★★	€70–€185
18TH ARRONDISSEMENT				
Terrass Hôtel	★★★★	★★★★½	★★★	€280–€410

Accommodations on the Right Bank

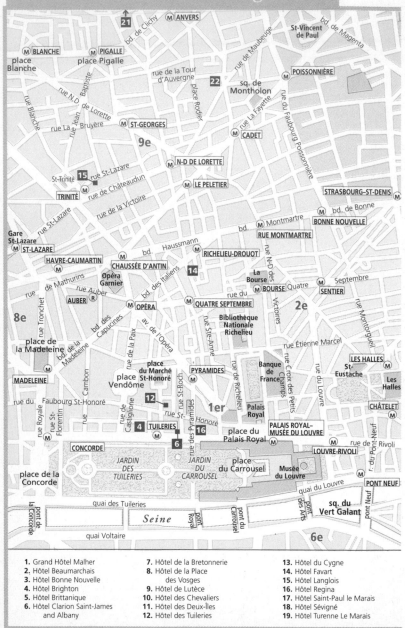

1. Grand Hôtel Malher
2. Hôtel Beaumarchais
3. Hôtel Bonne Nouvelle
4. Hôtel Brighton
5. Hôtel Brittanique
6. Hôtel Clarion Saint-James and Albany
7. Hôtel de la Bretonnerie
8. Hôtel de la Place des Vosges
9. Hôtel de Lutèce
10. Hôtel des Chevaliers
11. Hôtel des Deux-Îles
12. Hôtel des Tuileries
13. Hôtel du Cygne
14. Hôtel Favart
15. Hôtel Langlois
16. Hôtel Regina
17. Hôtel Saint-Paul le Marais
18. Hôtel Sévigné
19. Hôtel Turenne Le Marais

(1er–4e, 8e–12e, and 18e)

Gare de l'Est
GARE DE L'EST Ⓜ
JARDIN
VILLEMIN
Hôpital
St-Louis
rue St-Maur
bd. de Belleville
BELLEVILLE Ⓜ
COURONNES
Ⓜ Belleville
MÉNILMONTANT Ⓜ

10e
rue du Faubourg St-Martin
Canal St-Martin
av. Parmentier
GONCOURT Ⓜ
St-Joseph
Fontaine au Roi
du Temple

bd. de
Strasbourg
Ⓜ
CHÂTEAU
D'EAU
Ⓜ JACQUES BONSERGENT
rue du Faubourg
rue de la
PARMENTIER
Ⓜ
ST-MAUR
Ⓜ

Nouvelle
RÉPUBLIQUE
Ⓜ
place de
la République
av. de la République
rue Oberkampf
11e

rue St-Martin
bd. St-Martin
3
bd. St-Martin
bd. Voltaire
OBERKAMPF
Ⓜ
ST-AMBROISE
Ⓜ

Conservatoire
des Arts et
Métiers
rue de Turbigo
Ⓜ TEMPLE
bd. du Temple
2
FILLES DU CALVAIRE
Ⓜ
rue St-Sébastien
RICHARD
LENOIR
Ⓜ

RÉAUMUR-
SÉBASTOPOL
Ⓜ
rue Réaumur
sq.
du Temple
rue du Temple
ARTS ET MÉTIERS Ⓜ
3e
rue Charlot
rue de Turenne
ST-SÉBASTIEN
FROISSART
Ⓜ
rue St-Sabin
bd. Richard
BREGUET
SABIN
Ⓜ
rue Sedaine

ÉTIENNE MARCEL Ⓜ
rue Beaubourg
rue des Archives
rue Vieille du Temple
Musée
Picasso
rue Amelot
bd. Beaumarchais
rue du Chemin Vert

13
bd. de Sébastopol
Ⓜ Rambuteau
RAMBUTEAU
rue
du Renard
rue
Musée
Carnavalet
rue des Francs Bourgeois
CHEMIN VERT Ⓜ
10
place
des
Vosges
rue des Tournelles
BASTILLE
Ⓜ

Centre
Pompidou
7
1 **17** **19**
8
BASTILLE Ⓜ
place
de la
Bastille
BASTILLE
Ⓜ

rue St-Denis
5
HÔTEL DE VILLE Ⓜ
Hôtel
de Ville
rue St-Antoine
4e
ST-PAUL Ⓜ
18
rue St-Paul
BASTILLE
Ⓜ
Opéra
Bastille
20
12e

av. Victoria
St-Germain
l'Auxerrois
quai des Célestins
bd. Henri IV
bd. Bourbon
bd. de la Bastille

Ste-
Chapelle
CITÉ Ⓜ
quai au
Change
pont
au Change
pont
Notre-
Dame
pont
d'Arcole
l'Hôtel de Ville
ÎLE DE
LA CITÉ
pont
Louis
Philippe
pont
Marie
PONT MARIE
Ⓜ
ÎLE
ST-LOUIS
SULLY-MORLAND Ⓜ
bd. de Sully

r. de la Cité
r. d'Arcole
Notre-
Dame
9 **11**
pont
St-Louis
pont
des
Deux Ponts

20. Le Pavillon Bastille
21. Terrass Hôtel
22. La Tour d'Auvergne

Ⓜ Métro Stop
Ⓡ RER Stop
— Railway

0   0.2 mi
0   0.2 km
N

17e 18e 19e
8e 9e 10e
16e 2e 3e 20e
1er 4e 11e
7e 6e 5e
15e 14e 13e 12e

Accommodations on the Left Bank (5e–7e)

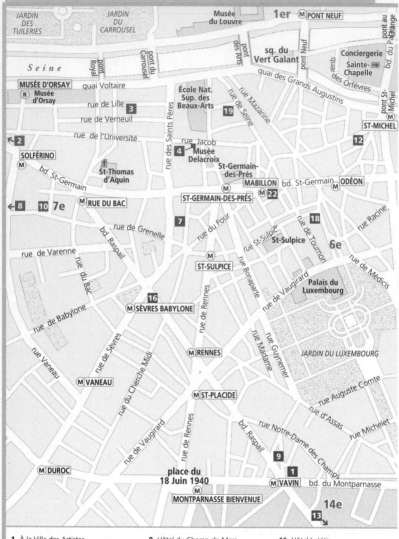

1. À la Villa des Artistes
2. Grand Hôtel Lévêque
3. Hôtel Bersolys
4. Hôtel d'Angleterre
5. Hôtel de Notre-Dame
   Maître-Albert
6. Hôtel des Grandes Écoles
7. Hôtel des Saints-Pères

8. Hôtel du Champ-de-Mars
9. Hôtel du Danemark
10. Hôtel Duc de Saint-Simon
11. Hôtel Esméralda
12. Hôtel Eugénie
13. Hôtel Istria
14. Hôtel Le Colbert
15. Hôtel les Jardins du Luxembourg

16. Hôtel Lutétia
17. Hôtel Parc Saint-Séverin
18. Hôtel Récamier
19. L'Hôtel
20. Les Rives de Notre-Dame
21. Timhôtel Jardin des Plantes
22. Welcome Hôtel

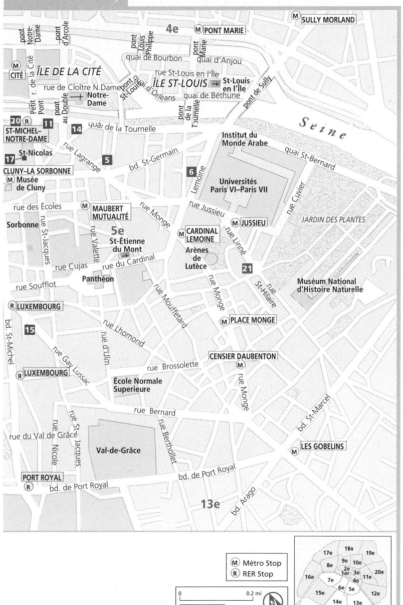

and 13e–14e)

M SULLY MORLAND

pont Notre-Dame
pont d'Arcole
4e
M PONT MARIE

pont Louis Philippe
pont Marie

quai de Bourbon
quai d'Anjou

M CITÉ
r. de la Cité
ÎLE DE LA CITÉ
rue St-Louis en l'Île
ÎLE ST-LOUIS
St-Louis en l'Île

rue de Cloître N.Dame
pont au Double
Petit Pont
Notre-Dame

pont St-Louis
quai d'Orléans
quai de Béthune

pont de la Tournelle
pont de Sully

S e i n e

20 R
11
14
quai de la Tournelle
M ST-MICHEL-NOTRE-DAME
17 St-Nicolas

rue Lagrange
5
bd. St-Germain

Institut du Monde Arabe
quai St-Bernard

CLUNY-LA SORBONNE
M Musée de Cluny

6
Lemoine
Universités Paris VI–Paris VII

rue Cuvier

rue des Écoles
M MAUBERT MUTUALITÉ
rue Monge
rue Jussieu
M JUSSIEU

JARDIN DES PLANTES

Sorbonne
rue St-Jacques
rue Valette
5e
St-Étienne du Mont

CARDINAL LEMOINE

rue Linné

Arènes de Lutèce

rue Cujas
rue du Cardinal
21

Muséum National d'Histoire Naturelle

rue Soufflot
Panthéon

rue Mouffetard
rue Monge
rue St-Hilaire

R LUXEMBOURG

bd. St-Michel
15

rue Lhomond
rue d'Ulm

M PLACE MONGE

R LUXEMBOURG
rue Gay Lussac

rue Brossolette
CENSIER DAUBENTON
M

École Normale Superieure
rue Monge

rue Bernard
rue Berthollet
bd. St-Marcel

rue St-Jacques
rue du Val de Grâce
Nicole

Val-de-Grâce

M LES GOBELINS

PORT ROYAL
R
bd. de Port Royal
bd. de Port Royal

13e
bd. Arago

M Métro Stop
R RER Stop

0   0.2 mi
0   0.2 km

17e 18e 19e
8e 9e 10e
2e 3e 11e 20e
16e 1er
7e 4e
6e 5e 12e
15e 14e 13e

continued from page 93

The rooms above the fourth floor on the street side of rue Joseph-de-Maître at **Terrass Hôtel,** at the top of Montmartre, offer lovers a sublime experience, marrying an exquisite panorama with total privacy. Here, you're in Paris and you're in heaven.

Most Unusual

L'Hôtel, on rue des Beaux Arts, offers you the chance to sleep in the room that Oscar Wilde died in. The décor has been left in the same style it was when our talented bohemian lived here.

Best View

Hôtel Lutétia's Eiffel Tower Suite not only gives you a view of the world's greatest monument, but it also affords you a bird's-eye glance from every room in the suite, the bathtub included!

Best Air

Hôtel des Grandes Écoles has an exquisite garden that transforms an urban setting into the countryside.

HOTEL PROFILES

WE HAVE CAREFULLY SELECTED A WIDE VARIETY of hotels by choosing several from each price range, attempting to offer a choice of styles and sizes as well.

You'll find in most areas at least one profiled hotel that is inexpensive (under €90), two that are moderately priced (€90–€160), two that are expensive (€160–€240), and one that is very expensive (€250 and up). The profiled hotels are listed in alphabetical order.

REMINDER ON DEPOSITS

MOST PARISIAN HOTELS do not require that you send them a deposit. Instead, most ask that you fax them your request for reservations along with a credit-card number and card expiration date. Your number will be held for your arrival as a deposit. If you do not show up, usually you will be charged for one night's stay. If you cancel your reservations at least a day in advance, your card should not be charged.

À la Villa des Artistes   €199–€240

OVERALL ★★★   QUALITY ★★★★   VALUE ★★★★   6TH ARRONDISSEMENT

**9, rue de la Grande-Chaumière, 75006; ☎ 01 43 26 60 86;
fax 01 43 54 73 70; hotel@villa-artistes.com; villa-artistes.com**

ON A RELATIVELY QUIET STREET, the hotel is extremely well named given that it's not far from the Montparnasse cafés where myths were made—La Coupole, Le Dôme, Le Sélect, and La Rotonde—and, of course, La Closerie des Lilas up the street. Though for the most part the modern décor prevents you from realizing that the building is from the 18th century, the stone corridor walls give you a glimpse of the building's history. On the ground floor there seems no end to places to sit, converse, relax, ingest: the salon's intimately lit, comfy armchairs; the small bar's closely grouped stools; the breakfast room's informal tables and chairs; the little garden/courtyard's white wrought-iron furniture, where breakfast can be taken as well. A plus is the wonderfully welcoming, attentive, and professional staff, starting with the director herself.

SETTING AND FACILITIES

Location Montparnasse. **Nearest Métro station** Vavin. **Quietness rating** A on courtyard, B on street. **Dining** €15 buffet breakfast. **Amenities** Parking nearby. **Services** Laundry.

ACCOMMODATIONS

Rooms 55. **All** TV with satellite, direct-dial phone, free Wi-Fi access, individual safe-deposit box, hair dryer, minibar, air-conditioning. **Bathrooms** Bright and functional. **Comfort and décor** If you're lucky enough to get room 3—right on the garden—you'll think you've gone to the country for a bit of bucolic tranquility (as opposed to being in one of the most "animated," as the French say, areas of the city!). The room's glistening, warm colors and comfortable appointments (good closet space, minibar, TV) add to the atmosphere of simple luxury.

RATES, RESERVATIONS, AND RESTRICTIONS

Pricing Single or double rooms: Club €199, "Arty" €240, reductions for online bookings. **Credit cards** All major credit cards. **Check-in/out** 3 p.m./noon. **Not allowed** Pets. **Elevator** Yes. **English spoken** Yes.

Grand Hôtel Lévêque   €69–€144

OVERALL ★★★½   QUALITY ★★★½   VALUE ★★★★★   7TH ARRONDISSEMENT

29, rue Cler, 75007; ☎ 01 47 05 49 15; fax 01 45 50 49 36; info@hotel-leveque.com; hotel-leveque.com

THOUGH THE ENTRYWAY OF THIS HOTEL IS UNREMARKABLE, you'll be attracted by the sitting area's charming furnishings, including a ceiling fan. By the time you reach the large neighboring breakfast room, you'll think you've mistakenly wandered into a Parisian café—woven-straw chair seats and all! You'll appreciate the service-oriented attitude of the staff. Twenty of the rooms were renovated in 2008.

SETTING AND FACILITIES

Location Invalides. **Nearest Métro station** École Militaire. **Quietness rating** B in the back, C on the street during market hours. **Dining** €9 Continental breakfast.

ACCOMMODATIONS

Rooms 50. **All** Flat-panel TV with cable, direct-dial phone, Wi-Fi access, hair dryer, individual safe, air-conditioning. **Comfort and décor** Room 50, streetside, is bright and sunny though small; from its balcony you can glimpse the top of the Eiffel Tower. Ceiling fans and air-conditioning in all rooms.

Pricing Single without shower and WC €69–€74, double €99–€129, triple €139–€144. **Deposit** Required. **Credit cards** All major credit cards. **Check-in/out** 3 p.m./noon. **Not allowed** Pets. **Elevator** Yes. **English spoken** Yes.

Grand Hôtel Malher   €100–€190

OVERALL ★★★	QUALITY ★★★★	VALUE ★★★★	4TH ARRONDISSEMENT

5, rue Malher, 75004; ☎ 01 42 72 60 92; fax 01 42 72 25 37; ghmalher@yahoo.fr; grandhotelmalher.com

STAYING IN THE MARAIS IS ALWAYS A TREAT, and within a short time you'll start to feel like this is your neighborhood. Several small hotels are clustered near each other on rue Malher, but the Grand Hôtel Malher is the most comfortable and most cheerful. Mr. and Ms. Fossiez are the third generation of Fossiezes operating this establishment, and they're pleased to be the ones bringing the hotel into the next millennium. It's perfectly renovated in the Marais style, as evidenced by the exposed stone in the lobby, vaulted ceilings in the medieval breakfast room, and polished-stone floors. Of course, the location is ideal, in the Marais close to the Bastille and an easy walk to Châtelet and the Latin Quarter. An all-around great address.

SETTING AND FACILITIES
Location The Marais. **Nearest Métro station** Saint-Paul–Le Marais. **Quietness rating** B. **Dining** €9 breakfast.

ACCOMMODATIONS
Rooms 31. **All** Satellite TV, phone, minibar, hair dryer. **Bathrooms** Small but immaculate. **Comfort and décor** We visited room 30, which is typical of the hotel; it's smallish (which is typical of the Marais) but impeccably clean and perfectly comfortable and quiet, although the quietest rooms face the courtyard. Room 64 is a minisuite, well suited for three adults or a couple with a child.

RATES, RESERVATIONS, AND RESTRICTIONS
Pricing Single €100 off-season, €120 high season; double €120 off-season, €145 high season; junior suite €175 off-season, €190 high season. **Credit cards** DC, MC, V. **Check-in/out** After noon/noon. **Elevator** Yes. **English spoken** Yes.

Hôtel Beaumarchais   €75–€199

OVERALL ★★★	QUALITY ★★★½	VALUE ★★★★	11TH ARRONDISSEMENT

3, rue Oberkampf, 75011; ☎ 01 53 36 86 86; fax 01 43 38 32 86; reservation@hotelbeaumarchais.com; hotelbeaumarchais.com

ONE OF THE FIRST THINGS YOU NOTICE is the soft, summery color scheme (much yellow and salmon) of this hotel, not far from the Cirque d'Hiver, tastefully redone with attention to comfort. The effect of the salon's impressive winding metal staircase (actually usable from the second floor up) is a bit undone by the plastic furniture in the nearby breakfast room, but all looks quite accommodating. Artwork tends to be contemporary. You'll find a customer-oriented staff. A garden patio is available for breakfast during the summer months.

SETTING AND FACILITIES
Location Bastille/République. **Nearest Métro station** Oberkampf, Filles-du-Calvaire. **Quietness rating** B. **Dining** 310 buffet breakfast, 312 in the room. **Amenities** Parking nearby. **Services** Room service and breakfast available at all hours (no alcohol served).

ACCOMMODATIONS
Rooms 31. **All** Satellite TV, direct-dial phone, hair dryer, air-conditioning, safe, Wi-Fi. **Comfort and décor** Room 2, overlooking the garden, often doubles as the "bridal room"; its mirrored closet doors give the illusion of more space.

RATES, RESERVATIONS, AND RESTRICTIONS
Pricing Single 375–390, double 3110–3130, junior suite 3150–3170, triple 3190–3199 (depending on season). **Credit cards** ae, ec, mc, v. **Check-in/out** 1 p.m./noon. **Elevator** Yes. **English spoken** Some.

Hôtel Bersolys   €130–€170

OVERALL ★★★	QUALITY ★★★½	VALUE ★★★	7TH ARRONDISSEMENT

28, rue de Lille, 75007; ☎ 01 42 60 73 79; fax 01 49 27 05 55;
hotelbersolys@wanadoo.fr; bersolyshotel.com

A HOTEL SINCE THE 1970s, this 17th-century building still has its exposed beams and period wrought-iron staircase. Guests often gravitate to the sitting area, where they relax and read in period and flower-print furniture. Reproductions of well-known paintings line the white corridor walls.

SETTING AND FACILITIES
Location Invalides. **Nearest Métro station** Rue du Bac. **Quietness rating** B (soundproof windows). **Dining** 310 Continental buffet breakfast from 7 a.m. till noon (breakfast served in rooms 7–10 a.m.). **Amenities** Parking on rue de Poitiers (330 a day), bar.

ACCOMMODATIONS
Rooms 16. **All** TV, direct-dial phone, hair dryer, air-conditioning, safe-deposit box. **Comfort and décor** Each room is named for a famous painter (Gauguin, Van Gogh, Monet, and so on) and displays corresponding reproductions. (To see some of the real things, hop over to the Musée d'Orsay, not too far away.) Coffee- and tea-making facilities in rooms. Good closet space.

RATES, RESERVATIONS, AND RESTRICTIONS
Pricing Single (shower) €130, single (bath) €140, double (shower) €150, double (bath) €170. **Credit cards** AE, MC, V. **Check-in/out** Noon/11 a.m. **Elevator** Yes. **English spoken** Yes.

Hôtel Bonne Nouvelle €69–€149

OVERALL ★★½   QUALITY ★★★   VALUE ★★★★★   2ND ARRONDISSEMENT

17, rue Beauregard, 75002; ☎ 01 45 08 42 42; fax 01 40 26 05 81; info@hotel-bonne-nouvelle.com; hotel-bonne-nouvelle.com

QUIET IN A BUSY AREA, old-style 19th-century charm, great furniture, and a variety of rooms and suites are featured here. In an area of Paris whose glory days were the mid-to-late 19th century, this 1887 hotel has the unmistakable atmosphere of a Balzac novel. The sensation starts as you pass through the ocher- and multicolored blown-glass front door and continues as you settle into the ground floor's deep, dark colors that, far from being oppressive, make you feel warmly protected from a cold, cold world. The salon's street-side windows, leather furniture, and real armoire remind you of a sitting area in a private home. The guest-floor corridors' interesting touches include brown fabric on the walls, large posters of turn-of-the-19th-century snow scenes, and a table. Though the hotel is on a busy street, the rooms are calm—but don't expect total silence.

SETTING AND FACILITIES
Location Grands Boulevards. **Nearest Métro station** Bonne-Nouvelle. **Quietness rating** B (no soundproof windows). **Dining** Breakfast €7 in the breakfast room 7–10 a.m., €9 in your room; Continental, but you can also order eggs. **Amenities** Parking nearby. **Services** Room service 24 hours; free Wi-Fi access throughout hotel.

ACCOMMODATIONS
Rooms 20. **All** TV, minibar, phone, hair dryer, modem jacks, free Wi-Fi access. **Bathrooms** Some toilet bowls have a rather dirty appearance due to years of mineral buildup in the water, but the hotel has now installed water softeners. **Comfort and décor** Behind room 19's dark wooden door, you'll find variegated upholstery, yellow carpet, and a distinctively turn-of-the-19th-century painting of a nude. The maroon-tiled bathroom (with a red shower curtain) is in perfect condition, except for a bit of rust.

RATES, RESERVATIONS, AND RESTRICTIONS
Pricing Double €69–€79 (depending on size of bed and view), triple €95, quad €135–€149. **Deposit** Credit card. **Credit cards** All except AE. **Check-in/out** Noon. **Elevator** Yes. **English spoken** Yes.

Hôtel Brighton €180–€365

OVERALL ★★★   QUALITY ★★★   VALUE ★★★½   1ST ARRONDISSEMENT

218, rue de Rivoli, 75001; ☎ 01 47 03 61 61; fax 01 42 60 41 78; brighton@espritfrance.com; paris-hotel-brighton.com

CHECK-IN PERSONNEL are very service-oriented and "friendly" in a way you expect in only smaller, more intimate establishments. The entrance area is bright, but the reception desk is small for a hotel of this size. A plus is the tea/breakfast salon, to the left of the check-in area, lit by chandeliers, graced by marble columns, furnished with charming little square tables, and protected by curtains from any indiscreet gawking by rue de Rivoli passersby. In 2005 the hotel was upgraded to four stars after major renovation work.

SETTING AND FACILITIES
Location Concorde/Champs-Élysées. **Nearest Métro station** Tuileries. **Quietness rating** A with windows closed and rooms on the courtyard, C otherwise. **Dining** €10 Continental breakfast, €16 buffet breakfast, 7–11 a.m. **Services** Room service 7 a.m.–7 p.m., Airport shuttle.

ACCOMMODATIONS
Rooms 61. **All** TV with satellite, direct-dial phone, free Wi-Fi access, air-conditioning, hair dryer, minibar. **Favorites** Rooms with view of the Tuileries garden; junior suites and standard double or deluxe double. **Comfort and décor** Old-world style, turn-of-the-19th-century lamps, and carved wooden wall panels. Imagine Somerset Maugham staying here.

RATES, RESERVATIONS, AND RESTRICTIONS
Pricing Superior double €180–€235, Tuileries double €220, deluxe €310–€390, Prestige €310–€340, junior suite €290–€365. **Deposit** Credit card. **Credit cards** AE, JCB, MC, V. **Check-in/out** 1 p.m./noon **Not allowed** Dogs. **Elevator** Yes. **English spoken** Yes.

Hôtel Britannique €160–€325

OVERALL ★★★★ QUALITY ★★★★½ VALUE ★★★ 1ST ARRONDISSEMENT

20, avenue Victoria, 75001; ☎ 01 42 33 74 59; fax 01 42 33 82 65; mailbox@hotel-britannique.fr; hotel-britannique.fr

YOU'LL FIND REMARKABLY customer service–oriented personnel (maybe because the hotel served as a Quaker mission during World War I). There is only a rather small (three-person) elevator, but some great touches, like the three clocks in the entryway indicating time in New York, London, and Victoria. Some rooms (usually the doubles) overlook the courtyard. There is one junior suite that can sleep two adults plus two children.

SETTING AND FACILITIES
Location Châtelet–Les Halles. **Nearest Métro station** Châtelet. **Quietness rating** A (when windows are closed). **Dining** €13 for a generous breakfast. **Amenities** Public parking nearby (Hôtel de Ville). **Services** Room service (breakfast).

ACCOMMODATIONS
Rooms 39. **All** Flat-panel TV with satellite, air-conditioning, Internet access, direct-dial phone, minibar, safe-deposit box, hair dryer, soundproof windows; broadband and Wi-Fi on request. **Bathrooms** Generally large. **Comfort and décor** Décor tends toward the British, with wooden furniture whose cushions nicely match the red carpets in hallways, and well-lit rooms.

RATES, RESERVATIONS, AND RESTRICTIONS
Pricing Single €160, double €190–€221, junior suite €279 for 2 persons and €325 for 4 persons, extra child's bed €30. You can get major discounts online

and by telephone. Discounts can reach 25 percent, but it depends on availability and season. **Credit cards** AE, DC, MC, V. **Check-in/out** 2 p.m./noon. **Elevator** Yes. **English spoken** Yes.

Hôtel Clarion Saint-James & Albany €425–€585

OVERALL ★★★★½ QUALITY ★★★★½ VALUE ★★★★ 1ST ARRONDISSEMENT

202, rue de Rivoli, 75001; ☎ **01 44 58 43 21;**
reservations ☎ **01 44 58 43 00; fax 01 44 58 43 11;**
hotel@ saintjames.com; hotels-francepatrimoine.com

PART OF THE HOTELS FRANCE PATRIMOINE CHAIN, this lovely mansion was once the home of the Ducs de Noailles, in-laws of Marquis de la Fayette who in 1779 hosted Marie Antoinette within its walls. You'll get a good taste of the Paris of dukes and duchesses in this stylish yet accessible institution. The large check-in area is adjacent to an interior courtyard and several salons—some rather spacious and all with their own mood: mirrors and beige armchairs in one, chandeliers and black-leather chairs in another. Pleasingly though not remarkably decorated, with pictures on the walls and often double closets. The rooms are all well designed and decorated although a bit stiff and formulaic. The dining room and the gardens convey the former high-society social life for which they were once used. Guests at the hotel have free access to its luxury health club, Saint-James Organic Spa, complete with a 15m pool and fitness and beauty centers. All guest rooms and reception areas have recently been refurbished.

SETTING AND FACILITIES

Location Concorde/Champs-Élysées. **Nearest Métro station** Tuileries. **Quietness rating** A with windows closed for rooms with view on rue de Rivoli. **Dining** Restaurant le Noailles; €24 buffet breakfast. **Amenities** Parking, Bar Saint-James, meeting facilities, ballrooms. **Services** Room service 24/7.

ACCOMMODATIONS

Rooms 184, including 9 executive rooms and 11 suites. **All** TV with cable, direct-dial phone, hair dryer, minibar, safe-deposit box, air-conditioning, Wi-Fi. **Bathrooms** All. **Comfort and décor** Regal, royal, aristocratic, and filled with antiques. The executive rooms are in a separate wing with a private lounge, PCs, and Internet access.

RATES, RESERVATIONS, AND RESTRICTIONS

Pricing Standard double €425, superior room €455, junior suite €525, executive suite €525, other suites €585. A selection of packages and special deals are available on the Web site. **Deposit** Fax credit-card number to hold reservation. **Credit cards** All major credit cards. **Check-in/out** 3 p.m./noon. **Elevator** Yes. **English spoken** Yes.

Hôtel d'Angleterre   €140–€320

OVERALL ★★★★   QUALITY ★★★★½   VALUE ★★★   6TH ARRONDISSEMENT

44, rue Jacob, 75006; ☎ 01 42 60 34 72; fax 01 42 60 16 93; reservation@ hotel-dangleterre.com; hotel-dangleterre.com

ERNEST HEMINGWAY ONCE LIVED in this former British embassy, with its high, wainscoted ceilings, exposed beams, period furniture, and canopy beds. You'll enjoy being on rue Jacob in the heart of the Saint-Germain-des-Prés area, with an easy walk to the Seine, the city's best galleries, and the most-famous cafés.

SETTING AND FACILITIES

Location Saint-Germain-des-Prés. **Nearest Métro station** Saint-Germain-des-Prés. **Quietness rating** A (rooms on the courtyard, all with windows closed). **Dining** Continental or buffet breakfast served in the restaurant or guest room, included in room rate. **Services** Room service (8 a.m.–8 p.m.); reservations for theaters, restaurants, shows, chauffeured limousine, Internet access.

ACCOMMODATIONS

Rooms 27, including 3 suites. **All** Satellite TV, direct-dial phone, Wi-Fi, safe-deposit box, hair dryer. **Some** View of garden. **Comfort and décor** Each room is spacious, and no two are alike. The best rooms overlook the garden.

RATES, RESERVATIONS, AND RESTRICTIONS

Pricing Single €140, double €200–€240, suite €295–€320, extra bed €45 in certain rooms. Online discounts offered periodically. **Deposit** First-night deposit requested. **Credit cards** AE, DC, JCB, MC, V. **Check-in/out** 3 p.m./noon. **Not allowed** Pets. **Elevator** Yes. **English spoken** Yes.

Hôtel de la Bretonnerie   €135–€215

OVERALL ★★★★   QUALITY ★★★★½   VALUE ★★★★   4TH ARRONDISSEMENT

22, rue Ste-Croix-de-la-Bretonnerie, 75004; ☎ 01 48 87 77 63; fax 01 42 77 26 78; hotel@bretonnerie.com; bretonnerie.com

THIS FAVORITE HOTEL of North Americans is in the heart of the Marais. Discreet from the outside, the 17th-century building surprises you as you enter. The delightfully decorated lobby is bathed in warm light streaming through yellow glass panes. Exposed beams frame a new décor in raspberry tones. The breakfast room is in the vaulted cellar furnished with low chairs and cushions. The labyrinth-like hallways are covered in stretched fabric in a delightful rose hue. Note that the hotel has a new owner.

SETTING AND FACILITIES

Location The Marais. **Nearest Métro station** Hôtel de Ville. **Quietness rating** A. **Dining** €9.50 breakfast.

ACCOMMODATIONS

Rooms 29, including 7 suites. **All** TV with satellite, direct-dial phone, free Wi-Fi access, minibar, hair dryer, safe. **Some** Duplex. **Bathrooms** Perfectly modern.

Comfort and décor Four rooms are furnished with very impressive baldaquin canopy-covered beds, perfectly in line with the 17th-century motif. All rooms are very inviting, cozy, and country-style. There are three rooms set up as duplexes. Dark wooden stairs and beams, with the sleeping space upstairs, make these feel like small apartments. Ask for the room called "Route du thé," which is decorated in warm rust tones.

RATES, RESERVATIONS, AND RESTRICTIONS

Pricing Double (bath, WC) €135, double "*charme*" €165, suite €215, extra bed €25, baby crib free. **Credit cards** MC, V. **Check-in/out** Noon/11 a.m. **Elevator** No. **English spoken** Yes.

Hôtel de la Place des Vosges   €90–€200

OVERALL ★★★★   QUALITY ★★★★   VALUE ★★★★★   4TH ARRONDISSEMENT

12, rue de Birague, 75004; ☎ 01 42 72 60 46; fax 01 42 72 02 64; contact@hpdv.net; hotelplacedesvosges.com

A FAVORITE LITTLE HOTEL in Paris, the Hôtel de la Place des Vosges exudes charm and high quality, although with small hotels, the quality of the experience depends on the service on the days you are there. The hotel enjoys an occupancy rate of 97 percent year-round. Americans (primarily from California) make up a large majority of the guests, and the marketing works mostly by word of mouth. The hotel sits on the quiet rue de Birague, which dead-ends into the Place des Vosges. Decorated in Louis XIII–epoch furniture and covered in regal tapestries, the exposed-beam lobby feels more like a salon than a hotel. The proprietor's calm and intelligent approach to inn-keeping carries over into the relaxed elegance of her place. "Our guests feel like they're at home. And that's how we like it," she says. The building dates back to the end of the 16th century, when it was a stable set up for the rental of mules. The other point of historical interest is that the novelist Georges Simenon lived here while writing his crime story *The Outlaw*. The prices used to be incredibly cheap but have now doubled after a full renovation; they are still reasonable for the location and comfort.

SETTING AND FACILITIES

Location The Marais. **Nearest Métro station** Saint-Paul–Le Marais, Bastille. **Quietness rating** A. **Dining** €8 Continental breakfast.

ACCOMMODATIONS

Rooms 16, including 1 suite. **All** Flat-panel TV with satellite, direct-dial phone, minibar, hair dryer, Wi-Fi. **Comfort and décor** Each room is a bit different, both in décor and size, but all are bright and carefully decorated, right down to the great beds with firm mattresses. The suite and many of the rooms have exposed beams, parquet floors, marbled bathrooms; the suite has a Jacuzzi.

RATES, RESERVATIONS, AND RESTRICTIONS

Pricing Standard double €90–€120, deluxe double from €155, suite €200 (up to 4 beds). **Credit cards** All major credit cards. **Check-in/out** Noon. **Elevator** Yes. **English spoken** Yes.

Hôtel de Lutèce   €155–€230

OVERALL ★★★   QUALITY ★★★★   VALUE ★★★   4TH ARRONDISSEMENT

65, rue Saint Louis en l'Île, 75004; ☎ 01 43 26 23 52; fax 01 43 29 60 25; info@hoteldelutece.com; paris-hotel-lutece.com

THE RECEPTION DESK IS JUST THAT—a desk, small and simple—chosen expressly so as not to scream "hotel" and to help guests feel that they have entered a very warm, welcoming private home. The service, on the other hand, is huge and screams, "We want to cater to your every wish!" In keeping with the noble ancientness of the Île Saint Louis—around which all of Paris grew out and up—the wood-beamed downstairs is reminiscent of a château in winter, its colors whispering warmth and comfort, its green plants (actually, there are plants all over the hotel) bringing nature in through the front door. Try to take the period staircase (with wrought-iron banister) instead of the elevator to stay within the mood of the hotel and of the *île* in general. And be sure not to leave the neighborhood without a stop (or several) at the legendary—and we do mean legendary!—Berthillon ice-cream parlor down the street at number 31.

SETTING AND FACILITIES
Location Islands. **Nearest Métro station** Pont-Marie. **Quietness rating** B. **Dining** €13 buffet breakfast. **Services** Reservations for theaters, trains, and so on; free Wi-Fi access.

ACCOMMODATIONS
Rooms 23. **All** TV with cable, direct-dial phone, free Wi-Fi access, air-conditioning, hair dryer, safe. **Comfort and décor** Many rooms have exposed beams (the top floor is mansard-roofed), and all are alike in most features; though rather dark (especially courtyard-side), they're not depressing. To save space, armoires have been sacrificed for simple white closets. Interestingly, curtains and bedspreads are in a loud, flower-patterned yellow, which tends to detract from the atmosphere.

RATES, RESERVATIONS, AND RESTRICTIONS
Pricing Single €155, double €195, triple €230; cancellation 48 hours before arrival without charge. **Credit cards** AE, V. **Check-in/out** Noon/11 a.m. **Not allowed** Dogs. **Elevator** Yes. **English spoken** Yes.

Hôtel de Notre-Dame Maître-Albert   €122–€165

OVERALL ★★★★   QUALITY ★★★★   VALUE ★★★★   5TH ARRONDISSEMENT

19, rue Maître-Albert, 75005; ☎ 01 43 26 79 00; fax 01 46 33 50 11; ma@hotel-paris-notredame.com, hotel-paris-notredame.com

THIS IS ONE OF OUR FAVORITE LITTLE STREETS in the Latin Quarter. It's close to everything, yet so private and tucked away. At the bend in rue Maître-Albert, which cuts from the Place Maubert to the Seine, this renovated medieval structure houses a classy little hotel. The street contains a number of antique shops, plus Atelier Maître Albert restaurant at the end of the street near the Seine. The lobby captures the style of the establishment with a statue of the Duchess of Richelieu, who is often mistaken for Marie Antoinette. The large tapestry hanging on the wall is a favorite possession of the owner, Mr. Fouhety. The exposed stone and earth-toned stone floors set the mood. The comfort, style, and location make this a prime choice.

SETTING AND FACILITIES

Location Latin Quarter. **Nearest Métro station** Saint-Michel, Maubert-Mutualité. **Quietness rating** B. **Dining** €7 Continental breakfast. **Amenities** Parking facilities, sauna.

ACCOMMODATIONS

Rooms 34. **All** TV, direct-dial phone, hair dryer, safe, minibar. **Comfort and décor** The rooms are tastefully decorated in bright hues from the south of France, period furniture, and new fabrics. Number 50, at the top of the house, affords a great view of nearby Notre-Dame. Try to stay in room 30, 31, 50, or 54, all of which are a bit more money but larger.

RATES, RESERVATIONS, AND RESTRICTIONS

Pricing Double €122–€165. **Credit cards** All major credit cards. **Check-in/out** Noon. **Elevator** Yes. **English spoken** Yes.

Hôtel des Chevaliers   €155–€190

OVERALL ★★★   **QUALITY** ★★★½   **VALUE** ★★★★   **3RD ARRONDISSEMENT**

30, rue de Turenne, 75003; ☎ 01 42 72 73 47; fax 01 42 72 54 10; info@hoteldeschevaliers.com; hoteldeschevaliers.com

ON A NOISY STREET not far from the Place des Vosges, this was, like so many establishments in the neighborhood, a 17th-century *hôtel particulier* (private town house). Fresh flowers seem to wink at the yellow walls and ceiling of the bright check-in area. Drinks are available in a small ground-floor salon. Down a wooden staircase, the cellar hosts breakfasting guests in an atmosphere warmed by yellow tablecloths, a "western-style" ceiling fan, and upholstered chairs. The showpiece of this room is the ancient stone well, now of course decorative only. All rooms have fresh-cut flowers, and guests who stay at least several days receive a box of chocolates or a basket of fresh fruit. The hotel was renovated in 2008.

SETTING AND FACILITIES

Location Bastille/République. **Nearest Métro station** Chemin Vert, Saint-Paul–Le Marais. **Quietness rating** A, with windows closed. **Dining** €13 Continental/buffet breakfast, 7–10:30 a.m. **Services** Laundry, room service 7 a.m.–8 p.m., reservations for shows, restaurants, taxis.

ACCOMMODATIONS

Rooms 24. **All** Flat-panel TV with cable, direct-dial phone, minibar, Wi-Fi access, safe-deposit box, hair dryer, air-conditioning. **Bathrooms** All. **Favorites** Quietest are 10, 11, 16, 21, 25, 31, 35, 41, 45, 51. **Comfort and décor** Bright and well-lit, this hotel speaks of good manners and simple elegance. The fresh flowers everywhere set the tone. Room 11, very well lit, is decorated in stately tones of gray throughout, accented at certain points with bordeaux.

RATES, RESERVATIONS, AND RESTRICTIONS

Pricing Single €150, double €190. Special deals available through the Web site. **Deposit** Fax credit-card number to hold reservations. **Credit cards** AE, EC, MC, V. **Check-in/out** 11 a.m. **Elevator** Yes. **English spoken** Yes.

Hôtel des Deux-Îles   €165–€195

OVERALL ★★★   QUALITY ★★★★   VALUE ★★★   4TH ARRONDISSEMENT

59, rue Saint Louis en l'Île, 75004; ☎ 01 43 26 13 35; fax 01 43 29 60 25; info@hoteldesdeuxiles.com; deuxiles-paris-hotel.com

YOU COULD ALMOST SPEND your entire Paris stay here and not be bored. From the cellar's main salon, wander off into an adjoining, comfortably furnished, even more intimate room where you can chat in semiprivacy or enjoy some of its mini-library's guidebooks and beautifully bound 19th- and 20th-century works. A highly enjoyable mix of Anglo-Saxon solidity and the exoticism of the unexpected. Pluses include the stone-walled cellar, with its warm greens and browns (also found throughout the hotel's common areas); the very cozy bar area (with hunting-lodge-esque pictures of ducks); and a private-club atmosphere straight from a 1940s Hollywood film.

SETTING AND FACILITIES

Location Islands. **Nearest Métro station** Pont-Marie. **Quietness rating** A in the back, B in the front. **Dining** €13 Continental breakfast. **Services** Wi-Fi.

ACCOMMODATIONS

Rooms 17. **All** TV with cable, direct-dial phone, Wi-Fi access, air-conditioning, hair dryer. **Some** Bathtubs. **Comfort and décor** Bright rooms in greens and yellows, but not especially spacious. The little blue tiles in the bathrooms do a great job of reflecting light.

RATES, RESERVATIONS, AND RESTRICTIONS

Pricing Single (shower, WC) €165, standard double (bathtub, WC; or shower, WC) €195; cancellation 48 hours before arrival without any charge. **Credit cards** AE, MC, V. **Check-in/out** Noon. **Elevator** Yes. **English spoken** Yes.

Hôtel des Grandes Écoles   €115–€140

OVERALL ★★★★   QUALITY ★★★★   VALUE ★★★★★   5TH ARRONDISSEMENT

75, rue du Cardinal-Lemoine, 75005; ☎ 01 43 26 79 23; fax 01 43 25 28 15; hotel.grandes.ecoles@wanadoo.fr; hotel-grandes-ecoles.com

THIS FORMER MONASTERY is astonishingly pleasant. It's easy to miss if you don't know there is a hotel behind the green doors. You enter a little cobblestone driveway and find yourself in a charming park in front of a late-19th-century building. A sublime mixture of country and city, the Hôtel des Grandes Écoles, with its main building (newly renovated) and two annexes, is one of Paris's best addresses. Breakfast is served in the parquet salon, complete with piano and freshly cut flowers. Weather permitting, you can have your breakfast in the garden. The service is so friendly, you feel like you belong to the family. Reserve three or four weeks in advance.

SETTING AND FACILITIES

Location Latin Quarter. **Nearest Métro station** Cardinal-Lemoine, Monge. **Quietness rating** A. **Dining** €8 breakfast. **Amenities** Parking (€30 a day). **Services** Wi-Fi.

ACCOMMODATIONS

Rooms 51, 3 with disabled access. **All** TV, phone, hair dryer, safe, bathtub/ shower, WC. **Bathrooms** Spacious, decorated in pastels and white. **Comfort and décor** Here, you feel like a private guest in a private mansion at the end of the 19th century. Lacework and delicate décor surround you. Classy and rustic. For Paris, the rooms are very spacious.

RATES, RESERVATIONS, AND RESTRICTIONS

Pricing Double €115–€140, extra bed €20. **Credit cards** MC, V. **Check-in/out** Noon/11 a.m. **Elevator** In 2 of 3 buildings. **English spoken** Yes.

Hôtel des Saints-Pères   €175–€370

OVERALL ★★★★   QUALITY ★★★★½   VALUE ★★★★   6TH ARRONDISSEMENT

65, rue des Saints-Pères, 75006; ☎ 01 45 44 50 00; fax 01 45 44 90 83; hsp@espritfrance.com; paris-hotel-saints-peres.com

THIS 17TH-CENTURY PRIVATE TOWNHOUSE belonged to one of Louis XIV's architects, who had the salon decorated by one of the artists from the Château de Versailles. Today this *chambre à la fresque* or fresco room is a spacious guest room (number 100), understandably much in demand and one of the main reasons many visitors seek out this hotel; charmingly, it is said to be reserved for couples as there is nothing but a simple screen—as opposed to a door—separating the bathroom (it has a round bathtub) from the bedroom. Of further historical note: From the first to the third floor, the staircase is original. As is often the case in this neighborhood, the entryway is deceptive, giving the impression from the exterior of a rather small establishment, only to seem to expand as soon as the visitor crosses the threshold. A highlight is the garden, visible through glass walls from the check-in desk and surrounding area, where breakfast is served on rattan furniture from 9:30 a.m. (so as not to disturb the guests in the 32 of 39 rooms that overlook this little treasure) to 11:30 a.m. A ground-floor bar and tearoom with comfortable caramel-colored leather furniture is open until 8 p.m. daily. Reserve one month in advance.

SETTING AND FACILITIES

Location Saint-Germain-des-Prés. **Nearest Métro station** Saint-Germain-des-Prés, Sèvres Babylone. **Quietness rating** A (triple-glazed windows). **Dining** €14 Continental breakfast served from 7–11:30 a.m. **Services** Room service 6 p.m.– dawn.

ACCOMMODATIONS

Rooms 39. **All** TV with satellite, direct-dial phone, Wi-Fi access, minibar, hair dryer. **Some** View of the little garden, air-conditioning. **Comfort and décor** Although room 114 is the least favorite because of its placement (its view is of the garden's floor tiles rather than the garden itself, and its ceiling is somewhat low), it has some unique features: a "raised" bedroom (once in the room, you have to go up several steps), exposed beams, two large windows (the other overlooks the street), and an 18th-century desk and engraving. As in many French houses and apartments, the WC is separate from the rest of what Americans call the bathroom.

RATES, RESERVATIONS, AND RESTRICTIONS

Pricing Double standard €175, twin €215, suite €305, *chambre à la fresque* €370. Special deals available through the Web site. **Credit cards** AE, CB, MC, V. **Check-in/out** 12:30 p.m./noon. **Not allowed** Dogs. **English spoken** Yes.

Hôtel des Tuileries   €140–€250

OVERALL ★★★½   QUALITY ★★★★   VALUE ★★★★   1ST ARRONDISSEMENT

10, rue Saint-Hyacinthe, 75001; ☎ 01 42 61 04 17; fax 01 49 27 91 56; htuileri@aol.com; hotel-des-tuileries.com

THE WELCOME IS WARM AND FAMILY-LIKE (the hotel enjoys a good amount of repeat business), and once you're at the check-in desk, the soft light from its big lamp makes you forget the entryway's rather dark appearance. The guest-floor corridors are not well lit either, but they are pleasant nonetheless. There is a breakfast salon and, in the cellar, a sitting room with stone walls and a vaulted ceiling. The lively neighborhood boasts many Paris "musts," including the Louvre. Ask for rooms with a view of the courtyard if you want silence. Rooms on the street are a little noisy during the summer months, but you have a wonderful view on a calm little street.

SETTING AND FACILITIES

Location Champs-Élysées/Concorde. **Nearest Métro station** Tuileries, Pyramides. **Quietness rating** B. **Dining** €15 buffet breakfast served until 11 a.m. **Amenities** Parking nearby (open 24 hours). **Services** Laundry, room service, Internet access.

ACCOMMODATIONS

Rooms 26. **All** TV with cable, phone, minibar, safe, hair dryer, trouser press, Wi-Fi access, air-conditioning. **Some** Family friendly. **Comfort and décor** The more traditional rooms, whose décor varies according to room size, are generally done in pastels, with paintings above headboards; modern rooms have striped curtains with touches of red, and wooden ceilings in the bathroom. Doubles are truly doubles, featuring two bedrooms separated by their own corridors and are usually reserved for families.

RATES, RESERVATIONS, AND RESTRICTIONS

Pricing Single €140–€200, double €150–€230, triple €230–€250, dog €10. Reductions for online booking. **Credit cards** AE, DC, JCB, MC, V. **Check-in/out** Noon/11 a.m. **Elevator** Yes. **English spoken** Yes.

Hôtel Duc de Saint-Simon   €225–€390

OVERALL ★★★★½   QUALITY ★★★★½   VALUE ★★★   7TH ARRONDISSEMENT

14, rue Saint-Simon, 75007; ☎ 01 44 39 20 20; fax 01 45 48 68 25; duc.de.saint.simon@wanadoo.fr; hotelducdesaintsimon.com

IN THE OTHERWISE NONSTOP-NOISE SECTION of Saint-Germain-des-Prés, this hotel's quiet street puts you in a vacation mood before you've even set your bags down. You reach the 18th-century building by crossing a large, well-lit, cobblestoned courtyard whose proliferation of plants casts an agreeable green glow. Converted to a hotel in 1905, the establishment was enlarged in 1950 by combining with an even older neighboring structure, then redone 30 years later. Furnishings are a mélange of the classics (Louis XIV, XV, XVI, and Napoléon III). Chandeliers (even in the guest rooms) and fresh flowers abound, and the check-in area looks like a room in a private home. Breakfast is served in a huge, colorful, well-lit vaulted cellar composed of refreshment-specific rooms (drinks, afternoon tea) with stone walls. Though some guest rooms have no minibar, the hotel will provide bottled water and other beverages on request. If you stay more than three days, you receive a box of chocolates from the management. Interestingly, the hotel created its own set of dishes, their decoration designed to go with the curtains and furniture of the common areas. A full range of tableware, fabrics, and household linen is available at their nearby shop at 92, rue de Grenelle. Service is excellent; the German director, characteristically refined and customer-oriented, leaves no doubt in her guests' minds that she is there to make their stay as perfect as possible.

SETTING AND FACILITIES
Location Saint-Germain-des-Prés. **Nearest Métro station** Rue-du-Bac. **Quietness rating** A. **Dining** Bar where you can order breakfast, tea, or a light snack or enjoy a drink; €15 Continental breakfast. **Amenities** Parking nearby. **Services** Room service 7 a.m.–10 p.m.

ACCOMMODATIONS
Rooms 34, including 5 suites. **All** Phone, satellite TV, hair dryer, individual safe, Internet access. **Some** Showers with bath, private terrace. **Bathrooms** Only 4 rooms have a shower stall in addition to the bathtub. **Comfort and décor** Specify whether you want a room overlooking the garden (16 rooms—no air-conditioning here as these rooms tend to remain cool) or courtyard (5 rooms). All rooms are different: number 7 (in the 17th-century wing) has a king-size bed and spacious closets; number 6—with garden view—a European-style bed, exposed beams, and a towel dryer.

RATES, RESERVATIONS, AND RESTRICTIONS
Pricing Classic double €225–€290, superior double €285–290, suite €385–€390; extra bed plus 30 percent; special rates available. Rooms not vacated by noon or guests who depart prematurely will be charged an extra night. **Deposit** First night; cancellation must be received 48 hours before arrival. **Credit cards** AE, EC, MC, V. **Check-in/out** 2 p.m./noon. **Not allowed** Dogs. **Elevator** Yes. **English spoken** Yes.

Hôtel du Champ-de-Mars €89–€119

OVERALL ★★★★ QUALITY ★★★★ VALUE ★★★★★ 7TH ARRONDISSEMENT

7, rue du Champ-de-Mars, 75007; ☎ 01 45 51 52 30; fax 01 45 51 64 36; reservation@hotelduchampdemars.com; hotel-du-champ-de-mars.com

NEAR A LIVELY, OUTDOOR MARKET/pedestrian street, the hotel's warm, homey atmosphere is best reflected by the sitting area, where magazines are available to guests relaxing in red-and-yellow-striped armchairs. Of course, the absolute main attraction is the hotel's proximity to the Eiffel Tower. Reserve early because this little hotel fills up well in advance.

SETTING AND FACILITIES

Location Invalides. **Nearest Métro station** École-Militaire, RER Pont de l'Alma Invalides. **Quietness rating** A and B (soundproof windows). **Dining** €8 Continental breakfast.

ACCOMMODATIONS

Rooms 25. **All** TV with cable, direct-dial phone, free Wi-Fi access, hair dryer. **Comfort and décor** While the décor of the small cellar/breakfast room (only 3 tables) is a bit busy and less attractive than that of the rest of the hotel, the comfort factor does not suffer for it—unless you're a smoker: a blackboard reminds you that this is a nonsmoking area!

RATES, RESERVATIONS, AND RESTRICTIONS

Pricing Single €89, double €95, twin €89, triple €119 (all with bath or shower and WC). **Credit cards** All major credit cards. **Check-in/out** Noon. **Not allowed** Large pets. **Elevator** Yes. **English spoken** Yes.

Hôtel du Cygne €75–€165

OVERALL ★★★ QUALITY ★★★½ VALUE ★★★★★ 1ST ARRONDISSEMENT

3, rue du Cygne, 75001; ☎ 01 42 60 14 16; fax 01 42 21 37 02; contact@hotelducygne.fr; hotelducygne.fr

THIS IS A FRIENDLY PLACE. You may not love the old-fashioned aesthetics and the 1950s décor, but you will feel welcome and comfortable. The most pleasant spot in the hotel is the bright and cozy breakfast nook, which feels like a veranda and is filled with plants. From the lobby, a 17th-century staircase with original beams leads up to the five floors. The hallways are covered in coffee-colored fabric, which darkens the atmosphere but goes well with the staircase and is not offensive. This hotel is well run, the service is friendly, and the owner attempts to please. A surprisingly good deal for central Paris.

SETTING AND FACILITIES

Location Châtelet–Les Halles. **Nearest Métro station** Étienne-Marcel, RER Châtelet–Les Halles. **Quietness rating** B. **Dining** €8.50 Continental breakfast.

ACCOMMODATIONS

Rooms 20. **All** TV, direct-dial phone, hair dryer, safe, Internet access by power line communication. **Some** Safe, shower, and WC, 2 with sink only. **Comfort**

and décor The rooms are spacious for Paris. Room 35 is by far the prettiest, and the owner assigns it only to the most "deserving" guests (we have no idea how one becomes deserving). We like the little salon with its red sofa, which folds out into a third bed. Up a step, you'll find the bedroom and another roomy, white bedroom. Room 41, under the eaves, is very pleasant, with a sunroof window. The bathroom, though, has only a swinging barroom door, so privacy is limited.

RATES, RESERVATIONS, AND RESTRICTIONS
Pricing Single (shower, WC) €75, double (shower, WC) €120, twin (bath, WC) €130, triple €165. **Credit cards** AE, DC, MC, V. **Check-in/out** 1 p.m./noon. **Elevator** No. **English spoken** Yes.

Hôtel du Danemark   €158–€178

OVERALL ★★★   QUALITY ★★★½   VALUE ★★★   6TH ARRONDISSEMENT

21, rue Vavin, 75006; ☎ 01 43 26 93 78; fax 01 46 34 66 06;
paris@hoteldanemark.com; hoteldanemark.com

LIKE BEAUTIFUL SERVING PIECES in a Scandinavian tableware shop, the entryway is all in blue. The basement breakfast room features the fun of café-style tables and chairs. Smack in the middle of Lost Generation territory (where American literary notables lived after World War I), the hotel boasts a Hemingway sighting—on a visit to Simone de Beauvoir, who lived in the hotel and ate in the restaurant now called Le Vavin (Le Pagès in her day) on the nearby square.

SETTING AND FACILITIES
Location Montparnasse. **Nearest Métro station** Notre-Dame-des-Champs. **Quietness rating** B (soundproof windows). **Dining** €11 Continental breakfast. **Amenities** Parking nearby.

ACCOMMODATIONS
Rooms 15. **All** Satellite TV, direct-dial phone, Wi-Fi access, hair dryer, minibar, safe. **Comfort and décor** An interesting juxtaposition of the old exposed-stone walls and the sleek, modern, all-black check-in area. Rooms are spotless and freshly renovated. Bright tones, quilted beds, recessed wall fixtures. Several deluxe rooms have their own Jacuzzi.

RATES, RESERVATIONS, AND RESTRICTIONS
Pricing Single €158, double or twin €158, superior room €178. **Credit cards** All major credit cards. **Check-in/out** Noon. **Elevator** Yes. **English spoken** Yes.

Hôtel Esméralda   €65–€140

OVERALL ★★½   QUALITY ★★★½   VALUE ★★★★★   5TH ARRONDISSEMENT

4, rue Saint-Julien le Pauvre, 75005; ☎ 01 43 54 19 20; fax 01 40 51 00 68

WHAT'S IMPRESSIVE ABOUT THIS spot is its Middle Ages ambience. Dark and gloomy but very authentic, with exposed stone, beams, and aged wood. Informal service may be a plus or a minus for you. Situated at the edge of

Notre-Dame, this is a perfect spot for poets and bohemians. Shakespeare & Co. Bookshop is just around the corner. Some visitors love staying here, but claustrophobics should go elsewhere. The good news is that all rooms now have toilets and showers or bathtubs. In keeping with its style, the hotel is not yet online, but we were told their Web site will be ready in 2010.

SETTING AND FACILITIES
Location Latin Quarter. **Nearest Métro station** Saint-Michel. **Quietness rating** B. **Dining** €6 Continental breakfast.

ACCOMMODATIONS
Rooms 16. 4 have a shower and WC; 12 have a bath and WC. **Bathrooms** Tiny and not well equipped. **Comfort and décor** Due to the age of the building, the hotel tends to be dusty and poorly aired. The green tapestry in the corridors is sad and a bit tasteless, and the rooms are very cramped. Room décor leaves a lot to be desired. Old and musty.

RATES, RESERVATIONS, AND RESTRICTIONS
Pricing Single €65, double €85, luxury double with view on Notre-Dame €105, triple €120, quad €140. **Deposit** Reserve 3 months in advance. **Credit cards** Not accepted. **Check-in/out** Noon. **Elevator** No. **English spoken** Some.

Hôtel Eugénie   €115–€165

| OVERALL ★★★ | QUALITY ★★★ | VALUE ★★★★ | 6TH ARRONDISSEMENT |

31, Saint-André-des-Arts, 75006; ☎ 01 43 26 29 03; fax 01 43 29 75 60; eugenie.hotel@wanadoo.fr, eugenie-paris-hotel.com

THE STAFF AND THE DÉCOR ARE BRIGHT, warm, and welcoming. A TV salon makes you feel like you're at home, and a grand stairway makes you feel like you're away. Often ignored by the guides, this address, newly renovated, merits the attention of people who care about feeling comfortable as opposed to being engulfed in material comfort. Two steps from Saint-Michel, the busy pedestrian street on which this hotel is perched, is one of Paris's liveliest, cluttered with bars, restaurants, boutiques, and galleries. Make reservations three weeks in advance.

SETTING AND FACILITIES
Location Saint-Germain-des-Prés. **Nearest Métro station** Saint-Michel. **Quietness rating** B. **Dining** €8.50 Continental breakfast.

ACCOMMODATIONS
Rooms 28. **All** Flat-panel TV with cable and satellite, direct-dial phone, air-conditioning, minibar, hair dryer, safe, free Wi-Fi access. **Bathrooms** Contemporary. **Comfort and décor** The caramel-colored wooden furniture adds a pleasant note throughout.

RATES, RESERVATIONS, AND RESTRICTIONS
Pricing Single €115, double €140, twin €150, triple €165. **Credit cards** AE, DC, JCB, MC, V. **Check-in/out** After noon/11 a.m. **Not allowed** Pets. **Elevator** Yes. **English spoken** Yes.

Hôtel Favart   €97–€200

OVERALL ★★★   QUALITY ★★★½   VALUE ★★★★   2ND ARRONDISSEMENT

5, rue Marivaux, 75002; ☎ 01 42 97 59 83; fax 01 40 15 95 58;
favart.hotel@wanadoo.fr; hotel-favart.com

WE LOVE THE FACT that the Spanish painter Goya stayed here. There is even a room called the *chambre Goya*. The area is characterized by its theatrical past, and you'll enjoy both the calm of a small street and the bustle of central Paris. The street and the hotel were named after the eponymous 18th-century playwright who influenced Voltaire greatly. You are equidistant from the Grands Boulevards and the Palais-Royal, making shopping, theatergoing, and late-night strolls easy and pleasurable. The spacious lobby is studded with marble columns and a stairway that leads to the rooms.

SETTING AND FACILITIES
Location Châtelet–Les Halles. **Nearest Métro station** Châtelet–Les Halles. **Quietness rating** B. **Dining** Continental breakfast included in room rates. **Services** Laundry.

ACCOMMODATIONS
Rooms 38. **All** TV, direct-dial phone, radio, minibar, Internet access. **Bathrooms** Modern and comfortable, although a bit oddly decorated with trompe-l'oeil motifs. **Comfort and décor** Try to get a room higher than the second floor, where the rooms are large and bright.

RATES, RESERVATIONS, AND RESTRICTIONS
Pricing Single €97–€150, double €128–€180, triple €135–€200, quad €155–€200. **Credit cards** All major credit cards. **Check-in/out** Noon/11 a.m. **Elevator** Yes. **English spoken** Yes.

Hôtel Istria   €70–€185

OVERALL ★★★★   QUALITY ★★★★   VALUE ★★★★   14TH ARRONDISSEMENT

29, rue Campagne-Première, 75014; ☎ 01 43 20 91 82;
fax 01 43 22 48 45; reservation@istria-paris-hotel.com;
istria-paris-hotel.com

WHEN YOU CHOOSE a hotel in Montparnasse, it's not easy to avoid bumping into the ghosts of its most celebrated denizens. In this case (an establishment mentioned in the Michelin and Hôtels de Charme guides), you'll be rubbing spiritual elbows with some of the best of 'em—Man Ray, Josephine Baker, Erik Satie, all of whom lived here. As if the guardian angel of them all, a little statue of Charlie Chaplin graces the charming, well-lit salon. Monsieur Cretey and his fine, customer-oriented team keep everything in very good condition.

SETTING AND FACILITIES
Location Montparnasse. **Nearest Métro station** Raspail. **Quietness rating** A and B (soundproof windows). **Dining** €10 buffet breakfast. **Amenities** Parking nearby. **Services** Reservations for theaters, restaurants.

ACCOMMODATIONS

Rooms 26. **All** TV, direct-dial phone, Wi-Fi access; hair dryer, individual safe, minibar, air-conditioning. **Bathrooms** Rather small (triangular shower stalls save space). **Comfort and décor** Rooms are decorated in a simple, pleasant style.

RATES, RESERVATIONS, AND RESTRICTIONS

Pricing Single or double €70–€185 according to season; promotional rates available through Web site. **Deposit** 1-night deposit is requested for all reservations. **Credit cards** All major credit cards. **Check-in/out** Noon/11 a.m. **Elevator** Yes. **English spoken** Yes.

Hôtel Langlois   €110–€190

OVERALL ★★★½   QUALITY ★★★★   VALUE ★★★★★   9TH ARRONDISSEMENT

63, rue Saint-Lazare, 75009; ☎ 01 48 74 78 24; fax 01 49 95 04 43; info@hotel-langlois.com; hotel-langlois.com

WHETHER YOU TAKE THE LITTLE, two-person elevator (it's the original) or the carpet-covered staircase, it's not hard to imagine a day in the early life of this 19th-century hotel. One experienced guest remarked that his bathroom was large enough "to play racquetball in." Formerly the Hôtel des Croisés, the establishment is perfect for seasoned travelers who don't mind being in a less chic neighborhood but appreciate the excellent price-quality relationship. Surprisingly, the Langlois is closer to the heart of town than you'd think, and an easy walk brings you to Place de la Madeleine and Concorde. The Métro is a 30-second jump from your front door. This hotel is frequented by French people from the provinces who've been staying here for years, as well as knowledgeable tourists. For a room half the size, you'd pay three times as much in the Marais or in Saint-Germain-des-Prés. This is the kind of place you'd have a hard time finding on your own, but once you've been, you'll return.

SETTING AND FACILITIES

Location Grands Boulevards. **Nearest Métro station** Trinité. **Quietness rating** B and A (when windows are closed). **Dining** €13 buffet breakfast 7 a.m.–11 a.m. **Services** Room service 7 a.m.–7 p.m., free Internet access available after 11 a.m. in breakfast room.

ACCOMMODATIONS

Rooms 27, including 3 suites. **All** TV with satellite, direct-dial phone, air-conditioning, hair dryer, large bathtubs. **Some** Only 1 room with shower. **Comfort and décor** The ceilings are high, and, though no longer used, there is a fireplace in every room. Room 7, overlooking a courtyard, has red carpet, 2 red armchairs, and a well-lit, spacious bathroom whose toilet is separated by a partition from the bathtub and sink. Though its all-white bathroom is a bit smaller, room 8 is basically the same. The street-side room 10, decorated in greens and gray, is a suite that has a fireplace in both the salon and bedroom but a relatively small bathroom. However, the upper floors sport rooms with spacious bathrooms with original tiles and massive footed bathtubs.

RATES, RESERVATIONS, AND RESTRICTIONS
Pricing Single €110–€120, double €140–€150, twin €150, suite €190, extra bed €20 (depending on season). **Credit cards** MC, V. **Check-in/out** 2 p.m./noon. **English spoken** Yes.

Hôtel le Colbert   €179–€490

OVERALL ★★★★   QUALITY ★★★★½   VALUE ★★★   5TH ARRONDISSEMENT

7, rue de l'Hôtel Colbert, 75005; ☎ 01 56 81 19 00; fax 01 56 81 19 02; melia.colbert@solmelia.com; solmelia.com

IF YOU ARE LOOKING for the utmost in small, discreet Left Bank hotels combined with perfect comfort and old-world elegance, and you don't mind paying dearly for them, you just found your place. The recently renovated Le Colbert is the only hotel in this category in the Latin Quarter. Tucked in beyond a quaint garden on the tranquil rue de L'Hôtel Colbert, this establishment (part of the Sol Meliá group) caters to an international clientele of sophisticated guests. The receptionist may speak not only English but also German, Spanish, or Italian. The breakfast buffet is copious and stylish, but at €28 a person it should be.

SETTING AND FACILITIES
Location Latin Quarter. **Nearest Métro station** Saint-Michel, Maubert-Mutualité. **Quietness rating** A. **Dining** €28 buffet breakfast or €16 Continental. **Amenities** Bar. **Services** Laundry.

ACCOMMODATIONS
Rooms 39, including 2 suites. **All** TV with satellite, direct-dial phone, Internet access, minibar, hair dryer. **Some** Good views. **Bathrooms** Mix of charm and modernity. **Comfort and décor** Earth tones, marble, and embroidered fabrics. If you desire a view of Notre-Dame from your room, ask for number 12, 13, 21, 22, 31, 32, or 33. If size is more important than a view (you don't need to see Notre-Dame from your room; the cathedral is a 30-second walk from the door!), ask for one of the larger rooms: 5, 7, 8, or 9. Suite 54 will make you feel presidential.

RATES, RESERVATIONS, AND RESTRICTIONS
Pricing Single or double €179–€299, suite €458–€490. **Deposit** Credit card. **Credit cards** AE, CB, DC, JCB, MC, V. **Check-in/out** 2:30 p.m./noon. **Elevator** Yes. **English spoken** Yes.

Hôtel les Jardins du Luxembourg   €143–€153

OVERALL ★★★   QUALITY ★★★½   VALUE ★★★   5TH ARRONDISSEMENT

5, impasse Royer-Collard, 75005; ☎ 01 40 46 08 88; fax 01 40 46 02 28; jardinslux@wanadoo.fr; les-jardins-du-luxembourg.com

FOR SOME, THE FACT THAT this was the hotel in which Sigmund Freud stayed in 1885 is an added delight. Others are charmed by the colorful and inviting environment. The lobby, which also serves as an informal lounge for drinks and coffee, is covered in contemporary paintings, wrought-iron furniture, a fireplace, and a stylish mirror and coatrack on which a straw hat is always hanging. A great advantage to this hotel is its proximity to the Jardins du Luxembourg—perfect for jogging, picnicking, and relaxing strolls. Off the lobby is an attractive spiral staircase that is primarily decorative.

SETTING AND FACILITIES

Location Latin Quarter. **Nearest Métro station** RER Luxembourg. **Quietness rating** B. **Dining** €11 Continental breakfast in your room, buffet downstairs. **Amenities** Small sauna. **Services** Laundry (if you ask for laundry service before 10 a.m. you can have your items back the same day).

ACCOMMODATIONS

Rooms 26, 1 with disabled access. **All** TV with satellite, direct-dial phone, Wi-Fi access, minibar, safe-deposit box, hair dryer, air-conditioning. **Some** Balconies. **Bathrooms** Tastefully decorated, capturing both contemporary design and turn-of-the-19th-century aesthetics. **Comfort and décor** Rooms face the street or a tiny, flowered courtyard. Street-facing rooms come with small balconies. The ground-floor room, number 12, has been equipped for disabled guests.

RATES, RESERVATIONS, AND RESTRICTIONS

Pricing Standard double with bathroom from €143, deluxe double with bathroom from €153. **Credit cards** AE, DC, JCB, MC, V. **Check-in/out** Noon. **Elevator** Yes. **English spoken** Yes.

Hôtel Lutétia   €600–€5,000

OVERALL ★★★★½   QUALITY ★★★★★   VALUE ★★★   6TH ARRONDISSEMENT

45, boulevard Raspail, 75006; ☎ 01 49 54 46 46; fax 01 49 54 46 00; lutetia-paris@lutetia-paris.com; lutetia-paris.com

ONCE YOU'VE PASSED UNDER the stately awning and through the gleaming revolving doors of this 90-year-old hotel, the real treat begins. As with all great classic hotel-palaces of Europe, the immense entrance hall, with its high ceiling and grand chandelier, will take your breath away. The word palace keeps coming to mind as the glitter from the numerous chandeliers highlights the richness of the red décor (furniture, marble columns, carpets) and the corps of uniformed receptionists busy themselves with your exigencies. Ask for a top-floor room for both quiet and view. This hotel served as Gestapo headquarters during World War II and, appropriately enough, as a post-Liberation center where families could inquire about and be reunited with loved ones who had been deported. For romantic occasions, ask for the Eiffel Tower suite, which affords a view of the tower from every window.

SETTING AND FACILITIES

Location Invalides. **Nearest Métro station** Sèvres-Babylone. **Quietness rating** A (windows closed), C (windows open). **Dining** Restaurant Paris and brasserie; €28, €10 children under age 12, supplement for breakfast in room. **Amenities** Fitness center, business center, parking nearby. **Services** Room service 24 hours.

ACCOMMODATIONS
Rooms 231, including 60 junior suites. **All** TV with satellite, direct-dial phone, Internet access, minibar, safe-deposit box, hair dryer, air-conditioning. **Comfort and décor** The Art Deco décor in the rooms is courtesy of Sonia Rykiel (whose workshop and boutique are not too far away). Spaciousness and marble bathrooms add to the allure. In Room 611, overlooking boulevard Raspail, there is a little salon with a television.

RATES, RESERVATIONS, AND RESTRICTIONS
Pricing Superior double €600, deluxe double €650, junior suite €850–€1,150, suite up to €5,000; extra bed free for those under age 12, then €90. **Credit cards** AE, DC, JCB, MC, V. **Check-in/out** 2 p.m./noon. **Elevator** Yes. **English spoken** Yes.

Hôtel Parc Saint-Séverin €156–€365

OVERALL ★★★★   QUALITY ★★★★   VALUE ★★★   5TH ARRONDISSEMENT

22, rue de la Parcheminerie, 75005; ☎ 01 43 54 32 17; fax 01 43 54 70 71; hpss@espritfrance.com; paris-hotel-parcsaintseverin.com

WALK IN AND YOU ENCOUNTER THE DÉCOR of an Agatha Christie novel set in the south of France—with a slightly contemporary, efficient touch. The open office area near the reception desk could double as a private library, and the warmth of the red carpet contrasts comfortably with the salon's citrus-colored cushions on airy white furniture and the floors of pastel (mostly orange) corridors. Hallways feature paintings, photos, and somewhat modern-looking gray doors.

SETTING AND FACILITIES
Location Latin Quarter. **Nearest Métro station** Cluny–La Sorbonne, Saint-Michel, RER Saint-Michel. **Quietness rating** B, A when windows are closed. **Dining** €13 Continental breakfast in rooms, buffet in the dining room.

ACCOMMODATIONS
Rooms 27. **All** Air-conditioning, TV with satellite, direct-dial phone, free Wi-Fi access, minibar, safe-deposit box, hair dryer. **Bathrooms** White and spacious, though not wheelchair-adapted. **Comfort and décor** Although the entrance is on the small rue de la Parcheminerie, many of the rooms offer a view of the place de l'Église Saint-Séverin. Sit in the yellow-upholstered white rattan furniture of Room 60—bright and unexpectedly spacious for a French hotel—and gaze out at the church itself, or enjoy the neighborhood rooftops, the Saint-Séverin cloister, and the Musée de Cluny gardens from a window on the fifth floor and up. Asking for a corner room on the top floor will get you a balcony as well. A plus is the quiet, whether due to the insulated windows or—even with windows wide open—the general calm of the immediate area, all the more surprising given the proximity to the lively boulevard Saint-Michel and rue Saint-Jacques.

RATES, RESERVATIONS, AND RESTRICTIONS
Pricing Classic double €156–€190, superior double €240–€265, double with large terrace €320–€365, extra bed €18. Special deals are available periodically on the Web site. **Credit cards** AE, DC, JCB, MC, V. **Check-in/out** Noon. **Not allowed** Dogs. **Elevator** Yes. **English spoken** Yes.

Hôtel Récamier €250–€420

OVERALL ★★★½ **QUALITY** ★★★★ **VALUE** ★★★★ 6TH ARRONDISSEMENT

3 bis, place Saint-Sulpice, 75006; ☎ 01 43 26 04 89; fax 01 46 33 27 73; contact@hotelrecamier.com; hotelrecamier.com

ITS VERY SLIGHT DISTANCE from the Place Saint-Sulpice affords the best of two worlds: the quiet of a side street and the advantages of being so close to shopping and cafés.

SETTING AND FACILITIES

Location Saint-Germain des Prés. **Nearest Métro station** Saint Sulpice. **Quietness rating** A. **Dining** Buffet breakfast €18. **Amenities** Parking nearby.

ACCOMMODATIONS

Rooms 24. **Comfort and décor** Each room is decorated in a different style; half of them look onto Place Saint-Sulpice. The hotel was totally refurbished in summer 2009.

RATES, RESERVATIONS, AND RESTRICTIONS

Pricing Single €250, traditional €280, luxury (with view) €320, club €420. **Credit cards** MC, V. **Check-in/out** Noon. **Not allowed** Big dogs. **Elevator** Yes. **English spoken** Yes.

Hôtel Regina €375–€3,160

OVERALL ★★★★½ **QUALITY** ★★★★½ **VALUE** ★★ 1ST ARRONDISSEMENT

2, Place des Pyramides, 75001; ☎ 01 42 60 31 10; fax 01 40 15 95 16; reservation@regina-hotel.com; regina-hotel.com

THE LOCATION OF THIS ABSOLUTE JEWEL of a hotel is ideal—on the Right Bank rue de Rivoli near the Louvre (at the edge of the Jardin des Tuileries), the Opéra Garnier, Châtelet—Les Halles, and Place de la Concorde, but just a short walk to the Left Bank, Saint-Germain-des-Prés, and the Latin Quarter. The turn-of-the-19th-century Regina, with its 120 rooms and suites furnished in original Louis XV, Louis XVI, and Directoire styles, has both the charm of a small hotel and the efficiency and grandeur of a large one. Why stay here? 1. Location. 2. Spacious rooms. 3. Sumptuous lobby and public spaces. 4. Original art nouveau décor. 5. Top-rated restaurant, the Pluvinel, and quaint tearoom/Bar Anglais.

SETTING AND FACILITIES

Location Right Bank. **Nearest Métro station** Louvre. **Quietness rating** A. **Dining** Award-winning restaurant Le Pluvinel serves classical French cuisine; seats 45. Open 7–10 a.m. for breakfast (€24 Continental, €32 buffet), noon–2:30 p.m. for lunch, and 7–10 p.m. for dinner. Drinks and snacks in sumptuously decorated Bar Anglais. **Amenities** Windows open out to either an unobstructed view of the Tuileries Gardens or a quiet, landscaped courtyard; air-conditioning. **Services** Room service and porter service, babysitting, laundry, Wi-Fi.

ACCOMMODATIONS

Rooms 120, including 13 suites. **All** Lovely bathrooms, authentic period-piece furniture, TV with satellite, direct-dial phone, Internet access, minibar, safe. **Some** Wheelchair access. **Bathrooms** Massive, original ceramic sinks. **Favorites** Rooms 118, 218, 318, 418, and 518 have spectacular views of the Tuileries Gardens and can open up into the next room to create suites. **Comfort and décor** Two-tone 1900s marble floors everywhere. Green original ceramic wall tiles on all the floors, plus copper beds, lovely coiffeuse (makeup tables), and tissue broché fabric on walls. Majestic high ceilings. The elegance of the age in which this hotel was built has been preserved, and here you feel princely (and princess-like). We love the abundance of Aubuisson tapestries, ceramic details, gold-plated stucco, the Louis XV chests of drawers, and the original painted-glass "vitrine" in the restaurant.

RATES, RESERVATIONS, AND RESTRICTIONS
Pricing Superior double €375–€450, deluxe double €515, suites €620–€3,160, €82 extra bed. Special deals and packages available on the Web site. **Deposit** Credit card. **Credit cards** AE, JCB, MC, V. **Check-in/out** Noon. **Elevator** Yes. **English spoken** Yes.

Hôtel Saint-Paul le Marais   €158–€390

OVERALL ★★★★   QUALITY ★★★★½   VALUE ★★★★   4TH ARRONDISSEMENT

8, rue de Sévigné, 75004; ☎ 01 48 04 97 27; fax 01 48 87 37 04; reservation@hotelsaintpaullemarais.com; hotel-paris-marais.com

HERE IS A HOTEL that has a lot going for it, with a dynamic, service-conscious, and particularly friendly owner who has run the show for over a decade. A bright, airy interior with contemporary paintings by an excellent local painter and black-leather armchairs dominate the lobby. Comfort reigns in this small *hôtel de charme,* and everything from the vaulted breakfast room downstairs to the flowering courtyard has been conceived to please its visitors. One of the best places we visited in the area at this price level.

SETTING AND FACILITIES
Location The Marais. **Nearest Métro station** Saint-Paul, Bastille. **Quietness rating** B. **Dining** €14 buffet breakfast. **Amenities** Parking nearby. **Services** Laundry.

ACCOMMODATIONS
Rooms 28. **All** TV with cable, direct-dial phone, safe-deposit box, air-conditioning, free Wi-Fi, tea- and coffee-making facilities, soundproof windows, hair dryer. **Comfort and décor** Some rooms offer spectacular features such as lots of space; 2 have a whirlpool tub; cloth wall covering, high ceilings, and other elegant touches.

RATES, RESERVATIONS, AND RESTRICTIONS
Pricing Single €158, standard double or twin €195, superior double and triple €253, apartment €390. Special deals available on the Web site. **Credit cards** MC, V. **Check-in/out** 3:15 p.m./noon. **Not allowed** Dogs (unless well behaved). **Elevator** Yes. **English spoken** Yes.

Hôtel Sévigné €68–€111

OVERALL ★★½ QUALITY ★★★ VALUE ★★★★ 4TH ARRONDISSEMENT

2, rue Malher, 75004; ☎ 01 42 72 76 17; fax 01 42 78 68 26; contact@le-sevigne.com; le-sevigne.com

IT'S OFTEN DIFFICULT finding an available room in the Marais, so it's good to keep a few trustworthy addresses on hand. The Sévigné enjoys an excellent location on rue Malher just off rue Saint Antoine, a stone's throw from the exquisite facade of the Saint Paul–Saint Louis Church. This is a reliable address at a very reasonable price in one of Paris's most popular areas. The lobby and reception area doubles in the mornings as the breakfast room, and the buffet breakfast is a good deal at €8. The hotel was named after the celebrated Marquise de Sévigné, best known for her letters and journal, which depict Paris under the reign of Louis XIV.

SETTING AND FACILITIES
Location The Marais. **Nearest Métro station** Saint-Paul, Bastille. **Quietness rating** B. **Dining** €8 breakfast (7–10 a.m.).

ACCOMMODATIONS
Rooms 29. **All** TV with satellite, direct-dial phone, air-conditioning. **Comfort and décor** The rooms are comfortable and clean but nothing special. The overall feel is functional. The hotel now has additional rooms with bathtubs.

RATES, RESERVATIONS, AND RESTRICTIONS
Pricing Single (shower, WC) €68, double (shower, WC) €82, double (bath, WC) €88, twin (shower, WC) €88, twin (bath, WC) €93, triple €111. **Credit cards** MC, V. **Check-in/out** Noon/11:30 a.m. **Elevator** Yes. **English spoken** Yes.

Hôtel Turenne le Marais €125–€250

OVERALL ★★★ QUALITY ★★★ VALUE ★★★★ 4TH ARRONDISSEMENT

6, rue de Turenne, 75004; ☎ 01 42 78 43 25; fax 01 42 74 10 72; hotel@turennemarais.com; turenne-marais.com

PREVIOUSLY PART OF THE LIBERTEL CHAIN, Hôtel Turenne is now part of the Hôtels France Patrimoine group. Rooms, all a bit different in blue and white or green and white, make attentive use of old etchings of Paris to remind visitors of the city's historical richness. Depending on the room, you can have a good view of l'Hôtel de Sully or its gardens or the Dôme de Saint-Paul. Several rooms are set aside for nonsmokers. Rooms are small, but in fact, the drawers and closet make up for the lack of space and are appreciable. Bathrooms are perfectly adapted to international standards and even have towel heaters.

SETTING AND FACILITIES
Location The Marais. **Nearest Métro station** Saint-Paul, Bastille. **Dining** €14 breakfast. **Amenities** Safe, parking nearby. **Services** Laundry, room service.

ACCOMMODATIONS

Rooms 41, 5 junior suites. **All** TV with satellite, phone, Wi-Fi access, minibar, hair dryer, double-pane windows. **Some** 6 with shower, WC. **Bathrooms** 35 rooms with bath. **Comfort and décor** Comfortable and modern, the décor leans toward the practical rather than the authentic.

RATES, RESERVATIONS, AND RESTRICTIONS

Pricing Single/double €125–€199, triple €165–€239, junior suite €250. Reductions offered on Web site. **Deposit** Fax credit card number to hold reservations. **Credit cards** AE, DC, MC, V. **Check-in/out** Noon. **Elevator** Yes. **English spoken** Yes.

L'Hôtel   €288–€740

OVERALL ★★★★½   QUALITY ★★★★★   VALUE ★★★   6TH ARRONDISSEMENT

13, rue des Beaux-Arts, 75006, ☎ 01 44 41 99 00; fax 01 43 25 64 81; stay@l-hotel.com; l-hotel.com

Both the best-kept and best-known secret among seasoned Paris travelers, this veritable institution relies on word of mouth. Now a four-star luxe establishment, l'Hôtel has long been a haven for celebrities looking for peace and quiet. The bell tower of the Église de Saint-Germain-des-Prés can be glimpsed from some windows. The most striking feature is the beehive-shaped dome over the ground floor—the building's former courtyard. Oscar Wilde died here. The hotel was refurbished by designer Jacques Garcia in 2006 to coincide with it joining the luxury chain, A Curious Group of Hotels. Reserve one month in advance in high season.

SETTING AND FACILITIES

Location Saint-Germain-des-Prés. **Nearest Métro station** Saint-Germain-des-Prés. **Quietness rating** B. **Dining** Le Restaurant, €18 Continental breakfast. **Amenities** Parking (rue Mazarine), small pool and steam bath, free Internet access. **Services** Room service, laundry.

ACCOMMODATIONS

Rooms 20. **All** TV with satellite, direct-dial phone, minibar, safe-deposit box, hair dryer, air-conditioning. **Comfort and décor** Room 16 has been redone in the style in which Oscar Wilde found it in 1900; Robert de Niro's favorite is Apartment 62 and its flower-kissed terrace. Rooms are rather small. Each has its own distinct style, but all have period furniture; photos of the rooms can be viewed on the Web site.

RATES, RESERVATIONS, AND RESTRICTIONS

Pricing Double (shower, WC) €288–€370, penthouse suite (big balcony, view) €640–€740. **Credit cards** AE, DC, JCB, MC, V. **Check-in/out** Noon. **Elevator** Yes. **English spoken** Yes.

Le Pavillon Bastille   €195–€390

OVERALL ★★★   QUALITY ★★★★   VALUE ★★★   12TH ARRONDISSEMENT

65, rue de Lyon, 75012; ☎ 01 43 43 65 65; fax 01 43 43 96 52; info@pavillonbastille.com; paris-hotel-pavillonbastille.com

TWO STEPS AWAY FROM THE BASTILLE, this hotel stands behind a gate. The spacious entryway has Greek-style columns, but the rest of the interior is done in a flowered motif, mostly of blues and yellows. The salon's modern furnishings make you think you've just come to visit your cousins in their New York loft. The staff of this privately owned hotel are true customer-service artists; they obviously know and love their trade.

SETTING AND FACILITIES
Location Bastille/République. **Nearest Métro station** Bastille. **Quietness rating** B. **Dining** €12 Continental, buffet breakfast. **Amenities** Bar, parking nearby. **Services** Laundry (except Sundays and public holidays), 24-hour room service, Wi-Fi.

ACCOMMODATIONS
Rooms 25, including 1 family suite. **All** TV with cable, direct-dial phone, hair dryer. **Comfort and décor** Elegant and contemporary, with neoclassical décor.

RATES, RESERVATIONS, AND RESTRICTIONS
Pricing Single and double €195, family suite €390. Special deals offered on the Web site. **Credit cards** AE, DC, JCB, MC, V. **Check-in/out** 2 p.m./noon. **Not allowed** Big dogs. **Elevator** Yes. **English spoken** Yes.

Les Rives de Notre-Dame   €150–€550

OVERALL ★★★★   QUALITY ★★★★½   VALUE ★★★   5TH ARRONDISSEMENT

15, quai Saint-Michel, 75005; ☎ 01 43 54 81 16; fax 01 43 26 27 09; hotel@rivesdenotredame.com; rivesdenotredame.com

THIS LITTLE GEM OF A HOTEL with its Mediterranean décor has a great reputation due to its classy style and incredibly strategic location in the heart of the Latin Quarter with a stunning view of the Conciergerie. With only ten rooms, Les Rives de Notre-Dame is almost always full, so when possible reserve as soon as you know your travel dates (at least two months in advance). As they are oversolicited, they tend to be a bit blasé with new inquiries, and the select clientele of regulars give the impression of being a bit standoffish. Don't be put off—this is a great address. On the far side of the flower- and ivy-covered lobby, notice the high, vaulted, hexagonal-glass roof. It's not old, but it drenches this hotel with original charm. Ceramic tile in earth tones and exposed stone dominate the décor.

SETTING AND FACILITIES
Location Latin Quarter. **Nearest Métro station** Saint-Michel. **Quietness rating** A (with windows closed). **Dining** €11 Continental breakfast in room, €14 buffet breakfast. **Services** Room service 24 hours; reservations for shows, cars, airport

transfer.

ACCOMMODATIONS

Rooms 10, including 1 suite. **All** TV with satellite, direct-dial phone, air-conditioning, hair dryer. **Comfort and décor** You enter each room through an arched doorway. The rooms are spacious, generally decked in blue tapestry, and are characterized by Provençal décor with a touch of chic. Furniture in wrought iron. Excellent soundproofing, necessary in this busy neighborhood.

RATES, RESERVATIONS, AND RESTRICTIONS

Pricing Single and double €215–€340, suite €350–€550. **Credit cards** All major credit cards. **Check-in/out** 1 p.m./noon. **Elevator** Yes. **English spoken** Yes.

Terrass Hôtel €280–€410

OVERALL ★★★★ **QUALITY** ★★★★½ **VALUE** ★★★ **18TH ARRONDISSEMENT**

12–14, rue Joseph-de-Maistre, 75018; ☎ 01 46 06 72 85;
fax 01 44 92 34 39; reservation@terrass-hotel.com;
terrass-hotel.com

ON A QUIET STREET, the hotel lives up to its four-star rating in terms of both service (excellent—there are at least four extremely customer-oriented, English-speaking receptionists on duty) and luxury (everything is large, well lit, and accommodating). A plus: the rooftop restaurant's superb view of Paris, including the Eiffel Tower (there's also a restaurant on the ground floor and a big salon for relaxing). We think this hotel is one of Paris's most romantic places to stay. Once you get back to your room, you won't feel like going out again! If the weather is clear, Paris unfolds beneath you and you'll be content to sip Calvados on the terrace in the cool months and pastis in the summers. If the distance from central Paris doesn't bother you, this is an exceptional address for visiting the City of Light. Reserve four months in advance during trade fairs and three weeks during the rest of the year.

SETTING AND FACILITIES

Location Montmartre. **Nearest Métro station** Place-de-Clichy, Abbesses, or Blanche. **Quietness rating** A. **Dining** 2 restaurants, 1 is on the rooftop and open in summer only; €17 breakfast. **Amenities** Parking, safe, conference rooms for rent. **Services** Reservations for shows, cars, tickets desk, laundry.

ACCOMMODATIONS

Rooms 98, including 15 junior suites. **All** TV with satellite, direct-dial phone, hair dryer, minibar, Wi-Fi. **Some** Air-conditioning. **Bathrooms** Sumptuous in the superior rooms. **Comfort and décor** Modern mixed with 19th-century elegance.

RATES, RESERVATIONS, AND RESTRICTIONS

Pricing Classic double €280, deluxe double €330, suite €380–€410; children under age 12 free in their parents' room; packages and special rates for online reservations. **Credit cards** AE, DC, JCB, MC, V. **Check-in/out** Noon. **Elevator** Yes. **English spoken** Yes.

Timhôtel Jardin des Plantes   €90–€140

OVERALL ★★★½   QUALITY ★★★★   VALUE ★★★★   5TH ARRONDISSEMENT

5, rue Linné, 75005; ☎ 01 47 07 06 20; fax 01 47 07 62 74; jardin-des-plantes@timhotel.fr; timhotel.com

THIS HOTEL OFFERS TWO CONTRASTING and equally engaging moods: the modern brightness of the entrance floor—where you check in, have breakfast, and dine amid floor-to-ceiling mirrors, light wood, flowery ceramic tiles, and summery yellow, blue, and orange fabrics—and the classic sobriety of the vaulted cellar, with its wrought-iron railing, ceiling beams, stone walls, a piano, café au lait–upholstered sofas, and low wooden tables. The top floor hosts a balcony with several tables and lots of flowers, but unfortunately a view in the wrong direction—of neighboring buildings rather than the glorious Jardin des Plantes. The corridor reflects the open, garden-style mood of the reception area. Though not overly friendly, the personnel do their job well.

SETTING AND FACILITIES
Location Latin Quarter. **Nearest Métro station** Jussieu. **Quietness rating** B. **Dining** €10 buffet breakfast. **Amenities** Public parking nearby. **Services** Room service for breakfast, laundry.

ACCOMMODATIONS
Rooms 33. **All** TV with satellite or cable, direct-dial phone, Wi-Fi, air-conditioning, hair dryer. **Some** 4 with shower, WC. **Comfort and décor** Room 52 is rather spacious and looks even more so due to its mirrored closet doors. Its furniture in light wood and white rattan as well as its greenhouse-colored fabrics give you the feeling of being away from it all. The bathroom is in white tile.

RATES, RESERVATIONS, AND RESTRICTIONS
Pricing Double €90–€140; discounts are available during trade fairs; special deals for online booking. **Credit cards** AE, DC, MC, V. **Check-in/out** 1 p.m./noon. **Elevator** Yes. **English spoken** Yes.

La Tour d'Auvergne   €145–€190

OVERALL ★★½   QUALITY ★★★½   VALUE ★★★★   9TH ARRONDISSEMENT

10, rue La Tour d'Auvergne, 75009; ☎ 01 48 78 61 60; fax 01 49 95 99 00; tourdauvergne@wanadoo.fr; hoteltourdauvergne.com

MODIGLIANI LIVED HERE. Near Métro Cadet, this attractive three-star hotel situated on a quiet street offers a good reception from the staff, and many inviting touches, including a particularly well-stocked table full of cultural and historic information useful during your Paris stay. You can have a drink in the small bar or relax in the little salon. The hotel underwent extensive renovation in 2008.

SETTING AND FACILITIES
Location Grands Boulevards. **Nearest Métro station** Cadet and Anvers.

Quietness rating B. **Dining** €12 Continental, buffet breakfast. **Services** Room service 7–10 a.m., reservations for restaurants, theater, airport transfer, taxi, and so on.

ACCOMMODATIONS
Rooms 24. **All** Satellite TV, phone, minibar, hair dryer, Wi-Fi. **Bathrooms** Modern and well equipped. **Comfort and décor** Relatively large and lavishly decorated rooms, all decked with canopy beds.

RATES, RESERVATIONS, AND RESTRICTIONS
Pricing Standard and deluxe double €145–190, extra bed €15. Special deals available on the Web site. **Deposit** Credit card. **Credit cards** AE, DC, MC, V. **Check-in/out** Noon. **Not allowed** Large pets. **Elevator** Yes. **English spoken** Some.

Welcome Hôtel   €85–€129

OVERALL ★★★½   QUALITY ★★★★   VALUE ★★★★   6TH ARRONDISSEMENT

66, rue de Seine, 75006; ☎ 01 46 34 24 80; fax 01 40 46 81 59; welcome-hotel@wanadoo.fr; welcomehotel-paris.com

A 17TH-CENTURY BUILDING in the heart of Saint-Germain-des-Prés, not far from the Odéon section with its famous pedestrian streets and markets. Hallways have beamed ceilings. Common-area carpets are green or orange. Reserve two months in advance.

SETTING AND FACILITIES
Location Saint-Germain-des-Prés. **Nearest Métro station** Mabillon. **Quietness rating** B (windows closed), C otherwise. **Dining** €11 Continental breakfast. **Services** Room service 7:30–10:30 a.m.

ACCOMMODATIONS
Rooms 29. **All** TV with satellite, direct-dial phone, Wi-Fi access, hair dryer. **Comfort and décor** Décor is pleasant but not remarkable (though the pictures of old Paris scenes are interesting), and bathrooms tend to be small and a bit drab. Room 53 (twin beds), overlooking boulevard Saint-Germain, gets plenty of light through lots of windows.

RATES, RESERVATIONS, AND RESTRICTIONS
Pricing Single €85, double €122–€129. **Credit cards** MC, V. **Check-in/out** Noon/11 a.m. **Not allowed** Pets. **Elevator** Yes. **English spoken** Some.

PART FOUR

ARRIVING, GETTING ORIENTED, *and* DEPARTING

YOUR TWO MOST STRESSFUL DAYS IN PARIS will be your date of arrival and date of departure. Most of the stress, however, can be eliminated with some planning and helpful tips, like knowing the best way to get to the airport, how early you should check in, how much luggage you are allowed to carry, and so on. If you read the following pages a few times and familiarize yourself with the process before traveling, you'll find getting in and out of Paris more or less manageable. It's true that Paris's fast-growing Roissy–Charles de Gaulle Airport and wildly busy terminals can be stressful, especially in the early mornings, when numerous flights arrive from and depart to North America. Security measures for travel to and from the United States and Canada require that you leave extra time for departing. You can find lots of information about the Paris airports on the Web at **parisinfo.com** and **aeroportsdeparis.fr.** For Roissy–Charles de Gaulle airport only, try **easycdg.com.**

BEATING JET LAG

PARIS TIME IS SIX HOURS AHEAD of the East Coast of the United States, and nine hours ahead of the West Coast. Most flights originating in North America arrive early in the morning, between 8 a.m. and 10 a.m. Thus, for your body it'll feel like the middle of the night. Everyone has his or her own theories on coping with jet lag. Here are a few time-tested tips of ours:

- Try to sleep at least a few hours on the plane.
- Drink plenty of water or juice and limit your alcohol consumption to the occasional glass of Champagne or wine with dinner.
- Set your watch to Paris time as soon as you take off. Psychologically, you'll be less disoriented when you arrive.
- Try not to go to sleep as soon as you arrive at your hotel. Go for a walk or begin with some lazy sightseeing. If you absolutely have to take a nap during the day, make it a brief one (just long enough to

keep you functioning through the rest of your day)—the goal is to keep yourself awake until evening and then have an early night on Paris time.

- Go to sleep a bit earlier than usual, but not too early. You'll be tired when you awake, but functional. Getting a good night of rest on your first night in Paris is essential and should "jolt" you into the correct time zone, even though it will be several more days until you feel "normal."
- Some people take melatonin tablets (consult your doctor first).

ARRIVING: *Day One*

THOSE FIRST MINUTES

TIRED, TIME-LAGGED, DISORIENTED, and unfamiliar with the new currency and exchange rate—the best piece of advice is to just relax, get your bearings, pinch yourself, observe the surroundings, inhale the wafts of strong coffee coming from the nearby cafés, and take a few deep breaths to get focused.

The differences will register immediately—the sound of the airport address system, the aesthetics of the signs and markings, the ethnic mix of travelers. Paris is a crossroads of movement and migration from not only Europe but its former colonies in Africa and Asia, and you will be amazed to see flights arriving from Antananarivo, Ouagadougou, Hanoi, and Marrakech. The colorful tails of aircraft from around the world on the tarmac at Charles de Gaulle alert you to the fact that you are far from home and that the world is a much larger place than you may have thought.

unofficial **TIP**
The best way to get totally immersed in the Paris ethos is to get oriented geographically and culturally from day one.

You'll want to feel comfortable as quickly as possible. You'll want to mix with the Parisians and take yourself to be one during your Paris stay. You don't mind being treated as a visitor, but you don't want to be shoved aside as an insensitive, ugly tourist.

PARIS AIRPORTS

PARIS HAS TWO INTERNATIONAL AIRPORTS, **Charles de Gaulle** (CDG), also known as **Roissy** because it's located in the suburb of Roissy about 18 miles (28 km) north of Paris, and **Orly** (ORY), located about 10 miles (18 km) south of Paris. Both are easily accessible by a commuter subway line called the RER (Réseau Express Régional), public buses, Air France buses, and taxis. Airport signs are mostly in French and English and are pretty clear.

Roissy–Charles de Gaulle Airport (CDG)

Charles de Gaulle Airport is large, expansive, modern, and not overly intimidating. There are three principle terminals: the older and circular **Aérogare 1,** which has recently been refurbished; **Aérogare 2,** newer and user-friendly, divided into seven halls or sections (2A, 2B, 2C, 2D, 2E, 2F, and the separate 2G), dominated by Air France, and where most U.S. and Canadian flights arrive; and **Aérogare 3** (formerly T9), which is principally used for charter flights and budget airlines such as Air Transat, which serves Canada.

AÉROGARE 1 If you're arriving from North America you'll probably be arriving in the morning and often very early. As you disembark you'll follow the glass corridors and the crowd onto a long and bouncy moving sidewalk that carries you and your hand luggage toward the core of Aérogare 1 and the waiting Immigration and Passport Control lines. Non-EU (European Union) citizens must fill out a simple yellow embarkation card; you should fill this out on the airplane to save you the time and aggravation of having to procure the form at the front of the line. (You'll be given a card onboard the plane.) Aérogare 1 is in the shape of a large circle, with numbered satellites branching out from the core. The lines to get past the immigration inspector are often long and somewhat unruly. You will notice that the French—who love form—are not too concerned with order and are not keen on civic education. Thus, there will be some jockeying for position in the line.

You'll be tired, and waiting in line is not fun. Instead of waiting in the line in front of you, walk around the circular Aérogare 1, and within two minutes you'll come to the next available Passport Control point. There will be many fewer people here. Go through. You can often avoid the big rush in a big way. Don't worry; you can't get lost; all Passport Control points converge on the same descending escalators toward the exit (*sortie* [soar-**tee**]). Follow the signs to the *bagages* (bah-**gahj**) claim area.

CLAIMING YOUR LUGGAGE Your luggage emerges from below and tumbles out onto a circular conveyor belt rather quickly. First, grab yourself a free luggage cart from the stacked line. There are usually plenty, but on days in which lots of flights arrive at once, you may have a problem finding a free cart. Special luggage such as animal cages, skis, oversize packages, bicycles, and so forth are brought into this area by hand on a large cart, so keep an eye out if you checked in anything of unusual dimensions.

If your baggage is missing or damaged, there are counters within this area for reporting this. Our experience is that trying to make claims on small damages is not worth it, just as it's rarely worth it back home. A report will be made and you may be sent to a luggage repair shop in the middle of Paris to have your American Tourister restitched. This will be a waste of time. If there is substantial damage, file a form nonetheless. You may be sent to the same shop for a replacement piece, or you may attempt to take this up with the airline upon returning. Some tourists have had success waiting to report the damage until they're back in the United States, as satisfaction was easier to obtain in the more customer-oriented U.S. offices.

With your bags, proceed to the *sortie*. Be careful: From the luggage carousels there are two exits, *sortie* 14 and *sortie* 36. If someone is picking you up or waiting for you, make sure that you exit from the *sortie* that is indicated for your flight, or you may end up waiting at the wrong spot. This happens. As you approach the sliding doors, you will spot customs officials in blue uniforms. There will be two sides and two signs. In green, meaning keep going, is "RIEN À DECLARER/ Nothing to Declare." In red, meaning stop, is "À DECLARER/To Declare." Chances are you'll have nothing to declare traveling into the country, so you should just ignore these people and keep walking. Do not slow down, hesitate, or make eye contact, or you might give them the chance to stop you and make a spot-check of your luggage. This doesn't happen too often, but people who are too hesitant or are lugging massive packages do get stopped on occasion. It may also help to keep your passport out and take on a bored, indifferent look as a visual reminder that they needn't bother you. In almost all cases, you won't even notice that you went through customs. Although the 2000 foot-and-mouth disease scare created more customs-consciousness, France does not pay particular attention to passengers arriving with food, fresh produce, flowers, or even dogs and cats.

If you're coming into Paris from another European Union (EU) country, there won't even be a Passport or Customs Control. You will have cleared that in your first country of entry.

Now in the outer part of this circular terminal, you'll see signs overhead in French and English for the many exits, parking, taxis, and buses.

AÉROGARE 2 The process of getting from the plane through the passport control and baggage claim area in Aérogare 2 is much simpler and faster than in Aérogare 1. The procedure is the same, but the lines are shorter and the luggage recovery tends to be quicker. There is no chance of exiting from the wrong *sortie;* follow the same general procedures here as with Aérogare 1. American Airlines uses a round pavilion that jets out from Aérogare 2A. Walking to and from with heavy luggage is rather inconvenient. In 2003 Air France and Delta opened their own Aérogare 2E exclusively for flights to the United States and South America.

When exiting, you'll see the **Aéroports de Paris (ADP) Information Stand,** clearly marked and open from 6 a.m. to midnight. Phone cards can be bought in the newspaper stand to your right and left. There are also ATM machines scattered around the different halls, for your convenience.

AÉROGARE 3 Formerly T9, this terminal is primarily used for charter flights and low-cost airlines. It is situated only a short walk from the RER station and is also served by taxis and the free CDGVAL airport interterminal rail shuttle, which also connects to the RER station at the airport. This free automated rail service replaced the bus shuttle at Charles de Gaulle Airport in 2007.

LOST LUGGAGE SERVICE ☎ 01 48 62 13 34 (Terminal 1) and ☎ 01 48 16 63 83 (Terminal 2). Call with questions about lost or damaged luggage.

ADP INFORMATION STANDS These information stands, marked in French as "Renseignements," provide lots of useful information and assistance in English. They distribute brochures and maps in English upon request. They also provide a little-known hotel-reservation service that can not only get you lodged in a choice hotel but can also give you substantial savings of up to 50 percent!

GETTING INTO PARIS FROM CHARLES DE GAULLE AIRPORT (AÉROGARE 1 OR 2) Your first big decision is how to get into Paris. Here's the drill:

If you don't have a lot of luggage, take the RER train (see below). It's fast and reliable, and there are no traffic snarls.

If you do have a lot of luggage and you'd rather not incur the cost of a taxi, take the Air France bus into Paris or arrange for a pickup service. If your hotel is near one of the Air France bus stops in Paris, you may prefer this option whether you have a lot of luggage or not.

If you're in a hurry and don't mind spending some cash, take a taxi. Note that, unfortunately, this is the only option for disabled travelers as none of the public-transport options mentioned below are equipped for wheelchair access.

RER (PARIS'S FAST COMMUTER TRAIN NETWORK) This is the fastest and most reliable access into Paris from Charles de Gaulle Airport. Count on about 40 minutes of travel time to central Paris. If you plan to buy the highly recommended five-zone Métro pass (Paris Visite), the trip into Paris will be included.

There is direct access by foot to the RER station at the airport from Terminals 2 and 3. Follow the signs for RER. From Terminal 1, you need to take the free airport rail shuttle (*navette*) CDGVAL to the RER station, which is only five minutes away.

*un**official* **TIP**
Show up with exact change, and you can buy your ticket from a machine without standing in line.

Trains run every 15 to 20 minutes from 5 a.m. until 11:45 p.m. and cost €8.40 per adult, €5.80 per child each way. If you change money at the airport, make sure to ask for some euro coins. Some machines will accept Visa or MasterCard, but we don't like risking a problem so early into the trip.

It's always best to ask your hotel in advance which RER stop you should get off at, but when in doubt, get off at Gare du Nord and either transfer to the Métro or take a taxi to your hotel. The RER stops in Paris at Gare du Nord, Châtelet–Les Halles, Saint-Michel–Notre-Dame, Luxembourg, Port Royal, Denfert-Rochereau, and Cité Universitaire. One way of selecting a hotel is by its convenience to one of these stops.

Above the platform you'll see a lit-up sign indicating which train will be the next to *départ* for Paris. The airport is the end of the line, so you can't possibly take the train the wrong way. The RER now connects with the TGV (*Train à Grande Vitesse*), France's famous high-speed train, to points north. In some cases you may be able to take the Brussels- or Amsterdam-bound train directly from the airport and not have to go into Paris. The TGV station is at the RER station called Charles de Gaulle 2.

AIR FRANCE AIRPORT BUS   This is a convenient and comfortable way to get in and out of town. It is accessible to everyone—you do not need an Air France plane ticket or need to be an Air France passenger to use the Air France airport bus service. From your terminal, follow the well-marked signs for buses to Paris. From Charles de Gaulle, take either Line 2 or Line 4, depending on where in Paris you'd like to be dropped off—Étoile–Porte Maillot, Gare de Lyon, or Montparnasse. The buses are air-conditioned, and there is a baggage handler at each stop. In compliance with recent legislation, they are also gradually being fitted with seatbelts. You do not need to prepurchase tickets; you pay onboard. Children ages 2 to 11 pay half-price, and a 15 percent discount is offered for groups of four or more passengers. Call ☎ 08 92 35 08 20 for recorded information in English (€0.34 per minute) or visit the Web site, **cars-airfrance.com.** If this is your preferred option, you may want to look at their combo card, Paris à la Carte, which gives discounts on boat and bus tours of Paris. Information is the same as above and at **parisalacarte.free.fr.**

LINE 2   Line 2 leaves from Terminals 1 and 2 and stops at Palais des Congrès at the Porte Maillot and at the Charles de Gaulle–Étoile RER/Métro stop (avenue Carnot exit). Service runs every 30 minutes from 5:45 a.m. to 11 p.m. Price: €15 per person each way, €24 round-trip.

LINE 4   Line 4 leaves from Terminal 1 but stops at Terminal 2 before leaving for Paris's Gare de Lyon train station (Métro: Gare de Lyon, boulevard Diderot) and Gare Montparnasse (Métro: Montparnasse, rue du Commandant Mouchotte). Service runs every 30 minutes from 6:30 a.m. until 9:30 p.m. Price: €16.50 per person each way, €27 round-trip.

ROISSYBUS This airport bus runs between all Charles de Gaulle Airport terminals and the Opéra (rue Scribe in front of the American Express office near the Place de l'Opéra; Métro: Opéra). Service is provided daily every 15 minutes between 6 a.m. and 7 p.m. and every 20 minutes between 7 and 11 p.m. Price: €8.60 for all passengers. Your Paris Visite pass is valid on this bus. For recorded information in English about this and other RATP (Régie Autonome des Transports Parisiens) airport links, call ☎ 011 33 8 92 69 32 46 from abroad and 3246 when in France (€0.34 per minute) or visit **ratp.fr.**

RATP BUSES (LOCAL CITY BUSES) Less known to out-of-town visitors, the RATP runs two lines between Paris and Roissy–Charles de Gaulle. These are the slowest and least convenient but cheapest form of public transportation between the city and the airport. If you're traveling light, have plenty of time, or are staying close to either the Gare de l'Est or Nation, you may opt for this service.

Bus 350 Leaves from the front of the Gare de l'Est.

Bus 351 Leaves from Place de la Nation.

Both make local stops and take 1 hour and 10 minutes. The trip costs three Métro tickets, about €4 if you buy a *carnet* of ten tickets. Your Paris Visite pass is valid on these buses too.

TAXIS Follow the signs for taxis and line up on the sidewalk as the next available taxi pulls up to the curb. Parisians do not share taxis, and drivers do not appreciate your attempts to make a deal with the people in front or in back of you in line. Paris taxi drivers are not known for their loquaciousness or general friendliness. Few speak English. They are entitled to smoke in their cab but only with the consent of the customer. Others drive around with a dog in the front seat. In terms of honesty, it's not common that a driver will try to rip you off, but nonetheless, you should check that the meter only starts once you've gotten in. You should have a rough idea where your hotel is situated and not appear hopelessly dependent. Look like you know the ropes and you shouldn't have to worry about getting "taken for a ride." From Charles de Gaulle Airport to central Paris, count on the ride costing €55–€60. You'll be charged €1 extra for each additional piece of luggage after the first one. Count on the ride taking an hour from the airport to the middle of Paris, depending on the time of day and traffic. For more details on Paris taxis, see Part Five, Getting Around.

SHUTTLES AND PICKUP SERVICES Aside from hotel services and limousines, there are several companies offering regular and reliable shuttle or pickup services. Some of the most popular services are PariShuttle, Blue Vans, and Paris Airports Service.

Blue Airport Shuttle (paris-blue-airport-shuttle.fr) operates seven days a week, year-round. Rates begin at €26 per person in a shared shuttle and €63 for a private shuttle for 2 passengers (children under age 3 are half price including an infant car seat). One of this company's bright blue-and-yellow eight-passenger minivans will be waiting for you at your terminal at Charles de Gaulle Airport or Orly Airport (for groups of four or more). There is no extra charge for luggage. Simply reserve ahead—online reservations only—through their Web site, stating your name, airport, flight number, and time of arrival. Returning home, reserve the Blue Vans through their Web site two days before your departure. Although Blue Vans promises not to make any more than three stops after yours to pick up other passengers, make sure you leave early enough to avoid close calls. Give yourself an hour and a half to get to the airport. So for a 10 a.m. flight from Charles de Gaulle, you'll want to check in between 8 a.m. and 8:30 a.m., meaning that, depending on the location of your hotel and the traffic patterns, you'll need to be picked up between 6:30 a.m. and 7 a.m.

PariShuttle (parishuttle.com) prides itself on its reliability and door-to-door service. Bilingual drivers also offer excursions to Versailles, Giverny, Disneyland Paris, and Fontainebleau; Paris sight-seeing tours; and VIP arrivals service. Shared airport shuttles start at €27 for one person, and €19 each for two to four people. You can make reservations online at **paris-anglo.com;** just click on the Paris Shuttle link.

Airport Connection (airport-connection.com) has been in business for more than 10 years and offers a similar kind of service. Their rates start at €24 per person to or from Orly and €28 per person to or from Charles de Gaulle, with some seasonal reductions such as 20 percent during the winter months. As a member of the global organization Go Airport Shuttle (**goairportshuttle.com**), they offer the added advantage that you can book transfers for both your city of departure and for your arrival in Paris at the same time.

CAR RENTAL Follow the signs for car rental (*Location de voiture*). For local car-rental phone numbers and a discussion of the pros and cons of renting a car in Paris, see Part Five, Getting Around.

A NOTE ON THE DRIVE INTO PARIS Chances are that it'll be early morning when you arrive, it'll be overcast and drizzly, and your taxi driver will be grumpy. It's not your fault, but he has just spent two to three hours waiting in line for your fare. Make sure that the meter does not already show some horrendous sum like €30 before you even get going. Some tourists have reported paying three times the correct fare due to this ruse. The areas between airports and cities are often ugly, and Paris's are no exception. The drive through the northern suburbs along the A1 or 13 highway from Charles de Gaulle Airport into Paris is ugly and industrial. You're likely to gasp, "This is Paris?!?"

For inter-airport buses between Charles de Gaulle and Orly Airports, take the **Air France Bus Line 3** (price: €19). Count on an hour of travel time. The Air France Airport Bus service operates an information number in French and English at ☎ 08 92 35 08 20. You can also take the RER B south in the direction of Saint-Rémy–lès-Chevreuse (not Robinson trains), and get off at Antony. There are several trains per hour that go direct between Roissy and Antony. From here, take the Orlyval to Orly Airport. The trip will take about 1 hour 20 minutes and costs €17.60, half for children ages 4 to 10.

Orly Airport

Orly Airport has two main terminals, **Orly Sud** and **Orly Ouest.** You'll most likely be arriving at Orly Sud. Both are equally served by ground transportation into Paris.

GETTING INTO PARIS FROM ORLY AIRPORT (SUD AND OUEST TERMINALS) Your first big decision is how to get into Paris. Here's how to solve this one.

If you don't have a lot of luggage, take the RER train. It's fast and reliable, and there are no traffic snarls.

If you do have a lot of luggage and you'd rather not incur the cost of a taxi, take the Air France bus into Paris or arrange for a pickup service. If your hotel is near one of the Air France bus stops in Paris you may prefer this option whether you have a lot of luggage or not.

If you're in a hurry and don't mind spending some cash, take a taxi.

One Paris-lover commented: "Instead of a taxi, I use the Air France bus departing Orly Sud and stopping at Orly Ouest every 15 minutes. There's a French and English video played on the 40-minute drive into town. I tried the Orlyval to the RER to the Métro once, but with luggage the bus is much easier."

RER/ORLYVAL Follow the signs for the RER/Orlyval. The trains are accessed directly from both terminals. The Orlyval is a fast, fully automated train offering an eight-minute connection service between Orly Airport and the RER (Line B) intersection at a station called Antony. The trip takes 25 minutes to Châtelet in the center of Paris. If you have bought the Paris Visite

unofficial **TIP**
Show up with local currency, and, if possible, enough coins to be able to buy your ticket from a machine and not have to stand in line.

five-zone pass, your trip into Paris is included. Follow the well-marked signs for the RER/Orlyval train toward Paris. The train stops in Paris at Cité Universitaire, Denfert-Rochereau, Port-Royal, Luxembourg, Saint-Michel–Notre-Dame, Châtelet–Les Halles, and Gare du Nord.

Orlyval runs daily, every four to seven minutes between 6 a.m. and 11 p.m. The price, including the connecting RER into Paris, is €9.60 per person each way and half-price for children between the ages of 4 and 10. The round-trip price is exactly double the one-way price, so there is no advantage to buying your return portion in advance.

AIR FRANCE AIRPORT BUS This is a very convenient and comfortable way to get in and out of town. It is accessible to everyone, so don't be confused—you don't need an Air France plane ticket or need to be an Air France passenger to use the Air France airport bus service. From your terminal, follow the well-marked signs for buses to Paris. From Orly Sud or Ouest, Line 1 takes you to Montparnasse (in front of the Hotel Meridien, 1, rue du Commandant Mouchotte, Métro: Montparnasse) and the Air France Terminal at the Invalides Métro station. Line 1* follows the same route then continues on to its terminus at Charles de Gaulle–Étoile RER/Métro stop (avenue Carnot exit). Both lines will also stop at Porte d'Orléans Métro station if you ask the driver, but only for passengers who do not have luggage stowed underneath.

All Air France buses are air-conditioned, and there is a baggage handler at each stop. In compliance with recent legislation, they are gradually all being fitted with seatbelts. You do not need to prepurchase tickets; you pay onboard. Children ages 2 to 11 pay half-price, and groups of four or more passengers receive a 15 percent discount.

LINE 1 Lines 1 and 1* leave Orly Sud (Gate L) and Ouest (Gate H) every 30 minutes between 6:15 a.m. and 11:15 p.m. and cost €11.50 per person each way. Round-trip is €18.50, so if you'll be using the service to get back to the airport, consider buying the round-trip ticket when you arrive (a saving of €7). A 24-hour information service in English can be reached at ☎ 08 92 35 08 20, (€0.34 per minute) or visit the Web site, **cars-airfrance.com.** If this is your preferred option, you may want to look at their combo card, Paris à la Carte, which gives discounts on boat and bus tours of Paris. Information is the same as above and at **parisalacarte.free.fr.**

ORLYBUS The RATP offers a regular Orly Airport bus service to the RER station at Denfert-Rochereau. You can get off at intermediate stops such as Jourdan Tombe Issoire and Alésia René Coty. Travel time is 30 minutes. Catch this bus at Porte H at quai 4 in Orly Sud or Porte G on Niveau 0 in Orly Ouest. The service runs daily every 15 to 20 minutes from 6 a.m. to 11:30 p.m. Cost: €6.30 per person each way. Your Paris Visite five-zone pass is valid on this service. Tickets are purchased on the bus or at the ADP window in the airport. Many travelers use this service to Denfert-Rochereau and then take a taxi or jump on the Métro to their hotel.

TAXIS Follow the signs for taxis and wait in line on the sidewalk as taxis pull up curbside. Expect to pay €40 to €45, depending on your Paris location and the traffic, as well as €1 for each additional piece of luggage after the first one. Be careful to check that the meter is started only when you get in the taxi. The best way to avoid being "taken for a ride" is to have a good idea where your hotel is situated. Taxis are also the only alternative for some disabled travelers as none of the public transport options described are adapted for wheelchair access.

SHUTTLES AND PICKUP SERVICES Aside from hotel services and limousines, there are several companies offering regular and reliable shuttle or pickup services, such as the Blue Vans, PariShuttle, and Paris Airports Service. See "Shuttles and Pickup Services" under Charles de Gaulle Airport information above, or go to **paris-anglo.com** and click on Airport Shuttles.

CAR RENTAL Follow signs for car rental (*Location de voiture*). For local car-rental phone numbers and a discussion of the pros and cons of renting a car in Paris, see Part Five, Getting Around.

LOST LUGGAGE SERVICE ☎ 01 49 75 34 10 (Orly Sud) and ☎ 01 49 75 42 34 (Orly Ouest). Call here with questions about lost or damaged luggage.

WI-FI ACCESS

IF YOU ARE TRAVELING with your laptop and want to connect to the Internet upon your arrival, Wi-Fi access is available throughout the public areas and boarding halls of the terminals. Just buy a Wi-Fi session at any of the Relay newsagents or online at the airport Web site **aeroportsdeparis.fr.** And some gates now have Internet terminals, which give you access in increments of 15 minutes for a reasonable fee.

CHANGING MONEY AT THE AIRPORT

IF YOU CAN AVOID IT, aside from using an airport ATM, don't change money at the airport (or train station). Your choices are limited, the exchange rate is lower than average, and you'll be wasting time. On the other hand, if you arrive without a euro in your pocket, you'll need some cash to get you into the city. If you can change $100, you'll be secure for the next few hours. American Express has 20 exchanges throughout Roissy–Charles de Gaulle airport and two at Orly. The exchange rate at the airport is not negotiable, regardless how much you change. Remember, of course, you can use the same euros in 16 countries, namely Austria, Belgium, Cyprus, Finland, France, Germany, Greece, Ireland, Italy, Luxembourg, Malta, Netherlands, Portugal, Slovakia, Slovenia, and Spain. To understand the posted rate card, note that the *vente* column represents the price at which they are selling the currency, while the *achat* column represents at what price they are buying your dollars. For a more detailed explanation, see "Changing Money" later in this chapter.

Our choice is to arrive with a minimal amount of euros and supplement this at an ATM (*guichet automatique*). There are lots of these in every hall of each airport terminal and train station. Have your PIN ready. When you do get your first bank notes, study the currency for a minute to get acquainted with its denominations.

DEPARTING

YOU'LL PROBABLY JUST WANT TO REVERSE your steps to get back to the airport. Don't forget your passport and airplane tickets! Keep them in a handy but secure place. Check your information twice for the airport and terminal you are leaving from. You'll almost always leave from the airport you arrived at, but occasionally airlines operating out of both airports change schedules. Check, just to be sure. Going to the wrong airport or the wrong terminal at the right airport is no fun.

Your options for Roissy–Charles de Gaulle Airport (CDG) are Terminal 1 (CDG 1) or Terminal 2 (CDG 2A, 2B, 2C, 2D, 2E, 2F, and 2G). CDG 3 is Charles de Gaulle Terminal 3 (formerly T9).

Your options for Orly (ORY) are Orly Sud (ORY SUD) or Orly Ouest (ORY OUEST).

Several budget European airlines operate flights out of Beauvais Airport (BVA) to Germany, Hungary, Ireland, Italy, Poland, Portugal, Romania, Spain, Sweden, and the UK. There is a one-hour shuttle-bus service to Porte de Maillot in Paris that costs €13.

CONFIRMING YOUR FLIGHT: REACHING THE AIRLINES

AIRLINE OFFICES DO NOT ANSWER THEIR PHONES around the clock like they do in North America. You either call them during working hours or call the airport information number for flight information and for direct airport telephone numbers for some airlines.

MAJOR AIRLINE OFFICES IN PARIS	
Air France	☎ 36 54
Air Canada	☎ 08 25 88 08 81
American Airlines	☎ 01 55 17 43 41
British Airways	☎ 08 25 82 54 00
Continental Airlines	☎ 01 71 23 03 35
Delta Air Lines	☎ 08 11 64 00 05
Northwest Airlines	☎ 08 92 70 26 08
United Airlines	☎ 08 10 72 72 72
U.S. Airways	☎ 08 10 63 22 22

Roissy–Charles de Gaulle Traveler Information
☎ 39 50 (€0.34 per minute)

Orly Airport Traveler Information ☎ 39 50 (€0.34 per minute)

Flight Update Hotline (Incoming and Outgoing) ☎ 39 50 or **aeroportsdeparis.fr.**

GETTING TO THE AIRPORT ON TIME

EVERY TRAVELER HAS HIS OR HER OWN STYLE. Some have nervous breakdowns if they aren't checked in three hours before the scheduled flight time. Others just seem to breeze in at the last minute before the flight is closed. On international flights we strongly suggest that you plan to be checked in at least two hours before the scheduled flight time. Air France and other airlines tend to be rather strict on closing flights at an announced time. You risk losing your seat if you are late. If you plan on claiming a VAT (value-added tax) refund on your purchases or visiting the duty-free shops, or you want to make sure you get good seats, plan to arrive more than two hours before departure, as the airlines instruct. It's better to avoid such stress.

unofficial **TIP**
As a rule, give yourself 1 hour and 15 minutes to reach Charles de Gaulle Airport and 1 hour to reach Orly Airport, regardless how you're getting there.

For a more detailed description of each of the following services, see the arrival information earlier in this chapter.

Roissy–Charles de Gaulle

To get to Roissy–Charles de Gaulle Airport from Paris, depending on the location of your hotel, the amount of luggage you have, and your budget, select the means that suits you best.

RER B This offers direct service to Roissy–Charles de Gaulle Airport from the following Paris stations: Gare du Nord, Châtelet–Les Halles, Saint-Michel–Notre-Dame, Luxembourg, Port Royal, Denfert-Rochereau, and Cité Universitaire.

Trains are frequent, but count on a 15-minute wait. Travel time is around 40 minutes, depending on where you get on. As you are waiting on the platform, note that the lit sign above the platform indicates the destination of the next train and the stops it makes. Make sure you get on a train heading toward Charles de Gaulle Airport. If your Paris Visite five-zone pass is still valid, then you can use it to return to the airport. Otherwise, you'll need a ticket. Trains run every 15 to 20 minutes from 5 a.m. until midnight and cost €8.10 per person.

AIR FRANCE AIRPORT BUS Line 2 leaves Paris's Étoile (1, avenue Carnot) every 20 minutes from 5:45 a.m. to 11 p.m. daily, and from Porte Maillot (boulevard Gouvion Saint-Cyr) every 15 minutes from

5:45 a.m. to 11 p.m. daily. This bus services Charles de Gaulle Airport Terminals 2A, 2B, 2C, 2D, 2E, 2F, 2G, and Terminal 1. The service costs €15 one way, €24 round-trip; children ages 2 to 11 travel half-price. Groups of four or more passengers are entitled to a 15 percent discount.

Air France Bus Line 4 leaves Montparnasse (rue du Commandant Mouchotte in front of the Meridian Hotel) and the Gare de Lyon (boulevard Diderot) every 30 minutes from 7 a.m. to 9.30 p.m. This bus services Charles de Gaulle Airport Terminals 2A, 2B, 2C, 2D, 2E, 2F, 2G, and Terminal 1. The cost is €16.50 one way, €27 round-trip; children ages 2 to 11 travel half-price. Groups of four or more passengers are entitled to a 15 percent discount. For recorded information in English 24 hours a day, seven days a week, call ☎ 08 92 35 08 20 or visit **cars-airfrance.com.**

ROISSYBUS This airport bus runs between Opéra (rue Scribe in front of the American Express office at the Place de l'Opéra) and Charles de Gaulle Airport daily every 15 minutes between 6 a.m. and 8 p.m., and every 20 minutes between 8 and 11 p.m. The price is €8.60 for all passengers. Your Paris Visite five-zone pass is valid for this trip. For recorded information in English call ☎ 011 33 8 92 69 32 46 from abroad and 3246 when in France or visit **ratp.fr.**

TAXIS You can either grab a taxi at a taxi stand near your hotel or you can have your hotel receptionist call a taxi for you. If a taxi is called for you, don't be surprised to see that the meter already has €4.50 to €6 on it when it arrives. If the sum seems exorbitant, don't accept the taxi. Savvy travelers note the phone number at the nearby taxi stand and call ten minutes before they want to be picked up. The amount on the meter will be considerably less. If you want to call one of the taxi companies yourself or arrange for your pickup the night before, try Taxis Bleus ☎ 08 91 70 10 10 (**taxis-bleus.com**). You can pay with Visa or MasterCard for fares over €15. Reservations can be made by phone or online up to a week in advance or as little as 15 minutes before the pickup time.

SHUTTLES AND DROP-OFF SERVICES If you use one of the pickup and drop-off services, call several days in advance to reserve. Always allow for an extra 30 minutes in case there is a delay, traffic, or an unforeseen problem. Allow an extra hour to get to the airport, since the minibuses often make a number of pickup stops around Paris before heading to the airport. We have heard of passengers missing their planes because of such delays. Don't assume that because the service specializes in getting people to the airport, the driver will manage your schedule well.

CAR RENTAL Inquire with the car-rental company on the procedures for returning vehicles. Upon arriving at the airport along the A1 highway, follow the signs for "*Location de Voiture.*" For early or late drop-offs, inquire about returning your car the day before your departure. See Part Five, Getting Around, for car-rental numbers.

Orly Airport

To get to Orly Airport (Sud and Ouest Terminals) from Paris, depending on the location of your hotel, the amount of luggage you are carrying, and your budget, select the means that suits you best.

RER/ORLYVAL Buy a ticket for Orly via the Orlyval at any Métro or RER station. If your Paris Visite five-zone pass is still valid, you may use it to get to Orly Airport. Take the RER B train, direction of Saint-Rémy-lès-Chevreuse, south to Orly, which stops in Paris at Gare du Nord, Châtelet–Les Halles, Saint-Michel-Notre-Dame, Luxembourg, Port-Royal, Denfert-Rochereau, and Cité Universitaire. Get off the train at the Antony station and transfer to the Orlyval train. It will be hard to miss because the airport connection is prominently announced in French and English. The Orlyval runs every four to seven minutes between 6 a.m. and 11 p.m. daily. The price of the combined ticket is €9.60 per person and half-price for children ages 4 to 10.

AIR FRANCE BUS The Line 1 bus leaves from the Air France Terminal at Invalides every 12 minutes between 5:45 a.m. and 11 p.m. It stops at Montparnasse (in front of Hotel Meridien, 1, rue du Commandant Mouchotte, Métro: Montparnasse). Line 1* starts from Charles de Gaulle–Étoile RER/Métro stop (avenue Carnot exit). The cost for both lines is €11.50 per person each way. Round-trip costs €18.50.

ORLYBUS The bus leaves from in front of the Denfert-Rochereau RER station every 15 to 20 minutes from 5:30 a.m. to 11 p.m. daily. You can buy tickets on the bus or use your Paris Visite five-zone pass if it's still valid. The price is €6.30.

TAXIS You can either grab a taxi at a taxi stand near your hotel, or you can have your hotel receptionist call a taxi for you. If a taxi is called for you, don't be surprised to see that the meter already has €4.50 to €6 on it when it arrives. If the sum is much higher than this, don't accept the taxi. Savvy travelers note the phone number at the nearby taxi stand and call ten minutes before they want to be picked up. The amount on the meter will be considerably less. If you want to call one of the taxi companies yourself or arrange for your pickup the night before, try Taxis Bleus, ☎ 08 91 70 10 10 (**taxis-bleus.com**). You can pay with Visa or MasterCard for fares over €15. Reservations can be made by phone or online up to a week in advance or as little as 15 minutes before the pickup time.

unofficial **TIP**
Don't assume that just because a service specializes in getting people to the airport that the driver will manage your schedule well.

SHUTTLES AND DROP-OFF SERVICES If you use one of the pickup and drop-off services, call several days in advance to reserve. Always allow an extra 30 minutes in case there is a delay, traffic, or an unforeseen problem. Allow an extra hour to get to the airport because the mini-buses often make a number of pickups around Paris before heading to the airport. We have heard of passengers missing their planes because of such delays.

CAR RENTAL When driving to Orly Airport from Paris along the A10 highway, make sure you keep to the left when the highway splits between Lyon and Orléans. If you miss the left-lane exit for Orly, you'll be stuck with a 20-minute detour to get back.

As you approach Orly Airport, you'll spot signs for the car-rental companies and "*Location de Voitures.*" Call your rental company in advance to inquire about special drop-off instructions. See Part Five, Getting Around, for car-rental numbers.

CLAIMING YOUR VAT REFUND ON PURCHASES

AT THE AIRPORT, DON'T FORGET TO CLAIM YOUR VAT REFUND on your purchases before proceeding to your gate. For detailed procedures on doing this, refer to Part Eight, Shopping. Note that the VAT refund can be claimed only in the last country you visit within the European Union. In other words, you can't "de-tax" your purchases in France when leaving for England.

ARRIVING *and* DEPARTING *by* TRAIN

TRAIN STATIONS

PARIS HAS SIX MAIN TRAIN STATIONS (*les gares*), so first make sure that you know which station you're coming into and which station you're departing from. There is nothing more stressful than showing up on time for a train that leaves from another station. All Paris train stations are accessible by at least two Métro lines.

FOR ALL STATIONS Information and ticket sales and recorded train times (in French) ☎ 36 35 and at **voyages-sncf.com** (in English).

GARE DU NORD 75010, Métro: Gare du Nord on Lines 4 and 5, RER B, and D. Served by bus lines 26, 38, 42, 43, 46, 48, 54, 56, 65, and 350. This enormous neoclassical train station was designed by Jacques-Ignace Hittorff in 1863 and was crowned with statues representing the larger cities of France. As its name suggests, it serves destinations in the north of France. It is also the departure point for the Eurostar (Brussels, London) and Thalys (Brussels, Amsterdam, Cologne, Düsseldorf) train lines.

GARE DE L'EST 75010, Métro: Gare de l'Est on Lines 4, 5, and 7. Served by bus lines 30, 31, 32, 38, 39, 46, 47, 56, 65, and 350. Originally one of the more modest stations in Paris, it recently underwent extensive refurbishment in preparation for the opening of the TGV line linking Paris to Strasbourg in only 2 hours and 20 minutes. It serves other destinations in the east of France, such as Nancy, Reims, and Metz, as well as Germany, Switzerland, and Luxembourg. An enormous *fresque* (fresco) by A. Herter illustrating French soldiers departing for the "Grande War," as World War I is called in French, is worth a look.

GARE MONTPARNASSE 75014/75015, Métro: Gare Montparnasse on Lines 4, 6, 12, and 13. Served by bus lines 28, 58, 88, 91, 92, 94, 95, and 96. This station lies beneath the 209-meter Tour Montparnasse and serves destinations west and southwest of Paris, such as Brittany, Poitiers, La Rochelle, Bordeaux, Toulouse, Biarritz, and Lourdes. It's organized into two areas; Montparnasse 2 is where the TGV departs.

GARE D'AUSTERLITZ 75005, Métro: Gare d'Austerlitz on Lines 5 and 10, RER C. Served by bus lines 24, 57, 61 63, 89, and 91. Trains leaving from this station link France with Spain and Portugal. It is presently undergoing extensive refurbishment in preparation for the arrival of a TGV line in 2012.

GARE SAINT LAZARE 75008, Métro: Gare Saint Lazare on Lines 3, 9, 12, 13, 14, and RER E. Served by bus lines 20, 21, 22, 24, 26, 27, 28, 29, 32, 43, 53, 66, 80, 81, and 95. This station has been called a "factory of dreams" because of its steel-and-glass architecture. It was built by J. Lisch in 1885 and acts as the commuter hub for most of the suburbs to the west of Paris. Note the bronze sculpture of piled-up battered suitcases in front of the station. It was here that thousands of homeless and uprooted Eastern Europeans arrived at the end of World War II.

GARE DE LYON 75012, Métro: Gare de Lyon on Lines 1 and 14 and RER A and D. Served by bus lines 20, 24, 29, 57, 61, 63, 65, 87, and 91. This station has been remodeled several times since its construction (1847–1852). It has had its present-day modern style since the arrival of the TGV. It serves destinations between Paris and the Midi (south of France), including Dijon, Lyon, Montpellier, Marseilles, and Nice. The nearby Gare de Bercy is also the departure point for Artesia trains linking France and Italy (you can reach Turin in 5.5 hours and Milan in 6.5 hours).

THE FAMOUS TGV (*TRAIN À GRANDE VITESSE*)

THESE HIGH-SPEED TRAINS have been influential in recent demo-graphic changes in France, allowing people who work in Paris to live in the less-crowded regions around the city without losing a lot of time commuting. Travel on the TGV, Thalys, or Eurostar requires a ticket and a reservation (*billet avec réservation*). For more information and to make reservations, visit **tgv.com, idtgv.com,** or call ☎ 36 35. You may be holding on the line for a while, though.

TRAIN RESERVATIONS AND TICKETS

ANY SNCF AGENCY, TRAIN STATION, or travel agent can sell you train tickets and reservations. Travel agents usually charge around €5–€7 above the ticket price as their service fee. This is often worth it, since you won't have to go to the train station or wait in lines prior to your departure. Better still, pop into one of the numerous Boutiques SNCF throughout the city, where you can also buy a ticket directly or obtain leaflets and other information. The SNCF has an information phone line, but you may spend a long time on hold and then the staff may not speak adequate English or may become impatient if you ask too many questions. Ask your hotel concierge if he can help you make reservations. For information: ☎ 08 91 67 10 08, Île de France; ☎ 36 35, Grandes Lignes. Or go to **voyages-sncf.com.**

LOCKERS AND OTHER SERVICES

ALTHOUGH ALL THE TRAIN STATIONS have lockers called *con-signe,* which will give you 24 hours of storage, it is best not to count on these because periodic security restrictions limit their access. But if you do end up relying on a locker, be equipped with euro coins. The stations also have a storage service for suitcases and larger items, although due to tightening security measures, regulations about their use may also change without notice. Definitely do not ever leave your baggage unattended; it risks being picked up by a security team and destroyed.

TAKING THE EUROSTAR

GETTING BETWEEN ENGLAND AND FRANCE has never been easier; the Eurostar Paris–London route via the 22-mile Eurotunnel takes just over two hours. The service runs between the Gare du Nord and Saint Pancras Station more or less hourly between 6:30 a.m. and 9 p.m. To make reservations in Paris, call ☎ 08 92 35 35 39 or visit **eurostar.com.**

One-way standard tickets cost around €330 for first class and €230 for second class. However, advance bookings can bring the price down to about €230 first class and €40 second class.

It's relatively easy to find special Eurostar prices at either end, with discounts of up to 50 percent off the published price. To inquire, call ☎ 08 92 35 35 39. For example, Eurostar offers "leisure" round-trip fares starting at as little as €77 in second class for travelers spending a Saturday night in London.

The ride is generally comfortable and smooth, with the 20-minute tunnel interlude passing by uneventfully. It just feels like you're traveling at night. Multilingual Eurostar attendants decked out in navy blue with yellow scarves or ties are very accommodating, and the onboard buffet car is convenient. The train also has public phones and power sockets in certain carriages.

Is It Worth Going First Class?

Not really. In terms of comfort, you don't really need the wide, reclining seat, similar to business-class airline seats, for a two-hour journey. But you might enjoy the elegant meal served at your seat, which is included in your ticket price, and the executive lounges at both Saint Pancras Station and Gare du Nord help reduce the wear and tear of travel. But we prefer saving the cash and having a better meal later.

ARRIVING *and* DEPARTING *by* CAR

IF YOU ARE DRIVING INTO PARIS, you'll feel the presence of the big city by the congestion you hit as you approach the beltway, the *périphérique*. It's generally easier to move east and west by car in Paris than north and south. Sunday evening Paris-bound traffic on the *autoroutes* is almost always jammed up. Here are our suggestions for getting into central Paris, depending on where your hotel is located.

If you're coming into Paris from the west, take the Voie Express, which follows the Seine on the Right Bank eastward from western Paris.

If you're coming into Paris from the east—get off the *périphérique* at Porte de Bercy and hug the Seine on the Right Bank to head west. (Note however that riverside routes are frequently closed to traffic on weekends and during the summer.)

If you're coming into Paris from the north or south—follow the *périphérique* either east or west depending on where your hotel is and then follow directions as if you were coming in from the east or west.

RULES OF THE ROAD

ALL YOU'LL NEED TO DRIVE IN PARIS are a valid U.S. driver's license and, preferably, an international driver's license (easily obtainable from any AAA office in the United States and valid for one year). Be aware, however, that some French rules of the road will be foreign to you. Please be certain to note the following:

- *Priorité à droite.* When there is no stop or yield sign present, you must yield to the car approaching from the right. That's the law, so be very careful to give way to traffic merging from the right.
- Do not cross a solid middle line in the road. This is taken far more seriously than in North America.
- Buckle up for safety. There is a €135 fine for driving or riding without a seat belt.

PARKING

PARIS PARKING CAN BE HAIR-RAISING. And you'll be amused to see how Parisian drivers can squeeze into anything. Since Parisians are taught to leave their parked cars in neutral (*point mort*), some drivers even push other parked cars forward and backward with their bumpers to make room for their vehicle. One Japanese tourist witnessed this bumper-to-bumper contact and with alarm exclaimed, "In Japan that would be considered an accident!"

unofficial **TIP**
Remember that when using a credit or debit card from a U.S. bank you will be charged an additional 2 percent or 3 percent, depending on the fee schedule of your bank.

At night around the crowded parts of town, cars will be parked on sidewalks and along the center line in the street.

If you are driving, we recommend that you use the underground parking lots marked everywhere with a large P. They are for the most part affordable (you can always pay with a Visa or MasterCard) and safe, and you will save yourself time and aggravation by avoiding street parking.

GAS

THERE IS NO PROBLEM FINDING GASOLINE IN PARIS, but the prices may jolt you, since European countries tax gasoline heavily in order to encourage people to use the excellent public-transportation system and to reduce the amount of car-related pollution. Count on paying roughly the same amount for a liter (about a quart) as what you pay in North America for a gallon. All rentals require lead-free gasoline (*sans plomb*). Unleaded gasoline (95 and 98 octane) will be marked in green. Larger model cars often use diesel, which is also called gasoil. Note that you'll get much better mileage when using diesel, which means less cost and fewer fill-ups. Leaded gasoline is now extinct. Visa and MasterCard are widely accepted. American Express is accepted in many but not all stations.

Note that there are gas stations as you approach and leave both Charles de Gaulle and Orly airports.

TRAFFIC

PARIS TRAFFIC IS REASON ENOUGH NOT TO DRIVE. Seriously, we recommend instead that you walk, use the Métro, and take taxis when necessary—public transportation in Paris is easy to use, efficient, and inexpensive. Otherwise, plan on being stuck in traffic along the *périphérique*, around Châtelet, or on rue de Rivoli. And traffic patterns around Étoile at the Arc de Triomphe and the Bastille, although not mean-spirited, may require you to take sedatives. The style of driving in Paris requires that you keep moving, yield only to your right, never honk, and don't hesitate. Parisians can be aggressive and impatient but generally refrain from demonstrating real anger. It's like a game of bumper cars—hopefully, without bumping. If you do bump into someone, though, remain calm and fill in the *Constat Amiable* ("friendly report") you'll find in the glove compartment of your vehicle. If in doubt, do not sign anything that you cannot read or understand.

UNDERSTANDING THOSE FIRST SIGNS *and* GETTING DIRECTIONS

YOUR FIRST ENCOUNTER WITH THE FRENCH LANGUAGE will probably occur when you need directions or instructions, so you may want to either write out the following dialogues for handy consultation or memorize a few key lines that will be useful for getting you out of the airport, into a taxi, or to your hotel, or for finding a toilet.

Excusez-moi. Où sont les toilettes, s'il vous plaît?
(Excuse-say **mwah.** Oo **sown** lay twa-**let,** see voo **play**?)
Excuse me. Where are the restrooms, please?

Excusez-moi. Où est-ce que je peux trouver un taxi, s'il vous plaît?
(Excuse-say **mwah.** Oo **eska** juh **puh** troo-**vay** uh **tax**-zi, see voo **play**?) **Excuse me. Where can I find a taxi, please?**

Excusez-moi. Où est-ce que je peux trouver le RER, s'il vous plaît?
(Excuse-say **mwah.** Oo **eska** juh **puh** troo-**vay** luh **air** euh air, see voo **play**?) **Excuse me. Where can I find the RER, please?**

Excusez-moi. Où est-ce que je peux trouver un guichet automatique, s'il vous plaît? (Excuse-say **mwah.** Oo **eska** juh **puh** troo-**vay** oon gee-**shay** auto-mat-**teek,** see voo **play**?) **Excuse me. Where can I find an ATM, please?**

TELEPHONES, E-MAIL, *and* POSTAL SERVICES

A PROMINENT WORD ON CALLING OR FAXING PARIS

DON'T YOU JUST HATE IT WHEN A GUIDEBOOK gives you a foreign phone number and you have to search all over the book for the country code! To avoid the delay and annoyance, note:

To make a call or send a fax to Paris from North America, dial 011 followed by 33 for France and 1 for Paris. Note that Paris-area numbers always begin with 01 and have ten digits. When dialing from outside of France you drop the 0. When dialing in France you keep the 0. So, to reach ☎ 01 48 59 66 68 from abroad, dial ☎ 011 33 1 48 59 66 68. The numbers for the rest of France begin with 02, 03, 04, and 05, and cellular phone numbers begin with 06. Toll-free numbers begin with 08 00. Be aware that any other 08 numbers will cost you anywhere from €0.02 to €1.20 a minute. Notice that the French recite phone numbers in twos. Example: 01 (*zero un*), 48 (*quarante huit*), 59 (*cinquante neuf*), 66 (*soixante six*), 68 (*soixante huit*), and that's how you should give phone numbers as well to avoid confusion.

CALLING HOME FROM YOUR HOTEL

YOU'D THINK THAT MAKING A SIMPLE PHONE CALL anywhere in the world today would be easy. But most visitors end up either fumbling for the right codes to reach their friendly stateside operator or settling for the hotel's internal direct-dialing service, resigning themselves to the fear that they're going to get royally fleeced. The instructions you get from your local carrier on using foreign telephones are usually spotty and often completely wrong.

The good news is that calling from Paris is not like it once was, and there are some real options to lighten both the emotional stress and the burden to your wallet.

First, you should know that the deregulation of the French state monopoly, France Telecom, opened up the market to every international concern as well as to the smaller and scrappy callback companies whose ubiquitous advertisements promise huge discounts when calling North America.

COME PREPARED

TO BE BEST PREPARED FOR A SHORT STAY, we strongly advise a small arsenal of communication tools: Bring your usual carrier's calling card with your code and your PIN or access number, a major credit card, and, if possible, a prepaid/prestocked calling card from your local carrier. You may pick up a handy France Telecom Ticket

Téléphone International upon arriving, which you can easily find at the airports, *tabacs* (tobacco shops), post offices, Métro stations, and newsstands (*kiosques*) marked "Télécarte en vente ici." The France Telecom Ticket Téléphone International comes with a code that you key in. There are two denominations: €7.50 and €15.

unofficial **TIP**
There are a lot of competitive telephone cards available, and they all work perfectly in any telephone booth in France.

In France, calls made via France Telecom on a private line are billed in minutes. A local call costs €0.78 for the connection, then €0.02 per minute in peak time (8 a.m. to 7 p.m.) and €0.01 in off-peak hours. The costs of calls from a phone booth will depend on which card you use. With a France Telecom Ticket Téléphone International, a call from Paris to North America costs €0.17 a minute at any time. From hotel rooms, the cost may be as much as two, three, or four times the base price, depending on the number of stars and the policy of the hotel. One Best Western hotel admitted to charging the equivalent of nearly €5 a minute! So beware.

To call from your room, your best bet is to call the operator of your home carrier. Access calls to your AT&T, MCI, or Sprint operators are free from hotel rooms. Most Paris hotels now offer direct-access dialing, so once you get an outside line, you can usually reach the operator of your home carrier. Otherwise, you have to ask the hotel front desk to get you an outside line.

unofficial **TIP**
It is generally advisable to avoid making collect calls from hotel rooms. Also, calling mobile and cell phones from hotel rooms may cost you more than dinner!

To reach your home carrier operator, call:

AT&T ☎ 08 00 99 00 11

MCI Worldwide Access ☎ 08 00 99 00 19

Sprint ☎ 08 00 99 00 87

Canada Direct ☎ 08 00 99 00 16 or 08 00 99 02 16

Note that calling the United States from Paris via your U.S. operator may not be your cheapest option.

USING PARISIAN TELEPHONES

THE COMMON FRENCH PUBLIC TELEPHONE BOOTH is called a *cabine téléphonique*. They are all over the place—street corners, Métro stations, train stations, and public places—and since they do not take coins, they are rarely broken. To use one you'll either need a France Telecom telephone card or the card of one of its many competitors. You may also access your home carrier and charge your call to your home account number or debit your prepaid card at these phones, without a telephone card.

Instructions in French telephone booths are also in English, but the writing is small and the steps are not perfectly clear. When using one of the many telephone cards, pick up the receiver, insert your card into the slot, wait for the dial tone, then dial. With the Ticket Téléphone International, dial 3089, tap in your code, and follow the voice instructions. To call the United States or Canada, dial 00 1, then the area code and number. To reach the United Kingdom, dial 00 44, then the city code and number.

Coins

The French used technology to combat vandalism and increase profit, replacing the coin-operated pay phone with the telephone-card pay phone. Coin-operated phones are only found in cafés and bars these days and are increasingly rare. You'll need coins (*pièces de monnaie*) to make a local call. Note that you can call internationally by simply dialing 00 and then the country code and number.

Prepaid Telephone Cards

All the major U.S. carriers issue prepaid telephone cards for domestic and international use. Make sure that the card you buy is coded for world service. You can order a prepaid telephone card from AT&T on their Web site (**consumer.att.com/prepaidcard**); however, the help desk refused to quote us their rates unless we purchased a card.

unofficial **TIP**
Though these prepaid cards sound like a pretty good deal, it is generally much easier and more economical to simply buy the France Telecom Ticket Téléphone International when you arrive.

ORDERING PREPAID PHONE CARDS

A NUMBER OF NEWLY CREATED INTERNATIONAL telephone companies have sprung up over the last several years, competing directly with both the local France Telecom and the leading American carriers by offering cut-rate access from France with the use of an access code. Otherwise, you can buy prepaid phone cards at newspaper stands, *tabacs,* Monoprix and other supermarkets, and in the numerous phone shops around the city. Even the French post office sells prepaid phone cards.

Other companies offering international access at competitive prices:

Alice Telecom ☎ 0 800 768 000   **Primus** ☎ 0 800 333 999

Budget Telecom ☎ 0 805 020 022

UNDERSTANDING THE BUSY SIGNAL

WHEN YOU DIAL A NUMBER in France and the line is busy, you will often get a recorded message in French stating in a pleasant feminine voice that the line is busy and asking you to stay on the line. This is the French equivalent of call waiting. Don't get confused and hang up.

USING CELL PHONES IN FRANCE

OTHER THAN SATELLITE-BASED PHONES, many American portable cellular phones will not work in France, so there's little point in bringing yours unless you have a GSM phone with tri-band capacity. If you do bring a GSM phone, be prepared: the roaming costs can be steep. Phones from the United Kingdom and the rest of Europe are capable of roaming France if you have a subscription that includes this feature. One solution is to rent a cell phone. Consider arranging this before you leave with the U.S.-based **Cellular Abroad** (☎ 800-287-5072; **cellularabroad.com**) or **Cellhire** (☎ 877-244-7242; **cellhire.com**). If you travel in Europe regularly, you may prefer to buy a cell phone in France and use a prestocked card with it. **Orange (France Telecom), SFR,** and **Bouygues** all provide these products.

INTERNET TELEPHONY

AS INTERNET TELEPHONY CATCHES ON and more and more users worldwide download the software, international travelers bringing laptops may opt to use Skype, I-Chat, and other free Internet telephone solutions as a means of calling home and staying in touch with family and office. We have had relative success with **Skype** (download free software at **skype.com**). This is worth exploring.

E-MAIL

IN TERMS OF THE NUMBER OF USERS, France, which had been behind the United States and other advanced countries using the Internet, has lessened the gap dramatically. Internet use continues to rise sharply in France, although public-school access is still lagging. If it's important for you to access your e-mail or get online in Paris, you can do so without too

unofficial **TIP**
Note that online traffic is particularly heavy in the late afternoons in Paris, and depending on your connection and modem, your experience may be painfully slow.

much difficulty. Most Paris hotels offer an Internet connection either in the public areas or in the guest rooms—some for free and others for a daily fee that is added to your bill, much like all hotels in the world today. The city also has many Internet cafés from where you can send and receive e-mail (see chart below). There are even Internet kiosks in more than 65 Métro and RER stations as well as in Monoprix supermarkets, but be prepared to queue. If you are traveling with a laptop, you'll be able to access any of the 400 free Paris Wi-Fi hotspots operated by the city authorities. These are located in public places such as libraries, museums, and parks. For other Wi-Fi locations, check out **free-hotspot.com**.

INTERNET ACCESS PROVIDERS Check with your Internet access provider before traveling about how to access your e-mail. If you're in an Internet café and you download your e-mail, you'll either want to save it to a disk or a USB drive or make sure you leave the mail on

unofficial **TIP**
France has recently emerged as the world leader in the number of online connections per inhabitant.

the host server. If all else fails, you can always have your modem make an international call to your access provider back home to access your mail, in which case you'll have to reset your access settings by adding 00 1 to the access number. Connecting from a hotel room is still tricky business in most establishments due to the access number you need to get an outside line. If you are traveling with your laptop and are staying in a four-star hotel, ask for a room with a Wi-Fi or direct modem connection.

Internet Cafés

Paris has its share of Internet cafés, which can be helpful for travelers wishing to send or download e-mail. Numerous hotels are now equipped for you to send and fetch your e-mail and use the Internet for a fee. See the chart below for your Internet café choices in Paris. For word processing on Macs or PCs, call ahead.

PARIS INTERNET CAFÉS			
NAME	ADDRESS	TELEPHONE NUMBER	MÉTRO
Baguenaude	30, rue Grande Truanderie	☎ 01 40 26 27 74	Les Halles
Côté Cyber Jardin	5, rue La Sourdière	☎ 01 42 60 79 04	Pyramides
Cyber Cube	5, rue Mignon	☎ 01 40 46 81 55	Odeon
Cyber Cube	9, rue d'Odessa	☎ 01 56 80 08 08	Montparnasse
Luxembourg Micro	81, boulevard Saint Michel	☎ 01 46 33 27 98 RER Luxembourg	
Milk	1, boulevard Sébastopol	☎ 08 20 00 10 00	Les Halles
Milk	20, rue du Faubourg Saint-Antoine	☎ 08 20 00 10 00	Bastille
Milk	53, rue de la Harpe	☎ 08 20 00 10 00	Saint Michel
Web 46	46, rue du roi de Sicile	☎ 01 40 27 02 89	Saint Paul

USING THE FRENCH POST OFFICE

POST OFFICES IN FRANCE ARE EASILY IDENTIFIABLE by their bright-yellow markings and the words "*La Poste*." Not unfriendly places, they'll nonetheless impress you with their agonizing slowness. Post offices also provide banking and financial services, and in fact, *La Poste* is now *La Banque Postale*. So although all you'll want to do is send a postcard, you'll find diverse services and a hefty line. The efficiency of the post office tends to vary from office to office, so if you find a good one, you're lucky. Some are organized like a bakery, where you need to take a number to be served; others have a single line feeding several counters. On the whole, try to avoid *La Poste* altogether by sending postcards and simple letters either from your hotel or by purchasing stamps at any tobacco shop (*tabac*) and posting them yourself. Postcards and letters under 20 grams (one or two sheets of paper) sent within France or the European Union require the same €0.56 stamp; it's €0.85 to the United States. For heavier letters, the rates jump to €1.70.

Mark your letters *prioritaire*, and don't forget to fill in the country. Be careful when writing numbers, since the French 1 and 7 differ from their Anglo-Saxon equivalents. Smart travelers buy the packs of prepostmarked envelopes, good for anywhere in the world. These cost €0.95 per standard envelope and €1.75 for larger envelopes with contents weighing up to 50 grams. Then, you just slip them into the *étranger* slot of any yellow mailbox, and off they go.

If you need to send packages, try to keep them under two kilos (4.4 pounds). Again, for small packages, your best bet is the prepostmarked (*poste export monde entier*) box, which for €19.50 (for up to two kilos) not only simplifies your life, but also gives your package first-class status. Count on priority-rate letters and packages to generally take a week to arrive at most major U.S. cities, although some letters make it in as little as five days or as much as two weeks.

You can also send faxes from post offices with their Postéclair service. The price is about €8 per page to the United States.

Similarly, mailboxes are bright yellow and are mounted on buildings and on posts outside of all Métro stations and tobacco shops (*tabacs*), where stamps—not just cigarettes—are sold.

Post offices also house public-telephone booths, copy machines, and often, ATMs. Most offer Internet access as well.

General operating hours are from 8 a.m. to 7 p.m., with the last mail going out for the day at around 6 p.m. Another good piece of info: The main Paris post office, Paris-Louvre, is open 24 hours a day. It is located at 52, rue du Louvre, 75001; Métro: Louvre.

La Poste also provides Chronopost service, part of the EMS express mail courier network. To North America, count on a minimum charge of €50. Otherwise, call Federal Express or DHL for hotel or home pickup. If you have a courier account already, your account will be charged back home at the American rates. If not, you'll need to pay in euros, in cash, at the time of pickup.

DHL Worldwide Express ☎ 08 20 20 25 25

FedEx Express ☎ 08 20 12 38 00   **UPS** ☎ 08 21 23 38 77

UNDERSTANDING EUROS

NOW THAT FRANCE AND 15 OF THE OTHER EUROPEAN UNION countries have opted for a single currency, the euro, the monetary scene has changed. Although the euro became the official currency of France on January 1, 1999, until 2002 the French franc continued to be widely used in everyday commerce. Today, you will see goods and services quoted in the euro.

The euro coins come in eight sizes and values: 1 euro cent, 2 euro cents, 5 euro cents, 10 euro cents, 20 euro cents, and 50 euro cents, and 1- and 2-euro coins. There are also new 5-, 10-, and 15-euro coins, but these are rarer. The paper bills include seven notes in denominations of 5, 10, 20, 50, 100, 200, and 500 euros. Avoid using bills over 50 euros when making small purchases.

CHANGING MONEY

IT NEVER FAILS. As unromantic as it seems, historically the exchange rate between the dollar and the local currency has always had a direct impact on the kind of experience visitors have in Paris. Obviously, the more euros you get for your dollar, the more mileage you get out of your budget. Although no tourist has ever been able to single-handedly regulate the strength of the dollar, there are tips for ensuring that you spend as little time as possible—and nab as many euros as you can— when converting your greenbacks into the coin of the realm.

It is essential that you ask for the rate and commission fees before you agree to exchange currency. Sometimes a heavy commission is camouflaged by an advantageous rate. Go slowly, and use your calculator. Remember that the more you exchange, the better the rate. But again, don't change too much too soon. And unless you have a particular objection, you should try to pay for your larger expenses (hotel, restaurants, gifts, and so on) with a major credit card. The exchange rates are better, you limit your risk of carrying cash, you benefit from built-in insurance, and in many cases you even earn frequent-flyer miles per dollar spent. In France, you'll even be able to pay for your entrance to the Louvre and your subway pass with your credit card.

Thinking in Euros

It's hard to "feel" the value of a currency you don't think in, and it's normal that you'll want to translate every price into the currency you best understand. But when you think in dollars, everything will seem much more expensive than it would be "back home." As a result you'll tend to spend less and do fewer things, and it will generally put a damper on your level of enjoyment. So "think euros" when determining value. Soon you'll be able to determine value by comparing euro prices at one place to euro prices at other place. Similarly, when it comes to changing money, compare your alternatives in euros.

ATMs

As for changing money, by far the easiest and most economical means is to use your Visa or MasterCard to pull cash out of the ubiquitous ATMs (*guichets automatiques*) found on nearly every corner. Most are connected to the Cirrus or PLUS networks, offer instructions in English, and are clearly marked. You'll need to bring along your PIN, of course. The great advantage is that money is available when you need it, the exchange rate is based on the bank-to-bank rate, and the transaction fee is usually a set $2 to $5 (ask your bank before leaving), which appears on your monthly statement, and is lower than what local banks often charge in commissions. To be safe, ask your bank for a duplicate card before leaving, so if your card gets gobbled by a French machine when the bank is closed, your trip won't be in jeopardy.

Hotels

The worst place to exchange money is at your hotel, where the rates are not competitive and service charges are often tacked on. Hotels are not banks and change money as an extra service. Avoid them when possible.

Local Banks

The second worst place to change money is a local bank. First, many branches do not have an exchange window and often hang up confusing signs on their doors stating "No exchange" or "No change." When they do offer foreign-currency exchange, you'll most often get killed by both the rate and the commission, which is always a percentage above a fixed minimum.

unofficial **TIP**
The HSBC bank (which has swallowed up scores of French banks seemingly overnight) has a huge branch on the Champs-Élysées and is the exception—the rates are advantageous. To figure this out, bring your calculator.

Change Bureaus

Better than banks are the numerous "change" bureaus that populate the touristy areas of town, such as Saint-Germain-des-Prés, the Champs-Élysées, Châtelet–Les Halles, and Montparnasse. They are often grouped, thus you can compare. Be careful not to get confused between the attractive "selling" rate and the less attractive "buying" rate. Remember, you're buying euros, and they're buying dollars; you are selling dollars, and they are selling euros. Most travelers never realize that the published rate hung up on the board outside is almost always negotiable, especially when you're changing larger sums, a few hundred dollars at least. Don't be afraid to ask for a better rate. Usually, by simply asking you'll obtain a few cents more per dollar, which can quickly add up to enough for another meal or a small gift.

The Best Street in Paris for Changing Money

Little known to visitors, there is one street near *la bourse* (stock exchange) where the professional money changers, gold merchants, and coin dealers have set up shop. For small amounts of cash it might not be worth going out of your way, but for larger sums the savings will be considerable. You may save up to 10 percent per dollar and not pay a commission. The published rates are better than you'll find in the banks and change bureaus, and on larger sums you can do better still. Get off the Métro at Grands Boulevards or Bourse and check out the change shops on rue de Vivienne.

unofficial **TIP**
Depending on the amount you are exchanging, the commission percentage is negotiable.

Cash for Cash

Another way to change money in Paris is by inserting your $20, $50, or $100 bills into special ATMs that convert foreign cash automatically. The exchange rates are clearly posted, so there are no surprises. These machines are found at 66, avenue des Champs-Élysées (Métro: George V); on the boulevard Saint-Michel at the corner of rue des Écoles near the Sorbonne (Métro: Cluny–La Sorbonne); and at other select locations.

La Poste

We often send friends to check the exchange rate in the "main" post offices of the arrondissement in which they are staying.

American Express

An old-time fixture in Paris, the American Express office has been a meeting point and landmark since the war. Today, it plays a less important role. For American Express card holders, it still serves as a point for getting cash advances, cashing checks, buying traveler's checks, and having lost or stolen cards and traveler's checks replaced. It even has a cash dispenser for card holders. 11, rue Scribe, 75009; ☎ 01 47 77 77 00; Métro: Opéra or RER Auber. But the exchange rate is not as advantageous as those on rue de Vivienne; plus, you'll have the commission to pay.

BANKING IN PARIS

AS A VISITOR, TRY TO SPEND LITTLE TIME or no time at all in a Paris bank. If you have a Citibank card, you can withdraw cash at any ATM connected to the Cirrus network. The fee depends on the amount you withdraw. No one at Citibank will be able to tell you how much that is, but we've been promised that the ATM will flash on the screen how much you'll be debited for the operation and will ask you if you authorize this. If you lose an American-issued Citibank card in France, call the United States toll-free at ☎ 800-950-5114.

Getting in the Bank Door

Don't get spooked by the strange doors of all banks in France. For security purposes, banks have opted for a system whereby you must push a green button to be let in. The outer door unlocks when the green button lights up "POUSSER," meaning push. You enter into a middle chamber between two doors. The door behind you must lock before the door in front of you can open. You push a second green button that unlocks when a bank employee buzzes you in. Don't panic if you find yourself in this no-man's-land for half a minute waiting to be buzzed in. The same process occurs when you try to leave. Annoying, but bank robberies are down in France since its implementation.

For your information, the largest commercial banks with the most branches include:

BNP-Paribas (Banque Nationale de Paris–Paribas)

CA (Crédit Agricole)

CL (Crédit Lyonnais)

HSBC (Hongkong and Shanghai Banking Corporation)

SG (Société Générale)

Getting Money Wired

If you need to have money sent to you or you need to send money to someone else, the French post office acts as an agent for Western Union Money Transfers. The system is simple. Someone contacts Western Union in the United States and wires an amount of dollars to you. They give you the transaction code by phone. You go into any French post office, say you want to pick up a Western Union Money Transfer, and give them the transfer code, and they give you the equivalent amount in euros. The sender pays for the service. Western Union has numerous storefront money shops all over the city.

USING CREDIT CARDS

MASTERCARD AND VISA ARE WIDELY ACCEPTED in restaurants, shops, hotels, Métro ticket offices, cinemas, and even the Louvre. In France, you'll see these logos, plus CB for Carte Bleue, which administers Visa and MasterCard transactions. American Express is accepted less and less, and it is not advised to travel only with an American Express card. Diners Club is accepted in many establishments. In France, credit cards have embedded chips built in and are used with a PIN code, meaning that users don't need to sign the purchase voucher. Your cards—with the magnetic strip on the back—require a swipe in the machine. French merchants don't always know how to do this. You may have to show them. Occasionally, your card will not seem to work in their machines. Keep trying. Just like anywhere else, how fast or slow you swipe your card may determine its effectiveness. Some French merchants unaccustomed to the magnetic strip–style cards may tell you that they don't accept such cards. Gently insist. The cards almost always work.

TRAVELER'S CHECKS

HOTELS AND LARGE RESTAURANTS USUALLY ACCEPT traveler's checks. If you pay a hotel bill with traveler's checks in U.S. dollars, the funds will be converted to euros first. It's better to pay directly in euros or euro traveler's checks. And a note on personal checks: If you do not have a euro account in a French bank, do not accept a personal check from someone else. You will not be able to cash it. In fact, you can never cash a check in France; you can only deposit it to the account of the person the check is payable to. And checks cannot be endorsed and countersigned, either.

TIPPING

TIPPING IN FRENCH IS *pourboire* (poor-**bwar**), literally "for a drink." Parisians in general are not highly service-oriented, and it has not been drummed repeatedly into the heads of employees and clerks in this city that the customer is always king. Thus, the relationship between services rendered and tips given is not omnipresent, as it is in the United States.

In fact, tipping habits in Paris are simple to understand. There are, however, a few nuances involved. For a detailed discussion on tipping in restaurants see Part Seven, Dining and Restaurants. There are a few points that must be understood from the start. France is not a tipping society in the way that you may be accustomed to back home. A few modest but correct tips placed at the right time will be appreciated and will enhance the service you're getting and will continue to get.

Here are a few guidelines:

- The gesture of tipping in Paris should be characterized by a naturalness and the elegance of the act. If a 10 percent tip on a taxi ride brings the total fare to €5.50, you'd obviously give €6. This can work in your favor as well. Try in all cases to maintain a fluidity and elegance without either overpaying or underpaying too much.

- **Waiters and Waitresses** A service charge of between 15 percent and 20 percent is included in almost all eating establishments. This means that the price of the service has been figured into the menu prices. It should not appear as an extra on your bill. The tip is only a small, ritual gesture of your pleasure with the person serving you. Parisians were accustomed to leaving a five- or ten-franc coin and maybe the small copper coins in the dish in which the bill is presented. Most Parisians now leave a euro coin or two on the plate. Do not leave 15 percent or 20 percent of the bill, ever. You'll only prove how easy it is to take advantage of ignorant tourists.

- **Taxi Rides** Give 10 percent or round out the sum on the meter when your driver has been efficient and you're satisfied. There is an automatic supplement for train station pickups, for luggage in the trunk, and so on. Don't calculate the tip on this. Calculate the tip only on what's on the meter.
- **Hotel Porters** A euro or two for each full-sized suitcase is standard.
- **Concierges** Nothing, unless they have rendered a particular service for you.
- **Hairdressers** One or two euros is fine, more if the place is chic.
- **Tour Guides** Play it by ear.
- **Ushers** Traditionally, ushers in concert halls and small, independent cinemas are tipped €0.30 or so per person for showing you to your seat. This very Parisian habit is disappearing.

THINGS *the* LOCALS ALREADY KNOW

GETTING AN ENGLISH-LANGUAGE NEWSPAPER

MANY PARIS HOTELS OF THREE STARS or more receive at least a few copies of the *International Herald-Tribune,* the *Financial Times,* or the European edition of the *Wall Street Journal.* You can find *USA Today* as well, but frankly, you're in Paris and you probably don't really need to know what's going on in Illinois. Smaller hotels may not offer newspapers at all. For general news, international and American news, and sports, you can find the Paris-based *IHT* at most newsstands (*kiosques*) in the city for €2.50. The Sunday *New York Times* can be found at the bookstores **W. H. Smith** (248, rue de Rivoli, 75001; Métro: Concorde) and **Brentano's** (37, avenue de l'Opéra, 75002; Métro: Opera).

For other English info, visit **parisinfo.com,** the Paris Tourist Office's Web site, or call them at ☎ 08 92 68 30 00.

OTHER PARIS PUBLICATIONS

PARIS VOICE **parisvoice.com.** Once the leading expat newspaper, this English-language community Web site covers topics of interest to the English-language residents of Paris, but the listings of cultural events and entertainment choices in English will certainly give visitors a great idea of how to spend their leisure time.

PARISCOPE For €0.40 you can pick up at any *kiosque* a thick weekly calendar of cinema, theater, exhibition, club, show, and concert listings in Paris. It's in French and comes out on Wednesdays.

L'OFFICIEL DES SPECTACLES Same idea as *Pariscope* but cheaper; also comes out on Wednesdays.

FUSAC Bimonthly free advertising supplement catering to the English-language community. Stuffed with classified ads, apartment offerings, employment, and so on. Check its Web site at **fusac.fr.**

IRISH EYES Monthly free community magazine focused on the Irish community in Paris; **irisheyes.fr.**

FREE DAILY NEWSSHEETS IN FRENCH *Le Métro, 20 Minutes, Direct Matin,* and *Direct Soir* are distributed at Métro exits. The free weekly *A Nous* magazine is available on racks inside the Métro. General news roundup and what's on in Paris.

OTHER FREE STUFF The Galeries Lafayette supply free city and Métro maps in their stores and in many Métro stations and tourist offices.

PUBLIC TOILETS

UNDERSTANDING WHERE TO FIND and how to use public toilets removes not only pressure from your bladder but also a burden from your mind. Thinking about this when you need a toilet is too late. Fortunately, Paris, the birthplace of the public *pissoir* (pees-**wahr**), offers easy, sanitary, and well-located solutions.

French law states that you have the right to enter any café and use the toilet without consuming anything. (*Note:* Don't use the word *pissoir.*) We suggest that you ask first: "*Est-ce que je peux utiliser les toilettes, s'il vous plaît?*" You might feel more comfortable stopping into a café, standing at the counter, ordering a coffee (the cheapest thing on the menu), and then before it even arrives following the sign to *les toilettes* or asking, "*Où sont les toilettes, s'il vous plaît?*"

Caution: Some Parisian cafés still have the old-style Turkish toilets. These porcelain throwbacks consist of merely a hole in the floor with two spots for your feet. For gentlemen executing Number One, there is no problem. For the uninitiated and all other scenarios, this is a bit crude and tricky in that you need to keep your coat, jacket, handbag, backpack, trouser bottoms, and so on clear of danger. Before you pull the chain, sending a torrent of water down to rinse the environs, make sure you get your feet out of the way. A truly Parisian experience, and character-building to boot. You'll thoroughly enjoy your awaiting coffee when you reemerge into the day in progress.

unofficial **TIP**
Toilet paper, although often rough, is usually available, but experienced travelers carry paper on them as standard procedure.

The Public-Toilet Compartments

In the late 1980s the city erected hundreds of rather futuristic free public toilets on the streets of Paris. A press of a button opens a sliding door. You enter. The door shuts and locks. The cabin, which resembles a large airplane toilet, is well lit and heated. The rest is self-explanatory; after each use, the cabin is automatically washed, disinfected, and dried before it can be used again. There is no time limit for each visit, but if you linger too long, you will likely arouse suspicions. In 2009 the city began replacing the older model with a new generation of cabin by designer Patrick Jouin. Check out his upbeat Web site at **patrickjouin.com** for an idea of how the French apply chic to even their toilets!

UNCURBED DOGS

PARIS'S REPUTATION FOR DOG EXCREMENT has outstripped contemporary reality, but the problem continues nonetheless. So look down. Dog owners are getting a bit better, but no steep fines or sense of civic duty keep the owners of Rex (the most common dog name in France) in line. Stiffer laws were introduced by the City of Paris in 2002, obliging dog walkers to clean up after their pet in any public area. There is now a minimum fine of €183 for people who do not curb their dogs, and undercover inspection teams target problems areas to enforce this. The once-tolerated practice of encouraging your dog to use the *caniveau* (gutter) is now forbidden.

DOING LAUNDRY

A QUICK SCENARIO: You're perched in your favorite Hugo Boss blazer, feeling as cool as spring on the Seine; you're in Paris, of course, and you're sitting *tête-à-tête* with your favorite person on earth, snuggled at your favorite table in your favorite bistro, devouring your favorite meringue desert, an *île flottante*. Then catastrophe hits: an unctuous glob of rich and unforgiving *crème anglaise* slips from your dessert spoon and free-falls down your jacket, landing everywhere in your lap. You try white wine, then salt. Nothing works; you need help. "And I was counting on wearing the same ensemble to the opera tomorrow night," you cry out. Help is not on its way.

unofficial **TIP**
French washing machines take more time than their American counterparts, as do the dryers.

Going to the cleaners in Paris sometimes feels more like being taken to the cleaners, and dry cleaning is still somewhat of a luxury in France. Be prepared to spend around €8 to have a single shirt, pair of pants, or pullover laundered and ironed (the verb "to iron" is *repasser*). T-shirts will cost you around €4.50, socks and underwear about €2.60. A suit or overcoat will cost between €15 and €30—everything depends on the neighborhood. If you expect one-hour service or to get your clothes back on wire hangers or with cardboard in your shirts, you may be disappointed. Often, fresh laundry is only wrapped neatly in thin paper. This is more a question of aesthetics and practicality than anything else. Timing is often a problem with neighborhood cleaners, since many do not have "on location" cleaning and need three days to get your clothes back to you. And, of course, plenty of cleaners are shut on Mondays and are closed between noon and 2 p.m. for lunch. Ask in advance, and *do not lose your ticket.*

More and more laundromats have cropped up around the city, and this may be your best or only option. Plan on bringing a pocketful of coins. You may want to pick up your own soap. In general, Parisians wash their clothes slowly and thoroughly but at lower temperatures. They do not overdry their clothes, since "cooking" your clothes too long weakens the fibers. They are more conscious of fabric fragility and expect garments to last longer. If you're used to a 25-minute wash cycle, count on twice that in Paris. Many laundromats include self-serve dry-cleaning machines, which are advantageous, especially for bulky coats and the like, but the results don't always cut the *moutarde* (mustard).

Your first stop for laundry will most likely be your hotel. Most of the larger and upscale hotels have their own in-house laundry services. The housekeeper is called the *gouvernante.* The Hôtel Meurice, for example, will press your suit in 30 minutes for about €27 or have it dry-cleaned for less than €43. If you're in a hurry, expect them to add a 30 percent charge for a three-hour service. The smaller hotels almost always farm out your soiled and wrinkled garments to a nearby "pressing." Usually, clothes sent out by 9 or 10 a.m. will be back in your room by the next afternoon. If this is not fast enough, ask for the local equivalent of rush, *service express* (sair-**vees** ex-**press**), which in most cases means "same-day service," again for a supplement of 30 percent. Really small hotels have no laundry services but will on occasion lend you an iron. Otherwise, it's either self-service in the sink or finding your own "pressing" or laundromat. Bring your own detergent.

UPDATE ON FRENCH SMOKING

ALTHOUGH THE SMOKING SITUATION in France has changed swiftly, if you're a smoker, there's no problem—there are lots of smokers on the sidewalks and no one will judge you. The truth about smoking in France is that more than 20 percent of the adult population has yet to kick the habit. However, a massive hike in taxes on tobacco and radical new legislation have been partially responsible for a marked decrease in tobacco sales and, with it, the number of smokers, who now number 13.5 million—down from 20 million only a few years ago. From January 2008 it became wholly illegal to smoke in any enclosed public place in France. Although there was initially some resistance, more and more individuals and establishments in France understand that fighting for smokers' rights is a lost cause. The French have traditionally loved their nicotine (named after the Frenchman who imported tobacco into France, Jean Nicot) and have preferred to view the act of smoking more as a source of pleasure and social accoutrement than as an addiction.

If you do smoke and are looking for a pack, you'll be obliged to duck into a neighborhood tobacco shop (*tabac*) for your cigarettes, cigars, or pipe tobacco. In France, sale of tobacco is a state monopoly licensed exclusively to these authorized cafés. The usual price is at least €6 per pack, and it's on the rise. You'll see the red leaf-shaped sign hanging above the sidewalk *tabac* sign. Also note that *tabacs* are official points of sale for postage stamps and other fiscal stamps. You'll always find a French mailbox (yellow and square and usually fixed to a wall) outside a *tabac*. As a service to customers, most restaurants and bars will have selected brands of cigarettes discreetly available at a marked-up price. Cigarette packs are now plastered with very ominous black-and-white warnings declaring that "Smoking Kills." This doesn't seem to dissuade the addicted, but it does indicate that there is a mounting political will to reduce the cost of tobacco-related illnesses. The real problem is that the state monopoly of tobacco generates (in the short term) massive amounts of revenue used to fund public spending. You see the problem.

In France there are two types of tobacco available, blonde and *brune*. The blonde, or refined, tobacco corresponds to the cigarettes North Americans usually smoke. The *brune* is darker and harsher, the "filterless" kind that beret-wearing Frenchmen in black-and-white films smoke. France's best-known brands are Gauloises and Gitanes. You'll also find all the major international brands of cigarettes, although some smokers contend that the Marlboro they buy in Europe does not taste like the same brand back home. When you consider that the state collects about 75 percent of the cover price in taxes, you'll begin to understand why the government's efforts to reduce smoking in France lack real teeth.

HEALTH

INTERNATIONAL TRAVELERS ARE ALWAYS NERVOUS about getting sick while they're away. You should put these fears aside concerning your Paris trip. French doctors and hospitals are excellent, and the public-health system, which is known as Securité Sociale, is one of the best in the world. A 24-hour emergency service (SAMU) is readily available. There are two major hospitals in which English is the mother tongue, several English pharmacies, and plenty of English-speaking and some U.S.-trained doctors and dentists in Paris. Having said that, be prepared for a different and somewhat less comforting aesthetic in doctors' offices or hospital waiting rooms, which are far less antiseptic-looking than their American equivalents. The public relations, marketing, and communications side of health care in France also tends to be less evolved, for mostly economic reasons. Public funding focuses on the health side of health care. So be careful not to judge the system by cosmetic indicators.

Tap Water

If you're hesitant about drinking the tap water (*eau du robinet*), eliminate that thought from your mind this instant. Although Parisians drink bottled mineral water incessantly, the tap water is 100 percent safe.

Doctors

If you need a doctor, ask the concierge at your hotel, and he'll either inform you where the closest doctor's office is located or call the *médecin de garde* (the neighborhood doctor on call) who'll make a house call to your hotel room. You'll quickly notice a difference in style and aesthetics, as French doctors come across as more professorial than clinical. Doctors do not dispense much medicine themselves. Nor do they administer tests or do any lab work. They'll give you a prescription (*ordonnance* [ordun-**nunce**]) for medication or lab tests, which you'll need to take to a local pharmacy or laboratory. A visit to the doctor's office (GP) will cost you €22—the government-regulated fee for a consultation—and a house or hotel-room call will cost from €40 to €60. Specialists may cost twice as much. Note, too, that many doctors divide their office hours between appointments and open hours, where you can simply walk in and wait your turn in the waiting room (*salle d'attente*).

unofficial **TIP**
Some hospitals accept credit cards, and the American Hospital can process some American insurance bills directly.

Health Insurance

It's a good idea to ask your health-insurance provider what the extent of your coverage is while you're traveling abroad and what procedures to follow in the case of illness or accident while you're in France. Bring a copy of your health-coverage card with you, and the phone and fax numbers of your health-insurance provider in case you have a problem. You will have to pay your French doctor's bill in cash. You'll get a standardized form called a *feuille de soins*, which you may be able to use for a reimbursement from your health-insurance provider when you get home.

By the way, the French wonder why there is so much resistance to health care reform in the U.S. and may ask you to comment on this. In France, universal health coverage is not seen as a sign of socialism or state control of your freedom of choice, but rather as a normal service in a civilized nation and a logical benefit use of your taxes.

Hospitals

In case of emergency or a late-night illness or accident, consult with your hotel concierge first. He'll either call a doctor (SOS Médecins for 24-hour house calls) or, in extreme cases, the SAMU or *pompiers* (pohm-**pyay** [fire department]), who'll rush you to the closest hospital.

SAMU 15	**Police** 17
Pompiers 18	**Emergency (Europe-wide)** 112

The **American Hospital of Paris** (Hôpital Américain de Paris; 63, boulevard Victor Hugo, 92200 Neuilly sur Seine; ☎ 01 46 41 25 25; fax 01 46 24 49 38; **american-hospital.org;** Métro: Pont de Levallois) is a famous private hospital that employs British, American, and French doctors. F. Scott Fitzgerald, among others, spent time here in the pre-renovation days drying out "on the wagon."

It is much more expensive than French hospitals, but it offers excellent health care with a style that you may recognize and appreciate. You can pay with dollars and major credit cards. Those insured by Blue Cross–Blue Shield have their hospitalization covered at the American Hospital, provided they fill out the appropriate paperwork first. Another hospital that employs English-speaking doctors and is noted for serving the Anglophone community is **Hertford British Hospital** (3, rue Barbès, 92300 Levallois Perret; ☎ 01 46 39 22 22 (24 hours); fax 01 46 39 22 26; **british-hospital.org;** Métro: Anatole-France).

You can find a full listing of doctors at **paris-anglo.com,** and in the Paris-Anglophone directory, found in most bookstores. The two hospitals listed above can also provide names of doctors and specialists.

If Your Children Become Ill

Either get the hotel to call for a doctor (Urgence Pédiatrique SOS ☎ 01 47 27 47 47) or, in the case of serious illness or accident, call the SAMU or *pompiers*. In the case of an emergency, go directly to the closest of the following hospitals. These are Paris's best pediatric centers.

- **Hôpital Armand Trousseau**
  26, avenue Dr. Arnold Netter, 75012
  ☎ 01 44 73 74 75

- **Hôpital Saint-Vincent-de-Paul**
  82, avenue Denfert-Rochereau, 75014
  ☎ 01 40 48 81 11

- **Hôpital Necker**
  149, rue de Sèvres, 75015
  ☎ 01 44 49 40 00

Dentists

If you need a dentist, ask at your hotel. Otherwise, call SOS Dentaire at ☎ 01 43 37 51 00. If you prefer an English-speaking dentist, you can request one.

Pharmacies

The pharmacist in Paris plays a more active role in curing his or her customers than do pharmacists back home. When in doubt, ask a local pharmacist. They are even trained to identify poisonous mushrooms! Every pharmacy has a sign on its window indicating the *pharmacie de garde*, the closest pharmacy open during nonbusiness hours. There is always one pharmacy in every area open at all times, and there are also three 24-hour pharmacies in Paris.

- **Grande Pharmacie Daumesnil**
  6, place Félix-Éboué, 75012
  ☎ 01 43 43 19 03
  Métro: Daumesnil

- **Pharmacie Européenne de la Place Clichy**
  6, place de Clichy, 75009
  ☎ 01 48 74 65 18
  Métro: Place Clichy

- **Pharmacie Les Champs**
  84, avenue des Champs-Élysées (passage des Champs), 75008
  ☎ 01 45 62 02 41
  Métro: George-V

PRESCRIPTIONS It's best you bring enough prescribed medication with you to last for the duration of your trip. In case you need more medication (or you lose your pills), it's a smart idea to bring copies of your prescriptions with you when you travel. We tell people who are very uptight about being ill away from home to have their local pharmacist write out the generic names of their medications, since the same drugs in Europe may be available under a different trade name. Take the phone and fax number of your doctor and pharmacist with you, too, in case you need a new prescription faxed to Paris. You may even want to leave copies of your prescriptions with your local pharmacist and inform him or her of your travel dates to Paris. In most cases, pharmacies in Paris will help you out even without a prescription (*ordonnance*).

unofficial **TIP**
French pharmacies are not to be confused with U.S.-style drugstores. They are purely medical, and the personnel are highly trained and knowledgeable about illness and treatments.

To know precisely what to ask for in a French pharmacy, we suggest you ask your hotel concierge. *Note:* Condoms are available in all pharmacies, in dispensers in Métro stations, outside pharmacies, and at the Monoprix. The French word for condom is *préservatif* (preh-zair-va-**teef**), and sanitary napkins and tampons are called *serviettes hygiéniques* (sir-vi-**yet** ee-jee-yen-**neek**) and *tampons*, respectively; both are available in department stores and pharmacies.

Glasses and Contact Lenses

It's always smart to travel with a backup pair of glasses or lenses. Also bring your prescription in case you have to have new glasses made. There are optometrists and eyeglass stores in every neighborhood.

AIDS

The French organization **SIDA Info Service** (☎ 08 00 84 08 00; **sida-info-service.org**) offers a free and anonymous help line for people who have questions or problems related to AIDS. Although there is no dedicated English help line, there will always been an English speaker on duty.

RELIGION AND HOUSES OF WORSHIP

PARIS HAS ITS SHARE OF CHURCHES and other houses of worship; to find services and mass in English by contacting the following:

EMMANUEL INTERNATIONAL CHURCH 56, rue des Bons Raisins, 92500 Rueil-Malmaison; ☎ 01 47 51 29 63; **eicparis.org.** Interdenominational Evangelical Fellowship; English services at 10 and 11:30 a.m., French service at 6 p.m.

ST. MICHAEL'S CHURCH 5, rue d'Aguesseau, 75008; ☎ 01 47 42 70 88; **saintmichaelsparis.org; Métro:** Concorde. Anglican services at 9:30 and 11:15 a.m. and 7 p.m. French service at 5 p.m.

TRINITY INTERNATIONAL CHURCH Église Réformée de Pentemont-Luxembourg, 58, rue Madame, 75006; ☎ 01 45 08 16 63; **trinity-paris.org; Métro:** Rennes. English service at 3:30 p.m.

THE AMERICAN CHURCH IN PARIS 65, quai d'Orsay, 75007; ☎ 01 40 62 05 00; **acparis.org; Métro:** Invalides. Protestant, interdenominational services, 9 and 11 a.m.

THE AMERICAN CATHEDRAL IN PARIS 23, avenue George-V, 75008; ☎ 01 53 23 84 00; **americancathedral.org; Métro:** George V–Alma-Marceau. Episcopalian and Anglican services, 9 and 11 a.m.

LA GRANDE MOSQUÉE 2, bis Place du Puits de l'Ermite, 75005; ☎ 01 45 35 97 33; **mosquee-de-paris.org; Métro:** Monge.

CHRISTIAN SCIENCE CHURCH 36, boulevard Saint-Jacques, 75014; ☎ 01 47 07 26 60; **Métro:** Denfert-Rochereau. English service at 11:20 a.m.

ST. JOSEPH'S ROMAN CATHOLIC CHURCH 50, avenue Hoche, 75008; ☎ 01 42 27 28 56; **stjoeparis.org; Métro:** Charles-de-Gaulle–Étoile. English mass at 9:30 and 11 a.m. and 12:30 and 6:30 p.m. (July and August: 10 a.m., noon, and 6.30 p.m.)

KEHILAT GESHER 10, rue de Pologne, 78100 Saint-Germain-en-Laye; **Métro:** RER Saint-Germain-en-Laye. 7, rue Léon Cogniet 75017; **Métro:** Courcelles; ☎ 01 39 21 97 19; **kehilatgesher.org.** French-Anglophone-Jewish congregation (Reform/Conservative). Friday service at 7 p.m. and Saturday at 10.30 a.m., alternating between Saint-Germain-en-Laye and Paris's 17th arrondissement. Phone for details or e-mail contact@kehilatgesher.org.

■ TRAVELERS *with* DISABILITIES

TRAVELERS WITH PHYSICAL DISABILITIES should not be discouraged from traveling to Paris, but they should be forewarned: France

HOTELS EQUIPPED FOR TRAVELERS WITH DISABILITIES

1ST ARRONDISSEMENT

Best Western Paris Louvre Opera ★★★ 1 disabled-adapted room
4, rue des Moulins; ☎ 01 40 20 01 10; FAX: 01 40 20 01 22
bestwestern-paris-louvreopera.com MÉTRO: Palais Royal

Novotel Paris Les Halles ★★★ 7 disabled-adapted rooms
8, place Marguerite de Navarre; ☎ 01 42 21 21 10; FAX: 01 42 21 92 92
novotelparisleshalles.com MÉTRO: Châtelet

3RD ARRONDISSEMENT

Tulip Inn Little Palace ★★★ 1 disabled-adapted room
4, rue Salomon de Caus; ☎ 01 42 72 08 15; FAX: 01 42 72 45 81
littlepalacehotel.com MÉTRO: Réaumur-Sébastopol

5TH ARRONDISSEMENT

Hôtel des Carmes ★★ 1 disabled-adapted room
5, rue des Carmes; ☎ 01 43 29 78 40; FAX: 01 43 29 57 17
hoteldescarmesparis.com MÉTRO: Maubert-Mutualité

6TH ARRONDISSEMENT

Holiday Inn Paris Saint-Germain-des-Prés ★★★
   2 disabled-adapted rooms
92, rue de Vaugirard; ☎ 01 49 54 87 00; FAX: 01 49 54 87 01
holiday-inn.com MÉTRO: St-Placide

Hôtel de Nantes ★★ 1 disabled-adapted room
33, boulevard du Montparnasse; ☎ 01 45 48 75 64; FAX: 01 42 84 00 57
MÉTRO: Duroc

8TH ARRONDISSEMENT

Arc Élysées ★★★ 2 disabled-adapted rooms
45, rue de Washington; ☎ 01 45 63 69 33; FAX: 01 45 63 76 25
MÉTRO: George-V

is still behind the United States in terms of both legislation and public awareness concerning the needs and rights of disabled persons, although progress has been made. Traveling to and from Paris in a wheelchair or on crutches may pose some serious obstacles that are surmountable only when you're well informed and adequately prepared. However, in recent years the regional authorities have been addressing the issue, and facilities for disabled persons are gradually improving.

One disabled Floridian who visited Paris with his wife during the summer found that even in the big hotel chains in Paris he couldn't confirm a room with an easy-access shower. Often the smaller hotels do not have elevators large enough to accommodate wheelchairs. Public buildings do not all have ramps, and some that

8TH ARRONDISSEMENT (*continued*)
Marriott International ★★★★ **3 disabled-adapted rooms**
70, avenue des Champs-Élysées; ☎ 01 53 93 55 00; FAX: 01 53 93 55 01
MÉTRO: George-V

10TH ARRONDISSEMENT
Ibis Gare du Nord Lafayette ★★ **3 disabled-adapted rooms**
122, rue de la Fayette; ☎ 01 45 23 27 27; FAX: 01 42 46 73 79
Ibishotels.com MÉTRO: Poissonnière

12TH ARRONDISSEMENT
Novotel Gare de Lyon ★★★ **6 disabled-adapted rooms**
2, rue Hector Malot; ☎ 01 44 67 60 00; FAX: 01 44 67 60 60
novotel.com MÉTRO: Gare de Lyon

Relais Mercure Paris Bercy ★★★ **7 disabled-adapted rooms**
77, rue de Bercy; ☎ 01 53 46 50 50; FAX: 01 53 46 50 99
mercure.com MÉTRO: Bercy

15TH ARRONDISSEMENT
Novotel Paris Tour Eiffel ★★★★ **17 disabled-adapted rooms**
61, quai de Grenelle; ☎ 01 40 58 20 00; FAX: 01 40 58 24 44
novotel.com MÉTRO: Charles Michel

20TH ARRONDISSEMENT
Suitehotel Paris Porte De Montreuil ★★★ **5 disabled-adapted rooms**
22, avenue du Professeur André Lemierre;
☎ 01 49 93 88 88; FAX: 01 49 93 88 99
suite-hotel.com MÉTRO: Porte de Montreuil

do still have a step or two at the top or bottom, making the access
hazardous. We've asked a young French woman, Frédérique Suchet,
who has been confined to a wheelchair since the summer of 1998, to
point out some of the obstacles that disabled tourists should expect
to encounter.

Despite the city's pride in restoring and maintaining its sites and
monuments, Paris today remains only moderately accessible and
friendly to wheelchair users. Your first worry
will be how to get around in a city that is so
vast, lively, and old. Your best bet is to have
a car at your disposal (preferably a taxi) and
be accompanied. The taxi firm **G7 Horizon**

unofficial **TIP**
We strongly recommend
taking a taxi (see left) to
your hotel.

(**taxisg7.fr**) runs a fleet of 40 specially equipped taxis that can be booked at no extra charge by calling their dedicated number ☎ 01 47 39 00 91 or by e-mailing service.clients@taxis-g7.com. Make sure you notify your airline when booking and reconfirming your flight that you're in a wheelchair and that you need assistance at both ends. This will activate the *service d'assistance* at the airport in Paris. Note that if you have an electric wheelchair, you should make sure that you remember to take care of the dry-cell batteries before leaving home. The liquid-electrolysis–type batteries must absolutely be emptied before boarding (emptying takes about an hour). Gel batteries pose no problem at all.

Upon your arrival at either Charles de Gaulle or Orly airport, a private assistance company will greet you at the exit of the plane and accompany you through immigration and customs and baggage claim. Consult the pages (in English) dedicated to disabled travelers on the Web site **aeroportsdeparis.fr.**

With the exception of the automated shuttle trains, CDGVAL at Charles de Gaulle and Orlyval at Orly, the public-transport options at the airports are only partially wheelchair accessible. Note that taxis are not supposed to charge you a supplement for the transport of your wheelchair.

If you're traveling by train, note that on all mainline routes, including the TGV (fast) trains, special disabled seating is often situated in first class but is open to you with a second-class ticket. Some trains are equipped with direct-access toilets for wheelchairs, but in others you'll have to ask a conductor for a *chaise de transfert,* a transfer chair. The conductor is supposed to know what this is and where to find one onboard.

Every SNCF station in France has an assistance service in the *accueil* area of the station, which will advise the destination station of your arrival. Use this. All the mainline Parisian stations also offer the Accès Plus service. Contact the help line before you travel at ☎ 08 90 64 06 50 or by e-mail at accesplus@sncf.fr to make your reservation and arrange assistance. Don't forget to mark your baggage with disabled stickers and bring your disabled card with you.

The SNCF has a dedicated Web site, **accessibilite.sncf.com** (in French only), to assist disabled travelers. It also publishes a guide (in French) titled *Guide du Voyageur Handicapé,* which you can obtain at all principal stations or download from the Web site. This guide gives detailed information regarding reservation procedures, seating arrangements, and assistance as well as a list of disabled services provided in individual stations throughout France. For door-to-door personalized assistance in Paris and throughout France, contact the association **Les Compagnons du Voyage** at ☎ 01 58 76 08 33;

info@compagnons.com; or **compagnons.com**. They will provide clients with a companion traveler; the hourly rate in Paris is €27. There is also a municipal service known as **PAM (Paris Accompagnement Mobilité)** that visitors to the city can use. Reservations are via the Web site, **pam.paris.fr**. You can also call ☎ 08 10 08 10 75 between 7 a.m. and 8 p.m. for information. This service operates through the Greater Paris area and rates start at €6 per trip.

The principal train stations are equipped with lifts, wheelchairs, ticket windows, toilets, and telephone booths reserved for the disabled traveler. In theory, railway staff should be on hand to assist you; however, you are asked to arrive 30 minutes before departure. All Eurostar and Thalys trains are equipped with disabled-adapted seats and toilets in first-class cars, and guide dogs ride for free on both services.

HOTELS EQUIPPED FOR TRAVELERS WITH DISABILITIES

THE LEGAL NORMS AND REQUIREMENTS for accessibility for disabled citizens in France are not as well respected as in the United States. Expect to find details that blatantly ignore all good sense. Regulated heights of steps are not respected, railings may be missing, and the like. The worst problem, though, is that in Paris the criteria for disabled accessibility have all been determined by nondisabled administrators. An official "Tourisme and Handicap" label was introduced in 2001 to classify the accessibility of accommodations, restaurants, cultural sites, and leisure facilities. However, in 2009 only 14 hotels in central Paris had earned this label. On pages 174–175 is a partial list of hotels, organized by arrondissement, that offer rooms that have been adapted for safe use by disabled visitors (such as bathrooms, toilets, sinks, and showers that conform to legal norms). We've indicated the number of rooms available to you. For a full list, including suburban locations, consult the Web site **parisinfo.com**.

USING THE MÉTRO

A FEW MÉTRO AND RER STATIONS, including all stations on Line 14, are wheelchair accessible. Also known as Méteor (Métro Est Ouest Rapide), Line 14 runs from Gare Saint Lazare to Olympiades, serving key stations such as Madeleine and Châtelet on the way. Disabled access is ensured by a series of elevators from street-level to train platforms at each of the nine stations.

The RATP is gradually increasing the number of buses that are wheelchair accessible and at present has 28 bus routes with total or partial accessibility. The most recent addition to the urban transport network, the tramway line to the south of the city, is also entirely accessible. Printed maps and additional information are available at any RATP information office or Métro station.

RESTAURANTS AND DISABLED ACCESS

NUMEROUS RESTAURANTS IN PARIS ARE ACCESSIBLE to people in wheelchairs. However, very few Paris restaurants are equipped with disabled-accessible toilets, with the exception of a few museum and chain-hotel restaurants. Check our list of profiled restaurants in Part Seven, Dining and Restaurants, or call ahead for details. If it's any comfort to you, note that all McDonald's restaurants are wholly accessible.

MONUMENTS AND DISABLED ACCESS

DON'T BE SHY ABOUT ATTEMPTING TO SEE EVERYTHING. There will be some minor obstacles, but on the whole you can visit most sights. You must go up the Eiffel Tower. On a clear day be prepared to see all of Paris and 40 miles beyond. The night view is splendid. Go up the north leg of the tower (Pilier Nord). You can go as far as the second level by elevator. The toilets on the ground, first, and second floors are all wheelchair friendly.

For disabled-access information on Paris's main attractions and monuments, see the attraction profiles in Part Six, Sightseeing, Tours, and Attractions.

A USEFUL CONTACT

Infomobi (**infomobi.com**; ☎ 08 10 64 64 64 in French only) is an information service provided by the regional authorities to assist the mobility of disabled travelers in the Paris area. Services offered include personalized itineraries based on each individual traveler's limitations and the limitations of the transport network. A map detailing transport options in the Paris region for wheelchair users can be downloaded from the Web site.

TRAVELING *with* CHILDREN

kids TRAVELING WITH CHILDREN IN GENERAL affords you great pleasures and joys in addition to daily problems to anticipate and solve. Visiting Paris with kids can be wonderfully gratifying but desperately frustrating if you don't plan ahead. On the positive side, Parisians are generally more tolerant than Anglo-Saxons when it comes to children. You'd never find condominium complexes in France for adults only, and you will often see children accompanying their parents in fancy restaurants. And although many restaurants and hotels are not as family-oriented as you may be used to finding back home, there are lots of wonderful activities for kids, big and small, that will enchant you.

EATING OUT WITH KIDS

RESTAURANTS ARE GENERALLY open for lunch between noon and 2 p.m. and for dinner between 7 and 10 p.m. If feeding time for your kids differs from this, you'd better bring along snacks. Fast food is always an option for hungry or finicky kids, but we don't encourage this. You're in Paris! Don't rush off to one of the scores of McDonald's (known in Paris as *McDoh*) that grace this city.

*un*official **TIP**
The services listed here all claim to provide carefully screened, bilingual babysitters, who are almost exclusively female university students.

Don't count on finding high chairs, paper bibs, crayons, or children's toys in restaurants. Your kids are welcome, but you had better bring along your own paraphernalia and amusements.

Meals take more time in Paris than you're probably accustomed to. You should ask for your children's food first. Kitchens do not always understand these special needs, so really insist on this, with a smile. If your 5-year-old is about to pull a tantrum if she doesn't get her noodles (*des pâtes* [day **paht**]), order the noodles before you order anything else. If your child is not going to like a sauce, ask for the *pâtes nature* (nah-**tur**). Memorize this sentence: *Excusez-moi. Est-ce qu'on peut avoir des pâtes pour le petit* (or *la petite*) *maintenant, s'il vous plaît?* (Excuse--say **mwah.** Es **kown puh ahv**-war lay paht por luh peh-tee [la peh-**teet**] met-**nawh,** see voo **play.**) You are asking, "Excuse me. May we have the noodles for the child now, please?"

Some restaurants will offer a *menu enfant,* which usually consists of a slice of ham or a *saucisse* (hot dog), *steak haché* (ground beef), french fries or pasta, an orange juice, and a yogurt or *crème caramel.* You may prefer to make up a plate from the good things you ordered.

For bigger kids, we strongly suggest that you let them explore freely. You are helping them develop their tastes and build their understanding of the world. Cuisine is a major part of this process of discovery.

There is no taboo in Paris against letting adolescents taste the wine.

BABYSITTERS

LARGER HOTELS MAY HAVE A LIST of local babysitters and may even arrange for one, but we've researched the subject for you and can recommend several highly reputable and reliable babysitting services. You don't need a lot of phone numbers; you need a state of mind. You need to be 100 percent confident about leaving your little ones in a hotel in a foreign city. Regardless of the age of your kids, you'll be able to step out for dinner or dash around town on a shopping spree without worry and without *les enfants* (lay zohn-**fohn**) in tow.

The hourly rate for babysitters in Paris ranges from €8 to €10 per hour, with a bit more for multiple kids and late at night. You can relax as you're sipping Champagne at Maxim's because your kids will be learning French from the babysitter.

BABYSITTING SERVICE 1, place Paul Verlaine, Boulogne Billancourt 92100; ☎ 01 46 21 33 16; fax 02 48 72 89 81; **babysittingservices. com.** Madame Marise Bloch's service has been providing babysitters since 1981. Her supply of about 100 young women includes English-speaking students. The hourly rate is €7.50, and there's a €12.90 agency fee, which is payable by credit card.

BABYCHOU 31, rue du Moulin de la Pointe, 75013; ☎ 01 43 13 33 23; **babychou.com** (in English). This agency provides a range of childcare solutions, including a bilingual babysitting service for hotels. Booking can be made just a few hours in advance. There is an agency fee of €16 payable by credit card at the time of booking, and the hourly rate, paid directly to the sitter, is €8 per hour for one child, €9 per hour for two, and €10 for three children.

SPECIAL PARKS FOR KIDS

FOR DETAILED DESCRIPTIONS, times, prices, and hours, see Part Six, Sightseeing, Tours, and Attractions.

Aquaboulevard Leisure Complex
4–6, rue Louis Armand, 75015. **Métro:** Balard, Porte de Versailles. ☎ 01 40 60 10 00; fax 01 40 60 18 39; **aquaboulevard.fr. Full price** €25; children ages 3 to 11, €10; children under 3 not admitted.

Jardin d'Acclimatation
Bois de Boulogne, 75016. **Métro:** Sablons or Porte Maillot. ☎ 01 40 67 90 82; **jardindacclimatation.fr. Cost** Entrance, €2.70; price per ticket per ride, €2.50; 15 tickets, €32; 25 tickets, €48; children under age 3, free.

Jardin du Luxembourg
Between rue Guynemer and boulevard Saint-Michel, 75006. **Métro RER:** Luxembourg. **Cost** Free entrance.

Jardin Sauvage de Saint-Vincent
14, rue Saint-Vincent, 75018. **Métro:** Lamarck-Caulaincourt. **Open** April–October, Saturday only, 10 a.m.–12:30 p.m., 1:30–6:30 p.m.

Parc de la Villette
Cité des Sciences, Parc de la Villette, Musée de la Musique, 211, avenue Jean Jaurès, 75019. **Métro:** Porte de la Villette. ☎ 01 40 03 75 75; **villette.com.**

Parc Floral de Paris
Bois de Vincennes–Esplanade du Château, Route de la Pyramide, 75012. **Métro:** Château de Vincennes. **boisdevincennes.com/site/parcfloral.php3. Cost** Free all year except Wednesday, Saturday, and Sunday between June 6 and September 21, when the following rates apply: adults, €5; children ages 7–26, €2.50; children under age 7, free.

THEME PARKS FOR KIDS

FOR DISNEYLAND PARIS AND PARC ASTERIX, see attraction profiles in Part Six, Sightseeing, Tours, and Attractions.

MUSEUMS FOR KIDS

ANY MUSEUM CAN BE A TREAT OR A HORROR STORY FOR KIDS. The key is to set realistic expectations and let your kids help you open your eyes to new things. With a museum pass (see "Absolutely Necessary: The Museum and Monument Pass" in Part Six, Sightseeing, Tours, and Attractions), which allows you to come back as many times as you like, you won't feel guilty spending only a few hours in the Louvre or Musée d'Orsay at a time. The **Rodin Museum** has an enchanting sculpture garden, and little children love to interact with the forms. They'll imitate *The Thinker* for the rest of their lives. The **Picasso Museum** is filled with wonderfully inventive works of art that tend to ignite the imaginations of kids. The scale of the museum is not overly intimidating, and you can easily see everything in two hours. The **Palais de la Porte Dorée** is a favorite for kids, with its impressive aquarium in the basement complete with crocodile enclosure. Upstairs is the rather new and controversial Museum of History of Immigration, which is worth a visit. The lake in the **Bois de Vincennes** is within walking distance and is perfect for picnics. Dog lovers will enjoy the Bois in the summer, especially on Sundays. Hundreds of dog owners promenade with their setters and spaniels and very French-looking poodles. Although a bit out of the way, the museum at **Le Bourget,** the Paris airport that preceded Orly for commercial flights, hosts a stunning collection of French airplanes, including the first models of the Concorde, which you can climb into.

unofficial **TIP**
We highly recommend a spin through the Egyptian section of the Louvre with kids. They can actually read hieroglyphics!

For all museum addresses, Métro stops, opening times, prices, and descriptions, see attraction profiles in Part Six, Sightseeing, Tours, and Attractions.

JARDIN DES ENFANTS AUX HALLES (LABYRINTH) A true highlight for kids in Paris, the outdoor labyrinth in the park at Les Halles is a wonderland of inventive and safe activities. Each hour a limited number of kids between ages 7 and 11 are allowed to move through a course of obstacles, illusions, doors, steps, tunnels, cliffs, slides, and more at their own pace, while curious (and envious) parents watch from behind the gates. There is no better way to spend an hour on a Saturday morning with your kids in Paris than at the Labyrinth. 105, rue Rambuteau, 75001; ☎ 01 45 08 07 18; Métro: Châtelet–Les Halles (exit Rambuteau); open Tuesday through Sunday. Times change seasonally. Closed when raining. Free admission.

LES MANÈGES AND LES GUIGNOLS   You'll still find lots of great old merry-go-rounds from the 1920s and 1930s here, as well as the wonderful French tradition of taking kids to ride them after school at 4:30 p.m. or on the weekends. Classical examples are found at Châtelet–Les Halles near the top of the RER entrance, at the riverfront by the Eiffel Tower, and in the Bois de Boulogne and Bois de Vincennes.

Similarly, there is a great French tradition of taking children to the 4 p.m. matinee of the famous Guignol marionettes. Don't worry that the program is in French; your kids will understand it and love it. Check the weekly *Pariscope* or *l'Officiel des Spectacles* for locations and times.

PUBLICATIONS AND LISTINGS

FOR A LISTING OF THINGS TO DO with kids during your stay, check the *Paris Voice* Web site or *Pariscope* (in French).

SAFETY *and* SECURITY

YOU'VE JUST ARRIVED AND YOU'RE CONCERNED about what is safe to do and what isn't. Paris is a safe city and cannot be compared with large American cities in terms of overall crime statistics. In central Paris, you can usually walk around day or night with little fear of aggression. However, Paris is a large city, and the crime rate has increased markedly over the last ten years. As in any city, women should be careful about venturing alone into unfamiliar areas. Most crime is located in the suburbs and occurs late at night in certain Métro stations and trouble spots. There are cases of muggings, sexual aggression, pickpocketing, vandalism, and car theft, but fortunately they are not common, and visitors should be prudent but not at all fearful or hesitant.

IF YOU'RE A VICTIM OF CRIME . . .

PARIS IS RELATIVELY SAFE—much safer than almost any American city. You will in all likelihood not encounter violent crime, and you should not feel insecure about walking around the city, even after dark. Having said that, Paris is a big place, and you should take certain precautions when you're out and about.

- Pickpockets exist in and around the flea markets and in certain crowded Métro stations. Make sure your money and passport are securely stored in a zipped portion of a daypack or in a secure pocket.
- Women should generally avoid riding the Métro or RER late at night (after midnight) alone.
- The area around Stalingrad Métro station can get a bit rough late at night since it is frequented by drug dealers and their clients. Similarly,

late night the Châtelet–Les Halles area should be approached with caution. Some of the nearby suburbs with large housing projects are best avoided late at night unless you are accompanied by someone who lives there.

- Parts of the Bois de Boulogne and the Bois de Vincennes become sex markets at night for female and transvestite prostitutes. These areas aren't particularly dangerous, but you might not want to be mistaken for a client when you thought you were just going out for a long walk.
- If in doubt about an area, ask your concierge for his or her opinion before setting out.
- If your wallet is stolen, it's probable that your money and credit cards will be gone forever, but the wallet itself and other papers may turn up at Paris's central Lost and Found. Call ☎ 08 21 00 25 25; see additional details below.

HOTEL SECURITY

PRACTICALLY ALL OF PARIS'S HOTELS ARE VERY SAFE, and it's rare to hear of break-ins, thefts, or attacks. Nonetheless, you should always lock your door when you're in your room, as well as when you leave it, and you should avoid leaving cash, jewelry, and obvious valuables exposed. Most hotels offer in-house safe-deposit boxes for your peace of mind. Standard stuff.

LOST AND FOUND

PARIS HAS A CENTRAL LOST-AND-FOUND CENTER (Prefecture de Police, Objets Trouvés [oh-**bjay** troo-**vay**]) located at 36, rue des Morillons, 75015; ☎ 08 21 00 25 25; Métro: Convention. Open 8:30 a.m. to 5 p.m. Monday to Thursday, and 8:30 a.m. to 4.30 p.m. on Friday. Call or ask your hotel to call for you if you lost something or left something in a taxi. Even stolen wallets turn up here (without the cash), and items can even be traced in the database over the phone if you can provide sufficient details. Limited English.

LOST CREDIT CARDS

Eurocard/MasterCard/MasterCharge ☎ 08 00 90 13 87

Carte Bleue or Visa ☎ 08 92 705 705

American Express ☎ 01 47 77 72 00

Diners Club ☎ 08 10 31 41 59

EMERGENCY NUMBERS

ON THE NEXT PAGE IS A QUICK REFERENCE LIST of emergency numbers. Note that you may not find English speakers at the other end of the line, so it may be necessary to have a French-speaking person call for you.

- Police: ☎ 17
- Fire: ☎ 18
- Medical Emergencies: ☎ 15
- Ambulance SAMU Service: ☎ 15
- Europe-wide number for all the above services: ☎ 112
- Anti-Poison Center (24 hours a day): ☎ 01 40 05 48 48
- SOS Médecins (24-hour emergency medical house calls): ☎ 01 47 07 77 77
- SOS Cardiologues (emergency service for heart patients): ☎ 01 47 07 50 50
- SOS Dentaire (emergency dental help): ☎ 01 43 37 51 00
- Emergency locksmith (24 hours a day): ☎ 08 00 80 15 40
- Rape Crisis Hotline: ☎ 08 00 05 95 95 (toll-free)
- Pregnancy Hotline: ☎ 01 45 82 13 14
- SIDA Info Service (AIDS Helpline): ☎ 08 00 84 08 00

YOUR EMBASSY OR CONSULATE

YOU MAY REGISTER YOUR LOCAL ADDRESS in Paris with your Paris consulate, although very few visitors do this on short visits, and it is not strictly necessary. On the other hand, if you are away during a sensitive time back home or you're in fragile health, the consulate can be helpful in locating you or contacting your family in case of an emergency.

- **U.S. Consulate**
  4, avenue Gabriel, 75008
  ☎ 01 43 12 22 22
  Métro: Concorde
- **Canadian Consulate**
  35, avenue Montaigne, 75008
  ☎ 01 44 43 29 00
  Métro: Franklin D. Roosevelt

- **Australian Embassy**
  4, rue Jean Rey, 75015
  ☎ 01 40 59 33 00
  Emergencies ☎ 01 40 59 33 01
  Métro: Bir-Hakeim
- **British Consulate**
  18 bis, rue Anjou, 75008
  ☎ 08 92 23 01 75
  Métro: Madeleine

PART FIVE

GETTING AROUND

▌ VISUALIZING *the* CITY

PARIS POSSESSES THE QUAINT CONTRADICTION of being organized according to no specific system or grid—aside from Baron Haussmann's 1850ish scheme for wide boulevards—but at the same time it has been developed on a scale that makes aimless exploring pleasurable without the risk of getting too lost. In essence, streets can be small and jumbled, but the city is user-friendly. You can always situate yourself in Paris by using the closest Métro stop as your mental and geographic crutch. Everything in Paris is accessible by the Métro—the veins through which the life of the city flows—and the system will inevitably become your best friend. Find a Métro station and you'll never be lost or too far from anything. You'll quickly get to know your Métro stop and a few local cafés, which you'll keep coming back to each day. Comfort and pleasure in Paris builds as you settle into these little routines. The other reference point is, of course, the Seine, the river that runs east–west across the city.

Using our arrondissement map in the Introduction, memorize the key areas of Paris and where they are in relation to each other and your hotel. This way, you'll always have your bearings, wherever you are. Memorize your closest Métro stop, the line that it's on, and the *direction* (the last station on the line heading in the direction of your hotel).

PARIS *PRATIQUE*

WE'VE MENTIONED ON SEVERAL OCCASIONS how to find free city and Métro maps. These will help you get around, except when you're looking for an obscure shop in the 13th arrondissement or a bistro that a friend raved about in the 12th arrondissement. With one of these handy map books, you'll be able to track down every street in Paris and its closest Métro stop. And as a tourist, you'll *unofficial* TIP

To get the shape of Paris clear in your head, think of a large egg lying on its side. The RATP public-transportation authority uses the shape of the city as its logo, with the path of the Seine River forming the profile of a face.

look like a local. You can find a selection of *L'Indispensable* map books in all stationery shops, most newsstands, and department stores priced from about €2.50 to €23 for a deluxe edition with waterproof cover. Michelin publishes a similar spiral-bound one for around €10. Trust us, this is a great value—you'll get very attached to your map book very quickly and will want to keep it for return journeys.

The arrondissements are organized clockwise in concentric circles starting in the city center. The street signs are posted on the corner of buildings and most of the time indicate the arrondissement as well as the street.

SPOTTING THE EIFFEL TOWER

"WHERE'S THE EIFFEL TOWER?" How often do we hear this from arriving visitors? For many, you're not really in Paris until you've spotted the world's most famous monument. Go satisfy the urge right away. If this is your first time in Paris, the single most dominant image in your mind is surely this spectacular hunk of metal. Most visitors don't feel like going to the Louvre or the Picasso Museum until they've first laid eyes on this larger-than-life icon, situated on the Left Bank of the Seine in a long and elegant garden called the Champ de Mars, in the 15th arrondissement. Aside from the top, the absolute best viewing point during the day—and especially at night—is the terrace at the Trocadéro on the Right Bank. To get to the Eiffel Tower, take either Line 6 of the Métro to the Bir-Hakeim station or Line C of the RER to the Champ-de-Mars–Tour Eiffel stop. For more information, you can call ☎ 01 44 11 23 23 or visit **tour-eiffel.fr.**

WALKING IN PARIS

THE BEST WAY TO EXPERIENCE PARIS is by foot (*à pied* [ah pee-**ay**]). The human scale of Paris permits you to move easily from the Latin Quarter, across the islands, into the Marais, along rue de Rivoli, past the Louvre, along the Seine, over the Pont Neuf, and into the Saint-Germain-des-Prés area and back to your centrally located hotel without any problem at all. Pause for lunch and stop at least once or twice for a coffee or glass of beer or wine in an inviting café.

Note: Traffic signals do not hang in the middle of intersections but are affixed to poles on the far side of intersections. Green and red have the usual universal meanings. Parisians are not a highly disciplined people, but they are not jaywalkers either. Don't cross in the middle of streets or ignore street signs like New Yorkers do. Drivers are not used to irresponsible pedestrians and do not usually slow down for them.

STREET ADDRESSES

IN PARIS, STREET SIGNS ARE FIXED to the sides of buildings, much higher than eye level. Traditional Parisian street signs are blue with green trim. The arrondissement is often shown above the name.

With regard to street numbers, don't be surprised if odd and even numbers are not located opposite each other on a street. Many Paris buildings have long and deep courtyards and passageways leading from the street. You'll often see numbers followed by *bis* or *ter*, like "37 bis" or "104 ter," simply indicating that this address is adjacent to number 37 or 104.

PUBLIC TRANSPORTATION

PUBLIC TRANSPORTATION IN PARIS IS EXTENSIVE, inexpensive, safe, and easy to use. Even if you've never used public transportation back home, or you're afraid you'll get lost or squeezed to death in crowds, in Paris, trust the RATP and use it—especially the Métro. The Métro will not only save you valuable time and lots of money, but it will quickly bring you to the heart of everyday Parisian life. The RATP also has an extensive public-bus system with multiple lines crisscrossing the city that links neighborhoods between Métro stops. And you might also want to try the affiliated Bat-o-Bus, which hosts regular river traffic on the Seine.

The RATP has a 24-hour telephone hotline for all questions concerning rates, itineraries, and hours. To reach a human being who speaks some English, call between 7 a.m. and 9 p.m.; you may need to ask for an English-speaking agent (☎ 3246); otherwise you'll get only recorded messages in French. You can also check their site (in English) at **ratp.fr.**

THE MÉTRO

THE BACKBONE OF THE RATP NETWORK is the **Métro,** one of the world's greatest subway systems, which was inaugurated in 1900 with the Porte de Vincennes–Porte Maillot Métropolitain line (hence the name "Métro"). Today the Métro includes 16 lines and a whopping 298 stations. Essentially every neighborhood in Paris is accessible by Métro. The Métro opens at 5:30 a.m. and closes around 1 a.m. An extended service operates Friday and Saturday nights and the eve of all public holidays until almost 2 a.m.—but don't cut it too close. Ask at the Métro station closest to your hotel when the last Métro runs. (*Excusez-moi, c'est quand le dernier Métro ce soir, s'il vous plaît?* [Ex-cu-say **mwa;** say **cah-wn luh dare-nyeh** Métro suh swah, see voo **play**?])

Each Métro line has an assigned number and is commonly referred to by the last station at the end of its line or direction. Each line is

MÉTRO LINES

Line 1	Château de Vincennes	La Défense
Line 2	Nation	Porte Dauphine
Line 3	Gallieni	Pont de Levallois–Bécon
Line 3 bis	Porte des Lilas	Gambetta
Line 4	Porte de Clignancourt	Porte d'Orléans
Line 5	Bobigny–Pablo Picasso	Place d'Italie
Line 6	Nation	Charles de Gaulle–Étoile
Line 7	La Courneuve 8 mai 1945	Mairie d'Ivry/Villejuif–Louis Aragon
Line 7 bis	Pré-Saint-Gervais	Louis Blanc
Line 8	Créteil Préfecture	Balard
Line 9	Mairie de Montreuil	Pont de Sèvres
Line 10	Gare d'Austerlitz	Boulogne Pont de Saint-Cloud
Line 11	Mairie des Lilas	Châtelet
Line 12	Porte de la Chapelle	Mairie d'Issy
Line 13	Châtillon-Montrouge	Asnières Gennevilliers Les Courtilles–Saint-Denis Université
Line 14	Saint-Lazare	Olympiades

MÉTRO TICKET PRICES

Single ticket T+, €1.60   *Carnet* (ten tickets), €11.40

Mobilis (one-day unlimited travel), €5.80 (1–2 zones) to €16.40 (1–6 zones)

also color-coded, but with 16 different lines, you'll find the numbers a better indicator. The colors help you follow a line across the map.

You'll want to pick up a map of the Métro and RER and keep it handy all the time. Free maps are available at all Métro and RER stations, as well as at the RATP information office in the massive Châtelet–Les Halles station, which acts as the central hub for the system and is the major intersection of numerous lines. You can also download a printed Métro map from the official RATP Web site at **ratp.fr** or directly onto your PDA, if you use one. In addition, the Galeries Lafayette department store prints millions of copies of colorful city and Métro maps, which are distributed free in their stores and at hundreds of points of contact for tourists.

Distances in Time

To determine how long it will take you to get from one station to another, roughly allow between one and two minutes per station,

PARIS VISITE PASS

	ONE-DAY ADULTS	CHILDREN	TWO-DAY ADULTS	CHILDREN
1–3 zones	€8.80	€4.40	€14.40	€7.20
1–6 zones	€18.50	€9.25	€28.30	€14.15
	THREE-DAY ADULTS	CHILDREN	FIVE-DAY ADULTS	CHILDREN
1–3 zones	€19.60	€9.80	€28.30	€14.15
1–6 zones	€39.70	€19.85	€40.40	€24.20

Children ages 4–11 pay half price; children under age 4 travel free.

Zones 1–3 include Paris and its nearby suburbs (La Défense, Saint-Denis Université, Le Bourget, Vincennes).

Zones 1–6 include Paris and the surrounding area (Versailles, Charles de Gaulle and Orly Airports, and Disneyland Paris at Marne la Vallée).

Charles de Gaulle Airport (Roissy) is in Zone 5 and costs €8.20 each way.

Orly Airport is in Zone 4 and, via Orlyval, costs €9.60 each way.

Disneyland Paris is in Zone 5; note that the Disneyland Passport (€51 adults, €43 children ages 3 to 11, under age 3 free) only covers your entrance to the resort. You will also have to purchase a ticket to Chessy–Marne la Vallée station at €6.45 each way.

Versailles is in Zone 4 and costs €2.90 each way.

Saint-Germain-en-Laye is in Zone 4 and costs €3.60 each way.

and add five minutes for each change of line (*correspondance*) you need to make. The high-speed RER trains come less frequently than the Métros but are faster and stop less. You can get from the center of the city at Châtelet–Les Halles to the Arc de Triomphe in less than 10 minutes by RER, which would take twice as long by Métro.

Buying Métro Tickets

Métro tickets will be one of your staple tools for navigating Paris. You have several ticket options, depending largely on how long you are staying and how many times you think you'll be using the Métro, RER, or buses. Paris public transportation is organized into six zones, each commanding its own fare, so a little calculating is necessary to make the best choice.

All public transportation (Métro, RER, and buses) within Paris city limits and all the Métro stops on all 16 lines (even those that go beyond the city limits) collectively constitute Zones 1 and 2 and require only a Métro ticket. Almost all of your travel, except perhaps to one of the airports or Disneyland Paris, will fall within these two

unofficial **TIP**
If you plan to use the RER between either airport and Paris, or to and from Disneyland Paris, it is definitely a good deal to buy a Paris Visite upon arrival. If you are not going to use public transportation to and from the airport or Disneyland Paris, you might consider simply buying a carnet of ten tickets at a time.

zones. You can buy tickets one at a time as you go, in a packet of ten called a *carnet*, or as a special one-, two-, three-, or five-day visitors pass called the **Paris Visite.** Prices do change periodically, so they might be a little different from what is listed here, but changes will be minimal and proportional.

As you can quickly calculate, it is very advantageous to buy a Paris Visite in many cases. Not only will you save money, you won't have to spend time in lines, and you won't have to figure out how, when, or where to get tickets. And, best of all, you won't hesitate over how or if you should go somewhere. With the pass in hand, you're more likely to use it and really explore Paris.

Advantages of the Paris Visite

If you do opt for the Paris Visite, we've listed below just some of the benefits offered at press time. Check the Web site, **ratp.info/touristes,** for the full list of partners and updated information.

BATEAUX PARISIENS 25 percent off each adult ticket.

PALAIS GARNIER Tour of the classic opera house for €5 instead of €8.

CITÉ DES SCIENCES Admission discounted by €2.

ARC DE TRIOMPHE Admission discounted by 20 percent.

ESPACE DALI Admission €6 instead of €10.

GALERIES LAFAYETTE Discount of 10 percent on purchases plus a free shopping bag.

OPEN TOUR BUS One-day pass at €25 instead of €29.

DISNEYLAND Admission discounted by 20 percent.

MUSÉE DU QUAI BRANLY Admission €6 instead of €8.50.

CHÂTEAU DE VINCENNES Admission discounted by 25 percent.

PANTHÉON Admission discounted by 20 percent.

LIDO Admission to Champagne-Revue shows discounted by 50 percent.

TOUR MONTPARNASSE Admission discounted by 35 percent.

Where to Purchase a Paris Visite

It's simple. Just go to almost any Métro or RER station ticket window and ask for a Paris Visite for the number of days and number of zones you wish. In all stations you'll be able to pay with your credit card. You don't need a photo or any identification, and you can buy the card on any day and begin using it on any other day. It automatically activates the first time you insert it into the turnstile. Note that the whole day will be billed, regardless of the time you start.

You can buy your card at the RER station at either airport, and you can even buy it from a ticket machine with your Visa or Master-Card and PIN number, which will save you time.

How to Use the Métro

THE TURNSTILE The Métro is very easy to use once you've mastered the symbols employed to indicate exits, transfers, and train directions. After you've bought your tickets or a pass, you slip the ticket into the slot in the turnstile. The machine will grab it and spit it out in another slot. You grab it and proceed through the turnstile. Keep your ticket until you exit the Métro system because you may be asked to show it while you're in transit. In the case of the RER, you'll need to reinsert the ticket to get past the turnstile at your exit as well as at any intersection between the Métro and RER, so don't lose it; if you do, you'll either have to explain, beg, jump over the turnstile, or pay a fine.

*un*official **TIP**
If you're caught going through a turnstile together on one ticket, be ready for a whopping €50 fine for each of you.

You will observe a number of people "cheating"—climbing over the turnstile, going in the exit door, or squeezing through the turnstile with another passenger (often strangers). Someone may even squeeze in behind you without asking. The RATP has *contrôleur* dragnets set up periodically throughout the system, attempting to catch or deter cheaters.

If you lose your ticket and have the bad luck of being noticed by a *contrôleur,* try to explain what happened. Most likely you'll gain no sympathy and have to either pay the €40 fine on the spot, or show your passport and agree to have an increased fine of €72 (payable within two months) mailed to you at home, with a copy sent to your consulate.

FOLLOW YOUR DIRECTION Métro lines are named after their endpoints, that is, Line 4 going north to Porte de Clignancourt is called Direction Porte de Clignancourt; the same line traveling in the opposite direction is called Direction Porte d'Orléans. Once you know which line your stop is on, head in the direction of the last station on that line. A large sign above the platform indicates direction.

TRANSFERRING FROM ONE LINE TO ANOTHER: CORRESPONDANCE For transferring from one line to another, color-coded signs on the *quai* (platform) marked "*Correspondance*" indicate the path to other platforms and other directions. This may be confusing because you sometimes need to follow the *correspondance* sign for your line through long corridors, moving sidewalks, and along platforms of other lines.

Make sure your direction is marked on the sign hanging above the platform at which you end up waiting. If you happen to get on a

Métro going the wrong way, don't panic. Get off at the next stop and cross over to the platform marked with the correct direction.

SORTIE (EXIT)/ACCÈS AUX QUAIS (ENTRANCE)   Blue signs marked *"Sortie"* point you in the direction of the exit, and often you'll have a choice of exits, all emerging onto different streets or different sides of the street. When meeting friends at a Métro station, make sure to specify which exit and whether you will meet underground or above ground. In every big station, you will find a *plan du quartier* (neighborhood map) on the platform, but all Métro stops have these maps at the ticket-office exit. When with a group, if one of you gets left behind, a good policy is to get off at the next stop and wait for your friend to arrive, and then continue on together.

A TIP ON AVOIDING LONG TRANSFERS   If you are changing from one Métro line to another, study your options to reduce the number of changes and stops you need to make to reach your destination. If you can avoid transferring at Châtelet and Montparnasse, you may be avoiding a very long walk through an endless corridor with a moving sidewalk. An experimental high-speed travelator was installed at Montparnasse but is frequently out of order.

First Class

First class in the Métro was abolished in the mid-1980s under the Socialist government. You may still find some RER cars marked first class. Just ignore the numbers and sit where you'd like. The SNCF trains still maintain a first-class service category, however.

Street People/Beggars/Musicians

For years the Paris Métro has been home to an odd mix of down-and-out individuals, street musicians, beggars, Gypsies, winos, and street people (called *clochards*). Quite often you'll spot a sad-looking person sitting on the cement in the Métro with a handwritten sign stating his or her story or problem—*"J'ai faim* [I'm hungry],*" "54 ans, trois enfants, et sans travail* [54 years old, three children, and out of work]*," "SVP, donnez-moi une pièce ou deux* [Please give me a coin or two].*"* The growing homeless population (referred to as SDF, for *sans domicile fixe*) of Paris publishes several magazines, guidebooks, crossword puzzles, and even a brief history of each Métro stop, which are sold on the Métro cars. Musicians play a song or two and then file through the moving Métro with a hat or cup. Recent immigrants, typically women, will sit with quiet infants for hours waiting for handouts. Others will give a desperate speech and come around looking for a few coins or a restaurant ticket. Don't feel intimidated or obliged to give anything. However, if you feel like helping someone, a few coins are always appreciated.

Occasionally you have to watch out for small bands of street kids roaming the carriages of the Métro on some of the busier lines and in the train stations. They are skilled pickpockets. They encircle their prey and distract them as one of them grabs the contents of pockets and purses. Hang on to everything, and don't be afraid to shoo them away.

Getting Back to Your Hotel

If you memorize your Métro stop, you'll never get lost. We suggest that you keep a card from your hotel in your pocket in case you must ask someone for directions and your French is still a bit rusty.

unofficial **TIP**
These solicitations may make you a bit uncomfortable at times, but, by and large, they do not represent any danger to passengers.

Heads Up: Keep to Your Right

When walking through the corridors, on the escalators, and along the long moving beltways in the Métro, the rule is for slower walkers to keep to the right. People have the right to pass on your left.

THE RER

THE RER (RÉSEAU EXPRESS RÉGIONAL) SYSTEM—also run by the RATP—is the high-speed city-suburb network that can zoom you across the city, out to Versailles or Saint-Germain-en-Laye, and even to Disneyland Paris in a short amount of time. The aesthetics are very different from the Métro, since the stations are vast tunnels with deep platforms and the trains are fast and silent. Note that the Métros approach each platform from your left while most of the RER trains approach from your right. There are five lines on the RER (A, B, C, D, E), forking out into numerous directions. The RER and Métro lines connect at various points, and although the RER is not designed to be used for very short distances, it makes longer-distance traveling across the city or from city to suburb incredibly easy and efficient. Key junction (*correspondance*) stations are Châtelet–Les Halles, Nation, Étoile, and Auber. Don't confuse Charles de Gaulle–Étoile, where the Arc de Triomphe is located, with Roissy–Charles de Gaulle, the suburban site of the airport.

On the platform there are lit panels indicating the precise direction and list of stations the next train will be serving, as well as the expected time of arrival of the next train. All trains stop at all Paris stations. Be careful at Nation and Étoile stations not to board a train on the correct line but the wrong branch; otherwise, you'll have to circle back and pay another fare. Note that you can go to the Château de Vincennes Métro stop with a Métro ticket, but in order to get off the RER at Vincennes you'll need an additional fare. Controllers often stake out the Vincennes RER station, catching hordes of violators.

unofficial **TIP**
If you continue on past the city limits (Zones 1 and 2), your Métro ticket will not work in the exit turnstile, and you'll be forced to jump over the turnstile and risk a fine.

The trains have funny four-letter names that are written in lights on the front of the first car. The stopping point for both the long and short trains is indicated by fixed signs suspended over the platforms at the points where the front (*tête*) and rear (*queue*) of the train will be when it stops. This is an important thing to notice, since you could be waiting for a train on the correct platform but be 100 meters behind or in front of the train's arrival point.

Unlike on the Métro, when using the RER, keep your ticket handy since you'll need it to get out of the turnstile at your destination. You may use the RER like the Métro—with the exact same Métro ticket—when traveling within Paris. Other tickets are needed when going beyond the city limits. Be careful here.

Here is a list of RER lines and some of their routes:

RER A1	Saint-Germain-en-Laye	RER C3	Argenteuil
RER A2	Boissy Saint Léger	RER C4	Dourdan La Forêt
RER A3	Cergy le Haut	RER C5	Versailles Rive Gauche
RER A4	Chessy–Marne La Vallée	RER C6	Saint-Martin d'Étampes
RER A5	Poissy	RER C7	Saint Quentin-en-Yvelines
RER B2	Robinson	RER C8	Versailles-Chantiers
RER B3	Roissy–Aéroport Charles de Gaulle	RER D1	Orry-la-Ville-Coye
		RER D2	Melun
RER B4	Saint-Rémy–lès-Chevreuse	RER D4	Malesherbes
RER B5	Mitry-Claye	RER E1	Haussmann Saint-Lazare
RER C1	Pontoise	RER E2	Chelles Gournay
RER C2	Massy-Palaiseau	RER E4	Tournan

BUSES

IT TAKES A WHILE TO GET THE HANG OF THE BUSES and where they go. The great advantage to hopping on a bus is that you're above ground and can take in the scenery while you get where you're going.

Try using the public bus as an unofficial tour bus. There is nothing quite as glorious as sitting in the back of a city bus, unhurried, unlike the commuters, and watching the city—all included in the price of your single ticket or Paris Visite. The buses run on a kind of honor system. When you get on flash your *carte* at the driver or scan it past the machine. If you are using Métro ticket T+, you must insert one in the validation machine located in the aisle. The machine validates your ticket and spits it back out, and you should keep it until you get off. Note that the same ticket can be used on more than one bus or tram on the same day, but not in the Métro. You may be asked to show it to *contrôleurs,* who periodically make spot-checks on buses. If you have a Paris Visite, do not insert it in the machine. You can download the Paris bus plan from **ratp.fr.**

Suggested Bus Routes

BALABUS On Sundays and public holidays from early April through September, the RATP offers a sightseeing line from 12:30 to 8 p.m. The bus runs between La Défense and the Gare de Lyon and costs a total of three Métro tickets if you stay on for the whole journey.

MONTMARTROBUS One of the new generation of electric buses, this daily service runs between Pigalle up and over the hill of Montmartre to the 18th arrondissement town hall.

#63 We suggest catching this bus at Boulevard Saint-Michel and riding it west past the Musée d'Orsay, the National Assembly, Les Invalides, and the view of the Louvre and Trocadéro. It then passes near the Eiffel Tower, where you should get off before it crosses Pont de l'Alma. When you're finished here, take the same #63 bus back in the other direction. The eastward route follows boulevard Saint-Germain past the chic Saint-Germain-des-Prés area, complete with galleries, shops, and the celebrated Café de Flore, Brasserie Lipp, and Les Deux Magots, and continues past the Carrefour de l'Odéon. Hop off at the Roman ruins of Cluny just after you cross boulevard Saint-Michel, not far from where you got on.

#82 This starts at Luxembourg Gardens, swings around the park to Montparnasse, then continues on past Les Invalides and École Militaire. The bus then passes under the Eiffel Tower, climbs up to Trocadéro, and continues out to Neuilly, ending at the famous Hôpital Américain.

#85 Start at Luxembourg Gardens, heading north toward the Seine. The bus will follow boulevard Saint-Michel past the famous fountain, across the Seine, and past the golden gates of the Palais de Justice and Notre-Dame Cathedral on its way to the dead center of Paris, Châtelet. From here it veers west past the Louvre before turning right and heading toward Pigalle and Montmartre.

Many Parisian buses run until midnight, although some less frequented routes stop running around 9 p.m. and do not run on Sundays. During the day most buses run every five to ten minutes. You can verify the schedules in the bus shelters along the routes.

Night Buses

For night owls who can't find a taxi, it's good to know that there is a comprehensive network of 42 night buses, called the **Noctilien** (marked by a letter N on a white background), that leave the center of the city and follow the major arteries out to the edges of Paris in every direction. This keeps late-night party hounds from becoming stranded. There are also two circular routes that link four of the main stations plus numerous nightspots such as Les Champs-Élysées,

Saint-Germain-des-Prés, Bastille, and Pigalle. The other radial routes operate from Gare Saint Lazare, Gare de l'Est, Châtelet, Gare de Lyon, and Gare Montparnasse. The service operates from 12:30 a.m. until about 5:30 a.m. at a frequency of anything from ten minutes to one hour, depending on the route and day of the week. All the usual RATP tickets are valid on this service, including the Paris Visite. Full information and the bus plan can be downloaded at **noctilien.fr.**

Batobus

Traveling on the Seine is scenic but slow. The RATP offers an affiliated boat service called the Batobus, which is a shuttle running from February through December, with eight stops departing every 15 to 30 minutes between the Eiffel Tower and the Hôtel de Ville. It does not take Métro tickets, nor can you use your Paris Visite here, but it does offer an all-day pass for €12 (half-price for children), allowing you to get on and off as often as you wish. For other Seine tours, refer to Part Six, Sightseeing, Tours, and Attractions.

Boarding points are found at:

- Tour Eiffel (Métro: Bir-Hakeim [Line 6]; RER: Champ de Mars [Line C])
- Musée d'Orsay (Métro: Solférino [Line 12]; RER: Musée d'Orsay [Line C])
- Saint-Germain-des-Prés (Métro: Saint-Germain-des-Prés [Line 4])
- Notre-Dame (Métro: Cité [Line 4]; RER: Saint Michel [Lines B and C])
- Jardin des Plantes (Métro: Gare d'Austerlitz [Lines 7 or 10]; RER: Austerlitz [Line C])
- Hôtel de Ville (Métro: Hôtel de Ville [Lines 1 or 11])
- Louvre (Métro: Palais Royal-Musée du Louvre [Lines 1 or 7])
- Champs-Élysées (Métro: Champs-Élysées–Clémenceau [Lines 1 or 13])

For more information, call ☎ 08 25 01 01 01 or visit **batobus.com.**

VOGUÉO

ANOTHER RIVER SHUTTLE BEGAN OPERATING in 2008 aimed at commuters traveling east of the city. It serves five stops upriver from Gare d'Austerlitz. Boats depart every 15 to 30 minutes daily and a ticket for a single journey costs €3. Visit **vogueo.fr.**

TAXIS

ALTHOUGH PARIS HAS ONE of the world's best subway systems, savvy visitors to the French capital need to master the ins and outs of *les taxis parisiens.* Taxis tend to be taxis, you're thinking, right? Well, almost. The quality of service is very uneven. You may have charming encounters with perfectly honest taxi drivers, or you may experience real grouches, or worse, the ones that "take you for a ride." The best protection is knowing where you're going and being alert.

If you're used to the frenzy of Manhattan and the competitive scuffs related to hailing cabs, chill out. In Paris, one rarely hails, whistles, flails at, or hustles cabs. Taxis are found at well-marked taxi stands scattered throughout the city. In fact, it is illegal for taxis to pick you up on the street if you're within at least 50 meters of an official taxi stand. Occasionally, you'll be able to jump into one in traffic, but this is a no-no and offenders risk heavy fines. So you've been warned.

Your other option is to call a taxi, and here you have a number of choices. If you're staying somewhere other than in a hotel where taxis usually line up and you use taxis regularly, it's wise and economical to note the telephone number of your nearest taxi stand. Why? Because in Paris the meter starts turning the moment you call, not the moment you hop into the backseat! When calling one of the citywide taxi companies, **Taxis Bleus** (☎ 08 91 70 10 10) or G7 (☎ 01 47 39 47 39) for

unofficial **TIP**
If the meter reads an exaggerated sum when your taxi arrives, you are completely within your rights to refuse the taxi altogether and not pay.

example, the dispatcher sends his or her closest available vehicle, but be prepared to find up to €8 already on the meter before the journey begins. Although this seems obnoxious, don't complain. *C'est comme ça ici* (That's how it's done here).

Paris has more than 16,000 taxis on its streets, and drivers are strictly regulated by the police. You'll notice a small digital counter on the back ledge of each vehicle indicating how many hours this driver has been behind the wheel. Parisian taxis by law cannot drive more than ten hours a day. There are few moonlighters.

Meters start at €2.10 during the day (10 a.m.–5 p.m.) and are calibrated on a base hourly rate of about €26, this rate is called Tarif A. *Naturellement,* the night rate, Tarif B (5 p.m.–10 a.m. and all day Sunday and public holidays), costs about €29 per hour. And Tarif C kicks in when you cross the *périphérique* (Paris's beltway) and venture into the near suburbs as well as from midnight Saturday until 7 a.m. Sunday morning in Paris. The *périphérique* itself, however, is still considered part of Paris, so don't let your driver click the meter onto Tarif C too soon (an old trick).

unofficial **TIP**
Call 01 45 30 30 30 to be put through to the nearest taxi rank; the driver who answers will come to collect you.

A taxi with a white "TAXI" light on is available; if darkened, there's a passenger on board or the driver is en route to one. You'll also notice on the dome of all taxis three small colored lights, marked A, B, and C. When lit these indicate that there is a fare en route and the tariff is being applied. When taxis are off duty, drivers strap a funky black-leather corset over the lights. Note that you'll never convince a Paris taxi driver to take you when he's off duty, and if his shift is almost over and you're not going his way, there is a good chance he'll turn you away. *Très parisien ça!*

If you climb in at an airport, expect a supplement. Any luggage, bikes, skis, and packages that are either oversized or weigh more than 5 kilos (12 pounds) also cost €1 after the first item. All charges and supplements are clearly noted on the inside passenger window in French and English for easy verification. *Note:* Since the taxi driver's strike in 2000, the minimum fare (even to go one block) is €5.60.

In general, you may not climb into a taxi with a dog (other than a guide dog), but don't be alarmed to find a bored-looking schnauzer curled up on the passenger's seat next to the driver.

Some of the larger taxi fleets accept Visa and MasterCard; almost none accept checks, and forget about using U.S. cash anywhere in Paris. As for tipping, taxi drivers don't view this as an obligation, so the rule is to add on what you feel like. Two or three euros to or from either airport is fine, and a few coins following a short Paris jaunt is perfectly acceptable. Don't overdo it. Note, though, that the *fisc* (French tax authority) automatically adds on 7 percent more than a driver's declared meter receipts. So a 7 percent tip simply covers costs. A 10 percent tip is always adequate and appreciated.

The real pleasure of Paris taxis, though, is the wide range of opinions, pop philosophy, and local commentary on French politics and Parisian life that many of Paris's animated chauffeurs provide free of charge.

TRAIN PASSES AND RESERVATIONS

IF YOU ARE CERTAIN YOU'LL BE STAYING ONLY in or around Paris, you won't need to concern yourself with train passes or advance reservations. If you change your mind while you're in Paris, you can always buy a round-trip train ticket at some travel agencies or at a French Railways (SNCF) train station or boutique. If you are over 60 years old, you'll be eligible for reduced fares on the condition that you obtain a **Carte Senior,** which you can get for €56 when buying your tickets in Paris. For SNCF information and reservations, call ☎ 36 35 (€0.34 per minute) or visit the Web site at **voyages-sncf.com.**

If you plan on using the Paris public-transportation system and making short, day excursions from Paris, you can deal with your ground transportation when you arrive. If, however, you plan to visit London, Brussels, Florence, Barcelona, Amsterdam, or other European cities on the same trip, you'll want to look into buying a Eurail train pass before you leave the United States.

The **Eurail Regional Pass** (starting at $79) allows for three to eight days rail travel in France plus one neighboring country during any one-month period. The **Eurail Select Pass** ($445–$639) allows for unlimited travel on any 5, 6, 8, 10, or 15 days within a two-month period, using the rail networks of 3, 4, or 5 adjoining Eurail countries. Finally, their **Global Pass** allows travel through a total of 21 Eurail countries. All adult passes entitle passengers to first-class travel, there is a Saver Pass offering a 15 percent discount for groups of 2 or more as well as a reduced Youth Pass for those under age 26. Children ages 4 to 11 travel at half price and children under 4 ride free. You can read about all these options and order tickets at **eurail.com.**

If you're considering a few days in the south of France, Normandy, Brittany, the Loire Valley, or the Alps, or a side trip to Brussels, Amsterdam, Barcelona, or Milan, for example, and you'd like to pre-arrange your travel schedule, you can consult the SNCF Web site or visit the Rail Europe Group Web site at **raileurope.com.**

RENTING *a* CAR

IF YOU ARE FLYING INTO PARIS and staying there, don't even think about renting a car. Even if you plan on taking side trips from Paris, you do not necessarily want or need a car. If, however, you plan on picking up a rental car in Paris and driving, for example, to the south of France or the Alps, you might consider taking the train to your destination and arranging to pick up your car there. The SNCF has a program with Avis for car rental pickups at many French train stations. If you are holding discounted train tickets, you are entitled to discounts at Avis, too. Additionally, if you arrive when the Avis office is closed, a local SNCF staff member will have been entrusted with the contract and keys of the vehicle for you. For details, visit the SNCF at **voyages-sncf. com** or Avis at **avis.com,** or call Avis in France at ☎ 08 20 05 05 05 or in the United States at ☎ 800-230-4849. If you want your car in Paris, consult a city map and arrange for your pickup at a location closest to your hotel. If you're staying in central Paris and you plan on driving south, avoid picking up a car at Roissy–Charles de Gaulle Airport, which is 30 miles to the north. The French carmaker Renault has a "Eurodrive" two-week rental or purchase program with 36 pickups and drop-offs all over Europe. In the United States call ☎ 888-532-1221 for details and prices, or check out **renault-eurodrive.com.**

unofficial **TIP**
If you're already in Paris and decide that you want to rent a car for a few days, it's better to make an international call back to a car-rental company in the United States to reserve your car for a Paris pickup—usually at one of the train stations (not the airports). You will benefit from the U.S. rates. There's no need to mention that you're already in Paris. You can access 800 numbers from France, but they will not be toll free. Replace 800 with 880.

RENTAL-CAR CONTACT INFORMATION IN THE UNITED STATES		
Alamo	☎ 877-222-9075	alamo.com
Avis	☎ 800-230-4849	avis.com
AutoEurope	☎ 888-223-5555	autoeurope.com
Budget	☎ 800-527-0700	budget.com
Dollar	☎ 800-800-3665	dollar.com
Hertz	☎ 800-654-3001	hertz.com
National	☎ 877-222-9058	nationalcar.com
Sixt	☎ 888-749-8227	e-sixt.com
Thrifty	☎ 800-847-4389	thrifty.com

If you do rent a car, make sure you reserve it before leaving home. North American rates are substantially lower than those offered in France for the exact same vehicle. To get an idea of prices and special offers, start with the international rental companies. Ask for a discount and see what they offer. Don't forget to pick up frequent-flyer miles, too. Then try some of the smaller or more economical companies such as Ada and AutoEurope.

Here are a few of the leading car-rental companies in Paris. They all have multiple pickup points. Call the company to inquire which location is closest to your hotel.

ADA ☎ 08 25 16 91 69   Autorent ☎ 01 45 54 22 45

Avis ☎ 08 20 05 05 05   Budget ☎ 08 25 00 35 64

Europcar ☎ 08 25 35 83 58   Hertz ☎ 08 25 00 11 85

Online travel sites offering car-rental deals with a Paris pickup include the following. You may find that the negotiated rates obtainable through one of these operators are less than what you are quoted directly from a car-rental company. It never hurts to give it a try. We like working with **france.com,** but explore a bit on your own for the best deals.

ebookers.com   **liligo.com**

webcarhire.com   **france.com**

sidestep.com

A TIP ABOUT PRICE QUOTES

HERE'S ONE DETAIL TO LOOK OUT FOR. You should be quoted prices with the sales tax included, and if you're booking from home, you'll be quoted in U.S. dollars. When you go to pay with your credit card in Paris, you may find that the French value-added tax (VAT) of 19.6 percent has been tacked on to the sum you expected to pay. Make sure that you request that the sales tax (VAT) is included on your reservation voucher.

CHAUFFEURED TOURING

INSTEAD OF RENTING A CAR, you can rent an English-speaking driver and guide if you're willing to pay for this lovely luxury. You can stay within Paris or make an excursion out of the city. Rates start at about €240 per half-day. You avoid the driving hassles, the gasoline prices, the insurance, the parking, and the stress, and you get your own guide and chauffeur included. To make a reservation, contact:

Baron's Limousine Service ☎ 01 45 30 21 21; **barons-limousines.com**

Executive Car ☎ 01 42 65 54 20; **executive-car.com**

Prestige ☎ 01 40 43 92 92; **prestige-limousines.fr**

PART SIX

SIGHTSEEING, TOURS, *and* ATTRACTIONS

PLANNING *for* PARIS TOURING

MANAGING YOUR TIME WILL BE YOUR GREATEST CHALLENGE while visiting Paris. There is so much you'll want to see and do in this city that you'll be forced to determine your own priorities and make some hard choices. We'll attempt to help you structure your days and nights, and we'll offer some time-tested suggestions and options.

OPENING AND CLOSING TIMES

YOU SHOULD KNOW FROM THE START that some smaller stores, retail businesses, and banks that are open on Saturdays are closed on Mondays. "Closed" in French is *fermé* (fair-**may**); "open" is *ouvert* (oow-**vair**). Almost all the public museums are closed on Tuesdays, so plan accordingly, and if necessary, call ahead.

Banks, businesses, and big stores usually open at 9:30 a.m. (remember that 9:30 a.m. is written in French as 9.30h, *h* meaning *heures* [hours]), and many close at lunch time for an hour or two—but usually not before 12:30 p.m. There is no set rule for this. Banks shut down at 4:30 p.m. (1630h) or 5 p.m. (17h), but businesses are usually open until 6 p.m. (18h), with retail shops and stores staying open until 7 p.m. (19h). Bread stores and other food-related shops stay open even later. Boutiques may open as late as 11 a.m. Although French law traditionally required most businesses to be closed on Sundays, this has loosened up over the last few years. A number of boutiques, especially in the Marais and Châtelet areas, remain open now on Sundays. Street markets are also open, and even the Monoprix remain open half days on Sunday. Don't expect too many 24-hour convenience stores in Paris. Sundays are great days, though, for museum visits, strolls in parks, rides on the Seine, and window-shopping. Many restaurants are closed on Sunday nights.

When the Lights Go Out

Paris's monuments, fountains, and facades glitter in the evenings, thanks to a municipal lighting system. But when do those lights go out? During winter months, the monuments and fountains stay lit until midnight during the week and on Saturday, and until 1 a.m. daily in the summer.

PLANNING VISITS OF THREE, FIVE, AND SEVEN DAYS

STATISTICALLY, MOST TRAVELERS TO PARIS STAY for a week or less. Of course, some stay longer, and if you're lucky enough to spend ten days or two weeks in the French capital, you'll be able to pace yourself differently. We've offered some flexible itineraries for the three-day, five-day, and seven-day visit. Pace is everything. If you do not give yourself enough time to savor what you are seeing—to wander, revel, mill around, and stroll—you will miss much of Paris's charm. You can't accomplish everything in a few tightly packed days, but you can see a lot, and the emotional strength of the experience can be powerful and indelible.

Here's a laundry list of *must* places to visit and the minimum time needed. Even if time is limited, try to get a taste of each of the following. These sites are discussed in detail in this chapter.

NOTRE-DAME CATHEDRAL Outside, inside, and if possible, a climb to the top; one hour.

SAINTE-CHAPELLE AND THE CONCIERGERIE At least a half hour.

EIFFEL TOWER Stand under it, then go up to the top; 90 minutes.

ARC DE TRIOMPHE Stand in front of it, then go up to the top; one hour.

THE LOUVRE Walk through the Cour Napoléon, enter the museum, and select a wing or two to visit; half a day.

MUSÉE D'ORSAY Study the facade from across the river; spend at least two hours inside.

ORANGERIE Reopened in 2006 after six years of renovation work, it is now home to Monet's *Water Lilies* series; 45 minutes.

PLACE DE LA CONCORDE Drive around in a taxi a few times. The mixture of lights and sculpture at night is nothing short of inspiring. Also stand at the foot of the obelisk where Marie Antoinette was guillotined; 15 minutes.

ÎLE SAINT-LOUIS Walk across the island along rue Saint-Louis en l'île and walk back either way along the quay; one hour.

LATIN QUARTER Deserves a daytime stroll and a late-night stroll with a café break and wine stop; one hour each.

MONTMARTRE Climb up to the Place du Tertre, visit the Sacré Cœur Basilica, rest on the steps, and take in the view, day or night. If you have the time and energy, walk down the hill; otherwise take the funicular; 90 minutes.

MONTPARNASSE CAFÉS A glass of wine or a bowl of onion soup at La Coupole or Le Dôme will do it, preferably at night; one hour.

BASTILLE Drive around the place by taxi. Walk down rue de la Roquette and the narrow rue de Lappe; stop for drinks, dinner, music, dancing; from one hour to the whole evening.

TROCADÉRO The view at night from the terrace is a must; minimum 15 minutes.

LUXEMBOURG GARDENS A leisurely stroll in the late afternoon or anytime on Sunday affords you both solace and a taste of timeless leisure, Paris-style. Sit on a wrought-iron chair and rest; one hour.

RODIN MUSEUM You can get a delightful taste of the genius of this sculptor in an hour; a walk through the sculpture gardens is a must.

POMPIDOU CENTER This mecca of contemporary culture and architecture should be seen. If you don't visit one of the exhibitions, at least take the escalators to the top for the view of central Paris. Hang out on the immense square in front and witness the impromptu carnival of counterculture, street music, and showmanship; one hour.

PLACE DES VOSGES A stroll under the vaulted arcade past Victor Hugo's house represents only 30 minutes of well-spent time.

PÈRE-LACHAISE CEMETERY If you can visit only one cemetery in Paris, let it be this one. Studded with two centuries of cultural luminaries and original ambience; 90 minutes. Add 30 minutes if you want to be with Jim Morrison for a while.

LA VILLETTE An impressive expanse of diverse buildings and activities located on the northeastern edge of the city. Some of the most interesting and innovative exhibitions of art and contemporary themes are staged here. It's also the site of the Cité des Sciences museum and the Cité de la Musique, where a constant flow of high-quality concerts are given. Great area for kids; give yourself a good two hours.

PALAIS DE VERSAILLES Out of town, but easy to get to by RER. Crowds can be intense, but a visit to the palace and a brisk walk in the gardens will be memorable; half a day with travel time.

Below are suggested time-based itineraries for getting in the essential sights. Remember that much of the pleasure of being in Paris is just walking around; leave time for that. Note that each day includes meals in two restaurants (consult the list of profiled restaurants in Part Seven for specific recommendations).

Touring Paris in Three Days

DAY 1 Visit Notre-Dame, Sainte-Chapelle, and Île Saint-Louis, walk through the Latin Quarter, and stroll through the Luxembourg

Gardens and the Saint-Germain-des-Prés area. See the Eiffel Tower at night.

DAY 2 Explore the Louvre, the Tuileries, and Châtelet-Les Halles; do a bit of shopping (window- or otherwise); and visit the Pompidou Center, Pont Neuf, Place de la Concorde, Champs-Élysées, and the Arc de Triomphe. Visit Montmartre at night.

DAY 3 See the Marais and the Place des Vosges, do some shopping in the Marais, spend some quiet time at the Père Lachaise cemetery, and cap off the day with a boat ride on the Seine. Visit the Bastille area at night.

Touring Paris in Five Days

Follow the three-day itinerary above and continue with:

DAY 4 Visit the Musée d'Orsay and/or the Rodin Museum, then see Les Invalides and do some shopping. Explore Montparnasse at night.

DAY 5 Spend time at the Picasso Museum and window-shop in the Place des Victoires area. Visit the theater or opera at night.

Touring Paris in Seven Days

Follow the three- and five-day itineraries above and continue with:

DAY 6 Have fun hunting for treasures in the Flea Market or La Villette, and visit the Catacombs, the Panthéon, and the Place de la Contrescarpe (rue Mouffetard). Enjoy a concert or the theater at night.

DAY 7 Take a half-day side trip to Versailles. Visit the bridges of Paris, and return to your favorite Parisian spots to say goodbye.

TOURS *and* GUIDES

CITY TOURS

IF YOU'D LIKE TO GET A QUICK OVERVIEW OF THE CITY, you may opt for a mass-market, two-hour coach tour in a huge, modern bus that swings by many of the essential Paris sights. There are several large companies that provide this round-the-clock service, including **Paris Vision** and **Cityrama,** a division of the Gray Lines. They seem to be busy, so either people like them or they don't know better. We do not advise taking a tour with 50 or more tourists of mixed nationalities in which the guided narration is either prerecorded or multilingual; there is no better way to become bored than hearing the condensed history of Notre-Dame Cathedral squeezed into English, German, Japanese, *and* Italian.

There are some high-quality options available, however, and they provide you with a good overview of the city. Specialized Paris minivan tours are ideal for getting a deeper view of different aspects of Paris society and history.

PARIS TRIP A variety of minibus tours for small groups ranging from €50 per person for a three-hour city tour to €332 for a half-day tour of Paris, a visit to Versailles, and a Moulin Rouge dinner and dance show. ☎ 01 56 79 05 23; **paris-trip.com.**

PARIS VISION A two-hour tour of the city; €41 adult fare and €21 children under 12. ☎ 01 42 60 30 01; **parisvision.com.**

Other City Tours

IXAIR See Paris from a different perspective. For €239 per person, you can take a 50-minute helicopter tour over Paris and Versailles with a stop at the Abbaye de Chaalis north of Paris. ☎ 01 30 08 80 80; **ixair.fr.**

PARIS L'OPEN TOUR A more flexible option, this service allows you to get on and off the bus when and where you please. Prices vary, but a typical one-day ticket is €29 for adults or €25 with a Paris Visite Pass; €15 for children ages 4 to 11. ☎ 01 42 66 56 56; **parislopentour.com.**

4 ROUES SOUS 1 PARAPLUIE For a novel tour of Paris, this company offers excursions in their fleet of 25 Citroen 2CV cars. From €19 per person for a 30-minute tour of the Champs-Élysées. ☎ 08 00 80 06 31 (toll-free in France); **4roues-sous-1parapluie.com.**

RIVER TOURS
Bateaux Mouches

Bateaux Mouches is the name of the most famous Seine riverboat-trip company, but it has also become the generic name for all Seine River excursion tours. There are a number of such companies offering river rides on a variety of large and small boats at comparable prices. With a carrying capacity of 21,000 passengers a day, the celebrated Bateaux Mouches gives the impression of being the "mastodon" of the river cruises, and you can be assured of finding a seat on board one of its 14 boats. Although it may seem a tacky thing to do, there's nothing quite like viewing the city from the Seine. We especially love cruising the Seine at night, when the strong beams of light stroke the 17th-century facades of the buildings on both banks of the river. Cruise duration: 1 hour and 10 minutes.

There are lunch and dinner cruises available, but they are pricey, and besides, who wants to look at a shrimp cocktail when passing the illuminated Louvre? We like cruising the Seine without the distraction of eating. Daily departures are every 45 minutes by day and every 20 minutes in the evening. Boarding point: Pont de l'Alma (Métro: Alma-Marceau; RER: Pont de l'Alma). For more information: ☎ 01 42 25 96 10 or see **bateaux-mouches.fr.**

Bateaux Parisiens (Seine Tours)

This company has a fleet of twelve vessels, including three trimarans with a capacity of 580 passengers, and more than 50 years of experience on the Seine. Guided tours in English of riverside monuments, the Eiffel Tower, Notre-Dame, and Parisian history and architecture.

Boats leave every 30 minutes during high season. Boarding points: Tour Eiffel trip, Port de la Bourdonnais (Métro: Trocadéro), year-round; Notre-Dame Cruise, quai de Montebello (Métro: Saint-Michel), from March to November only. For more information: ☎ 08 25 01 01 01 or visit **bateauxparisiens.com.**

Canauxrama (Canal Tours)

A romantic evening cruise along the canal of Saint-Martin, with an explanation of Paris's historical canal-lock system and its monuments. Cruises run from June to September and last two and a half hours. Departures leave from Bassin de la Villette (5 bis, quai de la Loire, 75019 Paris; Métro: Jaurès) at 6 p.m. and from Port de l'Arsenal (50, boulevard de la Bastille, 75012 Paris; Métro: Bastille) at 9 p.m. For more information: ☎ 01 42 39 15 00 or visit **canauxrama.com.**

BIKING AND WALKING TOURS

PARIS HISTORIQUE (ASSOCIATION FOR THE SAFEGUARD OF HISTORICAL PARIS) Walking tours of the historical districts of Paris, including the Père Lachaise Cemetery. Tours are in French, but an English-speaking guide can be arranged on request. Visit its offices at 44, rue François Miron, 75004, or its Web site **paris-historique.org,** for details of tours and pricing, or call ☎ 01 48 87 74 31.

FAT TIRE BIKE TOURS This is a fun way of visiting Paris, day or night, rain or shine, in English, bikes included! Count on around €26 for a four-hour daytime tour, including bike. Tours run year-round at 11 a.m. and 3 p.m. from April to October. The meeting point is the south leg (*pilier sud*) of the Eiffel Tower; look for their yellow sign. Forget buses, taxis, and vans—this is the way to see the city. The company also offers tours on those enticing Segway vehicles, walking tours (see below), trips to the D-Day beaches, and wine tastings. Visit **fattirebiketours paris.com** for details, or call ☎ 01 56 58 10 54.

unofficial **TIP**
Fat Tire Bike Tours operates its own English-speaking tourist office complete with Internet access, English satellite television, digital-camera services, refreshments, and even free luggage storage. It is located at 24, rue Edgar Faure, 75015, about a 10-minute walk from the Eiffel Tower.

CLASSIC WALKS A sister company of Fat Tire Bike Tours, this company offers guided walking tours of Montmartre and the Latin Quarter, as well as themed tours such as walks on World War II and the French Revolution, and a very popular *Da Vinci Code* tour. Call ☎ 01 56 58 10 54 or visit **classicwalksparis.com.**

PARIS À VÉLO A different way of seeing the city, with themes like Unusual Paris, Paris by Night, and, for the truly courageous, the 6 a.m. Dawn Paris. A three-hour tour costs €34. Call ☎ 01 48 87 60 01 or visit **parisvelosympa.com.**

PARIS WALKING TOURS A small company that offers a variety of walking tours (such as Hemingway's Paris, The French Revolution, and *Da Vinci Code* walks), day excursions, and museum visits in English to Anglophones living in Paris, their visitors, French people who like to see Paris in English from an Anglo-Saxon point of view, and other travelers who are clever enough to find them. Their guides are mostly Brits and Americans who live in Paris and know the city well, and the tours are informative and fun. Tours generally last for two hours and cost €12. Reservations are necessary for the more popular tours. For details call ☎ 01 48 09 21 40, or visit **paris-walks.com.**

POCKETVOX For the independent traveler looking for a more spontaneous form of tour, Pocketvox offers audio tour guides that you can download before you leave home. Visit **pocketvox.com** to view their selection of 13 audio guides of Paris. Each narration lasts about 90 minutes and costs €5.

CONTEXT TOURS For the traveler who wants a deeper cultural or intellectual experience while walking the city, Paul Bremmer's Context Tours is the Cadillac of the genre. Paul, an acclaimed writer on architecture, began his service of professor- and specialist-led walking tours in Rome before bringing the service to Paris in 2006. Context offers 15 distinct tours per week and includes painting workshops, culinary tours, and its classic Chocolate Walk. Prices vary; call ☎ 01 72 81 36 35, or visit **paris.contexttravel.com** for more details.

SUGGESTED WALKING ITINERARIES

Tour 1—Les Passages de Paris: Grands Boulevards

Take the Métro to the Grands Boulevards stop. Walk down rue Montmartre, heading south toward the Seine. Just before you get to rue Saint-Marc, you'll find an entranceway at number 11 to the **Passages des Panoramas.** Here you'll find a collection of cluttered boutiques, stamp shops, print shops, clothing stores, and *salons de thé* (tearooms, where you drink tea and eat cakes). Turn to your right and follow the passage out to boulevard Montmartre. Cross the street and enter **Passage Jouffroy** at number 10–12. Observe the tile motifs and the metalwork structure of the arcade. Here you'll find old bookshops, toy stores, the entrance to the **Hôtel Chopin,** and the main attraction, the **Musée Grévin,** Paris's celebrated wax museum. After making a quick left and a right turn, you'll follow the passageway to rue de la Grange Batelière. Cross the street and enter **Passage Verdeau** at number 6. Far less commercial, this arcade is a prime example of

unofficial **TIP**
Lunch at Chartier, 7, rue du Faubourg Montmartre, is a perfect way to conclude (or begin) this itinerary.

the architectural ideas of the mid-1800s. Lovers of old cameras and photos should check out **Photo Verdeau** at number 14. **Bonheur des Dames** at number 8 is perfect for needlepoint enthusiasts.

Exit on rue du Faubourg Montmartre, turn right, and continue back to boulevard Montmartre. Turn right, and at rue Richelieu cross the street. At number 97–99 you'll find the entrance to **Passage des Princes,** opened in 1860 on the authority of the city planner Haussmann. This was Paris's last covered arcade. Admire the décor, the lamps, and the wrought iron. Exit on boulevard des Italiens.

Tour 2—Les Passages de Paris: Étienne-Marcel Area

Take the Métro to Étienne-Marcel. Follow rue de Turbigo past rue Saint-Denis, and just before reaching boulevard Sébastopol, turn left at rue de Palestro. At number 3, on your left you'll find the entrance to **Passage Bourg-l'Abbé.** Don't confuse it with rue Bourg-l'Abbé, which was added afterward. Directly across the street, at 145, you'll find the beginning of the narrow **Passage du Grand-Cerf,** the tallest of all Paris arcades. Continue through the Place Goldoni and conclude on the busy and lively rue Montorgueil, a perfect spot for lunch. On the far side of Montorgueil, between rue Mandar and rue Léopold-Bellan, you'll find **Passage Ben-Aïad,** formerly Passage du Saumon. Built in 1828 at the peak of arcade construction, today this passageway is run-down and ill-kept, but it still gives visitors a good hint of the era. Take rue Mondar and at number 8 turn right, into the arcade. The passage continues on the other side of rue Bachaumont, so don't give up too quickly. Continue along the passage.

*un*official **TIP**
You'll end this tour in the heart of "immigrant" Paris, and the arcade is a busy thoroughfare of Turkish, Pakistani, and Indian restaurants, import-exporters, spice shops, and cut-rate merchandise.

You'll end up on rue Bellan. Turn left and then right on rue Montmartre, followed by a quick right on rue d'Aboukir. At the corner of rue du Caire enter the labyrinth-like **Passage du Caire** (Cairo) and enjoy a Middle Eastern Paris that you won't experience elsewhere. Cluttered with cut-rate clothes shops and sweatshops, it is in a state of dilapidation that masks the underlying handsomeness of Paris's largest arcade. But it's lots of fun to slum here. Exit on rue Saint-Denis and cross the street. At number 212 you'll find the mouth of **Passage du Ponceau,** an arcade that is dark and somber but worth a peek. At the far end, turn around and return to rue Saint-Denis. Turn right and follow it through the impressive arches at Porte Saint-Denis. On the other side of the arch, veer to turn right and enter **Passage du Prado** at 16, boulevard Saint-Denis. You'll find a lively right angle filled with wholesale clothes and barber shops. Exit on rue du Faubourg Saint-Denis, turn right, and continue to **Passage Brady** at number 46. Here you'll find yourself briefly in a wholly different Paris, filled with the spices and colors of India and Pakistan.

Tour 3—Les Passages de Paris: Louvre Area

Start at the Métro Louvre and walk north up rue du Louvre. In front of the round building, the Bourse du Commerce, at a little square, take a sharp left onto rue Jean-Jacques Rousseau. At number 19 you'll find the entrance to the lovely **Galerie Véro-Dodat,** built in 1826 in a neoclassical style. Note the black-and-white tiled flooring, the brass work, gold molding, and etched-glass facades. Visit the art galleries and antique shops. Stop in at the **Café de l'Époque** for a *café crème*.

Exit onto rue Croix-des-Petits-Champs and turn right. At the very elegant Place des Victoires, turn left on rue des Petits-Champs. On your right, at number 4, enter the exquisite **Galerie Vivienne,** the most beautiful of Paris's arcades. Stroll across the mosaic floor and take in the details of the arches, the lamps, and the windows until you reach the rotunda and its Empire décor. The tea shop **A Priori-Thé** is a perfect excuse to stop for a pot of Earl Grey. Fans of antique books will need more time.

unofficial **TIP**
Capping off your stroll with dinner at the nearby brasserie Le Colbert would be an excellent choice.

Turn left for a few steps and duck back into the same building at number 4. Here is the **Galerie Colbert,** the "sister enemy" of the Galerie Vivienne. It was built in 1826 to compete with the beauty and popularity of its neighbor. Soon you'll find yourself under a large rotunda, a stunning stained-glass dome. Exit to your right back to rue des Petits-Champs.

From here you can either cross the street and stroll in the **Jardin du Palais Royal** or turn right and track down **Passage de Choiseul** at number 40. The entrance to the famous theater **Bouffes-Parisiens** is found here.

EXPLORING POINTS *of* INTEREST

ANGLO-AMERICANS IN PARIS

THE ATTRACTION OF PARIS FOR AMERICANS is as old as the nation itself. Here is a partial list of leading American writers, artists, explorers, musicians, and politicians who have lived in Paris, followed by at least one of their Paris addresses. This can make for a fun self-crafted walking tour in itself. The best way to find these addresses is to print the detailed street map found at **pagesjaunes.fr** or **viamichelin.com.**

GETTING THE BEST VIEW: MICRO AND MACRO

THE DEEPEST LEVEL OF BEAUTY in the Parisian cityscape is in the details—the facades of buildings, the gold leaf, the grillwork, the sculpted window frames and ornate doorways, the gargoyles, the fountains, the design of the Métro entrances, and even the style of the old park gates, tree enclosures, sewer grates, park benches, and wrought-iron trash bins. That's the beauty of the city on a small-scale level. It takes a bit of discipline for enthusiastic tourists eager to take everything in to slow down and look around some. Don't rush. Digesting the little things is as valid a way to see Paris as is quick, broad-sweeping gallivanting around the city to all the major sights.

The big picture, of course, affords visitors a unique sensation of largesse and splendor. To get a panoramic view of the city you have to be elevated. Paris has only one skyscraper, fortunately, but nevertheless there are several ways of seeing Paris from above:

- **Eiffel Tower** Advantage: exciting going up
- **Tour Montparnasse** Advantage: highest point in Paris
- **Pompidou Center** Advantage: great view of Paris rooftops
- **Galeries Lafayette** (roof) Advantage: great break from shopping
- **Institut du Monde Arabe** (terrace) Advantage: unique view of Seine and Notre-Dame
- **Grande Arche de La Défense** Advantage: dramatic perspective of Paris axis
- **Ballon Air de Paris** Advantage: Views from a hot-air balloon in André Citroën Park (see Parks later in this chapter)

LITERARY AND ARTISTIC LANDMARKS

PARIS IS STUDDED WITH COMMEMORATIVE PLAQUES marking where writers, artists, and musicians lived, worked, and died. Often the house is not marked at all. There is no better way to feel connected to history than stumbling upon Gertrude Stein's apartment or passing by the very spot where Molière made his first appearance as an actor (at 12, rue Mazarine).

Bookstores

Paris is a joy for book-lovers. One of the most pleasant ways of passing time in the French capital is to *flâner* (stroll aimlessly) from *bouquiniste* to *bouquiniste* (bookseller to bookseller) along the Seine on both banks between Notre-Dame and the Pont-des-Arts. These stalls, owned and run by literary Parisians and brimming with good-quality used books, posters, and vintage postcards, are passed on from generation to generation.

For English-language bookshops, **Shakespeare & Company** at 37, rue de la Bûcherie on the Left Bank in front of Notre-Dame is by far the most colorful. Owner George Whitman, now in his late 90s, still lives above the shop. His daughter, Sylvia, manages the shop and has injected lots of creative energy into the literary landscape, such as Festivalandco, a biennial literary festival. Previous festival themes have been travel writing, memoirs, and biographies; the 2010 Festivalandco is on politics and storytelling. Three floors of great used

ANGLO-AMERICANS IN PARIS

Henry Adams   206, rue de Rivoli (Métro: Tuileries)

John Quincy Adams   97, rue Richelieu (Métro: Richelieu-Drouot)

Louis Armstrong   252, rue du Faubourg Saint-Honoré (Métro: Ternes)

Fred Astaire   10, place de la Concorde (Métro: Concorde)

Josephine Baker   32, rue Richer (Métro: Cadet)

James Baldwin   170, boulevard Saint-Germain (Métro: Saint-Germain-des-Prés)

P. T. Barnum   24, rue de Rivoli (Métro: Saint-Paul-le-Marais)

Sylvia Beach   18, rue de l'Odéon (Métro: Odéon)

Art Buchwald   52, rue Monceau (Métro: Monceau)

William Burroughs   9, rue Gît-le-Cœur (Métro: Saint-Michel)

Alexander Calder   60, boulevard du Montparnasse
(Métro: Montparnasse-Bienvenüe)

James Fenimore Cooper   59, rue Saint-Dominique (Métro: Invalides)

Harry and Caresse Crosby   2, rue Cardinale (Métro: Mabillon)

e. e. cummings   7, rue François (Métro: Alma-Marceau)

John Dos Passos   45, quai de la Tournelle (Métro: Saint-Michel)

Isadora Duncan   25, rue de Mogador (Métro: Trinité)

Thomas Edison   23, quai Conti (Métro: Pont-Neuf)

Dwight D. Eisenhower   133, avenue des Champs-Élysées
(Métro: Charles-de-Gaulle–Étoile)

T. S. Eliot   9, rue de l'Université (Métro: rue du Bac)

Duke Ellington   31, avenue George V (Métro: George V)

William Faulkner   26, rue Servandoni (Métro: Saint-Sulpice)

Lawrence Ferlinghetti   89, rue de Vaugirard (Métro: Saint-Placide)

F. Scott Fitzgerald   14, rue de Tilsitt (Métro: Charles-de-Gaulle–Étoile)

Benjamin Franklin   2, rue de l'Université and 56, rue Jacob
(Métro: Saint-Germain-des-Prés)

George Gershwin   19, avenue Kléber (Métro: Kléber)

books, first editions, and literary finds—this landmark exudes lore and poetry.

For a good dose of what's happening on the literary front in Paris today, a visit to Odile Hellier's **Village Voice Bookshop** at 6, rue Princesse (Métro: Mabillon or Saint-Germain-des-Prés) is in order. Here local writers and the Anglo-American literary community come to hear writers and poets read and to buy their books. The shop has renovated and added lots of new space for its remarkable collection of current titles. Another Anglophone literary bookshop is Brian Spence's **Abbey Bookshop** at 29, rue de la Parcheminerie (Métro:

Nathaniel Hawthorne   164, rue de Rivoli (Métro: Louvre)

William Randolph Hearst   10, place de la Concorde (Métro: Concorde)

Ernest Hemingway   74, rue du Cardinal Lemoine (Métro: Place Monge) and 12, rue de l'Odéon (Métro: Odéon)

Harry Houdini   28, boulevard des Capucines (Métro: Opéra)

Langston Hughes   15, rue Nollet (Métro: La Fourche)

Henry James   13, rue de la Paix (Métro: Opéra)

Thomas Jefferson   30, rue Richelieu (Métro: Palais-Royal) and 11, quai Conti (Métro: Pont-Neuf)

Eugene Jolas   6, rue de Verneuil (Métro: Rue du Bac)

Helen Keller   7, rue de Berri (Métro: George V)

John F. Kennedy   37, quai d'Orsay (Métro: Invalides)

Jack Kerouac   28, rue Saint-André-des-Arts (Métro: Saint-Michel)

Charles Lindbergh   12, avenue d'Iéna (Métro: Iéna)

Henry Miller   24, rue Bonaparte (Métro: Saint-Germain-des-Prés)

George Patton   25, avenue Montaigne (Métro: Franklin Roosevelt)

Ezra Pound   9, rue de Beaune (RER: Musée d'Orsay)

Man Ray   22, rue La Condamine (Métro: La Fourche)

Franklin D. Roosevelt   239, rue Saint-Honoré (Métro: Palais-Royal)

Teddy Roosevelt   Esplanade des Invalides (Métro: Invalides)

Gertrude Stein   27, rue de Fleurus (Métro: Rennes)

John Steinbeck   7, rue de Berri (Métro: George V)

Mark Twain   164, rue de Rivoli (Métro: Palais-Royal)

Edith Wharton   58, rue de Varenne (Métro: Varenne)

James Whistler   5, rue Corneille (Métro: Odéon)

Orville and Wilbur Wright   228, rue de Rivoli (Métro: Tuileries)

Richard Wright   1 bis, rue de Vaugirard (RER: Luxembourg)

Saint-Michel and Cluny), specializing in Canadian literature and offering a steady roster of events. The Right Bank's W. H. Smith at 248, rue de Rivoli (Métro: Concorde) is a large, popular bookshop for new books, guides, newspapers, and magazines. It hosts periodic readings and events as well. **Librairie Galignani,** at 224, rue de Rivoli (Métro: Tuileries) under the arcade in front of the Tuileries, is the oldest English-language bookstore on the continent. Other bookstores include the very lively and friendly **Red Wheelbarrow Bookstore** at 22, rue Saint-Paul in the 4th arrondissement, and **Tea & Tattered Pages** at 24, rue Mayet near Métro Duroc. Note that **Brentano's** on the avenue de l'Opéra closed in June 2009. The expatriate literary and art journal *Frank*, published in Paris since the early 1980s, began publishing for the iPad in 2010 (**readfrank.com**).

Exhibitions and Galleries

For art lovers, Paris will be a feast. Aside from the rich assortment of major and minor museums, the art scene presents lots of opportunities for gallery-hopping. Although the bottom has fallen out of the Paris art market, the number of art galleries and art openings (*vernissages*) (vhere-nee-**sahj**) in Paris defies this. There are primarily three major areas with high concentrations of galleries:

SAINT-GERMAIN-DES-PRÉS Especially the streets between Place de l'Odéon and the Seine. A mixture of avant-garde, established, and established avant-garde.

BASTILLE Between Place de la Bastille and Oberkampf—follow rue de Charonne. More innovative spaces and experimental work.

MIROMESNIL–SAINT-HONORÉ Highly established and renowned galleries showing artists of confirmed reputations and prices.

Your best bet for gallery-hopping is to pick up a copy of Paris's free gallery listings distributed in most galleries and cultural centers. To start out, we suggest a stroll down rue de Seine, rue Dauphine, and rue Guénégaud, followed by a glass of Beaujolais at the famous watering hole for artists and culture-mongers, **La Palette,** situated at the corner of rue de Seine and the tiny rue Jacques Callot.

TAKING CLASSES

AS A SHORT-TERM VISITOR you can hardly sign up for a semester at the Sorbonne, but you might enjoy an afternoon cooking class or a wine-tasting session. Some of you may even be up for a few hours of French conversation. Here are some fine options:

Cooking

Here are two classic choices for Paris visitors interested in spending a bit of time in an apron, learning the techniques of preparing and presenting French recipes. Inquire for specialized lessons in pastry cooking, sugar work, regional cuisine, and more.

LE CORDON BLEU 8, rue Léon Delhomme, 75015; ☎ 01 53 68 22 50; **cordonbleu.edu.** This classic landmark of French culinary education offers a wide array of short- and long-term courses and demonstrations.

RITZ ESCOFFIER ÉCOLE DE GASTRONOMIE FRANÇAISE 38, rue Cambon, 75001; ☎ 01 43 16 30 50. For program information visit **ritzparis. com** or e-mail ecole@ritzparis.com. Upscale and prestigious, the Ritz school has emerged as one of France's top institutions for training foreign visitors in the culinary arts. They offer a Wednesday afternoon class for kids that we highly recommend.

Wine Tasting

O CHATEAU 52, rue de l'Arbre Sec, 75001; ☎ 08 00 80 11 48; **o-chateau.com** for a wide selection of wine tastings in English.

French Lessons

Forcing yourself to actually practice the little bit of French you may know will be much appreciated by Parisians and will do wonders for your speaking confidence.

KONVERSANDO Offers conversation-exchange classes. Call ☎ 01 47 70 21 64 or visit **konversando.fr.**

For a list of other schools, consult **paris-anglo.com** or the advertising handout *FUSAC.*

GETTING TICKETS

FOR OBTAINING TICKETS TO CULTURAL EVENTS, try calling the **Office du Tourisme de Paris** at ☎ 08 92 68 30 00, or visit **en.parisinfo. com** or its offices at 25, rue des Pyramides, 75001. You can also purchase tickets at any of the six FNAC stores or at Virgin Mégastore, or book online at **fnacspectacles.com, virginmegastore.fr,** or France Billet at **paris.francebillet.com.**

PARIS FACADE-SPOTTING

THE BEST PIECE OF ADVICE FOR VISITORS hoping to really see Paris: Look up!

There are a zillion ways of visiting a city as spectacular as the one you're presently in. Perhaps the simplest, and surely one of the most pleasurable, is simply knocking around with no fixed itinerary.

And September—especially September—is sublime for just that. The light in late summer is mellow, the broad-leafed trees along the boulevards cast deep shadows, the air takes on the scent of nostalgia, and the surfaces of Paris buildings are bathed in rich hues. As Parisians hurry back to the craze of *la rentrée* (return from summer holidays) and the hordes of tourists retreat to jobs and schools and busy schedules, you're here, free to loll in a luscious state of linger, to partake in the simple joy of dallying in the capital of style. To be "unrushed" in the midst of urban scurry is a rare brand of luxury for international travelers. So indulge.

In the Paris of your imagination you are not being led around at a furious pace; you are out-of-step and reflective, receptive to emotions. Aesthetics take on new meaning. In truth, the special quality of the place is its unique ability to celebrate your solitude or, for visiting couples or families, that heart-lifting sensation of being two against the world.

In English, the word *facade* implies superficiality and imitation. In the Parisian context, however, when it comes to facades, nothing could be less true. In fact, the outer surfaces of most of Paris's buildings are a veritable feast of substance, thrilling aesthetics, historical references, architectural vision, poetic narration, and passionate attention to detail. The buzz that you get again and again from strolling Paris's boulevards and back alleys comes from the Seurat-like composition of all its stylish touches.

Despite the aesthetics of function and practicality captured in such monumental achievements as the Pompidou Center, the Louvre Pyramide, the Grande Arche at La Défense, and the Bibliothèque Nationale in the 13th arrondissement, the true statement of Parisian buildings is the public display of art in everything.

In the French capital, it's precisely the design and artfulness of the common surfaces, not the magnificent monuments and memorable museums, but the pastiche of quaint little things, that keeps us nourished and visually alert. The cupolas and gargoyles, the trimmed doorways, the stylized arches, the braided cement appliqués and iron railings, the carved banisters, molded-plaster balustrades, sculpted window frames, twirled cornices, ornate grillwork, layered moldings, and carved *pierre de taille* form a collective whole that translates seductively into beauty. Even the gates to the park squares, the wrought-iron trash cans, and the metal grates encircling the trees on the sidewalk reek of design.

unofficial **TIP**
There's an entire Paris waiting to be revealed in the facades of buildings never mentioned in the guidebooks and tours.

The key to enjoying Paris's streets is having nowhere to go and nothing in particular to see. The greatest tip anyone can ever give you on how to indulge in the aesthetic orgy of Parisian street life is to look up, to alter your viewing habits and zoom in on the gilded Art Deco floral touches around the seven-floor apartment buildings on boulevard Haussmann or the 19th-century headquarters of the old French supermarket chain Félix Potin on the corner of rue Réaumur and rue de Palestro, in the fashion designers' and textiles district.

Most *quartiers* in all of Paris's 20 arrondissements lend themselves brilliantly to this act of inspired milling. If you love to take pictures, be sure to take your camera as you facade-spot. We recently gleaned the sidewalks in the 2nd and 3rd arrondissements and were bowled over by the carved visages on the old **Théâtre de la Gaîté** on rue Papin just in front of the lovely Square Émile Chautemps. Nearby, the building at **61–63, rue Réaumur,** at the top of the ill-famed rue Saint-Denis, is surprisingly ornate, covered in Ravier and Jacquier sculptures and a colorful Art Nouveau clock. Along boulevard Saint-Martin, the facade of the **Théâtre de la Renaissance** is by Carrier-Belleuse and houses the very stage where Sarah Bernhardt played the works of Musset and Rostand. Even those who have walked past there a hundred times may have never noticed the ballet of sculpted figures on the west facade.

Walk down boulevard de Sébastopol and wander east into the Marais district, always looking up. The **Maison de Nicolas Flamel** and his wife, Pernelle, located at 51, rue Montmorency, sports its original medieval facade from 1407. Wander rue **des Francs-Bourgeois** past once-private mansions, and take note of the carved doorways and turrets, brass knockers, and iron window-railings, details that dance between baroque, Art Deco, and Neo-Rococo.

When you're tired, stop in a café for a *panaché* (draft beer with lemon soda) or *café noisette* (espresso with a dash of milk), something that only residents know to ask for. Then start off again. Avoid the widest boulevards and wander knowing nothing more than your general direction. Use Métro stations as your only guideposts. **Rue Saint-Dominique** area around rue Cler in the 7th arrondissement is well adapted for such facade-hunting. So are the back streets between Montparnasse and the Luxembourg Gardens in the 6th and 14th arrondissements. Ambitious walkers may opt for the hidden treasures and tucked-away *pavillons* (little houses) in the lesser-known 13th arrondissement between the Métro station Les Gobelins and Denfert-Rochereau. Some find the more proletarian side of the 17th arrondissement around La Fourche and Métro Guy-Môquet exciting to explore. And the elevated **Promenade Plantée** above the Viaduc des Arts, running from La Bastille eastward, affords a startling facade of mammoth neoclassical concrete nudes carved at the top of an otherwise banal building that houses the local police station at street level, just behind the Gare de Lyon on the avenue Daumesnil. The less-visited but perhaps last remaining areas of authentic Parisian neighborhoods are tucked away in the 20th arrondissement around Belleville, Ménilmontant, and Gambetta. The chestnut tree–lined **rue du Jourdain** at Métro Jourdain (not to be confused with boulevard Jourdan) is a delightful spot to check out facades and begin an afternoon of aimless exploration.

Remember that the key to strolling is the absence of purpose. You are not sightseeing. You are not ticking off the monuments that are considered "musts." You are simply looking up, profoundly enjoying the surfaces while those unfortunate others push by with seemingly important things to do.

CULTURAL PARIS

TO COME TO PARIS and not partake in its first-class spread of cultural events is like going to a five-star restaurant and not eating. Plan to eat heartily. Theater, opera, concerts, shows, dance performances, and cinema abound. Here's how to participate.

What's Going On

One of the best ways to find out what's going on in Paris is to call the Office du Tourisme de Paris, at ☎ 08 92 68 30 00. You'll be given the choice of hearing the information in English. Push 2 and wait for an operator to take your call. Alternatively, visit the What's On pages of its Web site at **en.parisinfo.com.**

ABSOLUTELY NECESSARY: THE PARIS MUSEUM PASS

REGARDLESS OF THE LENGTH OF YOUR STAY, we strongly suggest that you purchase one of Paris's greatest inventions for tourists, the Paris Museum Pass, which for one price affords you unlimited entry into more than 60 sites, museums, and monuments, representing a great savings of both money and time.

With the pass, there's no admission charge to pay, no waiting in lines, and no limit to the number of times you can visit any of the museums and monuments listed in their brochure.

The Paris Museum Pass is available for two, four, or six consecutive days.

Advantages to Pass Holders

Free direct entry (no waiting) to the permanent collections (passes do not permit entry to temporary exhibits). Unlimited visits, unlimited validity, and use of pass may begin any time after purchase.

Prices and Options

Paris Museum Pass for 2 days—€32

Paris Museum Pass for 4 days—€48

Paris Museum Pass for 6 days—€64

Admission into most museums and monuments for children under age 18 and for citizens of the 27 EU countries under age 26 is free. Note that the pass does not include entrance into special or temporary exhibitions within the included museums or monuments.

Getting a Pass and How to Use It

Visit the Web site **parismuseumpass.com** to purchase a pass online and for further details on where to obtain one in person. Outlets include the various addresses of the **Office du Tourisme de Paris** throughout the city, the Tourist Information desk in Terminals 1, 2C, 2D, and 2F in Charles de Gaulle Airport, FNAC stores, and all participating museums.

Clearly print your first and last name and the date of first use on the back of your card. (A brochure listing all the details is distributed with the card and can also be downloaded from the Web site.)

TOURING NEIGHBORHOODS

HERE ARE THUMBNAIL SKETCHES of each of the main areas covered in this guide and a list of attractions you'll find in each.

LATIN QUARTER

THE LATIN QUARTER LIES IN THE 5TH AND 6TH arrondissements. Roman expansion covered the Left Bank beginning in the third century; however, the quarter takes its name from the language of scholarship and religion centered around the famous Sorbonne since the 13th century. Several Roman vestiges remain from the second century, most notably the **Thermes de Cluny** (6, place Paul-Painlevé; Métro: Cluny–La Sorbonne) and the **Arena of Lutèce** (49, rue Monge; Métro: Place Monge). The Hôtel de Cluny, Paris's second-oldest residential building, has been the home of the **Musée National du Moyen-Age** (6, place Paul-Painlevé) since 1843. It boasts one of the most important collections of medieval finery, art, and architecture in the world.

The Latin Quarter's reputation as an avant-garde and rebel intellectual community dates from the 1950s and 1960s. It was the location of the first barricades erected by students in May 1968 and also the home of the hottest jazz clubs after World War II, showcasing musicians such as Miles Davis and Thelonius Monk. It has since lost much of its student and avant-garde population to become a high-traffic tourist stop. And as in most of these spots in Paris, prices are often inflated without a corresponding increase in quality.

THE MARAIS

LOVELY, QUAINT, MEDIEVAL, JEWISH, GAY—the Marais is many things to many people. One of the preferred areas of Paris for both visitors and Parisians, the Marais (meaning "swamp" or "marsh") offers wonderful museums, mansions, shops, cafés, galleries, boutiques, and restaurants. Narrow streets teem with people day and night.

CHÂTELET–LES HALLES

THE HEART OF THE CITY, CHÂTELET–LES HALLES is the transportation hub for the Métro and RER. Historically, Les Halles was the central wholesale market for produce, meat, fish, and dairy goods for Paris. Today, the market has been transformed into a lively shopping district and commercial mall. The area is filled with boutiques, restaurants, bars, clubs, and slightly seedy porn shops. At the northern edge of this area, you run into the fashion district, which is bustling with stores and workshops filled with creativity and trend-setting ideas. A major renovation project is planned for the mall and gardens, with work due to commence in 2010.

ÎLE SAINT-LOUIS–ÎLE DE LA CITÉ

UNLIKE ÎLE DE LA CITÉ, Île Saint-Louis was urbanized relatively recently, dating from the 17th century. Developers joined the two islands called Notre-Dame and Île aux Vaches with two bridges and constructed hotels there between 1627 and 1664, giving the island an architectural homogeneity unusual in Paris.

SAINT-GERMAIN-DES-PRÉS

THE LITERARY, PUBLISHING, AND INTELLECTUAL DISTRICT, Saint-Germain-des-Prés today is upmarket and chic. With classy stores and expensive and stylish cafés that come with a load of existential baggage (see the profiles for **Café de Flore** and **Les Deux Magots** in Part Seven)—this area is wonderful for milling around in, shopping, gallery-hopping, and browsing in the many bookshops. The hotels are quaint, but the prices reflect the style, design, and history of the area.

BASTILLE-RÉPUBLIQUE

THE BASTILLE LODGED ITSELF IN HISTORY and the consciousness of the French people in 1789, when six prisoners were freed from its walls, sparking a revolution. Although the prison was quickly broken up and made into jewelry—and even part of the **Pont de la Concorde**—today its name continues to evoke something of the revolutionary spirit. But don't expect any of the quarter's diverse habitués to define this revolutionary spirit in the same fashion.

In other words, there's something here for everyone at all times of the day or night. Check out rue du Faubourg Saint-Antoine for fine furniture, antiques, and lamps. Rue de Lappe and vicinity is still attracting crowds for its dancing and bars, just as it did at the turn of the century. Today there are even cheap tapas and a wide selection of sushi bars, Mediterranean cuisine, and a dozen other styles of restaurants from around the world presented *à la française*. Always *à la française*.

CHAMPS-ÉLYSÉES–CONCORDE

LARGE-SCALE ELEGANCE IS EASY TO SPOT, from the dramatic square at La Concorde—complete with the **Luxor obelisk,** near the spot where Marie Antoinette lost her head—along the Champs-Élysées axis to the **Arc de Triomphe.**

INVALIDES–EIFFEL TOWER

AN ELEGANT AND EXPENSIVE AREA OF PARIS, studded with government buildings, cultural centers, and some consulates. The hotels are generally of high quality, as are the restaurants, although visitors should be prepared to pay high prices. This is not an area for nightlife, but it is very pleasant, and what's missing in street life is made up in the architecture.

MONTPARNASSE

IN 1826 VICTOR HUGO RENTED AN APARTMENT on rue Notre-Dame-des-Champs for the quarter's quiet, rural charm. Several dance halls, such as the Grande Chaumière and La Closerie des Lilas, moved to Montparnasse soon after, along with a growing population of artists and intellectuals. Rousseau (the painter) followed Hugo in 1895. Up to World War I, the École de Paris group of artists that included Modigliani and Foujita, Russian rebels Trotsky and Lenin, Blaise Cendrars, Picasso, Marc Chagall, and Fernand Léger all animated the nightlife along boulevard Montparnasse or at the Carrefour

Vavin in now-famous cafés such as La Rotonde, Le Dôme, and Bal Nègre. The world wars did little to interrupt the artistic energy gathering in this quarter, although they brought new names, such as Miró, Calder, Giacometti, Ernst, Kandinsky, Fitzgerald, Hemingway, Stein, and many others, into the same cafés or new ones such as Le Sélect and La Coupole. Many of these cafés are still around today and still draw contemporary artists and writers from all over the world. Prices are usually somewhat inflated, but the cuisine is consistently good, to say nothing of the real reason we are there: to take in the ambience and history, and picture Fitzgerald getting tipsy or Lenin and Trotsky arguing and pounding red fists on the café's tables.

GRANDS BOULEVARDS

IN THE MID-19TH CENTURY, this was the place to stroll. Today, the area around this continuous beltway of wide busy boulevards is a mixture of bustling commercial life, ethnic Paris, and fascinating passageways affording visitors a glimpse of old Paris. There is lots to discover in this part of town.

MONTMARTRE

MONTMARTRE (HILL OF MARTYRS) GOT ITS NAME after Saint-Denis was decapitated there by the Romans in AD 272. It was outside the Parisian city limits until 1860, and its once-low-cost rent and rural charm attracted artists such as Toulouse-Lautrec, Eric Satie, Picasso, Modigliani, and Apollinaire in the first part of this century. The view from **Sacré Cœur** is particularly impressive at night, as is the excitement nearby in place du Tertre. The least demanding route to the top is from Métro Anvers. Ascend rue Steinkerque and take a left on rue Tardieu until you come to the funicular car that whisks you up to Sacré-Cœur for a Métro ticket.

OUTER ARRONDISSEMENTS

BEYOND THESE LIMITS, PARIS CONTINUES to offer visitors many points of interest. For example, ethnic Paris is at its greatest in the 10th, 13th, 18th, and 20th arrondissements. Don't hesitate to venture to the far edges of the city and beyond.

NEIGHBORHOODS FOR THE ADVENTUROUS

CHINATOWN Paris's largest concentration of residents from China, Hong Kong, Cambodia, Laos, Thailand, and especially Vietnam is located in a slice of the 13th arrondissement beginning at place d'Italie and running between Porte d'Italie and Porte d'Ivry. Here you'll find hundreds of Asian restaurants and a lively offering of Chinese supermarkets dominated by the Tang brothers, the largest importers of Asian goods into France. Take the Métro to place d'Italie and walk down avenue de Choisy all the way to avenue Masséna. Turn left and left again at avenue d'Ivry. There are inexpensive restaurants everywhere. A particularly good one is **Sinorama,** 118, avenue de Choisy (☎ 01 53 82 09 51). Start at Métro Porte de Choisy.

PIGALLE Between place de Clichy and Métro Barbès-Rochechouart on the edge of the 18th and 9th arrondissements, Pigalle, Paris's bawdy quarter, is found. Traditionally bohemian, noted for Toulouse-Lautrec's passion for the **Moulin Rouge** cabaret (still in full force although frequented only by tourists), today's Pigalle is dotted with flashing lights, bustling sex shops and live peep shows, and tacky window displays of leather objects and fluorescent underwear. In the summer, the area is mobbed with out-of-towners and gawking tourists bussed in from Germany, Holland, and the United Kingdom. There is nothing to be afraid of here, although you should keep your valuables securely stowed. The 18th arrondissement between Barbès-Rochechouart and the Métro stop Marcadet-Poissonnière is filled with back streets inhabited by many of Paris's African residents and a host of daunting-looking but absolutely friendly restaurants with local specialties from Senegal, Cameroon, Congo, and Ivory Coast. Start at Métro Pigalle.

BELLEVILLE This former village on the northwest edge of the **Père-Lachaise Cemetery** is today a lively mixture of North African, Eastern European, and Chinese residents, offering a wide range of both seedy and wonderful restaurants and bars. Paris's second Chinatown, Belleville, also offers a healthy assortment of couscous restaurants. Today, as Paris's nightlife, bar scenes, and artistic hangouts creep east (Bastille, Oberkampf, Ménilmontant), Belleville finds itself at the edge of some of the city's most creative funkiness. To get there, take the Métro to the Belleville stop and walk up to Ménilmontant.

BEYOND THE PÉRIPHÉRIQUE Although not too many visitors trek out beyond the city limits, delineated by the *périphérique* beltway, some of the most interesting cultural activities now occur in the nearby urban communities of **Montreuil, Saint-Denis, Bagnolet,** and **Malakoff.**

ATTRACTION PROFILES

PARIS ATTRACTIONS HAVE BEEN SPLIT into two main categories: Museums, Monuments, and Churches; and Parks, Gardens, City Squares, and Cemeteries. For attractions in Paris proper, the heading of each profile indicates the arrondissement where the attraction is found; more-specific information can be found in the maps that accompany this chapter. Following these profiles, you'll find a section describing Paris's picturesque bridges, and then a few suggestions for day trips immediately outside of Paris and environs. Our selection process is based on Paris's most interesting attractions. Additionally, knowing the way travelers travel, we wanted to make sure that each time you pass a building or monument and, quite naturally, ask yourself "What's that?" you'll be able to find the answer in this guidebook.

MUSEUMS, MONUMENTS, AND CHURCHE:

Arc de Triomphe 8th arrondissement

place Charles-de-Gaulle (access via underground passage);
☎ 01 55 37 73 77; arc-de-triomphe.monuments-nationaux.fr;
Métro: Charles-de-Gaulle–Étoile

Type of attraction Roman-style monument to the French armed forces. **Admission** €9 adults, €5.50 young adults (ages 18–25), free for those under age 18 and EU citizens under age 26. **Hours** 10 a.m.–11 p.m. daily, closes at 10:30 p.m. October–March (ticket office closes half an hour before). **When to go** Lunch hour. **Special comments** Less crowded during lunchtime; partial wheelchair access. **Author's rating** ★★★★★. **How much time to allow** 1 hour if you go up.

DESCRIPTION AND COMMENTS You'll never tire of seeing the arch, circling it, approaching it from the different sides, and finally climbing to its roof. Twelve majestic avenues spoke off from this celebrated landmark, forming a star shape and thus giving the bustling intersection its name, Étoile. True to Napoléon's original wishes in 1806, the Arc de Triomphe serves as a dramatic entry point into Paris used to honor and celebrate French military campaigns. Today the arch is the focal point for official parades and ceremonies, including November 11 in remembrance of the unknown soldier laid to rest at the end of World War I. Images of German soldiers marching through the arch and occupying Paris in 1940 still haunt elderly Parisians.

TOURING TIPS Don't try to cross the menacingly dangerous intersection to reach the arch! Take the tunnel found at the top of the Champs-Élysées. On sunny days the view is spectacular! Elderly people, disabled visitors, pregnant women, and children are permitted to take the elevator. Others walk.

OTHER THINGS TO DO NEARBY Stroll the Champs-Élysées.

Baccarat Gallery Museum 16th arrondissement

APPEAL BY AGE	PRESCHOOL –	GRADE SCHOOL –	TEENS ★
YOUNG ADULTS ★★		OVER 30 ★★★	SENIORS ★★★

11, place des États-Unis; ☎ 01 40 22 11 00; baccarat.fr; Métro: Boissière

Type of attraction Museum of the famous maker of glassware and crystal. **Admission** €5.50 adults, €3.50 students under age 26, free for children. **Hours** 10 a.m.–6:30 p.m. (closed Tuesday, Sunday, and public holidays). **When to go** Anytime. **Special comments** Wheelchair access. **Author's rating** ★★. **How much time to allow** 1 hour.

DESCRIPTION AND COMMENTS After a long history on a small, back street in the 10th arrondissement devoted to fine glassware, the Baccarat Museum moved to the much more upscale 16th arrondissement.

continued on page 226

Paris Attractions by Type

ATTRACTION NAME	AUTHOR'S RATING	ARRONDISSEMENT/ LOCATION
CEMETERIES		
Cimetière du Père-Lachaise	★★★★★	11, 20
Cimetière Montparnasse	★★★★	14
Cimetière de Montmartre	★★★½	18
CHÂTEAUX		
Château de Fontainebleau	★★★★	Fontainebleau
Château de Versailles	★★★★	Versailles
Château de Vincennes	★★	Vincennes
CHURCHES		
Cathédrale de Notre-Dame	★★★★	4
Sainte-Chapelle	★★★★	1
La Basilique du Sacré-Cœur	★★★	18
Église Saint-Sulpice	★★★	6
Église Saint-Eustache	★★	1
Église Saint-Germain-des-Prés	★★	6
La Madeleine	★★	8
CITY SQUARES		
Place de la Concorde	★★★★★	8
Places des Vosges	★★★★½	3, 4
Place de Fürstenberg	★★★★	6
Place Vendôme	★★★★	1
Trocadéro	★★★★	16
Place Dauphine	★★★½	1
Place des Victoires	★★★½	1, 2
MONUMENTS		
Arc de Triomphe	★★★★★	8
Les Catacombes	★★★★★	14
La Tour Eiffel	★★★★★	7
Tour Montparnasse 56	★★★★★	15
Champs-Élysées	★★★★	8
La Conciergerie	★★★	1
La Grande Arche la Défense	★★★	La Défense
Mémorial de la Shoah	★★★	4
Mémorial des Martyrs de la Déportation	★★★	4
Palais Royal	★★★	1
Place de la Bastille	★★★	11
Hôtel de Ville	★★	4
La Sorbonne	★★	5

ATTRACTION NAME	AUTHOR'S RATING	ARRONDISSEMENT/ LOCATION
MUSEUMS		
Le Louvre	★★★★★	1
Musée d'Orsay	★★★★★	7
Musée du Quai Branly	★★★★★	7
Centre Georges Pompidou (Musée National d'Art Moderne)	★★★★	4
Cité des Sciences et de l'Industrie	★★★★	19
Galeries Nationales du Grand Palais and Palais de la Découverte	★★★★	8
Musée de l'Orangerie	★★★★	1
Musée Jacquemart-André	★★★★	8
Musée Marmottan-Monet	★★★★	16
Musée National Picasso Paris	★★★★	3
Musée Rodin	★★★★	7
Muséum National d'Histoire Naturelle	★★★★	5
Pinacothèque de Paris	★★★★	8
La Cinémathèque Française— Musée du Cinéma	★★★	12
Galerie des Gobelins	★★★	13
Giverny	★★★	Giverny
Hôtel National des Invalides	★★★	7
Institut du Monde Arabe	★★★	5
Maison de Balzac	★★★	16
Maison Victor Hugo	★★★	4
Musée Carnavalet	★★★	3
Musée Cernuschi	★★★	8
Musée d'Art et d'Histoire du Judaïsme	★★★	3
Musée d'Art Moderne de la Ville de Paris	★★★	16
Musée de la Monnaie	★★★	6
Musée de la Musique	★★★	19
Musée des Arts Décoratifs	★★★	1
Musée du Moyen Age (Thermes de Cluny)	★★★	5
Musée Grévin	★★★	2
Musée National des Arts Asiatiques Guimet	★★★	16
Musée Zadkine	★★★	6
Palais de Chaillot	★★★	16
Palais de la Porte Dorée— Aquarium Tropical	★★★	12
Palais de la Porte Dorée–Cité Nationale de l'Histoire de l'Immigration	★★★	12
Baccarat Gallery Museum	★★	16
Égouts de Paris (sewers)	★★	7
Espace Montmartre–Salvador Dalí	★★	18

Paris Attractions by Type (continued)

ATTRACTION NAME	AUTHOR'S RATING	ARRONDISSEMENT/ LOCATION
MUSEUMS (CONTINUED)		
Musée Cognacq-Jay	★★	4
Musée de la Mode de la Ville de Paris– Palais Galliera	★★	16
Musée de l'Armée	★★	7
Musée Eugène Delacroix	★★	6
Musée Jean Moulin–Mémorial Leclerc	★★	15
Musée Nissim de Camondo	★★	8
Opéra Garnier	★★	9
Le Panthéon	★★	5
PARKS		
Bois de Boulogne	★★★★★	16
Bois de Vincennes	★★★★★	12
Jardin du Luxembourg	★★★★★	6
Jardin d'Acclimatation	★★★★	16

continued from page 223

Nowhere other than here can you admire a crystal evening gown: the Baccarat "chandelier dress." The more functional objects on view include chandeliers, crystal vases, glasses, carafes, and even liquor cabinets. This is luxury nudged beyond excess.

TOURING TIPS You break it, you bought it. Hang on to small children!

OTHER THINGS TO DO NEARBY Treat yourselves to lunch here at the swanky Baccarat Cristal Room Restaurant.

La Basilique du Sacré-Cœur 18th arrondissement

APPEAL BY AGE	PRESCHOOL –	GRADE SCHOOL ★	TEENS ★★★
YOUNG ADULTS ★★★	OVER 30 ★★★		SENIORS ★★★

35, rue du Chevalier-de-la-Barre; ☎ 01 53 41 89 00; sacre-coeur-montmartre.com; Métro: Abbesses

Type of attraction Famous basilica and landmark situated at the top of Montmartre. **Admission** Basilica and crypt, free; dome, €5 per person. **Hours** Basilica, daily, 6 a.m.–10:30 p.m.; dome and the crypt, midday–7 p.m. (6 p.m. in winter) daily. **When to go** Crowded on weekends and in the evenings. **Special comments** Guided tours on request. **Author's rating** ★★★. **How much time to allow** 1 hour.

DESCRIPTION AND COMMENTS Visible on clear days from many corners of Paris, La Basilique du Sacré-Cœur (Basilica of the Sacred Heart), with its

ATTRACTION NAME	AUTHOR'S RATING	ARRONDISSEMENT/ LOCATION
PARKS (CONTINUED)		
Jardin des Plantes	★★★★	5
Parc de la Villette	★★★★	19
Parc des Buttes-Chaumont	★★★★	19
Parc Monceau	★★★★	8, 17
Promenade Plantée and Viaduc des Arts	★★★★	12
Les Tuileries	★★★½	1
Parc André Citroën	★★★	15
Parc de Bagatelle	★★★	16
Parc Montsouris	★★★	14
Trocadéro Aquarium (Cinéaqua)	★★	16
THEME PARKS		
Disneyland Paris	★★★★	Marne-la-Vallée– Chessy
Parc Astérix	★★★★	Plailly

unmistakable white dome, is one of the city's most beautiful sights from both far off and up close. Overlooking the city from the pinnacle of Montmartre, this church was an undertaking of the French government in 1873 at the initiative of Catholic citizens. The church was designed in a Roman-Byzantine style by Paul Abadie, who died before seeing his plans completed. It was not finished until 1914 and is a destination for thousands of pilgrims each year. The stained-glass windows are not the originals—those were destroyed in 1944 during World War II. The inside of the church is kind of gloomy, but you can climb to the dome's peak and exit along a railed area, below which all of Paris can be seen. In the summer, the area in front of Sacré-Cœur and the steps that wind down through Square Willette below are usually cluttered with students, foreign backpackers, local riffraff with beer bottles and guitars, and vendors of cheap African carvings and leatherwork.

After visiting the church, take a spin around the very touristy but nonetheless charming Place du Tertre, celebrated for its now kitschy collection of street artists and caricaturists, postcard vendors, and postcards and cheap reproductions of Toulouse-Lautrec. The square is lined with pleasant but overpriced cafés and crêperies.

TOURING TIPS It gets crowded with tourists on summer nights, but no visit to Paris is complete without a hike up to Sacré-Cœur and Place du Tertre. From Métro Abbesses, take the funicular ride to the top for

continued on page 230

Paris Attractions by Location

1ST ARRONDISSEMENT

Le Louvre | Museum | ★★★★★
Musée de l'Orangerie | Museum | ★★★★
Place Vendôme | City square | ★★★★
Sainte-Chapelle | Collection of stained-glass windows | ★★★★
Place Dauphine | City square | ★★★½
Place des Victoires | City square | ★★★½
Les Tuileries | Park | ★★★½
La Conciergerie | Gothic structure and former prison | ★★★
Musée des Arts Décoratifs | Museum of French decorative arts | ★★★
Palais Royal | Architectural remnant of the French monarchy | ★★★
Église Saint-Eustache | Church | ★★

2ND ARRONDISSEMENT

Place des Victoires | City square | ★★★½
Musée Grévin | Wax museum | ★★★

3RD ARRONDISSEMENT

Places des Vosges | City square | ★★★★½
Musée National Picasso Paris | Museum | ★★★★
Musée Carnavalet | Museum on history of Paris | ★★★
Musée d'Art et d'Histoire du Judaïsme | Museum of Judaica | ★★★

4TH ARRONDISSEMENT

Places des Vosges | City square | ★★★★½
Cathédrale de Notre-Dame | Gothic cathedral | ★★★★
Centre Georges Pompidou (Musée National d'Art Moderne)
   Museum | ★★★★
Maison Victor Hugo | Historic home and museum | ★★★
Mémorial de la Shoah | Holocaust memorial | ★★★
Mémorial des Martyrs de la Déportation | Memorial to French Jews deported to
   Nazi death camps in World War II | ★★★
Hôtel de Ville | Paris's city hall | ★★
Musée Cognacq-Jay | Museum | ★★

5TH ARRONDISSEMENT

Jardin des Plantes | Park and zoo | ★★★★
Muséum National d'Histoire Naturelle | Natural history museum | ★★★★
Institut du Monde Arabe | Museum of Arab culture | ★★★
Musée du Moyen Âge (Thermes du Cluny) | Museum of Paris's Roman past
   ★★★
Le Panthéon | Mausoleum and museum | ★★
La Sorbonne | University | ★★

6TH ARRONDISSEMENT

Jardin du Luxembourg | Park | ★★★★★
Place de Fürstenberg | City square | ★★★★
Église Saint-Sulpice | Church | ★★★
Musée de la Monnaie | Museum of France's national mint | ★★★
Musée Zadkine | Museum | ★★★
Église Saint-Germain-des-Prés | Church | ★★
Musée Eugène Delacroix | Historic home and museum | ★★

7TH ARRONDISSEMENT

Musée d'Orsay | Best collection of Impressionist and Art Nouveau paintings and
    sculptures in the world | ★★★★★
Musée du Quai Branly | Primitive art | ★★★★★
La Tour Eiffel | Monument | ★★★★★
Musée Rodin | Museum | ★★★★
Hôtel National des Invalides | Military museum | ★★★
Égouts de Paris (sewers) | Underground museum | ★★
Musée de l'Armée | Military museum | ★★

8TH ARRONDISSEMENT

Arc de Triomphe | Roman-style monument | ★★★★★
Place de la Concorde | City square | ★★★★★
Champs-Élysées | Famous street | ★★★★
Galeries Nationales du Grand Palais and Palais de la Découverte
    Museum | ★★★★
Musée Jacquemart-André | Sublime private art museum | ★★★★
Parc Monceau | Park | ★★★★
Pinacothèque de Paris | Temporary art exhibitions | ★★★★
Musée Cernuschi | Museum of East Asian art | ★★★
La Madeleine | Church and monument | ★★
Musée Nissim de Camondo | 18th-century mansion and museum | ★★

9TH ARRONDISSEMENT

Opéra Garnier | Opera house and museum | ★★

11TH ARRONDISSEMENT

Cimetière du Père-Lachaise | Cemetery | ★★★★★
Place de la Bastille | Landmark | ★★★

12TH ARRONDISSEMENT

Bois de Vincennes | Park | ★★★★★
Promenade Plantée and Viaduc des Arts | Park | ★★★★ Promenade/
    ★★★½ Viaduc
La Cinémathèque Française–Musée du Cinéma | Museum of cinema | ★★★

ttractions by Location (continued)

ONDISSEMENT (CONTINUED)

Palais de la Porte Dorée–Aquarium Tropical | Aquarium | ★★★
Palais de la Porte Dorée–Cité National de l'Histoire de 'Immigration | History of immigration museum | ★★★

13TH ARRONDISSEMENT

Galerie des Gobelins | Antique tapestries and furniture | ★★★

14TH ARRONDISSEMENT

Les Catacombes | Collection of human bones stored under the city | ★★★★★
Cimetière Montparnasse | Cemetery | ★★★★
Parc Montsouris | Park | ★★★

15TH ARRONDISSEMENT

Tour Montparnasse 56 | Paris's only skyscraper | ★★★★★
Parc André Citroën | Park | ★★★
Musée Jean Moulin-Mémorial Leclerc | World War II memorial | ★★

16TH ARRONDISSEMENT

Bois de Boulogne | Park | ★★★★★
Jardin d'Acclimatation | Educational park | ★★★★
Musée Marmottan-Monet | Museum of impressionists | ★★★★
Trocadéro | Best open space for viewing Eiffel Tower | ★★★★
Maison de Balzac | Historic home and museum | ★★★
Musée d'Art Moderne de la Ville de Paris | Museum of 20th-century art | ★★★
Musée National des Arts Asiatiques Guimet | Museum of Asian art | ★★★
Palais de Chaillot | Museum | ★★★
Parc de Bagatelle | Park | ★★★
Baccarat Gallery Museum | Glassware and crystal museum | ★★

continued from page 227

only one Métro ticket and walk down if you feel up to it. You can also pick up the Montmartrobus at Métro Pigalle.

OTHER THINGS TO DO NEARBY Visit Dalí museum and Montmartre cemetery.

Cathédrale de Notre-Dame 4th arrondissement

APPEAL BY AGE	PRESCHOOL –	GRADE SCHOOL ★★	TEENS ★★★
YOUNG ADULTS ★★★	OVER 30 ★★★★		SENIORS ★★★★

Île de la Cité, 6, parvis Notre-Dame; tower ☎ 01 53 10 07 00;
crypt ☎ 01 55 42 50 10; notredamedeparis.fr;
RER: Saint-Michel–Notre-Dame, Métro: Cité

16TH ARRONDISSEMENT (CONTINUED)

Musée de la Mode de la Ville de Paris–Palais Galliera | Museum of fashion and costume design | ★★

Trocadéro Aquarium **(Cinéaqua)** | Underground audiovisual aquarium | ★★

17TH ARRONDISSEMENT

Parc Monceau | Park | ★★★★

18TH ARRONDISSEMENT

Cimetière de Montmartre | Cemetery | ★★★½

La Basilique du Sacré-Cœur | Basilica | ★★★

Espace Montmartre–Salvador Dalí | Museum | ★★

19TH ARRONDISSEMENT

Cité des Sciences et de l'Industrie | Contemporary museum | ★★★★

Parc de la Villette | Park and exhibition space | ★★★★

Parc des Buttes-Chaumont | Park | ★★★★

Musée de la Musique | Museum of music | ★★★

20TH ARRONDISSEMENT

Cimetière du Père-Lachaise | Cemetery | ★★★★★

DAY TRIPS AND EXCURSIONS

Château de Fontainebleau | Royal residence and gardens | ★★★★

Château de Versailles | Royal residence and gardens | ★★★★

Disneyland Paris | Theme park | ★★★★

Parc Astérix | Theme park | ★★★★

Giverny | Historic home and museum | ★★★

La Grande Arche la Défense | Massive archlike building | ★★★

Château de Vincennes | French château and moat | ★★

Type of attraction The most celebrated Gothic cathedral in the world. **Admission** Free; tower, €8 adults, €5 reduced price, free for those under age 18; Crypt, €4 adults, €3 ages 14–26, free for children age 13 and under. **Hours** Daily, cathedral 8 a.m.–6:45 p.m., and until 7:15 p.m. weekends; tower, April–September, daily, 10 a.m.–6:30 p.m.; October–March, daily, 10 a.m.–5:30 p.m.; extended hours until 11 p.m. weekends during June, July, and August; last tickets sold 45 minutes before closing; crypt, daily (except Monday), 10 a.m.–6 p.m.; last tickets sold 30 minutes before closing. **When to go** Midnight mass on Christmas, during any Sunday service, or for the free organ recitals on Sunday at 4:30 p.m. **Special comments** Crowded during mass but much more spiritual. **Author's rating** ★★★★. **How much time to allow** 1½ hours if you climb to the top; add 30 minutes if you visit the crypt.

continued on page 241

Top Paris Attractions

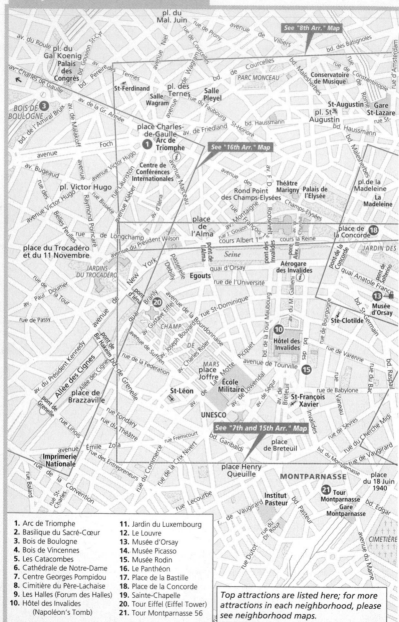

1. Arc de Triomphe
2. Basilique du Sacré-Cœur
3. Bois de Boulogne
4. Bois de Vincennes
5. Les Catacombes
6. Cathédrale de Notre-Dame
7. Centre Georges Pompidou
8. Cimitière du Père-Lachaise
9. Les Halles (Forum des Halles)
10. Hôtel des Invalides
    (Napoléon's Tomb)

11. Jardin du Luxembourg
12. Le Louvre
13. Musée d'Orsay
14. Musée Picasso
15. Musée Rodin
16. Le Panthéon
17. Place de la Bastille
18. Place de la Concorde
19. Sainte-Chapelle
20. Tour Eiffel (Eiffel Tower)
21. Tour Montparnasse 56

Top attractions are listed here; for more attractions in each neighborhood, please see neighborhood maps.

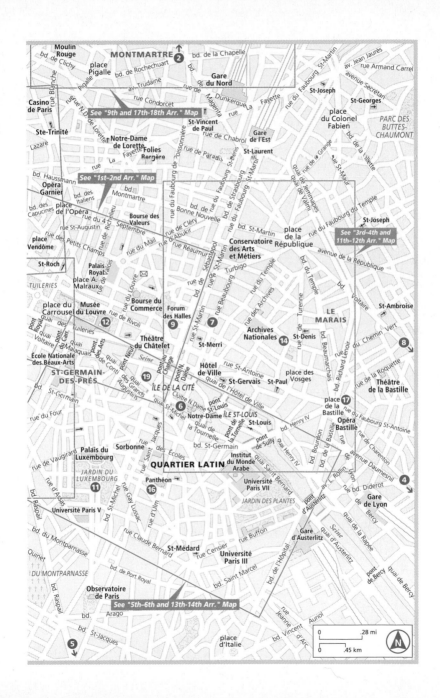

Attractions on the Right Bank (1er and 2e)

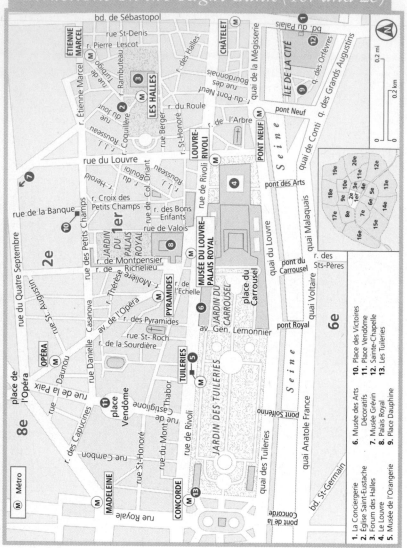

1. La Conciergerie
2. Église Saint-Eustache
3. Forum des Halles
4. Le Louvre
5. Musée de l'Orangerie
6. Musée des Arts Décoratifs
7. Musée Grévin
8. Palais Royal
9. Place Dauphine
10. Place des Victoires
11. Place Vendôme
12. Sainte-Chapelle
13. Les Tuileries

Attractions on the Right Bank (3e, 4e, 11e, and 12e)

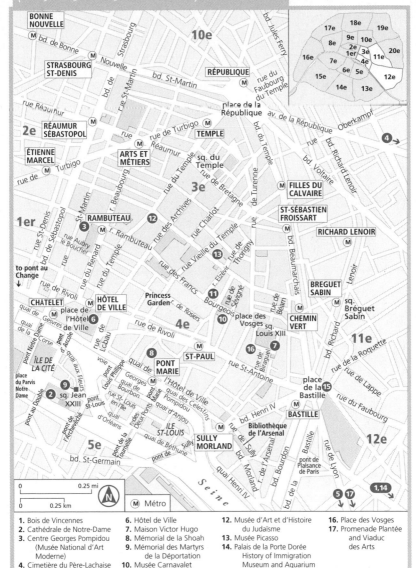

1. Bois de Vincennes
2. Cathédrale de Notre-Dame
3. Centre Georges Pompidou (Musée National d'Art Moderne)
4. Cimetière du Père-Lachaise
5. La Cinémathèque Française
6. Hôtel de Ville
7. Maison Victor Hugo
8. Mémorial de la Shoah
9. Mémorial des Martyrs de la Déportation
10. Musée Carnavalet
11. Musée Cognacq-Jay
12. Musée d'Art et d'Histoire du Judaïsme
13. Musée Picasso
14. Palais de la Porte Dorée History of Immigration Museum and Aquarium
15. Place de la Bastille
16. Place des Vosges
17. Promenade Plantée and Viaduc des Arts

Attractions on the Left Bank (5e, 6e, 13e, and 14e)

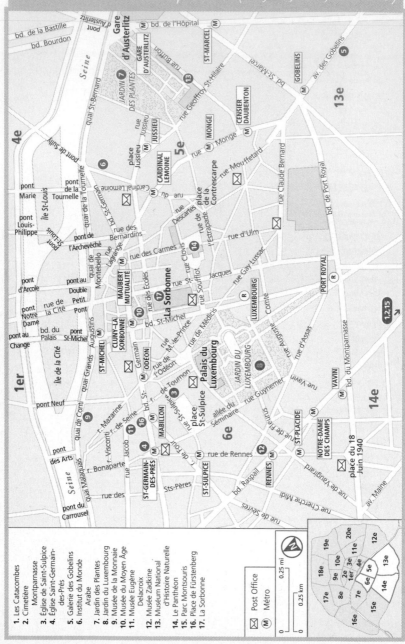

1. Les Catacombes
2. Cimetière Montparnasse
3. Eglise de Saint-Sulpice
4. Eglise Saint-Germain-des-Prés
5. Galerie des Gobelins
6. Institut du Monde Arabe
7. Jardin des Plantes
8. Jardin du Luxembourg
9. Musée de la Monnaie
10. Musée du Moyen Âge
11. Musée Eugène Delacroix
12. Musée Zadkine
13. Museum National d'Histoire Naturelle
14. Le Panthéon
15. Parc Montsouris
16. Place de Fürstenberg
17. La Sorbonne

Attractions on the Left Bank (7e and 15e)

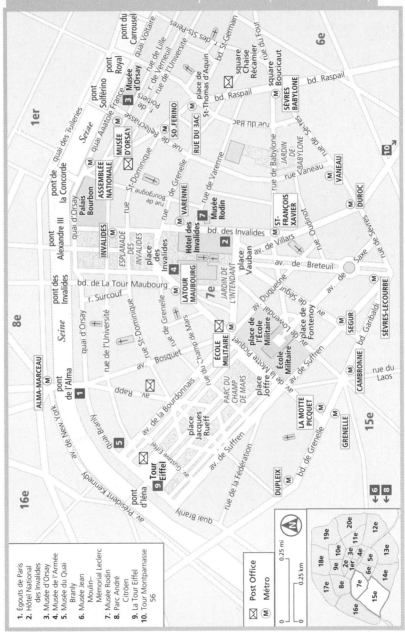

1. Égouts de Paris
2. Hôtel National des Invalides
3. Musée d'Orsay
4. Musée de l'Armée
5. Musée du Quai Branly
6. Musée Jean Moulin–Mémorial Leclerc
7. Musée Rodin
8. Parc André Citröen
9. La Tour Eiffel
10. Tour Montparnasse 56

⊠ Post Office
Ⓜ Métro

0   0.25 mi
0   0.25 km

Attractions on the Right Bank (8e)

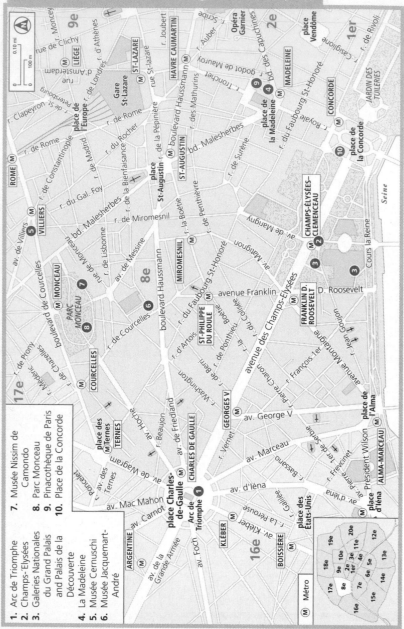

1. Arc de Triomphe
2. Champs-'Elysées
3. Galeries Nationales du Grand Palais and Palais de la Découverte
4. La Madeleine
5. Musée Cernuschi
6. Musée Jacquemart-André
7. Musée Nissim de Camondo
8. Parc Monceau
9. Pinacothèque de Paris
10. Place de la Concorde

Attractions on the Right Bank (9e, 17e, and 18e)

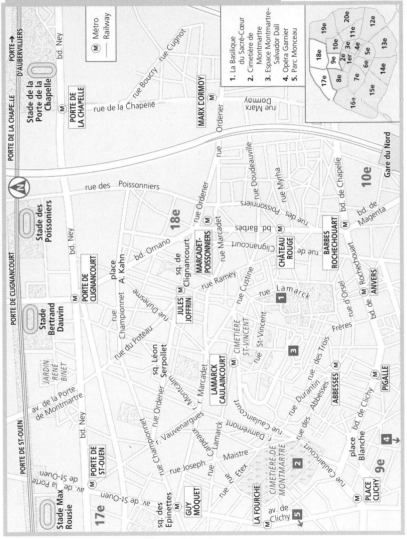

M Métro
— Railway

1. La Basilique du Sacré-Cœur
2. Cimetière de Montmartre
3. Espace Montmartre— Salvador Dalí
4. Opéra Garnier
5. Parc Monceau

Attractions on the Right Bank (16e)

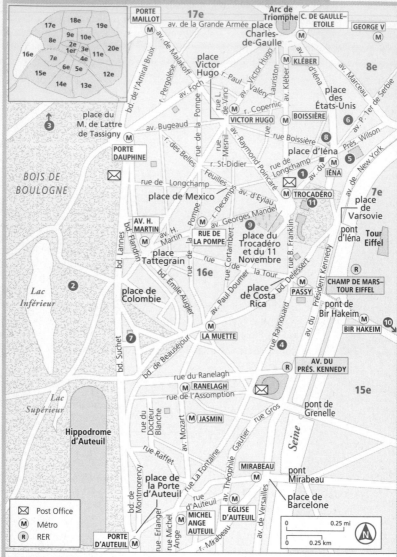

1. Baccarat Gallery Museum
2. Bois de Boulogne
3. Jardin d'Acclimatation
4. Maison de Balzac
5. Musée d'Art Moderne de la Ville de Paris
6. Musée de la Mode de la Ville de Paris—Palais Galliera
7. Musée Marmottan-Monet
8. Musée National des Arts Asiatiques Guimet
9. Palais de Chaillot
10. Parc de Bagatelle
11. Trocadéro and Trocadéro Aquarium

continued from page 231

DESCRIPTION AND COMMENTS Welcome to Kilometer Zero, the reference point for all distances to Paris from anywhere in the country. You'll be quickly reminded of Hugo's Hunchback. Notre-Dame, built on the île de la Cité, Paris's historical birthplace, is France's most celebrated cathedral. Initiated by Bishop Maurice de Sully in 1160, it was not completed until the 14th century. It was constructed on the site of a basilica dating from the 4th century, which was itself built on the site

Notre-Dame de Paris

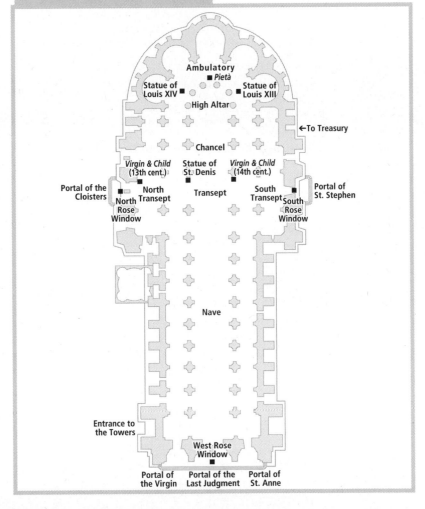

of a Roman temple dedicated to Jupiter. Its Gothic gargoyles, facade, and carved portals make it one of the best examples of the metamorphosis from Romanesque to Gothic style in European architectural history as the original plans for Notre-Dame followed the location's preceding edifices. The first schools in Paris were founded here, under Episcopal control. Before the renovation by Viollet-le-Duc in the 19th century, Notre-Dame had become so dilapidated that animals were sheltered there by nearby inhabitants, something hard to imagine today. You must climb 387 steps to reach the top of Notre-Dame and in addition pay €8. The view is worth it. The last few stairs are wooden, and they take you to the massive bronze bell in the tower. On busy days, the increasingly narrow stone steps cause a bit of claustrophobia.

TOURING TIPS In the summer months, go early to beat the crowds.

OTHER THINGS TO DO NEARBY Hôtel de Ville, Centre Georges Pompidou, Marais, Latin Quarter.

Centre Georges Pompidou   4th arrondissement (Musée National d'Art Moderne)

APPEAL BY AGE	PRESCHOOL –	GRADE SCHOOL ★★	TEENS ★★★★
YOUNG ADULTS ★★★★		OVER 30 ★★★★	SENIORS ★★★★

place Georges Pompidou; ☎ 01 44 78 12 33; centrepompidou.fr; Métro: Châtelet–Les Halles, Rambuteau, Hôtel de Ville

Type of attraction Innovative and lively museum and cultural center. **Admission** 1-day Museum & Exhibition Ticket with access to all current exhibitions, €10–€12 adults, €8–€9 reduced price, free for those under age 18. **Hours** Centre, daily (except Tuesday), 11 a.m.–10 p.m.; Atelier Brancusi, daily, 2–6 p.m.; museum and exhibitions, daily 11 a.m.–9 p.m.; library, Monday–Friday, noon–10 p.m.; Saturday and Sunday, 11 a.m.–10 p.m. **When to go** Avoid the weekends. **Special comments** Disabled access; avoid the queues by purchasing the 1-day Museum & Exhibition Ticket from the Web site. **Author's rating** ★★★★. **How much time to allow** 1–2 hours.

DESCRIPTION AND COMMENTS This highly original landmark perfectly marries function and style. Also known as "Beaubourg" because it is on rue Beaubourg, the Centre National d'Art et de Culture Georges Pompidou is located in the heart of Paris and acts as a major artery between Châtelet–Les Halles and the Marais. Richard Rogers and Renzo Piano designed the controversial structure (is there anything built in Paris in recent times that hasn't been controversial?) in 1977. The colors of its structure represent the internal systems (electricity, water, heat, and so on) of the building. It houses an impressive library, an enormous modern-art collection, research centers, cafés, and a cinema. All of this attracts more tourists and Parisians than any other monument or museum in all of France. The huge cobblestone plaza in front of the center functions as one of Paris's most popular public spaces, encouraging all sorts of pedestrians, street performers, musicians, and shoppers to linger and congregate, making it sort of the people's place.

TOURING TIPS Check for openings. Visit the rooftop veranda for its unique view or soak it in over a drink at the Café Restaurant Georges.

OTHER THINGS TO DO NEARBY Visit Les Halles, the Marais.

Château de Vincennes

APPEAL BY AGE	PRESCHOOL –	GRADE SCHOOL ★★	TEENS ★★
YOUNG ADULTS ★★		OVER 30 ★★	SENIORS ★★

1, avenue de Paris, 94300 Vincennes; ☎ 01 48 08 31 20; chateau-vincennes.fr; Métro: Château de Vincennes

Type of attraction Dramatic French château and moat. **Admission** Tour of the donjon: €7.50 adults, €4.80 students, free for those under age 18. **Hours** Daily, 10 a.m.–6 p.m.; closes at 5 p.m. September–April, tours last between 45 minutes and 1 hour 15 minutes. **When to go** When the weather is good. **Special comments** Combine visit with stroll in the Bois de Vincennes. **Author's rating** ★★. **How much time to allow** 2 hours.

DESCRIPTION AND COMMENTS At the eastern end of Métro Line 1 you come out at the Château de Vincennes, a surprisingly impressive 17th-century château with a moat and dungeon at the edge of the Bois de Vincennes. The 14th-century donjon was recently reopened after 12 years of renovation work. The dungeon with its turret-encased tower was used as the inspiration for *Twenty Years After,* Alexandre Dumas's sequel to *The Three Musketeers.*

TOURING TIPS Wear comfortable shoes.

OTHER THINGS TO DO NEARBY Combine a visit to the château with a picnic or visit to Parc Floral.

Cité des Sciences et de l'Industrie
19th arrondissement

APPEAL BY AGE	PRESCHOOL ★★★★	GRADE SCHOOL ★★★★	TEENS ★★★★
YOUNG ADULTS ★★★★		OVER 30 ★★★★	SENIORS ★★★★

Parc de la Villette, 30, avenue Corentin-Cariou; ☎ 01 40 05 80 00; reservations ☎ 08 92 69 70 72; cite-sciences.fr; Métro: Porte de la Villette

Type of attraction Highly contemporary museum and public space with captivating temporary and permanent exhibitions. **Admission** From €8 adults, €6 reduced rate, depending on combination chosen, free for children under age 2. **Hours** Tuesday–Saturday, 10 a.m.–6 p.m.; Sunday, 10 a.m.–7 p.m. **When to go** Very early or at mealtimes to avoid crowds. **Special comments** Referred to as "La Villette." **Author's rating** ★★★★. **How much time to allow** From 2 hours to a full day.

DESCRIPTION AND COMMENTS If you're traveling with kids, make sure you spend some time at La Villette, located at the edge of Paris's 19th arrondissement. Cité des Sciences et de l'Industrie is part of a complex that occupies the former slaughterhouses of the capital and includes the Musée de la Musique (see profile), the Zénith (a venue for pop and rock concerts), and a futuristic park. There's a full day of activities to choose from. The science museum has lots of hands-on exhibits, a planetarium, a simulator, 3D films, and permanent exhibits devoted to space, language, the environment, and technology. The Cité des Enfants is an interactive science lab for kids (2 to 12 years old); you can sign them up for sessions throughout the day. The Geode, a mirrored globe visible for miles, shows IMAX films, and a restored submarine just outside the museum is a great draw.

TOURING TIPS Get a schedule of activities from the information desk so you can plan your time around the planetarium shows, the inventorium science labs for kids (it's a good idea to reserve a time slot when you first arrive), the Geode films, and other activities.

OTHER THINGS TO DO NEARBY The park is great for picnics or summer naps. A free open-air film festival takes place several evenings a week in summer. Check *Pariscope* or online at **villette.com** for details.

La Cinémathèque Française–Musée du Cinéma
12th arrondissement

APPEAL BY AGE	PRESCHOOL —	GRADE SCHOOL ★	TEENS ★★
YOUNG ADULTS ★★	OVER 30 ★★★		SENIORS ★★★

51, rue de Bercy; ☎ 01 71 19 33 33; cinematheque.fr;
Métro: Bercy

Type of attraction Home to the largest archive of films, movie documents, and film-related objects in the world. **Admission** Cinema, from €6 adults, €3 under age 18; exhibitions, from €5 adults, €2.50 under age 18. **Hours** Sunday 10 a.m.–8 p.m.; Monday and Wednesday–Saturday, midday–7 p.m., with 10 p.m. closing on Thursday. **When to go** Weekdays. **Special comments** Disabled access. **Author's rating ★★★**, if you find that film you've been dying to see. **How much time to allow** Depends on film.

DESCRIPTION AND COMMENTS You must know that this Frank Gehry building began its life as the American Center, which went belly-up in 1996, only 19 months after it opened. The French Ministry of Culture saved this landmark, though, and devoted it to cinema. Paris is a film city, and Parisians take this art form very seriously. If you love cinema, check the schedule here not only for screenings but also *rencontres* with famous directors and actors. This is the real thing.

TOURING TIPS Definitely take the two-hour, behind-the-camera guided tour, which ends with a film showing or presentation of an experimental film.

OTHER THINGS TO DO NEARBY Stroll through Parc de Bercy to Bercy Village or visit Le Train Bleu Art Deco restaurant inside the Gare de Lyon train station.

La Conciergerie 1st arrondissement

APPEAL BY AGE	PRESCHOOL –	GRADE SCHOOL –	TEENS ★★★
YOUNG ADULTS ★★★	OVER 30 ★★★		SENIORS ★★★

**2, boulevard du Palais; ☎ 01 53 40 60 80;
conciergerie.monuments-nationaux.fr; Métro: Cité**

Type of attraction Gothic structure and former prison. **Admission** €7 adults,
€4.50 ages 18–26, free for those under age 18 and EU citizens under age 26;
€11 per person for Conciergerie and Sainte-Chapelle. **Hours** Daily, 9:30 a.m.–
6 p.m, March–October; 9 a.m.–5 p.m. November–February. **When to go** Crowded
during the tourist season. **Special comments** Daily guided tours at 11 a.m. and
3 p.m.; wheelchair access. **Author's rating** ★★★. **How much time to allow** 1 hour.

DESCRIPTION AND COMMENTS La Conciergerie will let you imagine medieval
   times with its 14th-century Gothic architecture and Reign of Terror
   prisons. In 1793 and 1794, more than 2,500 imprisoned men and
   women (including Marie Antoinette) were sent from here to be guillotined at various spots in Paris. It is said that 1,306 heads from La
   Conciergerie rolled in 40 days at Place de la Nation. From the outside,
   you should note the famous Tour de l'Horloge, which boasts the first
   public clock in Paris, built in 1370. It still runs! Inside, don't miss the
   Salle des Gens d'Armes, a masterpiece of Gothic architecture. (Note
   that Gens d'Armes, from which comes today's gendarmes, means
   men-at-arms.)

TOURING TIPS It's pleasant to walk along the upper quais of the Seine outside the Conciergerie.

OTHER THINGS TO DO NEARBY Visit Notre-Dame, Sainte-Chapelle, Saint-
   Michel, and Shakespeare & Co. Bookshop.

Église Saint-Eustache 1st arrondissement

APPEAL BY AGE	PRESCHOOL –	GRADE SCHOOL –	TEENS ★★
YOUNG ADULTS ★★	OVER 30 ★★		SENIORS ★★

**2, impasse Saint-Eustache; ☎ 01 42 36 31 05; st-eustache.org; Métro:
Châtelet–Les Halles**

Type of attraction Major church on the Right Bank with evening concert series.
Admission Free. **Hours** Monday–Friday, 9:30 a.m.–7 p.m.; Saturday, 10 a.m.–
7 p.m.; Sunday, 9 a.m.–7 p.m. **When to go** Anytime. **Special comments** Free
organ recitals on Sunday at 5:30 p.m. **Author's rating** ★★. **How much time to
allow** 30 minutes.

DESCRIPTION AND COMMENTS Best known for the organ and choral music
   recitals of first performances of works by Berlioz and Liszt, this Gothic
   and Renaissance church is worth a short detour when you're in the Les
   Halles area. Started in 1532 with Notre-Dame as the model, Saint-
   Eustace wasn't completed until 1754. Its size and central location have
   contributed to its importance. Cardinal Richelieu was baptized here, as
   was the playwright Molière, whose funeral also graced this church.

Near the front, to the left of the nave, you can spot an early Rubens painting, *The Pilgrims at Emmaüs*.

TOURING TIPS Take a break in the pleasant René Cassin Square in front of the church. Note the huge contemporary sculpture, *Tête*.

OTHER THINGS TO DO NEARBY Visit Forum des Halles, Châtelet, the Montorgueil quarter, the Louvre.

Église Saint-Germain-des-Prés 6th arrondissement

APPEAL BY AGE	PRESCHOOL –	GRADE SCHOOL –	TEENS ★★
YOUNG ADULTS ★★	OVER 30 ★★		SENIORS ★★

3, place Saint-Germain-des-Prés; ☎ 01 55 42 81 33; eglise-sgp.org; Métro: Saint-Germain-des-Prés

Type of attraction Prominent church in the heart of the Left Bank. Admission Free. Hours Daily, 8 a.m.–7 p.m. When to go Crowded at services, but otherwise quiet. Special comments Many classical music concerts are given in this church. The acoustics are only fair but the ambience is magical. Author's rating ★★. How much time to allow 30 minutes.

DESCRIPTION AND COMMENTS At the heart of the Saint-Germain-des-Prés area of the Left Bank lies this impressive abbey, an integral link in the prodigious line of the Benedictine order in Europe. The order produced 24 popes, 200 cardinals, and endless saints! In French, a pré is a field, and it was amid empty fields that the son of Clovis began building his religious shrine. Sacked by the Normans, the church was rebuilt several times over the centuries. The tombs of Descartes and other learned Frenchmen are found here.

TOURING TIPS The former bohemian character of this neighborhood has been supplanted by upscale shops, hotels, and cafés. Intellectual pretensions still prevail, though.

OTHER THINGS TO DO NEARBY Visit the legendary cafés of Saint-Germain—Les Deux Magots, Café de Flore, and Brasserie Lipp—and the Village Voice Bookshop.

Église Saint-Sulpice 6th arrondissement

APPEAL BY AGE	PRESCHOOL –	TEENS –	GRADE SCHOOL –
YOUNG ADULTS ★★	OVER 30 ★★★		SENIORS ★★★★

2, rue Palatine, Place Saint-Sulpice; ☎ 01 42 34 59 98; paroisse-saint-sulpice-paris.org; Métro: Mabillon, Saint-Sulpice

Type of attraction Important Left Bank church with Delacroix murals. Admission Free. Hours Daily, 7:30 a.m.–7:30 p.m. When to go Anytime; guided tours 3 p.m. every Sunday and two Fridays per month. Special comments F. Scott and Zelda Fitzgerald lived next door. Marcello Mastroianni's funeral services were held here. Author's rating ★★★. How much time to allow 30 minutes.

DESCRIPTION AND COMMENTS Aside from being an impressive 17th-century church with a massive antique facade, it draws most visitors with the murals of Delacroix (1849–1861) found inside. It's unlikely you'll be in the church at noon on the day of the winter solstice, but if you are, don't forget to observe the ray of sunlight passing through the tiny hole in the upper window in the south transept as it strikes the designated point on the obelisk in the far transept. A religious experience! Enjoy the central "Fountain of the Four Bishops" in the square outside, erected by Visconti in 1844. After being featured in Dan Brown's *Da Vinci Code,* Saint-Sulpice has experienced a massive increase in visitors—even though the Catholic Church refused permission for scenes to be shot inside Saint-Sulpice.

TOURING TIPS Hang out on the square. Nearby cafés are excellent for spotting stars.

OTHER THINGS TO DO NEARBY Do some shopping on rue Bonaparte, or visit Jardin du Luxembourg.

Égouts de Paris (Sewers) 7th arrondissement

| APPEAL BY AGE | PRESCHOOL – | GRADE SCHOOL ★★★ | TEENS ★★★ |
| YOUNG ADULTS ★★★ | | OVER 30 ★★ | SENIORS ★★ |

Pont de l'Alma opposite 93, quai d'Orsay; ☎ 01 53 68 27 81; RER: Pont de l'Alma

Type of attraction Paris's sewer system is an underground museum. Admission €4.30 adults, €3.30 children ages 6 to 16, free for children under age 6. Hours Saturday–Wednesday, 11 a.m.–5 p.m. (until 4 p.m. October–April); closed two weeks in January. When to go It's never too crowded. Special comments Read the printed descriptions in the exhibit. Author's rating ★★. How much time to allow 1 hour.

DESCRIPTION AND COMMENTS It is fascinating to note that every Paris street address has its equivalent address underground in the Paris sewers and is accessible by footpaths, some of which are lit. The Paris sewers have a celebrated history that goes far beyond the remarkable process in which Paris's water is used, filtered, cleaned, and recycled. The network empties at Archères in the northern suburbs, one of the world's largest water-purification systems. Initially part of Napoléon III's engineering project for the capital, the sewer system today includes more than 1,300 miles of tunnels and underground waterways that can be visited with guides by descending an ominous stairway at the foot of Pont de l'Alma on the Left Bank. The tour is a bit dark and musty, and although the air has been sanitized and deodorized, it's still a little funky. But the network and its historic use during World War II for hiding French resistance fighters excites the imagination. Note, too, the massive pipes for transporting fresh water, electric power, telecommunications lines, and, more recently, fiber-optic cable. An unusual but very interesting and uniquely Parisian attraction.

TIPS Perfect for rainy days.
THINGS TO DO NEARBY See the Eiffel Tower, Les Invalides.

Espace Montmartre–Salvador Dalí 18th arrondissement

APPEAL BY AGE	PRESCHOOL –	GRADE SCHOOL –	TEENS ★★
YOUNG ADULTS ★★	OVER 30 ★★		SENIORS ★★

9–11, rue Poulbot; ☎ 01 42 64 40 10; daliparis.com; Métro: Anvers or Abbesses

Type of attraction Private museum dedicated to the Father of Surrealism. **Admission** €10 adults, €7 seniors and teachers, €6 ages 8–26; free for children under age 8. **Hours** Daily, 10 a.m.–6 p.m. **When to go** Early, just after opening. **Special comments** Bookshop includes full range of Dalí posters and postcards. **Author's rating** ★★. **How much time to allow** 1 hour.

DESCRIPTION AND COMMENTS Just steps from the flourishing tourist trap of Place du Tertre is this small museum, with almost 350 works by the surrealist master Salvador Dalí. Voice recordings of the painter and sculptor play as you wander through the collection. Works by other 20th-century masters such as Picasso and Chagall are exhibited in the Galerie Montmartre.

TOURING TIPS Take a moment to enjoy the marvelous view from the tiny Place du Calvaire just in front of the museum.

OTHER THINGS TO DO NEARBY Mill about Place du Tertre; explore the quieter side streets; enjoy the view at Sacré-Cœur; stop by Saint-Pierre Church.

Galerie des Gobelins 13th arrondissement

APPEAL BY AGE	PRESCHOOL –	GRADE SCHOOL –	TEENS –
YOUNG ADULTS ★	OVER 30 ★★		SENIORS ★★★

42, avenue des Gobelins; ☎ 01 44 08 53 49; mobiliernational.culture.gouv.fr; Métro: Les Gobelins

Type of attraction Collection of antique tapestries and State furniture collection. **Admission** €6 adults, €4 reduced rates, free for children under age 7. **Hours** Tuesday–Sunday, 12:30–6:30 p.m. **When to go** Afternoons. **Special comments** If tapestries are your thing, don't miss this. **Author's rating** ★★★. **How much time to allow** 1 hour.

DESCRIPTION AND COMMENTS Reopened in 2007 after 35 years, the gallery is located at the Manufacture Nationale des Gobelins, the home of France's state weaving company. If this sounds dull, you are mistaken. The newly revealed woven masterpieces include four centuries of France's finest work, including the *tenture d'Artémise,* commissioned by Henry IV.

TOURING TIPS If you're traveling with a digital camera, bring it along and photograph details of tapestry. They make beautiful holiday cards.

OTHER THINGS TO DO NEARBY Picnic in the surprising Roman ruin, the Arènes de Lutèce, on rue Monge.

Galeries Nationales du Grand Palais and
Palais de la Découverte 8th arrondissement

APPEAL BY AGE	PRESCHOOL ★	GRADE SCHOOL ★★★	TEENS ★★★
YOUNG ADULTS ★★★		OVER 30 ★★★	SENIORS ★★★

3, avenue du Général Eisenhower; Galeries du Grand Palais
☎ **01 44 13 17 30; Palais de la Découverte** ☎ **01 56 43 20 21;**
grandpalais.fr and palais-decouverte.fr;
Métro: Champs-Élysées–Clémenceau

Type of attraction Leading museum complex for temporary and permanent exhibits in the realms of art and science. **Admission** Galeries du Grand Palais: Varies according to exhibition, free for children under age 13. Palais de la Découverte: €7 adults, €4.50 under age 18, students, and seniors over age 60. Planetarium €3.50 for all visitors. **Hours** Grand Palais: Thursday–Monday, 10 a.m.–8 p.m. (box office closes at 7:15 p.m.); Wednesday, 10 a.m.–10 p.m. (box office closes at 9:15 p.m.). Palais de la Découverte: Tuesday–Saturday, 9:30 a.m.–6 p.m., Sunday and public holidays, 10 a.m.–7 p.m. **When to go** The Palais de la Découverte is closed Mondays; Grand Palais hours and dates depend on exhibition. **Special comments** For prebookings (at least 48 hours in advance, with a fee of €1.50) go to the Virgin Mégastore (Métro: Franklin Roosevelt), Galeries Lafayette, Bon Marché, BHV, Printemps, or any FNAC store (☎ 08 92 68 46 94; **fnac.com**); often, there are 2 exhibitions happening at once, and you can buy a single ticket for the 2. Wheelchair access. **Author's rating** ★★★★. **How much time to allow** 2 hours.

DESCRIPTION AND COMMENTS This giant iron-and-glass structure, built for the 1900 Universal Exhibition, now has two distinct sections: the Galeries Nationales and the Palais de la Découverte. The first is the venue for blockbuster temporary exhibitions; recent shows have included Picasso and Warhol. It is also one of the venues for the FIAC Art Fair held in Paris every autumn. The second houses a science museum and a planetarium, highly recommended for anyone traveling with children. Note, too, that after extensive renovation work, the vast glass-domed nave of the Grand Palais has reopened to the public and is also used for exhibitions. It is accessible from avenue Winston Churchill.

TOURING TIPS To avoid the long lines for the temporary shows, pre-purchase entry tickets at any of the ticket outlets listed above. Mornings are reserved for ticket-holders; if you haven't managed to book ahead, you can wait in line in the afternoon. The Palais de la Découverte has lost a few visitors since the Cité des Sciences opened at La Villette, but the planetarium and temporary exhibitions make it worth the trip, and kids love it.

OTHER THINGS TO DO NEARBY Dine on the terrace of the Mini Palais restaurant lounge overlooking the glittery Pont Alexandre III, built at the same time as the Grand Palais; wander up Champs-Élysées.

La Grande Arche la Défense

APPEAL BY AGE	PRESCHOOL –	GRADE SCHOOL ★★	TEENS ★★
YOUNG ADULTS ★★★		OVER 30 ★★★	SENIORS ★★★

1, Parvis de la Défense, 92044 La Défense; ☎ 01 49 07 27 13; grandearche.com; Métro: La Défense Grande Arche; RER: La Défense

Type of attraction Massive, archlike building at La Défense marking the western point of the longest urban axis in the world. **Admission** €10 adults, €8.50 children ages 7–18 and students, free for children age 6 and under and disabled visitors. **Hours** Daily, 10 a.m.–8 p.m. April–September; 10 a.m.–7 p.m. October–March. **When to go** The earlier in the day the better. **Special comments** Panoramic view of Paris, exhibitions, bookshop, restaurant, lots of modern sculptures. **Author's rating** ★★★. **How much time to allow** 1 hour if you go to the top.

DESCRIPTION AND COMMENTS The sprawling esplanade in front of La Grande Arche and the steep but wide steps that lead up to it reflect a very different look at Paris. From the arch, you can follow the axis that lines up the Arc de Triomphe, the obelisk at Place de la Concorde, the Pyramide at the Louvre, and extends onward to the column at the Bastille. Eight kilometers of perfect symmetry. La Défense is far from beautiful, but this outcrop of skyscrapers, malls, office towers, and apartments comprises the heart of Paris's contemporary corporate culture.

TOURING TIPS You don't have to go up the Grande Arche to get a feel for La Défense and appreciate the view. But make sure you climb the steps at least in front of the arch.

OTHER THINGS TO DO NEARBY Underground shopping mall accessible from the Esplanade.

Hôtel de Ville 4th arrondissement

APPEAL BY AGE	PRESCHOOL –	GRADE SCHOOL –	TEENS –
YOUNG ADULTS ★★		OVER 30 ★★	SENIORS ★★

place de l'Hôtel de Ville (main public entrance, 29, rue de Rivoli); ☎ 39 75 help desk; ☎ 01 42 76 50 49 to book a visit, one week in advance for individuals and several months ahead for groups; Métro: Hôtel de Ville

Type of attraction Paris's dramatic city hall with public exhibitions. **Admission** Depends on exhibitions. **Hours** Exhibition hours vary; salons by appointment only and subject to official events. **When to go** Exhibitions are rarely crowded; city hall offices are closed to the public. **Special comments** This building acts as the backdrop in the famous black-and-white photograph of a returning French soldier embracing a local lass at the end of World War II. **Author's rating** ★★. **How much time to allow** You can tour the Hôtel de Ville only on the Journée du Patrimoine in September each year, but you can hang out in the vast square in front of the city hall at leisure, day or night.

DESCRIPTION AND COMMENTS Visitors should note that in French the word *hôtel* means mansion or large private building, and that every French town has its *hôtel de ville,* or city hall. Paris's Hôtel de Ville, built between 1874 and 1882 in neo-Renaissance style, offers a stunning facade of nearly 150 statues depicting leaders from French history and celebrated French cities. The ornate Third Republic ballroom and reception areas reflect both Belle Époque and Renaissance décor, but unfortunately, unless you're invited by the mayor or happen to be in Paris on the Journée de la Patrimoine, when public buildings are opened to the public, you have no chance of seeing past the facade. The open square in front of the Hôtel de Ville is a pleasant place to rest. In winter, the area is used to erect a Christmas manger and an ice-skating rink.

TOURING TIPS Use the pedestrian underpass to get across the street separating the Hôtel de Ville and the Seine.

OTHER THINGS TO DO NEARBY Visit the BHV department store, Notre-Dame, Centre Georges Pompidou, the Marais, Île Saint-Louis.

Hôtel National des Invalides 7th arrondissement

APPEAL BY AGE	PRESCHOOL ★	GRADE SCHOOL ★★★	TEENS ★★★
YOUNG ADULTS ★★★		OVER 30 ★★★	SENIORS ★★★

6, boulevard des Invalides; ☎ 01 44 42 37 72; invalides.org; Métro: Latour-Maubourg, Varenne, or Invalides

Type of attraction France's most celebrated complex of military museums, including Napoléon's tomb. Admission Free to visit the grounds; entry to Napoléon's tomb and museum, including an audio guide, €8.50 adults, €6.60 age 25 and under, free for those under age 18 and EU citizens under age 26. Hours Daily, 10 a.m.–6 p.m.; until 9 p.m. on Tuesday (open until 5 p.m. October–March); museum partially closed on Monday; dome open until 7 p.m. July and August. When to go As early as possible; gets crowded in the afternoons. Special comments Some areas may be closed for renovation. Partial wheelchair access. Author's rating ★★★. How much time to allow 2 hours.

DESCRIPTION AND COMMENTS Although Hôtel des Invalides was built by Louis XIV in 1674 as a military hospital for aging veterans, Napoléon's spirit reigns now over this giant homage to French military might. He died in exile, but his nephew, Napoléon III, orchestrated the return of his remains to Paris in 1840 and transformed the crypt to house a grandiose tomb (there are actually six coffins, one inside the other, all placed in a red porphyry sarcophagus). Several other museums are housed in the buildings. The Army Museum is reputed to be one of the best military museums in the world. Be sure to visit the new rooms dedicated to World Wars I and II and the Charles de Gaulle Audiovisual Memorial, inaugurated in 2008. There are often school groups here, and the kids enjoy the old armor and military garb from around the world. Less well known is the Plan and Relief Museum, also a favorite with kids. It houses scale models (some up to 20 feet across) of fortified French towns and harbors, built over the last few centuries to help military leaders plan campaigns and design defense installations.

TOURING TIPS One ticket is valid for Napoléon's tomb, the Army Museum, and the Plan and Relief Museum. This is the place for those interested in all things military.

OTHER THINGS TO DO NEARBY Visit the nearby Rodin Museum or stroll along the Seine.

Institut du Monde Arabe 5th arrondissement

APPEAL BY AGE	PRESCHOOL –	GRADE SCHOOL ★★	TEENS ★★
YOUNG ADULTS ★★★	OVER 30 ★★★		SENIORS ★★★

1, rue de Fossés Saint-Bernard; ☎ 01 40 51 38 38; imarabe.org; Métro: Jussieu

Type of attraction Stunning museum and exhibition center devoted to Arab culture. **Admission** Varies according to exhibitions from €6 adults, €4 under age 25; free for children under age 12. **Hours** Tuesday–Sunday, 10 a.m.–6 p.m. **When to go** Crowded on Sundays. **Special comments** Often long queues for exhibitions. English guided tour available; ask for it when you buy your ticket. **Author's rating ★★★. How much time to allow** 1–2 hours.

DESCRIPTION AND COMMENTS This is a fascinating building, with exhibitions that will open your eyes to regions of the world you may not be familiar with. Not much in English. The ancient cultures and art forms of Islam are married with contemporary architecture and design. There is a lovely rooftop terrace that is often overlooked by visitors. In addition, there's a first-rate but pricey restaurant on the top floor with an exquisite view. The seventh floor hosts a display of art from the 9th to 19th centuries, covering Islamic art, scientific achievements, and ornaments of wood, ivory, bronze, glass, and carpets.

TOURING TIPS Check to see if the current exhibit interests you. Kids don't find this museum too enticing, but a visit to the nearby Jardin des Plantes zoo can be mixed into the same afternoon.

OTHER THINGS TO DO NEARBY See Jardin des Plantes, Musée National d'Histoire Naturelle, La Mosquée, Arènes de Lutèce, and Notre-Dame.

kids Le Louvre 1st arrondissement

APPEAL BY AGE	PRESCHOOL ★★	GRADE SCHOOL ★★★	TEENS ★★★★
YOUNG ADULTS ★★★★★	OVER 30 ★★★★★		SENIORS ★★★★★

99, rue de Rivoli (entrance through Pyramide, Cour Napoléon, or Galerie du Carrousel); ☎ 01 40 20 50 50; recorded information ☎ 01 40 20 53 17; louvre.fr; Métro: Palais-Royal

Type of attraction Arguably the world's most famous museum. **Admission** Permanent collections: €9 adults, €6 adults Wednesday and Friday after 6 p.m., free for children under age 18 and EU citizens under age 26, for everyone on the first Sunday of the month, and the 14th of July; admission to the Hall Napoléon for temporary exhibitions, €11. **Hours** Permanent collections: Monday, Thursday, Saturday, Sunday, 9 a.m.–6 p.m. (box office closes at 5:15 p.m.); Wednesday and Friday, 9 a.m.–10 p.m. (box office closes at 9:15 p.m.); closed on Tuesday. Temporary exhibitions: Hall Napoléon: daily, 9 a.m.–10 p.m. (box office closes at 9:30 p.m.). **When to go** Try to avoid going on Sunday, especially the first Sunday of the month. **Special comments** Audio guides in English (€6); guided tours in English; wheelchair access, post office, lectures, kid's workshops. **Author's rating** ★ ★ ★ ★ ★. **How much time to allow** 4–5 hours.

DESCRIPTION AND COMMENTS The Louvre is definitely a five-star Parisian draw, up there with the Eiffel Tower and the Arc de Triomphe. There's no scenic view but ample material to nourish your spirit and soul. Although I. M. Pei's Pyramid scandalized many people when it was inaugurated in 1989, innovation at the Louvre is nothing new. Indeed, the buildings have pretty much been under construction since the 12th century, when King Philippe-Auguste had a massive fortress constructed to guard the western edge of Paris. Various monarchs added wings, courtyards, and other flourishes, creating the largest royal palace in the world. In 1793 the Musée Central des Arts opened as the precursor to today's Louvre.

The collections are divided into seven departments, housed in three main sections: Sully (in the Cour Carrée), Richelieu (in the wing on the rue de Rivoli side), and Denon (the wing alongside the Seine). Much to the surprise and relief of longtime visitors, the museum has finally managed to create a legible, straightforward map of the collections and departments, available in multiple languages. Pick one up at the central desk under the Pyramid before setting off. Although most people make a beeline for the *Mona Lisa,* we suggest an alternative route: Start with the Sully wing and the foundations of Philippe-Auguste's medieval keep (it's a good way to keep the kids interested as well). This leads to the Louvre's newly restored Egyptian section; with more than 50,000 objects, it's the largest collection of its kind outside of Cairo. From here, you have two choices: the Richelieu wing or the Denon wing. Most people veer off to the latter because it houses the spectacular Greek collection (don't miss the *Winged Victory*) and the Roman and Etruscan antiquities. Upstairs is the best in 16th- and 17th-century Italian painting, especially in the Salle des États, which has the *Mona Lisa,* and a few often-overlooked masterpieces by such painters as Veronese, Titian, and Caravaggio.

Most of the French painting (with the exception of large works) is in the opposite wing (Richelieu), along with the impressive Persian section, the objets d'art (usually deserted), and the Dutch and Flemish artists. Another rarely visited area is the Napoléon III apartments. If you don't have time to go to Versailles, you can get a taste of the gilded royal style in these few rooms.

TOURING TIPS It's helpful to do a bit of preplanning before taking on the

The Louvre

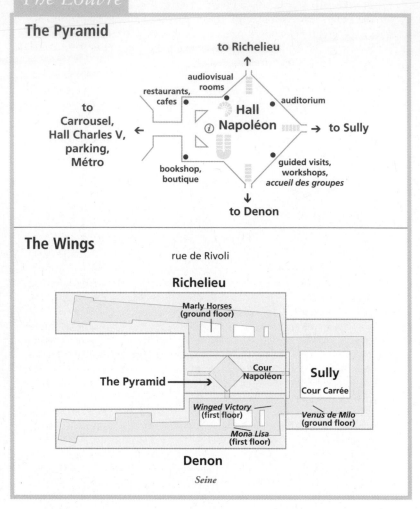

The Pyramid

to Richelieu

audiovisual rooms

restaurants, cafes

Hall Napoléon

auditorium

to Carrousel, Hall Charles V, parking, Métro

ⓘ

to Sully

bookshop, boutique

guided visits, workshops, *accueil des groupes*

to Denon

The Wings

rue de Rivoli

Richelieu

Marly Horses (ground floor)

The Pyramid →

Cour Napoléon

Sully

Cour Carrée

Winged Victory (first floor)

Venus de Milo (ground floor)

Mona Lisa (first floor)

Denon

Seine

largest museum in the world. Select an itinerary that suits your interests (or age group, if traveling with kids). The Louvre can be daunting, so for a first visit, choose just a few works of art or periods. The price drops after 6 p.m. on Wednesday and Friday; this still leaves plenty of time to explore the museum. If the lines are too long at the Pyramide, try the underground entrance through the shopping mall—but the best way to avoid the crowds is to prepurchase a ticket at the FNAC stores or online at **fnac.com** (with a booking fee); the tickets are valid anytime, and you can enter the museum directly through the Richelieu entrance.

OTHER THINGS TO DO NEARBY Have a snack or meal at Café Marly on the courtyard's northern leg—either sit on the terrace facing the Pyramide or inside overlooking the Richelieu wing's sculptures. After exploring the Louvre, walk through the Jardin des Tuileries and collapse into one of the green-metal chairs scattered throughout the park while your kids play with rented sailboats on the pond or you admire other people's kids sailing these adorable toys.

La Madeleine 8th arrondissement

APPEAL BY AGE	PRESCHOOL –	GRADE SCHOOL –	TEENS –
YOUNG ADULTS ★★★	OVER 30 ★★		SENIORS ★★

place de la Madeleine; ☎ 01 44 51 69 00; eglise-lamadeleine.com; Métro: Madeleine

Type of attraction Church and monument whose facade is a Paris icon. **Admission** Free. **Hours** Daily, 9:30 a.m.–7 p.m. **When to go** Anytime. **Special comments** Peering from La Madeleine, you see across the Place de la Concorde and the Seine what looks like the front door of the Assemblée Nationale, an optical effect created to give the impression of an axis between the two. **Author's rating** ★★. **How much time to allow** 20 minutes if you climb the tower.

DESCRIPTION AND COMMENTS This church, dedicated to St. Mary Magdalene, is a major landmark on the Right Bank located near the Place de la Concorde on rue Royale joining Paris's belt of grand boulevards. This Greek temple-like structure was completed in 1842 after many years of construction and Louis XVIII's 1814 orders to turn the temple into a church. Enter the church and climb the steps of the tower for a fine view of the posh rue Royale with its swanky shops, the famous Maxim's restaurant, and the obelisk in the majestic Place de la Concorde beyond.

TOURING TIPS If you go on a Saturday, you may get a glimpse of a society wedding. It is said that Paris's best families marry off their daughters at La Madeleine.

OTHER THINGS TO DO NEARBY Outside the church is a flower market with Paris's most famous gourmet caterers, Fauchon and Hediard, respectively, on opposite sides of the street. Visit the Maille mustard shop for excellent, original gifts. The same-day, half-price theater-ticket counter is located at number 15 on the square. The Pinacothèque de Paris art gallery is at number 28.

Maison de Balzac 16th arrondissement

APPEAL BY AGE	PRESCHOOL –	GRADE SCHOOL –	TEENS ★★
YOUNG ADULTS ★★★	OVER 30 ★★★		SENIORS ★★★

47, rue Raynouard; ☎ 01 55 74 41 80; balzac.paris.fr; Métro: Passy

Type of attraction Balzac's residence, commemorating the writer's life and work. **Admission** Free to the permanent exhibition. **Hours** Tuesday–Sunday,

10 a.m.–6 p.m. **When to go** Never really crowded. **Special comments** This is a good example of a writer's home turned into a museum, as is common in France. **Author's rating** ★★★. **How much time to allow** 1–1½ hours.

DESCRIPTION AND COMMENTS Overwhelmed by debt and pursued by his creditors, Honoré de Balzac moved in October 1840 to this house, where he lived under a pseudonym. The seven years he spent here were incredibly productive; you can see his writing desk, where he penned some of his masterpieces (*Une ténébreuse affaire, Splendeurs et misères des courtisanes*) and corrected the entire manuscript of *La comédie humaine.*

TOURING TIPS Though once considered a boring, bourgeois neighborhood, Passy now boasts many new restaurants and great boutiques.

OTHER THINGS TO DO NEARBY Wander around the nearby streets, or visit Passy Cemetery.

Maison Victor Hugo 4th arrondissement

APPEAL BY AGE	PRESCHOOL –	GRADE SCHOOL –	TEENS –
YOUNG ADULTS ★★★	OVER 30 ★★★		SENIORS ★★★

Hôtel de Rohan-Guéméné, 6, place des Vosges; ☎ 01 42 72 10 16; musee-hugo.paris.fr; Métro: Saint-Paul–Le Marais

Type of attraction Victor Hugo's home turned into a museum to commemorate the writer and his work. **Admission** Free to the permanent exhibition. **Hours** Tuesday–Sunday, 10 a.m.–6 p.m. **When to go** Avoid Sunday afternoons. **Special comments** You can also admire the view of Hôtel de Rohan-Guéméné. **Author's rating** ★★★. **How much time to allow** 1 hour, including a stroll under the arcade in Place des Vosges.

DESCRIPTION AND COMMENTS Victor Hugo spent 16 years, from 1832 to 1848, living and working on the second floor of this elegant house, the largest on Place des Vosges. It was here that he wrote *Les Misérables* and received famous friends, writers, and artists, including Balzac, David, and Dumas. Much of the museum's collection consists of memorabilia, books, and drawings, displayed in reconstructions of the rooms in which he and his family once lived. This is another specialist museum, great for French literature fans; others may want to explore the lovely Place des Vosges.

TOURING TIPS Keep an eye out for the plaques on many of the buildings indicating famous residents or events that occurred in or near Place des Vosges.

OTHER THINGS TO DO NEARBY Explore the Marais or Bastille areas.

Mémorial de la Shoah 4th arrondissement

APPEAL BY AGE	PRESCHOOL –	GRADE SCHOOL –	TEENS –
YOUNG ADULTS ★★★	OVER 30 ★★★		SENIORS ★★★

17, rue Geoffroy l'Asnier, 75004; ☎ 01 42 77 44 72; memorialdelashoah.org; Métro: Saint-Paul, Pont Marie, Hôtel de Ville

Type of attraction Historical monument and museum of particular interest to Jewish visitors. **Admission** Free, free guided tours. **Hours** Daily (except Saturday and public holidays), 10 a.m.–6 p.m.; Thursday open until 10 p.m. **When to go** Quieter in the morning. **Special comments** Wheelchair access. **Author's rating** ★★★. **How much time to allow** Minimum 1 hour.

DESCRIPTION AND COMMENTS A must for those interested in what transpired in France during World War II. Erected on the site of the Memorial to the Unknown Jewish Martyr, this emotional monument and museum bridges the generations who have a living memory of the Holocaust and those too young to remember it. The memorial also serves as a resource and archival center in addition to offering an active calendar of events, including debates, conferences, films, and workshops for children.

TOURING TIPS Although many of the programs are in French, the memorial offers a free guided tour in English at 3 p.m. on the second Sunday of every month to cater to the growing number of English-speaking visitors.

OTHER THINGS TO DO NEARBY Centre Georges Pompidou, Musée Picasso, Place des Vosges.

Mémorial des Martyrs de la Déportation
4th arrondissement

APPEAL BY AGE	PRESCHOOL –	GRADE SCHOOL –	TEENS –
YOUNG ADULTS ★★	OVER 30 ★★★	SENIORS ★★★	

Île de la Cité, Square de l'Île de France; ☎ 01 49 74 34 00; RER: Saint-Michel–Notre-Dame; Métro: Cité

Type of attraction Powerful memorial to Parisians deported to Nazi death camps. **Admission** Free. **Hours** Daily, 10 a.m.–noon, 2–7 p.m. (until 5 p.m. October–March). **When to go** Anytime before sunset. **Special comments** This is a somber reminder of one of the darkest chapters in French and European history. **Author's rating** ★★★. **How much time to allow** 15 minutes.

DESCRIPTION AND COMMENTS After visiting Notre-Dame, take few minutes to experience one of the most somber and moving memorial monuments in the world. At the tip of the Square de l'Île de France on the eastern edge of Île de la Cité, this monument, inaugurated by de Gaulle in 1962, commemorates the thousands of French Jews and resistance fighters deported to the Nazi death camps in the early 1940s. Strangely housed in an underground tunnel lit by candles, on the spot where Napoléon III built the municipal morgue, this tribute is a powerful, moving experience and a strong reminder of the horrors of the German occupation of Paris.

TOURING TIPS A visit to this memorial will sensitize you to the many plaques around town commemorating famous as well as unknown victims of Nazi aggression in Paris.

OTHER THINGS TO DO NEARBY Notre-Dame, Île Saint-Louis, Hôtel de Ville.

Musée Carnavalet   3rd arrondissement

APPEAL BY AGE	PRESCHOOL –	GRADE SCHOOL ★	TEENS ★★
YOUNG ADULTS ★★	OVER 30 ★★★		SENIORS ★★★

Hôtel Carnavalet, 23, rue Sévigné; ☎ 01 44 59 58 58; carnavalet.paris.fr; Métro: Saint-Paul

Type of attraction A comprehensive museum on the history of Paris. **Admission** Free to the permanent exhibition. **Hours** Tuesday–Sunday, 10 a.m.–6 p.m. (last ticket sold at 5:30 p.m.). **When to go** To beat the crowds, avoid weekends. **Special comments** Paris construction continues to unearth new archaeological finds, which are cataloged here. **Author's rating** ★★★. **How much time to allow** 1½ hours.

DESCRIPTION AND COMMENTS It is fitting that the museum devoted to the history of Paris be located in the former home of the Marquise de Sévigné, one of France's most famous chroniclers of day-to-day life in the city. Recently renovated, the museum encompasses two buildings; the collections are displayed chronologically, beginning with objects from Roman times through the present day. There are lots of portraits and objets d'art but most interesting here are the reconstructions of interiors and shop fronts, including Proust's bedroom and an extravagant 20th-century ballroom.

TOURING TIPS An excellent museum for those interested in the history of Paris, especially its architecture and interior design; others may want to explore the streets of the Marais neighborhood instead.

OTHER THINGS TO DO NEARBY Visit Place des Vosges, Musée Picasso, and Musée Cognacq-Jay, or stroll through the Marais area down to rue des Rosiers (Jewish quarter).

Musée Cernuschi   8th arrondissement

APPEAL BY AGE	PRESCHOOL –	GRADE SCHOOL ★★	TEENS ★★
YOUNG ADULTS ★★★	OVER 30 ★★★		SENIORS ★★★

7, avenue Velasquez; ☎ 01 53 96 21 50; cernuschi.paris.fr; Métro: Villiers

Type of attraction Gemlike museum of East Asian art and artifacts. **Admission** Free to permanent exhibitions. **Hours** Tuesday–Sunday, 10 a.m.–6 p.m. **When to go** Rarely very busy. **Special comments** Wheelchair access. **Author's rating** ★★★. **How much time to allow** 1½ hours.

DESCRIPTION AND COMMENTS Few people explore this museum devoted to East Asian art, with work ranging from Neolithic terracottas to 12th-century bronzes and some contemporary Chinese paintings, but it houses one of the most impressive collections of its kind in Europe. Like the nearby Nissim de Camondo, most of the works in this museum were put together by a single collector. Temporary exhibitions are held on the first floor. Recommended for those interested in Asian art. Others may prefer to skip it.

TOURING TIPS Guided tours available.

OTHER THINGS TO DO NEARBY Parc Monceau, Musée Nissim de Camondo.

Musée Cognacq-Jay
4th arrondissement

APPEAL BY AGE	PRESCHOOL –	GRADE SCHOOL –	TEENS ★
YOUNG ADULTS ★★	OVER 30 ★★		SENIORS ★★

Hôtel Denon, 8, rue Elzévir; ☎ 01 40 27 07 21; cognacq-jay.paris.fr;
Métro: Saint-Paul

Type of attraction Jewel of a private art collector's collection. **Admission** Free to permanent exhibitions. **Hours** Tuesday–Sunday, 10 a.m.–6 p.m. (last ticket sold at 5:30 p.m.). **When to go** Anytime. **Author's rating** ★★ **How much time to allow** 1 hour.

DESCRIPTION AND COMMENTS This museum, like the Jacquemart-André, was formed from one couple's personal collection. Louise Jay and her husband, Ernest Cognacq (founder of the Samaritaine department store), bequeathed their collection, which includes 18th-century artworks and objets d'art (paintings by Watteau, Fragonard, and Boucher, for example). It's in a charming old building that art lovers will adore.

TOURING TIPS Coordinate with nearby small attractions and museums.

OTHER THINGS TO DO NEARBY Visit Musée Carnavalet, Place des Vosges, and Jewish Quarter.

Musée d'Art et d'Histoire du Judaïsme
3rd arrondissement

APPEAL BY AGE	PRESCHOOL –	GRADE SCHOOL –	TEENS ★★
YOUNG ADULTS ★★	OVER 30 ★★★		SENIORS ★★★

Hôtel de Saint-Aignan, 71, rue du Temple; ☎ 01 53 01 86 60;
mahj.org; Métro: Hôtel de Ville

Type of attraction Museum of Judaica, religious and historic artifacts. **Admission** Permanent exhibition: €6.80 adults, €4.50 ages 18–26, free for those under age 18; temporary exhibitions: prices vary. **Hours** Monday–Friday, 11 a.m.–6 p.m.; Sunday, 10 a.m.–6 p.m. (last ticket sold at 5:15 p.m.). **When to go** Avoid Sundays. **Special comments** Wheelchair access, bookshop, library, audio guide included in admission price. **Author's rating** ★★★. **How much time to allow** 1 hour.

DESCRIPTION AND COMMENTS The Musée d'Art et d'Histoire du Judaïsme moved to this new headquarters in the Marais in 1998. Created in 1948, the museum has received generous donations from artists, including lithographs by Chagall and drawings by Soutine. The collection also includes religious artifacts and a fascinating room devoted to the architecture of the synagogue, with a rare 18th-century Italian tabernacle.

TOURING TIPS This is a special-interest museum; if you're not passionate about Jewish art and religion, you may prefer to skip this.

OTHER THINGS TO DO NEARBY Explore the Marais area.

Musée d'Art Moderne de la Ville de Paris
16th arrondissement

APPEAL BY AGE	PRESCHOOL –		GRADE SCHOOL ★	TEENS ★★
YOUNG ADULTS ★★★		OVER 30 ★★★		SENIORS ★★★

**11, avenue du Président Wilson; ☎ 01 53 67 40 00; mam.paris.fr;
Métro: Iéna**

Type of attraction The City of Paris's museum of 20th-century art. **Admission**
Free for permanent collection. **Hours** Tuesday–Sunday, 10 a.m.–6 p.m. (last
ticket sold at 5:20 p.m.); closes at 10 p.m. on Thursday for temporary exhibitions
only. **When to go** Early. **Special comments** Bookshop, wheelchair access.
Author's rating ★★★. How much time to allow 1–2 hours.

DESCRIPTION AND COMMENTS The museum's collection represents the major
movements in avant-garde art of the 20th century, including fauvism,
cubism, surrealism, and abstraction. The museum fosters new trends in
contemporary art and writing and organizes regular events. Some of
the most interesting canvasses belong to the Paris School painters.

TOURING TIPS Don't miss Dufy's *Fée Électricité* (*The Good Fairy Electricity*),
which is supposedly the world's largest painting, with 250 panels
depicting the story of civilization from the ancient Greeks to the inven-
tors of modern electricity.

OTHER THINGS TO DO NEARBY Explore the contemporary design space at the
Palais de Tokyo next door, Trocadéro, Musée Guimet, Eiffel Tower.

Musée de la Mode de la Ville de Paris–Palais
Galliera 16th arrondissement

APPEAL BY AGE	PRESCHOOL –		GRADE SCHOOL –	TEENS –
YOUNG ADULTS ★★		OVER 30 ★★		SENIORS ★★

**Palais Galliera, 10, avenue Pierre 1er de Serbie; ☎ 01 56 52 86 00;
galliera.paris.fr; Métro: Iéna**

Type of attraction Impressive museum of fashions and costume design.
Admission Varies with each exhibition. **Hours** Tuesday–Sunday, 10 a.m.–
6 p.m. **When to go** Crowds depend on the popularity of the temporary exhibits.
Special comments Check listings for temporary exhibits of interest. **Author's
rating ★★. How much time to allow** 1 hour.

DESCRIPTION AND COMMENTS The Musée de la Mode is, well, coming back
into fashion, with some popular recent exhibitions. Sadly, there is no
longer a permanent exhibition of their vast collection, which has a
strong emphasis on the 19th century, plus some more recent donations
by contemporary designers such as Balenciaga and fashion plates such
as Grace Kelly. A good place for fashion followers; there's also a
research library, open by appointment only. *Note:* The museum is open
only a few months of the year during temporary exhibitions.

TOURING TIPS Be sure to call ahead to check if the museum is open. Unless
everyone loves to look at clothes, don't take the whole family.

OTHER THINGS TO DO NEARBY Musée d'Art Moderne de la Ville de Paris, Trocadéro.

Musée de la Monnaie 6th arrondissement

APPEAL BY AGE	PRESCHOOL ★★	GRADE SCHOOL ★★★	TEENS ★★★
YOUNG ADULTS ★★★		OVER 30 ★★★	SENIORS ★★★

Hôtel des Monnaies, 11, quai de Conti; ☎ 01 40 46 56 66; monnaiedeparis.com; Métro: Pont Neuf

Type of attraction Museum of France's national mint and the history of money and currency. **Admission** €5 for all visitors, free for those under age 16. **Hours** Tuesday–Friday, 11 a.m.–5:30 p.m.; Saturday and Sunday, noon–5:30 p.m.; closed Monday. **When to go** Rarely crowded. **Special comments** Don't miss the excellent boutique, where you can buy commemorative coins marking the advent of the euro. **Author's rating** ★★★. **How much time to allow** 2 hours.

DESCRIPTION AND COMMENTS The elegant mansion standing on the Left Bank opposite the Louvre was not built by a rich aristocrat: Louis XV commissioned the building to house the National Mint, which operated here from 1775 to 1973. This is not just a linear display of coins under glass; the curators have designed a fascinating look at all aspects of coin and currency, from its fabrication to social and political aspects. Along the way, you'll pick up some great anecdotes—Louis XVI, for example, almost managed to avoid the guillotine by fleeing Paris but was apprehended at an inn when a man recognized the royal face from the image stamped on the coins then in circulation.

TOURING TIPS This is an underrated museum; few travelers have it on their list to see, but it's worth the trip.

OTHER THINGS TO DO NEARBY Explore the *bouquinistes* along the Seine; the Louvre is just across the river, and you're just steps from the Saint-Germain galleries and shops.

Musée de la Musique 19th arrondissement

APPEAL BY AGE	PRESCHOOL ★	GRADE SCHOOL ★★	TEENS ★★★
YOUNG ADULTS ★★★		OVER 30 ★★★	SENIORS ★★★

Cité de la Musique, 221, avenue Jean Jaurès; ☎ 01 44 84 44 84; cite-musique.fr; Métro: Porte de Pantin

Type of attraction Thoroughly enjoyable museum devoted to music and its history. **Admission** €8 adults, reduced rate €4–€6.40, free for childen under age 18 and EU citizens under age 26. **Hours** Tuesday–Saturday, noon–6 p.m.; Sunday, 10 a.m.–6 p.m.; closed Monday. **When to go** Crowded on Wednesdays and Sundays. Combine with meal or drink in the Café de la Musique and either a stroll through La Villette park or a visit to one of the temporary and topical exhibits. **Author's rating** ★★★. **How much time to allow** 2 hours, plus another 2 hours for picnics, exploring park.

DESCRIPTION AND COMMENTS The Cité de la Musique houses a recently renovated museum, concert hall, research center, and Gamelan orchestra (traditional Indonesian gongs). To visit the museum, don a headset, which is activated as you move within range of the various displays. The instrument collection ranges from obscure Renaissance instruments to Frank Zappa's synthesizer. Concerts of period musical scores with old instruments are held in the concert hall.

TOURING TIPS La Villette is not centrally located, but do not be dissuaded. It is completely worth your attention and energy. Leave yourself plenty of time.

OTHER THINGS TO DO NEARBY Try the other activities at La Villette. Also great for picnics.

Musée de l'Armée 7th arrondissement

APPEAL BY AGE	PRESCHOOL –	GRADE SCHOOL ★★	TEENS ★★★
YOUNG ADULTS ★★★		OVER 30 ★★	SENIORS ★★★

Place des Invalides, 129, rue de Grenelle; ☎ 01 44 42 38 77; invalides.org; Métro: Latour-Maubourg or Varenne

Type of attraction Military museum housed in Les Invalides. **Admission** €8.50 adults, €6.50 ages 18–26 and war veterans, free for those under age 18 and EU citizens under age 26. **Hours** April–September, daily, 10 a.m.– 6 p.m.; October–March, daily, 10 a.m.–5 p.m. (box office closes 30 minutes before); extended to 9 p.m. on Tuesday; museum partially closed on Monday. **When to go** Avoid Sundays. **Special comments** Some parts may be closed for renovation; partial wheelchair access. **Author's rating ★★. How much time to allow** 1½ hours.

DESCRIPTION AND COMMENTS See Hôtel des Invalides.

TOURING TIPS There are impressive military parades leaving from here in full regalia. Inquire for dates.

OTHER THINGS TO DO NEARBY Visit the Rodin Museum, Eiffel Tower, and Grand Palais.

Musée d'Orsay 7th arrondissement

APPEAL BY AGE	PRESCHOOL –	GRADE SCHOOL ★★★	TEENS ★★★
YOUNG ADULTS ★★★★		OVER 30 ★★★★★	SENIORS ★★★★

1, rue de Bellechasse; ☎ 01 40 49 48 14; musee-orsay.fr; RER: Musée d'Orsay

Type of attraction Converted train station houses the best collection of Impressionist and Art Nouveau paintings and sculptures in the world. **Admission** €8 adults, €5.50 ages 18–25 and all visitors after 4:15 p.m. (6 p.m. on Thursday); free for children under age 18 and EU citizens under age 26; free for all visitors on first Sunday of each month. **Hours** Tuesday–Sunday, 9:30 a.m.–6 p.m.; Thursday, open until 9:45 p.m.; last ticket sold one hour before closing; closed Monday. **When to go** Avoid on Sundays. **Special comments** English audio guide, guided tours, café-restaurant, bookshop, wheelchair access; immediate access with prebooking (available on the Web site, at FNAC stores, or at ticket kiosk outside the museum). **Author's rating ★★★★★. How much time to allow** 3 hours.

DESCRIPTION AND COMMENTS One of Paris's most important and pleasant art museums; no visit to Paris would be complete without a few hours at the Musée d'Orsay. This museum bridges the world of art between the Louvre and the Centre Pompidou. The space is superbly organized, the light is welcoming, and the work is well exhibited. Time passes painlessly. Victor Laloux completed this large steel-and-glass structure in 1900. It was originally a train station serving southwestern destinations in France, but new electric trains, longer than their predecessors, forced its closing by 1939. It has been a museum since 1986, housing France's impressive (and Impressionist) collection of paintings and sculpture from the period 1848 to 1914. The best examples of decorative and applied arts (jewelry, ceramics, furniture, and so on) are here. The museum is organized on three levels; the first floor is devoted to the 1840–1870 period. Art Nouveau works are on the middle floor, and Impressionist and Postimpressionist works are on the top floor. Don't miss Renoir's *Bal du Moulin de la Galette* and Van Gogh's *Church at Auvers*. It is particularly interesting to look out from behind the famous clock face over Paris and spot Sacré-Cœur in the distance. There is also an auditorium, restaurant, and movie theater.

TOURING TIPS We strongly recommend the inexpensive 2-course lunch in the museum restaurant.

OTHER THINGS TO DO NEARBY Explore Les Invalides and Place de la Concorde; walk along the Seine.

Musée de l'Orangerie 1st arrondissement

| APPEAL BY AGE | PRESCHOOL – | GRADE SCHOOL ★★★ | TEENS ★★★ |
| YOUNG ADULTS ★★★★ | OVER 30 ★★★★ | | SENIORS ★★★★ |

Jardin des Tuileries (Place de la Concorde); ☎ 01 44 77 80 07; musee-orangerie.fr; Métro: Concorde

Type of attraction Twin building to the Jeu de Paume houses spectacular Monets. Admission €7.50 adults, €5.50 ages 18–26 (plus an extra €2 for access to any temporary exhibitions), free for those under age 18, EU citizens under age 26, and for all visitors the first Sunday of the month. Hours Wednesday–Monday, 9 a.m.–6 p.m.; Fridays, open until 9 p.m. When to go Mornings. Special comments Wheelchair access, bookshop. Author's rating ★★★★. How much time to allow 1 hour.

DESCRIPTION AND COMMENTS The Orangerie—named because it was used to store the orange trees in the Tuileries gardens during the winter—houses the best collection of turn-of-the-19th-century and Impressionist paintings outside of the Musée d'Orsay. Amassed by Walter Guillaume, a pioneering supporter of his era's avant-garde artwork, the collection includes paintings by Soutine, Cézanne, Matisse, and Modigliani, among others. These are great reasons to visit, but most people know about the Orangerie because of Monet's famous *Water Lilies*, commissioned for the two oval rooms on the ground floor. During the course of the renovation work in 2004, a major archaeological find known as the *Fosses Jaunes* was unearthed in the crypt of the building; take a moment to view these extraordinary 16th-century remains, spanning the reigns of Henri III to Louis XIII.

TOURING TIPS English guided tours Monday and Thursday at 2:30 p.m.; audio guides also available in English for €5.

OTHER THINGS TO DO NEARBY Visit Jeu de Paume, Place de la Concorde, and the Louvre; stroll down to the Seine.

Musée des Arts Décoratifs 1st arrondissement

APPEAL BY AGE	PRESCHOOL –	GRADE SCHOOL ★★	TEENS ★★★
YOUNG ADULTS ★★★	OVER 30 ★★★		SENIORS ★★★

107, rue de Rivoli; ☎ 01 44 55 57 50; ucad.fr;
Métro: Palais-Royal or Tuileries

Type of attraction Massive museum collection of French decorative arts. **Admission** €8 adults, €6.50 students under age 26, under age 18 free. **Hours** Tuesday–Friday, 11 a.m.–6 p.m.; Saturday and Sunday, 10 a.m.–6 p.m.; extended opening until 9 p.m. on Thursday; closed Monday. **When to go** Popular on weekends. **Special comments** Wheelchair access; admission also gives access to the Musée de la Mode et du Textile and the Musée de la Publicité at the same address. **Author's rating** ★★★. **How much time to allow** 1½ hours.

DESCRIPTION AND COMMENTS Situated in the Rohan wing of the Louvre along rue de Rivoli, this museum is recommended to those interested in interior design. The museum covers every aspect of the decorative arts in France from the Middle Ages to the present. More than 200,000 objects, from ceramics to wallpaper, jewelry, and even toys, re-create everyday life through the ages. Highlights include the period rooms, such as the reconstruction of designer Jeanne Lanvin's apartment, and the Art Nouveau and Art Deco rooms. The Textile Museum and Poster Museum are also housed here. The Textile Museum presents temporary exhibits—everything from rare fabrics and accessories to works of avant-garde designers.

TOURING TIPS Some people may find this a less-daunting excursion than the mega-museum (the Louvre) next door. Combined ticket available if you also wish to visit the Musée Nissim de Camondo (see page 271), €10.50 adults.

OTHER THINGS TO DO NEARBY Visit the Louvre, Tuileries Gardens, and Palais Royal nearby.

Musée du Moyen Âge (Thermes de Cluny)
5th arrondissement

APPEAL BY AGE	PRESCHOOL –	GRADE SCHOOL ★★	TEENS ★★
YOUNG ADULTS ★★★	OVER 30 ★★★		SENIORS ★★★

Thermes de Cluny, 6, place Paul-Painlevé; ☎ 01 53 73 78 00;
musee-moyenage.fr; Métro: Cluny–La Sorbonne

Type of attraction A breathtaking reminder of Paris's Roman past. **Admission** €7.50; €5.50 ages 18–25, students, all visitors on the first Sunday of each month; free for those under age 18. **Hours** Wednesday–Monday, 9:15 a.m.– 5:45 p.m. (ticket office closes 30 minutes before). **When to go** Gets crowded on weekends. **Special comments** General guided tours Wednesday and Saturday and tours of the Roman baths Wednesday only. Check Web site for times. **Author's rating** ★★★. **How much time to allow** 1–2 hours.

DESCRIPTION AND COMMENTS Here's one of the more interesting architectural combinations in Paris: a 15th-century palace built on the ruins of
third-century Roman baths. The museum has lots of objets d'art for
those who like gilded altarpieces and crowns, but it's well worth visiting
for the series of six world-famous unicorn tapestries, which hang in a
specially designed circular room. Abutting the Gothic-style building are
the baths. The Romans knew what they were doing. The frigidarium,
the best preserved of the three, remains cool even during the muggiest
of Paris summers. Don't miss the King's Gallery. These are the heads
that were lopped off the figures lining the facade of nearby Notre-
Dame Cathedral during the French Revolution. And you can always
boast back home about seeing the oldest sculpture in Paris: the Pilier
des Nautes (Boatmen's Pillar), dated around AD 100.

TOURING TIPS Check out the weekly schedule of activities on the Web site.
This includes medieval music concerts and family activities.

OTHER THINGS TO DO NEARBY Explore the Latin Quarter, the Sorbonne, the
Panthéon, and Saint-Étienne du Mont Church.

Musée du Quai Branly 7th arrondissement

APPEAL BY AGE	PRESCHOOL ★	GRADE SCHOOL ★★★	TEENS ★★★
YOUNG ADULTS ★★★	OVER 30 ★★★★★		SENIORS ★★★★★

37, quai Branly; ☎ 01 56 61 70 00; quaibranly.fr; RER: Pont de l'Alma

Type of attraction Newly constructed museum dedicated to arts and civilizations from Africa, Asia, Oceania, and the Americas. Much of the collection has come from the former Musée des Arts d'Afrique et d'Océanie as well as the Musée de l'Homme and makes a larger statement about the way France sees much of its colonial past. **Admission** Permanent exhibition: €8.50 adults; free for those under age 18, EU citizens under age 26, and for all visitors the first Sunday of the month. **Hours** Tuesday, Wednesday, Sunday, 11 a.m.–7 p.m.; Thursday–Saturday, 11 a.m.–9 p.m. **When to go** Likely to be less crowded in mornings. **Special comments** Don't miss the vertical garden—15,000 plants of 150 species growing on a vertical surface of 800 meters. **Author's rating** ★★★★★. **How much time to allow** Minimum 2 hours.

DESCRIPTION AND COMMENTS Non-Western arts acquired a crucial place in
museum collections during the 20th century. This museum, designed
by celebrated French architect Jean Nouvel, is one of the city's highlights of the early 21st century. Ambitious in scope, the Musée du Quai

Branly officially recognizes the artistic contributions of African, Asian, and Oceanic civilizations, together with the heritages of peoples who are sometimes forgotten.

TOURING TIPS In good weather, plan to picnic by the Seine or in the Champ de Mars, beneath the Eiffel Tower.

OTHER THINGS TO DO NEARBY The Eiffel Tower, Trocadéro, boat trips on the Seine.

Musée Eugène Delacroix 6th arrondissement

| APPEAL BY AGE | PRESCHOOL ★ | GRADE SCHOOL ★★ | TEENS ★★ |
| YOUNG   ADULTS ★★ | OVER 30 ★★ | | SENIORS ★★ |

**6, rue Fürstemberg; ☎ 01 44 41 86 50; musee-delacroix.fr;
Métro: Saint-Germain-des-Prés**

Type of attraction Delacroix's home/museum commemorating his life and work. **Admission** €5 adults, free for those under age 18 and for all the first Sunday of the month. **Hours** Wednesday–Monday, 9:30 a.m.–5 p.m. (ticket office closes at 4:30 p.m.); open until 5:30 p.m. Saturday and Sunday, June–August. **When to go** Rarely crowded. **Special comments** A perfect example of how artists' homes are converted into public spaces in Paris. **Author's rating** ★★. **How much time to allow** 1½ hours.

DESCRIPTION AND COMMENTS This is the last place Delacroix lived; he moved here to be closer to Saint-Sulpice Church, where he was working on his final public commission. Seriously ill with tuberculosis, he nonetheless was able to complete the three large murals that you can see at the church. The museum contains some smaller works by the artist and copies of other major paintings in the Louvre and elsewhere. Most interesting about the museum, though, is the intimacy of the house and studio.

TOURING TIPS Although Place de Fürstenberg is in the heart of Saint-Germain, it is often overlooked by tourists. It's one of the most romantic little squares in Paris and is enchanting in the evening.

OTHER THINGS TO DO NEARBY Explore the Saint-Germain neighborhood.

kids Musée Grévin 2nd arrondissement

| APPEAL BY AGE | PRESCHOOL ★★★ | GRADE SCHOOL ★★★★ | TEENS ★★★★ |
| YOUNG   ADULTS ★★★★ | OVER 30 ★★★ | | SENIORS ★★★ |

**10, boulevard Montmartre; ☎ 01 47 70 85 05; grevin.com;
Métro: Rue Montmartre**

Type of attraction Paris's renowned wax museum. **Admission** €19.50 adults, €11.50 children ages 6–14, free for children under age 6. **Hours** Weekdays, 10 a.m.–6:30 p.m.; weekends and during French school holidays, 10 a.m.–7 p.m. (box office closes 1 hour before). **When to go** Avoid school holidays and weekends. **Special comments** At the turn of the 19th century, this is where the social elite came to be amused; wheelchair access. **Author's rating** ★★★. **How much time to allow** 1 hour.

DESCRIPTION AND COMMENTS This elaborately baroque Paris wax museum offers up the usual celebrities—Napoléon, President Clinton, Marilyn Monroe—along with quintessential modern-day French figures, such as the soccer heroes Zidane and Barthez. Not everything here is fake. The bathtub in which the effigy of the stabbed Marat lies is the genuine article. Don't miss the sound-and-light show held in the Palais des Mirages.

TOURING TIPS Kids will enjoy the Discovery Tour, where they will learn how the wax figures are made.

OTHER THINGS TO DO NEARBY Explore the 19th-century covered passages that crisscross this section of Paris.

Musée Jacquemart-André 8th arrondissement

APPEAL BY AGE	PRESCHOOL –	GRADE SCHOOL ★★	TEENS ★★
YOUNG ADULTS ★★★	OVER 30 ★★★★		SENIORS ★★★★

158, boulevard Haussmann; ☎ 01 45 62 11 59; musee-jacquemart-andre.com; Métro: Saint-Philippe-du-Roule

Type of attraction Sublime private art museum. **Admission** €10 adults, €7.50 for those under age 18 and students, free for children under 7. **Hours** Daily, 10 a.m.–6 p.m. (ticket office closes at 5:30 p.m.). **When to go** Avoiding weekends is always smart. **Special comments** Audio guide provided with each ticket; wheelchair access to ground floor only. **Author's rating** ★★★★. **How much time to allow** 1–2 hours.

DESCRIPTION AND COMMENTS For those who prefer intimate museums, this one is a gem. This lavish 19th-century home was built by Nélie Jacquemart and her husband, Édouard André, to house their personal art collection, with works by Rembrandt, Titian, and Uccello, and frescoes by Tiepolo.

TOURING TIPS Be sure to visit the austere upstairs bedroom of Nélie Jacquemart. Stop for an excellent light lunch at the museum's Café Jacquemart-André. Join the queue when it opens at 11:45 a.m. to be guaranteed a table (no reservations).

OTHER THINGS TO DO NEARBY Visit Parc Monceau and Nissim de Camondo Museum's art collection.

Musée Jean Moulin–Mémorial Leclerc 15th arrondissement

APPEAL BY AGE	PRESCHOOL –	GRADE SCHOOL ★	TEENS ★★
YOUNG ADULTS ★★	OVER 30 ★★		SENIORS ★★★

23, allée de la 2e DB (Jardin Atlantique); ☎ 01 40 64 39 44; ml-leclerc-moulin.paris.fr; Métro: Montparnasse

Type of attraction Museum and monument to French Resistance of World War II. **Admission** €4 adults, €2 under age 26, free for children under age 13. **Hours** Tuesday–Sunday, 10 a.m.–6 p.m.; closed Monday. **When to go** Anytime. **Special comments** Inaugurated in 1994 to mark the 50th anniversary of the liberation of Paris. Requires some French to appreciate. **Author's rating ★★. How much time to allow** 45 minutes.

DESCRIPTION AND COMMENTS These two museums explain and relate the history of the French Resistance and of the Liberation of Paris through the destinies of two exceptional men: Marshal Leclerc and Jean Moulin. Jean Moulin is one of France's greatest heroes and martyrs. Tortured and killed by the Germans, he refused to divulge what he knew to the enemy. A leader in the French Resistance against the occupying Nazis in World War II, Moulin's life and actions during the war are documented in this unusual but fascinating history museum on the rooftop garden complex above the Gare Montparnasse. If you are a war buff and appreciate old photos, newspapers, and objects from the 1940s, you'll find this rarely visited museum to be worth the effort.

TOURING TIPS Perfect place to kill an hour before catching a train nearby.

OTHER THINGS TO DO NEARBY Tour Maine-Montparnasse (Montparnasse skyscraper with 55th-floor observation deck) and Montparnasse Cemetery.

Musée Marmottan-Monet 16th arrondissement

APPEAL BY AGE	PRESCHOOL –	GRADE SCHOOL ★★	TEENS ★★★
YOUNG ADULTS ★★★	OVER 30 ★★★★		SENIORS ★★★★

2, rue Louis-Boilly; ☎ 01 44 96 50 33; marmottan.com; Métro: La Muette

Type of attraction Varied collection of work by Monet and other Impressionists. **Admission** €9 adults, €5 ages 8–25, free for children under age 8, audio guide €3. **Hours** Daily, 11 a.m.–6 p.m. (until 9 p.m. on Tuesday). **When to go** This is a good museum to save for a Tuesday, when most of the others, including the Louvre, are closed. **Special comments** Monet fans should visit this museum as well as l'Orangerie and Giverny. **Author's rating ★★★★. How much time to allow** 2 hours.

DESCRIPTION AND COMMENTS What began as a personal collection devoted to Napoleonic memorabilia gradually diversified through bequests to become a pilgrimage site for Monet lovers—especially after his son Michel left 65 canvases to the museum in 1971. Housed in a lavish mansion at the edge of the Bois de Boulogne, the Marmottan has superb Impressionist paintings, including Monet's *Impression,* the painting that when first shown was mocked by critics and gave a name to the Impressionist movement. Many of the works were painted at Giverny, in Normandy; the brilliant water-lily paintings are in a special room downstairs. Less well known is the Wildenstein bequest, more than 200 illuminated manuscripts from the 14th to the 16th century.

TOURING TIPS Most people come for the Monets, but the Marmottan has superb works by Gauguin, Corot, and Manet.

OTHER THINGS TO DO NEARBY Combine a trip to the museum with an afternoon exploring the Bois de Boulogne.

Musée National des Arts Asiatiques Guimet
16th arrondissement

APPEAL BY AGE	PRESCHOOL –	GRADE SCHOOL ★★	TEENS ★★
YOUNG ADULTS ★★	OVER 30 ★★★		SENIORS ★★★

**6, place d'Iéna; ☎ 01 56 52 53 00; museeguimet.fr;
Métro: Iéna or Trocadéro**

Type of attraction One of the world's most important museums for Asian art and artifacts. **Admission** €6.50 adults; €4.50 students and all visitors the first Sunday of each month; free for those under age 18. **Hours** Wednesday–Monday, 10 a.m.–6 p.m. (ticket office closes at 5:30 p.m.). **When to go** Mornings; crowded on Sundays. **Special comments** Wheelchair access. **Author's rating** ★★★. **How much time to allow** 1–2 hours.

DESCRIPTION AND COMMENTS One of the best collections of Asian art in the world. Great selection of Buddha heads. Key works from Cambodia, Vietnam, India, and China. The *Cosmic Dance of Shiva* is a noted bronze Hindu sculpture. If you have a particular interest in Asian history and culture, a visit here is a must. Others may feel that this is a lower priority for a Paris visit.

TOURING TIPS Audio guides available. Even if you don't think you're interested in Asian art, this one is really worth making an effort.

OTHER THINGS TO DO NEARBY Visit the Trocadéro and Musée d'Art Moderne de la Ville de Paris.

kids Muséum National d'Histoire Naturelle
5th arrondissement

APPEAL BY AGE	PRESCHOOL ★★★★	GRADE SCHOOL ★★★★	TEENS ★★★★
YOUNG ADULTS ★★★★	OVER 30 ★★★★		SENIORS ★★★★

**36, rue Geoffroy Saint-Hilaire; ☎ 01 40 79 54 79; mnhn.fr;
Métro: Jussieu or Gare d'Austerlitz**

Type of attraction Natural history museum with a spectacular dinosaur collection and Gallery of Evolution. **Admission** Grande Galerie, €9 adults, €7 children ages 5–13; other pavilions, each €8 adults, €6 reduced; zoo, €8 adults, €6 reduced; children age 4 and under free throughout. **Hours** Grande Galerie, Galerie de Minéralogie et de Géologie, and Galerie de Paléontologie, Wednesday–Monday, 10 a.m.–6 p.m.; zoo, daily, 9 a.m.–6 p.m. (6:30 p.m. Sunday). **When to go** Weekdays. **Special comments** Wheelchair access. **Author's rating** ★★★★. **How much time to allow** 1–1½ hours per pavilion.

DESCRIPTION AND COMMENTS For years, the Muséum National d'Histoire Naturelle was a dusty repository for old bones and scruffy stuffed animals. In 1994, however, the museum reopened with a spectacular new arrangement: a parade of stuffed animals cuts through the center of the exhibit like a modern-day Noah's Ark, and dramatic lighting throughout showcases the many exhibits. Marine animals hang suspended in the air—the great favorite is the 54-foot-long whale skeleton. Kids under age 12 will love the discovery room, which presents fossils and the natural sciences, and teenagers can explore the various displays in the science laboratory.

TOURING TIPS Combine this trip with the surrounding gardens and greenhouses and a visit to the small zoo, which retains a somewhat dilapidated charm. Explore the hard-to-find Alpine Garden (closed from October to February), where 2,000 types of plants thrive in a tiny microclimate.

OTHER THINGS TO DO NEARBY Cross the street toward the Seine and enjoy a stroll or picnic through the Tino Rossi open-air sculpture gardens; visit the Institut du Monde Arabe; take a break on the steps of the Arènes de Lutèce, which dates to Roman times.

Musée National Picasso Paris   3rd arrondissement
The museum will be closed for extensive renovation until at least 2011.

APPEAL BY AGE	PRESCHOOL –	GRADE SCHOOL ★	TEENS ★★★
YOUNG ADULTS ★★★★	OVER 30 ★★★★		SENIORS ★★★★

**Hôtel Salé, 5, rue de Thorigny; ☎ 01 42 71 25 21; musee-picasso.fr;
Métro: Saint-Paul or Chemin Vert**

Type of attraction An entire museum devoted to the life and work of Pablo Picasso. **Admission** Exhibition and museum, €8.50 adults, reduced rate €6.50, free for those under age 18, EU citizens under age 26, and all visitors on the first Sunday of each month. **Hours** April–September, Wednesday–Monday, 9:30 a.m.–6 p.m.; closes at 5:30 p.m. the rest of the year. **When to go** Show up early to beat the crowds. **Special comments** You can also appreciate the view of the Hôtel Salé. **Author's rating** ★★★★. **How much time to allow** 2 hours.

DESCRIPTION AND COMMENTS Housed in an elegant 17th-century *hôtel particulier,* Musée Picasso showcases the largest collection of works by this superstar artist. After his death in 1973 in southern France, the French government agreed to accept artwork in lieu of estate taxes. Although the curators had first pick of the enormous collection in Picasso's possession, they did not necessarily choose the best work; yet the 261 paintings, 198 sculptures, 88 ceramics, and more than 3,000 works on paper represent every phase of his artistic life, from the age of 14 until his death. The artwork is arranged chronologically, and detailed explanatory notes are provided throughout. Picasso amassed a large number of works by friends and contemporaries, and his personal collection of these, as well as his collection of primitive art, is exhibited on two floors.

TOURING TIPS This is an essential visit for art lovers; younger visitors may enjoy some of Picasso's more whimsical sculptures and ceramics.

OTHER THINGS TO DO NEARBY There are several other museums nearby (Carnavalet, Cognacq-Jay), but the best thing to do in this neighborhood is to simply wander through the streets, perhaps having coffee at Place des Vosges or falafel in the Jewish Quarter.

Musée Nissim de Camondo 8th arrondissement

APPEAL BY AGE	PRESCHOOL –	GRADE SCHOOL –	TEENS ★★
YOUNG ADULTS ★★	OVER 30 ★★		SENIORS ★★

**63, rue Monceau; ☎ 01 53 89 06 50; lesartsdecoratifs.fr;
Métro: Monceau or Villiers**

Type of attraction 18th-century mansion with an exquisite art collection.
Admission €8 adults, €6.50 ages 18–25, free for children under age 18; includes
audio guide. *Note:* If you intend to visit the Musée des Arts Décoratifs, there
is a combined ticket available for both museums. **Hours** Wednesday–Sunday,
10 a.m.–5:30 p.m.; closed Monday and Tuesday. **When to go** Rarely crowded.
Author's rating ★★. **How much time to allow** 1 hour.

DESCRIPTION AND COMMENTS Here's another opportunity to check out how
the rich lived in the 18th century, even though the mansion was built in
1914. Count Moise de Camondo was a rich banker who loved all things
French and amassed a collection of rare tapestries, furniture, and porcelain. He bequeathed the mansion and the collection to the government
in memory of his son Nissim, who was killed in World War I. Of interest
to history buffs and interior designers, perhaps; others may have had
their fill of gold leaf, marble, and objets d'art.

TOURING TIPS Take advantage of the combined ticket available to visit the
Musée des Arts Décoratifs (see page 264), €10.50 adults.

OTHER THINGS TO DO NEARBY Visit the Saint Alexander Nevsky Russian
Orthodox Cathedral, Parc Monceau, and Musée Cernuschi.

kids Musée Rodin 7th arrondissement

APPEAL BY AGE	PRESCHOOL ★★★	GRADE SCHOOL ★★★	TEENS ★★★
YOUNG ADULTS ★★★	OVER 30 ★★★★		SENIORS ★★★★

79, rue de Varenne; ☎ 01 44 18 61 10; musee-rodin.fr; Métro: Varenne

Type of attraction Lovely museum and gardens devoted to the life and work
of sculptor Auguste Rodin. **Admission** Museum: €6 adults, €4 ages 18–
25, free for those under age 18 and for all visitors on the first Sunday of the
month; gardens: €1 ages 18 and over. **Hours** Tuesday–Sunday, 9:30 a.m.–
5:45 p.m., gardens open until 6:45 p.m. (museum and gardens close at 4:45 p.m.
October–March); box office closes 30 minutes earlier than museum. **When
to go** Early or late to miss the lines during the summer months; try not to go
on Tuesday. **Special comments** English guided tours available but expensive;
you can use audio guides. **Author's rating** ★★★★. **How much time to allow**
1–2 hours.

DESCRIPTION AND COMMENTS The Rodin museum, also known as the Hôtel de
Biron, was created by Aubert and Gabriel in 1728 for the financier
Peyrenc de Moras and then sold to the Maréchal de Biron. It was a
convent until 1902 and now houses the best collection of Auguste

Rodin's work found anywhere in the world. Visit both inside the hotel and outside in the gardens. In the gardens behind the hotel is a cozy café with an affordable high-quality menu. All of Rodin's major works are here. A must for both the famous sculptor's fans and the newly initiated. Great photo op next to the original *Le Penseur* (The Thinker). The gardens are delightful in the spring and summer.

TOURING TIPS Let the kids play in the gardens and imitate the poses of the Rodin masterpieces. A great way to open their eyes to sculpture.

OTHER THINGS TO DO NEARBY Visit Les Invalides, Assemblée Nationale, and the Eiffel Tower.

Musée Zadkine 6th arrondissement

APPEAL BY AGE	PRESCHOOL –	GRADE SCHOOL ★★	TEENS ★★
YOUNG ADULTS ★★★	OVER 30 ★★★		SENIORS ★★★

100 bis, rue d'Assas; ☎ 01 55 42 77 20; zadkine.paris.fr; Métro: Port-Royal or Notre-Dame-des-Champs

Type of attraction Private museum created from the atelier of painter and sculptor Zadkine. **Admission** Permanent exhibition, free; temporary exhibitions, €4 adults, €3 ages 15–25, free for children under age 14. **Hours** Tuesday–Sunday, 10 a.m.–6 p.m. **When to go** Rarely crowded. **Special comments** It's fun running into other Zadkine enthusiasts here. **Author's rating ★★★. How much time to allow** 1–1½ hours.

DESCRIPTION AND COMMENTS What's interesting about this museum, which includes the house and studios where the Russian sculptor Ossip Zadkine lived and worked, is that it is almost exactly as he left it at his death in 1927. Although just a few blocks from the Jardin du Luxembourg, it is secluded, quiet, and usually tourist-free. The highlight of the museum is the sculpture garden.

TOURING TIPS After a visit here, stroll through the Luxembourg Gardens seeking other Zadkine sculptures.

OTHER THINGS TO DO NEARBY Stroll through the Jardin du Luxembourg.

Opéra Garnier 9th arrondissement

APPEAL BY AGE	PRESCHOOL –	GRADE SCHOOL –	TEENS –
YOUNG ADULTS ★★	OVER 30 ★★		SENIORS ★★

Palais Garnier, place de l'Opéra; ☎ 01 40 01 17 89; opera-de-paris.fr; Métro: Opéra

Type of attraction Paris's first and most illustrious opera house. **Admission** Free for individual visitors wishing to visit the foyers, staircase, museum, and auditorium. Guided tours (in English) of the opera and museum, €8 adults, €4 under age 26, children under age 10 free. **Hours** Daily, 10 a.m.–4:30 p.m. **When to go** To see the opera house, avoid performance times. **Special comments** Includes a branch of the Bibliothèque Nationale devoted to operatic history. **Author's rating ★★. How much time to allow** 30 minutes.

DESCRIPTION AND COMMENTS Whether you're an opera or ballet lover or not, a visit to the spectacular Opéra Garnier is well worth the time. The great staircase and the ornate chandeliers transport you into the splendors of the mid-19th-century Napoléon III style of architecture and décor. Named after the relatively unknown and young architect who built the house, the Opéra Garnier is considered by many to be the best monument of the Second Empire. An absolute must for visitors taking the tour is the ceiling of the main auditorium, consisting of opera-related frescoes by the modern painter Marc Chagall. The cheapest seats in the house afford you the best view of the ceiling.

TOURING TIPS Guided tours in English are offered daily during July and August, and on Wednesday, Saturday, and Sunday the rest of the year. Check Web site for times. There really is an underground lake (per *Phantom of the Opera*), though most tours do not include this.

OTHER THINGS TO DO NEARBY Tour La Madeleine, Grands Boulevards.

kids Palais de Chaillot 16th arrondissement

APPEAL BY AGE	PRESCHOOL ★★★	GRADE SCHOOL ★★★	TEENS ★★★
YOUNG ADULTS ★★★		OVER 30 ★★★	SENIORS ★★★

1, place du Trocadéro; ☎ 01 58 51 52 00; citechaillot.fr; Métro: Trocadéro

Type of attraction Large arts complex. **Admission** Different for each museum. **Hours** Different for each museum. **When to go** Avoid Sundays if possible. **Special comments** Check out the gardens on the sloping side of the complex. **Author's rating** ★★★. **How much time to allow** Different for each attraction.

DESCRIPTION AND COMMENTS The Palais de Chaillot, an immense winged structure built for the 1937 Universal Exhibition, houses the Musée de la Marine, Théâtre de Chaillot, and the Cité de l'Architecture et du Patrimoine. But first, linger on the parvis (square) and gaze across the river—this is the most spectacular view of the Eiffel Tower in Paris. There's always plenty going on: street performers, jugglers, and clowns, the inline skaters, who have colonized the lower level of the square with ramps, jumps, and other paraphernalia.

TOURING TIPS There are a lot of people hustling tourists here, especially in the summer; ignore them, avoid purchasing trinkets, and enjoy the view.

OTHER THINGS TO DO NEARBY Take your pick of one of the museums housed in the Palais; some are closed for renovation, but there's still something for everyone.

Palais de la Porte Dorée–Aquarium Tropical 12th arrondissement

APPEAL BY AGE	PRESCHOOL ★★	GRADE SCHOOL ★★★	TEENS ★★
YOUNG ADULTS ★★		OVER 30 ★★	SENIORS ★★

293, avenue Daumesnil; ☎ 01 53 59 58 60; aquarium-portedoree.fr; Métro: Porte Dorée

Type of attraction Aquarium. **Admission** €4.50 adults, €3 ages 4–25, free for children under age 4. **Hours** Tuesday–Friday, 10 a.m.–5:15 p.m.; Saturday and Sunday, 10 a.m.–7 p.m. (ticket office closes 30 minutes before). **When to go** Try to avoid Wednesdays; on Sunday, best hours are noon–2 p.m. **Special comments** Perfect if it's raining and you're traveling with children. **Author's rating** ★★★. **How much time to allow** 1–2 hours.

DESCRIPTION AND COMMENTS This aquarium is fun for the whole family and includes a large crocodile pit in the basement of the Palais. This building, which was originally built for the Colonial Exhibition of 1931, has recently been reopened as the Cité Nationale de l'Histoire de l'Immigration (see below).

TOURING TIPS Bring your lunch and picnic in the nearby Bois de Vincennes.

OTHER THINGS TO DO NEARBY Visit Bois de Vincennes.

Palais de la Porte Dorée–Cité Nationale de l'Histoire de l'Immigration 12th arrondissement

APPEAL BY AGE	PRESCHOOL —	GRADE SCHOOL —	TEENS —
YOUNG ADULTS ★★	OVER 30 ★★★		SENIORS ★★★

293, avenue Daumesnil; ☎ 01 53 59 58 60; histoire-immigration.fr; Métro: Porte Dorée

Type of attraction Immigration history museum. **Admission** €3, free for those under age 26. **Hours** Tuesday–Friday, 10 a.m.–5:30 p.m.; Saturday and Sunday, 10 a.m.–7 p.m. (ticket office closes 45 minutes before). **When to go** Anytime. **Author's rating** ★★★. **How much time to allow** 1½ hours.

DESCRIPTION AND COMMENTS This new museum of immigration history is of interest when considered in the context of contemporary French social tensions. It's particularly interesting for history and immigration and colonialization buffs.

TOURING TIPS Bring your lunch and picnic in the nearby Bois de Vincennes.

OTHER THINGS TO DO NEARBY See the aquarium in the basement.

Palais Royal 1st arrondissement

APPEAL BY AGE	PRESCHOOL —	GRADE SCHOOL —	TEENS ★★
YOUNG ADULTS ★★	OVER 30 ★★		SENIORS ★★

Place du Palais Royal; Métro: Palais-Royal

Type of attraction Regal architectural remnant of the French monarchy, perfect for strolling, sitting, sipping. **Admission** Free. **Hours** Daily, dawn to dusk. **When to go** When the weather is pleasant. **Special comments** Buildings are not open to public. **Author's rating** ★★★. **How much time to allow** 30 minutes.

DESCRIPTION AND COMMENTS An absolutely lovely thing to do is stroll through the gardens and along the arcades of the Palais Royal. The shops along the way characterize much of the old charm of Paris with antique books, bronze, toys, maps, stamps, and musical instruments. At the southern end of the gardens you'll find yourself hopping on contemporary pillars of varying heights that decorate the space outside the highly active French Ministry of Culture on rue de Valois, which in the 17th century had been Cardinal Richelieu's palace. Following Richelieu, the Palais Royal was bequeathed to Louis XIII. On the opposite side you'll find the illustrious Comédie Française on place Malraux, where Victor Hugo launched his career as a playwright and where to this day works by Molière, Corneille, Racine, de Musset, and Beaumarchais are performed. Molière enthusiasts will enjoy noting that the famed playwright lived at number 40 on the nearby rue de Richelieu; just up the street at 61, Stendhal, the novelist of *The Red and the Black* kept his residence.

TOURING TIPS Picnic in the gardens or stroll around the arcade at night after dinner. The famed gastronomical landmark, Le Grand Vefour, sits at the far end of the Palais Royal complex.

OTHER THINGS TO DO NEARBY Visit the Louvre and avenue de l'Opéra.

Le Panthéon 5th arrondissement

APPEAL BY AGE	PRESCHOOL –	GRADE SCHOOL –	TEENS –
YOUNG ADULTS ★★	OVER 30 ★★		SENIORS ★★

place du Panthéon; ☎ 01 44 32 18 00; pantheon.monuments-nationaux. fr; Métro: Cardinal Lemoine; RER: Luxembourg

Type of attraction Mausoleum and historic museum. **Admission** €8 adults, €5 students ages 18–25 and teachers, free for under age 18 and EU citizens under age 26. **Hours** daily, 10 a.m.–6:30 p.m. (April–September); closes at 6 p.m. the rest of the year (box office closes at 5:45 p.m.). **When to go** Rarely crowded. **Author's rating** ★★. **How much time to allow** 45 minutes.

DESCRIPTION AND COMMENTS When you spot the Panthéon you'll think of the U.S. Capitol building in Washington, D.C. Built on the highest point of the Left Bank, this attempt at the perfect marriage of Gothic and Greek architectural styles was ordered by Louis XV, after his recovery from a serious illness, in honor of Saint Geneviève, the Patron Saint of Paris. Initially a church, in 1791 it became the final resting place of great men who died in the name of French liberty. Thus, here in the crypt you'll find the tombs of Voltaire, Rousseau, Zola, Mirabeau, Hugo (historians estimate that 2 million people attended his funeral march from the Arc de Triomphe to the Panthéon), Louis Braille (the creator of the braille system for the blind), Pierre and Marie Curie (who was the first woman to be laid to rest here), and more recently André Malraux. If you've heard of Foucault's pendulum, you'll be delighted to note that it was from the massive dome of the Panthéon that physicist Léon Foucault suspended his iron pendulum in 1851, proving that the Earth rotates on its axis. (A replica is on display here; the original pendulum now resides in the Musée des Arts et Métiers, 60, rue Réamur, 75003, Métro: Arts et Métiers.)

TOURING TIPS Climb the stairs in the dome for a great view of central Paris.

OTHER THINGS TO DO NEARBY Visit la Sorbonne and Jardin du Luxembourg.

Pinacothèque de Paris 8th arrondissement

| APPEAL BY AGE | PRESCHOOL ★★ | GRADE SCHOOL ★★★★ | TEENS ★★★★ |
| YOUNG ADULTS ★★★★ | | OVER 30 ★★★★ | SENIORS ★★★★ |

28, place de la Madeleine; ☎ 01 42 68 02 01;
pinacotheque.com; Métro: Madeleine

Type of attraction Large exhibition space dedicated to temporary art exhibitions. **Admission** €9 adults, €7 ages 12–25, children under age 12 free. **Hours** Daily, 10:30 a.m.–6 p.m.; extended opening until 9 p.m. first Wednesday of the month. **When to go** To avoid crowds, avoid Wednesday. **Special comments** Family visits are organized on Sunday, 11 a.m.–3 p.m. **Reservations** required. **Author's rating** ★★★★. **How much time to allow** 1–2 hours.

DESCRIPTION AND COMMENTS This is one of Paris's newest and most accessible and user-friendly art museums, featuring well-presented exhibitions of classical and modern art. Recent exhibitons have included works from Rembrandt to Vermeer, Edvard Munch, Utrillo, Pollock, and Man Ray.

Place de la Bastille 11th arrondissement

| APPEAL BY AGE | PRESCHOOL – | GRADE SCHOOL – | TEENS ★★★ |
| YOUNG ADULTS ★★★ | | OVER 30 ★★★ | SENIORS ★★★ |

Place de la Bastille; Métro: Bastille

Type of attraction One of Paris's most celebrated landmarks. **Admission** Free. **When to go** Anytime, though it's wise to avoid the frequent demonstrations and rallie; at night, the area is teeming. **Special comments** One foreign dignitary, unaware that the original prison no longer stands, once asked how they fit all the prisoners into the obelisk that now stands at the center of the square. **Author's rating** ★★★. **How much time to allow** 10–20 minutes.

DESCRIPTION AND COMMENTS Nothing is left of the Bastille prison that was stormed on July 14, 1789, but the July Column in the center of this busy and popular intersection now marks this historic spot. Note the golden-winged Mercuryesque statuette at the top of the column, which has emerged as a symbol of Paris. Even today the Bastille remains an important public space for large demonstrations, marches, and rallies. Every Friday around 11 p.m., hundreds of motorcyclists on bikes of all sorts and sizes use the Place de la Bastille as the meeting point and point of departure for their noisy tour of the capital. A curious scene.

TOURING TIPS A canal boat trip leaves the basin at the Place de la Bastille and leads you under it.

OTHER THINGS TO DO NEARBY See Opéra Bastille, Place des Vosges, Place de la République, Promenade Plantée.

Sainte-Chapelle 1st arrondissement

| APPEAL BY AGE | PRESCHOOL – | GRADE SCHOOL ★★ | TEENS ★★ |
| YOUNG ADULTS ★★★★ | | OVER 30 ★★★★ | SENIORS ★★★★ |

4, boulevard du Palais; ☎ 01 53 40 60 80; sainte-chapelle.monuments-nationaux.fr.; Métro: Cité; RER: Saint-Michel–Notre-Dame

---

Type of attraction One of the most masterful assemblages of stained-glass windows in the world. **Admission** €8 adults, €5 reduced rate, free for those under age 18 and EU citizens under age 26; Sainte-Chapelle and Conciergerie, €10 per person. **Hours** March–October, daily, 9:30 a.m.–6 p.m.; November–February, daily, 10 a.m.–5 p.m. (box office closes 30 minutes before the chapel). **When to go** Early to beat the crowds and avoid the lines. **Special comments** Read the windows from left to right and from bottom to top. **Author's rating** ★★★★. **How much time to allow** 30 minutes.

DESCRIPTION AND COMMENTS If you have any affection for stained glass at all, this just may be one of your Paris highlights. This Gothic chapel, built within the confines of King Louis IX's private palace, was constructed in less than three years and finished in 1248. There are two super-imposed chambers forming the chapel, with a spiral staircase leading to the upper chapel. Here, the glass encasing becomes brilliantly illumi-nated, even when the light is low. Many of the relics of the chapel were pilfered or melted down during the French Revolution, and others have been stored in nearby Notre-Dame, but the original stained glass is the oldest surviving example of its kind in Paris. More than 700 of the 1,134 scenes represented on the 6,500 square feet of glass are original. Many of the same craftsmen from the Chartres cathedral worked on these windows. The main scenario in the glass is the celebration or Passion play as foretold by the prophets and John the Baptist. History buffs will be happy to note that Richard II of England married Isabel of France here in 1396.

TOURING TIPS Observe the worn floor to appreciate that seven centuries have passed since the church's construction.

OTHER THINGS TO DO NEARBY Visit Notre-Dame, the Latin Quarter, the Conciergerie, and Shakespeare & Co Bookstore.

La Sorbonne 5th arrondissement

APPEAL BY AGE	PRESCHOOL –	GRADE SCHOOL –	TEENS –
YOUNG ADULTS ★★	OVER 30 ★★		SENIORS ★★

47, rue des Écoles; ☎ 01 40 46 22 11; sorbonne.fr; Métro: Cluny–La Sorbonne

---

Type of attraction France's oldest and most celebrated university. Symbol of knowledge and enlightenment for more than seven centuries. **Admission** Limited public access; guided tour in French only, €9 per person. **Hours** Group tours organized by appointment, Monday–Friday; individuals can join the regular tour held one Saturday per month. **When to go** Weekdays or Saturday for a tour. **Special comments** The Latin Quarter gets its name from the fact that students used to study Latin at the Sorbonne. **Author's rating** ★★. **How much time to allow** 30 minutes.

DESCRIPTION AND COMMENTS The Sorbonne's reputation alone is reason to take note of this famed institution. Started in 1253 as a tiny college for poor students of theology, the Sorbonne was named after Robert de Sorbon, who came from a village in the Ardennes region. It was not until after Napoléon's reign, though, that the university grew into the institution of higher learning that it is known as. The chapel, in which the tomb of Cardinal Richelieu is located, is closed for renovation until 2012. For information regarding the guided tour call ☎ 01 40 46 22 11 or e-mail visites.sorbonne@ac-paris.fr. The meeting point for tours is at 46, rue Saint-Jacques.

TOURING TIPS Read up on the French educational system as a background for your tour. Take a peek into one of the lecture halls (amphitheatres).

OTHER THINGS TO DO NEARBY Visit Jardin du Luxembourg, Saint-Michel, Thermes de Cluny. Take a break at one of the many cafés on Place de la Sorbonne.

kids La Tour Eiffel 7th arrondissement

APPEAL BY AGE	PRESCHOOL –	GRADE SCHOOL ★★★	TEENS ★★★★★
YOUNG ADULTS ★★★★★		OVER 30 ★★★★★	SENIORS ★★★★★

Quai Branly, Champ de Mars; ☎ 01 44 11 23 23; tour-eiffel.fr; Métro: Bir-Hakeim; RER: Champs de Mars Tour Eiffel; buses: 42, 69, 72, 82, 87

Type of attraction The world's most recognizable landmark. **Admission** By stairs: first and second stories, €4.50 adults, €3.50 ages 12–24, €3 children ages 4–12; by lift to second story, €8 adults, €6.40 ages 12–24, €4 children ages 4–12; lift to top, €13 adults, €9.90 ages 12–24, €7.50 children ages 4–12; free for children under age 4. **Hours** January 1–mid-June and September 1–December 31: daily, 9:30 a.m.–11:45 p.m. (by lift), 9:30 a.m.–6:30 p.m. (by stairs); mid June–September 1: daily, 9 a.m.–12:45 a.m. (by lift or stairs). **When to go** Try to go an hour before sunset. **Special comments** Restaurants (first and second stories), souvenir shops. Wheelchair access to first and second stories only. **Author's rating** ★★★★★. **How much time to allow** 1–2 hours depending on the wait and the level you wish to climb to.

DESCRIPTION AND COMMENTS The Eiffel Tower is the superstar of Parisian monuments and most likely the world's best-known landmark. It was the largest construction in the world at 300 meters when it was inaugurated in 1889 by Gustave Eiffel to celebrate the centennial of the French Revolution. The tower exerts per square centimeter the equivalent of a person sitting in a chair, although its total weight is more than 7,000 tons. Its summit sways 12 centimeters only in the wind. Built first as a temporary structure, the tower was nearly knocked down in 1910, but due to its utility in radio and telegraph broadcasting it was saved from the scrap heap. The tower was re-electrified in 1989 for its centennial and the French bicentennial and stands today at 1,051 feet. The last days of the millennium (marked by an illuminated "J" for *jour*) were counted down on a huge electronic clock on the tower's front.

The tower consists of three platforms at 57 meters, 115 meters, and 276 meters. Go to the top. Don't try to save money here. From the third platform, you can see up to 40 miles when it's clear, although Parisian pollution sometimes veils the view. There is only one Eiffel Tower in the world. You've come this far; go to the top. For those of you afraid of heights, it's really not so bad. The elevator ride is scarier than the view. At the top you're enmeshed in protective cable. The best conditions are at sunset. If you're interested in the tower's utilitarian side, note that it is used as a radio and television transmitter, a weather station, and an aircraft navigational point. The tower hosts a culinary landmark, the Jules Verne, on the second level, which is terribly expensive but breathtaking (information ☎ 01 45 55 61 44; reservations online only at **restaurants-toureiffel.com**). Previously known as Altitude 95, the first-floor restaurant re-opened as 58 Tour Eiffel in 2009 (☎ 08 25 56 66 62). Going up the tower is always memorable regardless how many times you've done it. For returning visitors, it is worth renewing the pilgrimage at least once every decade.

TOURING TIPS Avoid midday, when the crowds are heaviest. Tickets can be purchased online at **tour-eiffel.fr.**

OTHER THINGS TO DO NEARBY Walk in the Champ de Mars, Trocadéro.

Tour Montparnasse 56   15th arrondissement

APPEAL BY AGE	PRESCHOOL —	GRADE SCHOOL ★★★★★	TEENS ★★★★★
YOUNG ADULTS ★★★★★		OVER 30 ★★★★★	SENIORS ★★★★

33, avenue du Maine; ☎ **01 45 38 52 56;**
tourmontparnasse56.com; Métro: Montparnasse-Bienvenüe

Type of attraction Paris's only modern skyscraper and France's tallest building. **Admission** Rapid elevator to the 56th floor: €10.50 adults, €7.50 ages 16–20, €4.50 children ages 7–15, free for children age 6 and under. **Hours** April–September, daily, 9:30 a.m.–11:30 p.m.; October–March, 9:30 a.m.–10:30 p.m. (until 11 p.m. Friday and Saturdays); last elevator 30 minutes earlier. **When to go** Early in the day or at night. **Special comments** The prices in the 56th-floor bar are as high as the view. **Author's rating** ★★★★★. **How much time to allow** 1 hour.

DESCRIPTION AND COMMENTS Atop Paris's sole skyscraper you are afforded a view of the city that truly is breathtaking. This is by far Paris's most underrated site. More spectacular than the view from the Eiffel Tower, from the top of the Tour Montparnasse you get to look down at the Eiffel Tower, and only from here can you really understand the scale and overall beauty of the city. The pattern and layout of the Montparnasse cemetery, literally beneath you, is revealed. The same is true for the Jardin du Luxembourg. On the 56th floor, you're in a windowed area where the view is great and there is even a small café for drinks and snacks. The fastest elevator in Europe carries you to the

56th floor in 38 seconds, but to reach the 59th-floor observation deck you need to walk up the stairs. Hold on to your hat and small kids. **TOURING TIPS** Walk up the stairs only on nice days.

OTHER THINGS TO DO NEARBY Visit Montparnasse Cemetery.

kids Trocadéro (Terrace or Esplanade) 16th arrondissement

APPEAL BY AGE	PRESCHOOL —	GRADE SCHOOL ★★★★	TEENS ★★★★
YOUNG ADULTS ★★★★		OVER 30 ★★★★	SENIORS ★★★★

Place du Trocadéro; Métro: Trocadéro

Type of attraction One of Paris's best open spaces for viewing the Eiffel Tower, especially at night. **Admission** Free. **When to go** Anytime, but late at night is spectacular. **Special comments** This hill was once used by the training cadets from the Right Bank École Militaire. **Author's rating** ★★★★. **How much time to allow** 30 minutes–1 hour.

DESCRIPTION AND COMMENTS Not only does Trocadéro merit a visit for the Palais de Chaillot and its Cité de l'Architecture et du Patrimoine, it is by far the single best place for viewing the Eiffel Tower. Go in the daytime, and then return at night before midnight when the lights on the tower go out. The square here and the park below are romantic and magical. Summer evenings are especially lively with excited crowds, bongo players and African dancers, inline skaters, and lovers hanging out.

TOURING TIPS Don't miss a late-night visit to this viewing point.

OTHER THINGS TO DO NEARBY Have a drink at Café de l'Homme, to your right as you face the Eiffel Tower.

kids Trocadéro Aquarium (Cinéaqua) 16th arrondissement

APPEAL BY AGE	PRESCHOOL —	GRADE SCHOOL ★★	TEENS ★★
YOUNG ADULTS ★★		OVER 30 ★★	SENIORS ★★

Jardin du Trocadéro, 2, avenue Nations Unies; ☎ 01 40 69 23 23; cineaqua.com; Métro: Trocadéro

Type of attraction Underground audiovisual aquarium. **Admission** €19.50 adults, €15.50 ages 13–17, €12.50 ages 3–12, free for children under age 3. **Hours** Daily, 10 a.m.–7 p.m.; last ticket 6 p.m. **When to go** Anytime. **Special comments** Wheelchair access throughout; café. **Author's rating** ★★. **How much time to allow** 2 hours.

DESCRIPTION AND COMMENTS This is an impressive state-of-the-art aquarium with a few dozen scary sharks and 9,000 fish. What's amazing is the mixture of live fish and high-definition animated films creating an experience called "Cinéaqua." Largest fish tank in France!

TOURING TIPS A definite winner with the kids. It might seem perverse, but there is an excellent Japanese restaurant, Ozu, here.

OTHER THINGS TO DO NEARBY Best view of the Eiffel Tower.

PARKS, GARDENS, CITY SQUARES, AND CEMETERIES

HERE IS A COMPLETE RUNDOWN OF PARIS PARKS, followed by a suggested list of quaint public places perfect for a rest, a picnic, a game of *boules,* some people-watching, and so on. Paris's open spaces and green spaces are thoroughfares for the city's history and architecture, as well as the venues for elegant relaxation and romance. A tour of the cemeteries reveals the city's intellectual, social, and political past—no trip to Paris is complete without at least a stroll in Père-Lachaise Cemetery.

Note that while the American concept of public park is participatory, in Paris uniformed guards protect the sanctity of many of these places and will not hesitate to whistle you off the grass. *Pelouse interdite* means "keep off the grass." Paris's mayor, Bertrand Deloanoë, has relaxed this custom somewhat, but only for green spaces of more than a hectare (around 2.5 acres).

kids Bois de Boulogne 16th arrondissement
Anchoring the city's western wing along and outward from the 16th arrondissement; Métro: Les Sablons

Type of attraction Paris's expansive green space and woods on the western edge of the city. **Admission** Free. **Hours** Daily, 24 hours. **When to go** Not after dark unless you know what you're looking for. **Author's rating** ★★★★★.

DESCRIPTION AND COMMENTS Paris's largest (over 2,000 acres) and most diverse green space, the Bois runs for miles at the western edge of the city. In the Bois you'll find two thoroughbred racetracks (Longchamps and Auteuil); the Jardin d'Acclimatation; the National Museum of Popular Arts and Traditions; the exquisitely landscaped Parc de Bagatelle, with Japanese water garden and water lilies and rhododendron garden; canoeing on the lakes, horseback riding, playing fields, picnic grounds, and jogging trails; the Roland Garros tennis stadium; the Pré Catalan, where Shakespeare is played in a garden planted with every flower, herb, and tree mentioned in his plays; and the Parc des Princes, Paris's most important sports stadium until the Stade de France was built for the World Cup in 1998.

Bois de Vincennes 12th arrondissement
Technically the 12th arrondissement, but outside city limits; Métro: Château de Vincennes

Type of attraction Paris's expansive green space and woods on the eastern edge of the city. **Admission** Free. **Hours** Daily, dawn–dusk. **When to go** Best when the weather is pleasant. **Author's rating** ★★★★★.

DESCRIPTION AND COMMENTS Paris's most significant green space on the eastern side of the city, the Bois de Vincennes offers a broad range of attractions, including picnicking, canoe rentals, jogging, a zoo (currently

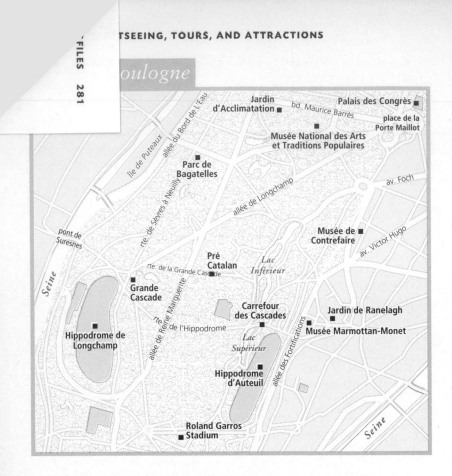

oulogne

closed for renovation), a château and dungeon, the Parc Floral, the Lac Daumesnil, the Hippodrome de Vincennes racetrack, a family farm, playing fields, merry-go-rounds, bike paths, and dense woods (perfect for mushroom hunting). One of our favorite pastimes is simply walking around the Lac Daumesnil or Lac des Minimes on a Sunday afternoon and observing Parisians as they stroll with their kids, play soccer, and frolic with hundreds of dogs.

Les Catacombes 14th arrondissement
1, place Denfert-Rochereau; ☎ 01 43 22 47 63; catacombes.paris.fr;
Métro: Denfert-Rochereau

Type of attraction A haunting but fascinating collection of human bones stored under the city. **Admission** €8 adults; €6 reduced rate, €4 ages 14–26, free for children under age 14. **Hours** Tuesday–Sunday, 10 a.m.–5 p.m. **When to go** Perfect for rainy days. **Author's rating** ★★★★★.

DESCRIPTION AND COMMENTS For some, this may be a highlight of their Paris trip. Many of the bones in Paris's public cemeteries are regularly raked out, sorted, lugged over, and stored in this maze of tunnels. You can descend into this dark world by climbing down the steep stairs at Denfert-Rochereau and visiting the miles of lined-up skulls, femurs, and crossbones. More than 6 million skeletons are down here. Originally opened to the public in 1810, the walkways today are well lit and the experience isn't oppressive. What you'll soon realize, though, is that Paris has a complex infrastructure of tunnels and ancient quarries beneath its streets. Kids and strange folks manage to get down into these tunnels, and it is believed that there is an entire universe of marginal activity down here. The French underground used the catacombs and other tunnels to organize its activities against the Nazis in World War II. Some readers advise visitors to bring their own flashlights because at times the paths are very dark. Allow about 90 minutes for a full visit.

Champs-Élysées 8th arrondissement
Between Place de la Concorde and the Arc de Triomphe;
Métro: Concorde, Charles-de-Gaulle–Étoile, George V

Type of attraction The most famous avenue on earth. **Admission** Free.
When to go Avoid New Year's Eve unless you want to be caught in the craze of hysterical crowds popping corks, honking horns, and kissing strangers on the lips. All major sporting victory celebrations tend to end up on the Champs-Élysées in pandemonium. **Author's rating** ★★★★.

DESCRIPTION AND COMMENTS The Champs-Élysées is studded with expensive stores, cafés, movie houses, airline offices, and clubs. Originally a field flanked by the most fashionable carriage path in the city, in the early 1700s rows of plane trees were planted and the peaceful stretch was renamed the Elysian Fields, or Champs-Élysées. Over the next century the road was lengthened to the Arc de Triomphe (Étoile) and finally all the way to Pont Neuilly (avenue de la Grande Armée and avenue Charles-de-Gaulle). In the 1800s, fountains and gaslights were added, and concerts were given in the streets. A musician named Sax played his newly invented instrument, the saxophone, for curious listeners. The Champs-Élysées became the symbol for the French nation, and military parades used its wide avenue. The Germans marched through the Arc de Triomphe in 1940. This was also the point of celebration for the liberation of Paris in 1944. The famous cycling event, Tour de France, finishes on the Champs-Élysées, and the Paris Marathon starts here. The July 14 parade moves along this avenue in an air of great triumph. When a head of state is visiting Paris, the flag of his or her country is raised with the French flag on every pole along the Champs-Élysées. Aside from the pomp and history of this great street, today there is little of interest in this overpriced and highly commercial area.

Cimetière de Montmartre 18th arrondissement
20, avenue Rachel, access by stairs from rue Caulaincourt;
☎ 39 75 (city hall help desk); Métro: Place de Clichy or Blanche

Type of attraction Celebrated Parisian cemetery, resting place for cultural stars. **Admission** Free. **Hours** Monday–Friday, 8 a.m.–6 p.m.; Saturday, 8:30 a.m.– 6 p.m.; Sunday, 9 a.m.–6 p.m.; closes at 5:30 p.m. November–March. **When to go** Before dark. **Author's rating** ★★★½.

DESCRIPTION AND COMMENTS   You have to like cemeteries in the first place to go out of your way to visit this one. Tucked in under an overpass at the base of Montmartre on the Clichy side, this cemetery is a pleasure to discover because few visitors make the effort—chances are it'll be deserted. As you walk across rue Caulaincourt, the stairway to your left brings you directly into the cemetery. You'll get a kick out of stumbling upon the graves of writer Émile Zola, composer Hector Berlioz, and poets Heinrich Heine and Théophile Gautier. Painter Edgar Degas and writers Alexandre Dumas and Stendhal rest here, too. More recent members of the club include the singer Dalída and the French filmmaker François Truffaut.

Cimetière du Père-Lachaise   11th, 20th arrondissements
Boulevard Ménilmontant; ☎ 39 75 (city hall help desk);
Métro: Père-Lachaise, Alexandre Dumas, Gambetta

Type of attraction Paris's most enchanting and star-studded cemetery. **Admission** Free. **Hours** Monday–Friday, 8 a.m.–6 p.m.; Saturday, 8:30 a.m.– 6 p.m.; Sunday, 9 a.m.–6 p.m.; closes at 5:30 p.m. November–March. **When to go** Before dark; and, for now, not on Jim Morrison's birthday. **Author's rating** ★★★★★.

DESCRIPTION AND COMMENTS   A lot more people these days visit the Paris grave site of Jim Morrison than those of Victor Hugo or Frédéric Chopin. In any case, almost everyone can find a mythic hero to visit in Paris's most celebrated and atmospheric cemetery, Père-Lachaise.

Tucked into the far corner of the 11th arrondissement lies a wild and hilly spread of 103 acres that is studded with stars, broken crypts, shifty cats, and a permanent guest list that will make your French teacher back home curse you from envy. Where else can you visit the resting spot of Marcel Proust, Honoré de Balzac, Édith Piaf, and Oscar Wilde in the same day? Even the remains of France's most important dramatist, Molière, are within reach. (Napoléon had Molière's bones transferred to Paris's most chic cemetery at its inauguration in 1803.)

You'll love hiking up the crooked alleys and narrow paths while getting lost in French cultural history. The mythic lovers Héloise and Abélard are here. So are the painters Corot, Daumier, Pissarro, David, Seurat, and Modigliani. The soul of Victor Hugo can be felt, and some claim that the brave voice of Maria Callas can be heard in the late afternoon. What an eclectic party: Laura Marx, Karl's daughter, is here, as well as Gertrude Stein and Alice B. Toklas. Sarah Bernhardt was buried at Père Lachaise in 1923, and more recently the philosopher Louis Althusser and actors Yves Montand and Simone Signoret have joined the posthumous cast.

Jim Morrison was buried in Père Lachaise in 1971; for the first decade there was no official stone, only graffiti, love letters, and empty bottles in his honor. Signs in chalk marked "Jim, This Way" lead you to the cult site. Several years back, a proper tomb was erected and a visit to the grave of the lead singer of the Doors has now become a must, the grave location having been added to the free map of the cemetery that you can ask for at any of the entrances. Most fans never realize that Morrison came to Paris to flee stardom and live as an obscure poet. After discussion of moving Morrison (his plot lease expired in 2001), the French government decided to immortalize the cult figure here.

One of our favorite places to get lost in Père Lachaise is at the base of Oscar Wilde's massive tomb, with a stone sphinx sculpted by Jacob Epstein. Wilde lived a number of truly decadent years in the French capital, and real Wilde fanatics can even stay in the Irish writer's room at the upscale l'Hôtel on rue des Beaux-Arts. The two great French pastimes, politics and sex, join here as visitors walk by the Mur des Fédérés, the wall where the last communard rebels were shot in 1871, an icon for die-hard left-wing sympathizers; and not far away, excited souls approach the life-sized statue of the 19th-century journalist Victor Noir. (Women come to touch, rub, and even lie on his prone, stone figure because it is supposed to embody amazing fertility power.)

It's doubtful that poor Père Lachaise, King Louis XIV's famed confessor, could have ever guessed what would become of his hilly parcel of land. Some tombs are marked *perpetuité,* meaning the plot was paid for for eternity; for other plots, the bones are gathered up and deposited in the catacombs every 300 years.

Cimetière Montparnasse 14th arrondissement
3, boulevard Edgar Quinet; ☎ 39 75 (city hall help desk); Métro: Edgar Quinet or Raspail

Type of attraction Paris's most important Left Bank cemetery. **Admission** Free. **Hours** Monday–Friday, 8 a.m.–6 p.m.; Saturday, 8:30 a.m.–6 p.m.; Sunday, 9 a.m.–6 p.m.; closes at 5:30 p.m. November–March. **When to go** Before dark. **Author's rating** ★★★★.

DESCRIPTION AND COMMENTS A visit to this cemetery is called for if you want to visit the grave site of the father of existentialism, Jean-Paul Sartre, or his companion, Simone de Beauvoir, whose classic work, *The Second Sex,* changed the way women saw themselves. Other stars in this orderly resting place, tucked behind Montparnasse, include Samuel Beckett, Guy de Maupassant, Man Ray, and Charles Baudelaire.

kids Jardin d'Acclimatation 16th arrondissement
Boulevard M. Barrès, Bois de Boulogne; ☎ 01 40 67 90 82; jardindacclimatation.fr; Métro: Les Sablons

Type of attraction Superb educational park for children in the Bois de Boulogne. **Admission** €2.70 per person, free for children under age 3. **Hours**

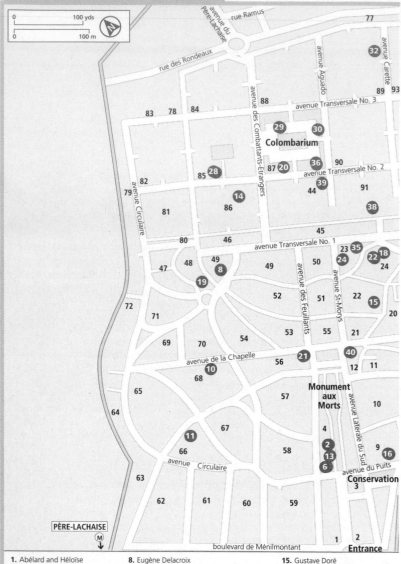

Père-Lachaise Cemetery

1. Abélard and Héloïse
2. Alfred de Musset
3. Amedeo Modigliani
4. Auguste Comte
5. Camille Pissarro
6. Colette
7. Édith Piaf
8. Eugène Delacroix
9. Frédéric Chopin
10. Georges Bizet
11. Georges Seurat
12. Gertrude Stein and Alice B. Toklas
13. Gioacchino Antonio Rossini
14. Guillaume Apollinaire
15. Gustave Doré
16. Hans Bellmer
17. Henri de Saint-Simon
18. Honoré Daumier
19. Honoré de Balzac
20. Isadora Duncan
21. Jacques-Louis David

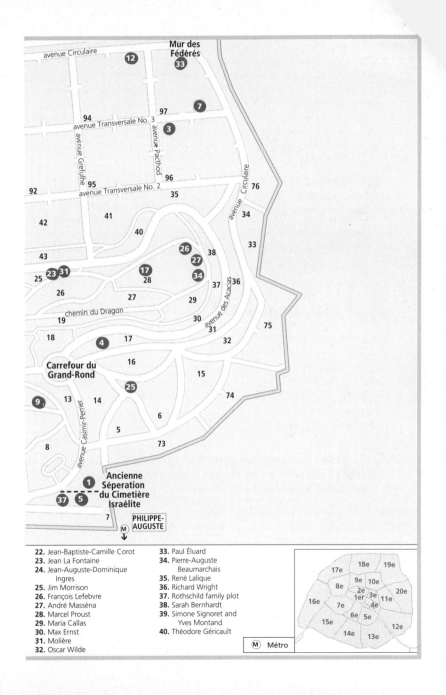

avenue Circulaire

Mur des Fédérés
33

12

97
7

94
avenue Transversale No. 3
3

avenue Grefulhe
avenue Pacthod

92
95
avenue Transversale No. 2
96
76

35

avenue Circulaire

42
41
34

40
33

26
38

27

43
17
34
37
36

25
23 **31**
28
29
avenue des Acacias

26
27
30

chemin du Dragon
31
75

19
32

18
4
17

16

Carrefour du Grand-Rond
15

25
74

9
13
14

avenue Casimir-Perier

6

5

8
73

Ancienne Séperation du Cimetière Israélite
1

37 **5**

7
PHILIPPE-AUGUSTE
Ⓜ

22. Jean-Baptiste-Camille Corot
23. Jean La Fontaine
24. Jean-Auguste-Dominique Ingres
25. Jim Morrison
26. François Lefebvre
27. André Masséna
28. Marcel Proust
29. Maria Callas
30. Max Ernst
31. Molière
32. Oscar Wilde
33. Paul Éluard
34. Pierre-Auguste Beaumarchais
35. René Lalique
36. Richard Wright
37. Rothschild family plot
38. Sarah Bernhardt
39. Simone Signoret and Yves Montand
40. Théodore Géricault

Ⓜ Métro

17e 18e 19e
9e 10e
8e 2e 20e
16e 1er 3e 11e
7e 4e
6e 5e
15e 12e
14e 13e

MAP 287

HTSEEING, TOURS, AND ATTRACTIONS

-7 p.m. May–September; rest of the year, daily, 10 a.m.–6 p.m. hen the weather is good. **Author's rating** ★★★★.

COMMENTS In the middle of the Bois de Boulogne you'll find diverse and pleasant park designed for children but also amusing and pleasant for the rest of the family. Take the tram outside Les Sablons Métro station right to the gate of the Jardin d'Acclimatation. There is an enchanted river ride and a miniature railway that traverses the park. You can play minigolf, ride minimotorcycles, attend a puppet show, or visit the Musée en Herbe, an ecological museum and workshop. Our favorite spot is the free-range petting zoo.

kids Jardin des Plantes 5th arrondissement
**Quai Saint-Bernard; ☎ 39 75 (city hall help desk);
Métro: Gare d'Austerlitz**

Type of attraction Lovely park and zoo on the Left Bank. **Admission** Free. **Hours** Daily, dawn–dusk. **When to go** Before dark. **Author's rating** ★★★★.

DESCRIPTION AND COMMENTS Site of Louis XIII's royal herb garden in the 1600s, today the Jardin des Plantes offers visitors a lovely respite from the urban experience without traveling far. Tucked into the eastern corner of the 5th arrondissement, this complex includes a very pleasant zoo, a botanical garden, a winter garden filled with exotic plants, and the world-renowned Grande Galerie de l'Evolution, part of the Natural History Museum, whose gallery of extinct species alone is worth a detour. Don't miss the turtles from the Seychelles Islands and the Tasmanian devil. The kids will love this. Not far from rue Cuvier entrance, you'll find a labyrinth of paths leading to the tomb of Daubenton, a gazebo hidden in the woods. This is an ideal hike or secret rendezvous spot for lovers.

kids Jardin du Luxembourg 6th arrondissement
**Place Edmond Rostand or place Auguste-Comte, rue de Vaugirard;
RER: Luxembourg; Métro: Rennes, Odéon**

Type of attraction The most Parisian of all Paris's parks. **Admission** Free. **Hours** Daily, dawn–dusk. **When to go** Before dark; the park is locked at night. **Author's rating** ★★★★★.

DESCRIPTION AND COMMENTS If you're in Paris for only a day, you'll want to spend part of it in this sprawling icon of the most Parisian Paris. There is something for everyone in this park: wooden-boat rentals on the pond for children, comfortable iron chairs for snoozing or reading, paths for jogging, pony rides for kids, basketball courts, a playground, a café beneath the shady trees, a perfect lawn reserved for babies under age 2, a Tuscan palace. Jardin du Luxembourg was created in 1617 by Boyceau de la Bareaudière after the wishes of Marie de' Medici. Its borders and design have been transformed through the centuries as much by its neighbors as its inhabitants. Even so, they remain an impressive oasis of nature and tradition that easily recalls historic Paris. The garden gives the impression that it was designed by a Parisian architect rather than Mother Nature, given all the straight lines, squares, and sharp angles found throughout most of it (even the trees). But it is a nice place to take a pause from the bustling streets of Paris. The garden is also the home of the French Senate building, where tours are available. To feel Parisian quickly, come here and sit.

Parc André Citroën 15th arrondissement
Rue Balard; Métro: Balard or Javel; RER: Javel

Type of attraction One of Paris's most innovative new parks. **Admission** Free. **Hours** Opens at 8 a.m. weekdays and 9 a.m. weekends; closes between 5:30 and 9:30 p.m., depending on time of year. **When to go** Before dark. **Author's rating** ★★★.

DESCRIPTION AND COMMENTS Seldom on the itineraries of visitors, this contemporary park is worth your time if you are staying nearby. On the site of the former Citroën car factory, which closed in the 1970s, the park now mixes marble, steel, plants, and, above all, water to create an unusual effect. In the Black Garden, you'll follow a circular path to an open space covered with 64 fountains, one of Paris's best-kept secrets for the hottest days of the year. Elsewhere, 100 water fountains perform a synchronized dance. The themes of the park are color-coded. A permanent fixture of the park is a hot-air balloon that rises 150 meters to give passengers a spectacular view over Paris. **Ballon Air de Paris;** ☎ 01 44 26 20 00; **aeroparis.com;** open daily 9 a.m. and closes 30 minutes before the park; weekends €12 adults, €10 ages 12–17, €6 ages 3–11; weekdays €10 adults, €9 ages 12–17, €5 ages 3–11, free for children under age 3.

Parc de Bagatelle 16th arrondissement
Route de Sèvres-à-Neuilly, route de la Reine-Marguerite; ☎ 01 53 64 53 80; Métro + Bus: Porte de Neuilly + Bus 43 or Porte Maillot + Bus 244

Type of attraction Park and flower gardens. **Admission** Free; exhibitions €5 adults, €2.50 ages 7–25, free for children under age 7. **Hours** Opens daily at 9:30 a.m.; closing times from 5 to 8 p.m., depending on the time of year. **When to go** Springtime is particularly pleasant. **Author's rating** ★★★. **How much time to allow** 1–2 hours.

DESCRIPTION AND COMMENTS Perfect for a Sunday stroll, this park within a larger park is guaranteed to please nature lovers. The most spectacular flowers follow the seasons, with May highlighting the iris garden, June through October the roses, and August being prime for the water lilies. Sculptures, fountains, bridges, and other bucolic details have been placed along the way.

Parc de la Villette 19th arrondissement
**211, avenue Jean Jaurès; ☎ 01 40 03 75 75; villette.com;
Métro: Porte de Pantin or Porte de la Villette**

Type of attraction Highly contemporary complex of green space, exhibition areas, recreation facilities for kids, music, and cultural events. **Admission** Free. **Hours** Daily, 24 hours. **When to go** Depends on what you're going to do or see there. **Author's rating** ★★★★.

DESCRIPTION AND COMMENTS Although a bit out of the way, visitors to the Parc de la Villette are never disappointed, and only the adventurous tourists make the effort. This is among Paris's largest parks, and it characterizes much of the best of the city's attitudes toward art, recreation, culture, and public space. The park is divided into sectors devoted to science and industry, music, film, and topical exhibitions of first-rate quality and originality contributing to the popular culture of the city. The Canal de l'Ourcq, which dates back to Napoléon and was used to bring fresh water into the city, flows through the center of the park. On the northern side, you'll find the Cité des Sciences et de l'Industrie, along with a real submarine you can visit, a dragon sliding board, and an unmistakable 118-foot-diameter steel globe called La Géode, in which an auditorium has been equipped with an 11,000-square-foot aluminum screen used for showing films with a 180-degree field of vision. Whatever is playing when you visit, try not to miss this experience.

On summer evenings, you can rent a reclining chair and view a classic film under the stars—delightful. Check out the entire program of outdoor summer activities on the Web site. If you're going to the Cité des Sciences or the Géode, get off the Métro at Porte de la Villette. If you are going to a temporary exhibit, the Cité de la Musique, or the Zénith concert hall, get out at Porte de Pantin.

Parc des Buttes-Chaumont 19th arrondissement
Rue Manin, rue de Crimée; Métro: Buttes-Chaumont

Type of attraction Rugged and beautiful park in a less-visited part of the city. **Admission** Free. **Hours** Daily, 7 a.m. until between 8 and 10 p.m., depending on the time of year. **When to go** Before dark. **Author's rating** ★★★★.

DESCRIPTION AND COMMENTS This is among the largest Parisian parks, English-styled and as beautiful as it is romantic. Created under Napoléon III by the designer Adolphe Alphand, it is a colorful landscape of about 5,000 acres with 600,000 trees. Wandering through the park, you can find Sibylle's temple atop an 89-meter cliff. One of the most secluded and peaceful spots in Paris is the cascade- and stalagmite-filled cave deep within the park. Joggers love it here.

Parc Monceau 8th, 17th arrondissements
**Boulevard de Courcelles at the place de la République Dominicaine;
☎ 01 42 27 58 30; Métro: Monceau**

Type of attraction Paris's most scenic *haute bourgeois* park. **Admission** Free. **Hours** Daily, 7 a.m.–8 p.m. (winter); 7 a.m.–10 p.m. (summer). **When to go** In pleasant weather, before dark. **Author's rating** ★★★★.

DESCRIPTION AND COMMENTS This park epitomizes the style and elegance of old-wealth bourgeois Paris. Artistically designed with a pagoda, temple, pyramid, windmill, and ornamental pond, Parc Monceau is surrounded by some of the finest and most exclusive apartments in the city. Nearby you'll find the Musée Nissim de Camondo and the Musée Cernuschi, which you can combine with a visit to the park.

Parc Montsouris 14th arrondissement
Boulevard Jourdan; Métro: Porte d'Orléans; RER: Cité Université; Tramway: T3

Type of attraction The finest park area in southern Paris. **Admission** Free. **Hours** Opens at 8 a.m. weekdays and 9 a.m. weekends, closes between 5:30 and 9:30 p.m., depending on time of year. **When to go** Before dark. **Author's rating** ★★★.

DESCRIPTION AND COMMENTS This is the finest park in the southern half of Paris. Opposite the Cité Universitaire, Parc Montsouris was designed by the famous city planner Haussmann in 1868 in an English style with an artificial lake. The tranquility of the park and its surroundings attracted numerous artists at the end of the 19th century, including Georges Braque and the Douanier Rousseau. Five minutes away, you'll stumble onto the Villa Seurat, a tiny dead-end alley on which Henry Miller lived in the studio of Artaud at number 18 and which he immortalized in his *Tropic of Cancer*. Anaïs Nin, Salvador Dalí, and Soutine also lived on this quaint alley.

Place Dauphine 1st arrondissement
Off the Pont Neuf, Île de la Cité; Métro: Pont Neuf

Type of attraction A perfectly charming and peaceful square at the western end of Île de la Cité. **When to go** At dawn when the sun's coming up over the Pont Neuf. **Author's rating** ★★★½.

DESCRIPTION AND COMMENTS Tucked in at the western tip of Île de la Cité behind the Palais de Justice, this quaint and discreet square dates back to the 1500s, when it stood as a muddy and damp area in the Seine. Henri IV conceived of a triangular square between the new Pont Neuf and the Conciergerie, and Place Dauphine is the result, named in honor of Louis XIII. Dotted with old eateries and legal bookshops.

Place de Fürstenberg 6th arrondissement
Center of Saint-Germain-des-Prés; Métro: Saint-Germain-des-Prés

Type of attraction Paris's most charming public square. **When to go** Anytime. **Author's rating** ★★★★.

DESCRIPTION AND COMMENTS A stroll through this tiny square in the heart of the Saint-Germain-des-Prés area transports you to the early 1700s. At number 6, you'll find the Delacroix Museum, where the Romantic painter worked and died.

Place de la Concorde 8th arrondissement
Where rue de Rivoli, rue Royale, and the quai all converge; Métro: Concorde

Type of attraction The most elegant and dramatic square in the city, and the site on which Marie Antoinette was guillotined. **When to go** Driving into the Place de la Concorde at night is breathtaking, but the driving is hazardous. **Author's rating** ★★★★★.

DESCRIPTION AND COMMENTS This square was built under Louis XV between 1755 and 1775. In 1793 a guillotine was installed there, and in 1833 Hittorf added the obelisk that was given to France by Mehemet Ali, viceroy of Egypt. This 2,300-year-old monolith is the most striking monument at Concorde, weighing 220 tons and measuring 23 meters high. In each of the eight corners of the Place there are statues honoring the great cities of France. It's difficult to walk around the Place, and it's treacherous driving here. At night, the Place is lit up, and a great regal presence is felt.

Place des Victoires 1st, 2nd arrondissements
Bridging 1st and 2nd arrondissements; Métro: Sentier or Étienne Marcel

Type of attraction Classy square in the heart of the fashion district. **When to go** During shopping hours. **Author's rating** ★★★½.

DESCRIPTION AND COMMENTS In the heart of Paris's most hip fashion district lies this very handsome square. Twentieth-century sweatshops where dresses and shirts, raincoats, and jackets are sewn sit just outside the square, abutting the 17th-century elegance. At the center is a fenced-in statue of Louis XIV on a horse, unveiled in 1822.

Place des Vosges 3rd, 4th arrondissements
Bridging 3rd and 4th arrondissements; Métro: Saint-Paul–Le-Marais

Type of attraction One of Paris's most elegant and royal squares. **When to go** Avoid the weekend crowds. **Author's rating** ★★★½.

DESCRIPTION AND COMMENTS One of only five prestigious *places royales* in Paris, Place des Vosges was created by Henri IV in 1605 and completed in 1612. It was highly frequented by the nobles of the epoch (when rich Parisians ended their squabbles through duels), then endured a period of relative dilapidation, only recently becoming once again a symbol of Parisian luxury. Today one can enjoy, besides greenery and a constant stream of the wealthy and famous, Victor Hugo's apartment, several art galleries, and some expensive but excellent restaurants.

Place Vendôme 1st arrondissement
1st arrondissement; Métro: Opéra or Tuileries

Type of attraction The only Paris square that can truly be called "ritzy." **When to go** Anytime. **Author's rating** ★★★★.

DESCRIPTION AND COMMENTS This square in the heart of Paris's most sophisticated fashion and design-driven neighborhood captures both the classical elegance of 17th-century style and the city's cutting-edge commercial chic. At the center of the posh and stately circle in 1810, Napoléon had the bronze Austerlitz Column erected, which was cast from the cannons used at the Battle of Austerlitz in 1805. In the Commune uprising, the column was destroyed, the painter Courbet was blamed and banished, and in 1871 a replica was finally erected. You'll find a handsome collection of arches supporting noble buildings. Today, the best known is the notorious Ritz Hotel, owned by the flamboyant millionaire Mohammed Al-Fayed, owner also of Harrods in London; his son was killed in a 1997 car crash with Diana, Princess of Wales. Although somewhat stuffy these days and having strong security—rumor has it that everyone entering the Place Vendôme is videotaped—you could slip into the Ritz for a cocktail at the famed Hemingway Bar, where the writer often sat and drank. At number 12 on the square, you'll note the house that Frédéric Chopin died in. (He's buried in Père Lachaise.)

Promenade Plantée (Elevated Level)
Viaduc des Arts (Ground Level) 12th arrondissement
**Begins at the intersection of avenue Daumesnil and
avenue Ledru Rollin; Métro: Reuilly Diderot or Bastille**

Type of attraction Paris's most original and longest park space. **Admission** Free. **When to go** Weekends tend to get painfully crowded. **Author's rating** ★★★★ (Promenade Plantée); ★★★½ (Viaduc des Arts).

DESCRIPTION AND COMMENTS Typical of Parisian priorities, instead of ripping down the old train viaduct that runs between the Bastille and the eastern edge of Paris, city planners converted the vaulted archways below into shops and cafés while transforming the wide rooftop into a planted walkway with benches and rest stops. You can stroll or jog all the way to the Bois de Vincennes or stop anytime along the way. A great vantage point from which to observe the facades of buildings in the 12th arrondissement.

Les Tuileries 1st arrondissement
**1, place Concorde; ☎ 01 40 20 90 43 (managed by the Louvre);
Métro: Concorde or Tuileries**

Type of attraction The most civilized of all of Paris's park spaces. **Admission** Free. **Hours** Daily, 7:30 a.m.–7 p.m. **When to go** In pleasant weather. **Author's rating** ★★★½.

DESCRIPTION AND COMMENTS Between the Louvre and Place de la Concorde on the Right Bank, Les Tuileries roll out in perfect splendor. This stretch of park is perfect for a tranquil stroll, a picnic, or simply as a route between the Louvre and points west. It is interesting to note that in the 1600s the area was dug up for its clay, which was used to make *tuiles* (tiles), from which this park gets its name. In the 18th century, public concerts were held in the château at the edge of the gardens, and even Mozart himself conducted here. The gardens have recently been renovated, and a collection of bronze nudes by Maillol have been added. The terrace overlooking the Seine affords visitors a lovely view of the river and the Musée d'Orsay on the Left Bank. Evenings and nights here now host Paris's most active and open gay cruising.

From the central pathway of the gardens, you enjoy a spectacular view of the obelisk in the Place de la Concorde and farther west along the Champs-Élysées to the Arc de Triomphe. The Café Réale is a pleasant spot for a light lunch.

The BRIDGES *of* PARIS

PARIS HAS A TOTAL OF 37 BRIDGES (the latest is the Simone de Beauvoir bridge, which opened in 2006) of greatly diverse sizes, styles, and materials arching over the Seine River between the east and west edges of the *périphérique* (the outer beltway). But there are only between five and ten magnificent *ponts* (bridges) that possess that special magic for transforming a mundane moment into a personal epiphany. New York or London may excite your mind or body, but Paris on the Seine is a purely emotional experience.

You might have to miss the Louvre or the Arc de Triomphe this time, skip a meal at that noted five-star restaurant you've been meaning to try, or sacrifice a run out to the *marché aux puces,* but whatever your time frame may be, don't visit Paris without stopping on a bridge in the City of Light! Miraculously, if you're not already in love in Paris, cross almost any bridge between Pont de Sully and Pont de l'Alma in the late afternoon or early evening, and you'll find yourself taking an inventory of the heart and realizing that being alive is, well, a glorious enterprise. What other city gives you that?

A TOUR OF PARIS BY BRIDGE

THE NICE THING ABOUT VISITING THE BRIDGES of Paris is that, depending on where you're staying, you can start your walking tour anywhere. You can follow the Seine east or west, descend from the street-level embankments called the *quais*, and strut along the water in either direction. Then you can climb back up to the street at the next bridge and continue on the *quai*. You can connect and disconnect from the buzz of city life as you please. You can use the frequent bridges to weave across the Seine, or you can keep walking for half as long as you want to be out, and then cross at the next bridge and return on the other bank.

Let's say you begin your stroll at Notre-Dame, a perfect point of departure in that the splendid Gothic cathedral not only is Paris's most central landmark but also the very point in Paris from which all distances in France are measured. From the little **Pont de l'Archevêché,** you are afforded a spectacular view of the spines and cornices of the back of Notre-Dame and its delightful park. (At the eastern tip of Île de la Cité, depending on your mood, you may wish to wander down into the somewhat hidden but terribly moving Mémorial de la Déportation commemorating those who were sent to death camps from Paris during the German occupation.)

From Île de la Cité, you have several attractive options. You can continue around to **Pont d'Arcole** and Hôtel de Ville, Paris's extraordinary city hall, or you can cross the pedestrian-only **Pont Saint-Louis,** which carries you over to the absolutely charming but somewhat overcrowded Île Saint-Louis. Assuming you do the latter, make sure you wait in line for a small, scrumptious ice-cream cone from Paris's most celebrated *glacier,* Berthillon. Then, either return to Pont Saint-Louis to watch the ducks, the colorful *péniches,* and the lovers, or explore Île Saint-Louis. From the foot of **Pont de la Tournelle,** Parisians tend to look up at the large window seats of Claude Terrail's culinary landmark, La Tour d'Argent, where the duck you order comes with registration papers.

From place Saint-Michel in the heart of the Latin Quarter, follow quai des Grands Augustins to **Pont Neuf,** one of Paris's loveliest bridges and the oldest means of crossing the Seine, finished in 1607 under the direction of Henri IV, who is immortalized in bronze on horseback on the bridge. Back in the mid-1980s, the eccentric artist Christo chose this bridge to wrap in miles of cloth and decorated the crossing with 100,000 begonias. The bridge cuts across the western tip of Île de la Cité, creating the secluded spit of land, the Square du Vert Galant, where you can sunbathe, picnic, and embrace while enjoying the most bizarre sensation of being totally alone yet wholly visible to every pair of eyes in the city. Continue on the other side of the bridge, past the massive bronze sculpture of a mounted Henri IV, and stroll through the private and shady Place Dauphine, which looks onto the majestic backside of the Palais de Justice, in which the unforgettable Sainte-Chapelle is housed.

On the Right Bank at the foot of Pont Neuf, you'll find the celebrated department store La Samaritaine, which was forced to close for major safety renovations (this mecca of Parisian commerce will not reopen before 2011).

A few hundred yards west, and you're at **Pont des Arts,** a wooden footbridge that attracts the city's funkier and more creative souls. The bridge is in line with the ornate, gilded dome of the world-renowned Institut, founded by Mazarin as the center of France's great science and art academies. On the Right Bank the bridge joins the Louvre, and with a little imagination, takes on metaphoric value suspended between creation and history. From the footbridge, you enjoy in every direction one of Paris's most copious visual feasts. Hang out here and rethink your life. Write a poem. Hold the hand of the person you married ages ago. Think about your kids . . . or forget them for the moment.

On both banks of the Seine you'll be amused to note the tiny green bookstalls of the merchants called *bouquinistes* permanently encrusted on the walls above the river. This literary vocation is passed from generation to generation, as it is virtually impossible to buy or rent a new space. Browse here; pick up an old copy of Éluard's poems or some Art Deco postcards.

Moving west, you'll strut past **Pont du Carrousel, Pont Royal,** and the innovative **Passerelle de Solférino,** one of the city's ambitious projects to join the Louvre complex with the Musée d'Orsay and create a direct liaison with the Jardin des Tuileries. The metal arch has a two-level walkway built in exotic wood, allowing pedestrians to cross the Seine here both from the river level and from the street.

Complementing the terrace in the Tuileries overlooking the Seine and an area known as the Plage de Paris, the walkway just opposite on the Left Bank—which is studded with statuary, greenery, and house-boat moorings—is a favorite meeting place for Paris's gay community.

THE BRIDGES BY NIGHT

FROM PONT DE LA CONCORDE AT NIGHT, you'll know why Paris is called the City of Light. On one end, the Assemblée Nationale is flooded in ochre tones, and the imposing structure of the Madeleine stands in the distance at the opposite end of the axis, with the sprawling Place de la Concorde glittering with wild traffic and 500 wrought-iron lamps. The etched obelisk, carried in one piece from Luxor, Egypt, towers in the center, in perfect symmetry with the Arc de Triomphe and the tip of the Pyramide at the Louvre. *Magnifique* is the only word that comes to mind. And for history buffs, it was precisely here that Queen Marie Antoinette was introduced to the guillotine.

The distance between Pont de la Concorde and Pont de l'Alma may be a bit much for some walkers, but the quiet **Pont des Invalides** offers a very romantic view of the river, and the Bateaux Mouches station, at night, of course, lights up the river in a dramatic way. The approach to **Pont Alexandre III** is priceless. Winged horses, cherubs, nymphs, gold-leaf swords (regilded for the 1989 bicentennial and recently repainted in gold) grace this Art Nouveau spectacle. Paris's most celebrated and most photographed bridge, Pont Alexandre III was built for the Universal Exhibition in 1900 and named after Russian Tsar Alexander III, who laid the first stone in 1896. The sidewalks on the bridge are wide, and there are no benches for sitting; so despite its elegance, this bridge is more for spectators than participants.

The area around **Pont de l'Alma** and the bridge that passes underneath is now heavily visited by tourists, who are fascinated to see where Princess Diana lost her life and to pay homage and leave written messages. The whole area has taken on a cultish appeal. At the foot of the bridge on the Right Bank, don't miss the gold-crusted flame of the Statue of Liberty. This was recast from the authentic mold used to build the original statue, which, given to the people of United States in 1812 as a gift from France, sits today at the mouth of the Hudson River in New York Harbor. A small imitation greets fluvial visitors to Paris as they sail under **Pont de Grenelle.**

Movie buffs won't want to miss the experience of stalking along the gray-metal stanchions of **Pont Bir-Hakeim** in the great style of Marlon Brando, who played a grieving American in the movie *Last Tango in Paris* and crossed that bridge repeatedly to rendezvous in amorous anonymity with an enticing Parisienne played by a young Maria Schneider.

On your way back toward the center, quai de la Mégisserie between Pont Neuf and Châtelet offers an amusing distraction. Aside from the extensive selection of house and garden plants, specialty shops roll cages with live ducks and geese, rabbits, snakes, lizards, Chinese newts, and other Parisian wildlife out onto the sidewalks. One always marvels at the sight of Parisian pigeons landing on the cages of their cousins in captivity.

Just on the other side of the Seine, on Île de la Cité, you'll find a wonderful bird market (open Sunday mornings), where the collectors and clientele are often as exotic as their Gabonese parrots or albino finches.

Let the bridges be your guide. The best way to find the romance of Paris is not only to cross the Seine but to also stop for a while suspended between both banks.

▌ DAY TRIPS *and* EXCURSIONS

TIME PERMITTING, YOU MUST SNEAK AWAY to the Palace and Gardens of Versailles or Fontainebleau, Chantilly, or Monet's Giverny, all within easy reach of Paris. But first, a few words about Le Mouse.

Disneyland Paris

APPEAL BY AGE	PRESCHOOL ★★★★	GRADE SCHOOL ★★★★	TEENS ★★★★
YOUNG ADULTS ★★★★		OVER 30 ★★★★	SENIORS ★★★★

Marne-la-Vallée–Chessy; ☎ 08 25 30 02 22; disneylandparis.com; RER Line A4: Marne-la-Vallée–Chessy

Type of attraction Classic Disney fare with a hint of Europe. **Admission** €62 adults, €54 children ages 4–11; 3-day pass, €139 adults, €118 children ages

NOT TO BE MISSED AT DISNEYLAND PARIS	
Frontierland	Big Thunder Mountain
	Phantom Manor
Adventureland	Pirates of the Caribbean
Fantasyland	Peter Pan's Flight
Discoverland	Buzz Lightyear Laser Blast
	Space Mountain Mission 2
	Star Tours
Walt Disney Studios	Cars Race Rally
	Crush Coaster
Main Street Electrical Parade	
La Parade Disney	

4–11; free for children under age 3. **Hours** Daily, 9 a.m.–11 p.m. (some seasonal variation; visit Web site for details). **Author's rating** ★★★★.

DESCRIPTION AND COMMENTS   We're not sure exactly why you'd come all the way to Paris to visit a Disney theme park. But if you can't get enough Disney in the States or want to see what became of all those dollars you've poured into the Disney coffers, Disneyland Paris (formerly Euro Disneyland) is a short train ride away.

Disneyland Paris opened in 1992 on a 5,000-acre tract surrounded almost exclusively by farms just 32 kilometers east of Paris. Located strategically in this vast expanse are the Disneyland Paris theme park, Walt Disney Studios park, five resort hotels, a convention center, an elaborate campground, a nighttime-entertainment complex, shopping arcades, almost 30 full-service restaurants, golf courses, several large interconnected lakes, and a transportation system consisting of four-lane highways, a train station, and a system of canals.

The theme park is a collection of adventures, rides, and shows drawn from Disney cartoons and films, and symbolized by Le Château de la Belle au Bois Dormant (Sleeping Beauty's Castle). The Disneyland Paris park is divided into five subareas, or "lands," arranged around a central hub. The first is Main Street, U.S.A., which connects the Disneyland Paris entrance with the central hub. Moving clockwise around the hub, the other themed areas are Adventureland, Frontierland, Fantasyland, and Discoveryland.

Disneyland Paris Guest Relations
Boite Postale 100
77777 Marne-la-Vallée, Cedex 4, France
calling from outside France ☎ **33 825 30 60 30**

In the United States, call the Disney Travel Company for information at ☎ 407-828-3232. Or visit **disneylandparis.com.**

ADMISSION OPTIONS One-day, two-day, and three-day admission passes are available for purchase for both adults (12 years and up) and children (3 to 11 years inclusive). All rides, shows, and attractions (except the Frontierland shooting gallery) are included in the price of admission. Multiday passes do not have to be used on consecutive days. If you are visiting Paris from the States, however, a one-day visit should suffice.

OPERATING HOURS It cannot be said that the Disney folks are not erratic when it comes to hours of operation for the park. They run several different operating schedules during the year, making it advisable to call ☎ 08 25 30 02 22 locally or check the Web site the day before you arrive at the theme park.

GETTING TO DISNEYLAND PARIS BY MÉTRO/RER You can reach Disneyland Paris in about an hour by taking the Paris Métro from wherever you are in the city and linking up with the RER Line A to Marne-la-Vallée–Chessy. You can purchase your Disney day passes at Métro and RER stations. For detailed tips on using the Métro and RER, see Part Five, Getting Around.

GETTING TO DISNEYLAND PARIS BY CAR Disneyland Paris is just 32 kilometers (19 miles) east of Paris, right off the A4 autoroute, sometimes known as the Autoroute de l'Est. Disneyland Paris is connected to the A4 autoroute by a direct access loop. Once on the loop, follow the signs to the park. Signs for the Parc Disneyland Paris exit appear on the autoroute, in both directions, way before you reach the general area.

Château de Fontainebleau

| APPEAL BY AGE | PRESCHOOL ★★★ | GRADE SCHOOL ★★★ | TEENS ★★★★ |
| YOUNG ADULTS ★★★★ | | OVER 30 ★★★★ | SENIORS ★★★★ |

77300 Fontainebleau, about 50 kilometers from Paris; ☎ 01 60 71 50 70; musee-chateau-fontainebleau.fr; Train: Gare de Lyon, Station Fontainebleau Avon (45 minutes plus 15-minute shuttle bus)

Type of attraction Excursion/day trip to this royal residence and gardens. **Admission** Gardens: free; château: €8 adults, €6 reduced rates (includes an audio guide), free for all visitors on the first Sunday of each month and for those under age 18. **Hours** Palace: June–September, 9:30 a.m.–6 p.m.; October–May, 9:30 a.m.–5 p.m.; closed Tuesday. **When to go** In pleasant weather only. **Special comments** A pleasant place for children, especially the gardens around the palace. **Author's rating** ★★★★. **How much time to allow** Half a day.

DESCRIPTION AND COMMENTS Revered by French kings for its proximity to great hunting, the Château de Fontainebleau makes for a delightful side trip from Paris. It is located about 40 miles south of the city and accessible by train in only 45 minutes; go in the morning and picnic on the grounds of the palace, or take a hike in the famous rock formations in the nearby forest. Plan on a good two hours visiting the palace, Napoléon's favorite residence. King François I turned the hunting lodge into a kingly palace and even hired the services of Italian artist Benvenuto Cellini. The ornate Louis XV staircase is one of the highlights of the tour. Of course, it's a thrill to visit the bedroom, throne room, and bathroom of Napoléon himself.

TOURING TIPS Buy a combined train, shuttle, and chateau ticket at Gare de Lyon. Bring a picnic.

SUGGESTED PLACE TO EAT Table des Maréchaux at the Hotel Napoléon, 9, rue Grande, 77300 Fontainebleau. ☎ 01 60 39 50 50, fax 01 64 22 20 87; **hotelnapoleon-fontainebleau.com**. Credit cards accepted. Elegant and quiet dining room with a pleasant terrace. Traditional French cuisine.

OTHER THINGS TO DO NEARBY Village of Barbizon.

Château de Versailles

APPEAL BY AGE	PRESCHOOL ★★★	GRADE SCHOOL ★★★	TEENS ★★★★
YOUNG ADULTS ★★★★	OVER 30 ★★★★★		SENIORS ★★★★★

78000 Versailles; ☎ 01 30 83 77 00; exhibitions ☎ 01 30 83 77 88; chateauversailles.fr; RER C: Versailles Rive Gauche station (40 minutes plus 8-minute walk)

Type of attraction Excursion/day trip to the most spectacular royal residence and gardens in France. **Admission** Gardens: free except during summer performances of the Grandes Eaux Musicales; palace (state apartments): €13.50 adults, free for those under age 18 and EU citizens under age 26; Marie Antoinette's Estate (which includes the Grand Trianon and Petit Trianon): €10 April–October, €6 rest of the year, free for those under age 18 and EU citizens under age 26; Passport day-pass with access to Palace, Marie Antoinette's Estate, and the Gardens: April–October, €20 adults, free for those under age 18 and EU citizens under age 26; November–March, €16 adults, free for those under age 18 and EU citizens under age 26. **Hours** Palace is closed on Monday, but the gardens and Marie Antoinette's Estate are open daily. Palace: Tuesday–Sunday, 9 a.m.–5:30 p.m. (open until 6:30 p.m. in summer; ticket office closes a half hour before palace). Marie Antoinette's Estate: July–October, indoor areas noon–6 p.m., outdoor until 7:30 p.m.; rest of the year, closes at 5:30 p.m. The gardens are open from 7 a.m. in summer, 8 a.m. in winter, and close at sunset. **When to go** As early as possible, preferably on weekdays. **Special comments** Audio guides in English included in entrance fee. **Author's rating ★★★★**. **How much time to allow** Half a day or full day.

DESCRIPTION AND COMMENTS If you'll be in Paris for five days or more, schedule a trip to Versailles. Easily accessible from central Paris via RER (under an hour), the palace and its gardens are guaranteed to impress you. The summer months attract a lot of foreign visitors, so try to go early and leave early. A complete tour of the château and gardens could take up to two days, but a good appreciation of the splendor of Versailles is possible in a half a day. Start with a tour of the interior apartments. On the first floor, do not miss the Chapelle Royale with its marble altar dedicated to Saint Louis, followed by the Grands Appartements, which include the royal bedrooms, a six-room suite occupied by Louis XIV from 1673 to 1682. Other highlights include the recently renovated Galerie des Glaces (Hall of Mirrors), where Louis XIV entertained foreign dignitaries. Seventeen windows and 17 glass panels with 578 mirrors illuminate the room. The hall, with its masterful view, was designed so that the last rays of sunlight each day fall here. Two major historical events subsequently transpired in this hall: the proclamation of the German Empire in 1871 and the signing of the Treaty of Versailles on June 28, 1919, marking the end to World War I. The Appartement de la Reine was Marie Antoinette's digs, and visitors should note her rococo touches. Nineteen royal births occurred here in the queen's bedroom; among them were Louis XV and Philip V of Spain. Then, go see the Appartement du Roi, Louis XIV's apartments, which wrap around the Marble Court. This should not be confused with the king's private apartments, which Louis XV reserved for his most intimate moments. The palace also includes the first oval opera house in France, inaugurated in 1770 for the marriage of the Dauphin—the future Louis XVI—and Marie Antoinette. *Note:* Some parts, including the Opéra Royale and Jeu de Paume, are closed for renovations.

After visiting the interior, you'll be ready for some air and open space. After viewing the front gardens, head out into the elaborate space around the Latona Basin and stroll through the groves. A walk around the grand and petit canals is a lovely way to take in the grandeur and elegance of this masterpiece of French landscaping in which nature has been organized according to classical principles. Of particular interest are the Grand and Petit Trianons (30 minutes by foot from the palace) and the Hameau de la Reine (15 minutes by foot beyond the Petit Trianon).

These country retreats from the official palace offer visitors a rare glance at a delightful thatched-roof hamlet of cottages built for Marie Antoinette. A great way to escape the crowds, too!

TOURING TIPS Get an early start. Bring good walking shoes. Avoid tours. Call ahead for information on English-language tours of the private apartments ☎ 01 30 83 78 00. All tickets can be purchased in advance at **chateauversailles.fr** and even printed at home before you leave. They can also be purchased in Paris from FNAC stores or combined with your SNCF train ticket at any station.

SUGGESTED PLACES TO EAT Potager du Roy, 1, rue Mar.-Joffre, 78000 Versailles; ☎ 01 39 50 35 34; fax 01 30 21 69 30. Closed Sunday and Monday. Credit cards accepted. Prewar décor. The cuisine puts the accent on vegetables since the restaurant is close to the Potager du Roi (King's vegetable garden). Set menu from €30 per person. Le Valmont, 20, rue au Pain, 78000 Versailles; ☎ 01 39 51 39 00 or **levalmont.com;** Closed Sunday evening and Monday. Credit cards accepted. A quaint and cheerful setting with Louis XVI–style chairs and paintings of île de France landscapes. Set menus start from €23 per person.

Giverny

APPEAL BY AGE	PRESCHOOL –	GRADE SCHOOL –	TEENS ★★★
YOUNG ADULTS ★★★		OVER 30 ★★★	SENIORS ★★★

Musée Claude Monet, 84, rue Claude Monet, 27620 Giverny, 1 hour from Paris; ☎ 02 32 51 28 21 (museum); fondation-monet.com; Train: Gare Saint-Lazare, Station Vernon (45 minutes)

Type of attraction Excursion/day trip to Monet's country residence and source of inspiration. **Admission** Fondation Claude Monet: €6 adults, €4.50 students, €3.50 children ages 7–12, under age 7 free. **Hours** April–November, daily, 9:30 a.m.–6 p.m. (box office closes at 5:30 p.m.); closed November–March. **When to go** Leave Paris early in the day; good weather only. **Special comments** Bring a picnic. **Author's rating ★★★. How much time to allow** 4 hours.

DESCRIPTION AND COMMENTS Fifty miles northwest of Paris on the way to Normandy, you can visit the house and gardens of Impressionist painter Claude Monet, who came to Giverny in 1883 when he was in his early 40s. This makes for a wonderful excursion in the spring and early fall. Connecting Monet's brilliant water lilies to the pond they floated in will be a spiritually fulfilling moment. Brace yourself for bucolic settings with wisteria hanging from a Japanese bridge, weeping willows, and vibrant rhododendrons. Between Monet's death in 1926 and 1977 the house and property were abandoned and fell into a decrepit state. Gerald van der Kemp, who had restored Versailles, took on the task of restoring Giverny, with the help of generous funds from Lila Acheson Wallace of *Reader's Digest*. Today, the property is managed by the Claude Monet Foundation. Set aside enough time to also visit the new Musée des Impressionnismes Giverny (formerly the American Art Museum), which opened in 2009 (☎ 02 32 51 94 65; **museedesimpressionnismesgiverny.com**).

TOURING TIPS If you don't have a car, you'll have to take the Paris-Rouen train from Saint-Lazare station (45 minutes). Get off at Vernon and take a taxi to Giverny (3 miles). There are bus excursions here, but you may not want to be part of a group when visiting this country setting. You can make a full day of it and go all the way to Madame Bovary's Rouen and stop at Giverny on the way back.

Parc Astérix

APPEAL BY AGE	PRESCHOOL ★★★★	GRADE SCHOOL ★★★★	TEENS ★★★★
YOUNG ADULTS ★★★		OVER 30 ★★★	SENIORS ★★★

60128 Plailly, 40 minutes north of Paris; ☎ 08 26 30 10 40; parcasterix.fr; direct shuttle bus leaves daily from the Carroussel du Louvre (Métro: Palais Royal); RER: B3 to Roissy–Charles de Gaulle 1, then take the Astérix shuttle bus to the park

Type of attraction Excursion/day trip to this Gallo-Roman theme park. **Admission** €39 adults, €29 children ages 3–11, free for children under age 3.

Promotional sales sometimes offered on the Web site. **Hours** April–August, daily, 10 a.m.–6 p.m. Only partially open the rest of the year, so be sure to check the Web site calendar before setting off. **When to go** Start out early and arrive at 9:30 a.m. **Special comments** A perfect way to mix history and entertainment. **Author's rating** ★ ★ ★ ★. **How much time to allow** 1 day.

DESCRIPTION AND COMMENTS If you want to enchant the kids, this theme park is a perfect way to combine amusement and French history and culture. An excellent alternative to Disneyland Paris, this park is studded with the popular Roman and Gaulois cartoon characters. Historical figures are interspersed with roller coasters and other theme rides, typical Gaulois houses, and re-created streets from Paris of the Middle Ages. Ponies, camels, and horses partake in the Olympic games in the ancient arenas, and the Menhir Express rafting ride through cascades and rapids will cool down the kids. There is a dolphin and otter show, plus other surprises. For a theme park, you'll be delighted with this original cultural attraction.

TOURING TIPS Go when it's gray or overcast to beat the heat and the crowds.

PART SEVEN

DINING *and* RESTAURANTS

BON APPÉTIT!

BRACE YOURSELF. One of your greatest sources of pleasure during your days and nights in Paris will be sublimely culinary. Of course, there is a huge difference between what you eat in a simple restaurant and what is served at a *restaurant gastronomique* (a gourmet or fine-dining establishment). Nonetheless, it is in the food in France at all levels that art and aesthetics, science and sustenance, meet. Indulging in Parisian cuisine requires more than tasting and swallowing; you must observe and contemplate.

unofficial **TIP**
Parisians do nearly everything around the lunch and dinner table, so never, ever think of a long, languorous meal in Paris as a waste of time. Try not to be rushed when in a restaurant, and approach each meal as an event as important as visiting a museum or exploring a monument.

There is no better way to learn about Parisian culture, language, social attitudes, style, and aesthetics, French agriculture and geography, and Parisian habits than *à table* (ah **tah**-bluh), or "at the table." Go slowly, and never forget that you are in the capital of pleasure and sensual gratification, so indulge and, for at least a few days or evenings, suspend all finickiness, guilt, waistline worries, and calorie and cholesterol counting. Try to add one new culinary adventure to every meal. There are lots of common local specialties that may be wholly new to you. Keep a little notebook of your savory discoveries, such as *cèpe* mushrooms or fiddleheads, periwinkles, snails, crayfish, beef muzzle, goose foie gras . . . and, with 450 types of cheese in France, it's going to be hard to avoid a high-butterfat adventure. If you select your restaurants well and know how to handle yourself, your dining experiences in Paris will be very memorable . . . and enriching. If you choose badly or just go for the quick and easy solution, eating in Paris can be both overpriced and disappointing. You

HOW PARISIANS STAY SO SLIM

The crude truth is that Parisians aren't as slim as they once were. In fact, nearly 10 percent of the population is now considered overweight. Why? The growth of fast food, the higher incidence of driving, and the increase of choice in school lunches (kids opt for the sweet and fatty stuff and grow up with fewer nutritious culinary habits than their parents). That said, Parisians still look pretty good. Why? On the whole . . .

- They do a lot of walking.
- They eat balanced and diverse meals.
- They eat little processed food with few additives.
- They eat few snacks and consume little between meals.
- Their food contains few hidden fats and sugars.
- They prefer water to soft drinks.
- They take plenty of time to digest their food.
- They eat modest portions.

don't mind a splurge once in a while, but you want the meal to overwhelm you with flavor, presentation, and ambience.

While Paris is studded with great restaurants, it is also packed with all sorts of mediocre cafés, bars, bistros, brasseries, fast-food establishments, and sidewalk stands. Without some good leads, coaching, or recommendations, you'll easily find yourself unsure of where to go and what to choose. The last thing you want is to end up staying in your hotel or just walking across the street to the closest restaurant because it's convenient. Similarly, returning to the same place you've been before because it's comforting to stick with a known entity is a shame. Adventure, explore, take risks. . . .

The sheer number of places at which you can eat in Paris is certain to make you wonder how they all manage to stay in business. Well, Parisians eat out a lot and per capita spend more money on food consumed away from home than the residents of most other European cities.

WHEN TO EAT

THE IDEA OF EATING WHEN YOU'RE hungry isn't quite French. Rather, custom and habit in Paris require that you be hungry when you're supposed to be dining. So, although you can always satisfy a growling stomach and yield to that pang for something *très chocolat,* keep in mind that lunch at a restaurant is served between noon and 2 p.m. and dinner is between 7:30 or 8 p.m. and 10 p.m. In Paris, a large city, there are plenty of exceptions and alternatives for the less traditional, but by and large these should be your dining hours. Although you can always eat something at a café, do not plan on having your midday meal at a restaurant at 3 p.m. Impossible. Don't even try. Similarly, if you're used to the early-bird special at 5:30 p.m., you'd better grab a snack, a coffee, and a piece of cake at a *salon de thé*—or a *chocolat chaud* (hot chocolate) at Chez Angelina or Café de Flore, for example—to hold you over until the Parisian dinnertime.

GENERAL HOURS

Breakfast 7 to 9 a.m.   Lunch noon to 2 p.m.   Dinner 8 to 10 p.m.

SIMILARLY, IF YOU WANT TO EAT SOMETHING after 10 p.m., you can, but your field of choices is drastically reduced. (See restaurant profiles later in this chapter for late dining hours.)

The other problematic meal in the week is Sunday-night dinner. Many Paris restaurants are closed on Sunday nights, but you still have to eat. (Again, see restaurant profiles later in this chapter for Sunday dining.)

A WORD ABOUT TOILETS AND TELEPHONES

ALL CAFÉS HAVE PUBLIC TOILETS AND TELEPHONES inside, usually at the back and often downstairs. The toilets are almost always free, but some of the larger and classier cafés may have an attendant sitting in the doorway with a suggestive plate of coins. You're guaranteed a higher level of hygiene here, and you can leave a tip if you wish. Paris café toilets are known for their uneven degrees of cleanliness: most are acceptable; some are impeccable; others are a bit funky and ill-equipped. It's a good rule of thumb when traveling to carry toilet paper with you as a precaution.

One of the great character-building experiences left in Paris is the Turkish toilet (more irreverently known as the "squat and pray"). Be prepared. Don't just turn around and leave before you give it a shot (pardon the pun). The Turkish toilet is a glorified hole in the ground. Position your feet on the porcelain platform, squat, and aim for the hole. To flush, you pull a chain that sends a torrent of water over the platform. To avoid soaking your feet, get ready to move out of the way before you yank the chain. This may seem primitive, but it's a totally hygienic, no-contact experience, and one you shouldn't miss.

unofficial **TIP**
Public telephones in cafés are often coin operated, but increasing numbers of cafés have card-operated phones.

PARIS RESTAURANTS:
Defined and Explained

JUST BECAUSE AN ESTABLISHMENT SELLS FOOD DOESN'T—in Paris—make it a restaurant. And similarly, don't expect to be able to walk into a restaurant (even if it has something that looks like a bar) to order a drink. The bill of fare, habits, hours, and expectations are all different. A restaurant is where the tables are set, there is a menu, and you're expected to order a full meal—to eat (*manger*), to dine. Gobbling down a sandwich is not considered dining. Here's a rundown of the ins and outs of Paris's eating and drinking options.

CAFÉ AND *CAFÉ TABAC*

THE CAFÉ IN PARIS IS FAR MORE THAN A PLACE TO DRINK COFFEE, although it is that, too. It is a place to rest, to read a novel or write one, to think, to meet friends, to do business, to glance over the sports page of the *Herald Tribune*, and to hang out and people-watch. It's probable that you'll find a café that you like, maybe even a table that you'll quickly grow attached to, and you'll return periodically. The delights are endless, but there are some basic customs you absolutely need to master before you can consider yourself a "regular."

- Cafés on the main avenues and boulevards are expensive, with even a simple espresso-style coffee costing more than €3. The smaller cafés on the back streets are more intimate and a bit more reasonable.

- There are three different price structures in a café. In essence, it's not the drinks you're paying for, but your location. When you sit at a sidewalk table on the terrace outside, you pay top price; when you sit at an inside table, you pay slightly less. The most economical place in a café is the counter, called the *zinc* (the counters in Paris cafés were traditionally made of shiny zinc). Here, you stand or lean, have your coffee or glass of wine, or even grab a quick sandwich. But if you want to linger, you'd be better off taking a seat.

- Don't sit at an inside table set for lunch if you only want a coffee or drink. You'll be asked to move; these tables are for dining only.

- Standing at a bar in Paris has none of the negative stigma or connotations of hard drinking that exists in the Anglo-Saxon world. In fact, although the French lead the world in alcohol consumption, most of this is in the form of wine drunk at meals. Underage drinking is not a real problem here, and you'll rarely see adolescents attempting to drink in public.

- If the price of drinks at a café seems overwhelmingly expensive to you, we recommend that you stop thinking in dollars. This will reduce the pain. Secondly, as one resident American travel writer puts it, "Don't think of the price of a coffee as the price of a coffee. Think of it as the cost of renting a prime piece of Paris real estate for an hour. Four dollars an hour is a bargain, and you get a good strong espresso thrown in as well."

- You can order a simple coffee and sit for as long as you like and no one will rush you or bother you. Take your time. No one will pressure you to order more or get moving.

- Don't call your waiter *garçon* ("boy")—that went out a generation ago and is no longer appropriate or appreciated. To get the waiter's attention, just motion with your hand or discreetly say, *"S'il vous plaît, monsieur"* (see voo **play**, miss-**yer**).

- When your waiter brings you your coffee or drinks, he'll leave a little cash-register receipt on a small plastic dish. This is your bill. Sometimes he'll leave this with you until you're ready to leave. However, when he's about to go off duty, he'll ask if he can *encaisser* (settle up) right away. You pay him directly, and he has a pouch from which he makes change. Then he'll give the slip of paper a little rip, which means you've paid your bill.

- As is the case with everything that you eat or drink in France, the "service," or tip, is included. So don't leave 15 percent on top of your bill. You can leave a few small coins though, which is a local habit.

- There are certain drinks you can only order at the *zinc,* such as a glass of draught lemon soda, which is used as well in a popular summer drink called a *panaché,* a blend of draft beer and lemon soda. A refreshing variation is the Monaco, a draft beer with grenadine syrup.

- In the past, the smoking might have stunned and discouraged you at first. As of 2008 there was a gust of fresh air when a law came into effect banning smoking in all enclosed public places.

- Liquid portions are measured in liters and divided into centiliters (cl). A beer glass has a little line indicating where the 33-cl or 50-cl level is. Bottled beer usually comes in 33-cl or 25-cl bottles. It's the measured quantity in France, not the full or almost-full glass, that counts.

unofficial **TIP**
What culinary ingredient kills the taste buds for wine? Chocolate!

CAFÉ TABAC

THE CAFÉ TABAC (OR TABAC FOR SHORT), easily spotted by its red-neon sign, is a café with a few extra features. Primarily, these establishments have been state licensed to sell cigarettes and other tobacco products to the public. Only a *café tabac* can sell tobacco products, and often you'll see a stream of smokers coming out the door. The *tabac* also sells postage stamps, lottery tickets, telephone cards, street-parking cards, and fiscal stamps needed for licenses, parking tickets, and other official documents. You'll always find a yellow mailbox for all your letters outside a *tabac.*

WHAT TO ORDER IN A CAFÉ

COFFEE Frequenting a café doesn't necessarily mean you're thirsty, but nonetheless you have to order something. (To simply quench your thirst, carry a bottle of mineral water with you during your sightseeing.) Your feet will thank you for each café stop, and there is no better way to drink up the atmosphere than simply hanging out at a marble-topped café table on a Paris sidewalk.

So, what to order? The most obvious choice is coffee, and it's the cheapest, too. Many Americans order *café au lait* at every chance. Ask for a *café crème* if you want to impress them with your expertise (don't worry, it'll be made with 2 percent milk, not cream). A simple coffee is called *un café* or *un express* (*espresso* is the Italian word.) This comes in a

unofficial TIP
Café au lait is usually consumed by Parisians in the morning, but you can order one whenever you like; Parisian waiters are used to this.

tiny cup, half-filled or less, with a nice layer of aromatic foam on the surface, a tiny spoon, and a sugar cube in the saucer. It is not unusual to ask for a glass of water with your coffee (*un verre d'eau, s'il vous plaît*) [ahn vair **doh,** seel voo **play**)]). If you want a bigger shot of caffeine, ask for a *double express* (**doo**-bla ex-**pres**), which is served in a larger cup and costs twice as much.

There are lots of lovely little variations and nuances to ordering coffee, a few of which we'll share with you. If you like your coffee intensely strong, ask for a *café serré* (cah-**fay** sai-**ray** [condensed coffee]), and you'll get the same dose of caffeine in about half as much water. Or if you don't want a big, creamy *café au lait* but do like a bit of milk in your coffee, ask for a *noisette* (nwa-**zet**), literally meaning "hazelnut," because a tiny splash of milk is dropped into your espresso, forming a white shape like a hazelnut.

Hot chocolate is always an option as well, and because the quality of chocolate is excellent in France, you'll most likely be pleased. But most of the big cafés today have opted for the powdered chocolate instead of the real old-fashioned melted chocolate, so be forewarned.

If you're used to a huge mug of coffee à la Starbucks, you can ask for a *café long* (cah-**fay lohng**) or a *café américain* (cah-**fay** a-mair-ree-**kainh**), which will contain more water and be substantially weaker. Hotel coffee will be brewed, but not café-style, coming instead out of a steam-pressured espresso machine. Note that although France and its "French roast" have a good reputation, this is not a coffee-producing nation, and the quality of café coffee is not particularly excellent. (It is strong, though.) What is excellent is the atmosphere and culture in which you can sit with your coffee.

Lastly, there is virtually no such thing as "take-out" coffee, and hardly anyone will be seen drinking the stuff from plastic or Styrofoam containers or transportable goblets with spill-proof covers, except just maybe if you happen to be in the vicinity of one of the 35-odd Starbucks that have mushroomed here in recent years. No one in Paris drinks coffee on the street, on the subway, all morning long at their desks, or in their cars. Don't even think of it. Just take a seat and relax.

TEA If you drink tea—or *thé* (tay)—you should know that you cannot order just a cup of tea; you also have to get a little pot of it, which you can order with either lemon or milk. Don't be furious to learn that the wedge of lemon costs extra: Parisians are not too astute on the public-relations aspect of delivering value to customers. No one complains about these sorts of things. However, you can ask the waiter to add more hot water to the pot to give yourself another cup, and this is free.

BEER A highly popular drink to order in a café is a draft beer (*bière* [**bee**-yair]), popularly called a *demi,* indicating the size of the glass, a half pint. When you ask for a beer, Parisian café waiters will often seize the opportunity to try to sell you one of the more expensive beers in bottles or on tap. If you just want basic local beer, just ask for a *bière normale* (nor-**mahl**). French beers are all brewed in the eastern region of Alsace, including Kronenbourg and its premium beer, 1664. Dutch and Belgian beers are widely served as well. If you've never had a Belgian Leffe, treat yourself to a frothy *demi.* Be prepared to have a hard time going back to Bud or Miller Lite after you've consumed a few pints of the flavorful and hearty European suds.

Cafés also serve draft beer in a pint glass called a *formidable.* The price is formidable as well.

WINE You can order wine (*vin* [**vaah**-n]) by the glass at all cafés. The simple standard fare is called a *ballon de rouge* (bah-**lown de rooj**) or *ballon de blanc* (bah-**lown de bloh**-n), after the bulbous round glass that the house red or white wine is served in. The bar wine is drinkable, but you'd do better asking for a *ballon* of Côtes-du-Rhône or Beaujolais (red), or Sauvignon or Sancerre (white).

Bottles of wine and Champagne are also available but usually overpriced in cafés. There are, of course, wine bars, which are another story. Read on.

APÉRITIFS In the late afternoon and early evening, cafés come alive with regulars having an *apéritif* (ah-per-a-**teef**) before going home for dinner. Aside from a beer or glass of wine, one of the most popular drinks in France is *kir,* white wine with a dash of *crème de cassis* (blackcurrant liqueur), a delightful cocktail. Without a doubt you should order a *kir* or two while you're in Paris. An even more delightful spin-off is the *kir royal* in which Champagne is substituted for the white wine.

CHAMPAGNE You can never go wrong with a glass of Champagne as an apéritif, but be prepared to pay at least €10 for a flute of the bubbly stuff. Sparkling wine from outside the Champagne appellation is called *blanc de blancs* or *crémant.*

WHISKEY AND MIXED DRINKS Parisians drink whiskey before dinner, and the stigma of whiskey as reserved for heavy drinkers does not exist in France. In fact, whiskey, either the good Scottish stuff or the mythic American brands, is prestigious but expensive when consumed as a cocktail. True gourmets know, too, that drinking hard liquor before a meal is a sure way to deaden the taste buds.

In the summer, you'll want to sit outside in the shade, pretend you're somewhere along the Mediterranean, and order a *pastis*. As you add an ice cube and some water to your shot of clear-amber licorice-tasting liqueur, the substance goes foggy and milky. Sip this refreshing libation and slide slowly into a stupor of relaxation.

After-dinner (or lunch) drinks are called *digestifs*. Here your choices are numerous. Try a Cognac or an Armagnac. Late in the afternoon or in the evening, you may opt to nurse one of these while you relax in a café. To feel really part of the scene, order a Calvados (apple liqueur from Normandy) with a coffee. In the colder months, this is the best way to warm yourself up from the inside

SYRUPS AND SOFT DRINKS Parisians drink a variety of beverages in which yummy syrups are added to either sparkling water or milk. It may seem silly to stand at a bar and order a *lait fraise* (strawberry milk) or *lait grenadine* (pomegranate milk), but it is done. Orange juice is expensive and comes in tiny bottles, and thus tends to be a disappointment for tourists. Tomato juice comes with a saltshaker and celery powder.

Vittel *menthe* is an excellent choice for a hot day. You'll be served a small bottle of Vittel spring water and a glass with a dash of mint syrup. Be careful not to order the similar *menthe à l'eau,* which is served with mint liqueur and costs twice as much.

Very popular in the warm months is the *citron pressé,* simply a lemon squeezed into a glass, served with ice cubes, packets of sugar, and a *carafe* of water, all of which you mix in your glass according to your taste.

Young French clubbers who don't drink alcohol opt for a Coke, referred to in French as a *coca*. This will not come with ice unless you ask for it. Tourists often yearn for those refreshing liquid common denominators, Coke and Pepsi, and they are readily available at all Parisian cafés and fast-food restaurants. Coke, still basking in its reputation as a foreign status symbol, continues to be disproportionately expensive, so be prepared to pay a lot more for it than for a glass of beer or wine. Tourists often make this mistake and order a Coke thinking it'll be the most common and cheapest drink on the menu. Wrong. Diet Coke is called Coca-Cola Zéro, and Diet Pepsi is called Pepsi Max. Since we're talking about calories, bring your own artificial sweetener, to be on the safe side.

*un**official* **TIP**
Never order a Coke with your meal at a restaurant. Parisians cannot understand how Americans can drink something that has nine spoonfuls of sugar in it with a well-prepared dinner.

ICE CUBES Although this is changing somewhat, ice cubes (*glaçons* [glah-**sown**]) are generally not provided or easy to find unless you ask for them specifically. Parisian waiters know that Americans have a fixation on ice, so they'll be accommodating, but they will probably roll their eyes too. Generally, Parisians do not require their drinks to be excessively cold or hot, believing that, aside from it being unhealthy to drink freezing-cold drinks before going back out into the heat, the flavor of drinks is truer when they're served at room temperature. Don't confuse the words *glaçons* and *glace,* the latter meaning "ice cream."

Eating in Cafés

When you find yourself hungry between official French mealtimes— before noon (too early for lunch), after 2 p.m. (too late for lunch), before 7:30 p.m. (too early for dinner), or after 10 p.m. (too late for dinner), the café will be your savior. Additionally, you may not wish to take two hours to eat, spend a lot of money, or be obliged to consume a large amount of heavy food before strolling around the Louvre. Again, the café is your answer. You may (we stress the conditional) eat well in a café, but then again you may not. You may be wholly satisfied, but in Parisian culinary terms, this has not been a proper French meal. You may not care. And that's fine, as long as you know the difference between having something acceptable to eat in a café and having a real meal, *un repas* (uh ruh-**pah**), in a Parisian restaurant. We hear a fair number of tourists claiming to have had a delicious meal in a particular café, and without sounding too pretentious, we must correct this notion. You may have had a nice salad or a tasty *plat du jour* (daily special), but you didn't dine.

unofficial **TIP**
A sandwich eater in Paris is not considered to be someone who is dining.

At any time of day or evening you can order a *sandwich* (sahnd-weech), a *croque monsieur* (croak miss-**yer** [grilled cheese with ham on toast]), or often a salad. *Caution:* Cafés also serve a lunch meal. You'll notice that tables set with placemats are for people who are dining. If you are stopping in for a coffee or a drink, you cannot sit at one of these spots. If you are just having a quick sandwich or *croque monsieur,* these spots are not for you either. You must sit at one of the "unset" café tables. Hey, don't knock it; join in.

SANDWICHES AND OTHER LIGHT CHOICES The choice of café sandwiches is almost always identical from café to café. You can choose ham (*jambon* [dzahm-**bown**]), cheese (*fromage* [froh-**maj**]), *pâté* (pah-**tay**), hard sausage (*saucisson sec* [saw-see-**sown** sec]), or *rillettes* (ree-**yet**), a tasty, high-fat pork or duck spread served on a long *baguette* (bag-**get**). One tourist complained that when he asked for a piece of lettuce on his ham sandwich, he was charged extra. This was not a case of lettuce extortion; the café owner just called this simple variation from the norm a *sandwich fantaisie,* and the price was adjusted accordingly. Note that it's not common to make special requests, and the guy behind the counter is not going to be very accommodating. When in doubt, we recommend the sandwich *jambon avec cornichons* ([cor-nee-**shown**], a ham sandwich with vinegar pickles). And spread your baguette with dabs of Dijon mustard—delicious! Mustard, by the way, makes for an excellent, original, inexpensive gift.

A very Parisian sandwich is the *croque monsieur,* or its variation, the *croque madame.* Simply, this is a ham sandwich topped with a slice of Gruyère (a Swiss cheese also known as Emmental), grilled in the broiler, and eaten with a knife and fork—the *croque madame* is the same with a sunny-side-up egg sitting on top. For about €6, you may enjoy this simplest item of Paris café cuisine. Other options include a slice of quiche or one of the many variations of *tarte* (savory pie), such as the *tarte à l'oignon* (onion) or *tarte au poireau* (leek). The classic quiche lorraine is made with cheese and *lardons* (chunks of smoked bacon, sometimes fatty and studded with crunchy cartilage; Parisians just chew and swallow).

In addition, café restaurants almost always offer a few salads, which have caught on over the last ten years as more and more Parisians want to eat lighter meals at lunch. Two standard salads to choose from are the *salade niçoise,* which is a combination of lettuce, tomato, tuna, egg, green beans, black olives, and often rice or corn, served with a vinaigrette dressing. The other is the *salade de crottin de chèvre chaud,* which is a bed of lettuce on which two disks of warmed goat cheese sit—a simple delicacy. A salad, a glass of wine, a hunk of baguette, maybe a slice of *tarte au citron* (lemon meringue pie), and *un express café,* and voilà, you've had a lovely and very Parisian lunch. Formerly, this would have constituted a bare-bones minimum lunch—a meal that is not hot is not a meal. But habits are changing. You'll start to understand this the more meals you eat in Paris.

Cafés with restaurant sections, sometimes referred to as *cafés-brasseries,* will also offer a *plat du jour* (a daily special), which may be a meat or fish dish and may be ordered without an appetizer or dessert.

Restaurant Tickets

If you see Parisians paying for lunch with little coupons, note that many companies offer this widely accepted form of payment to their employees, who pay half the value—usually €4 or €5.

RESTAURANTS, HAUTE CUISINE, AND *LA GASTRONOMIE*

THERE IS NO SHORTAGE OF FOOD IN PARIS or of fine places to wine and dine, and dining will certainly be included in your top-priority list of essential things to do, along with sightseeing, museum visiting, and shopping. If you count each day in Paris as an opportunity for essentially two great meals, you can decide how many of those opportunities you want to turn into memorable culinary occasions. You may determine that one serious restaurant

unofficial **TIP**
If you wish to try one or more of the starred, highly celebrated, and stunningly expensive restaurants, you may opt for the more reasonable lunch experience to compensate.

a day is plenty, and you may want to alternate visits between lunch and dinner. In any case, your culinary exploits need to be somewhat planned and quantified. What is particularly fun is to mix your eating schedule with informal restaurants, a few classic *brasseries,* a serious *haute cuisine* haunt or two, or a stop at some interesting regional or ethnic places, combined with a stint of Parisian street-food slumming and open-air-market shopping, and, weather permitting, a picnic or two in the Luxembourg Gardens or along the Seine.

We've attempted to select restaurants that offer a truly Parisian experience, in which the menu is interesting and varied, the service is attentive and elegant, the décor and style reinforce the fare, and the quality-to-price ratio assures you great value and a memorable moment, whether it's a magical evening at one-star landmark **Jacques Cagna** or a cheap but savory lunch at the raucous proletarian eatery **Chartier.**

Paris restaurants vary in style and form, and to our way of thinking the only things that matter are that your experiences are truly Parisian and you have a good time. The rest is merely pretense. Fortunately, France has one overriding rule when it comes to food: anything you do that increases your pleasure and enjoyment at the table is permissible and encouraged. We love repeating this. Anything you do that increases your pleasure and enjoyment at the table is permissible and encouraged.

Brasseries and Bistros

What's the difference? Don't be bashful; everyone asks. Today the two types of restaurant have gotten confused, and the terms are used incorrectly.

Most cafés that serve lunch have the word *brasserie* printed on their outside awnings. But for history buffs, brasseries were originally the late-night eating halls owned and operated by the beer makers of Alsace. The verb *brasser* in this sense means "to brew." And, thus, brasseries have always been loud open spaces for informal eating and consuming numerous kinds of brewed beer. These days they're more like regular restaurants, but they still have an eastern-French flavor, are open late, and often serve *choucroute,* the regional sauerkraut dish, and other Alsatian specialties and seafood. Many of these establishments were conceived in the brasserie style but postdate the era of true brasseries themselves. Some brasseries are among Paris's most celebrated and popular restaurants today, such as **Bofinger, La Coupole, Chez Jenny, Brasserie Balzar, Brasserie Flo,** and **Brasserie Lipp.** Plan to eat in one.

The word *bistro* or *bistrot* has been grossly corrupted over time. Although you'll read that *bistro* derives from the Russian word for "Hurry up," which hungry soldiers occupying Paris screamed in the cafés, this is an old and tired-out story. Traditionally, a bistro was simply a modest and simple restaurant, often a small family-run eatery with an intimate cluster of tables, hearty French cuisine, and good but common wines. The menu was scribbled on a chalkboard because the fare changed every day. Today a bistro is often just a café in which simple dishes are also served. Because of the great charm and simplicity of this old style of establishment, restaurateurs have usurped the name for their eateries and chains. Bistro Romain is as much a bistro as Kentucky Fried Chicken is a quaint country diner. True bistros do still exist, though, and we recommend them for their atmosphere. More recently, young creative chefs have opted to open small, bistro-like restaurants for imaginative high cuisine, attracted to the idea that offering smaller-scale, higher-quality cooking in simpler but aesthetically attractive décor (small wooden tables sans tablecloths) is a more satisfying endeavor than launching more costly, commercially riskier establishments.

OYSTER BARS At bistros and brasseries, you'll often see an impressive wet bar outside the restaurant on the sidewalk, adorned with huge platters of crushed ice and seaweed, on which raw oysters, clams, *langoustines,* and other unidentifiable shellfish (*fruits de mer* [fwee duh mair]) are being shucked and placed by hearty men in rubber aprons. There is a lot of ritual and pageantry in ordering and eating a platter like this, and if you are a shellfish fanatic, it is worth doing this once during your Paris stay.

You'll never understand all the sizes, grades, and types of oysters offered on the menu, but here are a few simple pointers.

The *creuses* are the fatter oysters in the deeper, rougher shells; the *plates* are the leaner ones in the flatter, smoother shells. The pens or beds in the oyster parcs in which the shellfish are raised are called *claires*. In restaurants, the *creuses* and *plates* are offered on the menu in several sizes—*creuses: huîtres de parc* (the smallest), *fines de claires* (medium), *spéciales* (the largest); *plates: belons* (small and elegant) and *marennes* (greenish).

> *unofficial* **TIP**
> When in doubt, go for 6 or 12 *fines de claires* for starters. White wine is a must.

Crêperies

Although France is famous for its *crêpes,* the celebrated pancakes eaten with both sweet and savory toppings (the latter called *galettes*) actually originated in the Brittany region of northwest France. In the area around the Montparnasse train station, a community of Bretons settled long ago, and today the neighborhood is teeming with *crêperies*—restaurants that specialize in crêpes.

Crêpes are made with *froment* (wheat) flour; the sweet versions are garnished with chocolate, jam, chestnut spread, powdered sugar, nuts, and other toppings. The *galette* is a crêpe in which the batter is made with *sarrasin* (buckwheat) flour and salted butter. The dark pancake is then topped with ham, mushrooms, cheese, eggs, and the like. Don't forget that crêpes are washed down with bowls of Normandy *cidre,* which is more like apple wine than apple cider.

Other excellent crêperies:

CRÊPE DENTELLE 10, rue Léopold Bellan, 75002; ☎ 01 40 41 04 23; Métro: Sentier or Les Halles.

CRÊPERIE LE PETIT JOSSELIN 59, rue du Montparnasse, 75014; ☎ 01 43 22 91 81; Métro: Montparnasse.

Salons de Thé

All over Paris you'll find small, informal tearooms offering sandwiches, warm slices of savory pies, salads, flavorful pieces of cake and *tartes aux fruits,* and, of course, a selection of teas and coffees. These are perfect places for lighter lunches and snacks. The tartes and cakes are usually displayed, so if a wedge of salmon-and-spinach tarte or a plate of watercress salad with fresh beets catches your eye, go for it. There are scores of delightful *salons de thé* in Paris, too numerous to note here, but we've listed two highly recommended establishments to visit if you happen to be exploring their neighborhoods.

ANGELINA (226, rue de Rivoli, 75001; ☎ 01 42 60 82 00; Métro: Tuileries) The atmosphere is a bit old-fashioned, but this is an address not to miss. Famous for its soupy-rich hot chocolate. You can bring a sack of the dark powder home with you.

LA CHARLOTTE DE L'ISLE (24, rue Saint-Louis-en-L'Isle, 75004; ☎ 01 43 54 25 83; **pagesperso-orange.fr/la-charlotte/index.htm;** Métro: Pont Marie) A quaint spot on the Île Saint-Louis known for delicious cakes and chocolates.

LADURÉE (16, rue Royale, 75008; ☎ 01 42 60 21 79; **laduree.fr;** Métro: Madeleine; four other locations) A busy spot between the Place de la Concorde and the Madeleine. Perfect for a coffee, tea, and *gâteau* (cake) break.

THE BAGUETTE AND BOULANGERIE

THE STAPLE OF THE FRENCH TABLE is the nightly baguette, regulated in weight and price by law. Each boulangerie (bread shop) bakes baguettes at least four times a day, with the first bread coming out early in the morning and the last late in the afternoon. Currently, a 250-gram baguette costs between €0.85 and €1. You'll notice that regular customers are accustomed to asking for the bread loaf either crusty (*bien cuit*) or softer and lighter (*pas trop cuit*), and some ask for it cut in half (*coupé en deux*). A heavier baguette (400 grams) is called a pain. And a skinny baguette, weighing half the grams, is called a ficelle.

unofficial **TIP**
Buy your baguettes only from a local *boulangerie,* not a supermarket.

Don't be alarmed that bread is handled with bare hands, is rarely bagged, and is often just wrapped slightly in a twisted piece of paper and carried under the arm and in the Métro. No one has ever gotten sick from a contaminated baguette. The real, old-fashioned baguette (not really old-fashioned, since baguettes only came into fashion in the 1920s; the 18th-century French bread whose shortage provoked Marie Antoinette to foolishly say "Let them eat cake!" was flat and loaf-like) has been challenged by the industrially kneaded bread stick that looks like a baguette and is called a baguette, but according to true bread-eaters, tastes nothing like the real thing. With health consciousness on the rise in France, you'll now find numerous other choices—multigrain, muesli, and other breads.

Croissants

Good croissants (kwas-**sahn**) are great, and you'll undoubtedly munch quite a few of these quintessentially French flaky delights during your Paris stay. Note, though, that it is now easy to find rather mediocre croissants—less rich, less flakey. The insistence on uncompromising quality when it comes to *viennoiserie* (the generic term in France for puff pastry and other breakfast pastries such as *pain au chocolat, pain aux raisins, chausson aux pommes,* and so on) has slipped in the big cities. When you find a memorably delightful croissant at a local patisserie, stick with the address. Croissant aficionado Julia Alvarez writes: "A good croissant must have layers of pastry that are dry, brittle, flakey, and slightly crunchy. The buttery flavor bleeds through with a delicately balanced mix of salt and sugar. The baking should be equal on the top and bottom of the croissant. Also important is the sound that the buttery crescent makes when bit into. I can almost hear its cry when ripped in half. Breakfast pastry is a living substance. It's the soul of the pastry chef." *Figaro Magazine* named the purveyors of Paris's best croissants:

unofficial **TIP**
It was a French pastry chef who created the first croissant for the rulers of the Ottoman Empire, shaping the light puff pastry after the crescent star of the Turkish flag.

1. Pierre Hermé
2. Triomphe
3. L. Duchêne
4. Mulot
5. Lenôtre
6. Boulangerie de Monge
7. Vandermeersch
8. Julien
9. Delmontel
10. Grande Épicerie
11. A. Poilâne
12. M. de la Vierge

But you may be wondering what the difference is between the croissants whose ends point straight out and those whose points are turned in. Well, the straight ones, called *croissants au beurre*, are made with pure butter. They are richer and cost about €0.10 more. The

PARIS STREET FOOD AND WHERE TO FIND IT

- **Crêpes** You'll find crêpe stands in most busy areas of town, usually attached to cafés, although these aren't the best. You'll also find dozens of crêpe restaurants (crêperies) throughout the city, with a high concentration around rue de Montparnasse (Métro: Montparnasse-Bienvenüe), noted for its large Breton community.

- **Falafel** rue des Rosiers (Marais)

- **Ice cream Berthillon** on Île Saint-Louis, and high-quality spinoffs such as Italian ice-cream maker **Amorino,** whose gelato is made daily with fresh fruit. There's plenty of Häagen-Dazs and even Ben & Jerry's, but you didn't come to Paris for ice cream you could eat at home, did you?

- **Sandwich grec** Latin Quarter

crescent-shaped ones, croissants *ordinaires,* are made with margarine and offer a few less calories.

Croissants are eaten almost exclusively in the morning, so if you crave one in the late afternoon, you'll look a little odd and the offerings won't be as fresh as the morning's choices. *Pain au chocolat,* however, is the traditional snack of choice for kids of all ages on their way home from school. For sweet delights to satisfy your afternoon sugar urges, see Part Eight, Shopping.

FAST FOOD AND FRENCH CHAINS

YOU CAN'T HELP BUT NOTICING that "McDo," as Parisians call McDonald's, is everywhere, from the Champs-Élysées to the Latin Quarter. The lines can be long and the prices relatively steep. Even if you're tempted, stay away. There is no reason to eat here unless you are desperately homesick and need a Big Mac fix to reestablish your mental balance, in which case we'll consider this digression to be of therapeutic value and forgive you . . . grudgingly. McDo has understood that in France it makes sense to localize some of its offerings, like adding goat cheese to its salads. They don't do that in Pittsburgh or Manchester.

kids France has its own fast-food chains as well. They're interesting to observe, and you may even like them, but they are hard to recommend. The McDo knock-off is a Belgian-owned chain called Quick—trust us, this can be missed. A few family-style restaurant chains obviously cannot compare with real cuisine, but they can come in handy when your time is limited or you're traveling as a family. There is more space, the setting is casual, the menus are well conceived and inexpensive, and the portions are generous. Here are a few other fast food–type places that we recommend for the kids:

BISTRO ROMAIN Known for its all-you-can-eat plates of *carpaccio* (thin slices of raw beef or salmon), French fries, or green beans, and chocolate mousse, served in tacky ancient Rome–inspired surroundings. The kids will like it.

HIPPOPOTAMUS Essentially a steak-house chain; popular with younger French couples and singles. It's fine if you know you just want a piece of meat, some fries, and a beer. Each meal counts when you're on a trip, so if necessary, digress wisely.

LÉON DE BRUXELLES The specialty is mussels and French fries; can be a lot of fun for those who don't get to eat massive bowls of fresh mussels all the time. Inexpensive.

STREET FOOD

EACH CITY HAS ITS OWN STREET-DINING SPECIALTIES, and it's amazing how a €4 detour can end up being the highlight of a trip. In the past, Parisians rarely ate while walking, but since the pace of working life has intensified in recent years, you'll now see Parisians wolfing sandwiches while strutting to the Métro. You still won't, however, see waves of white-collar workers lined up on a wall or around a fountain outside their office buildings eating salads out of plastic take-out containers with plastic forks as you often do in American cities.

A GOURMAND'S PARADISE

THE MOST FAMOUS GOURMET SHOP IN PARIS IS **Fauchon.** Founded in 1886, this icon of catered extravagance—with products ranging from Iranian caviar to handpicked choice lychees from Madagascar, thinly sliced *saumon fumé,* sugar work that approaches the aesthetics of fine jewelry, and much, much more—should be treated more like a gallery than a grocery store. Never walk in hungry or you'll walk out broke, although you should try a pastry in the Fauchon café next door. In the last few years, Fauchon has developed its own brand of almost everything, which it sells in its decked-out subterranean store and cafeteria. The quality is high, but the prices top everything. Across the Place Madeleine you'll find another great Parisian culinary institution, **Hediard.** Visit both.

FAUCHON 24–26, place de la Madeleine, 75008; ☎ 01 70 39 38 00; **fauchon.com;** Métro: Madeleine.

HEDIARD 21, place de la Madeleine, 75008; ☎ 01 43 12 88 88; **hediard.fr;** Métro: Madeleine. There are six other addresses throughout Paris; check the Web site for details.

ETHNIC FOOD

IF YOU HAVE TIME, you should diversify your eating experiences by going ethnic. Paris is a cosmopolitan city and a former colonial

CLASSIC FRENCH DISHES TO TRY

- *andouillettes*—chitterling sausages. The "A. A. A. A. A." is a marking on the menu to indicate that this sausage has been found to be of supreme quality by the Chitterling Sausage Association. It owes its reputation to the spices, condiments, coatings, and wine used in its preparation.

- *blanquette de veau*—pieces of veal stewed in an egg-and-cream sauce

- *café gourmand*—a sampler dessert of two or three small portions from the dessert menu served with an espresso café

- *cassoulet*—white-bean casserole with duck, sausage, pork, or goose

- *choucroute*—Alsatian sauerkraut dish with sausage, pork, ham, and potatoes

- *coq au vin*—rooster stewed in red wine

- *lapin chasseur*—wild rabbit, often cooked with mushrooms

- *couscous*—North African dish of steamed semolina, broth, chickpeas, carrots, and assorted vegetables served with grilled lamb, beef, chicken, or merguez sausage

- *magret de canard*—sliced breast of fattened duck

- *moules marinière*—mussels cooked in white wine, onions, shallots, and herbs

- *pot-au-feu*—boiled beef served with carrots, leeks, and turnips

- *poulet basquaise*—Basque-style chicken cooked with tomatoes and sweet peppers

capital, with large communities of immigrants from North Africa and Maghreb (Morocco, Algeria, and Tunisia), southeast Asia (Vietnam, Cambodia, and Laos), sub-Saharan west Africa (Mali, Cameroon, Senegal, Ivory Coast, Congo, and Benin), the Indian Ocean (Réunion, Mauritius, and Comoros), and the French West Indies (Martinique and Guadeloupe). Additionally, there are many immigrants from China and Hong Kong, Turkey, Greece, Portugal, Italy, Eastern Europe, and Latin America. Lastly, about 100,000 Anglo-Americans live permanently in Paris. All these people contribute widely to the culinary offerings of the city. In fact, you can have some of the best African and Vietnamese food in the world in Paris.

Couscous: North African Cuisine

One of Paris's greatest resources is its cultural diversity, which extends to a wide range of culinary delights. Within this fabulous pastiche that makes Paris "more than French," you'll find a vibrant North African presence.

Moroccan cuisine is some of the world's finest, most flavorful, and most colorful, and many of the best restaurants for *tagines* and *couscous* are right in the French capital. If you've never had couscous, you haven't lived fully! This typical dish, ubiquitous across the Maghreb, is a feast of steamed semolina; a rich vegetable stew with carrots, turnips, and chickpeas; and an assortment of grilled lamb, chicken, and spicy red sausage (veal and lamb) called *merguez*. *Tagines* are actually earthenware crocks in which broiled meat, fish, fowl, vegetables, fruit, nuts, and spices are baked and are served simmering. Meals are followed by delicious mint tea and pine nuts served in painted glasses.

Couscous can be found in almost every Parisian neighborhood and at all prices. Here are three excellent suggestions for elegant North African and Lebanese dining:

LE SOUK 1, rue Keller, 75011; ☎ 01 49 29 05 08; Métro: Bastille. Reservations recommended.

MANSOURIA 11, rue Faidherbe, 75011; ☎ 01 43 71 00 16; Métro: Faidherbe-Chaligny. Run by a noted Moroccan anthropologist, Mansouria offers elegant dining amid attractive traditional Moroccan décor. Set menu from €30; reservations recommended.

What to Avoid: Pizza and Chinese

Unless it comes highly recommended, be wary of the glut of Italianate pizza restaurants and mixed-Asian "Chinese" restaurants. Every day, Parisians eat tons of unsliced, individual-sized pizza (with a knife and fork) and Cantonese rice. There are a number of good Italian and Chinese restaurants, but there are even more mediocre ones, and Parisians don't know the luxury of top-quality cheap pizza and Chinese food. You didn't come to Paris to order Pizza Hut or Domino's (both are here). However, for a word on great Vietnamese food in Paris, see "Ethnic Food" on the previous page. For a better Chinese experience, take the Métro to Place d'Italie and walk down to the Porte d'Ivry and Paris's Chinatown. You'll find a second, smaller Chinatown at Métro Belleville, where Asian restaurants are mixed in with the North African Arab fare.

unofficial **TIP**
There are 450 kinds of cheese in France.

VEGETARIAN PARIS

Parisians eat not only lots of meat but a stunning variety of animals ranging from guinea hen (*pintade*) to wild baby boar (*marcassin*). It's not all that easy to get away from meat, but the good news for vegetarians is that Parisians also eat an amazing range of fresh vegetables and fruits. Plus, the breads are excellent, the wine impeccable, the pastries sinfully good, the selection of fresh fish wonderful, and the dairy products diverse and tasty. Open-air markets are ubiquitous, and there is a small number of very good vegetarian restaurants in the city. So it's not all that difficult to survive in Paris as a vegetarian. Here are a few veggie establishments:

AQUARIUS 40, rue de Gergovie, 75014; ☎ 01 45 41 36 88; Métro: Pernety. Fixed menus: lunch and dinner, €12–€15. Hours: Monday–Saturday, noon–2:15 p.m. and 7–10: 30 p.m.; Friday and Saturday, till 11 p.m.

LE GRAND APPÉTIT 9, rue de la Cerisaie, 75004; 01 40 27 04 95; Métro: Sully-Morland. A macrobiotic treat.

LE GRENIER DE NOTRE-DAME 18, rue de la Bûcherie, 75005; ☎ 01 43 29 98 29; Métro: Saint-Michel. Fixed menus: €12.50 lunch; €14.50 dinner. Hours: noon–2 p.m. and 7–10:30 p.m., until 11 p.m. on weekends.

LEMONI CAFÉ 5, rue Hérold, 75001; ☎ 01 45 08 49 84; Métro: Sentier or Palais Royal. Fixed menus: lunch, €11–€13.50. Hours: Monday–Friday, noon–3:30 p.m.

LA VICTOIRE SUPRÊME DU CŒUR 29, rue du Bourg Tibourg, 75004; ☎ 01 40 41 95 03; **vscoeur.com;** Métro: Saint-Paul or Hôtel de Ville. Fixed menus: lunch, €13.50; dinner, €19.50; brunch €19.50. Hours: Monday–Friday, noon–3 p.m. and 6:30–10:30 p.m.; Saturday, noon–11 p.m. Sunday buffet brunch, noon–4 p.m. and dinner 6:30–10:30 p.m.

A Word on *La Viande* (Meat)

The mad-cow crisis a decade ago, followed by the foot-and-mouth scare, helped elevate the general awareness about the meat supply and food chain. Standards—already high in France—have steadily increased. French *charolais* beef will delight meat eaters. The "bio" marking on beef in supermarkets guarantees that the meat was raised on organically grown natural feed. The French are less obsessed by the tenderness of meat and in fact often prefer their beef a bit chewy. If you need "tender," make sure you ask for this.

UNDERSTANDING FRENCH RESTAURANTS

BE PREPARED . . .
- to find menus only in French. Some restaurants will have translated menus. Some dishes don't translate too well and sound far more delicious in French. It's better having the waiter strain to explain the French menu than have an English one laid out for you. Avoid all restaurants with multilanguage menus depicted by little country flags (they're mostly tourist traps).
- to spend more time at the table than you expected. Don't rush. And in any case, you'll have a hard time speeding up the service. Never leave yourself less than an hour to eat, and try to allocate at least two hours for any sit-down meal. Don't be surprised to spend at least three hours when dining in a particularly fine establishment.

- to budget more money on food in France than you would for travels elsewhere, although on the whole you should find the price–quality ratio to be excellent. Hotels may be comparatively inexpensive (if you come from a large city such as New York or Los Angeles), but eating well will be proportionally more expensive. The French understand the value of culinary arts, choice ingredients, and the time and imagination needed to create wonderfully tasty dishes and artful presentations, and they're ready to pay for this.

- to have less space than you might be accustomed to. Restaurants in Paris are often crowded, with tables pushed close to each other. This doesn't seem to bother Parisians, but it may feel too close for comfort to you. And the waiters will not be very accommodating when you ask to move to a table set for four when there are only two of you. This will be true even when the dining room is empty. Two people don't get to sit at tables meant for four—that's just how it is in Paris.

- to be served water only when you ask for a *carafe d'eau* (cahr-**raf doh**). No one will be regularly topping up your glass with a pitcher of ice water as is common in restaurants back home. And forget the ice in any case. You may order bottled water (*eau minérale* [**oh** min-air-**rahl**]), either sparkling (*eau gazeuse* or *pétillante* [**oh** ga-**zooz** or pey-tee-**yahnt**]) or nonsparkling (*eau plate* [oh **plaht**]). Note that at many restaurants, other than the fancy starred establishments, you will not receive a water glass unless you ask for one, since Parisians typically use the same glass for their water and wine, alternating between the two.

- to wait forever for the check (*l'addition, s'il vous plaît* [la-di-si-**youn**, see voo **play**]). The waiter will only bring you the check when you ask for it. This is a matter of local politeness. You should not be rushed. You can take quite some time after you've finished your meal before you actually leave. You may order a second coffee or a digestif or two, while you relax, digest, talk, and, if on the terrace, smoke. Of course, in smaller restaurants, if you see another party waiting to be seated, it's polite to not overdo your lingering.

- to peruse the menu outside before deciding to go in. French law requires all eating establishments to post their menus and prices prominently outside. You'll now see that many menus indicate lower prices since the French VAT (sales tax) was dropped in 2009 from 19.6 percent to 5.5 percent. This gives you the chance to review the offerings and prices before committing yourself. It is very rare to see people get up and leave a restaurant once they've been seated. Try to avoid changing your mind once inside. On the other hand, if the place's atmosphere doesn't please you or the table you've been offered doesn't cut the mustard, you should feel perfectly comfortable in politely leaving right away.

MESSAGE FROM FRENCH RESTAURANT OWNERS TO AMERICAN VISITORS

WE LOVE YOUR CASUALNESS, but please don't wear shorts to our restaurants. And leave the Rollerblades in your hotel.

Sorry that we can't feed you as early as you'd like. Some of you want dinner before we've even cleaned up from lunch!

We know you love escargot, but if you don't like kidneys or brains, please don't order *les rognons* or *la cervelle!*

A NOTE FOR NONSMOKERS

AS WE'VE INDICATED THROUGHOUT THIS GUIDE, as of January 2008, it is illegal to smoke in any enclosed public place in France, and thus the hazard of passive smoking should be seriously reduced.

MANNERS

THE SERVICE YOU RECEIVE IN A RESTAURANT depends greatly on the way you act. In some cases, service that you would classify as poor is the result of a waiter's repeated experiences with culturally insensitive visitors. You might not understand why you can't have something prepared "your way," and they don't understand why so many Americans expect customized preparations for dishes. These are conflicting concepts of "service." Queries and requests that are commonplace in the United States, like "Can I have the dressing on the side?" "Is the salmon cooked in oil or butter?" "Is it fried or broiled?" "Can I have the beef without the sauce?" or "Bring us our Cokes with the dinner," are strange and annoying to Parisian waiters. And then their disposition annoys you, which further annoys them. Try to nip these silly types of cultural misunderstandings in the bud.

HOW TO SETTLE A DISPUTE

IT DOESN'T HAPPEN OFTEN, but as anywhere, it can happen. If you have a problem with your food or wine, signal to the waiter or manager (*le responsable* [le rays-pown-**sahbl**]) right away. Be extremely polite and calm, and explain that your steak is very tough or that your soup is cold. The situation is more unfortunate when you misunderstood what you were ordering and you are very unhappy with what is now staring up at you from your plate. *Steak tartare* is served raw, spiced, and cold. So is *carpaccio. Ris de veau* is sweetbreads, and *cervelle* is brains.

It's better not to err from the start and order only dishes you're quite confident you'll enjoy, but if you do err, the rule is simply to not eat what's on your plate. You'll have a very hard time getting any satisfaction if you eat half of it and then complain. The Parisian mindset is very different from the American one. You may be used to a "Sorry that you don't like your dinner, ma'am. Would you like to choose something else?" response, but you won't find that here. We've heard of managers taking a bite out of your steak to determine whether it's tough or not and then defending the perfectly acceptable condition of your *entrecôte* (the French appreciate their meat a bit chewy). If you refuse a wine, again, you'd better be right. Again, the best solution is simply to not consume the food or drink in question. If you don't eat it, you'll have a better chance of not being asked to pay for it. On the other hand, if in fact there is a problem with your dish—if it is cold or burned, tastes bad, is smothered in cheese when you asked for

***unofficial* TIP**
Be careful to note the pricing on dishes that are marked on the menu "for two" (*pour deux*) or "for each person" (*par personne*). Is the price per person, or for the whole dish? Make sure you understand and agree that the price indicated is either for each person or for the two people *before* you order it.

none, or the like—it will, in most cases, be taken away and replaced or fixed. Don't get mad. Don't threaten. And don't break anything, even if you're dying to. Parisians respond poorly to aggression, and your evening will be ruined. Calmly and politely refuse what you've been served. If the dish in question appears on your bill, calmly and politely state that it is not customary to pay for something you didn't eat. Don't be rude, but don't be bullied either. In the worst-case scenario, in which you are obliged to pay for a dinner that you consider to be a total rip-off (which would be highly unusual in Paris), use your credit card and contest the bill when you get home. Visa, MasterCard, American Express, and Diners Club do not want dishonest establishments to use their services.

⚘ THE RESTAURANT RATINGS: STARS, FORKS, TOQUES, AND MORE

EVEN PARISIANS DON'T ALWAYS UNDERSTAND the system of awarding stars and *toques* to restaurants, and we venture to guess that most, if not all, of your excellent eating experiences in Paris will be at unstarred or "untoqued" establishments. Unlike hotels, which are awarded stars according to nationally regulated standards, restaurants are privately awarded stars by the *Michelin Guide* judges, who set the bar for the culinary world until Monsieur Gault and Monsieur Millau started assigning French chefs toques, or hats (instead of stars), to the best and the brightest. The pluralistic Zagat approach to rating restaurants arrived in Paris only in 1998, and a score of other critics have applied their own numbers, letters, hats, and forks to the establishments of the world's top culinary capital. It's still largely the stars, though, that continue to maintain the highest level of international prestige.

When Michelin gives two or three stars, a restaurant has been canonized (though with one slip of the knife a restaurant can find itself demoted and shamed). A three-starred chef such as Michel

Bras, who was awarded a third star for his mountaintop restaurant in Auvergne, compares his cooking to jazz "for its architecture, its fluid elegance, its silences." In other words, don't go to a three-star if you want good, standard French fare such as *canard à l'orange* or *steak au poivre*. Be prepared for *gargouillou de jeunes légumes,* literally meaning a "bubbling of young vegetables." Starred establishments live in perpetual vulnerability, as witnessed by the Chinese restaurant Chen Soleil d'Est, which suffered the misfortune of losing its lone Michelin star in 2007.

Michelin's three stars indicate "exceptional cuisine worth a special journey." There are 10 three-stars in Paris and only 25 in the whole of France. Michelin's two stars indicate "excellent cooking, worth a detour," and there are 14 two-stars in Paris. Michelin's one star indicates "a very good restaurant in its category"—there are 41 one-stars in Paris.

Michelin now awards the Bib Gourmand—using a representation of Bib, the Michelin Man, instead of a star—indicating "good meals at moderate prices" (at under €35), of which there are 60 in Paris. Additionally, Michelin awards forks (one to five) indicating the level of luxury and comfort the establishment offers. The more forks, the more luxurious, and thus the more expensive.

unofficial **TIP**
The key to finding the best price-to-quality ratio in gourmet restaurants is to select those with the most stars and the fewest forks.

The Two- and Three-star Experience

This needs some explaining. Dining at a two- or three-star establishment is a serious and formal experience. The atmosphere may feel very formal, and the service may be overly attentive for your comfort. Theatricality and staging, manners, codes, and gestures are combined with a refinement and cultivation of ingredients, tastes, and aesthetic presentation, all crafted to create a total effect. This may be precisely one of your main motivations for coming to Paris. On the other hand, you may find it intimidating and uncomfortable. The price, in any case, will be memorable, and only you can decide what represents good value. Reservations are always required. The Web site **bestrestaurantsparis.com** offers a free online-reservation service for the restaurants it features, many of which are starred. In Paris, the service can be accessed by phone Monday through Friday from 9 a.m. to 6 p.m. by calling ☎ 01 42 25 10 10. To call from outside of France, dial ☎ 33 1 42 25 10 10.

Unstarred Restaurants

All the restaurants in Paris with ambitious owners and chefs aspire for stars, but hundreds of fabulous restaurants go unstarred or untoqued for decades for numerous reasons, often related to décor or service, politics, or the personalities of their owners. Lots of restaurants never even aim for the big league, where the stress to remain brilliant is intense, and instead live happily serving wonderful dishes night after night to a loyal clientele of locals and their friends. We've attempted to direct you to tables that you will enjoy, period. The degree of innovation required for stars often produces dishes that go way beyond the enjoyment level of relative debutantes in French haute cuisine, whereas well-executed traditional French dishes, deemed far too ordinary and mundane for the star keepers, are likely to be highly pleasurable to you much of the time. (Everyone enjoys visiting an avant-garde art exhibition once in a while, but at the end of the day, there's nothing like the Louvre!)

unofficial **TIP**
When you decide which menu you want, you order by referring to its price, such as the €18 menu or the €25 menu. Americans sometimes hesitate here, thinking that it's gauche or tacky to call the menu by its price, but that's how it's done.

The highest level of gourmet dining applies criteria to a meal that some of you may value, but in our experience what most people want from a restaurant are a lovely evening and delicious food presented with style and grace in a pleasant and friendly setting. That's what we've kept in mind when selecting restaurants to profile.

THE MENU VERSUS *LA CARTE*

EVEN IF YOU DON'T SPEAK A WORD OF FRENCH, you certainly know the term *à la carte,* meaning that you order freely from the menu. In Paris, no one will understand what you mean if you use this in its English context. The word for the menu in French is *la carte.* To ask for the menu, say "*Excusez-moi, est-ce que je peux voir la carte, s'il vous plaît*" (excuse-**say mwah, eska** juh puh **vwar** lah **cart,** see voo **play**). It is easy to confuse the English concept of "menu" (that is, *la carte*) with the French phrase *le menu,* or the suggested fixed menu—which is the opposite of your understanding of *à la carte.* There will usually be several menus offered at different prices. The more expensive the menu, the more choices and the more complex or finer the selections it will include. A typical menu will list an appetizer (*entrée*), a main dish (*plat principal*), and dessert (*dessert*). Depending on how the menu is composed, wine or bottled water may or may not be included. Menus in fancier and finer restaurants may include an additional course, and a *menu dégustation* (tasting menu), which will be the top of the line, allowing you to sample the best of the entire *carte.*

Many Parisian restaurants understand that not everyone wants a long, expensive, and filling meal, especially at lunch, and thus have played with marketable variations on the theme. Now you can find menus that let you select either an appetizer and a main dish or just a main dish and a dessert. Coffee is seldom included in the menu price, but tax and service are. Restaurants will often have menus that are applicable only at lunchtime or during the week. It can be frustrating to read a menu that seems perfect, only to be told that you can't order this now.

On the whole, a menu often offers a good deal and a decent choice of what's best at the restaurant. You may be bothered to see a sign out front advertising the Tourist Menu at, say, €18. Tourists, especially North Americans, translate this as an invitation to be gouged and think the word *tourist* should be avoided at all costs. Although we agree that restaurants offering "tourist menus" are probably not the most charming and authentic, the term doesn't necessarily mean worse quality or an exploitative price.

unofficial **TIP**
The French don't necessarily use *tourist* as a pejorative term.

SIZE OF PORTIONS

ALTHOUGH IN PARIS YOU WILL EAT WELL and never complain of going hungry, French portions are not meant to overwhelm you. Your dinner is not a Disney production. Your *blanquette de veau* is designed for one human being, and your plate of salad should not be made of three heads of lettuce. The key to the French meal is balance, and the symmetry of the dinner takes into account the three principal courses. Dessert is not just a €5 add-on—it's as important as the rest of the meal. Likewise for the appetizer; it's not a routine house salad that comes with the prime-rib platter. Be prepared for smaller but balanced courses. Lastly, Parisians do not confuse quantity with quality, and although they are greatly impressed by the size and value of portions in the United States, they see these as a marketing device, and they continue to opt for proportion and taste over size.

COOKING INSTRUCTIONS

WHEN ORDERING RED MEAT, you'll be asked for the *cuisson* (**kwee**-sown) of your meat. The French eat beef much rarer than their American counterparts. People generally believe that beef, to be fully appreciated, should be eaten fairly rare, and Parisian cooking instructions correspond to this practice. Since there are three main choices—rare, medium, and well done—you'd think that the French medium (*à point* [ah **pwahn**]) would be the same as the Yankee medium, but no, it's usually far too rare for American tastes. Here's how to translate the differences:

UNITED STATES	FRANCE
very rare (bloody)	*saignant* (sen-**yohn**)
medium rare	*à point* (ah **pwahn**)
medium	between *à point* and *bien cuit* (byen **kwee**)
well done	*très bien cuit* (tray byen **kwee**)

Even with this knowledge, problems sometimes occur. Paris restaurants that are accustomed to serving American tourists and having beef regularly sent back tend to compensate for the cultural difference automatically, but not all restaurants do. Sort it out with your waiter. If you order in French, your meat should come out according to French standards.

A NOTE ON FRENCH BEEF

NOTE THAT IN FRANCE CUTS OF BEEF do not resemble the cuts you're used to back home. You won't find sirloin, T-bone, prime rib, or tenderloin. What you will find are the following:

bavette (skirt steak)

entrecôte (rib steak)

steak (beef steak)

pavé (thick slab of boneless beef)

steak haché (chopped steak)

Although you probably won't be buying and cooking meat in Paris, you should spend a few minutes at a *boucherie* (butcher shop) observing how they prepare and dress the beef, liver, lamb, veal, chickens, ducks, rabbits, and venison. And though you won't find any in restaurants, every neighborhood has its own shop selling prime cuts of lean horse meat (*chevaline*).

ORDERING AND TASTING WINE

IF YOU ARE AN EXPERIENCED WINE DRINKER, you need no introduction here: you know what to do and what you like. The rest of you may enjoy wine but aren't all that comfortable about choosing the right bottle at the right time for the right price. At good but not special or starred restaurants, the selected house wine or carafe wine is usually a very sound and reliable choice. At lower-end establishments such as pizza restaurants and cafés, the carafe (*pichet*) is neither good nor a good value. At very elegant restaurants, you may solicit a recommendation from a wine steward, or sommelier, but the problem here is that he may strongly advise an excellent 1995 St-Émilion at a cool €100 when you were hoping not to exceed €35 for your wine. It can then be a bit uncomfortable to say, "Oh, yes, I'm sure that's a great choice, but we'll take the 2007 Hermitage at €20." It's better to say from the start that you'd like a wine that's "*sympathique mais pas trop cher* (**sam-pa-teek may pah** trow **share**)." In other words, a pleasant but reasonably priced wine.

unofficial **TIP**
Especially in the warmer months, it's very pleasant to select a light red wine that is drunk chilled, such as a Gamay, Brouilly, or Saumur, all excellent with meat or fish.

Of course, you may want to go for some well-known names in French wines, but what's wonderful about Paris is that you can drink at very affordable prices some lovely wines that are never exported.

The tasting of the wine is customary and ceremonial. Get into it. Take your time. Sniff. Roll your glass slightly. Observe the rich burgundy or ruby tone. Take a mouthful (*gorgée*) and roll it around your tongue. Concentrate. Let the warmth of the 11-year-old Hospice de Beaune warm your cheeks. Then nod approvingly, and smile ever so slightly at your waiter and the lovely people with whom you're dining. Of course, if you sincerely find the wine lacking, or if it is too cold or not cold enough, share this information with the waiter. You're in control.

When it comes to matching wines with cheeses, it is said that if you take three or more kinds of cheeses at your *fromage* course, the choice of wine becomes moot. No wine can be matched with more than two cheeses.

You may wish to take a wine-tasting course during your stay in Paris. See "Taking Classes" in Part Six, Sightseeing, Tours, and Attractions.

For a selection of wine bars, see our restaurant profiles.

Excellent Vintages

The years 2001, 2003, and 2005 were very good, and in many cases exceptional, for red and white Bordeaux, red and white Burgundy, and Alsatian wines. The year 2005 was an excellent Côtes-du-Rhône year.

THE STRUCTURE OF THE MEAL

TO DINE SUCCESSFULLY IN PARIS, you must understand one basic concept: cuisine in France, although a constantly evolving art form and culture in and of itself, is bound by tradition and form. Respect the basic form of the French meal and customs, and you will be thoroughly delighted. Disrespect, ignore, or fiddle with the basic conventions of the meal, and you will disrupt the flow, elegance, and deliberate balance of the experience. It is this very rigidity that is at the backbone of a sustained common culture, and it is precisely this that many Americans have a hard time understanding, since their culture is a relatively new one, driven by the more contemporary values of change, flexibility, and mobility. The more you start to feel the history that presents itself in the dish in front of you, the gestures with which you're being served, and the way in which the table is set, the more you'll start reflecting on your own society and self. This, from the appetizer onward, is the true beauty of international travel.

The meal begins with an apéritif or cocktail, which you may quite easily and elegantly choose to decline. On the other hand, a *kir* is a very pleasant start to a meal.

A dinner roll or bread will be set out either in a basket or on a bread plate. Usually, butter is not served with the bread in France. You may ask for butter, but Parisians don't.

Carefully review the menu and wine list, and order only when you're ready. Feel free to ask your waiter for explanations. Some restaurants have English menus prepared, but it's often a good sign if they don't. If French is a problem for you, ask about the dishes. You might wish to carry a small pocket dictionary along for the occasion. Berlitz publishes a menu reader that allows you to know that *bigorneaux* are periwinkles and *museau* is beef muzzle, if that's helpful. But recognize that some delicious ingredients just don't translate well if they don't exist in an English-speaking country.

Select an Entrée (Appetizer)

Note right away how backward Anglo-Saxon habits are. Logically, the entrée is the entry into the meal, or the appetizer—not the main dish, as *entrée* has come to mean in American English. You may decide to let your wife or husband taste your foie gras, and she or he may be delighted to offer you an oyster (*huître*), but if you want to avoid annoying your waiter and ruining the service from the word go, don't order one starter for two people. "We're going to share the leek salad" will grate on the ears of your *serveur*. If you think your waiter's exasperation has to do with the fact that you'll be spending less money and thus he'll make a smaller tip on the meal, you're wrong. Splitting a dish simply violates the normal symmetry of a dinner. Sharing two choices is OK, but splitting one doesn't work too well.

Select a Main Dish

Don't try to have your endive salad, which is an appetizer, served at the same time as your salmon steak just because you like salad with your fish. Parisians do not eat meat very well done, but restaurants do understand the nuances here, so be very specific about how you'd like your meat cooked. For instructions on ordering meat, see "Cooking Instructions" earlier in this chapter.

The Cheese Course

In gourmet restaurants, you'll be offered a cheese course at the end of the meal but before dessert. If it's included in your menu, accept it even if you're stuffed full. You can have a sliver of a number of fascinating cheeses that will contribute to your culinary education.

In restaurants, if the cheese plate is brought to your table for you to serve yourself, remember that you're not expected to eat everything.

unofficial **TIP**
Note that cheese in France is always eaten after the main course and before the dessert, not as an hors d'oeuvre with white wine as is common in North America. Cheese is considered too heavy to eat before a meal.

Take a normal slice or wedge of what you know you like, and a few tiny slivers of others so you can test them.

Remember that it's considered gauche and awkward to cut the point off any wedge of cheese such as Brie or Camembert. Slices or wedges are cut out of the larger wheel of cheese, and you should cut along one of the existing edges.

WHEN DO YOU EAT THE RIND? Tourists have a tendency to want to cut off too much from the cheese, thinking that when in doubt, it's better not to eat the rind. The French approach would be: when in doubt, eat it. Every part of the cheese is edible except the thick, hard rinds of hard cheeses such as Emmental and Tomme de Savoie, which won't hurt you but are not pleasant to chew or digest. Dark plastic or woven straw wrappers along the edges of soft or crumbly cheeses should obviously be removed, but everything else is fair game. The ashes *(cendres)* on fresh goat cheese are inseparable from the cheese. You may sometimes prefer removing some of the darker, funkier, and more pungent parts of very ripe cheese, but even these are wholly edible. And, in any case, don't worry—even the advanced patches of mold on some cheeses won't hurt you.

It is generally believed that the smellier the cheese, the better it is. Some classics you should try include Crottin de Chavignol (a type of goat cheese that's often served warm on a bed of salad), Camembert, Brie de Meaux, Pont l'Évêque, Reblochon, and Roquefort. Many guidebooks list a few noted cheese shops, but we prefer to send you to the *fromagerie* or *crèmerie* in the neighborhood in which you're staying or at any open-air market. Ask, point, taste. Have your local cheese merchant write down the names of the cheeses you've bought. Buy small quantities *(juste un petit peu, s'il vous plaît* [joost ah pe-**tee** puh, see voo **play**]), and a baguette, and plan your own cheese-tasting party in your hotel room or in a park. *French Cheeses,* by Kazuko Masui and Tomoko Yamada, can help cheese enthusiasts visually orient themselves.

Select a Dessert

Yes, you're having dessert. Skip tomorrow's lunch if need be, but tonight you're having a warm wedge of *tarte tatin,* caramelized-apple tart, or a plate of *profiteroles,* ice cream–infused pastry puffs smothered in warm chocolate sauce. You can start your diet when you get home. Parisians feel no guilt by being self-indulgent—when "in the act," they do not consider things like calories, bank accounts, or marriage oaths—so to really get the most out of your Paris trip, shed all pangs of guilt immediately.

Coffee and Tea

These are usually taken after dessert, although some Parisians ask for their coffee with their dessert. Often it'll be served along with a dish of dainty chocolates or nougat wafers, to put the icing on the cake. Following that, you may just sit back and contemplate your wonderful evening, or you may feel like a snifter of Courvoisier or a shot of Calvados. If you're afraid the caffeine will keep you up at night, you can order either an *infusion* (ahn-few-**zyown**), a soothing herbal tea (try *verveine* [verbena] or *tilleul* [linden]), or a decaffeinated espresso, commonly called a *déca* (day-**cah**).

THE BILL (*L'ADDITION*)

THE BILL WILL ARRIVE WHEN YOU ASK for it. You may discreetly check whether it's more or less what you expected, but don't be overly obvious about tallying up the columns. Never take out a calculator—this just isn't done. In places frequented by tourists, however, it's not a bad idea to make sure you haven't been charged €20 for the duck dish that reads €14 on the menu; but again, be tasteful, since recalculating your bill translates as "we don't trust you" to the restaurant staff. French friends or couples don't usually split the bill, and they almost never divide up and pay according to what each person ordered. This is considered far too vulgar. One person usually pays this time, and the other will pay the next time. The person who invites or organizes the dinner outing is usually the person who pays. So if you suggest to French friends, "Why don't you have dinner with us?," be prepared to pick up the tab that evening.

unofficial **TIP**
Credit cards with a magnetic strip that you swipe through the machine sometimes pose a problem at restaurants in which their use is uncommon. You may have to show the waiter how to do it, or insist that your Visa or MasterCard will work on his or her machine. American Express is not as widely accepted as you might wish.

If you are paying with a credit card, you'll notice that the waiter will bring a slick little debit machine to your table and insert your card on the spot. The French have chip-embedded smart cards and a PIN code to punch in. There is nothing to sign, but you'll probably still have to sign a tiny slip of paper that resembles a cash-register receipt. If you are presented with the old-fashioned form with the numbers written in by hand, make sure that you put a line through the "Service" or "Tip" line and fill in the total at the bottom. Do not add a 15 percent or 20 percent gratuity, since the service has been included in the price of your food. Again, for a dinner that costs you between €30 and €100 for two people, you could leave €3 or €4 extra as a gesture of appreciation. For a bill under €30, leave €2. For a more expensive meal in which you were very satisfied with your service, you may leave what you like. There is really no rule here. Customarily, you leave something in cash, typically no less than a €1 coin. Don't gather up all the tiny coins in your pocket to get rid of them in this manner—that is perceived as rude. Leave something, be elegant and understated about it, and don't draw too much attention to yourself doing it. There is still an unsaid cultural value in France that money (which everyone wants anyway) is vulgar.

DOGGIE BAGS

ATTITUDES ARE CHANGING A BIT REGARDING the removal of uneaten food from restaurants. In general, though, the doggie bag is still not an accepted concept in Paris. Not that long ago, we heard the story of a tourist who asked for a doggie bag when he left a strip of sirloin on his plate. The waiter came back with a five-kilo sack of scraps from the kitchen. Parisians love their dogs, and this bag would have made at least ten pups happy. The word "to take out" or "take away" is *à emporter* (ah om-por-**tay**). In fine restaurants, you should abandon the idea totally, but if you left half a pizza or an entire plate of steamed dumplings at a restaurant in Chinatown, don't be timid. Get your goodies to go. Restaurants will not have neat and discreet bags ready for you, and if you really insist on taking something with you, they'll have to scramble in the back and find some plastic and a bag. You get the picture. Besides, delicate sauces do not travel well, so be sure you're trying to "take out" only something highly portable.

DRESSING FOR DINNER

IN PARIS, INFORMAL (*décontracté*) means being dressed nicely with taste and style, but not necessarily a tie and jacket for men or an evening dress for women. Informal does *not* mean shorts, Dallas Cowboys T-shirts, and so on. On the whole, this should be your model dress code: for gentlemen, a jacket and an open-collared shirt or polo shirt are perfectly appropriate in most establishments. We are calling this look "informal nice."

unofficial **TIP**
When we suggest that you dress more formally, we have labeled the look "comfortably formal."

Being dressed up with serious suits, evening dresses, and your best jewelry is almost never required. Elegantly dressed in Paris requires a touch of understatement and a well-selected accessory.

RESTAURANT BLOG

FOR FURTHER INSIGHT INTO FRENCH CULTURE, and in particular French gastronomy, check out Mayanne Wright's **Joie de vivre** at **mayannetravels.blogspot.com.** Mayanne, a Texan with an almost anthropological eye when observing culture, has a love affair with the fine things from France and blends useful information with her own experiences at Parisian restaurants, markets, wine cellars, and agricultural trade fairs.

The RESTAURANTS

HERE IS A LIST OF RECOMMENDED RESTAURANTS selected on the basis of their quality, particular style, value, reputation, and price–quality relationship. The list is organized in alphabetical order by restaurant name. Remember that *le menu* is a fixed menu (or prix fixe) and *la carte* is the menu itself. A fixed menu usually consists of an appetizer, a main dish, and a dessert for a set price. This often represents a good value overall. Wine and coffee usually cost extra, but not always.

PARIS RESTAURANTS RATED AND RANKED

WE HAVE DEVELOPED PROFILES FOR THE BEST and most interesting restaurants (in our opinion) in town. Each profile features a prominent heading that allows you to quickly check out the restaurant's name, cuisine, overall rating, cost, quality rating, and value rating.

CUISINE This is actually less straightforward than it sounds. A few years ago, for example, "pan-Asian" restaurants in Washington, D.C., were serving what was then generally described as "fusion" food—Asian ingredients with European techniques, or vice versa. Since then, there has been a pan-Asian explosion, but nearly all specialize in what would be street food back home: noodles, skewers, dumplings, and soups. Once-general categories have become subdivided—French into bistro fare and even Provençal, "new Continental" into regional American and "eclectic"; others have broadened and fused—Middle Eastern and Provençal into Mediterranean, Spanish and South American into Nuevo Latino, and so on. In some cases, we have used the broader terms (that is, "French") but added descriptions to give a clearer idea of the fare. Again, though, experimentation and "fusion" are ever more common, so don't hold us, or the chefs, to too strict a style.

OVERALL RATING This encompasses the entire dining experience, including style, service, and ambience in addition to the taste, presentation, and quality of the food. Five stars is the highest rating possible and connotes the best of everything. Four-star restaurants are exceptional, and three-star restaurants are well above average. Two-star restaurants are good. One star is used to indicate an average restaurant that demonstrates an unusual capability in some specialty—for example, an otherwise unmemorable place that has great foie gras.

COST In the middle of the heading is an expense description that provides a comparative sense of how much a complete meal will cost. A complete meal for our purposes consists of a main dish with vegetable or side dish and choice of soup or salad. Appetizers, desserts, drinks, and tips are excluded.

Inexpensive (Inexp)	€30 or less per person
Moderate (Mod)	€30–€60 per person
Expensive (Exp)	More than €60 per person

QUALITY RATING The food quality is rated on a scale of one to five stars, five being the best rating attainable. The quality rating is based expressly on the taste, freshness of ingredients, preparation, presentation, and creativity of food served. There is no consideration of price. If you want the best food available and cost is not an issue, you need look no further than the quality ratings.

continued on page 347

taurants by Location

	OVERALL RATING	PRICE	QUALITY RATING	VALUE RATING
SSEMENT				
Le Grand Véfour *French Haute Cuisine*	★★★★★	Exp	★★★★★	★★★★★
Chez Adrienne *Old-time French Bistro*	★★★★	Mod	★★★★	★★★★
L'Escargot Montorgueil *French snails*	★★★★	Exp	★★★½	★★★
Au Chien Qui Fume *French*	★★★½	Mod	★★★½	★★★
Café Reale *Garden Café/Italian*	★★★	Inexp	★★★	★★★★
2ND ARRONDISSEMENT				
Le Grand Colbert *French*	★★★★	Mod	★★★★	★★★★
Drouant *French Haute Cuisine*	★★★½	Exp	★★★½	★★
3RD ARRONDISSEMENT				
L'Auberge Nicolas Flamel *French*	★★★★	Mod	★★★★	★★★★
Chez Jenny *Alsatian Brasserie*	★★★★	Mod	★★★★	★★★
404 *Moroccan*	★★★★	Mod	★★★★	★★★★
L'Ambassade D'Auvergne *French Regional*	★★★½	Mod	★★★★	★★★★
4TH ARRONDISSEMENT				
L'Ambroisie *French Haute Cuisine*	★★★★★	Exp	★★★★★	★★
Bofinger *Classic Brasserie*	★★★★★	Mod	★★★★★	★★★
Les Côtelettes *French Bistro*	★★★★	Mod	★★★★	★★★★
Les Philosophes *French*	★★★★	Mod	★★★	★★★★
Le Vieux Bistro *French Bistro*	★★★½	Mod	★★★★½	★★★★
Le Dos de la Baleine *French*	★★★½	Mod	★★★★	★★★★
La Victoire Suprême du Cœur *Vegetarian*	★★	Inexp	★★★★	★★★★
5TH ARRONDISSEMENT				
La Rôtisserie du Beaujolais *Country-style Rôtisserie*	★★★★	Mod/Exp	★★★★½	★★★★
Le Balzar *Classic Brasserie*	★★★★	Mod	★★★★	★★★★
Ziryab *Gourmet Arabic*	★★★★	Mod/Exp	★★★★	★★★★
Le Jardin des Pâtes *Homemade Organic Pasta*	★★★½	Inexp	★★★	★★★★
6TH ARRONDISSEMENT				
Hélène Darroze *French Regional/Haute Cuisine*	★★★★★	Exp	★★★★★	★★★

ARRONDISSEMENT NAME | CUISINE	OVERALL RATING	PRICE	QUALITY RATING	VALUE RATING
6TH ARRONDISSEMENT (CONTINUED)				
Jacques Cagna *French Haute Cuisine*	★★★★★	Exp	★★★★	★★★★
Chez Marcel *French*	★★★★½	Mod	★★★★½	★★★★
La Bastide Odéon *French Bistro*	★★★★	Mod	★★★★★	★★★★
Fish! *Mediterranean*	★★★★	Mod	★★★★	★★★★
Roger la Grenouille *French Bistro*	★★★★	Mod	★★★	★★★
Chez Gramond *French*	★★★½	Exp	★★★★½	★★★
Brasserie Lipp *Classic Brasserie*	★★★	Mod	★★★	★★★
Le Comptoir du Relais Saint-Germain *Brasserie/French Bistro*	★★	Mod	★★★★	★★★★
7TH ARRONDISSEMENT				
Le Petit Bordelais *French Southwest Bistro*	★★★★	Mod	★★★★	★★★★
Restaurant du Musée d'Orsay *Traditional French*	★★★★	Mod	★★★	★★★★
La Cigale Récamier *Traditional French*	★★★	Exp	★★★★	★★★
8TH ARRONDISSEMENT				
Ladurée *French/Tearoom*	★★★★	Mod	★★★★½	★★★★
La Cantine du Faubourg *French Contemporary Fusion*	★★★★	Exp	★★★★	★★★★
Spoon *French*	★★★★	Exp	★★★★	★★★
9TH ARRONDISSEMENT				
Chartier *French*	★★★★	Inexp	★★★	★★★★★
10TH ARRONDISSEMENT				
Les Deux Canards *French Bistro*	★★★★	Mod	★★★★	★★★★
Julien *Art Nouveau Brasserie*	★★★★	Mod	★★★★	★★★
Le Verre Volé *Wine Bar*	★★	Inexp	★★★	★★★★
11TH ARRONDISSEMENT				
Astier *French Bistro*	★★★★½	Mod	★★★★½	★★★★★
Chez Ramulaud *French*	★★★★	Mod	★★★½	★★★★
Le Villaret *French*	★★★½	Mod	★★★★½	★★★★
Au Trou Normand *Neighborhood Bistro*	★★★	Inexp	★★★★	★★★★★

Paris Restaurants by Location (continued)

ARRONDISSEMENT NAME | CUISINE	OVERALL RATING	PRICE	QUALITY RATING	VALUE RATING
12TH ARRONDISSEMENT				
Les Zygomates *French Bistro*	★★★½	Inexp	★★★★	★★★★★
Le Square Trousseau *French*	★★★½	Mod	★★★	★★★
14TH ARRONDISSEMENT				
Les Petites Sorcières *French Bistro*	★★★★	Mod	★★★★½	★★★★
La Régalade *French Regional*	★★★★	Mod	★★★★	★★★★★
La Coupole *Classic Brasserie*	★★★★	Mod	★★★	★★★
Monsieur Lapin *French/Rabbit*	★★★½	Mod	★★★★	★★★★
15TH ARRONDISSEMENT				
Le Grand Pan *French Bistro*	★★★★★	Inexp	★★★★	★★★★★
Goldoni's Ristorante *Italian*	★★★★	Mod/Exp	★★★★	★★★★
L'Os à Moëlle *French Bistro*	★★★½	Mod	★★★★	★★★★
Le Père Claude *French*	★★★½	Mod/Exp	★★★½	★★★

Paris Restaurants by Cuisine

CUISINE NAME | ARRONDISSEMENT	OVERALL RATING	PRICE	QUALITY RATING	VALUE RATING
BRASSERIE, ALSATIAN				
Chez Jenny | 3rd	★★★★	Mod	★★★★	★★★
BRASSERIE, ART NOUVEAU				
Julien | 10th	★★★★	Mod	★★★★	★★★
BRASSERIE, CLASSIC				
Bofinger | 4th	★★★★★	Mod	★★★★★	★★★
Le Balzar | 5th	★★★★	Mod	★★★★	★★★★
La Coupole | 14th	★★★★	Mod	★★★	★★★
Brasserie Lipp | 6th	★★★	Mod	★★★	★★★
Le Comptoir du Relais | 6th Saint-Germain	★★	Mod	★★★★	★★★★
COUNTRY-STYLE RÔTISSERIE				
La Rôtisserie du Beaujolais | 5th	★★★★	Mod/Exp	★★★★½	★★★★

ARRONDISSEMENT NAME | CUISINE	OVERALL RATING	PRICE	QUALITY RATING	VALUE RATING
16TH ARRONDISSEMENT				
Vin & Marée *Seafood*	★★★	Mod	★★★★	★★★★
17TH ARRONDISSEMENT				
Caïus *French*	★★★★	Mod	★★★	★★★★★
18TH ARRONDISSEMENT				
Le Restaurant *French*	★★★★	Mod	★★★★	★★★★★
Rendez-Vous des Chauffeurs *Home-style French Bistro*	★★★	Mod	★★★★	★★★★★
20TH ARRONDISSEMENT				
Café Noir *Neighborhood Bistro*	★★★	Mod	★★★★	★★★★

CUISINE NAME | ARRONDISSEMENT	OVERALL RATING	PRICE	QUALITY RATING	VALUE RATING
CONTEMPORARY FUSION				
La Cantine du Faubourg | 8th	★★★★	Exp	★★★★	★★★★
FRENCH				
Chez Marcel | 6th	★★★★½	Mod	★★★★½	★★★★
Le Restaurant | 18th	★★★★	Mod	★★★★	★★★★★
L'Auberge Nicolas Flamel | 3rd	★★★★	Mod	★★★★	★★★★
Le Grand Colbert | 2nd	★★★★	Mod	★★★★	★★★★
Spoon | 8th	★★★★	Exp	★★★★	★★★
Chez Ramulaud | 11th	★★★★	Mod	★★★½	★★★★
Caïus | 17th	★★★★	Mod	★★★	★★★★★
Chartier | 9th	★★★★	Inexp	★★★	★★★★★
Les Philosophes | 4th	★★★★	Mod	★★★	★★★★
Chez Gramond | 6th	★★★½	Exp	★★★★½	★★★
Le Villaret | 11th	★★★½	Mod	★★★★½	★★★★

Paris Restaurants by Cuisine (continued)

CUISINE NAME | ARRONDISSEMENT	OVERALL RATING	PRICE	QUALITY RATING	VALUE RATING
FRENCH (CONTINUED)				
Le Dos de la Baleine | 4th	★★★½	Mod	★★★★	★★★★
Au Chien Qui Fume | 1st	★★★½	Mod	★★★½	★★★
Le Père Claude | 15th	★★★½	Mod/Exp	★★★½	★★★
Le Square Trousseau | 12th	★★★½	Mod	★★★	★★★
FRENCH BISTRO				
Le Grand Pan | 15th	★★★★★	Inexp	★★★★	★★★★★
Astier | 11th	★★★★½	Mod	★★★★½	★★★★★
La Bastide Odéon | 6th	★★★★	Mod	★★★★★	★★★★
Les Petites Sorcières | 14th	★★★★	Mod	★★★★½	★★★★
Chez Adrienne | 1st	★★★★	Mod	★★★★	★★★★
Les Côtelettes | 4th	★★★★	Mod	★★★★	★★★★
Le Petit Bordelais | 7th	★★★★	Mod	★★★★	★★★★
Les Deux Canards | 10th	★★★★	Mod	★★★★	★★★★
L'Os à Moëlle | 15th	★★★½	Mod	★★★★	★★★★
Roger la Grenouille | 6th	★★★★	Mod	★★★	★★★
Le Vieux Bistro | 4th	★★★½	Mod	★★★★½	★★★★
Les Zygomates | 12th	★★★½	Inexp	★★★★	★★★★★
Rendez-Vous des Chauffeurs | 18th	★★★	Mod	★★★★	★★★★★
Café Reale | 1st	★★★	Inexp	★★★	★★★★
FRENCH HAUTE CUISINE				
L'Ambroisie | 4th	★★★★★	Exp	★★★★★	★★
Le Grand Véfour | 1st	★★★★★	Exp	★★★★★	★★★★★
Jacques Cagna | 6th	★★★★★	Exp	★★★★	★★★★
Drouant | 2nd	★★★½	Exp	★★★½	★★
FRENCH REGIONAL				
Hélène Darroze | 6th	★★★★★	Exp	★★★★★	★★★
La Régalade | 14th	★★★★	Mod	★★★★	★★★★★
L'Ambassade D'Auvergne | 3rd	★★★½	Mod	★★★★	★★★★
FRENCH SNAILS				
L'Escargot Montorgueil | 1st	★★★★	Exp	★★★½	★★★

CUISINE NAME | ARRONDISSEMENT	OVERALL RATING	PRICE	QUALITY RATING	VALUE RATING
FRENCH TRADITIONAL				
Restaurant du Musée d'Orsay | 7th	★★★★	Mod	★★★	★★★★
La Cigale Récamier | 7th	★★★	Exp	★★★★	★★★
FRENCH/RABBIT				
Monsieur Lapin | 14th	★★★½	Mod	★★★★	★★★★
FRENCH/TEAROOM				
Ladurée | 8th	★★★★	Mod	★★★★½	★★★★
GOURMET ARABIC				
Ziryab | 5th	★★★★	Mod/Exp	★★★★	★★★★
ITALIAN				
Goldoni's Ristorante | 15th	★★★★	Mod	★★★★	★★★★
Café Reale | 1st	★★★	Inexp	★★★	★★★★
MEDITERRANEAN				
Fish! | 6th	★★★★	Mod	★★★★	★★★★
MOROCCAN				
404 | 3rd	★★★★	Mod	★★★★	★★★★
NEIGHBORHOOD BISTRO				
Au Trou Normand | 11th	★★★	Inexp	★★★★	★★★★★
Café Noir | 20th	★★★	Mod	★★★★	★★★★
PASTA				
Le Jardin des Pâtes | 5th	★★★½	Inexp	★★★	★★★★
SEAFOOD				
Vin & Marée | 16th	★★★	Mod	★★★★	★★★★
VEGETARIAN				
La Victoire Suprême du Cœur | 4th	★★	Inexp	★★★★	★★★★
WINE BAR				
Le Verre Volé | 10th	★★	Inexp	★★★	★★★★

Restaurants and Nightclubs on the Right Bank

1. L'Ambassade d'Auvergne
2. L'Ambroisie
3. Astier
4. L'Auberge Nicolas Flamel
5. Au Chien Qui Fume
6. Au Duc des Lombards
7. Au Trou Normand
8. Les Bains Douches
9. Le Balajo
10. Bofinger
11. Café Beaubourg
12. Café Reale
13. La Cantine du Faubourg
14. La Chapelle des Lombards
15. Chartier
16. Chez Adrienne
17. Chez Jenny
18. Chez Ramulaud
19. Le China
20. Clown Bar
21. Les Côtelettes
22. Crazy Horse Saloon
23. Les Deux Canards
24. Le Dos de la Baleine
25. Drouant
26. L'Escargot Montorgueil
27. La Favela Chic
28. 404
29. Folies Bergère
30. Le Grand Colbert

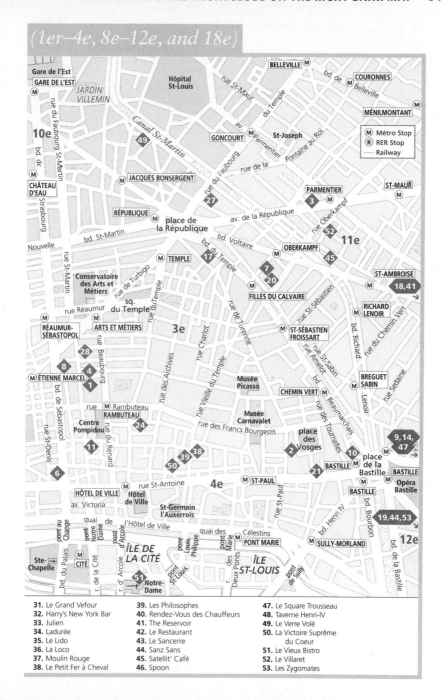

(1er–4e, 8e–12e, and 18e)

31. Le Grand Vefour
32. Harry's New York Bar
33. Julien
34. Ladurée
35. Le Lido
36. La Loco
37. Moulin Rouge
38. Le Petit Fer à Cheval

39. Les Philosophes
40. Rendez-Vous des Chauffeurs
41. The Reservoir
42. Le Restaurant
43. Le Sancerre
44. Sanz Sans
45. Satellit' Café
46. Spoon

47. Le Square Trousseau
48. Taverne Henri-IV
49. Le Verre Volé
50. La Victoire Suprême
du Coeur
51. Le Vieux Bistro
52. Le Villaret
53. Les Zygomates

Restaurants and Nightclubs on the Left Bank

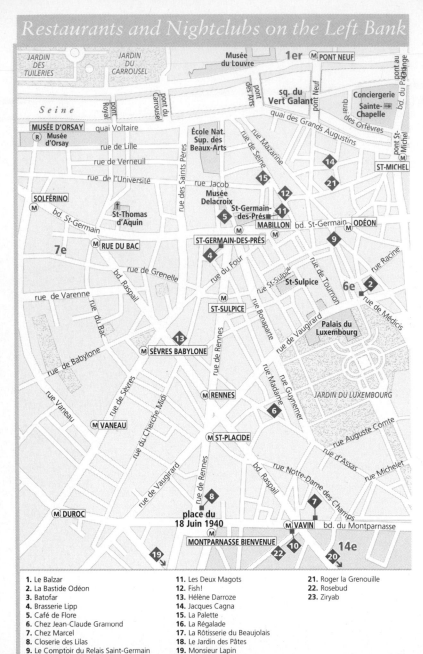

1. Le Balzar
2. La Bastide Odéon
3. Batofar
4. Brasserie Lipp
5. Café de Flore
6. Chez Jean-Claude Gramond
7. Chez Marcel
8. Closerie des Lilas
9. Le Comptoir du Relais Saint-Germain
10. La Coupole

11. Les Deux Magots
12. Fish!
13. Hélène Darroze
14. Jacques Cagna
15. La Palette
16. La Régalade
17. La Rôtisserie du Beaujolais
18. Le Jardin des Pâtes
19. Monsieur Lapin
20. Petites Sorcières

21. Roger la Grenouille
22. Rosebud
23. Ziryab

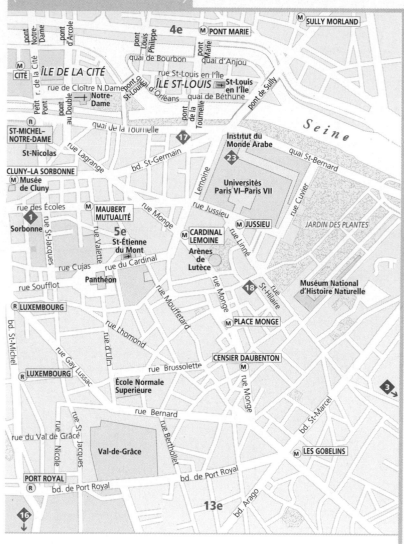

(5e–6e and 13e–14e)

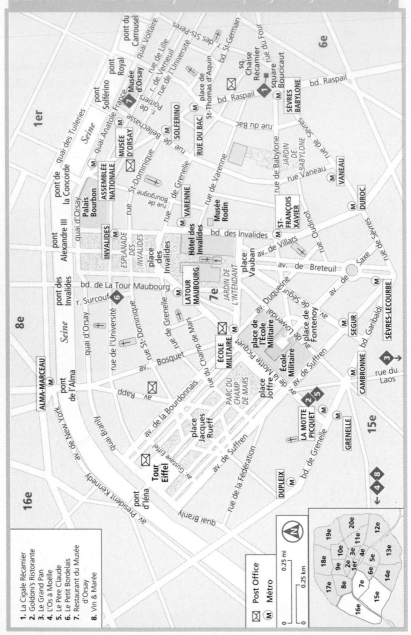

Restaurants on Left Bank (7e, 15e, and 16e)

1. La Cigale Récamier
2. Goldoni's Ristorante
3. Le Grand Pan
4. L'Os à Moelle
5. Le Père Claude
6. Le Petit Bordelais
7. Restaurant du Musée d'Orsay
8. Vin & Marée

continued from page 335

VALUE RATING If, on the other hand, you are looking for both quality *and* value, then you should check the value rating. The value ratings are defined as follows:

★★★★★	Exceptional value; a real bargain
★★★★	Good value
★★★	Fair value; you get exactly what you pay for
★★	Somewhat overpriced
★	Significantly overpriced

PRICING Here we supply an average price per person to eat a full meal at the profiled restaurant. We'll also tell you if the restaurant offers prix fixe menus (or only prix fixe menus), and how much they cost. offers

PAYMENT We've listed the type of payment accepted at each restaurant using the following code: AE equals American Express, CB equals Carte Blanche, D equals Discover, DC equals Diners Club, MC equals MasterCard, and V equals Visa.

RESTAURANT PROFILES

L'Ambassade d'Auvergne ★★★½

**FRENCH REGIONAL (AUVERGNE)   MODERATE   QUALITY ★★★★   VALUE ★★★★
3RD ARRONDISSEMENT**

22, rue du Grenier-Saint-Lazare, 75003; ☎ 01 42 72 31 22; ambassade-auvergne.com; Métro: Rambuteau

Customers Mixed. **Reservations** Not needed. **When to go** Sundays for lunch and dinner. **Pricing** Average per person, €35; prix fixe, €20 (weekday lunch only) and €28. **Payment** AE, JCB, MC, V, traveler's checks in euros. **English spoken** Yes. **Bar** None. **Wine selection** Wines from the Auvergne, Bordeaux, and Bourgogne. **Dress** Informal chic. **Disabled access** No. **Hours** Daily, noon–2 p.m. and 7:30–10 p.m.

SETTING AND ATMOSPHERE Warm environment. The first-floor dining room is rustic and cozy.

HOUSE SPECIALTIES Regional dishes. *Aligot* (a wonderful mix of mashed potatoes, cheese, and garlic), filet of beef from Salers, garlic-roasted guinea fowl, chocolate mousse.

SUMMARY AND COMMENTS Once you've eaten here, you'll swear to return every time you come back to Paris. The Auvergne is one of France's most noted regions in terms of cuisine, and here you find the best of the region. For a group of friends looking to dine together, this is a perfect spot; the two-story restaurant has special rooms for groups of ten or more. This is a good choice for Sunday dining. The *andouillette* sausage is famous here. If you've never tried an Auvergnat wine, this is your chance. And, of course, try the regional cheeses.

L'Ambroisie ★★★★★

FRENCH HAUTE CUISINE   EXPENSIVE   QUALITY ★★★★★   VALUE ★★
4TH ARRONDISSEMENT

9, place des Vosges, 75004; ☎ 01 42 78 51 45; ambroisie-placedesvosges.com; Métro: Saint-Paul

Customers Fine diners. **Reservations** Book as far in advance as possible (a minimum of 1 month) and reconfirm before showing up. **When to go** Not too late. **Pricing** Average per person, €250. **Payment** AE, MC, V, traveler's checks in euros. **English spoken** Yes. **Bar** None. **Wine selection** 500–600 vintage wines. **Dress** Casual chic, sober elegance. **Disabled access** Some tables only. **Hours** Tuesday–Saturday, noon–2 p.m. and 8–9:30 p.m.

SETTING AND ATMOSPHERE The tapestries on the walls set the tone for the meal. Two extended dining rooms are very pretty and help Danièle and Bernard Pacaud accommodate the demand to eat here.

HOUSE SPECIALTIES Langoustine tail *feuilletine* with sesame seeds and curry sauce, baby pigeon with caramelized onion and fresh peas, *tarte fine sablée* with Bourbon-vanilla ice cream.

SUMMARY AND COMMENTS Excellent food and less pretension than some of Paris's other top gastronomic addresses, but be prepared for a serious meal and a hefty bill. We've only profiled a few gastronomic superstars, and this is one of them. Perfect elegance abounds. You're in the hands of true artists who love to please and to surprise. Let them. A dinner here will be more than a meal; it'll be a refined cultural event.

Astier ★★★★½

FRENCH BISTRO   MODERATE   QUALITY ★★★★½   VALUE ★★★★★
11TH ARRONDISSEMENT

44, rue Jean-Pierre Timbaud, 75011; ☎ 01 43 57 16 35; restaurant-astier.com; Métro: Parmentier or Oberkampf

Customers Mixed regulars and tourists. **Reservations** Required in advance for dinner. **When to go** Not too late. **Pricing** Average per person €35; prix fixe €18.50–€32. **Payment** MC, V. **English spoken** Yes. **Bar** None. **Wine selection** 400 wines, good-quality value. **Dress** Casual. **Disabled access** No. **Hours** Daily, 12:15–2:15 p.m. and 7–10:30 p.m.

SETTING AND ATMOSPHERE Upscale bistro, linen tablecloths and napkins.

HOUSE SPECIALTIES Different dishes daily, about 50 specialties each year, depending on season.

SUMMARY AND COMMENTS Hip Paris has been creeping steadily into the Oberkampf area, where Astier has been for years. Here, you'll feel like you're making a real find and that the Paris of unpretentious local life is still attainable. This bistro is almost always packed with an active and lively crowd that looks like they eat here each week. The décor is plain; all the energy and life of the place have gone into the cuisine, which is varied, fresh, and plentiful. For the €32 menu, you get a four-course feast that you'll have to walk off later. Everyone says that if you go to Astier, bring your appetite. You can start off with a salad or plate of succulent white asparagus with a tangy vinaigrette. Or you could dive in right away with a pasta dish. We loved the *gigot d'agneau de lait persillé* (leg of lamb in parsley with homemade mashed potatoes). There is always a fish dish or two. Astier is also renowned for its copious and yummy selection of cheeses, served on a sprawling platter. All you can eat! Whether you're already stuffed or not, you must take at least a sliver from many of the two dozen choices. But leave room, if you can, for dessert. You'll talk for days about their magnificent dark rum baba with whipped cream. Others may be cowardly and opt for the cool sorbets or the fresh fruit. The wine list is extensive; ask for help.

L'Auberge Nicolas Flamel ★★★★

FRENCH   **MODERATE**   QUALITY ★★★★   VALUE ★★★★
3RD ARRONDISSEMENT

51, rue de Montmorency, 75003; ☎ 01 42 71 77 78; auberge-nicolas-flamel.fr; Métro: Rambuteau

Customers Curious tourists. **Reservations** Advised. **When to go** Anytime, better at night. **Pricing** Average per person, €60; prix fixe, €18.50 (lunch only), €31 and €46. **Payment** AE, DC, JCB, MC, V. **English spoken** Yes. **Bar** None. **Wine selection** More than 200 wines. **Dress** Casual. **Disabled access** No. **Hours** Monday–Saturday, noon–2:30 p.m. and 7–10:30 p.m.

SETTING AND ATMOSPHERE It's always a thrill to eat in Paris's oldest house. Once an almshouse, the medieval building is a historic monument dating to 1407. The 17th-century interior has been preserved, and the exposed stone and massive wooden beams create a cozy atmosphere that's perfectly authentic. The restaurant is dark and candlelit, making it particularly nice in the cold months. The upstairs dining area is called the Salon Pernelle.

HOUSE SPECIALTIES Lobster *mille feuille*, *gigot de sept heures* (leg of lamb cooked for seven hours), *lingot chocolat-or* (warm chocolate cake with melted chocolate at the core).

SUMMARY AND COMMENTS A change of management mid-2007 and the arrival of a new chef-owner has brought a change of style. Previously know for its hearty medieval-type dishes, the cuisine is wholly young, new, and contemporary in a traditional setting.

Au Chien Qui Fume ★★★½

FRENCH   MODERATE   QUALITY ★★★½   VALUE ★★★   1ST ARRONDISSEMENT

33, rue du Pont-Neuf, 75001; ☎ 01 42 36 07 42; auchienquifume.fr; Métro: Châtelet–Les Halles

Customers Mixed, professionals, tourists. **Reservations** Required. **When to go** Anytime, even late. **Pricing** Average per person, €40; prix fixe, €21.90–€37. **Payment** AE, D, DC, JCB, MC, V, traveler's checks in euros. **English spoken** Yes. **Bar** Yes. **Wine selection** 45 wines. **Dress** Casual. **Disabled access** No. **Hours** Daily, noon–midnight and until 2 a.m. Saturday.

SETTING AND ATMOSPHERE Warm and inviting. If you love dogs, you'll love this quirky but famous Paris bistro, where porcelain and ceramic hounds and poodles grace the shelf space. Yes, the "Dog Who Smokes" has original character.

HOUSE SPECIALTIES Fish, seafood, and traditional dishes.

ENTERTAINMENT AND AMENITIES Belle Époque décor, jazz music in the background; air-conditioned on the second floor.

SUMMARY AND COMMENTS This is one of the few reliable places to eat and enjoy yourself in and around the Châtelet–Les Halles commercial wasteland—clearly not our favorite part of town for culinary discoveries. That said, the terrace is pleasant in the summer, although the service tends to be either too fast or too slow. This bistro is best late at night.

Le Balzar ★★★★

CLASSIC BRASSERIE   MODERATE   QUALITY ★★★★   VALUE ★★★★
5TH ARRONDISSEMENT

49 rue des Écoles, 75005; ☎ 01 43 54 13 67; brasseriebalzar.com; Métro: Cluny–La Sorbonne

Customers Very Parisian (classy types, Sorbonne lecturers), English-speaking tourists in the summer. **Reservations** Essential for the evening, 24 hours in advance. **When to go** Early or late. **Pricing** Average per person, €38; prix fixe, only after 10 p.m., €17.20. **Payment** AE, MC, V, traveler's checks in euros. **English spoken** Some; English menu. **Bar** No. **Wine selection** Large; most under €30 a bottle. **Dress** Informal. **Disabled access** No. **Hours** Daily, noon–midnight.

SETTING AND ATMOSPHERE Situated right next to the Sorbonne on rue des Écoles, this landmark has a touch of literary and intellectual ambience. Not a very large place, and the tables fill up quickly; without reservation you're likely to wait awhile. The narrow window box of a café-bar is a very pleasant place to sip an apéritif while waiting for your table.

HOUSE SPECIALTIES Foie gras, roast leg of lamb, ray fish in butter, profiteroles.

SUMMARY AND COMMENTS One of Paris's staple brasseries attracts Parisians and adoring Francophiles. Legend has it that Balzar, now part of the Flo group, was created by a feuding family member who controlled Brasserie Lipp (see pages 352–353). Of the two today, we prefer Balzar. For starters, try the classic herring and warm potatoes or the leek vinaigrette, followed by a steak tartare (if you like perfectly lean, seasoned raw beef) or the *raie au beurre* (ray fish in melted butter). To remain perfectly classic, opt for the warm *tarte tatin* (caramelized-apple tart) for dessert or the *tarte au citron* (lemon tart with powdered sugar). This is eating Parisian-style.

La Bastide Odéon ★★★★

FRENCH BISTRO   MODERATE   QUALITY ★★★★★   VALUE ★★★★
6TH ARRONDISSEMENT

**7, rue Corneille, 75006; ☎ 01 43 26 03 65;
bastide-odeon.com; Métro: Odéon**

Customers Before- and after-theater crowd, regulars. **Reservations** Required for dinner, 72 hours in advance. **When to go** Early is better. **Pricing** Prix fixe, €22.90 (lunch only) or €45.80. **Payment** AE, MC, V, traveler's checks in euros. **English spoken** Yes. **Bar** None. **Wine selection** Rhône, Provence, Loire, and southeastern France. **Dress** Casual to dressy. **Disabled access** No. **Hours** Tuesday–Saturday, 12:30–2 p.m. and 7:30–10:30 p.m.; closed first 3 weeks in August and 1 week from Christmas to New Year's.

SETTING AND ATMOSPHERE One of Paris's "in" restaurants, located at the side of the Théâtre de l'Odéon and a minute's walk from the Jardin du Luxembourg. Split between two floors, the restaurant's warm Mediterranean interior was completely renovated in 2005.

HOUSE SPECIALTIES Mediterranean cuisine: Lettuce hearts and *poivrade* artichokes in olive oil; scallops risotto with tomato and parsley; and hot Valrhona chocolate cake, vanilla ice cream, or coffee custard cream for dessert.

SUMMARY AND COMMENTS This address has captured the art of marrying fine ingredients and traditional cuisine with contemporary tastes and mildly innovative presentations. A highlight for us was the mysteriously crafted dessert that somehow captured warm melted chocolate inside a star-shaped cake covered with a spoon of vanilla ice cream and a lacing of coffee sauce.

Bofinger ★★★★★

CLASSIC BRASSERIE	MODERATE	QUALITY ★★★★★	VALUE ★★★
4TH ARRONDISSEMENT			

5–7, rue de la Bastille, 75004; ☎ 01 42 72 87 82; bofingerparis.com; Métro: Bastille

Customers Tourists, regulars, and oyster lovers. **Reservations** Advised. **When to go** Early and late. **Pricing** Average per person, €45; prix fixe, €22.50–€27 (lunch and dinner). **Payment** AE, D, JCB, MC, V, traveler's checks in euros and dollars. **English spoken** Yes; menu in English. **Bar** Yes. **Wine selection** Bordeaux, Beaujolais, Côtes-du-Rhône; diverse cellar. **Dress** Nicely dressed, relaxed. **Disabled access** Yes. **Hours** Monday–Friday, noon–3 p.m. and 6 p.m.–1 a.m.; Saturday, Sunday, and holidays, noon–1 a.m.

SETTING AND ATMOSPHERE   The décor isn't décor—it's original Art Deco and Belle Époque hardware, brassware, stained glass, and carved wood-work. When you reserve, ask to sit under the cupola downstairs. Nonsmokers' requests are respected here, too. Everyone who works here is proud of the restaurant, which has been carefully restored and is a protected national monument. Regular diners reserve a small alcove upstairs, where they're not disturbed by the stream of foreign visitors. Peek upstairs at the dining room and the works of art. And make sure you check out the Art Deco men's urinal with the carved dolphin head.

HOUSE SPECIALTIES   Oysters, foie gras, *choucroute,* seafood.

SUMMARY AND COMMENTS   One of Paris's top brasseries, Bofinger is a feast in every sense of the word. The selection of seafood is a great kickoff. Go for a plate of chilled oysters or, if you want a sensual experience, the plateau of mixed shellfish. Take your time and learn the nuances of withdrawing the tiny bit of periwinkle with a straight pin. The foie gras is always a great starter. The meats and fish are all fresh and well pre-pared. Nothing overly experimental or exotic, just good French brasserie fare served with a friendly formality. If you're wondering about dessert, definitely go for the profiteroles—a chocolate delight.

Across the street, Bofinger has a simpler bistro-style sister restau-rant, Le Petit Bofinger. The food is good and the prices a bit more moderate, but our suggestion is if you've come this far, go for the real thing. The savings are not worth the sacrifice in atmosphere.

Brasserie Lipp ★★★

CLASSIC BRASSERIE	MODERATE	QUALITY ★★★	VALUE ★★★
6TH ARRONDISSEMENT			

151, boulevard Saint-Germain, 75006; ☎ 01 45 48 53 91; brasserie-lipp.fr; Métro: Saint-Germain-des-Prés

Customers Showbiz and TV crowd, politicians, literary celebrities, tourists seeking out celebrities. **Reservations** Advised. **When to go** Late. **Pricing** Average per person, €50. **Payment** AE, DC, MC, V, traveler's checks in euros and dollars. **English spoken** Yes. **Bar** No. **Wine selection** 40 vintage wines, 10 Bordeaux. **Dress** Nice but not formal. **Disabled access** No. **Hours** Daily, 11–1 a.m.; closed evening of December 24 and December 25.

SETTING AND ATMOSPHERE A legendary brasserie for regulars, locals, television personalities, government ministers, and curious tourists, Lipp is a Saint-Germain-des-Prés landmark. The 1920s décor, tiled floors, sculpted woodwork, and etched glass characterize the period. Lipp is always bustling. You'll feel a bit crowded and rushed. But this is an authentic Paris brasserie.

HOUSE SPECIALTIES *Choucroute,* stuffed pig's trotters, fish.

SUMMARY AND COMMENTS The food is competent and plentiful, but that's it. If you'd like to take part in this living tradition and aren't motivated only by the food, certainly try Lipp. Kill two birds with one stone and order the *choucroute,* an Alsatian dish of sauerkraut, pork, and potatoes eaten with dabs of tangy mustard and a flavorful Alsatian wine. You'll be amused (or you should be) to note that written on the menu in English is "No salad as a meal." They're not kidding. So if you aren't into respecting the integrity of the three courses (two, at the least), then move on.

Café Noir ★★★

NEIGHBORHOOD BISTRO   MODERATE   QUALITY ★★★★   VALUE ★★★★
20TH ARRONDISSEMENT

15, rue Saint Blaise, 75020; ☎ 01 40 09 75 80; cafenoirparis.com; Métro: Porte de Bagnolet

Customers Neighborhood crowd; about three-fourths are regulars. **Reservations** Advised for dinner on weekends. **When to go** Early or late. **Pricing** Average per person, €40; prix fixe, lunch only, €17. **Payment** MC, V. **English spoken** Some. **Bar** Yes. **Wine selection** 120 wines, some available by the glass for €5–€7; German white wines available. **Dress** Casual. **Disabled access** No. **Hours** Monday–Friday, noon–2:30 p.m.; Monday–Saturday, 7:30–11 p.m.

SETTING AND ATMOSPHERE Old-style (circa 1900), decked out with hanging hats, coffeepots, bric-a-brac, French and Italian movie posters, stone sculptures from the 1930–1950 period, and a lot more. It looks like an old thrift store with ancient coffee machines, antique hats, old cinema posters, and random statues everywhere. A terrace is available in the summer.

HOUSE SPECIALTIES Filet of beef with foie gras, sea bass in a salt crust and *pain d'épices* (spiced honey bread). Delicious ice creams, unusual flavors (bulgar yogurt, wild strawberry). Appetizers are the strong point of the menu and include traditional French ingredients such as beef marrow and foie gras fresh from local markets. Numerous main dishes are accompanied by sweet garnishes like pear compote, sweet potato purée, or lime sorbet, which tend to overshadow the flavors of the rest of the dish. In keeping with its name, the café also offers an extensive range of coffees.

SUMMARY AND COMMENTS   Café Noir is a great introduction to bric-a-brac chic. The food is lovely and fragrant. Loud music, hyper-friendly waiters, and a young clientele make for a relaxed night out. This is a great place to lose your sense of time and while away the hours with a decent bottle of red wine. You'll not find a lot of other out-of-town visitors here, and you're certain to have one of the most authentic Parisian evenings of your stay. It's a bit hard to find, but you can easily walk from the Porte de Bagnolet Métro station. You'll love the pedestrian street on which the restaurant is found.

Café Réale   ★★★

GARDEN CAFÉ/ITALIAN	INEXPENSIVE	QUALITY ★★★	VALUE ★★★★
1ST ARRONDISSEMENT			

Jardin des Tuileries, 75001; ☎ 01 42 96 63 03; Métro: Tuileries

Customers Tourists and locals. **Reservations** No. **When to go** Lunch. **Pricing** Average per person, €30; prix fixe, €16. **Payment** AE, MC, V, traveler's checks in euros and dollars. **English spoken** Yes. **Bar** No. **Wine selection** Italian and French wines. **Dress** Casual. **Disabled access** Yes, except restrooms. **Hours** Daily, 9 a.m.–9 p.m., closes at 6:30 p.m. October–May

SETTING AND ATMOSPHERE   Modern, 120 seats.

HOUSE SPECIALTIES   Parma ham, aubergine lasagna, ricotta and orange blossom tart. Children's menu, €8.

SUMMARY AND COMMENTS   There are three important things to mention about Café Réale: location, location, and location. Note that Café Réale is the former Café Véry.

Caïus   ★★★★

FRENCH	MODERATE	QUALITY ★★★	VALUE ★★★★★
17TH ARRONDISSEMENT			

6 rue d'Armaillé, 75017; ☎ 01 42 27 19 20; jmnotelet@gmail.com; Métro: Étoile or Argentine

Customers Tourists, well-dressed Parisians, and European clientele. **Reservations** Recommended. **When to go** Before 9 p.m. **Pricing** Average per person, €20; prix fixe, €39. **Payment** MC, V. **English spoken** Some. **Bar** No. **Wine selection** Adequate selection of inexpensive wines, with the Cuvée

Chartier (Burgundy) at €6.50, a dirt-cheap, reliable choice. **Dress** Casual. **Disabled access** Yes. **Hours** Monday–Friday, noon–2:30 p.m. and 7:30–10:30 p.m. Closed on weekends.

SETTING AND ATMOSPHERE An excellent and innovative fusion restaurant with a French mindset and an exotic touch that offers a fixed menu of unexpected yet delicious dishes, such as the gratin of Swiss chard (*blette*) with seafood. A cozy bar and a good selection of wines by the glass at reasonable prices help make this a place to recommend.

HOUSE SPECIALTIES The menu includes a large selection of fish dishes and seafood and a variety of well-seasoned meat dishes.

SUMMARY AND COMMENTS The service here is impeccable and the suggestions of the day on the slate are always a good choice. At the time of this writing, Caïus is a favorite of Paris's local culinary critics.

La Cantine du Faubourg ★★★★

CONTEMPORARY FUSION   EXPENSIVE   QUALITY ★★★★   VALUE ★★★★
8TH ARRONDISSEMENT

105, rue du Faubourg Saint-Honoré, 75008; ☎ 01 42 56 22 22; lacantine.com; Métro: Saint-Philippe du Roule

Customers Local business crowd at lunch, well dressed, sophisticated; minor celebs. **Reservations** Advised. **When to go** Anytime. **Pricing** Average per person, €80. **Payment** AE, D, MC, V. **English spoken** Yes. **Bar** Yes. **Wine selection** Extensive and excellent. **Dress** Nicely dressed but classic. **Disabled access** Yes. **Hours** Daily, 8 p.m.–1 a.m.; Monday–Friday, noon–3 p.m.

SETTING AND ATMOSPHERE La Cantine represents the best of contemporary Paris cuisine and comfort. Large, sprawling space with low Japanese-style seating, lots of wood, and attractive upholstery. Very un-French.

HOUSE SPECIALTIES Soft-boiled eggs with caviar, creamy squid risotto, mango milkshake with passionfruit sorbet.

SUMMARY AND COMMENTS La Cantine captures a new spirit among Parisian restaurateurs tired of traditional quality and old-time French rigidity. Here the room is spacious, the service respectful yet friendly, the presentation innovative yet not over the top. This is what sophisticated Parisians not afraid to spend money but uninterested in long, heavy, and traditional meals are keen on today. Even the opening hours reflect this: La Cantine is rare in that it offers service until 3 p.m.—unusual in France, and popular with professionals who like the flexibility. Filled with art dealers from the local galleries and journalists from *Les Échos*, the establishment attracts an interesting crowd of personable people. World music mixes with the French-inspired fusion cooking to create another type of Parisian experience. Art exhibitions in La Cantine's Gallery 105, themed *soirées*, and charity events are also held at La Cantine.

Chartier   ★★★★

FRENCH   INEXPENSIVE   QUALITY ★★★   VALUE ★★★★★
9TH ARRONDISSEMENT

7, rue du Faubourg Montmartre, 75009; ☎ 01 47 70 86 29; restaurant-chartier.com; Métro: Rue Montmartre

Customers Tourists, neighborhood regulars. **Reservations** Not accepted. **When to go** Before 9 p.m. **Pricing** Average per person, €20. **Payment** MC, V. **English spoken** Some. **Bar** No. **Wine selection** Adequate selection of inexpensive wines, with the Cuvée Chartier (Burgundy) at €6.50 a dirt-cheap, reliable choice. **Dress** Casual. **Disabled access** Yes. **Hours** Daily, 11:30 a.m.–10 p.m.

SETTING AND ATMOSPHERE At Chartier, time stopped somewhere around the turn of the 20th century. This noisy and spacious restaurant, situated behind a revolving door at the back of an indecorous alleyway near the Grands Boulevards, seats you where it can, sometimes with strangers, at simple tables set with paper napkins and paper menus that change daily.

HOUSE SPECIALTIES Pepper steak, beef stew, chocolate mousse.

SUMMARY AND COMMENTS One of Paris's most written-about restaurants, Chartier continues to be a favorite eatery for visitors and residents after years of operation. The food is not gourmet, the service ranges from stiff and unfriendly to jocular and amusing, the prices are about as low as you'll find in the city, and the atmosphere is a perpetual time warp. The bread and water are plentiful, the carafe wine is cheap and red, and life is beautiful. It's like what eating at home might have been like if you were a working-class Parisian in the early part of the 20th century. In fact, the little wooden drawers in the walls where the restaurant's daily customers kept their linen napkins are reminders of yesteryear. The *steak au poivre* is good, although you must be clear if you want your meat cooked anything other than rare. It always comes out rare. We usually take the *plat du jour,* regardless of what it is. The waiters, in worn-out white shirts and black bow ties, write down your order on the paper tablecloth and tally it up in front of you.

Chez Adrienne   ★★★★

OLD-TIME FRENCH BISTRO   MODERATE   QUALITY ★★★★   VALUE ★★★★
1ST ARRONDISSEMENT

37, rue de L'Arbre-Sec, 75001; ☎ 01 42 60 15 78; Métro: Louvre-Rivoli

Customers Knowledgeable tourists, Parisians, and professionals. **Reservations** Required. **When to go** Early. **Pricing** Average per person, €45; prix fixe, €23.50 (lunch). **Payment** AE, V, traveler's checks in euros. **English spoken** Yes. **Bar** None. **Wine selection** 25 from all regions. **Dress** Casual to dressy. **Disabled access** No. **Hours** Monday–Friday, noon–2:30 p.m.; Thursday and Friday 7–9 p.m.

SETTING AND ATMOSPHERE An excellent address where savvy Parisians sit at tables next to savvy travelers.

HOUSE SPECIALTIES Pot-au-feu, kidneys, calf's liver, *terrine maison*.

SUMMARY AND COMMENTS Traditional French bistro cuisine with a very friendly, casual touch. Generous portions and a copious assortment of hors d'oeuvres and terrines. Arrive hungry or you'll feel frustrated. We like the pot-au-feu (served only in winter) and the calf's liver with shallots (served anytime).

Chez Gramond ★★★½

FRENCH   EXPENSIVE   QUALITY ★★★★½   VALUE ★★★   6TH ARRONDISSEMENT

5, rue de Fleurus, 75006; ☎ 01 42 22 28 89; Métro: Saint-Placide

Customers Bourgeois, well-to-do tourists, editors, and writers. **Reservations** Advised. **When to go** Not too late. **Pricing** Average per person, €65. **Payment** MC, V. **English spoken** Some. **Bar** None. **Wine selection** Excellent cellar, vintage wines. **Dress** Comfortable. **Disabled access** No. **Hours** Monday–Saturday, noon–3 p.m. and 7–10 p.m.; closed in August.

SETTING AND ATMOSPHERE This small and quaint restaurant with only 25 seats serves classical French cuisine to adoring customers. They own a painting by John Wayne!

HOUSE SPECIALTIES All forms of small game, including partridge, Scottish grouse, and roast duck with figs. Seafood includes scallops Saint Jacques.

SUMMARY AND COMMENTS A bit formal and stiff, but the restaurant owner and staff are adorably accommodating. The dishes are beyond reproach, although the prices can be a bit hard to stomach.

Chez Jenny ★★★★

**ALSATIAN BRASSERIE   MODERATE   QUALITY ★★★★   VALUE ★★★
3RD ARRONDISSEMENT**

**39, boulevard du Temple, 75003; ☎ 01 44 54 39 00;
chez-jenny.com; Métro: République**

Customers *Choucroute* lovers, tourists. **Reservations** Advised. **When to go** Late. **Pricing** Average per person, €35; prix fixe, from €17.20 for express lunch menu to €52 for dinner. **Payment** AE, DC, JCB, MC, V, traveler's checks. **English spoken** Yes. **Bar** No. **Wine selection** 40 wines (Alsatian, Pays de Loire, Bordeaux). **Dress** Casual to good. **Disabled access** Yes, except restroom. **Hours** Daily, noon–midnight; Friday and Saturday, noon–1 a.m.

SETTING AND ATMOSPHERE Terrace and garden seating, five dining rooms, 600 seats, 1930s sculptures, a museum of inlay work.

HOUSE SPECIALTIES *Choucroute* and other Alsatian dishes, chicken in riesling, and seafood.

SUMMARY AND COMMENTS Owned by the same people who own the Grand Café Capucines and the Procope, Chez Jenny is worth the trip only if you order one of the Alsatian specialties, particularly *choucroute,* the massive platters of sauerkraut, assorted pork cuts, sausage, and potatoes. A delicious variation is the *choucroute,* with smoked haddock served with a *beurre blanc* sauce. You must order a fruity bottle of Alsatian wine or a few strong mugs of beer to wash this down.

Chez Marcel   ★★★★½

FRENCH	MODERATE	QUALITY ★★★★½	VALUE ★★★★
6TH ARRONDISSEMENT			

7, rue Stanislas, 75006; ☎ 01 45 48 29 94;
Métro: Saint-Placide, Montparnasse

Customers Regulars, local people, and the well informed. **Reservations** Advised. **When to go** Anytime with reservations, early or late without. **Pricing** Average per person, €40; prix fixe, €16.50 (lunch). **Payment** MC, V. **English spoken** A few charming words. **Bar** No. **Wine selection** Excellent small vintages. **Dress** As you like. **Disabled access** No. **Hours** Monday–Friday, noon–2 p.m., 7:30–10 p.m.; closed in August.

SETTING AND ATMOSPHERE Small, quaint restaurant that captures all the French ambience you'll ever want. Tables are a bit tight, but the atmosphere is charming and intimate. The owner serves in the restaurant.

HOUSE SPECIALTIES Traditional dishes from Lyon: coq au vin, lamb, and duck.

SUMMARY AND COMMENTS This is one of those places you'd never find on your own, but once you've eaten here you'll return on every occasion and will be hesitant to tell other people about it. Tiny in size, Chez Marcel (no longer owned by Marcel) is a true *bistrot lyonnais,* serving up freshly made, traditional dishes. Don't hesitate to order the *plat du jour* and the *vin de jour.* Always satisfying. The coq au vin, served in a copper casserole, is sumptuous and plentiful. The *pâté en croûte* is an excellent starter. Whatever the owner-waiter tells you to drink with your meal, comply.

Chez Ramulaud   ★★★★

FRENCH	MODERATE	QUALITY ★★★½	VALUE ★★★★	11TH ARRONDISSEMENT

269, rue du Faubourg Saint-Antoine, 75011; ☎ 01 43 72 23 29;
Métro: Nation, Faidherbe Chaligny

Customers Regulars, local people, and the well informed. **Reservations** Advised. **When to go** Anytime with reservations. **Pricing** Average per person, €40; prix fixe, €16 (lunch) and €29 (dinner). **Payment** MC, V. **English spoken** No. **Bar** No. **Wine selection** Excellent and moderately priced. **Dress** As you

like. **Disabled access** No. **Hours** Monday–Friday, noon–3 a.m., Monday–
Saturday, 7:30–11 p.m.

SETTING AND ATMOSPHERE Small restaurant filled with locals and regulars.
Simply decorated, with emphasis on the food. Noisy at lunch.

HOUSE SPECIALTIES Seasonal menu *du marché.*

SUMMARY AND COMMENTS This family-run bistro is not in the guidebooks or
frequented by many tourists, but Chez Ramulaud captures the best of
French regional cooking. Here, it is as if you've been invited for lunch
or dinner at your aunt's country house. But the menu changes every
two months.

La Cigale Récamier ★★★

| TRADITIONAL FRENCH | EXPENSIVE | QUALITY ★★★★ | VALUE ★★★ |
| 7TH ARRONDISSEMENT | | | |

4, rue Récamier, 75007; ☎ 01 45 48 86 58; Métro: Sèvres-Babylone

Customers Publishing world, politicians, journalists (lunch); Parisians and
international set (dinner). **Reservations** Advised. **When to go** Early dinner.
Pricing Average per person, €55. **Payment** AE, DC, MC, V, traveler's checks in euros.
English spoken Yes. **Bar** Yes. **Wine selection** Extensive. **Dress** Dressy. **Disabled
access** Yes. **Hours** Monday–Saturday, noon–2:30 p.m. and 7:15–11 p.m.

SETTING AND ATMOSPHERE A former literary salon once known simply as Le
Récamier, this is a landmark restaurant for elected officials and leaders in the publishing industry, including best-selling authors. Political
life meets intellectual life on the spacious terrace that flanks this
Parisian institution.

HOUSE SPECIALTIES Soufflés in all shapes and forms: spinach and mozzarella
soufflé, mussel soufflé, black-pudding soufflé, orange-blossom soufflé
with pistachio ice cream.

SUMMARY AND COMMENTS The menu, décor, and name have all changed,
but the chef, Gérard Idoux, and his staff have remained, as has the
clientele. Sit on the outdoor terrace or the covered terrace; they're
both delightful.

Le Comptoir du Relais Saint-Germain ★★

| BRASSERIE/FRENCH BISTRO | MODERATE | QUALITY ★★★★ | VALUE ★★★★ |
| 6TH ARRONDISSEMENT | | | |

**9, carrefour de l'Odéon, 75006; ☎ 01 44 27 07 97;
hotel-paris-relais-saint-germain.com; Métro: Odéon**

Customers Professionals, knowledgeable tourists, Parisians. **Reservations**
Required months in advance for dinner during the week. First come, first serve
lunch and weekends. **When to go** Lunch, late. **Pricing** Prix fixe, €50 (dinner)

and €18–€30 (lunch). **Payment** AE, DC, MC, V. **English spoken** Yes. **Bar** None. **Wine selection** 60 wines, great quality from small producers. **Dress** Nice but not formal for dinner, casual for lunch. **Disabled access** Yes. **Hours** Weekdays, noon–6 p.m. and 8:30–11 p.m.; weekends, noon–11 p.m.

SETTING AND ATMOSPHERE Casual and sunny brasserie by day, this eatery transforms into a sophisticated bistro by night with one five-course gastronomic menu on offer. Diners sit elbow-to-elbow, spilling out onto a delightful terrace in the summer, perfect for watching Parisian trendsetters stroll by. The yellow-and-red trimming on the wood-paneled walls give the space a cheerful appearance, despite the harried manner of the waiters.

HOUSE SPECIALTIES Pressed foie gras and pear confit, beef cheeks, green lentil soup with foie gras, roasted saddle of lamb with couscous.

SUMMARY AND COMMENTS Le Comptoir's chef-owner Yves Cambord, formerly of La Régalade, is credited with helping revive the Paris bistro by providing delicious traditional French food at affordable prices. Consequently, he has become the darling of both the French and American media. He and his bistro live up to the hype. Dishes range from the traditional, such as salade Niçoise, homestyle paté, and thick slabs of steak with fresh veggies, to the wildly innovative chilled lentil soup with sheep's milk cheese and mint. Only fresh market ingredients are used, and although portions are a bit small, they will not disappoint. For a gastronomical experience that won't break the bank, this is the place.

Les Côtelettes ★★★★

FRENCH BISTRO	MODERATE	QUALITY ★★★★	VALUE ★★★★
4TH ARRONDISSEMENT			

4, impasse Guéménée, 75004; ☎ 01 42 72 08 45; lescotelettes.com; Métro: Bastille

Customers Locals and tourists. **Reservations** Advised for dinner, especially for the terrace. **When to go** Early or late. **Pricing** Average per person, €45; prix fixe, €15 (lunch only); €40 and €45 (lunch and dinner). **Payment** AE, DC, MC, V. **English spoken** Yes. **Bar** No. **Wine selection** 100 wines. **Dress** Casual. **Disabled access** No. **Hours** Monday–Friday, noon–2:30 p.m. and 8–10:30 p.m.; Saturday, 8–10:30 p.m.; closed the month of August.

SETTING AND ATMOSPHERE Classic bistro décor with exposed stone and beams, marble bar.

HOUSE SPECIALTIES Foie gras *terrine,* spiced duck with parsnip purée, ice cream with crystallized ginger and pumpkin.

SUMMARY AND COMMENTS Les Côtelettes is a local restaurant and neighbors in the Marais come back regularly, including some international film stars and writers. We prefer lunch here, but don't be in a hurry. The kitchen takes the time to prepare its fare.

La Coupole   ★★★★

| CLASSIC BRASSERIE | MODERATE | QUALITY ★★★ | VALUE ★★★ |

14TH ARRONDISSEMENT

102, boulevard du Montparnasse, 75014; ☎ 01 43 20 14 20; flobrasseries.com; Métro: Vavin

Customers Regulars, artists, Parisians, tourists. **Reservations** Advised. **When to go** Great late. **Pricing** Average per person, €55; prix fixe, €17, €21, and €30. **Payment** AE, DC, JCB, MC, V, traveler's checks in euros. **Bar** Yes. **Wine selection** 80 vintage wines. **Dress** Relaxed. **Disabled access** Yes, except restroom. **Hours** Daily, 8:30–10:30 a.m. (Continental breakfast) then nonstop restaurant service 11:30 a.m.–1 a.m. and until 1:30 a.m. Friday and Saturday.

SETTING AND ATMOSPHERE Large space with open bar area on the side.

HOUSE SPECIALTIES *Choucroute,* lamb curry, seafood platters.

SUMMARY AND COMMENTS You can't say you know Paris until you've eaten at least twice at La Coupole. Now part of the illustrious Flo group, La Coupole has played a significant role in the life of literary and artistic Paris for a century. Immortalized by Hemingway and Fitzgerald, Kiki of Montparnasse, and the throngs of expatriate writers and artists who frequented Montparnasse and enshrined Paris as the eternal mythic capital of culture and decadence, La Coupole was their faithful watering hole. The cultural set—artists, actors and the theater crowd, writers, poets with some money, journalists, and out-of-town visitors—buzz into this huge and bustling brasserie day and night. The food is fine but not high-end gourmet. Perfect for a bowl of onion soup with bubbling melted Gruyère or a plate of oysters, a pepper steak, or their special, lamb curry. All the clichés about Paris prove true here. It's one of the French capital's few venues where being a short-term visitor makes you a quintessential Parisian. Just keep your guidebook in your pocket and your daypack under the table.

Les Deux Canards   ★★★★

| FRENCH BISTRO | MODERATE | QUALITY ★★★★ | VALUE ★★★★ |

10TH ARRONDISSEMENT

8, rue du Faubourg Poissonnière, 75010; ☎ 01 47 70 03 23; lesdeuxcanards.com; Métro: Bonne-Nouvelle

Customers Locals and regulars. **Reservations** Advised. **When to go** Early evening. **Pricing** Average per person, €30; prix fixe, €20 (lunch only). **Payment** AE, DC, MC, V. **English spoken** Yes. **Bar** None. **Wine selection** 20 vintage wines, and the house special. **Dress** Casual. **Disabled access** No. **Hours** Tuesday–Friday, noon–2:30 p.m. Monday and Saturday, 8–11 p.m.; closed 2 weeks in August.

SETTING AND ATMOSPHERE Warm surroundings, small restaurant.

HOUSE SPECIALTIES Fried foie gras with blueberries, sea snails in garlic butter, chestnut and chocolate fondant with vanilla cream.

SUMMARY AND COMMENTS If you don't know any Parisians who can invite you around to their apartment to eat, this is the next best thing. Dinner at Les Deux Canards feels like supper at a friend's place. The *patron*, Gérard Faesch, is a jolly chap, determined to make sure that everyone is relaxed, happy, and having a great time. His specialty, the classic dinner-party standby duck à l'orange, is as good as you'll find anywhere, and the warm welcome he extends is far better than you'll find in most places. If you compliment him enough and ask nicely, he might even give you the recipe.

Drouant ★★★½

FRENCH HAUTE CUISINE	EXPENSIVE	QUALITY ★★★½	VALUE ★★
2ND ARRONDISSEMENT			

18, place Gaillon, 75002; ☎ 01 42 65 15 16;
drouant.com; Métro: 4 Septembre

Customers Parisian intellectuals with money. **Reservations** Advised. **When to go** Not too late. **Pricing** Average per person, €60; prix fixe, lunch only, €43 (2 courses); dinner, €54.30. **Payment** AE, DC, MC, V, traveler's checks in euros. **English spoken** Yes. **Bar** Yes. **Wine selection** 100 vintage wines. **Dress** Casual chic. **Disabled access** No. **Hours** Daily, midday–2:30 p.m. and 7 p.m.–midnight.

SETTING AND ATMOSPHERE When Antoine Westermann took over in 2006 he completely renovated the interior. The café décor is in the style of the 1930s and was particularly beloved by Jean Cocteau. Soft lighting, a low rumble of conversation, well-spaced tables.

HOUSE SPECIALTIES Acclaimed Alsatian chef Antoine Westermann likes to surprise, mixing sensibilities and geographic influences, and playing with foie gras, truffles, and lobsters from Brittany.

SUMMARY AND COMMENTS If you come to Paris with literary aspirations and a large expense account, indulge yourself in the illustrious surroundings of Drouant, the haute cuisine restaurant where the judges of France's most prestigious literary prize (Le Prix Goncourt) meet for dinner and discussion once a month. The restaurant was bought in 2006 by Westermann, who has designed a menu "that offers freedom to our guests so that they can come with different appetites." This means you are at liberty to choose a series of four appetizers followed by a four-dessert taster rather than the classic three-course formula. Only a supper menu is served after 10:30 p.m.

L'Escargot Montorgueil ★★★★

FRENCH SNAILS	EXPENSIVE	QUALITY ★★★½	VALUE ★★★
1ST ARRONDISSEMENT			

38, rue Montorgueil, 75001; ☎ 01 42 36 83 51; escargot-montorgueil.com; Métro: Châtelet–Les Halles

Customers Parisians, show-business workers. **Reservations** Highly recommended. **When to go** Early. **Pricing** Average per person, €70; prix fixe, €35 or €45 (lunch only) and menu dégustation €90 (lunch and dinner). **Payment** AE, JCB, MC, V, traveler's checks in euros. **English spoken** Yes. **Bar** None. **Wine selection** 100 vintages. **Dress** Well dressed but not formal. **Disabled access** Yes. **Hours** Daily, noon–2:30 p.m. and 7–10 p.m. and until 11 p.m. on Saturday; closed August and first 2 weeks of January.

SETTING AND ATMOSPHERE The rue Montorgueil is one of the most animated and festive walkways in central Paris, deserving a visit in any case. Why not combine your stroll with a meal in this very atmospheric bistro, where meats are flamed and cut in front of you? In 1832 this building became a protected historic monument, and the décor feels more like museum than restaurant. Note the painting of Sarah Bernhardt.

HOUSE SPECIALTIES Snails in various butters and sauces.

SUMMARY AND COMMENTS Go here for snails, otherwise don't. If you go for the snails and a glass of wine, you'll be delighted. Try the *colimaçon* of mixed flavors of butter. You can share the 36-snail platter, soak up the butter with bits of baguette, and call it a meal! Don't worry about the rest, and don't feel pressured to order more. If you do, though, stay with the exotic, the stuff you can't get back home, such as the frogs' legs, which are bony but tasty. Look like you know what you're doing.

Fish! ★★★★

MEDITERRANEAN	MODERATE	QUALITY ★★★★
VALUE ★★★★ 6TH ARRONDISSEMENT		

69, rue de Seine, 75006; ☎ 01 43 54 34 69; Métro: Odéon

Customers Loyal regulars and tourists. **Reservations** Recommended for dinner. **When to go** Tourists show up at 7 p.m.; Parisians turn out at 9 p.m. **Pricing** Prix fixe only, lunch: Flying Fish menu €12.50 or €25.50; dinner: €31.50 and €35. **Payment** MC, V. **English spoken** Yes. **Bar** Wine bar. **Wine selection** Large, 250+ wines. **Dress** Casual. **Disabled access** No. **Hours** Tuesday–Sunday, 12:30–2:30 p.m. and 7–10:45 p.m. Closed last week of August. Open afternoons for wine, snacks, and sweets.

SETTING AND ATMOSPHERE A cozy restaurant with a comfortable and lively bar.

HOUSE SPECIALTIES Seasonal menu, gazpacho, anchovy and calamari risotto, roasted salmon with orange and fennel, lemon tart, pears poached in red wine.

SUMMARY AND COMMENTS This *boissonnerie*, as it is called, continues to gain popularity with both customers from the *quartier* and those from abroad. Featured in *Gourmet* and *Bon Appétit* magazines, Fish! is known for its freshness and creativity, and for the quality of its wine selection supplied by Le Dernier Goût, a wine store just around the corner. Without leaving Paris, here you're afforded an authentic taste of the Mediterranean in a warm ambience. The American and New Zealand owners are on site and lend a particularly cheery touch to this successful Parisian eatery. Leave room for dessert and, of course, a glass of dessert wine!

404   ★★★★

MOROCCAN	MODERATE	QUALITY ★★★★	VALUE ★★★★
3RD ARRONDISSEMENT			

69, rue des Gravilliers, 75003; ☎ 01 42 74 57 81; Métro: Arts et Métiers

Customers Youngish and professional. **Reservations** Required. **When to go** Early or late. **Pricing** Average per person, €40; prix fixe, €17 (lunch); Sunday brunch, €21. **Payment** AE, DC, JCB, MC, V, traveler's checks in euros. **English spoken** Yes. **Bar** None. **Wine selection** Tunisian, Moroccan, Algerian, French wines from Bordeaux and Burgundy. **Dress** Casual. **Disabled access** No. **Hours** Daily, noon–2:30 p.m. and 8:30 p.m.–midnight; Berber brunch, Sunday, noon–4 p.m.

SETTING AND ATMOSPHERE When it comes to atmosphere, you'll not find more or better than 404, a small but inviting Moroccan restaurant with low, crowded tables, an open kitchen, exotic North African décor, candlelight, Arab music, and the aura of spices.

HOUSE SPECIALTIES Duck tagine, vegetable couscous.

SUMMARY AND COMMENTS Dishes are rushed to you in piping-hot clay pots. Casual and exotic perfectly describe 404, where regulars return and bring their friends. The tagines are excellent.

Goldoni's Ristorante   ★★★★

ITALIAN	MODERATE	QUALITY ★★★★	VALUE ★★★★
15TH ARRONDISSEMENT			

53, avenue de la Motte-Picquet, 75015; ☎ 01 42 19 94 08; Métro: La Motte-Picquet

Customers Mixed; neighborhood crowd. **Reservations** Recommended for dinner. **When to go** Late. **Pricing** Average per person, €50; prix fixe, €15 (lunch only) and €30. **Payment** MC, V. **English spoken** Yes. **Bar** None. **Wine selection**

Large, primarily Italian regional wines. **Dress** Casual. **Disabled access** No. **Hours** Daily, noon–2:30 p.m. and 7–11 p.m.

SETTING AND ATMOSPHERE A chic and upbeat restaurant with a lot of style.

HOUSE SPECIALTIES Artichoke heart fritura, homemade pasta with foie gras and courgettes, chocolate truffles in coffee sauce.

SUMMARY AND COMMENTS An Italian restaurant in the lively area around La Motte-Picquet. A short walk from Les Invalides and the Eiffel Tower. Goldoni's serves an authentic North Italian cuisine, and the Chiantis are lovely.

Le Grand Colbert ★★★★

| FRENCH | MODERATE | QUALITY | ★★★★ | VALUE | ★★★★ |
| 2ND ARRONDISSEMENT | | | | | |

2–4, rue Vivienne, 75002; ☎ 01 42 86 87 88; legrandcolbert.fr; Métro: Bourse

Customers Parisian regulars, after-theater crowd, tourists. **Reservations** Advised. **When to go** Early or late. **Pricing** Average per person, €50; prix fixe, €29.50 (lunch) and €36.50 (dinner). **Payment** AE, MC, V, traveler's checks in euros or dollars. **English spoken** Yes. **Bar** Yes. **Wine selection** 60 vintage wines. **Dress** Casual to dressy. **Disabled access** No. **Hours** Daily, noon–1 a. m.

SETTING AND ATMOSPHERE If we asked you to imagine what a traditional Parisian brasserie looks like, we reckon that this is what you'd come up with. The Belle Époque–style building, classified as a historic monument, is really quite stunning and definitely worth a visit.

HOUSE SPECIALTIES Onion soup, Indian-style lamb curry, and hot chocolate profiteroles.

ENTERTAINMENT AND AMENITIES Air-conditioning, parking, wet bar, near theaters.

SUMMARY AND COMMENTS Friendly, efficient waiters serve late at Le Grand Colbert, and there's guaranteed to be something on the long menu to make your mouth water. Fans of steak tartare will not be disappointed, but if that's not your thing, then go for the excellent cod with puréed potatoes or the tasty lamb curry.

Le Grand Pan ★★★★★

| FRENCH BISTRO | INEXPENSIVE | QUALITY | ★★★★ | VALUE | ★★★★★ |
| 15TH ARRONDISSEMENT | | | | | |

20, rue Rosenwald, 75015; ☎ 01 42 50 02 50; Métro: Plaisance/ Convention

Customers Neighborhood crowd, out-of-town and local regulars. **Reservations** Book by phone a day ahead. **When to go** Lunch and early dinner. **Pricing**

€13–€25 (lunch), €20–€25 (dinner) per person. **Payment** DC, MC, V. **English spoken** Yes, but don't expect any translations. **Bar** Yes. **Wine selection** 33 wines from different regions, several wines by the glass or carafe. **Dress** Casual. **Disabled access** There's one step, but manageable. **Hours** Monday–Friday, noon–2 p.m. and 7:30–11 p.m.

SETTING AND ATMOSPHERE Cozy and intimate, eating here is like dining with your long-lost French family. Tables sit close together inside and outside on the sidewalk; some must be shared with other diners. Nonsmoking inside.

HOUSE SPECIALTIES Ever-changing seasonal food with a Basque twist, beef rib steak, veal chops and pork chops for two people.

SUMMARY AND COMMENTS On a nondescript street, off the beaten tourist path, this gem warrants a detour. All ingredients on the menu come from small purveyors, and many items change daily. Although not extensive, the menu is well rounded, featuring fowl, fish and seafood, beef and pork, and some excellent cured meats and homemade terrines. The dishes for two could really feed three people. Our favorites were the beef cheeks and tail terrine and the tender beef rib steak. Warning: Vegetarians will find nothing to feast upon here.

Le Grand Véfour ★★★★★

FRENCH HAUTE CUISINE   EXPENSIVE   QUALITY ★★★★★   VALUE ★★★★★
1ST ARRONDISSEMENT

17, rue du Beaujolais, 75001; ☎ 01 42 96 56 27; grand-vefour.com; Métro: Tuileries

Customers Wealthy diners, Parisians, curious tourists. **Reservations** Advised, at least 6 weeks in advance. **When to go** Lunch is a better deal. **Pricing** Average per person, €300; prix fixe, €88 (lunch) and €268 (*menu plaisir*). **Payment** AE, DC, JCB, MC, V, traveler's checks in euros and dollars. **English spoken** Yes. **Bar** None. **Wine selection** 600+ vintage wines. **Dress** Jacket mandatory, dresses recommended. **Disabled access** Yes, except restrooms. **Hours** Monday–Thursday, 12:30–1:45 p.m. and 8–9:45 p.m.; Friday, 12:30–1:45 p.m.; closed August, Christmas week, and Easter week.

SETTING AND ATMOSPHERE 19th-century style with an 18th-century ceiling. Opened as the Café de Chartres in 1784.

HOUSE SPECIALTIES Grilled red peppers with tofu, shoulder of lamb with baby corn and yogurt, crispy strawberries with herb sorbet and tomato jam.

SUMMARY AND COMMENTS If you are going for a serious gourmet meal and you're not sure which of Paris's culinary landmarks to choose, let us help you. If you're after the latest and the height of Paris chic, go elsewhere. If you want high visibility and pretension, go elsewhere. If you want to be treated like a duke and duchess, sit among the royal collection of art and objects, and dine in the utmost of timeless French gastronomy under the arches of the Palais Royal, reserve at Le Grand Véfour. This is the best of Paris's old wealth. Pigeon Prince Rainier III is a house specialty. Do we need to say more? Give yourself three to four hours and get a babysitter for the kids.

Hélène Darroze ★★★★★

FRENCH REGIONAL/HAUTE CUISINE   EXPENSIVE   QUALITY ★★★★★   VALUE ★★★
6IH ARRONDISSEMENT

4, rue d'Assas, 75006; ☎ 01 42 22 00 11; helenedarroze.com; reservation@helenedarroze.com; Métro: Sèvres-Babylone

Customers Fine diners. **Reservations** Book as far in advance as possible, best by phone, and reconfirm a few days to a week before. **When to go** Lunch is a better deal. **Pricing** Lunch prix fixe, €25, €55, €72; dinner prix fixe, €175 and à la carte, €38–€78 per person. **Payment** AE, MC, DC, V. **English spoken** Yes. **Bar** None. **Wine selection** Ranges from rare vintages (setting you back more than €2,000!) to fine regional bottlings, but the real treat is the exquisite collection of Bas Armagnac. **Dress** Casual chic. **Disabled access** No. **Hours** Tuesday–Saturday, 12:30–2:30 p.m. and 7:30–10:30 p.m.

SETTING AND ATMOSPHERE The orange and burgundy tones, blond hardwood floors, and plush chairs invite you to sit back, relax, and enjoy the feast to come. The contemporary and unassuming décor allows you to completely focus on the food before you. You can count on the waitstaff and sommelier to put you immediately at ease, providing excellent and detailed guidance in your food and wine selections.

HOUSE SPECIALTIES Foie gras from Landes, blue lobster roasted with tandoori spices, spit-roasted Racan pigeon.

SUMMARY AND COMMENTS Excellent service and inventive cuisine emphasizing fresh seasonal ingredients from the southwestern part of France make for a memorable dining experience. However, if you indulge in more than one course, wine, and an after-dinner Armangnac, be prepared to pay the piper. Much controversy exists over whether owner–executive chef Hélène Darroze deserves her two Michelin stars, but one bite of the whole foie gras steamed in fig leaves, doused with three different types of figs, and the Tandoori-spiced crayfish put an end to any doubts we might have had. Dinner here will not only delight your palate, it will provide a fine introduction to another region of France.

Jacques Cagna   ★★★★★

FRENCH HAUTE CUISINE   EXPENSIVE   QUALITY ★★★★   VALUE ★★★★
6TH ARRONDISSEMENT

**14, rue des Grands-Augustins, 75006; ☎ 01 43 26 49 39;
jacquescagna.com; Métro: Saint-Michel**

Customers Serious culinary buffs. **Reservations** Required for dinner. **When to go** Early dinner. **Pricing** Average per person, €120; prix fixe, €45 (lunch) and €95 (dinner). **Payment** AE, DC, JCB, MC, V, traveler's checks in euros and dollars. **English spoken** Yes. **Bar** None. **Wine selection** An impressive list of more than 500 wines. **Dress** Casual chic. **Disabled access** No. **Hours** Wednesday–Friday, noon–2 p.m. and 7:30–10:15 p.m.; Tuesday and Saturday, 7:30–10:15 p.m.; closed 3 weeks in August.

SETTING AND ATMOSPHERE *Hôtel particulier* from the 17th century; wooded area, one of the most beautiful collections of 17th-century Dutch paintings.

HOUSE SPECIALTIES Fresh snails *petit gris en surprise* "Jacques Cagna," Breton lobster risotto; spiced roast duck with raspberry sauce; roast pigeon pie with green Chartreuse; tiramisu with chocolate sauce and Irish coffee ice cream.

SUMMARY AND COMMENTS Be prepared to forfeit a chunk of change here, but you'll get the real deal. You'll love your meal, and you'll be enchanted by the flavors, the presentation, the originality of the experience, and the delightful mix of nonpretension and utmost sophistication. Bring a dictionary and note what you've eaten. You won't remember the details by yourself. Cagna loves to surprise and to invent. He's one of Paris's best, so remember that you're paying for the art, not just the ingredients.

Le Jardin des Pâtes   ★★★½

HOMEMADE ORGANIC PASTA   INEXPENSIVE   QUALITY ★★★   VALUE ★★★★
5TH ARRONDISSEMENT

4, rue de Lacépède, 75005; ☎ 01 43 31 50 71; Métro: Jussieu

Customers The health-conscious, pasta lovers, students, a few tourists. **Reservations** Encouraged. **When to go** Anytime. **Pricing** Average per person, €20. **Payment** MC, V. **English spoken** Limited. **Bar** No. **Wine selection** Limited. **Dress** Casual. **Disabled access** No. **Hours** Daily, noon–2:30 p.m. and 7–11 p.m.

SETTING AND ATMOSPHERE Simple, well-lit wooden tables and softly shaded walls. Wholesome feel.

HOUSE SPECIALTIES Barley pasta with fresh salmon, vegetarian rice pasta with tofu and caramelized ginger, fruit clafoutis.

SUMMARY AND COMMENTS After a stroll through the glorious Jardin des Plantes, why not amble over to the aptly named Jardin des Pâtes (that's "pasta garden") for a super-filling noodle feast? Here on a quiet side street, you'll discover a small menu of homemade dishes that attract mostly locals. This is fresh pasta, too: each dish is prepared from various organic flours the staff grinds themselves. You may not feel obligated to order a first course: ours weren't spectacular (an avocado-and-melon-sherbet salad struck us as the wrong combination, and an ordinary chèvre-tomato-green salad cried out for fresher ingredients). Luckily, the massive portions of pasta pleased everyone at the table. We sampled the chestnut pasta with duck in a mushroom-nutmeg cream sauce, the vegetarian rice pasta with tofu and ginger, a tomato-mozzarella-basil sauce over wide wheat fettuccine, and noodles and scallions held in place by an omelet. Try a shot of Farigoule, a thyme liqueur, to finish off: we guarantee you've never tasted a *digestif* so unusually luscious. With our cereal-based fake coffee, we took in a fresh cherry *clafoutis,* an egg-based tart bathed in cream. This isn't a place to offer many wines, but its decent prices and generous plate sizes are rare in Paris.

Julien ★★★★

ART NOUVEAU BRASSERIE   MODERATE   QUALITY ★★★★   VALUE ★★★
10TH ARRONDISSEMENT

16, rue du Faubourg Saint-Denis, 75010; ☎ 01 47 70 12 06; julienparis.com; Métro: Strasbourg–Saint-Denis

Customers Mixed, regulars, tourists, couples, professionals. **Reservations** Advised on weekends. **When to go** Late. **Pricing** Average per person, €45; prix fixe, €23 (lunch) and €28 (dinner). **Payment** AE, DC, JCB, MC, V, traveler's checks in euros and dollars. **English spoken** Yes. **Bar** Yes. **Wine selection** 60 vintage wines. **Dress** Casual to dressy. **Disabled access** No. **Hours** Daily, noon–3 p.m. and 7 p.m.–1 a.m.

SETTING AND ATMOSPHERE Beautiful stained glass, wonderful flowers, antique hats hanging from ornate hat stands, and fabulous mirrors reflecting the Art Nouveau splendor surrounding you set the scene for tourists and smart French to treat themselves.

HOUSE SPECIALTIES Duck foie gras sautéed with lentils, filet of sole, Castelnaudary goose cassoulet, hot chocolate profiteroles.

SUMMARY AND COMMENTS Part of the Flo group of restaurants, Julien is a magnificent brasserie. The formally dressed waiters whiz around at high speed, delivering competently made (if slightly overpriced) dishes. Its position close to several theaters makes it a good choice for a late supper.

Monsieur Lapin   ★★★½

FRENCH/RABBIT   MODERATE   QUALITY ★★★★   VALUE ★★★★
14TH ARRONDISSEMENT

11, rue Raymond-Losserand, 75014; monsieur-lapin.fr;
☎ **01 43 20 21 39; Métro: Gaîté**

Customers International. **Reservations** Advised for dinner. **When to go** Anytime.
Pricing Average per person, €45; prix fixe, €35. **Payment** MC, V. **English spoken**
Yes. **Bar** No. **Wine selection** More than 70 wines. **Dress** Casual. **Disabled access**
No. **Hours** Tuesday–Friday and Sunday, noon–2 p.m. Tuesday–Sunday, 7:30–
10:30 p.m.; closed 3 weeks in August.

SETTING AND ATMOSPHERE   Intimate. Situated just behind the Montparnasse
cemetery, this is a good spot for dinner after paying homage to Sartre,
de Beauvoir, and friends.

HOUSE SPECIALTIES   Rabbit terrine in strawberry jelly, crispy rabbit with
mushroom and dried fruits, hot praline soufflé.

SUMMARY AND COMMENTS   Monsieur Lapin (Mister Rabbit) is keen to offer
you many different ways of enjoying his particular charms. Although
this restaurant serves more than its name indicates, you should use the
occasion to explore the delicacies of rabbit.

L'Os à Moëlle   ★★★½

FRENCH BISTRO   MODERATE   QUALITY ★★★★   VALUE ★★★★
15TH ARRONDISSEMENT

3, rue Vasco de Gama, 75015; ☎ 01 45 57 27 27; Métro: Lourmel

Customers Professionals, locals, Anglophones. **Reservations** Advised. **When
to go** Not too late. **Pricing** Average per person, €50; prix fixe, €36. **Payment**
MC, V, traveler's checks in euros. **English spoken** Yes. **Bar** Yes. **Wine selection**
100 wines. **Dress** Casual. **Disabled access** Yes. **Hours** Tuesday–Saturday, noon–
2 p.m. and 7:30–11:30 p.m.; closed Sunday and Monday and all of August.

SETTING AND ATMOSPHERE   Red booths, lovely cellar with 17 seats for dining.

HOUSE SPECIALTIES   Market-driven menu, soups, homemade ice creams
and sorbets.

SUMMARY AND COMMENTS   People talk of L'Os à Moëlle as a real find; it is,
although it suffers from having been discovered and claimed by everyone else before you get there. The four-course menu is a good value for
the money; it changes daily, and the quality is always high. The chef,
Thierry Faucher, is very interested in ice cream, making this a good
choice of dessert and his restaurant a good place to satisfy any cravings.
The only problem with the L'Os à Moëlle is that it's a little hard to get
excited about, as they seem to have relaxed into a winning formula. It's
a steady, safe choice in a sleepy neighborhood, which is great if that's
what you're looking for.

Le Père Claude ★★★½

FRENCH   MODERATE/EXPENSIVE   QUALITY ★★★½   VALUE ★★★
15TH ARRONDISSEMENT

51, avenue de la Motte-Picquet, 75015; ☎ 01 47 34 03 05; lepereclaude.com; Métro: La Motte-Picquet, Grenelle

Customers Celebrities, politicians, friends of the owner. **Reservations** Recommended. **When to go** Late is more fun; it's packed after 9 p.m. **Pricing** Average per person, €60; prix fixe, €31 and €39.50. **Payment** AE, V. **English spoken** Yes. **Bar** Yes. **Wine selection** Good. **Dress** Informal to eccentric. **Disabled access** No. **Hours** Daily, noon–3 p.m. and 7 p.m.–midnight.

SETTING AND ATMOSPHERE Friendly, bright, casual elegance, memorabilia and signed photographs on the walls. A bit loud.

HOUSE SPECIALTIES Homemade *terrines,* sautéed frogs' legs, roast pigeon, *rôtisserie.*

SUMMARY AND COMMENTS Le Père Claude is a Paris institution. This small but accessible restaurant near the Eiffel Tower and the École Militaire is a favorite of politicians, stars, business magnates, and friends of the flamboyant owner who want to let their hair down. The food is good, but the atmosphere of Parisians enjoying themselves makes this dining choice worth it. A good place for a late-night dinner when you want to be in loud, well-dressed company.

Le Petit Bordelais ★★★★

FRENCH SOUTHWEST BISTRO   MODERATE   QUALITY ★★★★   VALUE ★★★★
7TH ARRONDISSEMENT

22, rue de Surcouf, 75007; ☎ 01 45 51 46 93; le-petit-bordelais.fr; Métro: Plaisance/Convention

Customers Neighborhood crowd, tourists, food-loving Parisians, out-of-town and local regulars. **Reservations** Recommended. **When to go** Lunch and dinner. **Pricing** €30 (lunch), €45 (dinner) per person. **Payment** AE, MC, V. **English spoken** Yes. **Bar** Yes. **Wine selection** Broad selection of wines chosen carefully, many from choice small vineyards. The chef and owner, Philippe Pentecôte, son of a wine merchant, grew up in the Bordeaux region. Don't hesitate to ask for suggestions. Wine by the glass available for €6–€7. **Dress** Casual-chic. **Disabled access** No. One big step in front. **Hours** Daily noon–2:30 p.m. and 7:30–10:30 p.m.

SETTING AND ATMOSPHERE Warm and inviting atmosphere with décor that is both chic and simple. Primarily red design, including the dinner plates. The atmosphere reflects attention to style but is comfortable and not stiff.

HOUSE SPECIALTIES Lobster charlotte with peppers and preserved eggplant; duck stew in red wine; monkfish à la ventrèche with matelote sauce;

panacotta with coconut, pineapple, and passion fruit gazpacho.

SUMMARY AND COMMENTS Very pleasant service. Philippe Pentecôte opened his restaurant in 2007 and he's managed to dig out a place for himself among the truly great tables of Paris, including Dodin Bouffant and the Grand Véfour. He has succeeded in preserving a grand simplicity in his fare, and he personally likes to come out to talk about his passion for his cuisine, wine, and France's southwest.

Les Petites Sorcières ★★★★

FRENCH BISTRO   MODERATE   QUALITY ★★★★½   VALUE ★★★★
14TH ARRONDISSEMENT

12, rue Liancourt, 75014; ☎ 01 43 21 95 68; Métro: Denfert-Rochereau

Customers Locals and curious seekers. **Reservations** Essential. **When to go** Early or late. **Pricing** Average per person, €50; prix fixe, €20 and €24 (lunch only). **Payment** MC, V. **English spoken** Yes. **Bar** Yes, for customers. **Wine selection** 30 wines. **Dress** Casual. **Disabled access** Yes, except restrooms. **Hours** Tuesday–Friday, noon–2:30 p.m. and 8–10:30 p.m.; Monday and Saturday, 7:30–10:30 p.m.; closed 3 weeks in August.

SETTING AND ATMOSPHERE The tables are too close, but the atmosphere is pleasant and you'll feel right at home. Modern witch motif!

HOUSE SPECIALTIES Modern French cuisine with an emphasis on Flemish cuisine: monkfish *waterzoo* (Flemish stew), cod in Trappist beer sauce, waffles with vanilla ice cream.

SUMMARY AND COMMENTS The restaurant changed hands in 2008 and is now run by a talented female chef, Ghislaine Arabian. The menu reflects her northern roots.

Les Philosophes ★★★★

FRENCH   MODERATE   QUALITY ★★★   VALUE ★★★★   4TH ARRONDISSEMENT

28, rue Vieille-du-Temple, 75004; ☎ 01 48 87 49 64; cafeine.com; Métro: Hôtel-de-Ville

Customers Locals, regulars, and informed visitors. **Reservations** Not required. **When to go** Lunch or late night. **Pricing** Average per person, €30; prix fixe, €17–€31; brunch, €21. **Payment** MC, V, traveler's checks in euros and dollars. **English spoken** Yes. **Bar** No. **Wine selection** 60 choice wines, many directly from the vineyards, €18 to a whopping €720! **Dress** Informal. **Disabled access** Yes. **Hours** Daily, 9 a.m.–1:15 a.m.; brunch from 9 a.m.; restaurant open from noon.

SETTING AND ATMOSPHERE For those of you who know about the Petit Fer à Cheval bar, café, and restaurant in the Marais (see Part 10), you know that its owner is capable of creating excellent atmosphere for his guests. This is what Xavier Denamur has done with Les Philosophes. The large terrace is pleasant in the warm months for simple savory dining and people-watching.

HOUSE SPECIALTIES *Tatin à la tomate* (an original creation), roast monkfish with fresh thyme, strawberry Basque cake.

SUMMARY AND COMMENTS If you're planning a big meal in the evening, a light lunch here is an excellent idea, and the two-course set menu allows you to select the main course and either an appetizer or dessert. We like the tomato tart and the lamb.

La Régalade ★★★★

FRENCH REGIONAL   MODERATE   QUALITY ★★★★   VALUE ★★★★★
14TH ARRONDISSEMENT

49, avenue Jean Moulin, 75014; ☎ 01 45 45 68 58; Métro: Alésia.

Customers Parisian couples, U.S. and Asian tourists, businesspeople. **Reservations** Advised. **When to go** Anytime. **Pricing** Average per person €32 prix fixe. Some dishes have a small supplement. **Payment** MC, V. **English spoken** Yes. **Bar** No. **Wine selection** Small; 70 labels. **Dress** Casual. **Disabled access** Yes, but small. **Hours** Monday, 7–11 p.m., Tuesday– Friday, noon– 2 p.m. and 7–11 p.m.

SETTING AND ATMOSPHERE Calm and quaint yet warm and lively room. This small restaurant offers fine French (mainly southwest) cuisine in a traditional bistro genre (wooden furniture, red-and-white tablecloths, only one glass type). Reserving is highly recommended since this place only serves 40 at a time.

HOUSE SPECIALTIES Huge *terrine de campagne* with crusty French bread and vinegar pickles keep you occupied while you wait for your first course. Spectacular appetizers include the seasonal sautéed wild mushrooms (*poelée de girolles*) and the *jambon cru* (prosciutto) or the *mi-cuit de thon* (rare tuna) with zucchini and a green salad. If you're in the mood for something standard but succulent, go for the French beef *entrecôte,* with homemade mashed potatoes and green salad. For dessert, don't miss the chocolate quenelles. Good wine list, but only one choice for wine by the glass.

SUMMARY AND COMMENTS Small, intimate, and reliable regional cuisine. The service is friendly and you'll find some of the staff speak some English. A totally reliable address for a dinner experience that will help you feel French.

Le Restaurant ★★★★

FRENCH	MODERATE	QUALITY ★★★★	VALUE ★★★★★
18TH ARRONDISSEMENT			

32, rue de Véron, 75018; ☎ 01 42 23 06 22; lerestaurant.fr; Métro: Abbesses

Customers Young and multicultural, artists, trendy people. **Reservations** Advised. **When to go** Anytime. **Pricing** Average per person €30; prix fixe €16 (lunch), €22 (dinner). **Payment** AE, JCB, MC, V, traveler's checks in euros. **English spoken** Yes. **Bar** Yes, for diners. **Wine selection** Small; 70 labels. **Dress** Casual. **Disabled access** Yes, except restrooms. **Hours** Daily, noon–2:30 p.m. and 7:30–11:30 p.m.

SETTING AND ATMOSPHERE Decorated in interesting bric-a-brac with lots of wood surfaces and candles. Friendly waitresses. Lots of chairs and tables of differing sizes and shapes.

HOUSE SPECIALTIES Green pea soup with gambas, rabbit with juniper berries, hot chocolate tart with vanilla ice cream and cacao beans.

SUMMARY AND COMMENTS Le Restaurant is convivial and original. Owner Yves Peladeau continues to provide original French dishes with style and a lack of pretension.

Restaurant du Musée d'Orsay ★★★★

TRADITIONAL FRENCH	MODERATE	QUALITY ★★★	VALUE ★★★★
7TH ARRONDISSEMENT			

Musée d'Orsay, 1, rue de Bellechasse (median level), 75007; ☎ 01 45 49 42 33; RER: Musée d'Orsay

Customers Mostly tourists. **Reservations** No. **When to go** Lunch or Sunday brunch. **Pricing** Average per person, €40; prix fixe, €16.50 for 2 courses at lunch (children €7.50); Thursday dinner €42, including entrance to the museum; Sunday brunch, €24. **Payment** AE, MC, V, traveler's checks in euros. **English spoken** Yes. **Bar** Yes. **Wine selection** Classical but small selection; Beaujolais, Bourgogne, Bordeaux. **Dress** Relaxed. **Disabled access** Yes. **Hours** Tuesday–Sunday, 11:45 a.m.–2:30 p.m.; Thursday, 7–9:30 p.m.; tearoom Tuesday–Sunday, 3:30–5:30 p.m.

SETTING AND ATMOSPHERE Much of the enjoyment of eating here is simply the fact that you're in one of France's most celebrated and stunning museums. The restaurant is in what used to be the deluxe eatery of the Hôtel de la Gare d'Orsay.

HOUSE SPECIALTIES *Terrines*, salads, beef, duck, fish, *pâtisseries*.

SUMMARY AND COMMENTS The cuisine is traditional French, the preparations are perfectly competent, and the price is fair. One of the great tips for travelers is to tour the museum and then break here for lunch. Note that the restaurant is accessible only from inside the museum.

Roger la Grenouille ★★★★

FRENCH BISTRO　　MODERATE　　QUALITY ★★★　　VALUE ★★★
6TH ARRONDISSEMENT

**26–28, rue des Grands-Augustins, 75006; ☎ 01 56 24 24 34;
Métro: Saint-Michel**

Customers Fun-loving internationals, after-work crowd, Parisians who've been coming here for years. **Reservations** Required for dinner. **When to go** Early or late. **Pricing** Average per person, €50; prix fixe, €23 (lunch) and €29.50 (lunch and dinner). **Payment** MC, V. **English spoken** Yes, with the heaviest accent on the Left Bank. **Bar** Yes (2 bars). **Wine selection** Red wines from the Var, rosés, and inexpensive Burgundy. **Dress** Informal. **Disabled access** No. **Hours** Monday–Saturday, noon–2:30 p.m. and 7:30–11:30 p.m.

SETTING AND ATMOSPHERE　A mythic place. Tucked into a tiny courtyard on a street off rue Saint-André-des-Arts, behind a window display of hundreds of assorted toy frogs, this very informal joint captures Parisian 19th-century bawdiness like nowhere else. The same waitresses have been there forever and love to aggressively tease the male customers, many of whom have danced on the tables before leaving their neckties pinned to the wall. The walls are covered in irreverent love notes and small bank notes from all continents.

HOUSE SPECIALTIES　Fresh frogs' legs (cooked nine different ways), fillet of beef in Sichuan pepper sauce, duck tournedos with cinnamon and orange caramel sauce, rum baba.

SUMMARY AND COMMENTS　Roger the Frog is a great little find that makes for great conversation for years. The food is country-style French with generous portions of coq au vin and a delicious *canard à l'orange*. The house prides itself on a very naughty and sexist dessert, which causes hilarious embarrassment when ordered secretly for unsuspecting women. Just tell your waitress that you want the dessert special, and she'll hurry one over—served with no spoon. When it's not overly crowded, Roger le Grenouille is a lot of fun. When stuffed to its gills, the service is slow and the kitchen can't keep up.

La Rôtisserie du Beaujolais ★★★★

COUNTRY-STYLE *RÔTISSERIE*　　MOD/EXP　　QUALITY ★★★★½　　VALUE ★★★★
5TH ARRONDISSEMENT

**19, quai de la Tournelle, 75005; ☎ 01 43 54 17 47;
Métro: Maubert-Mutualité or Pont Marie**

Customers Mixed, foreigners. **Reservations** Required. **When to go** Early or late. **Pricing** Average per person, €60. **Payment** MC, V, traveler's checks in euros. **English spoken** Yes. **Bar** Yes. **Wine selection** Beaujolais, Bordeaux, good selection of wine from Burgundy, Côtes-du-Rhône. **Dress** Informal chic. **Disabled access** No. **Hours** Daily, noon–2:15 p.m. and 7:30–10:15 p.m.

SETTING AND ATMOSPHERE One of Paris's first *rôtisserie* haunts is both sumptuous and relaxing for a busy bistro. You're sitting on street level by the Seine with a view of the illuminated Notre-Dame. The atmosphere is warm and lively.

HOUSE SPECIALTIES Lamb in puff pastry, rabbit fricassee, spit-roasted pigeon and chicken.

SUMMARY AND COMMENTS Situated next to the famed La Tour d'Argent, this very reliable and *très* Parisian restaurant is owned and operated by the Terrail family, which owns La Tour d'Argent and other Parisian restaurants, and it rarely disappoints. Fans keep coming back. The food is excellent although straightforward, centering around the impressive grill, which you can watch from your table. The beef *entrecôte* is excellent. A lot of people rave about the oven-steamed duck, which you can only order for two. We found the flavor succulent but the portions a bit lacking. This is a good place to sample coq au vin, stewed in Beaujolais. For non–beef eaters, the cod is very good, as is the sea-bass gratin. Even if you're stuffed, sample the cheeses.

Spoon ★★★★

FRENCH   EXPENSIVE   QUALITY ★★★★   VALUE ★★★   8TH ARRONDISSEMENT

14, rue de Marignan, 75008; ☎ 01 40 76 34 44; spoon.tm.fr; Métro: Franklin Roosevelt

Customers The trendy, the curious, tourists. **Reservations** Required 1 week in advance for dinner. **When to go** Early. **Pricing** Average per person, €90; prix fixe, €33 (lunch only). **Payment** ae, DC, JCB, MC, V, traveler's checks in euros and dollars. **English spoken** Yes. **Bar** No. **Wine selection** Extensive. **Dress** Creative and trendy. **Disabled access** No. **Hours** Monday–Friday, 12:15–2:30 p.m. and 7:30–10:30 p.m.; closed in August.

SETTING AND ATMOSPHERE We like the fact that the walls are white by day and purple by night; the fact that you can order a BLT with homemade ice cream for dessert and eat it out of a bizarre, angled dish; the fact that only a tenth of the wine list is French (and over half of the rest is American); and the fact that everyone is slightly bemused but definitely enjoying themselves and the food.

HOUSE SPECIALTIES Meat and fish.

SUMMARY AND COMMENTS Eating at Spoon is an enjoyable if slightly surreal experience. So much has been said about this place that it's difficult not to talk in quotation marks. It is a "designer eatery" with a "celebrity chef" famed for his "gastronomic marvels" and fabulously "creative" and "innovative" menu. Hype aside, Spoon is a really great place to eat. Following the trend for world food—that is, fusion of various elements, ingredients, and styles from around the globe—über-cook Alain Ducasse comes up with innovative taste combinations that work surprisingly well. The menu is rather avant-garde and very confusing, but the staff is happy to explain.

Le Square Trousseau ★★★½

FRENCH   MODERATE   QUALITY ★★★   VALUE ★★★   12TH ARRONDISSEMENT

1, rue Antoine Vollon, 75012; ☎ 01 43 43 06 00; fax 01 43 43 00 66; Métro: Ledru-Rollin

Customers Locals and tourists. **Reservations** Required. **When to go** Early or late. **Pricing** Average per person, €45. **Payment** AE, MC, V. **English spoken** No. **Bar** Yes. **Wine selection** 300 bottles. **Dress** Casual. **Disabled access** No. **Hours** Daily, noon–2:30 p.m. and 8–midnight.

SETTING AND ATMOSPHERE 1900s bistro.

HOUSE SPECIALTIES Fresh, market-based cooking; homemade duck foie gras, spaghetti with clams, chestnut tiramisu.

SUMMARY AND COMMENTS This early-20th-century bistro will delight you. It's so typical, you'll think it was made from a kit. But no, it's the real thing, and what's more, Le Square Trousseau is located on a lovely square just outside the range of the throngs of tourists. If it's full, you'll be among Parisians enjoying themselves. The wines are good, but there's no reason to go beyond the house wines, which are reasonable and which pair well with everything from the cold cuts to the duck, beef, and fish.

Le Verre Volé ★★

WINE   BAR   INEXPENSIVE   QUALITY ★★★   VALUE ★★★★
10TH ARRONDISSEMENT

67, rue de Lancry, 75010; ☎ 01 48 03 17 34; leverrevole.fr; Métro: Jacques Bonsargent

Customers Hip, young crowd, tourists who know their wine. **Reservations** Recommended, book a day in advance. **When to go** Early for lunch, either seating for dinner. **Pricing** €7.50–€13 per person. **Payment** DC, MC, V. **English spoken** Yes. **Wine selection** 300 wines from different regions; €7 corkage fee. **Dress** Casual. **Disabled access** No. **Smoking** Nonsmoking. **Hours** Tuesday–Saturday, 12:15–2:30 p.m. and 8 p.m.–1:00 a.m.

SETTING AND ATMOSPHERE Wine bottles line the walls, plain wooden tables and chairs bump into each other on the concrete floor, a miniscule kitchen sits at the back of the tiny room. This wine bar and cellar rolled into one matches the energy of the trendy area running along the Canal Saint Martin. Some might find the bubbling conversation, music, and enthusiastic service somewhat overwhelming.

HOUSE SPECIALTIES Family and traditional food, such as rillettes, cassoulet, cured meats and cheeses; artisan and organic wines.

SUMMARY AND COMMENTS Wine lovers usually rank this spot high among their favorite wine bars in Paris. Most of France's wine-growing regions (except Bordeaux) are well represented. Bottles are reasonably priced, some downright cheap. Appetizers and dishes range from mozzarella and figs with balsamic vinegar to black boudin sausage with caramelized onions. An evening here, although it might wear you out, will allow you to experience Paris' wine world firsthand and make new oenological discoveries.

La Victoire Suprême du Cœur ★★

| VEGETARIAN | INEXPENSIVE | QUALITY ★★★★ | VALUE ★★★★ |

4TH ARRONDISSEMENT

27–31, rue du Bourg-Tibourg, 75004; ☎ 01 40 41 95 03; vscoeur.com; Métro: Hôtel-de-Ville

Customers Mixed, not too young, French, and tourists. **Reservations** Recommended for dinner. **When to go** Lunch or 6:30–8 p.m. **Pricing** €10.50–€15.00 (lunch), €14.50–€18.50 (dinner) per person. **Payment** MC, V. **English spoken** Yes. **Wine selection** 10 wines by the glass, carafe, bottle. **Dress** Casual. **Disabled access** Yes. **Hours** Daily, noon–3 p.m. and 6:30–10:30 p.m. (until 11 p.m. Saturday).

SETTING AND ATMOSPHERE The muted colors and minimalist décor create a relaxing retreat from the hustle and bustle of the Marais. Ganesha, the Hindu god for overcoming obstacles, sits in the entryway under a chalkboard where diners leave comments and messages to their friends, setting a friendly tone.

HOUSE SPECIALTIES Seitin steak with mushroom sauce, mushroom roast with creamed sweet potatoes, vegan dishes made from non-GMO (no genetically modified organisms) fresh products.

SUMMARY AND COMMENTS This is the place to go if you are vegetarian, or just plain tired of eating all that meat. Vegans and those on gluten-free or raw food diets will also find tasty options here. The all-you-can-eat lunch buffet is a fantastic value. You get two soups, fresh salad makings (baby spinach, grated carrots and cabbage, steamed broccoli, quinoa), several types of legumes, rice, and scrumptious veggie lasagna, all for just €12.50. Although service is slow, it's friendly, and you don't have to ask for water.

Le Villaret ★★★½

| FRENCH | MODERATE | QUALITY ★★★★½ | VALUE ★★★★ |

11TH ARRONDISSEMENT

13, rue Ternaux, 75011; ☎ 01 43 57 89 76; Métro: Parmentier

Customers 25-to-40s crowd, cultivated. **Reservations** Advised. **When to go** Late. **Pricing** Average per person, €45; prix fixe, menu *dégustation* €50. **Payment** MC, V. **English spoken** Yes. **Bar** No. **Wine selection** Carefully selected wines from small vineyards; many under €25; 500 wines. **Dress** Casual. **Disabled**

access Yes, except restrooms. **Hours** Monday–Friday, 12:15–2 p.m. and 7:30–11:30 p.m.; Saturday, 7:30 p.m.–midnight; closed in August and for Christmas.

SETTING AND ATMOSPHERE   Le Villaret is a popular spot that's always packed with a youngish crowd enjoying a noisy evening out. The tables are tightly packed together, and the volume levels can be unbearable at times. This is best left off the list when you're choosing a romantic spot for an intimate dinner, but it's a good choice with a group of raucous friends.

HOUSE SPECIALTIES   Cream of mushroom and foie gras soup, swordfish steaks with white beans, peppered filet of beef, roast apricots in amaretto. Menu changes according to season.

ENTERTAINMENT AND AMENITIES   Air-conditioning.

SUMMARY AND COMMENTS   The menu changes daily according to what the chef finds in the market that morning and tends to be just okay rather than really good. Watch out for the steak, which is only served rare; unless you like your beef practically still mooing, this isn't the place for you. If you enjoy a cheese course, this is the place to indulge. The wine list is interesting, especially the selection of *grand cru* wines, which are offered at reasonable prices.

Vin & Marée   ★★★

SEAFOOD	MODERATE	QUALITY ★★★★	VALUE ★★★★
16TH ARRONDISSEMENT			

183, boulevard Murat, 75016; ☎ 01 46 47 91 39; vin-et-maree.com; Métro: Porte de Saint-Cloud

Customers Regulars and locals. **Reservations** Advised. **When to go** Early or late. **Pricing** Average per person, €50; prix fixe, €18.50 and €35 (lunch and dinner). **Payment** AE, DC, JCB, MC, V. **English spoken** Yes. **Bar** No. **Wine selection** List changes regularly. **Dress** Casual to understated elegance. **Disabled access** No. **Hours** Daily, 12:30–2:30 p.m. and 7:30–10:30 p.m.

SETTING AND ATMOSPHERE   Modern, bright, and intelligent, filled with people who love to eat, talk, and flirt, surrounded by good contemporary paintings, lots of glasses of white wine, and fumes of garlic and butter.

HOUSE SPECIALTIES   Fish and seafood, rum baba Zanzibar (an absolute must).

SUMMARY AND COMMENTS   At Vin & Marée, the philosophy behind the food is freshness, great quality, and low prices. There are four restaurants in the group (the others are in Montparnasse, near the Eiffel Tower, and by Métro Nation) that churn out good fish with heartening regularity. It looks and feels a little chain-restauranty, albeit a good-natured one trying not to be too predictable. They serve only fish, so don't come here for a meat feast. The wine list is a little dull, although it does feature some perfectly respectable bottles, and they try to make it all a little more exciting by changing the list regularly. Look like you've been there before and talk to the waitresses, and you'll have a great time.

Ziryab ★★★★

GOURMET ARABIC   MODERATE/EXPENSIVE   QUALITY ★★★★   VALUE ★★★★
5TH ARRONDISSEMENT

Institut du Monde Arabe, 9th floor, 1, rue des Fossés Saint-Bernard, 75005; ☎ 01 55 42 55 42; noura.com; Métro: Jussieu

Customers Professionals (lunch), politicians, show business, international (dinner). **Reservations** Required 2–3 days in advance for lunch, 1 week for dinner. **When to go** Not too late. **Pricing** Average per person, €60; prix fixe, €48–€72 (dinner only). **Payment** AE, MC, V, traveler's checks in euros. **English spoken** Yes. **Bar** No. **Wine selection** North African (red, rosé), Lebanese cocktails. **Dress** Elegant. **Disabled access** Yes. **Hours** Tuesday–Saturday, noon–2:30 p.m. and 7:30–11 p.m., with last orders at 10 p.m.; tearoom, Tuesday–Sunday, 3–6 p.m.

SETTING AND ATMOSPHERE Cultivated and formal in style, this restaurant requires that you dress up; consequently, it's not the best choice for family dining and is too formal for small children. The view from the terrace over the Seine and Notre-Dame is gorgeous.

HOUSE SPECIALTIES Lebanese and Moroccan cuisine, couscous, tagine.

SUMMARY AND COMMENTS Although you'll probably want to concentrate on French cuisine while you're in Paris, this culinary detour will be both original and memorable. Located on the ninth floor of the Institut du Monde Arabe on the Left Bank, Ziryab is an example of the finest Franco-Arab cuisine you'll find in the world. The food is exotic, filled with delicate nuance. If you have to ask what a tagine is, order one (it's a type of stew cooked in a clay pot). Friendly service.

Les Zygomates ★★★½

FRENCH BISTRO   INEXPENSIVE   QUALITY ★★★★   VALUE ★★★★★
12TH ARRONDISSEMENT

7, rue de Capri, 75012; ☎ 01 40 19 93 04; leszygomates.com; Métro: Michel-Bizot

Customers Regulars and tourists. **Reservations** Advised. **When to go** Anytime. **Pricing** Average per person, €30; prix fixe, €15 (lunch), €31 (lunch and dinner). **Payment** MC, V. **English spoken** Yes. **Bar** None. **Wine selection** 110 wines. **Dress** Casual. **Disabled access** Yes. **Hours** Monday–Saturday, noon–2 p.m. and 7:30–10:30 p.m.; closed August.

SETTING AND ATMOSPHERE Inside a late-19th-century delicatessen.

HOUSE SPECIALTIES Scallop tartare with beetroot, beef in truffle sauce, raspberry tiramisu.

SUMMARY AND COMMENTS It's easy to see why Les Zygomates is always busy. Low prices, friendly service, seasonal cuisine, and excellent quality make it well worth a visit. The prix fixes are always good and modestly priced. This place used to be a pork butcher's shop, and the quality of the meat dishes reflects its previous incarnation. The specialty *queue de cochon farcie aux morilles,* or pig's tail stuffed with morel mushrooms, may not sound too tempting and is maybe not for the squeamish, but it is succulent and tasty and well worth the bravery involved in the choice. Make sure to leave room for the Zygomates Sweet-tooth Platter (*Assiette Gourmande des Zygomates*), which boasts a selection of their delicious desserts.

PART EIGHT

SHOPPING

 A **BROWSER'S PARADISE**

WHEN A RECENT POLL ASKED WHAT ATTRACTED Paris-bound travelers the most, the second-most popular answer was shopping. Ahead of museums and restaurants, even. And it's true that although Paris shopping is not always the most economical, it is fun. The city is perpetually rejuvenating itself with the creative spirit of new boutiques. Paris windows (*les vitrines*) are a feast in themselves. The key to shopping in Paris is to know the difference between where to look and where to buy. The great thing about Paris shopping is that the activity is as much cultural as it is commercial. You actually learn a lot about contemporary and historic France by stalking its boutiques and bundling up its finest products.

You'll want to mix and match your shopping time between the five main venues for making Parisian purchases:

- the little boutiques (*petites boutiques*)
- the department stores (*grands magasins*)
- the supermarkets (*supermarchés*)
- the museum shops (*boutiques des musées nationaux*)
- the flea markets (*marchés aux puces*)

AN UNOFFICIAL SUGGESTION

IN TODAY'S GLOBAL MARKETPLACE, there are fewer and fewer truly original things to buy that are indigenous to a place. Many of the famed French brand names—Chanel, Yves Saint Laurent, Christian Dior, Hermès, Louis Vuitton, and others—are not only sold and distributed internationally, but their products are likely to be less expensive back home and are probably available online. We tell friends and travelers to apply the following rule: If you can find it at home or order it online, don't buy it in Paris. If it's made in France and can be found only in France, and you like it and can afford it and can carry it home, buy it.

There are two types of great Parisian shopping: the kind in which you spend money and the kind that costs you nothing—window shopping. Observing shop windows in Paris can be like gallery hopping.

VAT TAX REFUNDS ON YOUR PURCHASES

THE SALES TAX IN FRANCE, or VAT (value-added tax—known as the TVA in French), is 19.6 percent of the retail price. The tax is always built into the price that you see on price tags. When goods and merchandise are purchased for export, meaning that you will be taking them out of France with you, you have the legal right to request a refund of a part of the tax. However, there are specific conditions that must be met to qualify for this refund:

- You must spend €175 or more in the same store on the same day; your purchases are cumulative.
- You must be a resident of a country outside of the European Union.
- You must not have remained in France or in the European Union for more than six months.
- You must be age 15 or older.

If you meet these criteria, tell a sales clerk in the store where you have made your purchases that you want to receive a VAT refund on your purchases. The department stores do this a thousand times a day and have staff in dedicated customer service areas who will instruct you on the procedures in English.

You need to show your passport and your sales receipts. You'll fill in a VAT refund form, and you'll be asked how you wish to be refunded. The easiest way is to have your credit card credited. You may also have a check sent to you or have the money deposited to a bank account.

The form you'll be given has three copies and will be accompanied by an addressed and stamped envelope. One copy is for the customs inspector at the airport, one will be sent by mail to the store issuing the refund, and the third copy is for your records.

If you are heading home from a Paris airport, present yourself to the customs office (*douane*) in order to receive your VAT refund on your purchases. This window is clearly marked in all terminals of both airports. Note that you are supposed to show the items you have purchased to the customs officer in order to receive your VAT refund on them—so do

unofficial **TIP**
Remember that you can receive VAT refunds only on purchases at your final destination inside the European Union. So if you're going from Paris to London before flying back to San Francisco, you cannot claim your tax refund in Paris (but you can claim it in London).

not pack them in your suitcase! If you plan to place them in your checked luggage, make sure that you receive your VAT refund before you check in. If you check your luggage first, you will not be able to benefit from the refund because the customs police have no way of verifying that the goods are in your bags. The lines at this window can be long. Give yourself an extra 30 minutes at the airport to comfortably allow time to receive your VAT refund.

The customs inspector will ask you for your plane ticket, your passport, your VAT refund form or forms, and the goods. He or she will stamp the threefold form, then keep one, place one in the pre-addressed envelope, and give you the third to keep. Seal the envelope and post the letter in the yellow mailbox that will be in the vicinity. As soon as the store receives their copy, proving that the goods were VAT refunded by customs, it'll process your refund, which adds up to 12 percent of the 19.6 percent you paid. Either your credit card will be credited or you'll receive a check. One firm, Global Refund, will process your refund on the spot for a small commission. Our experience is that the credit-card credit is the best and fastest means of reimbursement.

This is an excellent way of reducing your shopping costs. It is also an incentive to group your purchases in one store, since as long as your purchases are more than €175 in the same store you're entitled to this sizable refund. Most clerks will mention this refund to you as soon as they realize you're a tourist (in about three seconds), but don't forget to ask for it just in case and complete the formalities before you leave the store. Always keep your passport with you when you're shopping.

Customs Restrictions

Returning U.S. residents are allowed to bring back up to $800 of retail purchases per person, including children. Canadians are allowed up to $750.

MAILING OR SHIPPING HOME YOUR PURCHASES

DEPARTMENT STORES WILL SHIP YOUR PACKAGES HOME for you and will automatically deduct the VAT even if you do not spend €175. The service is costly, though. A better bet, especially on small, not-too-heavy, and inexpensive items, is to send them yourself in preposted mailers or boxes at any post office (refer to Part Four, Arriving, Getting Oriented, and Departing). Remember that U.S. Customs strictly prohibits the importation of any food or agricultural items. So if you're sending a strand of fresh garlic cloves to your aunt who loves to cook, you're taking a chance. Also note that the $800 duty exemption doesn't apply on packages; the rule is "personal shipments worth up to $200 and gift packages worth up to $100" are exempt. Go to **cbp.gov** for more information.

USING CREDIT CARDS

YOU'LL BE PLEASANTLY SURPRISED at how widespread credit-card use is in Paris. Actually, almost all of the cards you see being used in Paris are really debit cards connected to the user's bank account. The bottom line, though, is that you can pay for everything from underground parking lots to museum admissions with your plastic money. Parisians use cards for paying tolls on the highway, paying for their groceries, and paying for cinema tickets. The preferred card is called the Carte Bleue (CB), which is the French banking administration for Visa and Mastercard (your Visa or Mastercard will be accepted widely). American Express and Diners Club are accepted widely, but not to the same extent as CB. If you plan to use your debit card while in Paris, contact your card's company before you leave to find out if your PIN will be valid in France—sometimes you just need to be given a different PIN to enable international-debit access. Smart travelers carry at least two different cards with them, in case one doesn't work.

One major complaint with visitors is that some merchants are less familiar with the swiping mechanism and think that their machines do not accept cards without PIN codes. Gently insist, and in some cases offer to pass the card through their machine yourself. They almost always work.

Also, the credit-card payment form in France that gets spit out with each purchase does NOT allow you to fill in tips and gratuities by hand. Service is included in all restaurants and bars, and thus any additional euros you'd like to leave must be in cash.

Note that some smaller establishments will accept credit cards for purchases only over, say, €10 or €15. If you beg and implore, occasionally you'll be allowed to use the card for smaller sums.

For lost or stolen cards or other problems while in France, here are your local contact numbers:

Visa/MasterCard ☎ 08 92 70 57 05. You'll get a voice-mail recording in French. Push 2 and hold the line for an English-speaking operator.

American Express ☎ 08 00 83 28 20.

Diner's Club ☎ 08 10 31 41 59

RETURNS AND REFUNDS

PARIS BUSINESSES RARELY if ever give cash refunds (*rembourse-ments*). In fact, it's only rather recently that you could even get store credit. The "customer is king" concept never really caught on in France, and although refund policies are a bit more flexible now than before, it's better to try to avoid exchanges or returns (*retours*). Ask what the store's policy on returns and exchanges is before you buy anything. The arrival of the American clothing chain, the Gap, sort of revolutionized the concept of retail public relations in France. You can buy a sweater at the Gap on rue de

Rivoli and return it for a full cash refund in Houston, Texas. *Très rare* in Paris.

Usually, if something doesn't fit or doesn't work, you'll be able to exchange it for another size or another one on the condition that you have the sales receipt and the original packaging. Be aware that French clothing sizes vary from those in North America.

DUTY-FREE SHOPS

THE DUTY-FREE SHOPS AT PARIS'S airports do not really offer many advantages to international shoppers. Duty-free shopping for European Union travelers has been abolished since the European Union is legally considered one single market. Prices are not all that attractive. There are plenty of touristy shops in the center of Paris advertising duty-free shopping, especially around rue de Rivoli near the Louvre. The prices here for perfume, scarves, and other popular tourist items are in line with the duty-free shops at the airport or better, but these gifts tend to lack imagination and personality.

unofficial **TIP**
The only advantage you'll find in making duty-free purchases at the airport is the convenience, for example, of not having to lug that bottle of Champagne to the airport that you wanted to bring back for your brother-in-law.

MUSEUM GIFT SHOPS AND BOOKSTORES

ONE OF PARIS'S GREATEST SOURCES OF INTERESTING, original, culturally enriching, and cost-effective gifts is the museum boutique and bookstore. There are 12 boutiques in Paris, and one at Terminal 2F at Charles de Gaulle Airport, offering quality reproductions of many of the museums' masterpieces. The museum shops also offer online services at **boutiquesdemusees.com.** So if you don't have time to make your purchases before leaving, don't feel like carrying a poster on the plane, or are unsure if that Monet reproduction will fit on your kitchen wall, you can wait until you get home to order. For general information on the boutiques visit the Web site.

The best and most complete shops include:

GALERIES NATIONALES DU GRAND PALAIS 3, avenue du Général Eisenhower, 75008; Métro: Champs-Élysées–Clémenceau; ☎ 01 44 13 17 42.

MUSÉE DE LOUVRE Under the Pyramide, Palais du Louvre, 75001; Métro: Louvre; ☎ 01 40 20 68 84.

MUSÉE D'ORSAY 62, rue de Lille, 75007; Métro: Rue du Bac; RER: Musée d'Orsay; ☎ 01 40 49 43 90.

MUSÉE QUAI BRANLY 220, rue de l'Université, 75007; Métro: Alma Marceau; RER: Pont de l'Alma; ☎ 01 47 53 60 23.

SHOPPING AREAS *and* FAVORITE STREETS

THE FOLLOWING AREAS AND HIGHLIGHTED STREETS in Paris offer prime shopping opportunities:

PLACE DES VICTOIRES/RUE ÉTIENNE MARCEL

A PREFERRED HUB FOR FASHION DESIGN HOUSES and trendsetters. Here you'll find **Jean-Paul Gaultier, Adolfo Dominguez, Kenzo,** and more. Don't miss the Galerie Vivienne covered passageway, rue Étienne Marcel, rue du Louvre, and rue Jean-Jacques Rousseau. The streets around the post office and rue Montmartre are cluttered with wonderful, original finds.

LES HALLES

IN THE HEART OF THE CITY, LES HALLES is so trendy that no guidebook can keep up with the openings and closings. There are lots of great little finds mixed in with a lot of tackiness. We prefer the little streets in the area adjacent to the multilevel indoor mall, except for the fact that inside you'll find the **FNAC** for books, CDs, and concert tickets. Check out rue Montmartre, rue du Jour, rue de Turbigo, rue Pierre Lescot, and rue Saint-Denis.

LE MARAIS

MORE OLD-WORLD THAN LES HALLES, the Marais is studded with great boutiques offering clothes, objects, art, and accessories. Stroll along rue Vieille du Temple, rue Sainte-Croix-de-la-Bretonnerie, rue du Roi de Sicile, rue des Écouffes, rue des Rosiers, rue Pavée, rue de Sévigné, Place des Vosges (where you will find Issey Miyake), and, without fail, rue des Francs-Bourgeois, which is one of Paris's best shopping streets.

SAINT-GERMAIN-DES-PRÉS

ELEGANT, UPMARKET SHOPS FOR THE VERY CHIC. Visit rue du Bac, rue Bonaparte, rue de l'Ancienne Comédie, rue de Sèvres, boulevard Raspail, rue Jacob, rue des Saints-Pères, Cour du Commerce Saint-André, rue de Grenelle, rue du Cherche Midi, rue Madame, rue du Vieux Colombier, rue du Four, rue de Rennes, rue Saint-Sulpice, rue de Seine, and, of course, the boulevard Saint-Germain. You'll find **Hugo Boss, Sonia Rykiel, Miki House, Lacoste, Apostrophe,** and the cosmetics wizard **Shu Uemura.** The area surrounding the Place Saint-Sulpice offers a wealth of great fashion and household delights.

BOULEVARD HAUSSMANN, RUE SAINT-HONORÉ, LA MADELEINE

WELCOME TO THE TOP-OF-THE-TOP, the chic-of-the-chic. In this area, also referred to as the Golden Triangle, you'll find all the world's leading haute couture fashion brands as well as Paris's top department stores.

Along the boulevard Haussmann you can't help but find the **Galeries Lafayette** and **Printemps.** Stroll rue de la Paix and enter the Place Vendôme. Here, aside from the Ritz, you'll find **Dior** and **Chanel.** Around the Madeleine you'll encounter **Ralph Lauren, Cerruti 1881,** and the catering meccas **Fauchon** and **Hédiard.** We like the **Maille** mustard shop on the Place for very original and affordable savory gifts. **Lanvin** is on rue du Faubourg Saint-Honoré, along with **Hermès,** makers of those famous silk scarves, and **Yves Saint Laurent** and fashionista havens such as **Colette.** We won't stoop to say that these shops are expensive, but one visiting woman from Boston eager to buy herself a new leather jacket in Paris was shocked by the sales tax for the price on the jacket she picked out; the 19.6 percent tax alone was already beyond her budget.

THE CHAMPS-ÉLYSÉES

THE AVENUE IS STILL IMPRESSIVE DESPITE the repeated invasions of **Häagen-Dazs, McDonald's,** the **Disney Store, Virgin Mégastore,** and **Planet Hollywood.** The spokes off avenue host some of the most elegant old-money names in the fashion industry. Wander down avenue George V and rue François 1er, where you will find **Paule Ka.** Then stroll along avenue Montaigne, where **Valentino** and **Christian Dior** and **Nina Ricci, Chanel,** have set up shops and studios. The forever inimitable **Louis Vuitton** has its flagship store at 101, avenue des Champs-Élysées.

PASSY—AVENUE VICTOR HUGO

THIS IS AN UPSCALE SHOPPING HAVEN in the lively part of the 16th arrondissement. **Kenzo, Chipie** (rue de la Pompe), and others, such as the famous gourmet caterers **Lenôtre,** are here.

THE BASTILLE

NEW AND INNOVATIVE FASHION DESIGNERS have progressively moved east. The Bastille is still the hub of the east, but the more interesting trendsetters have ventured farther east by now: Oberkampf, Nation, Ménilmontant, Montreuil. . . . Start at the Bastille and follow rue de la Roquette and rue de Lappe, head up rue de Charonne, and wander down alleys and lanes like the Passage Thiéré. Back at the Bastille, head out past the Opéra to avenue Daumesnil, where you can visit some 50 modern artisans at work in their studios at the **Viaduc des Arts** (**viaduc-des-arts.com**). The eclectic array of workshops include that of the chandelier maker **Baguès** at number 73, porcelain painter **Atelier le Tellec** at number 93, and laser engraver **Zephyr** at number 127.

BERCY VILLAGE

TAKE THE METRO LINE 14 still farther east of the Bastille to Cour Saint Émilion to visit this shoppers' paradise set in a tranquil, paved courtyard. Bercy Village (**bercyvillage.com**) boasts more than 15 boutiques housed in beautifully restored wine warehouses. The wide range of names include **agnès B, Résonances,** and **Oliviers & Co.**

▌ DEPARTMENT STORES

PARIS DEPARTMENT STORES (*grands magasins*) are famous and historic. Only in Paris could a department store also be a registered national monument. Such is the case with **Printemps** on boulevard Haussmann, which dates to 1865 and boasts an exquisite stained-glass dome. Even nonshoppers don't mind wandering through this Paris landmark. All the stores offer special services for international shoppers—service in English, gifts, maps, fashion shows, and, of course, shipping and VAT-refund services. Both **Galeries Lafayette** and the **BHV** next to the Hôtel de Ville are accessible directly from the Métro. You don't even have to go out into the street.

If you get to your last day in Paris and haven't bought your gifts yet, give yourself a few hours in one or several of these stores. If you group your purchases from the same store and on the same day, you will be able to benefit from a VAT refund—assuming your purchases total at least €175. See "VAT Tax Refunds on Your Purchases" above for details on the VAT refund for tourists.

BHV (BAZAR DE L'HÔTEL DE VILLE) 52–64, rue de Rivoli, 75004; ☎ 01 42 74 90 00; **bhv.fr;** Métro: Hôtel de Ville. Open Monday–Saturday, 9:30 a.m.–7:30 p.m.; Wednesday until 9 p.m. This department store is convenient if you're in the Marais or Latin Quarter. What's really special about the BHV is the basement, Paris's largest and most complete hardware and housewares store. Visitors have less reason to go here, but if you're imaginative you'll find all sorts of great ideas for your house and for gifts, like new handles or knobs for your doors back home, traditional blue enamel street numbers, or brass fittings and trim for your kitchen.

LE BON MARCHÉ 22 and 38, rue de Sèvres, 75007; ☎ 01 44 39 80 00; **treeslbm.com;** Métro: Sèvres-Babylone. Open Monday–Wednesday, 10 a.m.–7:30 p.m.; Thursday, 10 a.m.–9 p.m.; Saturday, 9:30 a.m.–8 p.m. This is Paris's oldest department store, and it prides itself on being the only one on the Left Bank. The ground-floor emporium of cosmetics called the **Théâtre de la Beauté** has among the best selections in the city. The **Grande Épicerie** supermarket is gourmet heaven and is open Monday–Saturday, 8:30 a.m.–9 p.m.

GALERIES LAFAYETTE 40, boulevard Haussmann, 75009; ☎ 01 42 82 34 56; **galerieslafayette.com;** Métro: Chaussée d'Antin; RER A: Auber; RER E: Haussmann–Saint-Lazare. Open Monday–Thursday and Saturday, 9:30 a.m.–9:30 p.m.; Friday closes at 8 p.m. You can also get a haircut or a facial or have your nails done. The **Lafayette Gourmet** supermarket (same hours as the main store) is not only a great place to stalk the finest produce in the city, it's a great place to buy unique culinary gifts or step up to one of ten counters for a specialty lunch.

PRINTEMPS 64, boulevard Haussmann, 75009; ☎ 01 42 82 57 87; **printemps.com;** Métro: Havre-Caumartin; RER A: Auber; RER E: Haussmann–Saint-Lazare. Monday–Saturday, 9:35 a.m.–8 p.m.; Thursday until 10 p.m.

SAMARITAINE 75, rue de Rivoli, 75001. This Paris landmark, owned by the LVMH luxury group, was closed in June 2005 for major renovation. Sadly, the latest estimated date for its relaunch is now 2011. Call ☎ 0800 010 015 or visit **lasamaritaine.com** for updated information.

A **SELECTION** of **SPECIAL SHOPS**

 THE FOLLOWING SELECTION OF SHOPS AND BOUTIQUES combines both the most interesting of Paris content and the most innovative contemporary architecture and design. Although the Paris stores of well-known chains such as Conran's and Habitat are worth visiting, we've tried to steer you into establishments unique to Paris, and to those with things to buy that you can actually carry home. Whether you're a buyer or not, after a visit to some of these boutiques you can boast of being at the cutting edge of what's new.

ALAIN MIKLI DIFFUSION 74, rue des Saints-Pères, 75007; ☎ 01 45 49 40 00; **mikli.com;** Métro: Saint-Germain-des-Prés. Designer eyewear, including the Starck Eyes collection of frames and sunglasses.

ART DU BUREAU 47, rue des Francs-Bourgeois, 75004; ☎ 01 48 87 57 97; Métro: Saint-Paul. Very cool and funky office interior stuff, including modular diaries and Watchpeople, Graves, Mondaine, and Milus watches.

AVANT-SCÈNE 4, place de l'Odéon, 75006; ☎ 01 46 33 12 40; **avantscene.fr;** Métro: Odéon. New talent in the field of art objects and interior design.

COLETTE 213, rue Saint-Honoré, 75001; ☎ 01 55 35 33 90; **colette.fr;** Métro: Tuileries or Pyramides. Paris's original temple of fashion, style, design, art, and food. The goods are displayed like art in a museum. Downstairs the restaurant and water bar features a vast choice of bottled waters from around the world.

COMME DES GARÇONS 54, rue Faubourg Saint-Honoré, 75008; ☎ 01 53 30 27 27; Métro: Madeleine. 23, Place Marché Saint Honoré, 75001; ☎ 01 47 03 15 03; Métro: Pyramides. Rei Kawakubo's boutique of stark minimalism, black garments, and other highly original avant-garde wear is located in rue Faubourg Saint-Honoré. You will find her perfume boutique, which sells her signature fragrance, Odeur 53 located nearby in the Place du Marché Saint-Honoré.

DOM 21, rue Sainte-Croix-de-la-Bretonnerie, 75004; ☎ 01 42 71 08 00; Métro: Hôtel de Ville. A huge and popular shop frequented by gay Parisians offers parodies of design objects, fake fur, heart-shaped lights, and other kitsch objects. Open until 9 p.m., including Sunday.

HERMÈS 24, rue du Faubourg Saint-Honoré, 75008; ☎ 01 40 17 47 09; Métro: Madeleine. 42, avenue Georges V, 75008; ☎ 01 47 20 59 60; Métro: Georges V. **hermes.com.** Hermès is an institution. An emblem of virtue, history, and class. For a really good time, try to be here during one of Hermès' bargain-basement sales (twice a year for a week each time). Watch the most demure Paris ladies scratch, bite, and kick to get their hands on Hermès scarves marked down 50–70 percent off the retail price. The sales are usually during January and July, but call first and sharpen your nails. Credit cards happily accepted.

ISABEL MARANT 16, rue de Charonne, 75011; ☎ 01 49 29 71 55; **isabelmarant.tm.fr;** Métro: Ledru Rollin. A melting pot of fun and elegant clothes that strings together North Africa, India, and Paris with its own integrity. Check Web site for other addresses.

LAGUIOLE 29, rue Boissy d'Anglas, 75008; ☎ 01 40 06 09 75; **laguiole .com;** Métro: Madeleine. The famous Laguiole knife is exhibited and sold in a Philippe Starck–designed boutique. When you get ready to pack, remember all knives must travel in checked-in baggage or they will be confiscated. There is nothing more heart-breaking than losing your Laguiole blade to the security folks.

LIEU COMMUN 5, rue Filles du Calvaire, 75003; ☎ 01 44 54 08 30; **lieucommun.fr;** Métro: Filles du Calvaire. Welcome to outer space. You'll find ergonomically designed clothing from jeans to suits and accessories in this boutique shared by four designers.

LOUIS VUITTON 54, avenue Montaigne, 75008; ☎ 01 45 62 47 00; Métro: Franklin D. Roosevelt. 101, avenue des Champs-Élysées, 75008; ☎ 0 810 810 010; Métro: George V. 6, place Saint-Germain-des-Prés,

75006; Métro: Saint-Germain-des-Prés; **vuitton.com.** Right from the start when it opened in 1914, Vuitton's flagship store on the Champs-Élysées was heralded as the largest travel accessory boutique on earth. Recently renovated, this immense space is still the largest of the brand's stores worldwide and sells the whole Vuitton line, including items you may not have seen before.

MARIE PAPIER 26, rue Vavin, 75006; ☎ 01 43 26 46 44; **mariepapier .fr;** Métro: Vavin. More than 400 different kinds of paper, colors, textures, and formats of writing stationery as well as scrapbooking accessories.

PAUL SMITH 22, boulevard Raspail, 75007; ☎ 01 42 84 15 30; **paul smith.co.uk;** Métro: Rue du Bac. 3, rue Faubourg Saint-Honoré, 75008; ☎ 01 42 68 27 10; Métro: Madeleine. Unless you come from England, you'll want to take in the art and wit of this British clothing designer in his original shop, redesigned every two weeks.

LA QUINCAILLERIE 3–4, boulevard Saint-Germain, 75005; ☎ 01 46 33 66 71; **laquincaillerie.com;** Métro: Maubert Mutualité. Yep, door and window furniture from all over the world.

RÉSONANCE Carrousel du Louvre, 75001; ☎ 01 42 97 06 00; Métro: Palais-Royal. Musée du Louvre, 3–5, boulevard Malesherbes, 75008; ☎ 01 44 51 63 70; Métro: Madeleine. 9, cour Saint-Émilion, 75012; ☎ 01 44 73 82 82; Métro: Cour Saint-Émilion; **resonances.fr.** A design emporium for the home.

SALONS SHISEIDO DU PALAIS ROYAL 25, rue Valois, 75001; ☎ 01 49 27 09 09; **salons-shiseido.com;** Métro: Palais Royal. A haven of sublime scents; here you find rosewood, violets, iris, and such inexplicable fragrances as "femininity of the woods." You can even have your bottles engraved with your initials.

SÉPHORA 70–72, avenue des Champs-Élysées, 75008; ☎ 01 53 93 22 50; **sephora.fr;** Métro: George V. France's leading distributor of perfumes and cosmetics displays the entire line in a vast den of fragrances among a video wall, a perfume organ, 654 fiber-optic heads, and endless ways to experience perfume. In addition to this flagship store, check out the Web site for the 21 other addresses in Paris.

SMART CENTER PARIS 27–33, avenue Paul Doumer, 75016; ☎ 01 56 91 50 00; **smart.com;** Métro: Trocadéro. You won't be bringing home one of these very smart electric cars, but you'll love what you see. The vehicle of urban tomorrow shown in a compact tower of aesthetics and economy of space. No more exhaust or gas bills.

SWATCH STORE 104, avenue des Champs-Élysées, 75008; ☎ 01 56 69 17 07; **swatch.com;** Métro: Franklin D. Roosevelt. The company's showcase. Over 1,000 models on display with interactive capabilities! Includes limited editions designed by noted artists.

COOL CHEAP SHOPPING

COMMON AND EVERYDAY OBJECTS IN PARISIAN LIFE become unusual conversation pieces back home. We love to shop in the kitchen-utensil section of the **Galeries Lafayette Maison** or **BHV** department stores. A globe-shaped sugar-cube dispenser found on the bar counter of every Parisian café becomes a stroke of genius for gift-giving when taken out of its context.

- A knife set from the **Cordon Bleu Cooking School** is a perfect gift.

- A French chef's professional apron and toque pleases.

- Women's lingerie! This is a win-win situation. Men love to buy this for their wives or girlfriends. Women love to buy it for themselves. Some of the sexiest underwear and bras in the world include the labels **Aubade,** known for their advertisements that teach women the art of seduction; **La Perla,** known for its form-fitting cuts; and **Chantal Thomass,** whose ruffled panties are known to inspire. Your best bet is shopping for these items in the department stores, where most brand names are found.

- Children's clothes and baby clothes. Aside from the prices—which may dissuade you—children's and baby clothing in Paris is kilometers ahead of its North American counterparts. So cute, so elegant, so original, so European. The leading stores include **Tout Compte Fait, Du Pareil au Même, Petit Bateau, Catimini,** and **Natalys.**

HAUTE COUTURE: DISCOUNTED AND MARKED DOWN

THE CLOTHING IN PARIS IS EXQUISITE. The prices can be through the roof. If you want to come home with an haute couture souvenir, you might want to track down one of these recommended discount shops. Note that a sign on a shop window marked *soldes* means "Sale." *Dégriffé* means marked down. A discount is a *remise*. The government-regulated sales periods in France are in January and July, although legislation introduced in 2009 has now given retailers added flexibility.

ANNA LOWE 104, rue du Faubourg Saint-Honoré, 75008; ☎ 01 42 66 11 32; **annalowe.com;** Métro: Champs-Élysées–Clémenceau. Dior, Gucci, Valentino, and other names at 40–60 percent off the retail price. This place has been written up in the *Chicago Tribune* as the "best of the off-price shops."

ANNEXE DES CRÉATEURS 19, rue Godot de Mauroy, 75009; ☎ 01 42 65 46 40; **annexedescreateurs.com;** Métro: Madeleine. Cocktail dresses, evening gowns, hats, and jewelry at up to 70 percent discounts.

CHERCHEMINIPPES 102, rue du Cherche Midi, 75006; ☎ 01 45 44 97 96; **chercheminippes.com;** Métro: Duroc. An outstanding range of fashions and home accessories, spread across six shops on the same street.

EMBELLIE 11, bis rue Vauquelin, 75005; ☎ 01 43 31 43 51; Métro: Censier Daubenton. Wide range of hip designer labels such as Sonia Rykiel, Kenzo, and Yohji Yamamoto.

GERZANE 9, rue Scribe, 75009; ☎ 01 49 24 03 18; Métro: Opéra. Menswear by Cerruti, Versace, Armani, and others.

MISS GRIFFES 19, rue de Penthièvre, 75008; ☎ 01 42 65 10 00; Métro: Miromesnil. Haute couture, prêt-à-porter, and season ends from top designers.

Take a trip to **rue d'Alésia,** 75014 (Métro: Alésia), where you will find a number of "stock," or end-of-season clothing stores such as **Cacharel** (at number 114), **Zapa** (number 82), **Dorotennis** (number 74), and **Baylaud** (number 149), all of which discount many different labels such as Daniel Hetcher, Guy Laroche, and Diesel.

Another way to buy designer clothes at knock-down prices is through the numerous consignment stores in the city where Parisians cash in last season's Dior, YSL, and Chanel.

VIOLETTE ET LÉONIE 22, rue de Poitou, 75003; ☎ 01 44 59 87 35; **violette leonie.com;** Métro: Saint-Sébastien Froissart. An Ali Baba's cave of designer labels, including Prada, Zadig et Voltaire, and Miu Miu.

OPEN-AIR MARKETS

ALMOST AS GRATIFYING AND INTERESTING AS MUSEUMS, Paris's open-air markets require some of your valuable time. You'll be impressed with the selection of fresh fruits and vegetables, meats, cheeses, and fish, as well as the colorful vendors that scream out their specials to attract shoppers. Although supermarkets have gained a significant amount of market share, most Parisians still rely on their local *marché* several times a week for their fresh produce. One of the fun aspects of these markets is the identification of products you don't find at home. Some visitors have a hard time with the hanging ducks and unplucked hens, the slippery eels, and the little containers of veal brains, while others are in their element. Note the variety of lettuces Parisians consume—dandelion (*pissenlit*) leaves and *mâche;* the size of the artichokes, fennel, and endives; and the long thick stalks of leeks. Every season has its share of produce, and in Paris much joy comes from seeing the first strawberries or cherries or melons of the season.

Autumn brings with it an awesome range of wild mushrooms, *cêpes,* chanterelles, pleurotes, and bolets. In the summer you should really try some mirabelles and quetsches. As a tourist, you probably won't be buying fish in the market, but you'll certainly be wowed by the urchins and *tourteaux,* the mountains of mussels, and the slabs of salmon and monkfish. Parisians not only eat a lot of fish, they eat a large variety of fish. Each quarter has its own fish market. Ask at your hotel for the closest one and its days of operation. Most are open either in the morning (until 1 p.m.) or in the afternoon (from 3 to 7 p.m.).

TIPS FOR SHOPPING IN THE OPEN-AIR MARKETS

THERE ARE TWO KINDS OF OPEN-AIR produce markets: the permanent ones (every day) and the roving ones (several times a week at the same location).

- Vendors can be loud and impatient. You may be interested in trying a sliver of a creamy-looking cheese; they're trying to make their living and tend not to like selling tiny slivers of anything.

- Try to figure out in what dimension and denominations produce is sold. Ham, cold cuts, and pâtés are sold by the slice (*tranche*), not weight. You must indicate how many slices and how thick—don't leave this up to the vendor. And always say *"un peu moins, s'il vous plaît"* (ahn puh **mwahn,** see voo **play**)—a little less please—to compensate for their heavy-handed suggestions.

- Fruit and vegetables are usually sold by weight—a kilo of *clémentines,* for example, or 300 grams of *champignons de Paris.*

- It's not a bad idea to discreetly count your change.

- If you wish to buy a bundle of goods, remember to bring your own bag or basket.

Here are a few outstanding and particularly colorful outdoor markets:

PERMANENT MARKETS

MAKE SURE YOU VISIT AT LEAST ONE or two of these permanent markets (*rues commerçantes*). Following each listing you'll find a suggested picnic spot nearby, a perfect place to taste the rewards of your marketing.

MARCHÉ MONTORGUEIL Rue Montorgueil, 2nd arrondissement, in the heart of Paris, Métro: Les Halles. This is the closest you can get to the old and authentic market that nearby Les Halles once was. Check out the regional products displayed as in the good old days; open daily. Picnic possibility: on the sloped garden in front of **Church Saint-Eustache.**

MARCHÉ MOUFFETARD Beginning at rue de L'Épée-de-Bois in the 5th arrondissement, Métro: Monge. Although the street is narrow and the market is frequented by lots of visitors, rue Mouffetard is one of Paris's great features. Don't miss this very colorful market, where you can even join in the spontaneous choir singing of traditional Parisian tunes

unofficial **TIP**
Borrow a knife and fork and some extra napkins from the breakfast room at your hotel, or travel with a basic Swiss army knife or Opinel (a French all-purpose "picnic" knife—another great souvenir idea for your gourmet friends back home). Plastic cutlery is hard to come by in Paris.

at the corner of rue de l'Arbalète. If the weather is good, definitely plan to while away an hour on the terrace of one of the cafés on the **Place de la Contrescarpe.** Picnic possibilities: **Arènes de Lutèce** or the **Jardin des Plantes.**

RUE CLER Rue Cler beginning at avenue de La Motte-Picquet in the 7th arrondissement, Métro: École Militaire. Here, you're in the heart of a stylish, traditional, and wealthy neighborhood, and the street market conveys the tastes and aesthetics of the local shoppers. You'll love the fish market and the pastries. Picnic possibilities: in the **Champs de Mars,** under the **Eiffel Tower,** or on the lawn in front of **Les Invalides.**

RUE DE LEVIS Beginning at the boulevard des Batignolles in the 17th arrondissement, Métro: Villiers. The great advantage to this bustling market is that you'll feel far from anything touristy. The famed food critic Patricia Wells raves about the Belle Époque baguettes at **Couasnon Boulangerie.** Picnic possibility: definitely in the **Parc Monceau.**

RUE LEPIC Wonderful, lively street that climbs the hill starting at the Place Blanche next to the famous Moulin Rouge. Picnic possibility: in the **Cimetière de Montmartre.**

ROVING MARKETS

THESE ROVING MARKETS (*marchés volants*) are open from about 7 a.m. to around 2:30 p.m. on certain days only. Below is a selection of addresses, a complete list of Paris markets is available on the city hall Web site: **paris.fr.**

MARCHÉ D'ALIGRE Place d'Aligre in the 12th arrondissement, Métro: Ledru-Rollin. This working-class neighborhood hosts a highly cosmopolitan market with some of the best prices in Paris. Tuesday–Saturday, 9 a.m.–1 p.m. and 4–7:30 p.m.; Sunday, 9 a.m.–1 p.m. Picnic possibility: **Square Trousseau.**

MARCHÉ GRENELLE Along the boulevard de Grenelle beginning at rue Lourmel and finishing at rue du Commerce in the 15th arrondissement, Métro: Dupleix or La Motte-Picquet-Grenelle. Wednesday and Sunday, 7 a.m.–2:30 p.m. Lively market in a commercially vibrant area. Picnic possibility: **Place Dupleix.**

MARCHÉ MAUBERT At Place Maubert in the 5th arrondissement, Métro: Maubert-Mutualité. Thursday and Sunday, 7 a.m.–2:30 p.m. A perfect spot to both shop and observe merchants, fresh produce, and local shoppers. Picnic possibility: either in the little park at the end of rue Lagrange or along the quai by the Seine.

MARCHÉ MONGE Place Monge, Métro: Monge. Wednesday, Friday, and Sunday, 7 a.m.–2:30 p.m. Excellent selection of regional ingredients and prepared recipes. Picnic possibility: Take your goodies across the street and picnic in the Roman ruins, **Arènes de Lutèce.**

MARCHÉ RASPAIL Along the boulevard Raspail between rue de Rennes and rue du Cherche-Midi, Métro: Rennes or Sèvres-Babylone. Tuesday and Friday, 7 a.m.–2:30 p.m. Picnic possibility: around the **Place Saint-Sulpice** fountain.

MARCHÉ SAXE-BRETEUIL From avenue de Ségur to the Place Breteuil along avenue de Saxe, Métro: Ségur. Thursday and Saturday, 7 a.m.–2:30 p.m. Impressive open-air market in a very bourgeois neighborhood. Picnic possibility: anywhere in the middle of avenue Breteuil or behind **Les Invalides.**

ORGANIC MARKETS

IN FRENCH, *marché bio* stands for *biologique,* meaning organic and organically grown produce.

BATIGNOLLES On the boulevard des Batignolles between numbers 27 and 48 in the 8th arrondissement, Métro: Rome or Place Clichy. Saturday, 7 a.m.–3 p.m. A bit out of the way, but a large market worth exploring if you're staying in the area.

BRANCUSI On the place Constantin Brancusi in the 14th arrondissement, Métro: Gaîté. Saturday, 9 a.m.–3 p.m. The most recently established organic market with about 60 stalls.

RASPAIL Along the boulevard Raspail between rue de Rennes and rue du Cherche-Midi in the 6th arrondissement, Métro: Rennes or Sèvres-Babylone. Sunday, 9 a.m.–3 p.m. You'll find a joyful crowd of environmentally conscious shoppers and New Age and health-food enthusiasts.

FLEA MARKETS

CHINER—to wander around lazily, poking around piles of *brocante* (old stuff to them— antiques to us), slumming, and strolling at a relaxed pace—in the *marché aux puces* is a popular Parisian weekend activity; unearth antiques and all kind of *bric-à-brac* as well as second-hand clothing. If you're wondering about bargaining, *marchander* (mar-shon-**day**), the answer is yes. Expect to spend about 30 percent less than what you're asked for at the start. On small, inexpensive items, you can manage a symbolic discount, but don't count on much. If the merchant asks €5 for a beer mug, you'll probably get it for €4 or €4.50. Here are your main choices.

unofficial **TIP**
Warning: Keep your money securely stashed; pickpockets rove some of these markets, and foreign visitors make for easy prey.

MONTREUIL Located at the Porte de Montreuil, this lively flea market is open every Saturday, Sunday, and Monday, 7 a.m.–7:30 p.m. From the Porte de Montreuil Métro station, walk over the *périphérique* and you'll stumble on a wide variety of tables and stalls of old clothes, secondhand goods, old tools, postcards, mirrors, plates, car parts, kitchenware, chairs, and similar junk or treasure, depending on your point of view. Early risers are certain to find a few collectibles to take home. Something of little value locally, like an old plaque from a Parisian café or an ashtray from Maxim's, may make for an excellent souvenir or conversation piece back home. Montreuil is known for its used clothes, so if you have the patience to mill through huge heaps of shirts and pants and ties, and you have an eye for vintage digs, you can go home with a sack of original items that cost you only a few dollars each.

PORTE DE VANVES Saturday and Sunday, 7 a.m.–7:30 p.m.; **puces devanves.typepad.com;** Métro: Vanves. The quality of the objects— real bric-a-brac, Art Deco mirrors, brassware, earrings and pendants, and drawings—is superior to what's found at the other flea markets, but the prices reflect this.

SAINT-OUEN From Porte de Saint-Ouen to Porte de Clignancourt in the 18th arrondissement; Saturday, Sunday, and Monday, 7 a.m.–7:30 p.m.; **parispuces.com;** Métro: Porte de Clignancourt. The oldest and most popular flea market of Paris is divided into several markets, secondhand or brand-new clothing, military surplus in **Marché Malik,** antiques in **Marché Serpette,** and others. There is a full range of new and old items, ranging from trinkets to luxurious antiques. You have to wade through a lot of junk to find the good stuff, and you have to arrive early if you hope to find something great at a low price.

SPECIALIZED MARKETS

MARCHÉ AUX FLEURS (FLOWER MARKET) Parisians enjoy several flower markets, open Tuesday–Saturday. Although you won't be able to carry flowers home with you, you'll enjoy the colors and varieties. The most famous markets are located at:

- Place Louis Lépine on the Île de la Cité, 4th arrondissement, Monday–Saturday, 8 a.m.–7:30 p.m.; Métro: Cité.
- Place de la Madeleine, 8th arrondissement, Monday–Saturday, 8 a.m.–7:30 p.m.; Métro: Madeleine.
- Place des Ternes, 17th arrondissement, Wednesday–Sunday, 8 a.m.–7:30 p.m.; Métro: Ternes.

MARCHÉ AUX LIVRES (BOOK MARKET) Old (antique) books at 87, rue Brancion, 15th arrondissement; Saturday and Sunday, 9:30 a.m.– 6 p.m.; Métro: Porte de Vanves.

MARCHÉS AUX OISEAUX (BIRD MARKET) If you really want to feel like you're in Europe, take a stroll through Paris's bird market.

- Place Louis Lépine, Île de la Cité, 4th arrondissement, next to the flower market, Sunday, 8 a.m.–7 p.m.; Métro: Cité.
- Quai de la Mégisserie, 1st arrondissement (on the Right Bank); Métro: Châtelet. A series of pet shops open every day.

MARCHÉ AUX TIMBRES (STAMP MARKET) At the corner of avenue Marigny and avenue Gabriel, 8th arrondissement; Thursday, Saturday, Sunday, and public holidays, 10 a.m.–sunset; Métro: Champs-Élysées–Clémenceau. This is where philatelists, postcard and coin collectors, and professionals and amateurs display, buy, and sell their collections.

FABRIC AND CLOTH MARKETS

CARREAU DU TEMPLE Rue Perrée, 3rd arrondissement; Tuesday–Sunday, 9 a.m.–noon; Métro: Temple or Arts et Métiers. A traditional covered market with a Middle Eastern feel and good bargains.

MARCHÉ ART & CRÉATION BASTILLE Boulevard Richard Lenoir, 11th arrondissement; Saturday, 10 a.m.–7 p.m.; **artistesparisbastille.fr;** Métro: Bastille. A melting pot of more than 250 artists exhibit and sell their work at this weekly arts and crafts market.

MARCHÉ SAINT-PIERRE 2, rue Charles Nodier, 18th arrondissement; Monday–Saturday, 10 a.m.–6:30 p.m. (closed on Monday during July and August); **marchesaintpierre.com;** Métro: Abbesses. This famous Montmartre covered market spreads out over five floors offering clothing, tapestry, bolts of African cloth, and hundreds of fabrics for curtains, pillows, and wall coverings. If you're handy with a sewing machine and you want to bring back a highly original souvenir, go out of your way to visit this market. Bring a calculator to convert lengths from meters to yards.

GREAT PARISIAN GIFTS
and WHERE *to* FIND THEM

ANTIQUES

ANTIQUES (*antiquités*) are a major shopping draw in Paris.

LE LOUVRE DES ANTIQUAIRES 2, place du Palais Royal, 75001; ☎ 01 42 97 27 27; **louvre-antiquaires.com;** Métro: Louvre. Tuesday–Sunday, 11 a.m.–7 p.m.; closed Sunday in July and August. For high-end antiques of the finest furniture, art objects, paintings, sculptures, and old jewelry, the best address in Paris is right across the street from the Louvre. The selection is so fine that you'll think you're in the museum.

VILLAGE SAINT-PAUL 23–27, rue Saint-Paul, 75004; **village-saint-paul. com;** Métro: Saint-Paul. If you'd like to bring home a piece of turn-of-the-19th-century jewelry, an Art Deco mirror, a carved picture frame, or something else old, a spin through the 70 shops in this one quaint location may be just what you're looking for. The prices are on the high side, but you're sure to be getting high-quality goods.

APRONS AND KNIVES

THE FAMOUS CORDON BLEU COOKING SCHOOL sells its own line of cooking and baking utensils, aprons, and knives, which make great gifts for others and are a good way to spoil yourself. The school is not centrally located, but it makes for a pleasant detour to one of Paris's residential neighborhoods.

LE CORDON BLEU 8, rue Léon Delhomme, 75015; ☎ 01 53 68 22 50; **cordonbleu.edu;** Métro: Vaugirard.

BATHROOM ACCESSORIES

THESE SORTS OF SMALL AND UNIQUE accessories—such as knobs, vanity accoutrements, mirrors, and the like—are perfect for design-conscious bathers.

BATH BAZAAR 23, boulevard Madeleine, 75001; ☎ 01 40 20 08 50; Métro: Madeleine. 6, avenue Maine, 75015; ☎ 01 45 48 89 00; Métro: Falguière. **bathbazaar.fr.**

BISCUITS AND CANDY

THIS STORE OFFERS A RANGE OF TRADITIONAL French sugary delights such as *Calissons d'Aix* and *Nougat*. You can make up your own selection or purchase one of their gift packs.

LA CURE GOURMANDE Cour Saint Emilion, 75012; ☎ 01 43 40 13 34; **la-cure-gourmande.com;** Métro: Cour Saint Emilion.

BREAD

FRANCE'S MOST FAMOUS BAKERY by far is Poilâne, whose famed sourdough loaves are flown to New York daily. Wait until your last day, and then fill in the empty space in your luggage with a Pain Poilâne. The company is run by Apollinia Poilâne, granddaughter of the founder, who became CEO in 2002 at the tender age of 18, after the tragic death of her parents.

POILÂNE 8, rue du Cherche-Midi, 75006; ☎ 01 45 48 42 59; Métro: Saint-Sulpice or Sèvres-Babylone. 49, boulevard de Grenelle, 75015; ☎ 01 45 79 11 49; Métro: La Motte-Picquet–Grenelle; **poilane.fr.**

CAFÉ TABLES AND OTHER AUTHENTIC ITEMS

AMONG THE GREAT SOURCES OF ORIGINAL GIFTS are the shops connected to the famous cafés and restaurants. Next to La Tour d'Argent you'll find the **Comptoir Tour d'Argent.** Next to the famous caterer **Fauchon,** you'll find Fauchon's emporium of specialty goods. We like the little store next to **Café de Flore,** where you can buy placemats, espresso cups, and even wicker café chairs. An extravagant gift item is the Café de Flore "Gueridon" sidewalk café table, a 50-centimeter round table with a green enameled top and brass edges, with the center leg in black cast iron. The cost? €640, plus the same again to ship it home. It weighs 18 kilos and is packed in three parts. The good news is that you'll get the VAT refunded and you'll have a permanent souvenir of Parisian café life right in your kitchen.

CAFÉ DE FLORE BOUTIQUE 26, rue Saint-Benoît, 75006; ☎ 01 45 44 33 40; Métro: Saint-Germain-des-Prés. Tuesday–Saturday, 10 a.m.–2 p.m. and 3–7 p.m. Closed Sunday, Monday, and three weeks in August.

CHEESE

ANY *FROMAGERIE* WILL BE MORE than able to supply a broad variety of interesting cheeses. True cheese lovers, though, will want to check out Paris's most celebrated cheese shop, **Androuët,** in business since 1909:

ANDROUËT 134, rue Mouffetard, 75005; ☎ 01 45 87 85 05; Métro: Censier Daubenton; plus five other stores throughout Paris and one at Roissy-Charles de Gaulle, Terminal 2E. Check **androuet.com** for addresses.

Note on Cheeses

Charles de Gaulle was noted as saying, "How can anyone govern a country that has over 450 kinds of cheese?" Make it a point to try as many as you can during your Paris stay. Remember that not only cow's milk is used for cheese—try some goat cheese and sheep cheese, too. You should try any of the highly flavorful raw milk (*lait cru*) cheeses, since these are not exported to the United States due to U.S. agricultural regulations, and thus you won't find them at home.

Taking Cheese Home

Carrying most food product or agricultural goods into the United States is strictly forbidden. We know of a friend who was fined $50 at Newark Airport for carrying an apple off the plane. The U.S. Department of Agriculture employs dogs to sniff out your food items at Logan Airport in Boston and other international points of entry. So take this seriously. For a list of what you *can* bring back, see **cbp.gov.**

kids CHILDREN'S BOOKS IN FRENCH

WHAT A GREAT WAY TO INITIATE THE KIDS into French. Check out the selection of illustrated books for children here. Note that the price of books in France is high, but the quality of production and the reproductions explain a lot. Parisians are used to paying more for their cultural products.

CHANTELIVRE 13, rue de Sèvres, 75006; ☎ 01 45 48 87 90; **chantelivre.fr;** Métro: Sèvres-Babylone.

CHOCOLATE

YOU'LL NEVER GO WRONG bringing high-quality chocolate home. Consider this: American chocolate bars contain around 2 percent cocoa. The chocolate bars you'll find even in Paris supermarkets contain between 35 percent and 80 percent cocoa. After experiencing European chocolate, it won't be easy going back to Hershey's. As an experiment, try melting any American chocolate bar in a saucepan. Watch what happens. It doesn't melt into a rich smooth sauce the way real chocolate does. The massive French, Swiss, or Belgian chocolate bars, which you'll find in any supermarket for between €3 and €6, make terrific gifts to take back to your family and friends.

At the high-end "art chocolate" milieu is **Virginie Duroc-Danner.** Virginie is passionate about her artistry and original creations. In fact, she is an artist first and considers chocolate to be her medium. She offers highly original gifts and customized works of art in chocolate. The only hitch is that Virginie sells her sweets only by phone or online. Call ☎ 01 41 96 84 15 or visit **virginieduroc-danner.com.**

For original chocolates and macaroons, visit **Christophe Roussel's** Chocolate Bar at the recently opened Hotel Cadran near the Eiffel Tower.

CHRISTOPHE ROUSSEL 10, rue du Champ de Mars, 75007; ☎ 01 40 62 67 00; **paris-hotel-cadran.com;** Métro: École Militaire.

Other chocolate connoisseurs, though, may be satisfied elsewhere. Try one of **Maison du Chocolat**'s eight locations (call or check the Web site following for the store closest to your hotel) or **Jadis et Gourmande,** which offers a large gift selection or will help you design your own. Note that fresh chocolate needs to be kept cool and will spoil if left out for several days.

JADIS ET GOURMANDE 49, bis avenue Franklin D. Roosevelt, 75008; ☎ 01 42 25 06 04; Métro: Franklin D. Roosevelt; check Web site for other addresses in Paris.

MAISON DU CHOCOLAT 225, rue du Faubourg Saint-Honoré, 75008; ☎ 01 42 27 39 44; Métro: Ternes; visit **lamaisonduchocolat.com** for other stores.

DISHES

SAVVY TRAVELERS BOAST OF GREAT FINDS on rue de Paradis in the 10th arrondissement near Métro Château d'Eau. The street is packed with china and porcelain shops.

kids DOLLS, BEARS, AND PUPPETS

FOR BEAUTIFUL PORCELAIN DOLLS and collector bears, visit either **Automates et Poupées** or **Jeanne et Jérémy.**

AUTOMATES ET POUPÉES 97, avenue Daumesnil, 75011; ☎ 01 43 42 22 33; **automatesetpoupees.fr;** Métro: Gare de Lyon.

JEANNE ET JÉRÉMY Village Suisse, 78, avenue de Suffren, 75015; ☎ 01 46 33 54 54; **jeannejeremy.com;** Métro: La Motte-Picquet–Grenelle.

FOIE GRAS, ESCARGOTS, CAVIAR, AND SAUMON FUMÉ

AGAIN, WITH VERY FEW EXCEPTIONS, it's too risky to take these luxury gourmet items home with you—you'll risk forfeiting the items and paying stiff fines if you're caught. Some adventurous travelers recommend wrapping these goodies in dirty laundry and placing them deep inside a huge piece of luggage. We suggest instead that you consume these things in Paris, enjoying them in context. For a good selection and easy access, shop for these items at one of six **Comtesse du Barry** stores in Paris or the **Lafayette Gourmet** supermarket in the Galeries Lafayette department store.

COMTESSE DU BARRY 13, boulevard Haussmann, 75009; ☎ 01 47 70 21 01; Monday–Saturday, 10 a.m.–7 p.m.; **comtessedubarry .com;** Métro: Chaussée d'Antin; RER A: Auber. Check the Web site for other locations.

LAFAYETTE GOURMET 40, boulevard Haussmann, 75009; ☎ 01 42 82 34 56. Monday–Saturday, 9:30 a.m.–8:30 p.m.; Thursday open until 9 p.m. Métro: Chaussée d'Antin; RER A: Auber.

GENERAL GROCERIES

FOR JAMS, COFFEES, TEAS, BISCUITS, candy, and other packaged gourmet edibles, try the supermarket at **Granterroirs,** which offers a full range of French regional produce, or **Galeries Lafayette**.

GRANTERROIRS 30, rue de Miromesnil, 75008; ☎ 01 47 42 18 18; **granterroirs.com;** Métro: Miromesnil.

LAFAYETTE GOURMET 40, boulevard Haussmann, 75009; ☎ 01 42 82 34 56; Métro: Chaussée d'Antin; RER A: Auber.

GOLD JEWELRY

THE CLOTHING CHAIN **Tati** sells an impressive line of high-quality gold jewelry at some of the lowest prices around. A gold Eiffel Tower charm bracelet makes a very special gift for someone.

TATI 18, boulevard Rochechouart, 75018; ☎ 01 55 29 50 00; **tati.fr;** Métro: Barbès-Rochechouart. Check the Web site for other Paris stores.

HARDWARE

HERE'S ONE OF OUR FAVORITE SUGGESTIONS. Rummage through the basement of the **BHV** department store to add really original touches to your kitchen, bathroom, or office. Banal little details like molding, brass drawer handles, or cabinet hinges—very typical and ordinary in France—really stand out back home.

BHV 52–64, rue de Rivoli, 75004; ☎ 01 42 74 90 00; **bhv.fr;** Métro: Hôtel de Ville.

KITCHEN, COOKING, AND DINING ROOM SUPPLIES

EASILY ONE OF THE MOST ENJOYABLE MOMENTS you'll have shopping will be while rummaging through the aisles of a Parisian restaurant- and culinary-supply shop. Just about everything will be a potential gift. You can spend €25 for a mustard crock or oyster shucker and delight someone back home.

A. SIMON 48, rue Montmartre, 75002; ☎ 01 42 33 71 65; **simon-a. com;** Métro: Les Halles or Étienne Marcel.

LINEN

FRENCH LINEN, SHEETS, PILLOW CASES, and towels make excellent gifts. Your best bet is to comb the department stores for these. Why not visit **Le Bon Marché** this time? For motifs from Provence, stalk the nearby boutiques on rue de Bonaparte in the Saint-Germain-des-Prés area.

LE BON MARCHÉ 24, rue de Sèvres, 75007; ☎ 01 44 39 80 00; **trees lbm.com;** Métro: Sèvres-Babylone.

LINGERIE

READY-MADE LINGERIE AND CUSTOM-MADE bras and panties can be found at the boutique listed below or at department stores—just think what you'll be doing to spice up your friends' lives back home!

ALICE CADOLLE 255, rue Saint Honoré, 75001; ☎ 01 42 60 94 94; **cadolle.com;** Métro: Concorde.

MUSIC AND FRENCH CDS

A VERY ORIGINAL GIFT IS A CD by one of France's leading groups or singers. France produces talent in the hip-hop and rap genres particularly. One store will have everything you need and allows you to listen before purchasing. Any FNAC store will have a healthy selection.

FNAC 74, avenue des Champs-Élysées, 75008; ☎ 08 25 02 00 20; **fnac. com;** Métro: Georges V; Monday–Saturday, 10 a.m.–11:45 p.m.; Sunday, noon–11:45 p.m. Check the Web site for other Paris addresses.

MUSTARD

THERE ARE REAL TRADE-OFFS in contemporary France. It's true that the banks and business climate often disappoint sophisticated visitors used to the no-nonsense atmosphere of New York or Tokyo, but where else besides Paris are your pickles and mustard made from the same recipe as back in 1747? It is definitely worth a few minutes to visit the **Boutique Maille,** which not only offers its full line of the finest pickles and vinegars in elegant jars, but also serves its famous mustard on tap. Fill up and take with you a hand-painted earthenware crock with Maille's tangy delight! An excellent, original gift at a modest price.

BOUTIQUE MAILLE 6, place de la Madeleine, 75001; ☎ 01 40 15 06 00; Monday–Saturday, 10 a.m.–7 p.m.; **maille.com;** Métro: Madeleine.

ORIGINAL READY-TO-WEAR AND MORE

ANTOINE ET LILI 95, quai de Valmy, 75010; Boutique: ☎ 01 40 37 41 55; Interior design: ☎ 01 40 37 34 86; **antoineetlili.com;** Métro: Gare de l'Est or Jacques Bonsergent. There are three stores here: Rose for women's wear, Green for the children's range, and the Yellow home decoration store on the corner, offering colorful kitschy objects and furniture for home and garden. Check the Web site for six other boutique locations.

BUBBLE 43, rue de la Folie-Méricourt, 75011; ☎ 01 48 87 02 60; Métro: Saint-Ambroise. A great address for original clothes for kids with a fantastic selection of slogan T-shirts in French.

PENS

ONE OF THE MOST CLASSIC GIFTS coming out of France is, of course, the Montblanc fountain pen. Why not go to the source and check out the latest Meisterstück, selling for around €250 to €485. Remember, you can *détaxe* it! (That is, receive your partial VAT refund.)

MONTBLANC 60, rue du Faubourg Saint-Honoré, 75008; ☎ 01 40 06 02 93; **montblanc.com;** Métro: Saint-Philippe du Roule. Check the Web site for other Paris boutiques.

PERFUME AND FINE COSMETICS

unofficial **TIP**
If you're just after a half ounce of some famous fragrance available in any duty-free store in the world, you should probably shop in a duty-free store or order it on the Internet.

YOU HAVE TO THINK OF THE MAKING of perfume and fine cosmetics as forms of high art, like wine-making and cheese-making and other acts of high culture. To understand France and its history at the deepest level, you must think of its perfume and cosmetics not as products of vanity but as potions marking the crossroads of science and art, passion and reason, sensuality and the land. If you're open to another type of sensual experience, then visit one of the following perfumeries and *maquillage* shops and bring along all your senses. For an individualized approach, visit **Nez à Nez,** where Christa Patour and her daughter will design your own bespoke perfume while you wait.

L'ARTISAN PARFUMEUR 24, boulevard Raspail, 75007; ☎ 01 42 22 23 32; **artisanparfumeur.com;** Métro: Sèvres-Babylone. Check the Web site for the other Paris boutiques.

GUERLAIN 68, avenue des Champs-Élysées, 75008; ☎ 01 45 62 52 57; **guerlain.com;** Métro: Franklin D. Roosevelt. Call or check the Web site for other locations.

NEZ À NEZ 40, rue Quincampoix, 75004; ☎ 01 42 71 11 76; **nezanez .net;** Métro: Rambuteau.

PARFUMS CARON 34, avenue Montaigne, 75008; ☎ 01 47 23 40 82; **parfumscaron.com;** Métro: Franklin D. Roosevelt.

STATIONERY

IN THE DIGITAL AGE, paper continues to be sacred in France. There are scores of fine *papeteries* around the city, and they offer lots of inexpensive and original gifts. Here's one we like—which is perfect for supplying the kids with back-to-school items that no one has back home.

LAVRUT 52, Passage Choiseul, 75002; ☎ 01 42 96 95 54; Métro: Quatre Septembre.

TRENDY CLOTHING

AGNÈS B. Depending on which collection you're after, 2 or 19, rue du Jour, 75001; ☎ 01 40 39 96 88; Métro: Étienne Marcel or Les Halles. Visit **agnesb.com** for the addresses of the other Paris stores.

The French know that **agnès b.** symbolizes contemporary French style to foreigners. There's something here for women, children, and men in each of their collections: *femme, enfant, bébé,* and *homme* (women, children, baby, and men).

JEAN-PAUL GAULTIER 6, rue Vivienne, 75002; ☎ 01 42 86 05 05; **jean paulgaultier.com;** Métro: Bourse. Other addresses available on the Web site. Jean-Paul Gaultier typifies the innovation and audacity that many associate with Paris today. Take a look for yourself! Clothes and perfumes for both men and women.

WINE AND SPIRITS

ALTHOUGH YOU WON'T BE ABLE TO CARRY large quantities with you, a few select bottles of wine make either a great gift or a great way to remember your trip. Every neighborhood has a **Nicolas** wine shop, France's largest chain (over 250 stores). The selection is broad and the prices are reasonable. The manager will be able to direct those with no or limited wine experience or knowledge on a suitable purchase.

Aside from wine, a bottle of old Cognac, Armagnac, or Calvados also makes a wonderful gift. One Plymouth, Massachusetts, resident whose son brought him a bottle of 20-year-old Calvados writes that every snifter reminds him both of France and his son.

More serious wine tasters and collectors may wish to spend an hour at a well-stocked showcase. Visit **Caves Augé,** 116, boulevard Hauss-mann, 75008; ☎ 01 45 22 16 97; **cavesauge.com;** Métro: Miromesnil.

Tips for Buying Wine and Spirits

Serious wine collectors need not read this. The rest of us may find it helpful to know that French wine with a blue metal wrapper around the cork indicates that the wine is a mixture or blend of collected vineyards. Perfectly fine for drinking at the table, but wholly inadequate to either take home or collect.

- The Beaujolais nouveau, which comes out every November, is fun and light to consume when it comes out. It is not made to age, and some Beaujolais nouveau will turn to vinegar in a matter of weeks. Don't bring it home unless you plan to drink it right away.

- Some of the best buys are smaller, lesser-known Bordeaux that are not exported to North America.

- The greatest pleasure comes from bringing home a few bottles of a wine you've discovered at a vineyard, a tasting, or a bistro. A good bottle of red wine makes an excellent gift and may cost you as little as €15.

- It's better to buy your wines in a wine store before leaving and not rely on the duty-free shops at the airport, where the selection is limited and the prices are high. Champagne, however, is often on promotion at duty-free shops.

- An old bottle of Armagnac, Cognac, or Calvados is a great souvenir of your trip to France. When given as a gift it will endear you for life . . . or at least until the last drop.

PART NINE

EXERCISE *and* RECREATION

SPORTS *and* FITNESS

SINCE MANY TRAVELERS TODAY LIKE TO EXERCISE even when they're on the road, we have researched this subject for the Paris-bound visitor. Parisians have become more fitness-conscious over the last ten years but still do not care as much about recreation and health as they do about pleasure. International hotels have followed the American model and have tried to incorporate exercise rooms and health centers into their facilities, but these will seem to you like afterthoughts.

Although you'll probably spend more time exploring cultural Paris, you should know that the city offers plenty of resources for the athletic crowd. For all sports-related questions, call the city hall hotline, ☎ 39 75.

For sports equipment in Paris, two main chains provide everything athletes need: **Décathlon** (28, avenue Wagram, 75008; ☎ 01 45 72 66 88; **decathlon.fr**) and **Go Sport** (Forum des Halles, 75001; ☎ 01 53 00 81 70; **go-sport.com**). Check both Web sites for other Paris locations.

unofficial **TIP**
If you love to jog, one of your most memorable jogs will be lapping around the pond and palais in the Jardin de Luxembourg in the Latin Quarter.

For specialized sporting equipment for cycling, jogging, swimming, climbing, camping, and other activities, go to **Au Vieux Campeur** at 48, rue des Écoles, 75005, and a number of smaller shops nearby; Métro: Cluny or Maubert Mutualité, ☎ 01 53 10 48 48; **auvieuxcampeur.fr**.

JOGGING AND RUNNING

PARIS AIR QUALITY IS NOT WONDERFUL, ALTHOUGH it is getting better. With less smoking among the inhabitants and the growing presence of "eco buses," which run on biofuel, the city is reducing its carbon footprint. Additionally, although Paris is a relatively clean city, Parisians are not all that disciplined, and many wouldn't bat an eye before tossing a candy wrapper or cigarette butt onto the sidewalk. This is surprising to many tourists. The notorious problem with "uncurbed" dogs has been improved by on-the-spot fines for transgressions, although vigilance is still recommended, particularly in the less-wealthy areas of town, where inspectors' presence is rare. Joggers are best advised to run in Paris streets with great caution, unlike the example of former U.S. President Bill Clinton, who insisted on jogging through Place de la Concorde at rush hour on his state visit to France in 1996. (George W. Bush helicoptered over the city in 2000, whereas Barack Obama quietly dined with his family at a bistro near the Eiffel Tower.) For your safety and the future of your lungs, you may prefer to jog in one of Paris's lovely parks or in either of the two large forests at the eastern and western edges of the city, Bois de Vincennes and Bois de Boulogne. Both are easily accessed by Métro.

A SPECIAL REPORT FOR SERIOUS RUNNERS

ONE AMERICAN FICTION WRITER, marathon-runner, and long-term Paris resident, Shari Leslie Segall, shares some of her secrets with our readers.

Where to Run

Paris is the most beautiful place in the world to run. It is possible, in one single (relatively lengthy) straight line, moving eastward along the upper quays of the Seine from the 15th arrondissement to the 5th, to pass before or through—or catch a distant flash of—almost every monument, cathedral, statue, structure, and patch of nature for which Paris (and much of Western civilization) is known and loved. Along this route, the river threads through its monuments like a silk cord through precious stones: the Eiffel Tower; the golden Invalides dome (don't forget to wave to Napoléon); Place de la Concorde (don't forget a kind word for Louis and Marie—this is where they had their "epiphany"); Sacré Cœur staring from the far north; the Tuileries Gardens; the Musée d'Orsay; the Louvre and its pyramid (run through that courtyard—it's a gas!); the bridges where midnight trysts among famous figures took place during wartime; Notre-Dame; the Tour d'Argent restaurant; all the way (with a couple of zigzags) to the Bois de Vincennes if you have the right shoes, stamina, and sense of history.

The city is anchored in the west by the Bois de Boulogne (*bois* means woods) and in the east by the Bois de Vincennes (which is why the Paris Marathon, which partially follows a version of the above-mentioned route, includes both); it's punctuated by patches of perfect running pockets: the **Luxembourg Gardens** (at 6 mph, you'll go around the perimeter in about 11 minutes), the **Champ de Mars** under the Eiffel Tower (about 14 minutes around the perimeter at 6 mph), the **Parc Monceau** (beautiful but kind of small—you'll need a lot of loops and patience), and the **Parc Montsouris** (ditto). For the mega-masochists among us, there's the legendary hilly **Buttes-Chaumont.**

The Best-Kept Secret

Runners who know about the **Promenade Plantée** keep the news to themselves for fear of invasion by the uninitiated. But you've just gotta know about this. From the Opéra de la Bastille (take the steps at the corner of avenue Daumesnil and avenue Ledru-Rollin) to the entrance to the Bois de Vincennes (the entrance is a street or so away, so check a very recent map if you want to continue into the Bois), roughly 3.5 kilometers (2 miles) of old railroad tracks have been turned into a sort of linear public park. At times, the park, as did the train, takes you giddily high above the street, dips to ground level, and rolls in and out of totally tunnel-dotted greenery to an occasional residential or commercial block. The path features what always seems like the first lush roses of the summer and the first russet leaves of the fall, and generally looks and feels like you made it all up, and you feel as though, if you open your eyes, it's all going to disappear. Do it. Go there. Run there. But . . . don't tell a soul!

Where to Buy Gear

As with most goods and services in Paris, with the exception of the occasional loaf of bread or bus ride, the price of running gear is so astoundingly high that you'll think they must have made a mistake. Your impulse is to go over to the nice cash-register lady and point out that there is one too many zeros on her nice price tag. Shoes, especially, can be as much as 75% more expensive than in the United States. If you need to bring a souvenir back from Paris, stick to Eiffel Tower statuettes rather than running gear.

MARATHON   26, rue Léon Jost, 75017; ☎ 01 42 67 49 44; **boutique marathon.com;** Métro: Courcelles. Open Tuesday, Wednesday, Friday, and Saturday, 10 a.m.–7 p.m.; Thursday, 10 a.m.–8 p.m. Shoes, clothing, accessories, books, and so on. Prices are still outrageous, but the owner is a longtime marathoner (she ran New York costumed as Wonder Woman), all the employees know their stuff, they speak enough of at least running-specific English to keep the transaction alive, they have a stock of which other Paris running stores can only dream, they cheerfully give out free running and gear-maintenance advice, and they let you take the shoes out for a test-drive around the block.

As elsewhere in the world, no running-department employees got hired because they needed a job in a chain or department store. Unless they were runners who needed a job. Running-specific chains abound (and compete with each other) in Paris, but are more often than not staffed by kids who could just as easily be stocking shelves at the local yarn-supply boutique, and whose only exercise consists of chewing gum.

What to Take Seriously

DOGS Paris is a true love-me-love-my-dog town. (One theory is that this gives the French something to kick after having received their own kicking for the past two millennia from tribes, Church, monarchy, and disagreeable civil servants.) You will probably encounter more dogs along your route than you ever have in all your years of running in your home country. The dogs will behave like dogs behave with runners anywhere else: The ones liable to get agitated will get agitated; the urbane, blasé ones will pretend not to notice you're there. The difference is, in Paris, you're the one expected to go out of your way to avoid the dog—not the other way around. And if the dog starts getting funny on you and you react accordingly (fear, aggression of your own, a comment to the owner), you're the one who's seen (and usually soundly reprimanded by the owner as well as tag-along members of the seemingly citywide dog-walking club) as the insensitive brute. All this, of course, while you're trying to keep running.

TRAFFIC LIGHTS *Rouge* may mean "red" in French, but it sure doesn't seem to mean "stop." Or, "stop right away." Never assume that once the light turns green for you and red for the crossing traffic, the crossing traffic will cease moving forward. It won't; several more cars will graze your nose before anything resembling stopping takes place. Never assume that now it's relatively safe (is it ever safe?) to cross, or that there will be no other vehicular activity in your particular intersection until the light turns red for you. There will be; cars will be making right and left turns into your path from what seems like streets all the way to the suburbs. Never assume that some smart-aleck motorcyclist won't start savagely revving his engine just as you're halfway across, mortifying you into thinking that the light's changed and you're dead. He will: the smaller his bike, the louder his rev. All this, of course, while you're trying to keep running.

SWIMMING

IF YOU FEEL LIKE GOING FOR A SWIM, you'll find excellent public facilities in almost every arrondissement. Entry to one of the 38 municipal pools is €3; privately run pools charge about €4. The

Piscine Suzanne-Berlioux in the Forum des Halles, impressively located underground in the center of Paris, offers rink hockey, handball, basketball, volleyball, badminton, tennis, dance courses, yoga, and martial arts, in addition to its pool facilities. For a great location, check out the municipal pool **Piscine Joséphine Baker**, a permanent floating pool located on the Seine. It has a 25-meter pool, fitness complex, and sun deck. Both facilities are accessible to the disabled.

Consult the sports page of the city hall Web site, **paris.fr,** for a complete list of other locations and opening times, bearing in mind access is often limited during the day when local schools use the pools. *Note:* Males are supposed to wear swimsuits rather than just baggy trunks. Here is a selection of addresses:

PISCINE ARMAND-MASSARD 65, boulevard du Montparnasse, 75015; ☎ 01 45 38 65 19; Métro: Montparnasse.

PISCINE SAINT-GERMAIN 12, rue Lobineau, 75006; ☎ 01 56 81 25 40; Métro: Mabillon.

PISCINE SAINT-MERRI 16, rue du Renard, 75004, with a solarium; ☎ 01 42 72 29 45; Métro: Hôtel de Ville or Rambuteau.

PISCINE SUZANNE-BERLIOUX 10, place de la Rotonde, 75001; ☎ 01 42 36 98 44; Métro: Les Halles.

PISCINE JOSÉPHINE BAKER Quai François Mauriac, 75001; ☎ 01 56 61 96 50; Métro: Quai de la Gare.

Hotel Pools

A few Parisian hotels have indoor pools, but this is rare. The Ritz has a pool that'll make you feel like you're in an Otto Preminger film, but paying Ritz prices for the sake of the pool is not a great idea.

Aquaboulevard

During the summer months when the days are hot and heavy, or alternatively, on a cold, wet winter's day, an outing to **Aquaboulevard,** an elaborate complex of swimming pools, slides, and recreational facilities, may be just right. 4–6, rue Louis Armand, 75015; ☎ 01 40 60 10 00; **aquaboulevard.fr;** Métro: Balard.

FISHING AND BOATING

THERE IS SOME FISHING in the Seine and Marne rivers, as well as in the ponds at the Bois de Vincennes and Bois de Boulogne, but considering the need for licenses and the specific equipment needed to nab a *poisson,* we advise you to limit your fishing experiences to the restaurants. You can rent rowing boats in the Bois de Vincennes and Bois de Boulogne.

Barques du Bois de Boulogne

These medium-sized rowing boats on the Lac Inférieur fit a maximum of five people. Rental is €10 per hour, and a cash deposit of €50 is required. Boats are available from mid-February to late October, 10 a.m. to 6 p.m. This is a lovely way to cool down at the end of a summer afternoon.

HIKING

THERE IS MORE NATURE IN PARIS than you'd be able to discover on your own. Short side-trips await you in dense forests laden with royal history. One of the most attractive parks inside Paris is the **Buttes-Chaumont,** which has rugged hills and even a few stalactites in a cave. It is among the largest Parisian parks, arranged in the English style and equally beautiful and romantic. Created under Napoléon III by the designer Jean-Charles Alphand, it is a colorful landscape of roughly 61 acres with over half a million trees. Check out Sybille's Temple on the top of a 98-foot cliff. Take Métro Line 7 bis and get off at the Buttes-Chaumont or Botzaris stops. For a more energetic hike, two of the national hiking trails, or Chemin de Grands Randonnées, cross Paris alongside many of the capital's monuments. Check the English pages of **gr-infos.com** for details. For out-of-town excursions, see Part Six, Sightseeing, Tours, and Attractions.

PARKS AND CITY SQUARES

SEE THE PARKS SECTION in Part Six, Sightseeing, Tours, and Attractions.

TENNIS

EVER SINCE YANNICK NOAH emerged as a national tennis hero, tennis has shed much of its bourgeois connotation in France. You may be interested in tennis as a spectator or a player or as both. The game of tennis was exceedingly popular in late-medieval France, and by the early 17th century, there were at least 200 tennis courts in Paris alone. Warwick University's research on 17th-century Paris playhouses reveals, "These walled structures were built in roofed and unroofed forms. The ready availability of these buildings and the ease with which they might be converted into performance spaces made them very attractive to traveling companies working in Paris." Apparently, troupes such as Molière's played at the Jeu de Paume du Marais courts in the late 1650s. Paris has 43 municipal tennis centers with over 170 courts, which can be reserved by visitors and Parisians alike. Register on their Web site, **tennis.paris.fr** to receive your access codes by e-mail and then book your courts online. The cost per hour is €7.50 for an outdoor court and €14 for a covered court. You pay when you turn up to play and will need to show proof of identity. There are also a number of private clubs in Paris, but nonmember access is very limited.

For information on the **Roland Garros French Open,** call ☎ 01 47 43 48 48 or visit **rolandgarros.com.** Many Web sites specialize in ticket sales at hefty premiums. The event lasts for two weeks in June, and it is, in our experience, not difficult to buy tickets outside of the stadium for at least the earlier days of the event. Be careful, though; scalpers have been known to sell fake tickets.

GYM CLUBS

ALTHOUGH IT'S POSSIBLE TO GET A GOOD WORKOUT in Paris, don't expect to find all the amenities and services that you are used to. There are several prominent gym clubs with locations all over the city offering workout rooms, saunas, whirlpools, and other equipment. Most do not offer any daily or weekly passes, but some do, and we've found these options for tourists who can't survive a week without their dose of the StairMaster. Many hotels now do have in-house exercise rooms. In general, Parisians, who traditionally have not been very exercise-conscious and would rather eat, drink, or go to the cinema than sweat, are changing. A wave of health clubs, fitness centers, and exercise and dance courses have opened in recent years. There is no word in French for fitness, so Parisians say "*le fitness.*" Note that many do not supply towels, and if they do, they're not large, and you have to pay extra. Facilities tend to be less spacious than you're perhaps accustomed to. You'll find elliptical trainers, treadmills, and stationery bikes in most gyms.

Some of the municipal pools have workout equipment, but access to them requires an additional fee. For example, the **Piscine Club Pontoise-Quartier Latin** (19, rue de Pontoise, 75005; ☎ 01 55 42 77 88; **clubquartierlatin.com;** Métro: Maubert-Mutualité) costs €20 per day for their well-equipped gym and €4.20 per day for the pool. The **American Church** (65, quai d'Orsay, 75007; Métro: Invalides) offers "Aerobics American Style" with an American instructor on weekday evenings and Saturday mornings; €10 per class. Visit **parisfitness.com** for details.

ESPACE VIT'HALLES Place Beaubourg, 48, rue Rambuteau, 75003; ☎ 01 42 77 21 71; **vithalles.fr;** Métro: Rambuteau. Entry: €25 per day or €99 per week. Open Monday–Friday, 8 a.m.–10:30 p.m.; Saturday and Sunday, 10 a.m.–7 p.m. One of the best clubs in France, with a wide variety of programs with personalized training (weights and cardio training, stretching, yoga, Pilates). Visit the Web site for four other Paris locations.

CLUB MED GYM AND WAOU CLUB MED GYM 10, place de la République, 75011; ☎ 01 47 00 69 98; **clubmedgym.fr;** Métro: République. Entry:

€26 per day. Many Club Med instructors speak English. With 22 clubs in Paris, several with pools, this chain is one of the most convenient for short-term visitors. Avoid late afternoons, when it gets congested and sweaty. Open Monday–Friday, 7:30 a.m.–10 p.m.; Saturday, 9 a.m.–6 p.m.; Sunday, 9 a.m.–5 p.m. Check the Web site for other locations.

LE RITZ HEALTH CLUB 15, place Vendôme, 75001; ☎ 01 43 16 30 60; Métro: Opéra. Entry: €150 per day, although a reduced rate of €100 is offered in the summer. You don't have to be a hotel guest to enjoy all the services offered by Le Ritz Health Club: a 16-meter pool, squash, steam bath, Jacuzzi, free weights, circuit training, exercise and yoga classes, but the day pass just might be more than you're paying for your hotel room!

BODY AND MIND

ALTERNATIVE FORMS OF EXERCISE SUCH as Yoga and Pilates are readily available in Paris. Here are a few addresses where you will find competent, bilingual instruction:

PARIS YOGA 9, rue Magellan, 75008; ☎ 01 40 70 14 44; **parisyoga.com;** Métro: Georges V. Daily classes in Agni Yoga and Pilates, €25 per class. Ayurvedic massage is also offered. Visit the Web site for scheduling.

COREBODY 76 bis, rue des Saints Pères, 75007; ☎ 01 45 49 97 29; Métro: Saint-Germain-des-Prés; **corebodypilates.com.** Closed Sunday. Pilates mat classes, €30; private session of each, €80. Visit the Web site for scheduling.

ELÉMENT 16, rue de la Grande Chaumière, 75006; ☎ 01 53 10 86 00; Métro: Vavin. **elementparis.com.** Closed Sunday. Pilates mat and Yoga classes, €30; private Pilates session with machines, €80. Acupuncture, reflexology, Shiatsu, Ayurvedic, meridian, and hot-stone massage also offered. Visit the Web site for scheduling.

CYCLING

THE FRENCH ARE SERIOUS CYCLISTS and host the celebrated Tour de France in July each year. Lance Armstrong has become one of France's favorite Americans. In the last decade, Paris has seen a 48% increase in the number of cyclists on its roads. If you'd like to join them, your best bet is to plan your routes along the ever-increasing network of cycle lanes (the city aims to provide about 375 miles by 2013); otherwise inner-city cycling is still rather hazardous. In any case, wear a helmet. The latest map of Paris cycling lanes can be found on the city hall Web site, **paris.fr.** You will also find details there of the city's *Paris Respire* or Paris Breathes initiative, closing a number of roads across the city to all motor traffic on weekends and public holidays. Cycling in the Bois de Vincennes and Bois de Boulogne in the summer is heavenly. There are seasonal bike-rental shops open in both parks. And, of course, bike trips to other regions in France are known to be glorious.

Bike Rentals

If you'd like to use a bike for a short trip within the city, you can rent a Vélib bike from one of the numerous self-service stations throughout Paris and the near suburbs. You'll find a row of available bikes every 300 yards or so. You'll need to pay the daily subscription of €1 by credit card (the kind that has an embedded chip), and then your first half hour is free. There are also longer subscription periods available. The bikes are adjustable, comfortable, and equipped with lights for night riding. Information in English is available at all stations and on the Web site: **en.velib.paris.fr.** This is one of Paris's best innovations, introduced in 2008 by Paris's progressive mayor Bertrand Delanoe. Essentially, with the Vélib option, you'll never be stranded in Paris.

unofficial **TIP**
Note that in the summer months, the French railroad company, **SNCF,** rents bicycles at 15 of the largest national train stations, including Gare de Lyon in Paris. For more information, contact local SNCF stations.

For a longer and more leisurely rental, here is a list of reputable companies that also service and repair bikes. Most of them do tours (usually just for groups; ask when you call).

FAT TIRE BIKE TOURS This is a fun way to visit Paris, day or night, rain or shine, in English, bikes included! Count on around €26 for a four-hour daytime tour and bike. Tours are offered daily at 11 a.m. year-round, and from April to October, an afternoon tour departs at 3 p.m. No reservations are necessary. The meeting place is by the south leg, *pilier sud,* of the Eiffel Tower; look for the Fat Tire sign. There are also regular tours of Versailles and Monet's Garden, as well as Paris night tours. Forget buses, taxis, and vans—this is the way to see the city. They also offer tours on those enticing Segway vehicles, walking tours, and wine tastings. Visit **fattirebiketours paris.com** for more details or call ☎ 01 56 58 10 54.

PARIS À VÉLO 2, rue Alphonse Baudin, 75011; Métro: Saint Sébastien-Froissart; ☎ 01 48 87 60 01 45; **parisvelosympa.com.** Three-hour tour, €34; English tours available.

Shipping Your Bike

For information on taking your bike with you, call your airline. Charter companies tend to be stricter with baggage requirements and are not equipped with bike boxes. Once you get to Paris, you shouldn't have much problem transporting your bike around. All RER lines have dedicated carriages for travelers with bikes, which can be used any time outside of the weekday rush hour. Access to Line 1 of the Métro is also permitted on Sunday and public holidays before 4:30 p.m. Certain trains also allow bikes on board; check with the SNCF for details.

For tour operators specializing in cycling trips to France, visit the French Tourist office Web site at **franceguide.com** or contact their France-on-Call hotline in the United States at ☎ 514-288-1904. One travel service known for their high-quality bicycling tours in France (but not Paris) is **Bike Riders,** formerly Progressive Travels, P.O. Box 130254, Boston, MA 02113; ☎ 617-723-2354 or 800-473-7040; fax 617-723-2355; **bikeriderstours.com.**

INLINE SKATING

INLINE SKATING REMAINS A POPULAR Parisian urban sport. This is a fascinating, fast-paced, and original way to see the city by day and night. With the advent of roller mania, many associations and group outings have been organized to bring together practitioners of all levels and interests.The **Roller Squad Institute** (☎ 01 56 61 99 61, **rsi.asso.fr**) organizes four roller excursions per week leaving from Les Invalides; check the Web site for details. The association **Pari Roller** (**pari-roller.com**) also organizes a three-hour, 30-kilometer outing for more-advanced bladers that leaves from Gare Montparnasse every Friday night at 10 p.m.

If you are a beginner, rental and instruction options are available at stores such as **Nomades** (37, boulevard Bourdon, 75004; ☎ 01 44 54 07 44; **nomadeshop.com;** Métro: Bastille). Nomades rents skates for €8 and also offers 1.5-hour lessons for €17. If you want to practice your technique, consult the sports page of the city hall Web site, **paris.fr,** for a list of the 12 municipal roller parks.

GOLF

THE POPULARITY OF GOLF IN FRANCE has been growing wildly, with more than 400 courses in the country. There are more than 50 private and public golf courses in the Paris/Île de France area alone, although to get to most of them you'll need a car. But, if you can afford the greens fees, we're not worried about your ability to get to the course. Some courses require all players to purchase insurance before stepping up to the first tee. Greens fees can be a bit pricey, but if you're in France and you love to golf, why not splurge at Chantilly, for example, one of the finest inland courses on the continent. For course descriptions, visit **golfeurope.com.** If the idea of a golfing holiday appeals to you, the French-based company, **France Golf Tours,** offers a Golf and Paris package. Contact them at info@francegolf-tours.com or visit the Web site, **france-golf-tours.com.**

Minigolf courses can be found in the Bois de Vincennes and Jardin d'Acclimatation.

HORSEBACK RIDING

THERE ARE LOTS OF RIDING OPPORTUNITIES throughout France—even riding holidays and pony camps during the summer and school holidays that might interest you. However, there are only a few opportunities in Paris. A comprehensive Web site in English for horseback riding in France can be found at **tourisme-equestre.fr.** If you feel like riding during your Paris visit, contact the **Centre Equestre de la Cartoucherie** in the Bois de Vincennes, 75012, ☎ 01 43 74 61 25. **cartoucherie-equitation.com.** Check the Web site for times, prices, and conditions. There is also a second choice on the western side of Paris: **Société d'Equitation de Paris,** Route de la Muette à Neuilly, 75116, ☎ 01 45 01 20 06; **equitation-paris.com.**

DOWN AT THE BEACH: PARIS PLAGES

IF YOU ARE VISITING PARIS IN JULY AND AUGUST, you can always spend a day at the beach. Launched in 2002, **Paris Plages,** gets bigger and better every year. The main beach extends 3 kilometers along the Right Bank from the Louvre to Pont de Sully; a second location is to the northeast of the city, at the Bassin de la Villette. Under the shade of the palm trees you can relax in a sun lounger or hammock, borrow a novel from the five-language library, or have a free massage. If lazing in the sun is not for you, there's always beach volleyball, badminton, tai chi, fencing, or table tennis. Water sports, including sailing, canoeing, and rowing, are all available at la Villette, where instructors are on hand to help beginners. All activities are free of charge; the beach is open daily from 8 a.m. until midnight from the third week of July until the third week of August. Check out the City of Paris Web site **paris.fr** for details.

PART TEN

ENTERTAINMENT *and* NIGHTLIFE

◼ PARIS *by* NIGHT

WHAT TO DO AT NIGHT? ANYTHING YOU WANT. Paris is practically as active or passive as you choose. It's all here. Many visitors love to spend each evening at a new restaurant, tasting new wonders and discovering liquid miracles of great vintage, and then wandering back to their hotels on a late-evening stroll along cobblestone streets to an inviting, feathery bed. For others, dinner is just the beginning of a long night, since Paris's club scene only begins to crank up at midnight and regularly pulses until the first Métro just before dawn. Culturally, Paris is so rich that the problem is always having to say no to things you'd love to see. Every night there are a hundred plays produced, a half-dozen operas, a dozen concerts, and two dozen extravagant shows and performances. For the literary set, there are readings. For art aficionados, a score of openings called *vernissages* await you. Paris is the capital of cinema, with hundreds of movie houses playing countless films every night. Normally, you'd never think of seeing a movie in a foreign city, but in Paris, why not duck into one of the lush cinemas and get lost in a recent French film? And then there are the bars and cafés, the people-watching, and talking, smoking, and cognac sniffing. And, of course, walking the *quai* and cruising on the Seine. And finally, the greatest of the great Parisian pastimes, *draguer* (a curiously Parisian verb falling somewhere crudely between just flirting and flirting with the intent of not going home alone), will certainly entertain you. Political correctness was never taken seriously among Parisians, who on the whole love to admire and be admired and enjoy being judged by their looks, their bulges, and their curves. For the unsingle set free to *draguer* in Paris, why not *draguer* your husband or wife, boyfriend or girlfriend? In Paris, public affection is as natural as a good meal, and if love is involved, it's never wrong. In Paris you can live the clichés.

THE LIGHTS OF PARIS

THE MOST IMPRESSIVE MOMENTS you'll spend in Paris are after dark, when the sky goes black and the beams and spots illuminate the monuments and building façades. You will quickly understand why Paris is called the City of Light. Paris after 10 p.m. begins to feel like a huge, living theater or museum, and you'll begin to realize that the best thing you can do is simply drink up its beauty. Don't try to comprehend; simply feel. You may not be into poetry, but evenings in Paris when you're free to stroll are poetic.

The City by Foot

If you want to take an evening walk, start at the middle of **Pont Neuf** and watch the barges stroke the 17th-century buildings on both banks with their strong flood lights. Cross the bridge and follow the long textured edge of the **Louvre** on the Right Bank. Duck under the archway to your left and enter into the central courtyard of the Louvre. The Pyramide at night is spectral. With your back to the pyramid, spot the **Arc de Triomphe** in the distance as it lines up perfectly with the tip of the obelisk at **Place de la Concorde.** Quickly, you'll begin to feel the symmetry of the city, and the degree of artfulness that the architects have invested in creating this beauty through the ages. Walk back to the Seine, turn left, and follow the river to Châtelet. The **Palais de Justice** and the eerie **Hôtel Dieu,** Paris's oldest hospital, will be lit up, glittering gold and iridescent blue on the Left Bank. For information about guided walking tours, see Part Six, Sightseeing, Tours, and Attractions.

SELF-GUIDED NIGHT TOUR BY TAXI

FOR A HIGHLY ORIGINAL EXPERIENCE, jump into a taxi at Châtelet and tell the driver to follow the Seine all the way to Pont de Bercy. Indicate that you want him to take the Voie Express, which dips down to river level and swirls and turns under the bridges. The neck of the river between the **Hôtel de Ville** and the exit for the **Bastille** is enchanting as the oldest buildings on Île Saint-Louis come alive in the lights and shadows. After the Gare de Lyon, the highway will lose some of its charm as the new Paris comes into focus, with the **Ministry of Finance** building, the **Bercy OmniSport Stadium,** the modern **UGC Ciné Cité** movie complex in Bercy Village, and, spanning the river, the elegant **Passerelle Simone de Beauvoir** footbridge, leading to the four box-like towers of the **François Mitterrand National Library** (Bibliothèque Nationale).

Have the driver cross the river and head back along the *quai* on the Left Bank. As the back of **Notre-Dame** comes into focus, you'll know why you're in Paris. Get out at Saint Michel, trot down the stone steps that lead to the edge of the Seine, and continue on foot along the Left Bank until you're tired. For less than €30, you will have given yourself the tour of your life.

One variation on this tour is to stay in the taxi and continue along the Left Bank, past the **Musée d'Orsay,** with Place de la Concorde off to your right. Take the drive down along the river and don't come up until you're under the **Eiffel Tower.** Then cross over toward Trocadéro and have the driver loop you around toward the left and up to the top of Trocadéro. Get out, have your driver wait, and pinch yourself. You'll be bowled over at the awe-inspiring view of a bejeweled Eiffel Tower. If you're up for more, follow avenue Kléber to the Arc de Triomphe and swing down the lively-at-all-hours avenue Champs-Élysées. This is the only time of day that *Les Champs* is truly worth visiting.

CULTURAL EVENINGS

WHERE TO GO FOR LISTINGS?

IF YOU'RE LIMITED TO ENGLISH, visit **parisvoice.com, timeout. com/paris,** or the English pages of the Paris Tourist Office site, **parisinfo.com.**

For concerts and other live performances (other than theater), visit **FNAC (fnac.com)** or **Virgin Mégastore (virginmega.fr)** to review their box-office listings. For serious music aficionados, pick up a copy of *Le Monde de la Musique* in any kiosk. It's in French, of course, but you'll easily recognize dates, times, Chopin, *La Flûte Magique* (*The Magic Flute*), and similar phrases. If you are visiting Paris in the summer months, check out the program of the city's annual cultural festival at **quartierdete.com.**

For the Paris theater world, check out **theatreonline.com.**

MUSIC, OPERA, AND DANCE

PARISCOPE, THE WEEKLY LISTINGS MAGAZINE, comes out every Wednesday at a cost of €0.40 and is one of the most comprehensive listings. It is arranged by category (classical, world music, operas, dance, jazz-rock, and *variétés*–French variety shows) and includes addresses, Métro stops, phone numbers, hours, and prices of an extensive number of Parisian musical venues.

Below we've listed a number of venues that host regular events.

Classical Music

AMPHITHÉÂTRE RICHELIEU DE LA SORBONNE 17, rue de la Sorbonne, 75005; ☎ 01 40 46 33 72; agenda-culturel@paris-sorbonne.fr; Métro: Cluny–La Sorbonne.

AUDITORIUM DU LOUVRE Le Louvre, Cour Napoléon, 75001; ☎ 01 40 20 84 40; **louvre.fr;** Métro: Palais-Royal.

AUDITORIUM DU MUSÉE D'ORSAY 1, rue de la Légion d'Honneur, 75007; ☎ 01 40 49 47 57; Métro: Solférino or RER Musée d'Orsay.

CITÉ DE LA MUSIQUE 221, avenue Jean Jaurès, 75019; ☎ 01 44 84 45 00; reservations: 01 44 84 44 84; **cite-musique.fr;** Métro: Porte de Pantin.

IRCAM 1, place Igor Stravinsky, 75004; ☎ 01 44 78 48 43; **ircam.fr;** Métro: Rambuteau or Hôtel-de-Ville.

SAINTE CHAPELLE 4, boulevard du Palais, 75001; ☎ 01 53 40 60 80; Métro: Cité or Saint-Michel.

SALLE PLEYEL 252, rue du Faubourg Saint-Honoré, 75008; ☎ 01 42 56 13 13; **sallepleyel.fr;** Métro: Ternes.

THÉÂTRE DES CHAMPS-ÉLYSÉES 15, avenue Montaigne, 75008; ☎ 01 49 52 50 50; **theatrechampselysees.fr;** Métro: Alma-Marceau.

Opera and Dance

CENTRE POMPIDOU 19, rue de Beaubourg, 75004; ☎ 01 44 78 12 33; **centrepompidou.fr;** Métro: Rambuteau or Hôtel-de-Ville. The Paris Mecca for contemporary popular culture.

CHÂTELET-THÉÂTRE MUSICAL DE PARIS 1, place du Châtelet, 75001; ☎ 01 40 28 28 40; **chatelet-theatre.com;** Métro: Châtelet–Les Halles. Tickets: Pricing varies with each production. Major venue for high-quality productions.

OPÉRA BASTILLE Place de la Bastille, 75011; ☎ 08 92 89 90 90; **operadeparis.fr;** Métro: Bastille. This controversial modern opera house was created by Canadian Carlos Ott. Since its first performance in 1989, there has been a nearly constant storm of criticism of not only its architecture, but also its acoustics and prices. Part of this reaction can be attributed to the typical slamming of anything new by Parisians. There are actually more operas performed here than at its crosstown cousin, the **Opéra Palais Garnier** (see below). We can't guarantee it, but there are often discounted seats available for students and seniors 15 minutes before the curtain rises.

L'OPÉRA COMIQUE Place Boieldieu, 75002; ☎ 08 25 01 01 23 (reservations); **opera-comique.com;** Métro: Richelieu-Drouot. Specializes in operettas and new productions.

OPÉRA PALAIS GARNIER Place de l'Opéra, 75009; ☎ 08 92 89 90 90; **operadeparis.fr;** Métro: Opera. This is the granddaddy opera house of Paris, built during Napoléon III's empire by the then-unknown Charles Garnier. The interior is impressive, including an eclectic mix of architecture and adornment from Gobelin tapestries to a Chagall ceiling. A large part of its season is dedicated to ballet. Guided tours of the opera and its library and museum are available daily from 10 a.m. to 4:30 p.m. (€10).

THÉÂTRE DE LA VILLE 2, place du Châtelet, 75004; ☎ 01 42 74 22 77; **theatredelaville-paris.com;** Métro: Châtelet–Les Halles. Progressive program of French and foreign productions.

THÉÂTRE DES CHAMPS-ÉLYSÉES 15, avenue Montaigne, 75008; ☎ 01 49 52 50 50; **theatrechampselysees.fr;** Métro: Alma-Marceau. High-quality performances; a favorite recital venue.

Concert Halls

LE BATACLAN 50, boulevard Voltaire, 75011; ☎ 01 43 14 00 30; **le-bataclan.com;** Métro: Oberkampf. Small concert hall for both big names and emerging ones in the rock, hip-hop, reggae, and other scenes.

LA CIGALE 120, boulevard Rochechouart, 75018; ☎ 01 49 25 81 75; **lacigale.fr;** Métro: Barbès-Rochechouart. Small music hall used for eclectic performances, guitarists, reggae, and others.

CITÉ DE LA MUSIQUE 221, avenue Jean Jaurès, 75019; ☎ 01 44 84 45 00; reservations: 01 44 84 44 84; Métro: Porte-de-Pantin. Major venue for classical, modern, contemporary, baroque, and other serious concerts. A bit far out, but worth the visit. Good and inexpensive restaurant on the premises.

MAISON DE RADIO FRANCE 116, avenue du Président Kennedy, 75016; ☎ 01 56 40 22 22; **radiofrance.fr;** Métro: Ranelagh or Passy; RER: Kennedy/Maison de Radio France. You can attend classical concerts, operas, and performances of the Orchestre National de France, which are broadcast on France Musique.

L'OLYMPIA 28, boulevard des Capucines, 75009; ☎ 08 92 68 33 68; **olympiahall.com;** Métro: Madeleine. This is one of musical Paris's hallmarks. French singers such as Édith Piaf, Jacques Brel, and Yves Montand made themselves internationally famous here. Although the *chansons françaises* once dominated the Olympia's stage, more contemporary acts from a variety of backgrounds are now included.

PALAIS DES CONGRÈS 2, place Porte Maillot, 75017; ☎ 01 40 68 22 22; **palaisdescongres-paris.com;** Métro: Porte de Maillot. Large performance hall.

PALAIS OMNISPORTS DE PARIS-BERCY 8, boulevard de Bercy, 75012; ☎ 08 92 39 01 00 (€0.34/minute); **bercy.fr;** Métro: Bercy. Huge and impressive stadium and hall for big groups and international acts. Note that the outer dome of the stadium is covered with real grass!

SALLE GAVEAU 45, rue la Boétie, 75008; ☎ 01 49 53 05 07 37; **sallegaveau.com;** Métro: Miromesnil. Small and intimate music hall for chamber music and concert recitals.

SALLE PLEYEL 252, rue du Faubourg Saint-Honoré, 75008; ☎ 01 42 56 13 13; **sallepleyel.fr;** Métro: Ternes. Medium-sized concert hall, home of the prestigious Orchestre de Paris.

ZÉNITH 211, avenue Jean Jaurès, 75019; ☎ 01 44 52 54 56; **zenith-paris.com;** Métro: Porte-de-Pantin. Concert hall for some of the biggest and loudest domestic and international talent.

Church Concerts

There are weekly church concerts held in a number of the following churches: **La Madeleine, Saint-Sulpice, Saint-Séverin, Saint-Germain-des-Prés, Sainte-Geneviève, Sainte-Chapelle, Saint-Augustin,** and of course **Notre-Dame.** For more information about specific performances and times, your best bet is to check *Pariscope* or *l'Officiel des Spectacles* when you arrive.

THEATERS AND SPECTACLES

PARIS HAS MORE THAN 130 THEATERS, including 14 municipal theaters, offering French and foreign productions. Whether you speak French or not, you may choose to spend an evening at the theater. The following Paris theaters not only offer top-quality performances, they will enchant you with their style, décor, architecture, and history. For programs, details, times, and prices, consult *Pariscope* or *l'Officiel des Spectacles.*

ATHÉNÉE LOUIS JOUVET 4, square de l'Opéra Louis Jouvet, 75009; ☎ 01 53 05 19 19; **athenee-theatre.com;** Métro: Opéra. Classic venue.

BOUFFES DU NORD 37 bis, boulevard de la Chapelle, 75010; ☎ 01 46 07 34 50; **bouffesdunord.com;** Métro: La Chapelle. Home of Peter Brooke's company.

BOUFFES PARISIENS 4, rue Monsigny, 75002; ☎ 01 42 96 92 42; **bouffesparisiens.com;** Métro: Quatre Septembre or Pyramides. Comic and dramatic works.

LA BRUYÈRE 5, rue La Bruyère, 75009; ☎ 01 48 74 76 99; **theatre labruyere.com;** Métro: Saint-Georges. Traditional works.

LA CARTOUCHERIE DE VINCENNES rue du Champ-de-Manœuvre, 75012; ☎; **cartoucherie.fr.** Métro: Château de Vincennes. One of Paris's most innovative theaters—home to a number of theater companies, including the famed Théâtre du Soleil; ☎ 01 43 74 24 08; **theatre-du-soleil.fr.**

COMÉDIE DES CHAMPS-ÉLYSÉES 15, avenue Montaigne, 75008; ☎ 01

53 23 99 19; **comediedeschampselysees.com;** Métro: Alma-Marceau. Classic venue.

COMÉDIE FRANÇAISE 2, rue Richelieu, 75001; ☎ 01 44 58 15 15; **comedie-francaise.fr;** Métro: Palais Royal. Historic landmark— Molière's home.

GUICHET MONTPARNASSE 15, rue du Maine, 75014; ☎ 01 43 27 88 61; **guichetmontparnasse.com;** Métro: Montparnasse-Bienvenüe. Small comic productions.

LA MADELEINE 19, rue de Surène, 75008; ☎ 01 42 65 07 09; **theatre madeleine.com;** Métro: Madeleine. Performs mostly French classics.

ODÉON THÉÂTRE DE L'EUROPE—ATELIERS BERTHIER 1, rue André Suarès, 75017; ☎ 01 44 85 40 40; **theatre-odeon.fr;** Métro: Porte de Clichy. Major venue for contemporary European works in original languages.

SPLENDID SAINT-MARTIN 48, rue du Faubourg Saint-Martin, 75010; ☎ 01 42 08 21 93; **lesplendid.com;** Métro: Strasbourg–Saint-Denis. Musicals, mimes, and social comedy.

THÉÂTRE DE LA BASTILLE 76, rue de la Roquette, 75011; ☎ 01 43 57 42 14; **theatre-bastille.com;** Métro: Bastille. Contemporary theater and dance.

THÉÂTRE DE LA HUCHETTE 23, rue de la Huchette, 75005; ☎ 01 43 26 38 99; **theatrehuchette.com;** Métro: Saint-Michel. Small, intimate productions.

THÉÂTRE DE LA VILLE 2, place du Châtelet, 75004; ☎ 01 42 74 22 77; **theatredelaville-paris.com;** Métro: Châtelet–Les Halles. Classical French work.

THÉÂTRE DU PALAIS-ROYAL 38, rue Montpensier, 75001; ☎ 01 42 97 40 00; **theatrepalaisroyal.com;** Métro: Palais-Royal. Classical performances.

THÉÂTRE DU ROND-POINT 2 bis, avenue Franklin Roosevelt, 75008; ☎ 01 44 95 98 21; **theatredurondpoint.fr;** Métro: Franklin D. Roosevelt. Major theater on the Champs-Élysées.

THÉÂTRE DU VIEUX COLOMBIER 21, rue du Vieux Colombier, 75006; ☎ 01 44 39 87 00; **vieux.colombier.free.fr;** Métro: Saint-Sulpice. Modern and classical works.

THÉÂTRE MOGADOR 25, rue Mogador, 75009; ☎ 01 53 32 32 32; **mogador.net;** Métro: Trinité. Celebrated for its French comedies.

THÉÂTRE NATIONAL DE CHAILLOT 1, place du Trocadéro, 75016; ☎ 01 53 65 30 00; **theatre-chaillot.fr;** Métro: Trocadéro. Major venue for nationally noted talent.

THÉÂTRE NATIONAL DE LA COLLINE 15, rue Malte-Brun, 75020; ☎ 01 44 62 52 52; **colline.fr;** Métro: Gambetta. Great innovative works.

Comedy for English-Speakers

If you're in need of a dose of Anglo-Saxon humor, *Laughing Matters* regularly presents touring British, American, Canadian, and Australian stand-up comedians at **La Java** (105, rue du Faubourg du Temple, 75010; ☎ 01 53 19 98 88; **anythingmatters.com**). To get tickets, call the box office directly or go to the theater.

Paris also has three same-day ticket offices offering seats at half price.

LE KIOSQUE THÉÂTRE Place de la Madeleine; Métro: Madeleine

PARVIS MONTPARNASSE Métro: Montparnasse

PLACE DES TERNES Métro: Ternes

Open from Tuesday through Saturday from 12:30 to 7:45 p.m. and Sunday from 12:30 to 3:45 p.m.

These kiosks accept cash and credit cards. You pay half price plus a commission of about €3 per ticket, which is still very much worth it. Visit **kiosquetheatre.com** for more information.

unofficial **TIP**
It is written everywhere that these kiosks are open until 8 p.m. and 4 p.m., respectively, but this is not true; they close 15 minutes earlier!

Tickets to many concerts and sporting events are available from the ticket service at the **Virgin Mégastore** on the Champs-Élysées, **Galeries Lafayette,** and **FNAC** stores. You may also buy tickets online at **theatreonline.com** or **ticketac.com**.

READINGS AND LECTURES

IF YOU'RE INTERESTED IN WHAT'S HAPPENING in the literary scene (in English) in Paris these days, the best listening post is the **Village Voice Bookshop** (6, rue Princesse, 75007; Métro: Mabillon; ☎ 01 46 33 36 47; **villagevoicebookshop.com**). Chances are that there will be a reading on one of the evenings that you're in town. Book events are also held at the celebrated **Shakespeare & Co** (37, rue de la Bûcherie, 75005, Métro: Saint-Michel), as well as the Canadian store, **The Abbey Bookshop,** around the corner. **The Red Wheelbarrow** in the Marais located in the 4th arrondissement (22, rue Saint-Paul) is a very friendly bookstore with a vibrant list of events. Also check out **Tea & Tattered Pages** (24, rue de Mayet; Métro: Duroc). The **American Library in Paris** hosts free "Evenings with the Author" (10, rue du Général Camou, 75007; ☎ 01 53 59 12 60; **americanlibrary inparis.org;** RER: Pont de l'Alma). **W. H. Smith** hosts book signings and talks, but these bookshops may be too reminiscent of what you left back home to feel particularly Parisian or expatriate. Of course, if your French is up to snuff, there are readings and talks in French at numerous venues. Check *Pariscope, l'Officiel des Spectacles,* or the French daily *Libération,* whose cultural coverage is excellent.

CINEMA

PARIS IS A CINEMA-LOVER'S PARADISE, with more movie houses than any other city in the world. (Don't forget that the Cannes Film Festival and the Deauville Festival are in France!) On any given night, there are around 300 films to be seen in Paris. If you happen to notice that there is a great French film you've been dying to see, pick one of Paris's more illustrious movie houses and enjoy both the film and this very Parisian pastime. The beautifully stylized advertisements before the film are worth the hefty admission price alone. Plan to pay between €7 and €12 per entrance, depending on the cinema and the time. For listings, check the weekly *Pariscope* or *l'Officiel des Spectacles,* on sale at all newsstands. If you are visiting Paris in the summer months, check out some of the city's open-air film festivals such as *Cinema en Plein Air* at Parc de la Villette: **villette.com.**

Film times are listed in two ways: *séances* (the times when the shorts, coming attractions, and commercials begin) and *films* (the time the picture actually begins, usually 10–20 minutes later). Films usually play twice each night, around 7:30 p.m. and around 10 p.m., but obviously this depends on the length of the film. For late-night showings (11 p.m.–midnight) on weekends, check *Pariscope.*

To reserve seats at selected cinemas, check the listing in *Pariscope* and call the **Résa** number given (€0.34 per minute) followed by ☎ and the three-digit code found under the listing.

unofficial **TIP**
Be careful: If you are choosing an English-language film, make sure it is playing in VO (*version originale*), marked next to the listing. Otherwise, you'll be watching Woody Allen dubbed into French. If it's a Swedish film in VO, it'll be in Swedish with French subtitles. If it's in VF (*version française*), the film will be dubbed into French.

The **RED LIGHTS** *of* **PARIS**

ONE OF THE GREAT CLICHÉS that Paris cannot seem to shake is the city's nightlife proclivity for girlie shows, can-can, cabaret, and *le grand spectacle.* Much of this comes from the simple fact that there is a healthy selection of famous and flamboyant shows in this genre that are relentlessly promoted. Although the leading shows are primarily nourished by foreign visitors, tourists, and French people from the provinces, much of the continued popularity of these extravaganzas is rooted to a constant reality: The French love glamour and possess a guiltless adoration for the female body, preferably unclothed. Being outside the jurisdiction of Anglo-Saxon puritanical attitudes and the gnawing pressure to be politically correct, you may permit yourself to check out some very exciting costumes . . . and the loveliness that they conceal.

Depending on your own tastes, these shows may seem kitschy or tacky, but they are larger than life and can be a lot of fun. Beware: these shows are relatively expensive but promise to be unforgettable. Only you can decide if the outlay is worth it.

Paris also sports a very vibrant "private club" scene for fulfilling just about all your interests and fantasies, including lap dances, partner swapping, and more. If this interests you, ask your hotel concierge or check online.

TIPS *for* GOING OUT
on the TOWN

DRESS CODES FOR PARIS CLUBS

IF YOU SEE A LISTING FOR A PARIS CLUB and are wondering how to dress, here are a few suggestions to guide you.

tenue correcte nice but not too fancy; jacket for men, dress or pantsuit for women
chic dressed up with a touch of flair
free wear as you like
chemise et veste obligatoires jacket and tie required
mode stylish, fashion-conscious
folies wear extravagant, crazy, fantasy
ouest parisien conservative, dressy
fancy eveningwear
le plus fou sera le mieux! the crazier the better; as off-the-wall or bizarre as you please

PRICES AND ENTRANCE FEES (*PRIX D'ENTRÉE*)

ACCORDING TO NORTH AMERICAN STANDARDS, Paris clubs and bars are expensive, and at times, absurdly expensive. To get into a nightclub, count on spending about €15 per person on the *prix d'entrée,* although at some clubs on some nights, women don't have to pay admission. Most clubs offer you one drink (*consommation*) with a paid entrance. The prices of mixed drinks in these places are exorbitant, however. The price of drinks in bars depends greatly on the bar, the time, and the neighborhood (see the nightclub profiles later in this chapter).

SEXUALITY

WE'LL JUST SHARE A FEW THOUGHTS HERE. Public affection is both prevalent and embraced (sorry about the pun) in France. Being in love (short- or long-term) in Paris is the perfect excuse for just about anything. Nudity in the advertisements on billboards on the streets and in the Métro will quickly help you understand that there is an openness and comfort level with sexuality, sensuality, the body, and its desires and functions, that we simply don't have in the United States. Even prostitution and pornography are integrated comfortably into French culture, and more specifically, into that of Paris. It might interest you to know that the controversy over former President Clinton's behavior amused Parisians to no end, since they found the Puritanism of Americans and our culture's fascination with sexual "dirty laundry" to epitomize the ridiculous.

Don't be surprised when you see attractive women standing by the sides of the main avenues leading into Paris luring customers to the curb. Similarly, the **Bois de Boulogne** is famous for its variety of exotic prostitutes, male and female (and male as female), attracting clients for amorous liaisons in the suburban woods. A stroll down the colorful and perfectly harmless rue Saint-Denis in the heart of Paris affords you an excellent means of safely observing the world's oldest profession in practice with typical Parisian *laissez-faire*.

Gay and Lesbian Paris

Gay and lesbian travelers will be pleased to note that the gay community in Paris is large, lively, and visible. Over the last few decades the Marais has emerged as a popular area for gays, with a healthy selection of gay bars, shops, and bookstores, the best of which is **Les Mots à la Bouche** (6, rue Sainte Croix de la Bretonnerie, 75004; ☎ 01 42 78 88 30; **motsbouche.com;** Métro: Saint-Paul). Here you'll find French- and English-language books and publications of interest to gays and lesbians, and additional information on gay activities in Paris.

An excellent source of information is the *Guide Gai,* an annual publication that offers readers comprehensive listings of gay and lesbian bars, restaurants, hotels, activities, groups, and services. Useful Web sites in English are **paris-gay.com** and **parisinfo.com.** Parisians in general are highly tolerant or indifferent when it comes to people's sexual orientations and activities. If you are a gay tourist in Paris, you should feel no tension or discrimination because of your sexuality. The gay and lesbian center, **Centre Gai et Lesbien (C.G.L.)** (63, rue Beaubourg 75003; ☎ 01 43 57 21 47, **cglparis.org;** Métro: Rambuteau, Arts et Métiers, Les Halles or Hôtel de Ville), offers information on activities and social events. For information on issues related to HIV and AIDS, contact the **SIDA Info Service** (☎ 08 00 84 08 00; **sida-info-service.org**), which offers a free and anonymous help line. Although

Paris Nightclubs by Location

ARRONDISSEMENT
NAME | DESCRIPTION

1ST ARRONDISSEMENT

Au Duc des Lombards | Jazz club and pub

Taverne Henri-IV | Wine bar for professionals and regulars believing in the old France

2ND ARRONDISSEMENT

Harry's New York Bar | Celebrated American cocktail bar for expats

3RD ARRONDISSEMENT

Les Bains Douches | Paris's most talked-about celebrity nightclub

4TH ARRONDISSEMENT

Café Beaubourg | Stylish late-night café for the culture crowd

Le Petit Fer à Cheval | Café perfect for late-night drinks and local flavor

6TH ARRONDISSEMENT

Café de Flore | Literary café that's quaint day or night

Closerie des Lilas | Famous literary cocktail bar, café, and restaurant

Les Deux Magots | Famous literary café and late-night watering hole

La Palette | Café in the heart of the gallery district

8TH ARRONDISSEMENT

Buddha Bar | Late-night café and designer restaurant

Crazy Horse Saloon | Cabaret with some of the most beautiful nude women in the world

Le Lido | Top-of-the-line contemporary Parisian cabaret

there is no dedicated English help line, there is always an English speaker on duty. There's also a drop-in centre in the Marais, the **Kiosque Info SIDA** (36, rue Geoffroy l'Asnier, 75004; ☎ 01 44 78 00 00; **lekiosque.org;** Métro: Saint-Paul).

There are many popular gay bars in Paris. Gay visitors to Paris often praise the establishments along rue des Archives, rue Vieille du Temple, and rue Sainte Croix de la Bretonnerie.

ARRONDISSEMENT
NAME | DESCRIPTION

9TH ARRONDISSEMENT

Folies Bergères | World-famous cabaret club turned general musical venue

11TH ARRONDISSEMENT

Le Balajo | Classic Parisian landmark for ballroom dancing and salsa

La Chapelle des Lombards | Nightclub specializing in tropical music

Clown Bar | Historically registered wine bar filled with authentic charm

La Favela Chic | Brazilian bar and restaurant

The Reservoir | Popular Bastille bar/nightclub on the crawler circuit

Sanz Sans | Super-hot club for the rowdy and beautiful

Satellit' Café | Paris's first world music bar/club

12TH ARRONDISSEMENT

Le China | Stylish cocktail/jazz club, restaurant, and speakeasy with smoking room

13TH ARRONDISSEMENT

Batofar | Club on a barge in the Seine

14TH ARRONDISSEMENT

Rosebud | Relaxing and cozy cocktail bar

18TH ARRONDISSEMENT

La Loco | A Parisian institution offering a diverse range of music to please all tastes

Moulin Rouge | Famous Parisian cabaret

Le Sancerre | Late-night café and bar

Safe Sex

It took the French some time to take the news seriously and change their habits, but on the whole campaigns for safe sex in this age of AIDS have been successful. Condoms (*préservatifs*) are widely available at subsidized prices in pharmacies, supermarkets, and automatic dispenser machines in hundreds of public places around the city, including Métro stations. Condoms for women (*préservatif féminin*) are also commercially available although not widely used.

NOTABLE PARIS NIGHTCLUBS

JAZZY CLUBS
Au Duc des Lombards
La Chapelle des Lombards

LITERARY PLACES
Café Beaubourg
Café de Flore
Closerie des Lilas
Les Deux Magots
La Palette

HIP CLUBS
Les Bains Douches
Batofar
Le China
La Loco
The Reservoir
Sanz Sans

ETHNO-HIP
La Favela Chic

GOOD FOR A DRINK
Buddha Bar
Clown Bar
Harry's New York Bar
La Palette
Le Petit Fer à Cheval
Rosebud
Le Sancerre
Taverne Henri-IV

WORLD MUSIC
Satellit' Café

BALLROOM DANCING AND SALSA
Le Balajo

THE BIG SHOWS
Crazy Horse Saloon
Folies Bergère
Le Lido
Moulin Rouge

NIGHTCLUB PROFILES

NOTE ON THE MIX OF CLUBS

NIGHTLIFE IS A TRICKY THING. Every traveler has his or her own idea of a good time. There are wild, late-night swingers who want to discover the hottest, fastest, trendiest places for dancing, drinking, flirting, and seducing. That you can find in Paris. Then there are those who want charming, quiet, typically French spots for drinking good wines, observing people, and reflecting on the special moments of the day. That's Paris too. And there are those driven by avant-garde music or 1950ish jazz joints or literary hangouts where writers drink and smoke and discuss. That's also a choice. Then, of course, there are those who think that Paris wouldn't be complete without a cabaret show and can-can dancers with great-looking girls moving behind tinsel pasties. We've got it covered. In fact, we have tried to offer an eclectic cocktail of ways to spend your evenings and late nights. For some, the evening begins after dinner; for others, well, it'll be a snifter of cognac and then a comfortable yawn. We've included the exotic, the clichés worth visiting, the classical, the obvious, and a tad of the outrageous. The mix may seem odd, and this is deliberate, because not everybody is after the same Paris.

NOTE ON FOOD AT THE CLUBS

IN THE PROFILED SELECTION of nightlife venues, we have combined nightclubs, bars, cabarets, and late-night and special cafés. The Paris nightclub and bar scene starts late, and although food of some sort is often available, no one goes to these establishments to eat.

unofficial **TIP**
We have included information about food only when there is some particularly noteworthy culinary offering.

Au Duc des Lombards

JAZZ CLUB AND PUB

42, rue des Lombards, 75001; ☎ 01 42 33 22 88; ducdeslombards.fr; 1st arrondissement; Métro: Châtelet

Cover €25. **Prices** From €6. **Dress** Casual. **Food available** None. **Hours** Daily, 6:30 p.m.–3 a.m. Concerts at 8 and 10 p.m. Closed 3 weeks in August.

WHO GOES THERE Mixed jazz lovers.

WHAT GOES ON This popular jazz club offers not only great live music but also a very comfortable environment. You can even reserve tables here, something not many clubs permit. The jazz and admission price vary depending on the group, but you can count on a lot of free jazz. American pianist Bobby Few, who still plays here, introduced live music at the Duc des Lombards in the 1970s. Their house band, Le Duc des Lombards Jazz Affair, plays two Wednesdays per month.

SETTING AND ATMOSPHERE Low lighting with comfortable chairs and a pleasantly subdued atmosphere. The club recently underwent extensive renovation and reopened with improved acoustics and the new Croq' des Lombards Restaurant.

IF YOU GO Sometimes Monday is big-band night, but the mix always changes.

Les Bains Douches

PARIS'S MOST TALKED-ABOUT CELEBRITY NIGHTCLUB

7, rue du Bourg-l'Abbé, 75003; ☎ 01 53 01 40 60; lesbainsdouches.net; 3rd arrondissement; Métro: Étienne-Marcel

Cover €10–20. **Prices** Drinks about €12; restaurant set menu from €45 per person. **Dress** Star-studded, fantasy. **Food available** Restaurant upstairs, with a Japanese menu. **Hours** Tuesday–Sunday, 11:30 p.m.–7 a.m.; Sunday morning *matinale*, 7–10 a.m.; restaurant serves 8 p.m.–2 a.m.

WHO GOES THERE Young and beautiful, glittery people.

WHAT GOES ON The club has recently reopened with a new manager, Kurt

Zdesar, and its Famous Club glamour night, every Friday from 11:30 p.m., which attracts the chic and the wannabe chic. Go to the Web site to print out a VIP Pass, which gives you free admission before 1 a.m.

SETTING AND ATMOSPHERE Rich people and wannabe stars stop by here regularly to see each other and the real stars. Two spaces within the club have been entirely redesigned with dazzling décor and state of the art sound: l'Etage and the Club with new bars and new outside terraces for cooling down. And, there's a renovated, fantastic swimming pool. Regular gay nights on Saturdays.

IF YOU GO If you reserve in the restaurant, you'll avoid the bouncer scrutiny. The problem here is that you don't go to Les Bains to eat. Ladies get a free glass of Champagne before 1 a.m.

Le Balajo

CLASSIC PARISIAN LANDMARK FOR BALLROOM DANCING AND SALSA

9, rue de Lappe, 75011; ☎ 09 54 94 54 09; balajo.fr; 11th arrondissement; Métro: Bastille

Cover €10–€20 with 1 drink; €8 for afternoon dancing on Sundays. **Dress** Depends on event. **Food available** None. **Hours** Tuesday Thursday, 8 p.m.– 4 a.m.; Friday and Saturday, 11:30 p.m.–5 a.m.; Sunday, 7–11 p.m.; *bal musette*, Sunday, 3–7 p.m.

WHO GOES THERE Diverse crowd, depends on event.

WHAT GOES ON A true undying rose of a club, the Balajo—literally "Joe's ball" if you want the English translation—is a fantastic old ballroom from the turn of the 20th century. One of the few places that still caters and creates events for an older clientele in the afternoon and a younger crowd for salsa, often until sunrise. You can feel the ghost of Édith Piaf moving between the dances.

SETTING AND ATMOSPHERE Large dance floor with original feel from the 1930s. Tables scattered around the edges. A fascinating time warp. You'll see elderly couples waltzing one night, or middle-agers jitterbugging, tango aficionados doing their thing, and salsa-lovers moving to the beat.

IF YOU GO Go Sunday afternoon to rediscover the atmosphere of a long-lost Paris. Stroll along rue de Lappe before and after your visit.

Batofar

CLUB ON A BARGE IN THE SEINE

Facing 11, quai François-Mauriac, 75013; ☎ 01 56 60 17 30; restaurant ☎ 01 45 83 33 06; batofar.org; 13th arrondissement; Métro: Bibliothèque Nationale

Cover Free–€20, depending on the night. **Prices** €4 for a beer, €25 for dinner.

Dress Casual. **Food available** À la carte, canteen-style munchies and vegetarian available. **Hours** Club: Tuesday–Saturday, 10 p.m.–4 a.m.; Sunday, 6 a.m.–midday. Restaurant: service until midnight.

WHO GOES THERE Hip locals.

WHAT GOES ON The Batofar is the place to be in Paris. An intelligent and eclectic program is offered each month, including the best of European house, funk, electro, and techno. Live music of all sorts. The Batofar, whose name translates to "lighthouse boat," is exactly that. Completely restored with a very solid sound system, it fills up with people instead of water every night. Consistent and different. If you're still standing at dawn, come here for their popular post-party chill, every other Sunday from 4 a.m. until noon, or visit Sunday afternoons in the summer for their musical siesta. Another recent innovation is their summer Apéros du Batofar from 7 p.m. during the week and 4 p.m. on the weekend.

SETTING AND ATMOSPHERE You're on a hot, packed, and sweaty houseboat moored on the Seine. Wild, lively, and fun.

IF YOU GO Get there early if you don't want to feel like a refugee left ashore!

Buddha Bar

LATE-NIGHT CAFÉ AND DESIGNER RESTAURANT

8, rue Boissy d'Anglas, 75008; ☎ 01 53 05 90 00; buddha-bar.com; 8th arrondissement; Métro: Concorde

Cover No cover charge. **Prices** Cocktails €17. **Dress** Trendy. **Food available** Bar snacks, sashimi, tempura, teriyaki, sushi, Peking duck. **Hours** Monday–Friday, midday–3 p.m.; daily, 4 p.m.–2 a.m.

WHO GOES THERE Fashion, business, and film crowds; people-watchers.

WHAT GOES ON So you've got some cash to throw around, you're thinking of selling your Sony stock, and you need some Japanese advice on the matter with an enormous Buddha overlooking the conversation. This is the place for you! Excellent mixed drinks and good wine list. The food is mediocre. You'll hear beautiful mixes by DJ Ravin and David Visan.

SETTING AND ATMOSPHERE This is a place to be seen. Over-the-top décor dominated by Buddha icon.

IF YOU GO Don't eat. Too pricey and trendy.

Café Beaubourg

STYLISH LATE-NIGHT CAFÉ FOR THE CULTURE CROWD

100, rue Saint-Martin, 75004; ☎ 01 48 87 63 96; 4th arrondissement; Métro: Châtelet

Cover None. **Prices** Drinks €5 and up, dinner €35, brunch €22. **Dress** Casual. **Food available** Salads, pasta, seafood, sandwiches, traditional food. **Hours** Daily, 8 a.m.–1 a.m. (until 2 a.m. Thursday–Saturday).

WHO GOES THERE Writers, publishers.

WHAT GOES ON Literary musing and networking among publishers and media mavens.

SETTING AND ATMOSPHERE Maybe the old cafés make you uncomfortable. Or maybe you're in Paris for the umpteenth time and need to imagine that you're in some other city. Something more urban with an international airport feel to it. Something designed to work. Café Beaubourg, just opposite the Centre Georges Pompidou, is a large bar on two floors. It set out to be a literary café and is. A quiet, concentrated atmosphere prevails. Many newspapers in different languages are read. A bit more expensive than the average café, but you have extra space and aren't bothered if you linger. This is one of the few cafés that serves a glass of water with each espresso and serves milk on the side when you order a crème.

IF YOU GO Weather permitting, sit on the comfortable wicker chairs outside and people-watch.

Café de Flore

LITERARY CAFÉ THAT'S QUAINT DAY OR NIGHT

172, boulevard Saint-Germain-des-Prés, 75006; ☎ 01 45 48 55 26; cafe-de-flore.com; 6th arrondissement; Métro: Saint-Germain-des-Prés

Cover None. **Prices** Be prepared to spend €5 for a café crème. **Dress** Casual. **Hours** Daily, 7:30 a.m.–1:30 a.m.

WHO GOES THERE Regulars, tourists, intellectuals, neighbors.

WHAT GOES ON One of the key landmarks in literary Paris, Café de Flore was founded in 1865 and named after a statue to the goddess of flowers, which no longer sits outside. If you feel like watching Saint-Germain Parisians in an original Art Deco setting, come to the Flore and nurse a coffee or glass of wine. The prices are high, but it's not every day that you can hang out in the digs of Apollinaire, André Breton, Picasso, and above all Jean-Paul Sartre and Simone de Beauvoir, who wrote here regularly because it was heated. The tradition continues—intellectuals, filmmakers, and philosophers stop in often.

SETTING AND ATMOSPHERE This is a café, and the atmosphere varies depending on the time of day or night you visit. Mixed crowd of locals, intellectuals, letter-writers, hopeful literati, and foreign tourists.

IF YOU GO Weather permitting, sit on the terrace, order a café crème, and plan to while away a leisurely hour or two.

La Chapelle des Lombards

NIGHTCLUB SPECIALIZING IN TROPICAL MUSIC

19, rue de Lappe, 75011; ☎ 01 43 57 24 24;
la-chapelle-deslombards.com; 11th arrondissement; Métro: Bastille

Cover Free on Tuesday, Thursday, Sunday; €15 for men and free for women on Thursday; €20 Friday and Saturday (with 1 free drink). **Prices** Drinks are €6–€9. **Dress** Dress to get past the bouncers. **Specials** Latin and tropical nights Thursday–Saturday; Tuesday, Thursday, Sunday, R&B, reggae, and soul. **Hours** Tuesday–Sunday, 11:30 p.m.–6 a.m.

WHO GOES THERE Latin, African, and West Indian dance lovers.

WHAT GOES ON For decades now, this rue de Lappe mainstay has been on the circuit for a youngish dance crowd with a passion for World Music. Lots of singles come here to dance and mingle. The bouncers have been known to be overly discriminating when it comes to single men. Separate enclosed smoking area.

SETTING AND ATMOSPHERE Electrified atmosphere. You go here with high energy and great expectations to dance, flirt, and boogie. Very crowded.

IF YOU GO Concerts start from €12.

Le China

STYLISH COCKTAIL/JAZZ CLUB, RESTAURANT, AND SPEAKEASY WITH SMOKING ROOM

50, rue de Charenton, 75012; ☎ 01 43 46 08 09; lechina.eu;
12th arrondissement; Métro: Bastille or Ledru Rollin

Cover None. **Prices** Soft drinks €5, cocktails €8. **Dress** Casual chic, stylish. **Specials** Nonalcoholic fresh-fruit mixed drinks at €6. **Food available** Refined Chinese cuisine. **Hours** Monday–Saturday, 6 p.m.–2 a.m.; Sunday, midday–2 a.m.

WHO GOES THERE All ages, chic and well-dressed, romantics.

WHAT GOES ON Classy French Colonial–style Chinese restaurant with a very high-class cocktail bar upstairs and Tuesday to Saturday live music down in the cellar Club de China. If you do go upstairs to the *fumoir chinois,* you'll be seduced by the lacquered walls and very discreet and dark seating. You'll quickly forget you're in Paris; you could be in Hong Kong or New York. The cocktails are among the best in town. This is not the place to go if you feel more comfortable in your jeans and T-shirt. If you're meeting your sweetie's parents for the first time, this is a good bet.

SETTING AND ATMOSPHERE This hideaway has a feel of being out of time, a mysterious place filled with elegance and intrigue. You'll think you're in a spy novel turned into a film that was shot in Shanghai in the 1930s. Charlie Chan goes yuppie.

Closerie des Lilas

FAMOUS LITERARY COCKTAIL BAR, CAFÉ, AND RESTAURANT

171, boulevard du Montparnasse, 75006; ☎ 01 40 51 34 50;
closeriedeslilas.net; 6th arrondissement;
Métro: Vavin or Port-Royal

Cover None. **Prices** Small beers €9, cocktails €14, brasserie meals from €45 a person, restaurant meals around €100 without wine. **Dress** Casual to dressy. **Food available** Brasserie food all day; steak tartare, oysters, fish, salads. **Hours** Daily, noon–2:30 p.m. and 7–10:30 p.m. (restaurant); 7 p.m.–1:30 a.m. (piano bar); noon–1 a.m. (brasserie).

WHO GOES THERE Intellectuals with money, ultra-chic bourgeois clan, wannabe writers, snobs, artists, and tourists.

WHAT GOES ON One of Paris's most celebrated cafés, immortalized by Hemingway's *A Moveable Feast,* in which the writer states his disapproval of the 1923 change of policy in the café obliging the waiters to shave their mustaches in order to attract a higher-class clientele. The café nonetheless was frequented religiously by the likes of Verlaine, Lenin, Baudelaire, the Symbolist poets, the Surrealists, the Dadaists, F. Scott Fitzgerald, Archibald MacLeish, and so on. According to literary café biographer, Noël Riley Fitch, it was here that James Joyce celebrated Sylvia Beach's decision to publish *Ulysses* in February 1921. So if motivated by literary lore, come here for a drink or stay on for dinner in either the brasserie (better deal, known for its excellent steak tartare) or more formal restaurant, which is stylish but overpriced. The open-air terrace is pleasant, but the prices inhibit all but best-selling authors in today's upscale market. A drink at the elegant mahogany bar, however, by the brass plate marked "E. Hemingway" will prove to be a memorable moment.

SETTING AND ATMOSPHERE Superb décor that's warm and inviting. Great oak bar, studded with copper. See the engraved plaque to Hemingway. Polished wood chairs. Mosaic floors. Large piano.

IF YOU GO Eat on the brasserie side or simply nurse a drink and take in the historical vibes.

Clown Bar

HISTORICALLY REGISTERED WINE BAR FILLED WITH AUTHENTIC CHARM

114, rue Amelot, 75011; ☎ 01 43 55 87 35; clown-bar.fr;
11th arrondissement; Métro: Filles du Calvaire

Cover None. **Prices** €6 for a drink, €18 fixed menu. **Dress** Casual. **Specials** Côtes du Rhône wines. **Food available** Filet *mignon* (pork) with *gratin dauphinnois,* tarte tatin. **Hours** Monday–Saturday, noon–3 p.m.; daily, 7 p.m.–midnight.

WHO GOES THERE Mixed, thirties crowd, after-theater or cinema crowd.

WHAT GOES ON The Clown Bar is like a museum piece that should have been in Orson Welles's personal collection. Circus paraphernalia is everywhere. Good, simple food and drink are served in a laid-back but friendly style. The Bouglione Circus is just next door in the old Cirque d'Hiver, used by the Nazis to round up Jews and political prisoners during World War II. Slip inside and see the décor. Burt Lancaster made a fabulous movie here called *Trapeze*. Original and charming.

SETTING AND ATMOSPHERE Beautifully decorated walls with the clown motif. Very warm atmosphere. Great zinc bar. Painted tiles, starlit ceiling. Owned by an antique dealer. The staff could use a lesson in customer service.

IF YOU GO Start your evening off with a glass of recommended Côtes du Rhône wine.

Crazy Horse Saloon

CABARET WITH SOME OF THE MOST BEAUTIFUL NUDE WOMEN IN THE WORLD

12, avenue George V, 75008; ☎ 01 47 23 32 32; lecrazyhorseparis.com; 8th arrondissement; Métro: George V

Cover €100 seated without drinks, or €120 seated with a half bottle of Champagne. **Prices** Extra drinks start at €18. **Dress** Fancy. **Food available** Dinner in a selected restaurant nearby (Le Fouquet, Chez Francis, or De Vèz) plus show, €175–€195. **Hours** Daily, 7:30 p.m.–2 a.m.; show, Monday–Friday, 8:15 p.m. and 10:45 p.m.; Saturday, 7 p.m., 9:30 p.m., and 11:45 p.m.

WHO GOES THERE Tourists, out-of-town visitors.

WHAT GOES ON Founded in 1951, the Crazy Horse is unique in the world of girlie-show business. This French parody of an American western saloon, featuring its established "teasing" show, now hosts original acts like 12 paintings in motion, classical as well as contemporary, consisting of 20 exceptional dancers revolving in a nude rainbow of light. Each of these live "paintings" represents a sculptural and luminous masterpiece. This nude revue emphasizes the divine figure of the dancers and is undoubtedly the most beautiful and professional in the world, as per the vision of the late founder, Alain Bernardin, who gathered a corps of exquisite and well-paid beauties. Drinks are served during the show, but you can easily get away with the two that come with the entrance. Fully air-conditioned. Reservations required. The show lasts an hour and a half.

SETTING AND ATMOSPHERE Situated between traditional burlesque and the art of upscale sleaze, the Crazy Horse's shows give you a chance to gawk at some impressive female bodies without feeling politically incorrect. Stage lights, red curtains, and slinky costumes that come undone at the right moments characterize the show. Guests include lots of middle-aged, well-dressed tourists and out-of-town French visitors. Famous Mounties stand out front.

IF YOU GO Take in the show, but you can get a better deal eating on your own than if you spring for one of the club's dinner packages.

Les Deux Magots

FAMOUS LITERARY CAFÉ AND LATE-NIGHT WATERING-HOLE

6, place Saint-Germain-des-Prés, 75006; ☎ 01 45 48 55 25; lesdeuxmagots.fr; 6th arrondissement; Métro: Saint-Germain-des-Prés

Cover None. **Prices** €4.70 for a *café crème*. **Dress** Casual. **Food available** Café fare. **Hours** Daily, 7:30 a.m.–1:30 a.m.; closed one week in January.

WHO GOES THERE Locals and tourists.

WHAT GOES ON Opposite its rival, the literary Café le Flore, Les Deux Magots is deliciously situated at the corner of boulevard Saint-Germain facing the Saint-Germain church. One of Paris's most famous cafés, it was founded in 1875 and supposedly named after the two porcelain Chinese figures that remain on the center posts inside the café. The second home to many writers, artists, and cultural personalities throughout the 20th century, Les Deux Magots is noted as the café in which Picasso created Cubism and Breton and Aragon drafted the Surrealist manifestos. Hemingway, Sartre, de Beauvoir, and plenty of others drank and conversed here. Plan to linger for a while and let the past meet the present. The prices are absurdly high for a coffee or glass of wine, but think of it as the price to rent the space.

SETTING AND ATMOSPHERE Here you are in the heart of literary folklore that continues to ring true. People around you will be reading *Le Monde* and good books, writing in diaries, and having lively topical or philosophical discussions. The charming décor dates to World War I. The quality of the service has always been a point of great pride to the establishment.

IF YOU GO Nurse your drink for a while, and don't be in a hurry. Or go early in the morning for a splendid Parisian breakfast on the terrace (€20).

La Favela Chic

BRAZILIAN BAR AND RESTAURANT

18, rue du Faubourg du Temple, 75011; ☎ 01 40 21 38 14; favelachic.com; 11th arrondissement; Métro: République

Cover Free Tuesday–Thursday, €10 Friday and Saturday with 1 drink. **Prices** Cocktails from €8. **Dress** Casual. **Food available** Brazilian fare, tapas, and picanha. **Hours** Tuesday–Thursday, 8 p.m.–2 a.m.; Friday and Saturday, 8 p.m.–4 a.m.

WHO GOES THERE Hipsters and trendsetters of all colors.

WHAT GOES ON La Favela Chic is one of the true trendsetters in the emerging Ménilmontant area. It's a great bar and restaurant frequented by a younger crowd with a constant stream of newcomers and regulars walking in the door. In fact, its success led to the opening of a second Favela Chic in London. Inspiring international dishes (€14–€28), plus memorable caipirinhas (Brazilian cocktails) at €8. Their location is the former Cacharel showroom—large and industrial with lots of room for dancing.

SETTING AND ATMOSPHERE Very friendly atmosphere where it's easy to strike up a chat with your neighbors. The drinks are great, but the flavor of the venue is better than the food.

IF YOU GO Go for a Brazilian cocktail and to hear some authentic samba.

Folies Bergères

WORLD-FAMOUS CABARET CLUB TURNED GENERAL MUSICAL VENUE

32, rue Richer, 75009; ☎ 08 92 68 16 50; foliesbergere.com; 9th arrondissement; Métro: Cadet or Grands Boulevards

Cover €24–€90, depending on seats and show. **Dress** Anything goes, but better be overdressed than under. **Food available** None—the dinner shows have been discontinued. **Hours** Depends on each show.

WHO GOES THERE Tourists, fans of musicals, and out-of-town guests.

WHAT GOES ON Folies Bergères, renowned for lively burlesque entertainment, has been a Paris landmark since 1886. The risqué African American singer and dancer Josephine Baker made a name for herself at this club. If it's skin you're hoping to see beyond the feathers and glitter, you'll be disappointed. In fact, the dinner-show format has been scrapped, and a variety of not-necessarily-burlesque shows have been booked in, such as *Zorro* and *The Lion King*. Check the Web site carefully before buying tickets.

SETTING AND ATMOSPHERE Old-world ambience, musical venue.

IF YOU GO Don't be late. The doors shut as the show starts.

Harry's New York Bar

CELEBRATED AMERICAN COCKTAIL BAR FOR EXPATS

5, rue Daunou, 75002; ☎ 01 42 61 71 14; harrys-bar.fr; 2nd arrondissement; Métro: Opéra

Cover None. **Food available** Club sandwiches, chili con carne lunchtime only. **Prices** Drinks €9–€15; €12 for a Bloody Mary. **Dress** Respectable; loosened neckties, after-work look. **Hours** Monday–Saturday, midday–4 a.m. (cocktail bar); Friday and Saturday, 10 p.m.–2 a.m. and 3 a.m. (piano bar).

WHO GOES THERE Anglo-Franco literary and journalist scene, businessmen.

WHAT GOES ON You probably aren't interested in hanging out at an American bar in Paris, but this one is such a fixture on the Paris bar scene that you might want to make an exception. Established in 1911, Harry's Bar, then called New York Bar, the oldest cocktail bar in Europe, still retains much the same feel and décor. College banners on the wall, lots of dark varnished wood, and photographs of Ernest Hemingway fishing and hunting. Allegedly the birthplace of the Bloody Mary, which regulars swear by. In fact, the experienced bar staff does an impressive job with all the cocktails (mixing exactly the right measure effortlessly). A bit pricey, but a good value nevertheless. There's a piano bar downstairs, where George Gershwin played "An American in Paris" while F. Scott Fitzgerald drank until he collapsed. Harry's enjoys a regular clientele of expats, foreign journalists, and American-loving French who have great stories and share a common feeling of belonging here. The bar is famous for its phonetic spelling of its address: "Sank Roo Doe Noo," which was created to help English-speaking customers direct taxi drivers to the bar. Founded by a Scot, Harry McElhone, and now owned by his granddaughter, Isabelle, the place is legend. Stop in for a time warp and a Bloody Mary.

SETTING AND ATMOSPHERE Enjoy the nostalgia felt in the history of this landmark, although some tourists have complained about the pricey drinks and less-than-gracious service. Varnished, dark wooden walls, a charming wooden bar and stools. Black-and-white photographs everywhere. Downstairs there is a second room with a small bar—perfect for private parties and receptions and the occasional exhibit.

IF YOU GO Go after working hours and plan to drink with the regulars. You'll get a good earful of what's going on in Paris today.

Le Lido

TOP-OF-THE-LINE CONTEMPORARY PARISIAN CABARET

116 bis, avenue des Champs-Élysées, 75008; ☎ 01 40 76 56 10; lido.fr; 8th arrondissement; Métro: George V

Cover €140–€280 for dining and dancing including Champagne; floor show only, €90; bar seats available €45–€80; children's dinner for €30; matinee €115–€125 including Champagne; floor show only, €80. **Prices** Included in cover prices. **Dress** Dressy. **Specials** Dining/dancing at 7 p.m.; shows start at 9:30 p.m. and 11:30 p.m. daily. **Food available** French cuisine, menu and à la carte, by chef Philippe Lacroix. **Hours** Daily, 1 p.m.–5 a.m.

WHO GOES THERE International visitors and out-of-town guests.

WHAT GOES ON The famous Bluebell Girls, founded by Miss Bluebell, as everybody called her, are clothed in feathers and light-reflecting material and sometimes little else but the latest modern technologies (lasers and video), making for a breathtaking spectacle. The performance is timed to a second with fantastic special effects. But the Lido is also known for its top international stars (magicians, singers, dancers), who will enchant you. If the Lido claims to be a world-famous floorshow, it's because it knows just how to put on a magnificent show. This world-renowned venue presents its famous international revue in a 1.5-acre cabaret. As the show begins, the dining floor goes down with all the spectators, leaving the dance floor clear to become an elevated stage offering a perfect panoramic view. A lunch revue is offered every Sunday and Tuesday.

SETTING AND ATMOSPHERE Set on the Champs-Élysées, the Lido is the most elaborate cabaret show in the world today. A fanfare of costumes, lights, glitter, music, feathers, and so on, the aesthetics collectively impress and enchant, although the whole deal is a kicking cliché caught between the early 1900s and the now-not-too-new millennium.

IF YOU GO Reserve ahead.

La Loco

A PARISIAN INSTITUTION OFFERING A DIVERSE RANGE OF MUSIC TO PLEASE ALL TASTES

90, boulevard de Clichy, 75018; ☎ 01 53 41 88 89; laloco.com; 18th arrondissement; Métro: Blanche

Cover Sunday–Thursday, €12 without a drink, €14 with 1 drink, €19 with 2 drinks; Friday and Saturday, €15 without a drink, €20 with 1 drink, and €26 with 2 drinks. **Prices** €7–€10. **Dress** Casual. **Hours** Daily, 11 p.m.–6 a.m.

WHO GOES THERE Mostly 18–25 set.

WHAT GOES ON A famous rock club from the 1960s originally known as the Locomotive, it has been kicking up the scene in Paris for the last few years with its innovative mixes. The enormous club (by Paris standards) on three floors holds up to 2,000 guests. You're bound to find something to suit you here, from Latin sounds, to R&B, house, techno, '80s sounds, and heavy metal or Goth concerts during the week.

SETTING AND ATMOSPHERE On three bustling levels you'll get your fill of contemporary music. There are bars at every corner and every intersection. Purportedly the largest club in Paris.

IF YOU GO Wear whatever you like, but no baggies or baseball caps.

Moulin Rouge

FAMOUS PARISIAN CABARET

82, boulevard de Clichy, 75018; ☎ 01 53 09 82 82; moulinrouge.fr; 18th arrondissement; Métro: Blanche

Cover Floor show €102 at 9 p.m. and €92 at 11 p.m. (includes half-bottle of Champagne); show and dinner €150, €165, €180; show and lunch €130; show only €100. **Prices** Included in cover. **Dress** Formal. **Food available** Traditional French cuisine. **Hours** Daily, dinner before the show at 7 p.m.; shows begin at 9 p.m. and 11 p.m.; limited number of matinees, with lunch before the show at 1 p.m. and show at 2.45 p.m.

WHO GOES THERE Out-of-town visitors, tourists.

WHAT GOES ON Its very name breathes the mythical spirit of Montmartre and the Paris of painter Toulouse-Lautrec, the frilly *feminines,* and the French can-can dance, which is best seen here. The "formidable" floor show and the 100 Moulin girls will wow you. Try to count the number of times they change costume, or sit back and enjoy the perfection of dancing and their dynamic high-kicking French can-can in voluminous skirts and petticoats. Formal dress is required.

SETTING AND ATMOSPHERE Exactly like you've seen it in old French films. Everything is still in place, right down to the ostrich feathers that tickle your nose. A good excuse to get a dose of French can-can dancers.

IF YOU GO Reserve in advance. Not necessary to eat here as well.

La Palette

CAFÉ IN THE HEART OF THE GALLERY DISTRICT

43, rue de Seine, 75006; ☎ 01 43 26 68 15; 6th arrondissement; Métro: Mabillon or Odéon

Cover None. **Prices** Drinks €5–€11. **Dress** Casual. **Food available** Salads, sandwiches, *plats du jour.* **Hours** Café: Monday–Saturday, 8 a.m.–2 a.m.; Restaurant: Monday–Saturday, 11:30 a.m.–3 p.m.; closed August, 1 week in winter, November 1, Christmas, New Years Day, Easter Monday.

WHO GOES THERE An artsy crowd.

WHAT GOES ON This is a favorite meeting spot for painters, sculptors, photographers, art lovers, neighbors, and Americans. Always lively and rarely pretentious, La Palette represents the best of the area. The paintings on the wall in the back depict the ageless waiters. The wines are excellent and reasonably priced. This is one of the best spots to be at midnight when the Beaujolais Nouveau is legally released on the third Thursday of November. Good, traditional French food, and on warm days and evenings you can sit out on the sidewalk. Very friendly service if they know you; a bit cool if they don't. A mixed crowd of people from the galleries, the Beaux Arts nearby, and tourists.

SETTING AND ATMOSPHERE A nightspot that manages to be totally unpretentious while being perpetually frequented by an elite culture crowd. All in all, very Parisian. Simple décor with a room in the back for light lunches or just those wishing to hang out and drink with friends. The waiters have been there for centuries.

IF YOU GO Relax and drink in the atmosphere along with the wine.

Le Petit Fer à Cheval

CAFÉ PERFECT FOR LATE-NIGHT DRINKS AND LOCAL FLAVOR

30, rue Vieille-du-Temple, 75004; ☎ 01 42 72 47 47; cafeine.com; 4th arrondissement; Métro: Hôtel de Ville or Saint-Paul

Cover None. **Prices** Dinner €30 without wine. **Dress** Casual. **Food available** Good, simple bistro fare. **Hours** Daily, 9 a.m.–2 a.m.

WHO GOES THERE Mixed, regulars, visitors, late-nighters.

WHAT GOES ON Since the turn of the 20th century, this has been a local bistro where one feels good about coming back day after day. Stop in to have a drink, to nibble, to talk about nothing at all and the affairs of the heart. Good selection of lesser wines and pleasing background jazz.

SETTING AND ATMOSPHERE We've made many friends over the years at Le Petit Fer à Cheval by just putting our elbows on the horseshoe-shaped bar and keeping an open mind. The small restaurant behind the bar with its little window onto the kitchen only adds to the charm of this café. Xavier, the owner, collects art to decorate the rooms, constantly changes the wine list with nice discoveries, and keeps the staff sharp, friendly, and responsive

IF YOU GO Go anytime. A perfect meeting spot in the Marais.

The Reservoir

POPULAR BASTILLE BAR/NIGHTCLUB ON THE CRAWLER CIRCUIT

16, rue de la Forge-Royale, 75011; ☎ 01 43 56 39 60; reservoirclub.com; 11th arrondissement; Métro: Faidherbe-Chaligny or Ledru-Rollin

Cover Depends on concert. **Prices** Beer €5, cocktails €10. **Dress** Casual. **Specials** Jazz brunch on Sundays. **Food available** Restaurant, 8 p.m.–midnight; Sunday brunch, 11:30 a.m.–6:30 p.m., €24. **Hours** Tuesday–Saturday, 8 p.m.–late; Sunday and Monday nights, by invitation only; closed 3 weeks in August.

WHO GOES THERE Mixed bag of bar regulars, show-biz types, and hordes of pretty women.

WHAT GOES ON Showbiz, art, and media people define their dreams and ambitions to the eclectic sounds and rhythms programmed by host Marcello. Saturdays feature groove. Stars often make surprise appearances.

SETTING AND ATMOSPHERE This transformed storehouse with a fantastic Italian Renaissance décor is the place to be in Paris for the cool crowd.

IF YOU GO Go late or for the very popular Sunday jazz brunch. Reservations are essential.

Rosebud

RELAXING AND COZY COCKTAIL BAR

11 bis, rue Delambre, 75014; ☎ 01 43 35 38 54; 14th arrondissement; Métro: Vavin

Cover None. **Prices** Small beers €7, cocktails €12–€14. **Dress** Casual. **Food available** Yes. **Specials** Excellent cocktails. **Hours** Daily, 7 p.m.–2 a.m.; closed August, Christmas, and New Year's.

WHO GOES THERE 30 and up.

WHAT GOES ON At €12 for a Bloody Mary, it better be bloody good! A true American cocktail bar with real bartenders that shake up a storm of iced drinks that can whittle your wallet down. Ask to see where Jean-Paul Sartre used to sit. Today, the place has that "has-been" feel to it, but the way they hang onto days gone by has its own charm, and the piped-in jazz tunes are perfect for a melancholic trip to the bar. Some say this has become a haunt for middle-agers hoping not to go home alone.

SETTING AND ATMOSPHERE Ideal for recharging your batteries after a stressful day. Beautiful 1930s décor with bistro-style tables and filtered light.

IF YOU GO Order a cocktail and put up your feet.

Le Sancerre

LATE-NIGHT CAFÉ AND BAR

35, rue des Abbesses, 75018; ☎ 01 42 58 08 20; 18th arrondissement; Métro: Abbesses

WHO GOES THERE Locals, eccentrics, very hip individuals, and deadbeats.

WHAT GOES ON If you get fed up walking around and want a steak and French fries, some heady wine, or a choice of beers all served with a rock-and-roll attitude, then stop in at Le Sancerre. Named after the wine and its region, Le Sancerre is a large bar that is packed on weekend nights and spills out onto the terrace, which remains open and heated in winter. A great place to inhale the real *parfum* of Paris while listening to the loud music of the barman's choice.

SETTING AND ATMOSPHERE A simple neighborhood café to start with, this place quickly gained its reputation due to the generous and open-spirited owner and his good drinks and simple dishes.

IF YOU GO Tuesday night is especially fun.

Sanz Sans

SUPER-HOT CLUB FOR THE ROWDY AND BEAUTIFUL

49, rue du Faubourg Saint-Antoine, 75011; ☎ 01 44 75 78 78; sanzsans.com; 11th arrondissement; Métro: Ledru-Rollin

Cover None. **Prices** €5–€10. **Dress** Casual. **Food available** Yes, upstairs. **Hours** Monday–Saturday, 9 a.m.–5 a.m.

WHO GOES THERE Pretty, sexy, young, party crowd.

WHAT GOES ON Excellent French bar in the Bastille that's positively heaving on weekends. Other reviewers have reported a difficult door policy, but you may not notice this at all. They serve food upstairs in a more relaxed atmosphere, but this is not really a place you go to eat.

SETTING AND ATMOSPHERE The crowd is cosmopolitan, young, and friendly. DJs spin the discs, while the crowd enjoys the music and drinks. The bar staff have a great time dancing and banging the cymbal lampshades at strategic moments in hip-hop hits. It was extremely hot even in March when Paris was cold, so it could be unbearable in summer.

IF YOU GO Prepare for a full-court press of clubbers. On the same crawl, you can check out El Barrio Latino club across the street toward the Bastille.

Satellit' Café

PARIS'S FIRST WORLD MUSIC BAR/CLUB

44, rue de la Folie Méricourt, 75011; ☎ 01 47 00 48 87; satellit-cafe.com; 11th arrondissement; Métro: Saint-Ambroise or Oberkampf

Cover €12, women free. **Prices** €5–€10. **Dress** Casual. **Hours** Wednesday–Friday, 9 p.m.–dawn; Sunday, 6 p.m.–2 a.m.

WHO GOES THERE Very mixed, world-music crowd.

WHAT GOES ON This venue describes itself as the Parisian Ambassador of world music, with a collection of records large enough to make a radio station green with envy. There's an excellent sound system and a faithful clientele that chooses this large bar for the quality of its expression. You'll hear talent from North Africa, Kurdistan, the French West Indies, and French gypsy groups. Check out the 24-track mixing board! Live bands play at 9 p.m. Wednesday through Friday, and a skillful DJ spins on the weekends. No bands play in July or August.

SETTING AND ATMOSPHERE Friendly setting for excellent world music and a great mix of faces.

IF YOU GO Check the Web site to find out who's playing before you go.

Taverne Henri-IV

WINE BAR FOR PROFESSIONALS AND REGULARS BELIEVING IN THE OLD FRANCE

13, place du Pont-Neuf, 75001; ☎ 01 43 54 27 90; 1st arrondissement; Métro: Pont-Neuf

Cover None. **Prices** €3–€12 a glass, bottles start at €15; meals at around €30. **Dress** Casual. **Food available** Hot tartines, escargots, duck foie gras with fig chutney. **Hours** Monday–Friday, 11:30 a.m.–11:30 p.m.; Saturday, 11:30 a.m.–5 p.m.; food served at all times; closed in August.

WHO GOES THERE Lawyers, police inspectors, judges, ministry workers, and neighbors.

WHAT GOES ON This favorite old-world watering hole sitting pretty on Pont Neuf at the mouth of Place Dauphine is a great place to stop in the late afternoon after a day of sightseeing or shopping for a glass of wine and a taste of old France.

SETTING AND ATMOSPHERE The décor is rustic, and the bar is real copper.

IF YOU GO Go early.

ACCOMMODATIONS INDEX

Note: Page numbers of hotel profiles are in **bold face** type.

RESTAURANT INDEX

Note: Page numbers of restaurant profiles are in **bold face** type.

SUBJECT INDEX

Unofficial Guide Reader Survey

If you would like to express your opinion in writing about Paris or this guidebook, complete the following survey and mail it to:

> *Unofficial Guide* Reader Survey
> P.O. Box 43673
> Birmingham, AL 35243

Inclusive dates of your visit: _____

Members of your party.

	Person 1	Person 2	Person 3	Person 4	Person 5
Gender:	M F	M F	M F	M F	M F
Age:					

How many times have you been to Paris? _____
On your most recent trip, where did you stay? _____

Concerning your accommodations, on a scale of 100 as best and 0 as worst, how would you rate:

The quality of your room?   The value of your room?
The quietness of your room?   Check-in/check-out efficiency?
Shuttle service to the airport?   Swimming pool facilities?

Did you rent a car?   From whom?

Concerning your rental car, on a scale of 100 as best and 0 as worst, how would you rate:

Pick-up processing efficiency?   Return processing efficiency?
Condition of the car?   Cleanliness of the car?
Airport shuttle efficiency?

Concerning your dining experiences:
Estimate your meals in restaurants per day? _____
Approximately how much did your party spend on meals per day? _____
_____

Favorite restaurants in Paris: _____
_____

Did you buy this guide before leaving?   while on your trip?

How did you hear about this guide? (check all that apply)

Loaned or recommended by a friend ☐   Radio or TV ☐
Newspaper or magazine ☐   Bookstore salesperson ☐
Just picked it out on my own ☐   Library ☐
Internet ☐

What other guidebooks did you use on this trip?_____

_____

_____

On a scale of 100 as best and 0 as worst, how would you rate them?

_____

_____

_____

Using the same scale, how would you rate the *Unofficial Guide*(s)?

_____

Are *Unofficial Guides* readily available at bookstores in your area? _____

Have you used other *Unofficial Guides*? _____

Which one(s)?_____

_____

_____

Comments about your Paris trip or the *Unofficial Guide*(s):

9 Orsay
9 Orsay
9 Louvre
2 10 Dah
20 versa
20 Boat
$77
28 30
$105.30